All the Shah's Men

An American Coup and the Roots of Middle East Terror

STEPHEN KINZER

WILEY

John Wiley & Sons, Inc.

Published by John Wiley & Sons, Inc., Hoboken, New Jersey
Published simultaneously in Canada

Design and production by Navta Associates, Inc.

Song lyrics on pages 13–14 from "Luck Be A Lady" from *Guys and Dolls* by Frank Loesser, © 1950 (Renewed) Frank Music Corp. All rights reserved

For general information about our other products and services, please contact our Customer Care Department within the United States at (800) 762-2974, outside the United States at (317) 572-3993 or fax (317) 572-4002.

Wiley also publishes its books in a variety of electronic formats. Some content that appears in print may not be available in electronic books. For more information about Wiley products, visit our web site at www.wiley.com.

Library of Congress Cataloging-in-Publication Data

Kinzer, Stephen.
    All the Shah's men : an American coup and the roots of Middle East terror / Stephen Kinzer.
       p. cm.
  Includes bibliographical references and index.
    ISBN 0-471-26517-9
  1. Iran—Politics and government—1941–1979. 2. Mosaddeq, Mohammad, 1880–1967.
  3. United States—Relations—Iran. 4. Iran—Relations—United States. I. Title.
  DS318.K49 2003
  955.05'3—dc21   2003009968

Printed in the United States of America

10 9 8 7 6 5 4 3 2

For the People of Iran

*There is nothing new in the world except
the history you do not know.*

—HARRY TRUMAN

CONTENTS

PREFACE

One day I attended a book party for an older Iranian woman who had written her memoirs. She spoke for an hour about her eventful life. Although she never touched on politics, she mentioned in passing that her family was related to the family of Mohammad Mossadegh, who served as prime minister of Iran for twenty-six months in the early 1950s and was overthrown in a coup d'etat staged by the Central Intelligence Agency.

After she finished speaking, I couldn't resist the temptation to ask a question. "You mentioned Mossadegh," I said. "What do you remember, or what can you tell us, about the coup against him?" She immediately became agitated and animated.

"Why did you Americans do that terrible thing?" she cried out. "We always loved America. To us, America was the great country, the perfect country, the country that helped us while other countries were exploiting us. But after that moment, no one in Iran ever trusted the United States again. I can tell you for sure that if you had not done that thing, you would never have had that problem of hostages being taken in your embassy in Tehran. All your trouble started in 1953. Why, why did you do it?"

This outburst reflected a great gap in knowledge and understanding that separates most Iranians from most non-Iranians. In Iran, almost everyone has for decades known that the United States was responsible for putting an end to democratic rule in 1953 and installing what became the long dictatorship of Mohammad Reza Shah. His dictatorship produced the Islamic Revolution of 1979, which brought to power a passionately anti-American theocracy that embraced terrorism as a tool of statecraft. Its radicalism inspired anti-Western fanatics in many countries, most notably Afghanistan, where al-Qaeda and other terror groups found homes and bases.

These events serve as a stark warning to the United States and to any country that ever seeks to impose its will on a foreign land. Governments that sponsor coups, revolutions, or armed invasions usually act with the conviction that they will win, and often they do. Their victories, however, can come back to haunt them, sometimes in devastating and tragic ways. This is especially true in today's complex and volatile Middle East, where tradition, history, and religion shape political life in ways that many outsiders do not understand.

The violent anti-Americanism that emerged from Iran after 1979 shocked most people in the United States. Americans had no idea of what might have set off such bitter hatred in a country where they had always imagined themselves more or less well liked. That was because almost no one in the United States knew what the Central Intelligence Agency did there in 1953.

In his time, Mohammad Mossadegh was a titanic figure. He shook an empire and changed the world. People everywhere knew his name. World leaders sought to influence him and later to depose him. No one was surprised when *Time* magazine chose him over Harry Truman, Dwight Eisenhower, and Winston Churchill as its Man of the Year for 1951.

Operation Ajax, as the CIA coup against Mossadegh was codenamed, was a great trauma for Iran, the Middle East, and the colonial world. It was the first time the United States overthrew a foreign government. It set a pattern for years to come and shaped the way millions of people view the United States.

This book tells a story that explains a great deal about the sources of violent currents now surging through the world. More than just a remarkable adventure story, it is a sobering message from the past and an object lesson for the future.

ACKNOWLEDGMENTS

A small but dedicated group of scholars has devoted considerable effort to uncovering the truth about events surrounding the 1953 coup. Most persistent among them is Mark J. Gasiorowski, who has become the group's unofficial dean. Others who have accompanied him on his mission of discovery include Ervand Abrahamian, Fakhreddin Azimi, James A. Bill, Maziar Behroos, Malcolm Byrne, Richard W. Cottam, Farhad Diba, Mostafa Elm, James F. Goode, Mary Ann Heiss, Homa Katouzian, William Roger Louis, and Sepehr Zabih. Their work made this book possible.

The CIA prepared its own internal history of the coup, but it remained secret for many years. In 2000, a copy was leaked to the *New York Times*. It confirmed much of what was known about the coup and added many new details. The reporter who obtained it, James Risen, deserves much credit for his role in bringing it to light.

My research also owes much to the cooperation of librarians and archivists who freely shared their time and expertise. They include those at the public libraries in Chicago and Oak Park, Illinois; the Kent Law Library in Chicago; the Dwight D. Eisenhower Library in Abilene, Kansas, and the Harry S. Truman Library in Independence, Missouri; the National Archives in College Park,

Maryland; and the Public Records Office in Kew Gardens, Surrey, England.

Among those who read early drafts of the manuscript, in whole or in part, and made valuable comments were Janet Afary, David Barboza, Elmira Bayrasli, David Shuman, James M. Stone, and John E. Woods. They bear no responsibility for the final product but have my warm appreciation.

Most of the Iranians who helped me during my research in Iran asked not to be identified by name. They know who they are, and to them I extend deep thanks.

NOTES ON USAGE

There is no universally accepted system for transliterating Persian words into English. As a result, there are many variations in the English spellings of Iranian names and other words. English-language books and articles about Mossadegh, for example, spell his name in almost a dozen different ways.

I have chosen spellings that seem closest to the original pronunciation. For the sake of consistency I have standardized these spellings and changed alternate spellings that occur in quoted documents. I have also omitted diacritical marks that are unfamiliar to English-speaking readers.

At several points I have made minor adjustments in translation and punctuation. These have been made only to clarify meaning and do not in any case represent substantive changes.

The division of Britain's Secret Intelligence Service that conducts operations abroad is called MI6. To avoid confusion, I have referred to it by the former name throughout.

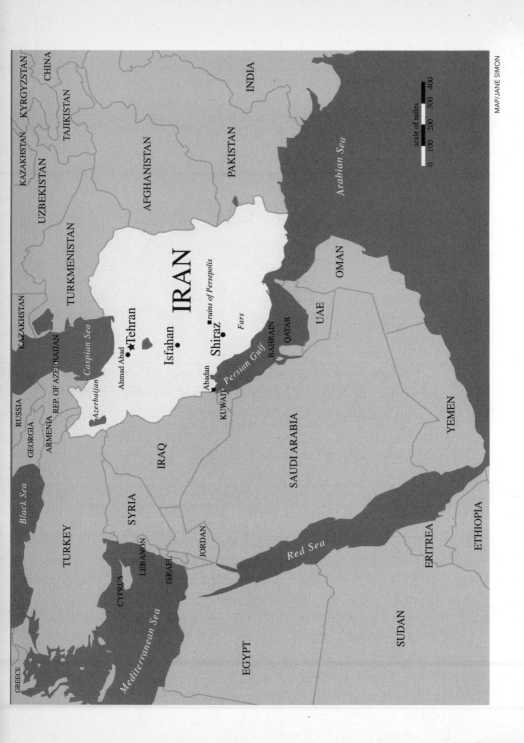

CHAPTER 1

Good Evening, Mr. Roosevelt

Most of Tehran was asleep when an odd caravan set out through the darkness shortly before midnight on August 15, 1953. At its head was an armored car with military markings. Behind came two jeeps and several army trucks full of soldiers. The day had been exceptionally hot, but nightfall brought some relief. A crescent moon shone above. It was a fine night to overthrow a government.

Sitting in the lead car, Colonel Nematollah Nasiri, the commander of the Imperial Guard, had reason to be confident. In his pocket he carried a decree from the Shah of Iran dismissing Prime Minister Mohammad Mossadegh from office. Nasiri was on his way to present this decree to Mossadegh and arrest him if he resisted.

The American and British intelligence agents who plotted this rebellion assumed that Mossadegh would immediately call out the army to suppress it. They had arranged for no one to be on the other end of the phone when he called. Colonel Nasiri was to stop first at the home of the military chief of staff and arrest him, then move on to deliver the fateful decree.

The colonel did as he was told. When he arrived at his first stop, however, he found something most unusual. Despite the late hour, the chief of staff, General Taqi Riahi, was not at home. Neither was anyone else. Not even a servant or a doorkeeper could be found.

This might have alerted Colonel Nasiri that something was amiss, but it did not. He simply climbed back into his armored car and ordered the driver to proceed toward his main objective, Prime Minister Mossadegh's home. With him rode the hopes of two elite intelligence agencies.

Colonel Nasiri would not have been foolhardy enough to attempt such a bold mission on his own. The decree he carried was of dubious legality, since in democratic Iran prime ministers could be installed or removed only with the permission of parliament. But this night's work was the culmination of months of planning by the Central Intelligence Agency and Britain's Secret Intelligence Service. The coup they were staging had been ordered by President Dwight Eisenhower and Prime Minister Winston Churchill.

In 1953 the United States was still new to Iran. Many Iranians thought of Americans as friends, supporters of the fragile democracy they had spent half a century trying to build. It was Britain, not the United States, that they demonized as the colonialist oppressor that exploited them.

Since the early years of the twentieth century a British company, owned mainly by the British government, had enjoyed a fantastically lucrative monopoly on the production and sale of Iranian oil. The wealth that flowed from beneath Iran's soil played a decisive role in maintaining Britain at the pinnacle of world power while most Iranians lived in poverty. Iranians chafed bitterly under this injustice. Finally, in 1951, they turned to Mossadegh, who more than any other political leader personified their anger at the Anglo-Iranian Oil Company (AIOC). He pledged to throw the company out of Iran, reclaim the country's vast petroleum reserves, and free Iran from subjection to foreign power.

Prime Minister Mossadegh carried out his pledges with single-minded zeal. To the ecstatic cheers of his people, he nationalized Anglo-Iranian, the most profitable British business in the world. Soon afterward, Iranians took control of the company's giant refinery at Abadan on the Persian Gulf.

That sent Iran into patriotic ecstasy and made Mossadegh a national hero. It also outraged the British, who indignantly accused Mossadegh of stealing their property. They first demanded that the

World Court and the United Nations punish him, then sent warships to the Persian Gulf, and finally imposed a crushing embargo that devastated Iran's economy. Despite this campaign, many Iranians were thrilled with Mossadegh's boldness. So were anticolonial leaders across Asia and Africa.

Mossadegh was utterly unmoved by Britain's campaign against him. One European newspaper reported that Mossadegh "would rather be fried in Persian oil than make the slightest concession to the British." For a time the British considered launching an armed invasion to retake the oil fields and refinery, but they dropped the idea after President Harry Truman refused his support. Only two options remained: leave Mossadegh in power or organize a coup to depose him. Prime Minister Churchill, a proud product of the imperial tradition, had no trouble deciding for the coup.

British agents began conspiring to overthrow Mossadegh soon after he nationalized the oil company. They were too eager and aggressive for their own good. Mossadegh learned of their plotting, and in October 1952 he ordered the British embassy shut. All British diplomats in Iran, including clandestine agents working under diplomatic cover, had to leave the country. No one was left to stage the coup.

Immediately, the British asked President Truman for help. Truman, however, sympathized viscerally with nationalist movements like the one Mossadegh led. He had nothing but contempt for old-style imperialists like those who ran Anglo-Iranian. Besides, the CIA had never overthrown a government, and Truman did not wish to set the precedent.

The American attitude toward a possible coup in Iran changed radically after Dwight Eisenhower was elected president in November 1952. Within days of the election, a senior agent of the Secret Intelligence Service, Christopher Montague Woodhouse, came to Washington for meetings with top CIA and State Department officials. Woodhouse shrewdly decided not to make the traditional British argument, which was that Mossadegh must go because he had nationalized British property. That argument did not arouse much passion in Washington. Woodhouse knew what would.

"Not wishing to be accused of trying to use the Americans to pull British chestnuts out of the fire," he wrote later, "I decided to emphasize the Communist threat to Iran rather than the need to recover control of the oil industry."

This appeal was calculated to stir the two brothers who would direct American foreign policy after Eisenhower's inauguration. John Foster Dulles, the incoming secretary of state, and Allen Dulles, the incoming CIA director, were among the fiercest of Cold Warriors. They viewed the world as an ideological battleground and saw every local conflict through the prism of the great East-West confrontation. In their eyes, any country not decisively allied with the United States was a potential enemy. They considered Iran especially dangerous.

Iran had immense oil wealth, a long border with the Soviet Union, an active Communist party, and a nationalist prime minister. The Dulles brothers believed there was a serious danger that it would soon fall to communism. The prospect of such a "second China" terrified them. When the British presented their proposal to overthrow Mossadegh and replace him with a reliably pro-Western prime minister, they were immediately interested.

Soon after President Eisenhower took office on January 20, 1953, John Foster Dulles and Allen Dulles told their British counterparts that they were ready to move against Mossadegh. Their coup would be code-named Operation Ajax, or, in CIA jargon, TPAJAX. To direct it, they chose a CIA officer with considerable experience in the Middle East, Kermit Roosevelt, a grandson of President Theodore Roosevelt.

Like other members of his famous family, Kermit Roosevelt had a penchant for direct action and was known to be decisive in times of crisis. He was thirty-seven years old, chief of the CIA's Near East and Asia Division, and an acknowledged master of his clandestine trade. The Soviet agent Kim Philby described him as the quintessential quiet American, "a courteous, soft-spoken Easterner with impeccable social connections, well-educated rather than intellectual, pleasant and unassuming as host and guest. An especially nice wife. In fact, the last person you would expect to be up to the neck in dirty tricks."

CIA agents in those days shared a profound idealism, a conviction that they were doing the vital dirty work of freedom. Many combined the best qualities of the thinker and the adventurer. None epitomized that combination more fully than did Kermit Roosevelt.

At the beginning of July, ignoring a CIA doctor's order that he first submit to urgent kidney surgery, he flew off on his secret mission. He landed in Beirut and from there set out by car across the deserts of Syria and Iraq. As he entered Iran at a remote crossing, he could barely contain his excitement:

> I remembered what my father wrote of his arrival in Africa with *his* father, T. R., in 1909 on the *African Game Trails* trip. "It was a great adventure, and all the world was young!" I felt as he must have felt then. My nerves tingled, my spirits soared as we moved up the mountain road. . . . As it turned out, on July 19, 1953, we encountered an unusually listless, stupid and semi-literate immigration/customs fellow at Khanequin. In those days US passports carried, as they do not now, some brief description of any notable features of the holder. With encouragement and help from me, the guard laboriously transcribed my name as "Mr. Scar on Right Forehead." This I found a good omen.

Roosevelt spent his first two weeks in Tehran conducting business from a villa rented by one of his American agents. Decades of British intrigue in Iran, coupled with more recent work by the CIA, gave him excellent assets on the ground. Among them were a handful of experienced and highly resourceful Iranian operatives who had spent years assembling a clandestine network of sympathetic politicians, military officers, clergymen, newspaper editors, and street gang leaders. The CIA was paying these operatives tens of thousands of dollars per month, and they earned every cent. During the spring and summer of 1953, not a day passed without at least one CIA-subsidized mullah, news commentator, or politician denouncing Prime Minister Mossadegh. The prime minister, who had great respect for the sanctity of free press, refused to suppress this campaign.

Iranian agents who came in and out of Roosevelt's villa knew him only by his pseudonym, James Lockridge. As time passed, they naturally developed a sense of comradeship, and some of the Iranians, much to Roosevelt's amusement, began calling him "Jim." The only times he came close to blowing his cover were during tennis games that he played regularly at the Turkish embassy and on the campus of the French Institute. When he missed a shot, he would curse himself, shouting, "Oh, *Roosevelt!*" Several times he was asked why someone named Lockridge would have developed such a habit. He replied that he was a passionate Republican and considered Franklin D. Roosevelt to have been so evil that he used Roosevelt's name as a curse.

The plan for Operation Ajax envisioned an intense psychological campaign against Prime Minister Mossadegh, which the CIA had already launched, followed by an announcement that the Shah had dismissed him from office. Mobs and military units whose leaders were on the CIA payroll would crush any attempt by Mossadegh to resist. Then it would be announced that the Shah had chosen General Fazlollah Zahedi, a retired military officer who had received more than $100,000 from the CIA, as Iran's new prime minister.

By the beginning of August, Tehran was afire. Mobs working for the CIA staged anti-Mossadegh protests, marching through the streets carrying portraits of the Shah and chanting royalist slogans. Foreign agents bribed members of parliament and anyone else who might be helpful in the forthcoming coup attempt.

Press attacks on Mossadegh reached new levels of virulence. Articles accused him not just of communist leanings and designs on the throne, but also of Jewish parentage and even secret sympathy for the British. Although Mossadegh did not know it, most of these tirades were either inspired by the CIA or written by CIA propagandists in Washington. One of the propagandists, Richard Cottam, estimated that four-fifths of the newspapers in Tehran were under CIA influence.

"Any article that I would write—it gave you something of a sense of power—would appear almost instantly, the next day, in the Iranian press," Cottam recalled years later. "They were designed to show Mossadegh as a Communist collaborator and as a fanatic."

As the plot gathered momentum, Roosevelt faced his most serious obstacle, Mohammad Reza Shah. The thirty-two-year-old monarch, only the second shah in the Pahlavi line, was timid and indecisive by nature, and he doggedly refused to be drawn into such an audacious plot. "He hates taking decisions and cannot be relied on to stick to them when taken," one British diplomat reported. "He has no moral courage and succumbs easily to fear."

More than personality traits held the Shah back. Mossadegh had been the most popular figure in modern Iranian history, and although Britain's campaign of subversion and economic sabotage had weakened him, he was still widely admired and beloved. It was not even clear that the Shah had the legal authority to remove him. The plot could easily backfire and endanger not only the Shah's life but the monarchy itself.

None of this daunted Roosevelt. To carry out his coup, he needed signed decrees from the Shah dismissing Mossadegh and naming General Zahedi in his place. Roosevelt never doubted that he would ultimately obtain them. His battle of wits with the Shah was unequal from the start. Roosevelt was clever and well trained, and behind him lay immense international power. The Shah was weak, immature, and alone.

Roosevelt's first gambit was to send emissaries who might have special influence over the Shah. First he arranged for the Shah's twin sister, Princess Ashraf, who was as sharp and combative as the Shah was dull, to visit her brother and try to stiffen his backbone. Ashraf's tongue-lashings of her brother were legendary, including one in the presence of foreign diplomats when she demanded that he prove he was a man or else be revealed to all as a mouse. She detested Mossadegh because he was an enemy of royal power. Her attacks on his government became so bitter that the Shah had felt it best to send her out of the country. From her golden exile in Europe, she watched events in her homeland with undiminished passion.

Ashraf was enjoying life in French casinos and nightclubs when one of Roosevelt's best Iranian agents, Asadollah Rashidian, paid her a call. He found her reluctant, so the next day a delegation of American and British agents came to pose the invitation in stronger terms. The leader of the delegation, a senior British operative named Norman Darbyshire, had the foresight to bring a mink coat and a packet of cash. When Ashraf saw these emoluments, Darbyshire later recalled, "her eyes lit up" and her resistance crumbled. She agreed to fly to Tehran and landed without incident under her married name, Madame Chafik. At first her brother refused to receive her, but after being not so subtly urged to change his mind by associates who were in touch with the CIA, he relented. Brother and sister met late on the evening of July 29. Their meeting was tense. She failed to persuade him to issue the crucial decrees, and to make matters worse, news of her presence leaked out and set off a storm of protest. To everyone's relief, she quickly returned to Europe.

Next Roosevelt turned to General H. Norman Schwarzkopf, who had spent most of the 1940s in Iran leading an elite military regiment and to whom the Shah felt deeply indebted. The CIA gave Schwarzkopf a "cover mission" of meetings and inspections in Lebanon, Pakistan, and Egypt so that his visit to Iran could be explained as a simple stopover. According to one account, he arrived there carrying "a couple of large bags" into which were stuffed several million dollars in cash. He met first with Roosevelt and then with Iranian principals in the operation, to whom he distributed much money. On the first day of August he called on the Shah at Saad Abad Palace.

It was a bizarre encounter. At first the Shah refused to say a word to his guest, indicating with gestures that he suspected hidden microphones. Then he led Schwarzkopf into a large ballroom, pulled a table into the center of the room, sat down on top of it, and invited the general to join him. There he whispered that he had still not decided whether to sign the decrees Roosevelt wanted. He doubted that the army would obey any order he signed, and he did not want to be on the losing side in such a risky operation.

Even as Schwarzkopf listened, he sensed the Shah's resistance weakening. One more visitor might be enough to bring the desired result, but it would have to be Roosevelt himself. This was a dangerous proposition. If Roosevelt was seen at the palace, news of his presence in Iran might leak out and compromise the entire operation. Schwarzkopf, however, told him there was no alternative.

Roosevelt expected this advice. "I had been sure from the beginning that a personal meeting would be necessary," he wrote afterward. "Securely and alone, the Shah and I could resolve the many difficult problems confronting us. This could only be done on a person-to-person basis. In all likelihood we would have to meet not once but several times. So the sooner we got to it, the better."

To prepare the way for his visit, Roosevelt sent his trusted agent Assadollah Rashidian to see the Shah on August 2. Rashidian's message was simple: the British and the Americans were planning a coup and would not be deterred. Under these circumstances,

Rashidian observed tartly, the Shah had little choice but to cooperate. The Shah nodded in silent agreement.

Only Roosevelt, however, could close the deal. He asked an agent in the royal court who was known by the code name Rosenkrantz to approach the Shah and say that "an American authorized to speak for Eisenhower *and* Churchill desired a secret audience." In a matter of hours the overture was made, and the Shah accepted it. He would send a car to Roosevelt's villa that night at midnight.

"Two hours to wait!" Roosevelt thought to himself after receiving the message. "I considered my costume. If not appropriate for a royal audience, it did seem good for these rather peculiar circumstances. I had on a dark turtleneck shirt, Oxford-gray slacks, and a pair of black-topped *givehs,* rope-soled cloth-covered Persian footwear somewhere between shoes and bedroom slippers. Not exactly smart but suitably unobtrusive."

Roosevelt, who had interviewed the Shah six years earlier while researching a book called *Arabs, Oil and History* and had met him again during subsequent visits to Iran, waited for the appointed hour with a handful of his agents. He thought it best not to drink, though his comrades had no such scruples. When midnight finally came, he walked through the front gate and out onto the street. A car was waiting. He climbed into the back seat.

Nothing stirred on the streets as Roosevelt was driven toward the stately palace. As his car began to climb the hill on which the palace sits, he decided that he should duck out of sight. His hosts had thoughtfully left a folded blanket on the car seat, and he put it to good use, lying down on the floor and pulling it over him.

There was no trouble at the sentry's gate, just a perfunctory wave. The car continued on for a few moments and then pulled to a stop well short of the palace's broad limestone steps. Roosevelt pulled off his blanket and sat up. A slim figure was walking down the steps toward him. The man, whom he recognized immediately as the Shah, approached his car, opened the door, and slid in beside him. Discreetly, the driver withdrew into the shadows.

"Good evening, Mr. Roosevelt," the monarch said, extending his hand. "I cannot say that I expected to see you, but this is a pleasure."

Roosevelt told the Shah that he was in Iran on behalf of the American and British secret services, and that this would be confirmed by a code word the Shah would be able to hear on the BBC the next night. Churchill had arranged that the BBC would end its broadcast day by saying not "It is now midnight," as usual, but "It is now *exactly* midnight." Such assurances were hardly necessary, the Shah replied. The two men understood each other.

Still, however, the Shah was hesitant to join the plot. He was no adventurer, he told Roosevelt, and could not take the chances of one. Roosevelt's tone sharpened. He told the Shah that leaving Mossadegh in power would "lead only to a Communist Iran or to a second Korea," which Western leaders were not prepared to accept. To avoid it, they had approved a plot to overthrow Mossadegh— and, incidentally, to increase the power of the Shah. He must embrace it within a few days; if he refused, Roosevelt would leave the country and devise "some other plan."

The Shah made no direct reply. Let them meet again the following night, he suggested. Then he turned to open the car door. Before stepping out into the darkness, he looked back at Roosevelt and said, "I am glad to welcome you once again to my country."

From then on, Roosevelt met with the Shah almost every midnight, entering the palace compound under the same blanket in the back seat of the same car. Before and after each session, he conferred with his Iranian operatives. When local police became suspicious of the villa he was using, he stopped conducting business there and devised another way to hold his conferences. He obtained a Tehran taxi, and at appointed times he would drive it to a quiet corner, always with the "On Call" sign showing. There he would park and begin walking until one or another of his agents, usually hyperactive and pumped on the adrenaline of the operation, picked him up in a Chrysler or a Buick. They planned their day-to-day tactics while careening through the hilly outskirts of town.

In his conversations with the Shah, Roosevelt said he had at his disposal "the equivalent of about $1 million" and several "extremely competent, professional organizers" who could "distribute pamphlets, organize mobs, keep track of the opposition—you name it, they'll do it." He described Operation Ajax as based on "four lines of attack." First, a campaign in mosques, the press, and the streets would undermine Mossadegh's popularity. Second, royalist military officers would deliver the decree dismissing him. Third, mobs would take control of the streets. Fourth, General Zahedi would emerge triumphantly and accept the Shah's nomination as prime minister.

It was an appealing but not entirely convincing plan, and the Shah continued to agonize. His mood turned to what Roosevelt called "stubborn irresolution." But it was "hopeless to proceed without the Shah," Roosevelt cabled to his CIA superiors, so he continued turning up the pressure. Finally, inevitably, the Shah's resistance broke. He agreed to sign the *firmans,* as the royal decrees were called, but only on condition that he be allowed to leave Tehran for some safer place immediately afterward.

Mohammad Reza Shah had never been known as a courageous man, so this latest show of prudence did not surprise Roosevelt. The two men decided that the safest place for the Shah to hide was a hunting lodge that the royal family maintained near Ramsar on the Caspian coast. There was an airstrip nearby, which the Shah found reassuring.

"If by any horrible chance things go wrong," he indelicately told Roosevelt, "the Empress and I will take our plane straight to Baghdad."

The two men met for the last time in the predawn of August 9. Before bidding the Shah farewell, Roosevelt felt it correct to thank him for his decision to cooperate, reluctant though it had been. This was a historic moment, and something beyond the ordinary was appropriate. Roosevelt came up with a wonderful way to embellish his message.

"Your Majesty, I received earlier this evening a cable from Washington," he prevaricated. "President Eisenhower had asked that I convey to you this word: 'I wish Your Imperial Majesty godspeed. If the Pahlavis and the Roosevelts working together cannot solve this little problem, then there is no hope anywhere. I have complete faith that you will get this done.'"

It was agreed that a CIA courier would bring the vital *firmans* to the palace early the next morning. The Shah would sign them and then fly immediately to his refuge at Ramsar. All seemed perfectly arranged.

When Roosevelt returned to his villa with the good news, he and his agents celebrated with an exuberant drinking binge. He finally made it to bed at five o'clock. A few hours later he was awakened by the cursing of an aide. There had been a last-minute failure. The courier who was to obtain the Shah's signature had turned up late at the palace. When he arrived, the royal couple was gone.

Whether this was a simple missed connection or a last-minute attempt by the Shah to run from signing the *firmans,* Roosevelt was determined that it not be allowed to upset his plan. These *firmans* played an indispensable role in the coup he had designed. They provided not just a fig leaf of legality but the operation's central organizing principle. If the Shah was not in Tehran to sign them, they would have to be brought to wherever he was.

The man best equipped to help at this moment, Roosevelt quickly realized, was Colonel Nasiri of the Imperial Guard. He was a strong royalist, could find and fly a plane, and was on intimate terms with the Shah. The arrangements were quickly made, and this time the connection worked. Nasiri flew to Ramsar, obtained the Shah's scribbled signature on both *firmans,* and then, because bad weather prevented him from taking off, sent them to Tehran by car.

Roosevelt and his comrades spent the day waiting impatiently around their pool, with no idea of what was taking Nasiri so long. When night fell, they took to smoking, playing cards, and drinking vodka with lime. Tehran was under a nine o'clock curfew, but after that hour passed, they still hoped someone would turn up. It was almost midnight when they heard shouts at the gate. They ran to open it. Outside was a small throng of unshaven and very excited Iranians, most of whom they did not recognize. They pushed a packet to Roosevelt, who opened it gingerly. Inside were the two *firmans,* duly signed by His Imperial Majesty.

After jubilantly embracing his new friends, Roosevelt considered how quickly he could now move. He was much dismayed when his agents told him there would have to be one more delay. The weekend, which Iranians observe on Thursday and Friday, was about to begin, and Iranians do not like to conduct business, much less overthrow governments, on weekends. Roosevelt reluctantly agreed to postpone the coup until Saturday night, August 15.

Confident of their plan but acutely aware that each passing hour increased the chance of betrayal, Roosevelt and his comrades spent three excruciating days at poolside. Saturday was the hardest to bear because the moment of truth was so near. Roosevelt later wrote that on that day, time moved "more slowly than anything we had ever before lived through."

By now Roosevelt had moved his command post to a basement

in the American embassy compound. His Iranian agents visited him less frequently, but they were busier than ever at their subversive work, as a CIA report on the coup makes clear:

> At this same time the psychological campaign against Mossadegh was reaching its climax. The controllable press was going all out against Mossadegh, while [DELETED] under station direction was printing material which the station considered to be helpful. CIA agents gave serious attention to alarming the religious leaders at Tehran by issuing black propaganda in the name of the [Communist] Tudeh party, threatening these leaders with savage punishment if they opposed Mossadegh. Threatening phone calls were also made to them, in the name of the Tudeh, and one of several sham bombings of the houses of these leaders was carried out.
>
> The word that the Shah would support direct action in his behalf spread rapidly through the "colonel's conspiracy" fostered by the station. Zahedi saw station principal agent, Colonel [DELETED], and named him as liaison officer with the Americans and as his choice to supervise the staff planning for the action. . . .
>
> On 14 August the station cabled that upon the conclusion of TPAJAX the Zahedi government, in view of the empty treasury of the country, would be in urgent need of funds. The sum of $5,000,000 was suggested, and CIA was asked to produce this sum almost within hours after the conclusion of the operation.

Now, in the words of that CIA report, "there was nothing that either the station or Headquarters could do except wait for action to begin." When dusk finally began falling over Tehran on August 15, Roosevelt climbed into his Hillman-Minx taxi, flipped down the "On Call" sign, and drove to a nearby safe house where his agents had gathered to await the news of victory. As vodka flowed, they sang along with records of Broadway show tunes. Their favorite was "Luck Be a Lady Tonight" from the musical *Guys and Dolls*. By acclamation, they adopted it as the official Operation Ajax theme song:

> They call you lady luck, but there is room for doubt;
> At times you have a very un-ladylike way of running out.
> You're on this date with me, the pickings have been lush,
> And yet before the evening is over you might give me the brush.

You might forget your manners, you might refuse to stay
And so the best that I can do is pray:
Luck, be a lady tonight.

As Roosevelt drove back to the American embassy later that evening, his route took him past the residence of General Riahi, the military chief of staff. He enjoyed the coincidence. If his plan worked, General Riahi would be behind bars in a few hours.

The officer Roosevelt had chosen to arrest the chief of staff and the prime minister that night, Colonel Nasiri, seemed ideal for the operation. He believed in the primacy of royal power and loathed Mossadegh. His command of the seven-hundred-man Imperial Guard gave him control of considerable resources. By successfully obtaining the vital *firmans* at a crucial moment, he seemed to have proven his reliability.

On the night of August 15, however, Nasiri was not thinking clearly enough. It was well after eleven o'clock when he arrived at General Riahi's home and found it abandoned. He was untroubled and simply ordered his men to proceed toward Mossadegh's residence. Unbeknownst to him, another military column was also on its way there. General Riahi had learned of the coup and sent troops to foil it.

The precise identity of the informant has never been established. Most guesses center on a military officer who belonged to a secret communist cell. There may have been more than one informant. In the end, what happened was precisely what Roosevelt feared. Too many people knew about the plot for too long. A leak was all but inevitable.

In the confusing hours around midnight, Tehran was bursting with plots and counterplots. Some rebellious officers learned of the betrayal in time to abort their missions. Others, not realizing that they were compromised, went ahead. One seized the telephone office at the bazaar. Another roused Foreign Minister Hussein Fatemi from bed and dragged him away barefoot and shouting.

The future of constitutional rule in Iran depended on which column of soldiers reached Mossadegh's house first. Shortly before one o'clock in the morning, the rebel column drove up Kakh Street, passed the corner of Heshmatdowleh, and stopped. Here Mossadegh lived with his wife in a small apartment, part of a larger complex that his family had owned for many years. The gate was closed. Colonel Nasiri stepped out to demand entry. In his hand he held the *firman* dismissing Mossadegh from office. Behind him stood several files of soldiers.

Colonel Nasiri had arrived too late. Moments after he appeared at the gate, several loyal commanders stepped from the shadows. They escorted him into a jeep and drove him to general staff headquarters. There General Riahi denounced him as a traitor, ordered him stripped of his uniform, and sent him to a cell. The man who was to have arrested Mossadegh was now himself a prisoner.

Roosevelt, who had no way of knowing that any of this was happening, was at his embassy command post, waiting for Colonel Nasiri to call. Tanks clattered by several times, but the telephone never rang. Roosevelt's apprehensions deepened as dawn broke. Radio Tehran did not begin its transmissions at six o'clock as normal. Then, an hour later, it crackled to life with a burst of military music, followed by the reading of an official communiqué. Roosevelt did not speak Persian but feared the worst when he heard the announcer use the word *Mossadegh*. Then Mossadegh himself came on the air, announcing victory over a coup attempt organized by the Shah and "foreign elements."

The Shah, cowering at his seaside villa, was also listening. As soon as he grasped what had happened, he roused his wife and told her it was time to run. They quickly packed two small briefcases, grabbed what clothes they could carry in their arms, and walked briskly out toward their twin-engine Beechcraft. The Shah, a trained pilot, took the controls and set a course for Baghdad. After arriving there, he told the American ambassador that he "would be looking for work shortly as he has a large family and very small means outside of Iran."

While the Shah was fleeing, military units loyal to the government were fanning out through Tehran. City life quickly returned to normal. Several conspirators were arrested and others went into hiding. A reward was offered for the capture of General Zahedi. CIA operatives made mad dashes back to the security of the American embassy or safe houses. Jubilant crowds took to the streets chanting, "Victory to the Nation!" and "Mossadegh Has Won!"

Inside his embassy compound, Roosevelt felt himself "close to despair." He had no choice but to send a cable to Washington saying that things had gone terribly wrong. John Waller, the head of the CIA's Iran desk, read it with great disappointment. Waller feared for the lives of his agents, and he sent Roosevelt an urgent reply. No copy of it is known to exist. According to CIA lore, it was an order that Roosevelt leave Iran immediately. Many years later, though, Waller said that it was not so categorical. Its message, he recalled, was: "If you're in a jam, get out so you don't get killed. But if you're not in a jam, go ahead and do what you have to do."

Things looked bleak for the plotters. They had lost the advantage of surprise. Several of their key agents were out of action. Their anointed prime minister, General Zahedi, was in hiding. The Shah had fled. Foreign Minister Fatemi, free after several hours in rebel custody, was making fiery speeches denouncing the Shah for his collaboration with foreign agents.

"O Traitor!" Fatemi railed before one crowd. "The moment you heard by Tehran Radio that your foreign plot had been defeated, you fled to the nearest country where Britain has an embassy!"

Operation Ajax had failed. Radio Tehran reported that the situation was "well under control," and so it seemed. Shock waves reverberated through CIA headquarters in Washington.

Then suddenly, around midevening, Roosevelt cabled a most unexpected message. He had decided to stay in Tehran and improvise another stab at Mossadegh. The CIA had sent him to overthrow the government of Iran, and he was determined not to leave until he had done it.

CHAPTER 2

Curse This Fate

Rising dramatically from the desert of southern Iran, with distant mountains adding to the majesty of the scene, the spectacular ruins of Persepolis testify to the grandeur that was Persia. This was the ceremonial and spiritual capital of a vast empire, built by Cyrus, Darius, and Xerxes, titans whose names still echo through history. Giant statues of winged bulls guard the Gate of All Nations, through which princes from vassal states passed once each year to pay homage to their Persian masters. The great Apadana, or Hall of Audience, where these princes knelt together before their dead sovereign, was the length of three football fields. Its roof was supported by thirty-six towering columns, some of which still stand. Two monumental staircases leading up to the hall are decorated with intricately detailed carvings depicting the annual ritual of obedience, which was held on the day of the vernal equinox. Today they offer a vivid picture of how completely Persian emperors once dominated the richest lands on earth.

The carvings show rulers of subject states filing past their supreme leader, each bearing gifts symbolizing the wealth of his province. Archaeologists have managed to identify most of them, and the very names of their cultures evoke the richness of antiquity.

The warlike Elamites, who lived east of the Tigris River, bring a lion to symbolize their ferocity. Arachosians from Central Asia offer camels and rich furs, Armenians a horse and a delicately crafted vase, Ethiopians a giraffe and an elephant's tusk, Somalis an antelope and a chariot, Thracians shields and spears, and Ionians bolts of cloth and ceramic plates. Arabs lead a camel, Assyrians a bull, Indians a donkey laden with woven baskets. All these tributes were laid before the King of Kings, a monarch whose reign spread Persian power to the edges of the known world.

Many countries in the Middle East are artificial creations. European colonialists drew their national borders in the nineteenth or twentieth century, often with little regard for local history and tradition, and their leaders have had to concoct outlandish myths in order to give citizens a sense of nationhood. Just the opposite is true of Iran. This is one of the world's oldest nations, heir to a tradition that reaches back thousands of years, to periods when great conquerors extended their rule across continents, poets and artists created works of exquisite beauty, and one of the world's most extraordinary religious traditions took root and flowered. Even in modern times, which have been marked by long periods of anarchy, repression, and suffering, Iranians are passionately inspired by their heritage.

Great themes run through Iranian history and shape it to this day. One is the continuing and often frustrating effort to find a synthesis between Islam, which was imposed on the country by Arab conquerors, and the rich heritage of pre-Islamic times. Another, fueled by the Shiite Muslim tradition to which most Iranians now belong, is the thirst for just leadership, of which they have enjoyed precious little. A third, also sharpened by Shiite beliefs, is a tragic view of life rooted in a sense of martyrdom and communal pain. Finally, Iran has since time immemorial been a target of foreign invaders, victim of a geography that places it astride some of the world's most important trading routes and atop an ocean of oil, and it has struggled to find a way to live with powerful outsiders. All these strains combined in the middle of the twentieth century to produce and then destroy the towering figure of Mohammad Mossadegh.

Migrants from Central Asia and the Indian subcontinent began arriving in what is now Iran nearly four thousand years ago, pushed out by a combination of resource depletion and marauding tribes from the north and east. Among them were the Aryans, from whose name the word *Iran* is taken. The emperor who united these migrant bands for the first time was Cyrus, one of history's most gifted visionaries and the figure who first conceived the idea of an empire based in the region known as Pars (later Fars).

After rising to power in 559 B.C., Cyrus launched a brilliant campaign that brought other leaders on the vast Iranian plateau under his sway. Some he conquered, but many he won to his side by persuasion and compromise. Today he is remembered for his conquests but also for the relative gentleness with which he treated his subjects. He understood that this was an even surer way to build a durable empire than the more common means of oppression, terror, and slaughter.

In 547 Cyrus marched into Asia Minor and captured the majestic Lydian capital of Sardis. Seven years later he subdued the other great regional power, Babylon. Over the decades that followed, he and his successors went on to more great victories, including one by Xerxes in which Macedon, Thermopylae, and Athens were taken by an army of 180,000 men, by far the largest seen in Europe up to that time. This dynasty, known as the Achaemenians, built the greatest empire of its era. By 500 B.C. it embraced the eastern Mediterranean from Greece through modern-day Turkey, Lebanon, Israel, Egypt, and Libya and stretched eastward across the Caucasus to the banks of the Indus. Cyrus called it Persia because it sprang from his own base in Pars.

The tolerant and all-embracing approach to life and politics for which Achaemenian emperors were known sprang in part from their connection to the Zoroastrian faith, which holds that the sacred responsibility of every human being is to work toward establishing social justice on earth. Zoroastrians believe that humanity is locked in an eternal struggle between good and evil. Theirs is said to have been the first revealed religion to preach that people must face judgment after death, and that each soul will spend eternity in either paradise or perdition. According to its precepts, God makes his judgment according to how virtuous one has been in life, measured by one's thoughts, words, and deeds. The prophet Zoroaster, later known to Europeans as Zarathustra, lived sometime between the tenth and seventh centuries B.C. in what is now northeastern

Iran, and preached this creed after a series of divine visions. Zoroastrianism has had a profound effect on Persian history not simply because Cyrus used it in his audaciously successful campaign of empire-building, but because it has captured the hearts of so many believers over the course of so many centuries.

The Zoroastrian religion taught Iranians that citizens have an inalienable right to enlightened leadership and that the duty of subjects is not simply to obey wise kings but also to rise up against those who are wicked. Leaders are seen as representatives of God on earth, but they deserve allegiance only as long as they have *farr,* a kind of divine blessing that they must earn by moral behavior. To pray for it, generations of Persian leaders visited Zoroastrian temples where holy flames burned perpetually, symbolizing the importance of constant vigilance against iniquity.

Cyrus and the other kings of his line bound their vast empire together with roads, bridges, uniform coinage, an efficient system of taxation, and the world's first long-range postal service. But eventually and inevitably, the tide of history turned against them. Their empire began to shake after Darius, Persia's last great leader, lost the decisive Battle of Marathon in 490 B.C. The death blow came from no less a conqueror than Alexander, who marched into Persia in 334 B.C. and, in a rampage of destruction, sacked and burned Persepolis.

For the next ten centuries, through periods of rule by three dynasties, Persians nurtured and deepened their strong feelings of pride and nobility. They flourished by assimilating influences from the lands around them, especially Greece, Egypt, and India, reshaping them to fit within the framework of their Zoroastrian faith. In the third century A.D. they began returning to the peak of world power on a scale that recalled the glory of the early emperors, capturing Antioch, Jerusalem, and Alexandria and pushing to the walls of Constantinople. Persian armies suffered a reverse at the hands of Byzantines in 626, but the great defeat was yet to come. A few years later, an army arose on the barren Arabian peninsula and turned toward Persia. These Arabs came armed not only with the traditional weapons of war, but with a new religion, Islam.

The invasion by the Arabs, who to the cultivated Persians seemed no more than barbarians, was a decisive turning point in the nation's history. Persia's fate paralleled that of many empires. Its army had been worn down by long campaigns, its leaders had slipped from what Zoroastrian priests would call the realm of light into that of darkness, and the priests themselves had become divorced from the masses. People fell into poverty as the greedy court imposed ever-increasing taxes. Tyranny tore apart the social contract between ruler and ruled that Zoroastrian doctrine holds to be the basis of organized life. By both political and religious standards, the last of the pre-Islamic dynasties in Persia, the Sassanians, lost the right to rule. The merciless logic of history dictated that it be overrun by an ascendant people fired by passionate belief in its leaders, its cause, and its faith.

Sassanian power was centered in Ctesiphon, the luxurious capital of Mesopotamia. This was not a city of stately columns like Persepolis but one bathed in excess. Its royal palace housed fabulous collections of jewels and was guarded by statuary of solid gold and silver. The centerpiece was the king's cavernous audience hall, which featured a ninety-foot-square silk carpet depicting a flowering garden and, metaphorically, the empire's wealth and power. Rubies, pearls, and diamonds were sewn into it with golden threads. When Arab conquerors reached Ctesiphon in 638, they looted the palace and sent the magnificent carpet to Mecca, where Muslim leaders ordered it cut to pieces to show their contempt for worldly wealth. They destroyed countless treasures, including the entire royal library. In an account of this conquest written by the tenth-century Persian poet Ferdowsi, a general laments: "Curse this world, curse this time, curse this fate / That uncivilized Arabs have come to force me to be Muslim."

Later in the same epic, the *Shahnameh*, which is four times as long as the *Iliad* and took thirty-five years to compose, Ferdowsi portrays the losing Persian commander, Rustam, lamenting the misfortune he sees ahead:

O Iran! Where are all those kings, who adorned you
With justice, equity and munificence, who decorated
You with pomp and splendor, gone?
From that date when the barbarian, savage, coarse
Bedouin Arabs sold your king's daughter in the street
And cattle market, you have not seen a bright day, and
Have lain hid in darkness.

By the time of the Arab conquest, Persians already had long experience in assimilating foreign cultures, and whenever they did so, they shaped those cultures to their liking or took certain parts while resisting others. So it was when they were forced to adopt Islam. They had no choice but to accept Mohammad as God's prophet and the Koran as God's word, but over a period of centuries they fashioned an interpretation of Islam quite different from that of their Arab conquerors. This interpretation, called Shiism, is based on a particular reading of Islamic history, and it has the ingenious effect of using Islam to reinforce long-standing Iranian beliefs.

About 90 percent of the one billion Muslims in the world today identify with the Sunni tradition. Of the remainder, most are Shiites, the largest number of whom are in Iran. The split between these two groups springs from differing interpretations of who deserved to succeed the prophet Mohammad as caliph, or leader of the Islamic world, after his death in 632. Shiites believe that his legitimate successor was Ali, a cousin whom he raised from childhood and who married one of his daughters. Ali was one of those to whom Mohammad dictated his revelations, which became known as the Koran, and he once slept in Mohammad's bed as a decoy to foil a murder plot. But another man was chosen as caliph, and soon Ali found himself in the position of a dissident. He criticized the religious establishment for seeking worldly power and diluting the purity of its spiritual inheritance. Economic discontent brought many to his side, and ultimately the conflict turned violent.

Ali was passed over twice more when caliphs died, and he devoted himself to preaching a doctrine of piety and social justice that won him many followers, especially among the lower classes. He finally won the supreme post in 656, but the conflict only intensified, and less than five years later he was assassinated while praying inside the mosque at Kufa, a Mesopotamian garrison town that was a cauldron of religious conflict. According to tradition, he knew he was to be murdered that day but refused to flee because "one cannot stop death." After being stabbed, he cried out, "O God, most fortunate am I!"

The mantle of resistance passed to Ali's son, Hussein, who was himself killed while leading seventy-two followers against an army of thousands in a suicidal revolt at Karbala in 680. Determined to suppress Hussein's legacy, the authorities ordered most of his family slain afterward. His body was trampled in the mud and his severed head taken to Damascus, where Shiites believe that it continued to chant the Koran even as the caliph beat it with a stick. Retelling these stories and others about Hussein, "the lord among martyrs," is what provokes the paroxysm of passion that spreads through Qom and other sacred Iranian cities every year on the anniversary of his death.

Hussein's embrace of death in a sacred cause has shaped the collective psyche of Iranians. To visit Qom during the mourning that commemorates his martyrdom is to be caught up in a wave of emotion so intense that it is hard for an outsider to comprehend. Processions of men and boys dressed in black move slowly, as if in a trance, toward the gate of the main shrine. All the while, they chant funereal verses lamenting Hussein's fate and flog themselves with metal-studded whips until their shoulders and backs are streaked with blood. In storefront mosques, holy men recount the sad tale with such passion that soon after they begin, worshipers fall prostrate with grief, weeping uncontrollably as if the most intimate personal tragedy had just crushed them. The breathtaking authenticity of this scene testifies to the success Iranian Shiites have had in formulating a set of religious beliefs that is within the Islamic tradition but still distinctly native.

Sunnis do not attribute great importance to the violent deaths of Ali and Hussein, but for Shiites, whose name comes from the phrase *Shi'at-Ali,* or "followers of Ali," they were cataclysmic events. To them, Ali and Hussein represent both the mystic spirituality of pure Islam and the self-sacrificing life that true Muslims must live. In this view, shaped by Zoroastrian tradition, the two heroes rebelled against an establishment that had become corrupt and thereby lost its *farr.* They are believed to have sacrificed themselves, as the truly pious must, on the altar of evil. By doing, so they embraced a pattern that still shapes Iran's consciousness. They bequeathed to Shiites a legacy of religious zeal and a willingness, even an eagerness, to embrace martyrdom at the hands of God's enemies. Ali remains the most perfect soul and the most enlightened leader who ever lived, excepting only the Prophet himself; Shiites still pore over his speeches and memorize his thousands of proverbs and aphorisms. Hussein epitomizes the self-sacrifice that is the inevitable fate of all who truly love Islam and humanity. His martyrdom is considered even more universally significant than that of Ali because it was inflicted by government soldiers rather than by a lone fanatic. Grasping the depth of this passion is essential to any understanding of modern Iran.

Iranian Shiites consider Ali to have been the first of twelve legitimate imams, or successors to Mohammad. The twelfth was still a youth when he passed into an occult state, apart from the world but aware of its suffering. For Iranian believers he is still vividly alive. They revere him as the Twelfth Imam, often called the Hidden Imam or the Imam of the Age, and many pray each day for his return to earth. When he does return, he will be the Mahdi, or messiah, who will right all wrongs and usher in an age of perfect justice. Until that time, it is the duty of temporal rulers to emulate his wisdom and righteousness. When they fail to do so, they trample not only on human rights but on the very will of God.

"The Imam watches over men inwardly and is in communion with the soul and spirit of men even if he be hidden from their physical eyes," the twentieth-century Shiite scholar Allamah Tabatabai has written. "His existence is always necessary, even if the time has not yet arrived for his outward appearance and the universal reconstruction that he is to bring about."

The profound hold that this tradition has on the souls of Iranian Shiites raises their beliefs above the level of traditional doctrine to what the anthropologist Michael M. J. Fischer has called "a drama of faith." They revere Mohammad but focus far more viscerally on Ali and Hussein, embracing what Fischer calls "a story expandable to be all-inclusive of history, cosmology and life's problems" and reinforcing it with "ritual or physical drama to embody the story and maintain high levels of emotional investment." Ali and Hussein gave them a paradigm that tells them not only how the moral believer should live, but also how he should die.

After Ali and Hussein met their worldly ends in the seventh century, the Arabian empire reached its peak and then began to weaken. Arabs who dominated Iran slowly melted into the country's already mixed population. As Arab power receded, Shiites gained strength, partly because their warnings about the corruption of worldly dynasties were borne out by the excesses of the conquering Seljuk Turks and the savagery of Genghis Khan's Mongol hordes, who ravaged Iran in the years after their invasion in 1220. When the Mongols began to lose control, power passed to the revolutionary Safavid dynasty, which was inspired by Shiite belief. The Safavid leader, Ismail, was a militant Shiite who sent his warriors into battle crying: "We are Hussein's men, and this is our epoch! In devotion we are slaves of the Imam! Our name is Zealot and our title is Martyr!"

After a series of victories won with the help of Shiites who flocked to his side from other lands, Ismail proclaimed himself shah, or king, in 1501. His first act after assuming the throne was to declare Shiism the official state religion. A famous miniature painting depicts the scene, with this caption: "On Friday, the exalted king went to the congregational mosque of Tabriz and ordered its preacher, who was one of the Shiite dignitaries, to mount the pulpit. The king himself proceeded to the front of the pulpit, unsheathed the sword of the Lord of Time, may peace be upon him, and stood there like the shining sun."

Far more than simply a religious act, this was the single most important step toward creating the Iranian nation. Ismail used Shiism to help him build an empire that within ten years of his coronation not only included most of modern-day Iran but extended from Central Asia to Baghdad and from the frosty Caucasus to the sands of the Persian Gulf. During Ismail's rule, today's Iran emerged not just politically but also spiritually. Iranians were already bound together by a shifting geography, a language, and a collective memory of ancient glory, but none of these ties evoked anything close to the unifying fervor of Shiism. By embracing this faith, Iranians accepted Islam but not in the way their Sunni Arab conquerors had wished. They rebelled while appearing to submit.

Perhaps most important, Iranians found an institution that would ultimately free them, at least spiritually, from the authority of the state. Ismail and the Safavid leaders who followed him thought they could control Shiism, and for most of the next two hundred years they did. But integral to Shiism, as to Zoroastrianism, is the belief that rulers may hold power only as long as they are just. Ultimately, this belief gave the Shiite masses, and by extension their religious leaders, the political and emotional power to bring temporal regimes crashing down.

By the time Ismail rose to power, Iranians had already reached great cultural pinnacles. As early as the ninth century, their intellectuals had traveled through the Islamic world in search of the wisest philosophers and the most learned scientists and had translated and studied the works of Plato, Aristotle, Archimedes, Euclid, Ptolemy, and other Greek thinkers. Artisans made breathtaking leaps forward in architecture and ceramic arts. Persian miniaturists established styles that were copied but never matched by masters from Constantinople to the steppes of Central Asia. Captivating poets composed works full of ecstasy and passion that are still read around the world. Many of them, like the thirteenth-century mystic Jelaluddin Rumi, reject orthodoxy of any kind:

> I hold to no religion or creed,
> am neither Eastern nor Western,
> Muslim or infidel,
> Zoroastrian, Christian, Jew or Gentile.
> I come from neither land nor sea,
> am not related to those above or below,
> was not born nearby or far away,
> do not live either in Paradise or on this Earth,
> claim descent not from Adam and Eve or the Angels above.
> I transcend body and soul.
> My home is beyond place and name.
> It is with the beloved, in a space beyond space.
> I embrace all and am part of all.

These cultural achievements meant that when Iranians finally achieved political unity, they were poised to enter the modern age confident of their creative, as well as of their military and spiritual, power. The Safavid king who inspired them to some of their greatest achievements as a people, Abbas Shah, is still revered as a hero. He sat on the throne for more than forty years, from 1588 to 1629. His success in unifying his people and giving them a sense of shared destiny was at least as profound as the success of his contemporaries, Elizabeth I in Britain and Philip II in Spain. He built roads that brought European traders into Iranian cities and established workshops to produce silk, ceramics, and other products those traders wanted to buy. His bureaucracy collected taxes, enforced justice, and organized life as it had not been organized since the era of Cyrus and Darius two thousand years before.

Abbas fit the archetype of Iranian rulers not only because he was dedicated to bringing the best of the world into his kingdom. He was also typical because he imposed cruel tyranny and brooked no challenge to his absolutism. Torture and execution were commonplace during his reign. For years he locked his own sons inside the royal palace, allowing them the pleasure of concubines but denying them access to the education and training that would prepare them for future leadership—or, Abbas feared, for rebellion against his rule. He had his eldest son murdered and two other sons, two brothers, and his father blinded.

The greatest physical legacy Abbas left to posterity was his glorious capital, Isfahan, which he transformed into one of the world's most splendid cities. To this day its soaring domes, intricately designed royal residences, and magnificently tiled prayer halls inspire awe in the visitor and justify what generations of Iranians have believed: *Isfahan nesf-i-jahan* (Isfahan is half the world). Abbas brought Armenian craftsmen to help build his city, Dutch traders to expand the reach of its grand bazaar, and diplomats from around the world to give it a cosmopolitan air. Half a million people lived there, and few cities on earth could compete with its grandeur. Yet Isfahan came to symbolize not just Iran's brilliance but also the dark sides of Abbas's rule.

"Everything, from the ornamental profusion of the faience decoration of the mosques to the ponds and flower beds round the royal pavilions, bears the hallmark of an art that not only aimed at pleasing but was enhanced by the might and majesty of the sovereign," one modern author has written. "Here we can best understand the peculiar mixture of cruelty and liberalism, barbarity and sophistication, magnificence and voluptuousness, that made up Persian civilization."

Given the savagery with which Abbas Shah treated potential heirs to his throne, it is not surprising that Iran fell into disarray after his death. Neighbors began to prey on it, and in 1722 Afghan tribesmen swept down and overran it, even sacking Isfahan itself. The Afghans were finally expelled by the last of Iran's great historical leaders, Nadir Shah, a Sunni Turk who then marched on to seize Delhi. One of the treasures he looted from Delhi was the jewel-encrusted Peacock Throne, which became a symbol of Iranian royalty. Nadir was assassinated in 1747, and after a series of power struggles that lasted nearly fifty years, a new dynasty, the Qajars, came to power.

The Qajars, a Turkic tribe based near the Caspian Sea, ruled Iran from the late eighteenth century until 1925. Their corrupt, small-minded kings bear heavy responsibility for the country's poverty and backwardness. As much of the world rushed toward modernity, Iran under the Qajars stagnated.

"In a country so backward in constitutional progress, so destitute of forms and statutes and charters, and so firmly stereotyped in the immemorial traditions of the East, the personal element, as might be expected, is largely in the ascendant," the British statesman Lord Curzon wrote toward the end of the Qajar period. "The government of Persia is little else than the arbitrary exercise of authority by a series of units in a descending scale from the sovereign to the headman of a petty village."

Had Iran been governed during the nineteenth century by a strong and sophisticated regime, it might have managed to fend off the ambitions of foreign powers. The pressures, however, would have been intense in any case. Geography placed Iran in the way of that era's two great imperial powers, Britain and Russia. When the British looked at Iran, they saw a nation that straddled the land route to India, their richest and most precious colony. The Russians, for their part, saw a chance to control a large swath of land across their exposed southern border. The fact that Iran was ruled by weak and self-involved monarchs made it too tantalizing for either empire to resist. Both rushed to fill the power vacuum left by the ignorant Qajars.

Qajar kings did not seem disturbed to see Iran slipping into subservience, or if they were, they determined to take what advantage they could of its seemingly unavoidable fate. In what turned out to be a great miscalculation, they presumed that the Iranian people would accept whatever their rulers dictated. But by their corruption and especially their willingness to allow Iran to slip under the domination of foreign powers, the Qajars fell out of step with their people and ultimately lost their right to rule, their *farr*. Armed with the Shiite principle that endows the ordinary citizen with inherent power to overthrow despotism, and with the ideals of the emerging new world, Iranians rebelled in a way their forefathers never had. Their demands were as astonishing as their rebellion itself: an end to the country's domination by outside powers and a parliament to express the popular will. This was the most radical program Iranians had ever embraced. It would spell the overthrow of the Qajar dynasty and define all of Iran's subsequent history.

CHAPTER 3

The Last Drop of
the Nation's Blood

Democracy dawned in Iran one day in December 1891, when the Shah's wives put aside their water pipes and vowed to smoke no more. It was no easy sacrifice. Tobacco was one of the great pleasures of harem life, and beauteous odalisques spent hours each day smoking it while reclining on lush divans. By renouncing it, they were defying the Shah, the institution of absolute monarchy, and the imperial system by which most of the world was ruled.

By the time the harem women took their fateful step, their husband, Nasir al-Din Shah, had been on the Peacock Throne for more than forty years. Like other Qajar rulers, he was famous for his excesses. His harem, where he spent much of his time, grew to sixteen hundred wives, concubines, and eunuchs. He fathered hundreds of princes, all of whom had free access to the national treasury. Garish clusters of jewels decorated his palaces. When he became bored by the pleasures of home, he would set out for Europe accompanied by a huge entourage. He demanded to be called not only Shah of Shahs but also Asylum of the Universe, Subduer of Climate, Arbitrator of His People, Guardian of the Flock, Conqueror of Lands, and Shadow of God on Earth. Those who refused to honor him were flogged, shot from cannons, buried alive, or set afire in public squares.

To support his lavish tastes, Nasir al-Din Shah sold government jobs, imposed oppressive taxes, and confiscated the fortunes of wealthy merchants. When there was no money left for him to take, he came up with the idea of raising cash by selling Iran's patrimony to foreign companies and governments. The British were his first customers. British officials were worried by native uprisings in India and wanted a telegraph line to their command posts there. In 1857 they bought a concession to build one across Iran. French, German, and Austrian groups bought a variety of other concessions. A German-born British subject, Baron Julius de Reuter, of news agency fame, won the most breathtaking one of all. In 1872, for a paltry sum and a promise of future royalties, he acquired the exclusive right to run the country's industries, irrigate its farmland, exploit its mineral resources, develop its railroad and streetcar lines, establish its national bank, and print its currency. Lord Curzon described this as "the most complete and extraordinary surrender of the entire industrial resources of a kingdom into foreign hands that has probably ever been dreamt of, much less accomplished, in history."

Many were angered by the extreme one-sidedness of the Reuter concession. Iranian patriots, of whom there were already quite a number, were naturally outraged. So were merchants and business-men, who saw their opportunities suddenly snatched away from them. Clerics feared for their status in a country so fully dominated by foreign interests. Russia, Iran's most powerful neighbor, was alarmed to see a British concern take so much power just across its southern border. Even the British government, which Reuter had not consulted in negotiating the concession, doubted its wisdom. Finally, Nasir al-Din Shah realized that he had overstepped the limits of the possible, and he revoked the concession less than a year after granting it.

The Shah's greed, however, did not allow him to abandon the idea of selling concessions. Over the next few years he sold three to British consortiums. One bought the mineral-prospecting rights that had briefly belonged to Reuter, another the exclusive right to establish banks, and a third the exclusive right to commerce along the Karun River, the only navigable waterway in Iran. Russia protested but was placated when the Shah sold Russian merchants the exclusive right to his caviar fisheries. Through these and other concessions, control over the nation's most valuable assets passed from the hands of Iranians to those of foreigners. The money they brought into the Iranian treasury sustained the Shah's lavish court for a while, but then, inevitably, it ran out. He raised more by borrowing from British and Russian banks.

As Iran sank ever deeper into the mire of poverty and dependence, a thirst for change gripped the population. Bazaars in large cities became hotbeds of protest. Religious reformers, Freemasons, and even socialists began spreading new and radical ideas. News about struggles for constitutional rule in Europe and the Ottoman Empire roused the literate classes. Provocative articles, books, and leaflets began to circulate.

Nasir al-Din Shah, isolated in the private world of the Qajar court, was oblivious to this rising discontent. In 1891 he sold the Iranian tobacco industry for the sum of £15,000. Under the terms of the concession, every farmer who grew tobacco was required to sell it to the British Imperial Tobacco Company, and every smoker had to buy it at a shop that was part of British Imperial's retail network.

Iran was then, as it is today, both an agricultural country and a country of smokers. Many thousands of poor farmers across the country grew tobacco on small plots; a whole class of middlemen cut, dried, packaged, and distributed it; and countless Iranians smoked it. That this native product would now be taken from the people who produced it and turned into a tool for the exclusive profit of foreigners proved too great an insult. A coalition of intellectuals, farmers, merchants, and clerics, such as had never before been seen in Iran, resolved to resist. The country's leading religious figure, Sheik Shirazi, endorsed their protest. In a shattering act of rebellion, he endorsed a *fatwa*, or religious order, declaring that as long as foreigners controlled the tobacco industry, smoking would constitute defiance of the Twelfth Imam, "may God hasten his appearance." News of his order flashed across the country through telegraph wires the British had built several decades earlier. Almost all who heard it obeyed. Nasir al-Din Shah was bewildered, frightened, and then overwhelmed by the unanimity of the protest. When his own wives stopped smoking, he realized that he had no choice but to cancel the concession. To add to the indignity, he had to borrow half a million pounds from a British bank to compensate British Imperial for its loss.

History changes course when people realize there is an alternative to blind obedience. Martin Luther's challenge to established Christianity, the storming of the Bastille during the French Revolution, and the Boston Tea Party were such moments. For Iran, the beginning of the end of absolutism came with the Tobacco Revolt. It ushered in a new political age. No longer would Iranians remain passive while the Qajar dynasty oppressed them and sold their nation's patrimony to foreigners.

After several years during which he drifted ever further from his royal duties and from reality itself, Nasir al-Din Shah was shot to death in 1896 while visiting a mosque near Tehran. Few mourned him. He left behind a country dominated by foreigners and plagued by widespread unemployment, crippling inflation, and serious food shortages. His son Muzzaffar, who succeeded him on the Peacock Throne, ignored his people's crying needs and wallowed in all the vices that led Iranians to hate the Qajars. Soon after ascending to the throne, he embarked on a lavish European tour, paid for with money borrowed from a Russian bank. Upon his return he took out another loan, this one from British financiers, and gave them in exchange a share of his customs revenue. Disgusted Iranians began denouncing him in public. When he responded by arresting some of the agitators, antigovernment riots broke out in Tehran and other cities.

Instead of trying to rally Iranians to his side, Muzzaffar al-Din Shah took a step that further inflamed them. In 1901 he sold William Knox D'Arcy, a London-based financier, the "special and exclusive privilege to obtain, exploit, develop, render suitable for trade, carry away and sell natural gas [and] petroleum . . . for a term of sixty years." It would be nearly a decade before D'Arcy struck oil and even longer before his concession turned into a blunt instrument of British imperial policy. Simply by granting it, however, Muzzaffar al-Din Shah shaped all of subsequent Iranian history.

In the decade since the Tobacco Revolt, the political consciousness of Iranians had grown enormously. Their belief that God requires leaders to rule justly, a central tenet of Shiite doctrine, led

many to embrace the ideals of popular sovereignty that were cours-
ing through society. By the time the twentieth century dawned,
some had even begun to doubt the very principle of monarchy.
Secret societies dedicated to subversion were formed in several
cities. Books about the French Revolution, including several that
glorified Danton and Robespierre, began passing from hand to
eager hand. A sense of unlimited possibility gained strength with
news that the supposedly invincible British were losing battles to
upstart Boers in South Africa. It was reinforced by the turmoil of
1905 in Russia, where military defeat at the hands of Japan led to a
revolt that forced Czar Nicholas II to accept a parliament. The stage
was set for revolution in Iran. All that was needed was a spark to set
the nation ablaze.

The spark came in December 1905, when a handful of merchants in Tehran were arrested in a dispute over sugar prices. They
were subjected to the *bastinado,* a favorite Qajar punishment in
which victims were hung by their wrists and thrashed on the soles
of their feet. The bazaar erupted in protest. At first, the rioters
demanded only dismissal of the local governor who had ordered
the beatings. Then, sensing their rising power, they began calling
for reduced taxes. Finally, at one of their climactic meetings, they
added an astonishing new demand: "In order to carry out reforms
in all affairs, it is necessary to establish . . . a national consultative
assembly to insure that the law is executed equally in all parts of
Iran, so that there can be no difference between high and low, and
all may obtain redress of their grievances."

This demand soon subsumed all others. With his people on the
brink of revolt, Muzzaffar al-Din Shah had no choice but to accept
the idea that Iran should have a parliament. After agreeing, however, he began to stall and for several months did nothing to bring
the idea to fruition. The protest movement swelled anew. Islamic
clerics took a leading role. Some invoked the authority of the Shiite
martyr Hussein, vowing to defend the poor even if it meant expos-
ing themselves, as he did, to the sword of evil. Thrilled by this
rhetoric, throngs of people took to the streets in the summer of
1906. Emotions reached a feverish pitch, and several hundred radicals, seeking to organize themselves in a place where troops could
not attack them, decided to take *bast,* or refuge, on the grounds of a
diplomatic mission. They chose the British Legation, a sprawling

compound with lands covering the space of sixteen city blocks. Most of the Legation staff was away on summer holiday, and its secretary told the protesters that although he wished they would find another sanctuary, he would not, "in view of the acknowledged custom in Persia and the immemorial right of *bast* . . . use, or cause to be used, force to expel them if they came." Before long, fourteen thousand Iranians were inside the compound. They lived in tents according to their guilds and ate from great cauldrons of food prepared in a common kitchen.

This assemblage quickly turned into a school at which the principles of democracy formed the core curriculum. Every day, articles from reformist newspapers were read aloud to the multitude, agitators gave speeches about social progress, and foreign-educated intellectuals translated the works of European philosophers. The Shah, disconcerted but still failing to grasp the intensity of the movement, offered to name a council that would help run the justice ministry. That was not nearly enough to satisfy the protesters. They wanted a Majlis, or parliament, with true power, not simply an advisory council.

"The law must be what the Majlis decides," they declared in one statement. "Nobody is to interfere in the laws of the Majlis."

The Shah finally agreed, although without enthusiasm and with the proviso that laws passed by the Majlis would require his signature before taking effect. This was a climactic moment, comparable in some ways to the signing of the Magna Carta in England seven centuries before. One British diplomat cabled his amazement back to London: "One remarkable feature of this revolution here—for it is surely worthy to be called a revolution—is that the priesthood have found themselves on the side of progress and freedom. This, I should think, is almost unexampled in the world's history. If the reforms which the people, with their help, have fought for become a reality, all their power will be gone."

Having won the Shah's reluctant assent, jubilant protesters left their sanctuary and set to work laying the groundwork for what many believed would be a new Iran. They produced a draft constitution based on Belgium's, which was considered the most progressive in Europe, and convoked national elections for a two-hundred-seat Majlis. Some members were directly elected and others chosen from guilds, one each for the grocers, blacksmiths, printers, butchers, watchmakers, doctors, tailors, and so on. They assembled for their historic first session on October 7, 1906.

A host of troubles faced the new Majlis. The haste with which the new system had been designed and the inexperience of those who now sought to help rule Iran threw it into discord. Many deputies were uneducated, and there were no political parties to forge them into blocs. Debates over the proposed constitution faltered because no one was quite sure how to divide the powers of government. To make matters worse, it had to be written in great haste because Muzzaffar al-Din Shah was dying and his crown prince, Mohammad Ali, was known to detest the very idea of democratization. It was finally adopted on December 30, 1906, setting Iran on what would be a century of highly uneven progress toward democracy. A week later Muzzaffar al-Din Shah died.

The new monarch, Mohammad Ali Shah, ridiculed and ignored the Majlis. Several deputies demanded that he be deposed if he continued his resistance. Monarchists bitterly counterattacked, and violent debate, often echoed by clashes in the streets, shook the capital. Regional and tribal factions, encouraged by bribes and corrupt arrangements, staged protests that greatly weakened the constitutional movement. Ordinary people began to associate the word *constitution* with upheaval and conflict.

Worst of all, the tenuous alliance between clerics and secular reformers began to unravel. Mullahs who had supported the reform movement became alarmed by the demands of radicals who they said had "thrown out the law of the Prophet and set up their own law instead." The Qajar court played adroitly on their concerns and managed to persuade many of them that their true interests lay with the monarchy.

"It is not advisable for the government of Iran to be constitutional, for in constitutional government all things are free, and in this case there must also be freedom of religion," one courtier asserted in a speech to the Majlis. "Certain persons will insist upon religious freedom, which is contrary to the interests of Islam."

Many clerics shared these fears. When the Majlis debated a bill to legalize secular schools, one asked, "Will entry into them not lead to the overthrow of Islam? Will lessons in foreign languages and the study of chemistry and physics not weaken the students' faith?" Others questioned the very premise of the reform movement: "By the use of two enticing words, justice and consultation, the freedom seekers have deceived our brothers into making common cause with atheists. . . . Islam, the most complete, the most perfect, took the world by justice and consultation. What has happened that we must bring our regulation of justice from Paris, and our plan of consultation from England?"

This clash between clerics and secular reformers would resonate through modern Iranian history. So would another clash that emerged during this period, the one that split the religious class itself. Some clerics believed that received religion was compatible with modern ideas, but others saw a contradiction and abandoned the reform movement. This debate reflected Iran's age-old conflicts: ancient versus modern, religious versus secular, faith versus reason. It pitted, in the words of one historian, "the Persian trait of openness and assimilation against the Islamic trait of insularity and traditionalism."

Confident that most of the country's religious leaders were with him, Mohammad Ali Shah began a campaign of terror and violence against the Majlis. In June 1908 his men assembled a gang of thugs and sent them rampaging through Tehran shouting, "We want the Koran! We do not want a constitution!" Then he ordered his elite Cossack Brigade to bombard and sack the building where the Majlis was meeting. Iranians rose up in protest in several cities, and many were killed in street fighting. For a time it seemed that full-scale civil war might break out, and at one point the Shah even took *bast* at the Russian Legation.

Both of the imperial powers that sought to dominate Iran, Britain and Russia, realized that the reform movement now threatened their dominant position in the country and encouraged the Shah to continue resisting it. Still the Majlis pressed on. One of its most decisive steps was its vote to hire an American banker, Morgan Shuster, as Iran's treasurer-general. Shuster arrived with a zealot's energy and set out to dismantle the elaborate systems of tax exemptions and back-room deals through which British and Russian syndicates were looting Iran. The governments of both countries demanded that he be removed, and in the fall of 1911 the Russians sent troops to enforce their will. When the Majlis defiantly refused to dismiss him, the royal court, immeasurably strengthened by the presence of foreign soldiers, shut it down and arrested many of its members. Iran's tumultuous five-year Constitutional Revolution, the first concerted attempt to synthesize Iranian tradition with modern democracy, was over.

The experience of these years profoundly reshaped Iran's collective psychology. Unlike the Tobacco Revolt, which had the narrow aim of defeating a single arbitrary law, the Constitutional Revolution aimed to establish an entirely new social and political order. It was crushed with the decisive help of foreign powers, but only after it had laid the foundation for a democratic Iran. A constitution had been written and adopted, and under its provisions there would be regular elections, which meant political campaigns and at least the semblance of open debate. In the years to come, Iranian rulers could and would ignore, overrule, and act against public opinion, but they would never manage to extinguish the people's conviction that they were endowed with rights no government could take from them. The lessons they learned during this burst of reformist passion shaped the peaceful revolution that Mohammad Mossadegh led nearly half a century later.

Iranians had flocked to the banner of democracy because they believed that establishing the rule of law in their country would help pull them out of poverty. They were also driven by mounting anger directed at two targets. One was the Qajar court, as exemplified first by the execrable Mohammad Ali Shah and then by his obese son, Ahmad, who ascended to the throne in 1909 at the age of twelve. The other was the suffocating role that foreign powers—Britain and Russia in particular—had come to play in Iran.

During the Constitutional Revolution, reformers tried repeatedly to pull Iran out of the orbit of foreign powers. At one point the Majlis went so far as to refuse a loan offered by Russian bankers. Soon afterward it voted to establish a national bank run by Iranians. These efforts, however, were in vain. Iran fell ever more deeply into bondage as the Qajars continued selling the country's assets.

In 1907 Britain and Russia signed a treaty dividing Iran between them. Britain assumed control of southern provinces, while Russia took the north. A strip between the two zones was declared neutral, meaning that Iranians could rule there as long as they did not act against the interests of their powerful guests. Iran was not consulted but was simply informed of this arrangement after the treaty was signed in St. Petersburg. What had long been informal foreign control of Iran now became an explicit partition, backed by the presence of Russian and British troops. When the treaty formalizing it came before the British Parliament for ratification, one of the few dissenting members lamented that it left Iran "lying between life and death, parceled out, almost dismembered, helpless and friendless at our feet."

As Russia was consumed by civil war and revolution, its influence in Iran waned. After the Bolsheviks seized power in 1917, they renounced most of their rights in Iran and canceled all debts that Iran had owed to Czarist Russia. The British, now at the peak of their imperial power, moved quickly to fill the vacuum. Oil was the new focus of their interest. The newly formed Anglo-Persian Oil Company, which grew out of the D'Arcy concession, had begun extracting huge quantities of it from beneath Iranian soil. Winston Churchill called it "a prize from fairyland beyond our wildest dreams."

Realizing the immense value of this new resource, the British in 1919 imposed the harsh Anglo-Persian Agreement on Ahmad Shah's impotent regime, assuring its approval by bribing the Iranian negotiators. Under its provisions the British assumed control over Iran's army, treasury, transport system, and communications network. To secure their new power, they imposed martial law and began ruling by fiat. Lord Curzon, who as foreign secretary was one of the agreement's chief architects, argued its necessity in terms that crystallized a century of British policy toward Iran:

> If it be asked why we should undertake the task at all, and why Persia should not be left to herself and allowed to rot into picturesque decay, the answer is that her geographical position, the magnitude of our interests in the country, and the future safety of our Eastern Empire render it impossible for us now—just as it would have been impossible for us any time during the last fifty years—to disinherit ourselves from what happens in Persia. Moreover, now that we are about to assume the mandate for Mesopotamia, which will make us coterminous with the western frontiers of Asia, we cannot permit the existence between the frontiers of our Indian Empire and Baluchistan and those of our new protectorate, a hotbed of misrule, enemy intrigue, financial

chaos and political disorder. Further, if Persia were to be alone, there is every reason to fear that she would be overrun by Bolshevik influence from the north. Lastly, we possess in the southwestern corner of Persia great assets in the shape of oil fields, which are worked for the British navy and which give us a commanding interest in that part of the world.

The Anglo-Persian Agreement removed the last vestiges of Iran's sovereignty, but it also infused the nationalist movement with new passion. Iranian patriots were inspired by the emergence of anti-colonial forces in other countries, including several under British rule. Radicals in northern provinces established a Communist party, and after Soviet troops landed on the Caspian coast and declared the surrounding area an "Iranian Soviet Socialist Republic," it seemed possible that two world powers might soon be waging war on Iranian soil. In much of the country, millions of people were living in worse conditions than they had ever known. Separatist movements gained force in several provinces. Iran was on the brink of extinction. Conditions were ripe for the rise of a charismatic leader. In 1921 he burst into the nation's consciousness, a rough man on horseback named Reza.

Born in the remote Alborz Mountains near the Russian border, Reza left home as a teenager to follow the family tradition of military service. Rather than join the private army of a local chief, he chose to enlist in the Cossack Brigade, the only unit in the country that was modern, disciplined, and well commanded. It had been founded by Russian officers dispatched by the Czar and served principally as a private guard for the interests of foreigners and the Qajar kings who served them. Reza signed on as a stable boy but was soon given a uniform and began rising through the ranks as Reza Khan. He was six feet four inches tall, as fierce a fighter with his scimitar as with his machine gun, and much admired for his bravery. Profane and hot-tempered, his face deeply pockmarked as a result of smallpox in childhood, he cut a fearsome figure.

During his years as a soldier, Reza had the chance to travel through Iran and see the misery in which most of its people lived. He participated in many operations against the tribes, gangs, and bandits who controlled much of the countryside. "Whenever an expedition was sent to any part of the country to round up brigands or quell a disturbance," one British diplomat reported, "he seems to have taken part in it."

Reza quickly came to share his people's disgust with their Qajar rulers. That made him a logical tool for the British, who had tired of dealing with mercurial tribal leaders and wanted a stronger central government. They saw in the Cossack Brigade the means to impose it. To seize control of the brigade and oust its Russian officers, they resolved to stage a coup and replace the Shah's prime minister with one of their choosing. Their candidate was a fiery ex-journalist, Sayyed Zia Tabatabai. To provide Sayyed Zia with the military power he needed, they approached Reza. He was willing. On the evening of February 20, 1921, he and a handful of his fellow officers led two thousand men to the outskirts of Tehran. He roused them with a passionate speech: "Fellow soldiers! You have offered every possible sacrifice in the defense of the land of your fathers. . . . But we have to confess that our loyalty has served merely to preserve the interests of a handful of traitors in the capital. . . . These insignificant men are the same treacherous elements who have sucked the last drop of the nation's blood."

The fervor in camp was intense, and Reza, not a patient man, seized on it. Before dawn the next morning, his soldiers entered Tehran and arrested the prime minister and every member of his cabinet. To the dissolute Ahmad Shah, Reza made two demands: Sayyed Zia must be named prime minister and he himself commander of the Cossack Brigade. The Shah had neither the will nor the means to resist. Within the space of a few hours, with almost no resistance, the coup had succeeded. It was a testament to the power of the British, the weakness of the dying Qajar dynasty, and the bold self-confidence of Reza Khan.

Cossack regiments immediately set about pacifying the country and suppressing tribal armies. Power flowed into Reza's hands. He dismissed Sayyed Zia just three months after the coup and then forced him to leave the country. Soon afterward he persuaded the Shah himself to leave, ostensibly on a temporary trip for health reasons. Soon this ambitious soldier was prime minister, army commander, and effective head of the resurgent Iranian state.

Reza had proclaimed himself a nationalist, but he recognized the power of his British backers and the debt he owed them. One study of the coup concluded: "There can be no doubt about the involvement of British army officers. . . . The day before the march to Tehran, Sayyed Zia had paid 2,000 tumans to Reza Khan and distributed 20,000 among his 2,000 men. No Iranian could have raised such a substantial amount of cash over a short period of time."

Once he had completed his drive to power, Reza had to choose a political framework in which to rule. He fervently admired the Turkish reformer Kemal Atatürk and for a time considered following Atatürk's example by declaring Iran a republic and installing himself as president. That idea terrified the religious class, which had been deeply shocked by Atatürk's decisions to abolish the sultanate and the Islamic caliphate. They insisted that Reza preserve the monarchy, and finally won him to their side.

Although Reza was uneducated and barely literate, he had a deep understanding of the Iranian style of politics. A couple of years after his coup, he conceived a theatrical drama that he correctly calculated would carry him to the pinnacle of power. He retired to a small village, supposedly to reflect and meditate, and resigned from all his government posts. Before departing, he had arranged to be bombarded by demands that he return to power. For a time Reza pretended to resist, but then, as he had hoped, the hated Ahmad Shah announced his intention to return home. The Majlis, which had reconstituted itself after the debacle of 1911 but never managed to accumulate any real power, was horrified at this prospect. United in rebellion, it pronounced the Qajar dynasty dead and offered the Peacock Throne to Reza. He assumed it on April 25, 1926, and proclaimed himself Reza Shah. His new dynasty, he announced, would be known by the family name Pahlavi, after a language that Persians spoke before the Muslim conquest.

Reza Shah was not averse to denouncing the British in public, but he and they had fundamental interests in common. He was the strongman they had sought, a reliable figure with whom they could bargain and whom they could, if necessary, depose. "The old Persia was a loose-knit pyramid resting on its base," observed the always-perceptive British diplomat Harold Nicholson. "The new Persian pyramid is almost equally loose, but resting on its apex; hence, it is much easier to overthrow."

It was impossible for Reza Shah to pull his country out of the orbit of foreign powers, especially the all-powerful British, but after consolidating his power, he worked steadily to limit their influence.

He accepted no loans from foreign financiers, banned the sale of property to non-Iranians, revoked a concession that gave the British-owned Imperial Bank of Iran the exclusive right to issue Iranian currency, and even forbade officials of his foreign ministry to attend receptions at foreign embassies. When the British insisted that he hire European engineers to build the rail line that was one of his grandest dreams, he did so on the condition that the engineers and their families agree to stand beneath each bridge they built when a train passed over it for the first time.

Subduing the vast expanse of Iran by military force would have required an enormous army. Instead, Reza Shah imposed his will by exemplary terror. Stories of his ruthlessness terrified and then pacified his people.

In 1935 religious leaders called a protest against Reza Shah's ban of the veil for women and his order that men wear billed caps that would prevent them from touching the floor with their foreheads during prayer. They gathered with several hundred believers in the sacred Khorasan mosque. As soon as Reza Shah learned of their assembly, he ordered soldiers to storm the mosque and massacre them. More than one hundred were killed. There were no further protests against his religious reforms.

Time and again, Reza Shah resolved problems with this brand of brutal decisiveness. Once during a visit to Hamedan in western Iran, for example, he is said to have learned that people there were going hungry because bakers were hoarding wheat in order to drive up prices. He ordered the first baker he saw thrown into an oven and burned alive. By the next morning, every bakery in town was filled with low-priced bread.

Many Iranians were appalled by stories like these, but many others, remembering that their country had enjoyed glory only when it was ruled by a powerful leader, remained silent or applauded. None could deny Reza Shah's achievements. He began by wiping out gangs of bandits that terrorized many parts of Iran. Then he embarked on a huge construction program that gave the country new avenues, plazas, highways, factories, ports, hospitals, government buildings, railroad lines, and schools for both boys and girls. He created the country's first civil service and the first national army it had known for centuries. He introduced the metric system, the modern calendar, the use of surnames, and civil marriage and divorce. Ever ready to scorn tradition, he restricted traditional clothing and forbade camel caravans to enter cities. He promulgated legal codes and established a network of secular courts to enforce them. In 1935 he announced that he would no longer tolerate references to his country as *Persia,* a word used mainly by foreigners, and would insist on *Iran,* the name by which its own citizens knew it. With typical resolve, he ordered that any mail from abroad addressed to Persia be returned unopened.

Yet for all Reza Shah's reformist passion, he did not manage a true social transformation. Under his rule, newspapers were strictly censored, labor organizing forbidden, and opposition figures murdered, jailed, or forced to flee. He forced nomadic tribes, which he considered relics of the past incompatible with a modern state, into barren settlements where thousands suffered and died. Commerce was centralized in the hands of the state and a small cadre of loyal entrepreneurs. The Shah himself became enormously wealthy by extracting bribes from foreign businesses and extorting money from tribal leaders. He confiscated so much land that at the peak of his power, he was the country's largest landowner.

"Reza Shah eliminated all the thieves and bandits in Iran," one member of the British Parliament observed, "and made his countrymen realize that henceforth there would be only one thief in Iran."

In 1934 Reza Shah traveled to Turkey to meet Atatürk. The two men got along famously, but as they toured the Turkish countryside, the Shah became depressed and frustrated as he realized how quickly Turkey was progressing toward modernity and secularism. He returned home determined to redouble his campaign to transform Iranian society. In his zeal, he charged ahead without regard to the country's long-established social patterns or its religious beliefs. Utterly lacking Atatürk's statesmanship and political skill, he turned much of the population against him.

Reza Shah was fascinated by the fascist movements that emerged in Europe during the 1930s. Mussolini, Franco, and Hitler seemed to him to be embarked on the same path he had chosen, purifying and uniting weak, undisciplined nations. He launched an oppressive campaign to obliterate the identity of minority groups, especially Kurds and Azeris, and he established a Society for Public Guidance to glorify his ideas and person. Baldur von Schirach, head of Hitler Youth, led a stream of Nazi dignitaries who visited Iran and spoke glowingly of the emerging German-Iranian alliance.

"The cardinal goal of the German nation is to attain its past glories by promoting national pride, creating a hatred of foreigners, and preventing Jews and foreigners from embezzlement and treason," one of the Shah's newspapers declared. "Our goals are certainly the same."

Partly because he needed a foreign friend who shared his growing enmity toward Britain and the Soviet Union, Reza Shah developed great sympathy for the German cause. When World War II broke out, he declared a policy of neutrality that tilted decidedly toward Germany. He allowed hundreds of German agents to operate in Iran. Many worked to build support networks among regional warlords. Western leaders feared that the Nazis were planning to use Iran as a platform for an attack across the Soviet Union's southern border that would greatly complicate the Allied war effort. To prevent that, British and Soviet troops entered Iran on August 25, 1941. Their planes dropped leaflets over Tehran. "We have decided that the Germans must go," they said, "and if Iran will not deport them, then the English and the Russians will."

Some Iranians must have appreciated the irony of these two countries positing themselves as Iran's friends and protectors, but there was little they could do. Iran's army yielded in a matter of days. After seizing strategic points around the country, Allied commanders demanded that Reza Shah sever his government's ties to Germany and allow the free use of his territory by their forces. If he had not alienated himself from almost every segment of Iranian society, and if he had kept a cadre of wise advisers around him instead of systematically exiling or murdering them, he might have been able to resist. Instead he found himself alone, his dreams shattered by his own narrow-mindedness, corruption, and boundless egotism.

Reza Shah did not wish to work for the Allies, and they had no use for him either. He abdicated on September 16, 1941. The next day his eldest son, twenty-one-year-old Mohammad Reza, was sworn in to succeed him. No more was heard from Reza, who died in Johannesburg three years later.

Although Reza Shah imagined himself a modernizing visionary, in fact he reinforced the tradition of *istibdad,* or absolute rule, that lies at the heart of Iranian history. His reforms were superficial and, because of the brutality with which they were imposed, deeply resented by his subjects. He made no progress toward creating the sense of shared enterprise and civic responsibility that is at the heart of successful societies. His efforts to rid Iran of foreign influence were praiseworthy in theory but disastrous in effect. In the end, his dictatorial impulses brought him down by driving him toward an alliance with fascist powers. His departure left Iran in the hands of foreigners and a weak, confused young king. Monarchy had once again failed to resolve the country's continuing crisis of development and identity. When World War II ended, Iranians were desperate for a new kind of leader.

CHAPTER 4

A Wave of Oil

Years in the rocky Iranian desert, where smallpox raged, bandits and warlords ruled, water was all but unavailable, and temperatures often soared past 120 degrees, might have driven lesser men than George Reynolds to madness or worse. Reynolds, however, was one of those legendary figures whose persistence and audacity have changed world history. He was a self-taught geologist and a petroleum engineer with several expeditions in the Sumatran jungle to his credit. During the first decade of the twentieth century, already in his fifties, he crisscrossed the barren wastelands of Iran in search of oil. To help him pull his wagonloads of equipment and dig his wells, he had at his service a ragged band that included a handful of Polish and Canadian drillers, a comically incompetent Indian doctor, and several dozen tribesmen who had trouble even understanding what oil is. "A more helpless crew I seldom saw," he lamented in one letter home.

Home for Reynolds was London, and there his patron, the millionaire dandy William Knox D'Arcy, waited anxiously for good news. D'Arcy had made a fortune prospecting for gold in Australia but was not satisfied. He sensed that oil would prove even more valuable than gold and knew that Iran was, in the words of one geologist who had surveyed its terrain, "unquestionably petrol-iferous territory." In 1901 he signed an agreement with the Shah of Iran, Muzzaffar al-Din, under which he assumed the exclusive right to prospect for oil in a vast tract of Iranian territory larger than Texas and California combined. To secure it, he gave the Shah, whom the British minister in Tehran described as "merely an elderly child," the sum of £20,000, an equal amount in shares of his company, and a promise of 16 percent of future profits.

D'Arcy, an elegantly mustachioed lion of London society known for extravagant gestures like hiring Enrico Caruso to sing at private parties in his Grosvenor Square mansion, never considered travel-ing to Iran himself. He hired Reynolds instead, and month after month, year after year, he wrote checks to support their venture. His spirits soared in January 1904 when Reynolds finally struck oil but crashed a few months later when the well ran dry. Bit by bit, his fortune slipped away. Finally he was forced to sell most of his rights to a Glasgow-based syndicate, the Burmah Oil Company, that was even wealthier than he was.

The Scottish financiers who took charge of the drive to find oil in Iran recognized that an epochal change was about to reshape Britain and the world. Internal combustion engines would soon revolutionize every aspect of human life, and control over the oil needed to fuel them would henceforth be the key to world power. Oil had been discovered around the Caspian Sea, in the Dutch East Indies, and in the United States, but neither Britain nor any of its colonies produced or showed any promise of producing it. If the British could not find oil somewhere, they would no longer be able to rule the waves or much of anything else.

By 1908 D'Arcy and his Scottish partners had sunk more than half a million pounds into their Persian venture and had come up with nothing. Finally they concluded that they must abandon their explorations and begin looking elsewhere. At the beginning of May they sent Reynolds a telegram telling him that they had run out of money and ordering him to "cease work, dismiss the staff, dismantle anything worth the cost of transporting to the coast for re-shipment, and come home."

It must have been a crushing moment for Reynolds, who had spent years in some of the most trying conditions imaginable looking for a treasure he knew could reshape the world. Desperate to buy whatever time he could, he told his men that in such a remote region, telegrams could not be trusted. They must continue working until the message was confirmed by post.

Reynolds was sleeping in his tent near an outpost in western Iran called Masjid-i-Suleiman when, at four o'clock on the morning of May 26, 1908, rumbling noises and wild shouting awakened him. He bolted up, ran across a stony plain, and saw oil spurting high above one of his derricks. In what might have been one of his last attempts, he had drilled into the greatest oil field ever found.

It did not take long for British leaders to grasp the scope and implications of this find. In the autumn of 1908 they arranged for a group of investors to organize a new corporation, the Anglo-Persian Oil Company, to absorb the D'Arcy concession and take control of oil exploration and development in Iran. Five years later, at the urging of First Lord of the Admiralty Winston Churchill, who saw world war on the horizon and knew he would need oil to power the ships that would win it, the British government spent £2 million to buy 51 percent of the company. From that moment on, the interests of Britain and the Anglo-Persian Oil Company became one and inseparable. "Mastery itself was the prize of the venture," Churchill asserted.

During its first few years in existence, Anglo-Persian drilled scores of wells, laid more than a hundred miles of pipeline, and extracted millions of barrels of oil. It established a network of filling stations throughout the United Kingdom and sold oil to countries across Europe and as far away as Australia. Most impressive of all, it began construction of what would for half a century be the world's largest oil refinery on the desert island of Abadan in the Persian Gulf.

Abadan, at the Gulf's northern end, had come slowly into existence over a period of a thousand years, built up by silt running from the rivers that meet to form the Shatt-al-Arab waterway. The first engineer Anglo-Persian sent there, twenty-eight-year-old R. R. Davidson, wrote home in 1909 that it was a place of "sunshine, mud and flies," totally flat and without a single stone bigger than a man's hand. It was also among the hottest places on earth. Nonetheless, within a couple of years Davidson had more than a thousand tribesmen at work building piers, barges, and brick buildings. Soon

Abadan boasted a power-generating station, several stores and workshops, a water filtration plant, and even a small railway. In 1911 the first pipeline from Fields, as the oil-producing region was called, was completed, and the next year oil began to flow.

Before long, Abadan was a bustling city with more than one hundred thousand residents, most of them Iranian laborers. From its private Persian Club, where uniformed waiters served British executives, to the tight-packed Iranian workers' quarters and the water fountains marked "Not for Iranians," it was a classic colonial enclave. Almost all of the technicians and administrators were British, and many enjoyed handsome homes with terraces and manicured lawns. For them and their families, Abadan was an idyllic place.

Life was much different for the tens of thousands of Iranian laborers. They lived in slums and long dormitories with only primitive sanitation. Shops, cinemas, buses, and other amenities were off limits to them. With their British employers, however, they shared life amid networks of giant pipes, beneath cavernous holding tanks, and in the shadow of towering smokestacks from which plumes of flame leapt up day and night. The air was heavy with sulfur fumes, a constant reminder of the vast wealth that was pouring from Iranian soil into Anglo-Persian's coffers.

Any doubts about the value of this new resource were resolved by the experience of World War I, in which, as Lord Curzon put it, the Allies "floated to victory on a wave of oil." Over the years that followed, the amount of oil flowing from Abadan increased steadily, from less than three hundred thousand tons in 1914 to five times that amount in 1920. Anglo-Persian gave first priority to the Royal Navy, which bought its oil at a great discount. What remained was sold to industrial customers and drivers in Britain and then, as supplies increased, to others around the world.

Oil could have made Qajar kings rich and powerful. They did not have the resources to find or exploit their deposits without foreign help, but with more foresight they could have struck a far better deal with their British partners. Instead they sold their birthright for a pittance. Iran's royalty payment for 1920, set according to the concession agreement at 16 percent of the company's net profit, was £47,000. Ahmad Shah considered it manna from heaven, but it was a small sum compared to what was pouring into the oil company's coffers.

The next year brought the fall of Qajar power and the rise of Reza Khan. As Reza consolidated his rule over Iran, he cast a scornful eye on Anglo-Persian and the D'Arcy concession that was its central asset. The company's profits were reaching astronomical levels, the means by which it calculated Iran's 16-percent royalty were becoming more questionable, and the gap between the living conditions of its British and Iranian employees widened steadily. In 1928 Reza, who was by then Reza Shah, directed his ministers to seek a new and more equitable accord with the company. The British did not take him seriously. For four years they turned aside his demands with a combination of refusals and delays. While he stewed, the worldwide depression spread and the royalties Anglo-Persian paid to Iran began to shrink. Finally and inevitably, Reza Shah exploded in anger. At a cabinet meeting on November 26, 1932, he cursed his ministers for their failure and then demanded to be shown the file of documents covering the four years of talks. When it was brought to him, he cursed some more and then threw the entire file into a blazing stove. The next day, he notified Anglo-Persian that he had canceled the D'Arcy concession.

This act, if allowed to stand, would have meant the end of Anglo-Persian's operations in Iran and, in effect, the death of the company. British officials were in turn shocked, outraged, and desperate. They appealed to the League of Nations, only to be met with a scathing counterattack from Iranian representatives who charged that Anglo-Persian had systematically falsified its accounts and cheated Iran out of its legitimate royalties. Sir John Cadman, Anglo-Persian's chairman, realized that he had to negotiate directly with Reza Shah, whose coronation he had attended eight years earlier. Cadman flew to Tehran, and the two old friends took only a few days to reach a compromise. Under its terms, the area covered by the D'Arcy concession was reduced by three-quarters, Iran was guaranteed payments of at least £975,000 annually, and the company agreed to improve working conditions at Abadan. In return, Reza Shah extended the concession, which was to expire in 1961, for an additional thirty-two years. It was also agreed that since the Shah did not like the name Persia, the company would henceforth be known as the Anglo-Iranian Oil Company.

"Am personally satisfied," Cadman wired home, "that new

Concession in every respect will open new era in our relations with Persia."

The 1933 accord stabilized the oil company's position for the rest of Reza Shah's reign. When the British forced him to abdicate eight years later, however, they removed the one leader who was strong enough to impose his rule by fiat on an increasingly restive country. Discontent over the company's privileged position grew steadily during the war years as the amount of oil it extracted rose from six and a half million tons in 1941 to sixteen and a half million tons in 1945.

In March 1946, less than a year after the guns finally fell silent, laborers at Abadan did something they would never have dreamed of doing in Reza Shah's time: they went on strike. Marching through the teeming streets, they carried signs and chanted slogans demanding better housing, decent health care, and a commitment by employers to abide by Iranian labor laws. Accustomed by long experience to challenges from restless natives, the British not only refused to negotiate but chose the path of active resistance. They organized ethnic Arabs and separatist tribesmen from nearby regions into a bogus union of their own and sent it to confront the strikers. Bloody rioting broke out, leaving dozens dead and more than one hundred injured. It ended only after Anglo-Iranian's directors grudgingly agreed to begin observing Iranian labor law. They never did, and to remind Iranians of their power, they arranged for two British warships to stage threatening maneuvers within sight of Abadan. With this show of force, they believed they had resolved the crisis. In fact, they had further inflamed public opinion and taken another step toward the abyss.

The Iranian labor movement was not the only long-dormant institution that came back to life after Reza Shah's departure. So did the Majlis. It had never ceased to exist, but Reza Shah had not allowed it to function freely. Now, angered like the rest of Iran by the rioting at Abadan, it began asserting itself. In 1947 it passed a bold law forbidding the grant of any further concessions to foreign companies and directing the government to renegotiate the one under which Anglo-Iranian was operating.

This law was the first blow in a long battle. It set Iran on the course of cataclysmic confrontation with Britain. The deputy who wrote it and pushed it through the Majlis had been an active nationalist in the early years of the century but was forced out of politics by Reza Shah and had lived in obscurity for twenty years. Now he was back, as fervent a defender of Iranian interests as ever. His name was Mohammad Mossadegh.

Two central beliefs shaped Mossadegh's political consciousness. The first was a passionate faith in the rule of law, which made him an enemy of autocracy and, in particular, Reza Shah. The second was a conviction that Iranians must rule themselves and not submit to the will of foreigners. That made him the nemesis, the tormentor, the implacable foe of the Anglo-Iranian Oil Company. In mid-twentieth-century Iran, he and the company faced off in an epic confrontation. Fate bound them together. The story of one cannot be told without the story of the other.

From the moment of his birth on May 19, 1882, Mossadegh had advantages that few of his countrymen enjoyed. His mother was a Qajar princess from a family that had produced governors, cabinet ministers, and ambassadors. The man she married came from the distinguished Ashtiani clan and served for more than twenty years as Nasir al-Din Shah's finance minister. He died when their son was still a child, but according to custom, young Mohammad was schooled in his father's profession. At the tender age of sixteen he was named to his first government post. It was no sinecure; he was chief tax auditor for Khorasan, his home province. This post introduced him not only to the complexity of public finance but also to the corruption and chaos that were eating away at the Qajar dynasty. By all accounts he performed brilliantly. A visitor who met Mossadegh soon after he assumed his post estimated that he was in his mid-twenties. The visitor wrote presciently in his journal:

> Among men of intelligence and learning, his decorum cannot be surpassed. He speaks, behaves, and receives people with respect, humility and courtesy, but without undermining his own eminence and dignity. He may at times have treated his colleagues, including high officials and finance ministers, with a measure of contempt, but in his dealing with other people he has shown warm human feeling, courtesy and humility. Such an impressive young man is bound to become one of the great ones.

Mossadegh came of age during a tumultuous time in Iranian history. He was eight years old when the Tobacco Revolt broke out, and considering how precocious he was and how involved his parents were in public life, it is safe to assume that he followed its course carefully. Several of his relatives, including his uncle, the formidable Prince Farman Farma, played important roles in the Constitutional Revolution. When elections for the first Majlis were convoked in 1906, Mossadegh became a candidate and won a seat from Isfahan. He could not assume it because he had not yet reached the legal age of thirty, but his political career was under way.

In those early years, Mossadegh developed more than a political perspective. He also began showing extraordinary emotional qualities. His boundless self-assurance led him to fight fiercely for his principles, but when he found others unreceptive, he would storm off for long periods of brooding silence. He did this for the first time in 1909, when Mohammad Ali Shah launched his bloody assault on the Majlis. Rather than stay and fight alongside his fellow democrats, he concluded that Iran was not ready for enlightenment and left the country. Like many Iranians of his class, he considered Paris the center of the civilized world, and he made his way there to study at l'Ecole de Sciences Politiques.

During his stay in France, Mossadegh suffered from illnesses that would plague him all his life. No one could precisely identify them. They were certainly real and periodically flared up to cause ulcers, hemorrhaging, stomach secretions, and other symptoms. But they also had a nervous component that led to fits and breakdowns. Neither purely medical nor psychosomatic, they both reflected and became a part of Mossadegh's persona. He was as dramatic a politician as his country had ever known. At times he became so passionate while delivering speeches that tears streamed down his cheeks. Sometimes he fainted dead away, as much from emotion as from any physical condition. When he became a world figure, his enemies in foreign capitals used this aspect of his personality to ridicule and belittle him. But in Iran, where centuries of Shiite religious practice had exposed everyone to depths of public emotion unknown in the West, it was not only accepted but celebrated. It seemed to prove how completely he embraced and shared his country's suffering.

The onset of illness forced Mossadegh to give up his studies in

France after a year and return to Iran. There he was able to rest, partly because the ruler he detested so viscerally, Mohammad Ali Shah, had been forced from the throne. After his recovery he returned to Europe, this time to the Swiss town of Neuchâtel, accompanied by his wife, their three small children, and his beloved mother. He entered the university there, earned his doctorate of law in 1914—the first Iranian to win such a degree from a European university—and decided to apply for Swiss citizenship. First, though, he would travel home to complete research for a book about Islamic law.

Mossadegh returned to a country ablaze with conflict. The Constitutional Revolution had given Iranians a taste of the forbidden fruit of democracy, and they were anxious for more of it. Qajar rule was crumbling. Most important, the outbreak of World War I had thrown all political certainties into question and made everything seem possible. Britain and Russia, having effectively divided Iran between them in 1907, still held the reins of true power, but resentment over their role was leading many Iranians to sympathize with the Kaiser's Germany. A group of intellectuals centered around Hasan Taqizadeh, who had been a key figure in the Constitutional Revolution, went so far as to set up a "liberation committee" in Berlin that published a radical newspaper and aimed ultimately to seize power in Tehran. Mossadegh was much encouraged by these developments, and instead of returning to Switzerland, he joined the faculty of the Tehran School of Law and Political Science, which was becoming Iran's first modern university. His book *Iran and the Capitulation Agreements* argued that Iran could develop modern, European-style legal and political systems if it took one vital step. It must impose the law equally on everyone, including foreigners, and never grant special privileges to anyone.

After Mossadegh had been home for less than a year, his uncle, Farman Farma, who had become prime minister, asked him to join the cabinet as minister of finance. Mossadegh declined because he did not want to be accused of rising to power through family connections. In 1917 he suffered an attack of appendicitis and was operated on in Baku, and while recovering, he received another offer, this time to become deputy finance minister. By this time his uncle was no longer prime minister, and at his mother's urging he accepted the offer. He upset his new colleagues by unearthing a series of corrupt schemes and insisting that the wrongdoers be punished, and after less than two years in office he was dismissed. Once again he decided that Iran did not deserve his services, and he returned to Neuchâtel. By doing so he showed, as he would show repeatedly throughout his life, that he was a visionary rather than a pragmatist, preferring defeat in an honorable cause to what he considered shameful compromise.

Mossadegh was in Neuchâtel when he received news of the infamous 1919 Anglo-Persian Agreement that effectively reduced Iran to the status of a British protectorate. He was outraged and did all he could to protest, as an Iranian biographer reported:

> He talked and corresponded with other prominent Iranians in Europe, published leaflets, and wrote to the League of Nations protesting against the agreement. He even traveled to Bern for the sole purpose of having a rubber stamp made for the Comité de Résistance de Nations in whose name the anti-agreement statements were issued. Anger, frustration and loneliness must have taken their toll on his nerves, for it is unlikely that, as he suspected, he was being watched by British agents—one of them in the shape of the "chic, pretty and bouncy" woman next door who called from her balcony, "Est-ce que vous voulez fumer ce soir?" and was disappointed when Mosaddegh answered, "Pardon, madame. Je suis malade. Je suis très occupé. Je suis fatigué. Excusez-moi. Je n'ai pas le temps."

Mossadegh was devastated by his countrymen's failure to rise up in righteous anger against the Anglo-Persian Agreement. The cause of Iranian patriotism, he concluded after a few months, was lost forever, and so there was no place for him in his homeland. He resolved to file his application for citizenship in Switzerland and spend the rest of his days practicing law there. Unfortunately Swiss immigration laws had been tightened since he had last considered this option, and his application was delayed. He came up with the idea of opening an import-export firm and decided to travel to Iran to make arrangements with merchants there. As soon as he set foot on his native soil, he found himself caught up again in politics. On his way to Tehran he passed through the southern province of Fars, and when local dignitaries learned of his presence, they offered him a large sum of money to stay there and become governor. He agreed, though he turned down the financial offer and even insisted on serving without salary.

After Reza Khan came to power in 1921, he tried to make use of Mossadegh's evident talents. Theirs was a short and unhappy partnership. Mossadegh first became minister of finance, a post for which he was eminently qualified, but upon taking office he launched an anticorruption campaign that threatened Reza and his friends, and was soon forced to resign. Next he was named governor of Azerbaijan province, where the Soviets were trying to stir up a separatist rebellion, but quit when Reza refused to give him authority over troops stationed there. Then he served for a few months as foreign minister. Finally he concluded that Reza shared neither his democratic instincts nor his anti-imperialist creed. He quit the foreign ministry, ran for a seat in the Majlis, and was elected easily. He was now a free agent, and soon he emerged as one of Reza's sharpest opponents.

By the time Mossadegh entered the Majlis in 1924, he was already a thoroughly political man. He had developed a deep understanding of his country, its political system, and above all its backwardness, much of which he attributed to the rapacity of foreign overlords. Yet he was never truly part of any establishment, political or otherwise. Many rich and influential Iranians considered him a class traitor because of his insistence on judging them by the letter of the law. Even some of his supporters chafed at the intense self-confidence that often led him to dismiss his critics as either rogues or fools.

Mossadegh's appearance was as strikingly unusual as his character. He was tall, but his shoulders slumped down as if they were bearing a heavy weight, giving him the image of a condemned man marching stoically toward execution. His face was long, marked by sad-looking eyes and a long, very prominent nose that his enemies sometimes compared to a vulture's beak. His skin was thin and pasty white. But for all that, he moved through life with a determination that many of his countrymen found impressive to the point of inspiration. In intellect and education he towered above almost all of them, a drawback for a politician in some countries but not in Iran, where those who do not live the life of the mind have always admired those who do. His arrival in the Majlis marked the beginning of a new stage in his remarkable career, as one of his cousins recalled in a memoir:

> With his droopy, basset-hound eyes and high patrician forehead, Mossadegh did not look like a man to shake a nation. . . . To his mind the parliament was the only mouthpiece of the people of Iran. No matter how rigged the election or how corrupt its members, it was the only body that did not depend for its power either on outside influence or on the [royal] court, but on the authority of the constitution. The Majlis became his soapbox. Elected to it time and again by the people of Tehran, he used it to denounce the misconduct of the British and the Russians, and later the Americans. When he said, "The Iranian himself is the best person to manage his house," he was stating not only a conviction but a policy that he was to pursue with unwavering purpose until his picture had appeared on the cover of *Time* magazine and he had thoroughly shaken the foundations of the world's oil establishment.
>
> Although Mossadegh championed Iranian self-determination, he had little faith in his fellow deputies, and few escaped the lash of his tongue. He accused them of cowardice, of lacking initiative, and worst of all being unpatriotic. His fulminations at the podium were both frightening and theatrical. Gesturing wildly, his hand unconsciously wiping away the famous tears that sprung unbidden from his eyes at times of nervousness or rage, he pilloried his listeners with the righteousness of a priest who suffers with his victims even as he unmasks them. . . . Distinguished, highly emotional, and every inch the aristocrat, he believed so totally in his own country that his words reached out and touched the common man. Mossadegh was Iran's first genuinely popular leader, and he knew it.

If Iran had faced only domestic problems, Mossadegh might still be remembered only as a vigorous advocate of reform and modernization. The country's main dilemma, however, centered around its relationship with outside powers, especially Britain and most especially the Anglo-Iranian Oil Company. Many Iranians resigned themselves to the imposition of these powers, but Mossadegh never did.

During his first few months in the Majlis, Mossadegh rose often to speak. He addressed topics ranging from military corruption to the need for new industries in Iran, but his central themes were always democracy and self-reliance. "If bringing prosperity to the country through the work of other nations were of benefit to the people," he asserted in one speech, "every nation would have invited foreigners into its home. If subjugation were beneficial, no subjugated country would have tried to liberate itself through bloody wars and heavy losses."

On October 29, 1925, the Majlis received one of the most far-reaching proposals it had ever considered. It was from supporters of Reza, asking that the Qajar dynasty be abolished and that Reza be named Shah. Mossadegh was horrified. When his turn came to speak on the proposal, other deputies fell into a hush. He began by producing a copy of the Koran and demanded that everyone in the chamber rise to acknowledge that they had sworn upon it to defend the constitutional system. All did so. Then, in the day's longest and most emotional speech, Mossadegh paid tribute to Reza's achievements but said that if Reza wanted to govern the country, he should become prime minister, not Shah. To centralize royal and administrative power in the hands of one man would be "pure reaction, pure *istibdad*," a system so perverse that it "does not exist even in Zanzibar." Darkly, Mossadegh warned of Reza's authoritarian tendencies and predicted that elevating him to the throne would lead the country back to absolutism.

"Was it to achieve dictatorship that people bled their lives away in the Constitutional Revolution?" he demanded. "If they cut off my head and mutilate my body, I would never agree to such a decision."

Mossadegh was under no illusion that he could prevent Reza from taking the throne. Reza was the rising power in a country that had been on the brink of extinction, and just two days after Mossadegh's fiery speech, the Majlis recognized that fact by agreeing to his coronation. At the ceremony, Reza placed the plumed and jeweled crown on his own head as Napoleon had done, symbolizing his determination to govern as he pleased. For a few months he ruled alone and then, having secured his power, named a prime minister and directed him to offer Mossadegh the post of foreign minister. It was an astute move. Mossadegh had a base of popular support and impeccable nationalist credentials that would serve the new regime well. To no one's surprise, however, he declined the offer. He enjoyed being a free agent and undoubtedly realized that his abhorrence of dictatorship would soon place him in conflict with the new Shah. Not satisfied with refusing an offer to join the cabinet, he denounced it when it was finally formed. In his speech he called two of the incoming ministers traitors for their role in negotiating the Anglo-Persian Agreement.

Over the months that followed, Reza Shah approached Mossadegh several more times with offers of high government posts, including chief justice and even prime minister. Mossadegh rejected them all. After he was reelected to the Majlis at the end of 1926, he went so far as to refuse to take his oath of office because it included a vow to respect the Shah's authority. That should have prevented him from taking his seat, but given the power of his presence and the force of his will, no one challenged him.

The Majlis, like every other institution in Iran, was soon reduced to the role of a rubber stamp for Reza Shah. He outlawed opposition parties and banned their leaders from public life. Once this repressive campaign began, there was no doubt that Mossadegh would soon be among the victims. When the 1928 election approached, Reza Shah ordered that votes be counted in such a way that no one who opposed him would win. Mossadegh was among the losers. At the age of forty-five, his political career seemed over.

Several possible courses lay open to the deposed statesman. He could soften his opposition to Reza Shah and try to work within the regime, but given the strength of his principles this was impossible. He could defy the regime by launching a campaign of subversion, which might have led to his murder; even several of Reza Shah's longtime allies suffered this fate when he began to suspect their loyalty. The remaining option fit best not only with the times but with Mossadegh's own personality. He simply dropped out of sight, retiring to his country estate at Ahmad Abad, sixty miles west of Tehran, and devoting himself to study and experimental farming. His name disappeared from the press and from public discourse. As Reza Shah's power grew, Mossadegh's image faded and then all but disappeared. Most Iranians presumed that his moment had passed. He believed so himself.

After the first few years of his self-imposed exile, weighed down by the travails of isolation and devastated by news of the 1933 accord under which Reza Shah reaffirmed Anglo-Iranian's right to run the country's oil industry, Mossadegh fell ill. He bled so profusely from his mouth that in 1936 he traveled to Germany to consult specialists; they could find no cause for his condition. Even in his weakened state, however, Reza Shah feared him. One day in 1940 soldiers appeared at his house in Ahmad Abad, ransacked it in search of evidence that might implicate him in subversion and then, although finding nothing, placed him under arrest. At the local police station, he protested indignantly to the chief, citing a law under which prisoners had to be charged with a crime or released within twenty-four hours. The chief replied that the only law he knew was Reza Shah's will and that Reza Shah had ordered Mossadegh imprisoned indefinitely without charge. This sent Mossadegh into a rage. He had to be dragged into the car that was waiting to take him to prison. On the way he took an overdose of tranquilizers, apparently a suicide attempt, but succeeded only in falling into a coma. In his cell he showed evidence of what his jailer called "chronic hysteria," trying to cut himself with razor blades and at one point embarking on a hunger strike. After several months, through the intercession of Ernest Perron, a Swiss-born friend of the Shah who had once been cured of an illness at a hospital endowed by Mossadegh's mother, he was allowed to return to Ahmad Abad under house arrest.

For twenty years, part of it spent in active politics and the rest in obscurity, Mossadegh saw Reza Shah and his regime as Iran's great enemy. Then, suddenly, Reza Shah was gone. That changed everything, both for the nation and for Mossadegh himself. The election of 1943 was the first free one in many years. Mossadegh emerged from his retreat, ran for his old seat in the Majlis, and was elected with more votes than any other candidate. But although his old enemy had been dethroned, a new and even more powerful one stood in the way of his dream for Iran. The British, and in particular the Anglo-Iranian Oil Company, dominated the country as never before. Now Mossadegh would turn his sights on them.

CHAPTER 5

His Master's Orders

During the late 1940s, when Iran was being torn by separatist rebellion and bled dry by the Anglo-Iranian Oil Company, the young Mohammad Reza Shah concentrated his attention on sports cars, race horses, and women. He became a fixture of the international party set, favoring London nightclubs and carrying on a string of affairs with second-level movie actresses like Yvonne De Carlo, Gene Tierney, and Silvana Mangano. Several times he tried to consolidate his shaky position at home through repression and vote-rigging, but succeeded only in making himself a figure of ridicule. Newspapers called him a lackey of the British. Public rallies were held to denounce him. He was blissfully unaware of the contempt in which many Iranians held him, however, and did not imagine he was in any danger when he visited the University of Tehran to attend an anniversary celebration.

Snow was falling on that day, February 4, 1949. The Shah had just stepped out of his car and was approaching a staircase when a young man posing as a photographer pulled out a pistol and began shooting at him. Just six feet separated the two, but the gunman proved a very poor shot. His first three bullets hit only the Shah's military cap. In a reflexive response, the Shah turned toward him, and as he turned, a fourth shot tore a hole in his right cheek. Body-guards, generals, and police officers, apparently not considering the Shah's life worth saving, dove for cover, leaving the two men facing each other for a second. The Shah ducked as a fifth shot rang out. It grazed his shoulder. With just one bullet left, the shooter pointed directly at the monarch's chest and pulled the trigger. There was only a light click. The pistol had jammed.

With the danger past, security agents jumped up and quickly clubbed and shot the would-be assassin to death. Mohammad Reza Shah, then twenty-nine years old, took a few minutes to recover. Still breathing heavily, he announced that he had been saved by divine intercession. He may have believed it. The next day he sent his bloodstained uniform to the Officers Club and ordered that it be placed in a display case. Soon afterward, he decided that it was time for him to impose his will on Iran as his father had done.

Iran had entered a new era when Reza Shah abdicated in 1941. Many of his former subjects were thrilled to see him gone, among them thousands of tribal families who immediately abandoned the wretched settlements into which he had herded them and returned to their ancestral mountains and nomadic life. Others, even some who had chafed under his harsh rule, feared that they had lost their country's only bulwark against chaos and the rule of foreigners. Most felt the mixture of relief and apprehension that rowdy school-children feel when a strict teacher suddenly takes ill. Newspapers, political parties, labor unions, and social organizations blossomed, but so did criminal gangs. The fear of authority that Reza Shah had instilled in people melted away. When one upper-class woman reprimanded her chauffeur for turning the wrong way into a one-way street, he replied, "Oh! It does not matter, now Reza Shah has gone."

After forcing the feared strongman to abdicate, the British had first considered restoring the discredited Qajar dynasty. Only after discovering that the pretender, who lived in London, spoke no Persian, did they decide to allow Mohammad Reza to take the throne. Immediately after his coronation, they directed him to appoint a pro-British politician, Mohammad Ali Furughi, as prime minister. Through Furughi they effectively ruled Iran. To secure their power, they revived the old formula under which the country was divided into three sectors. Soviet troops controlled the north, while the British held southern provinces that embraced oil fields, the refinery at Abadan, and the land route to India. Iranians were allowed to continue governing Tehran and the rest of the country's midsection, always under the occupiers' watchful eyes.

The Allies made good use of Iran during the war, not only extracting huge amounts of its oil but also building several large supply bases from which they launched military operations across the Middle East and North Africa. Ordinary Iranians, however, saw their standard of living fall precipitously. Much food was diverted from civilian to military use. Trucks and railroads were used mainly for military purposes. Prices rose as speculators thrived, and poor harvests left many people hungry. Furughi was dismissed when he became the target of public anger, but his successors fared no better.

As long as the war was on and Iran was under military occupation, dissent was muted. Slowly, however, political life resumed. Everyone understood that war and occupation were only temporary conditions. Once they were over, there would be a new nation to build.

Neither the young Mohammad Reza Shah nor his various prime ministers managed to capture the public imagination during the 1940s. The only figure who did was a flamboyant American soldier, General H. Norman Schwarzkopf, who arrived in 1942 as head of a military mission. Schwarzkopf was a West Point graduate who had become chief of the New Jersey State Police. He reached celebrity status while directing the investigation of the Lindbergh kidnapping and later spent several years as the voice of the radio drama *Gang Busters*. When World War II broke out, he rejoined the army and was sent to Iran. Allied commanders assigned him to transform the country's ragged rural police force into a crack unit, and he took to the task with gusto. For six years, including difficult periods when bread riots and other protests shook the country, he and his Imperial Iranian Gendarmerie turned up wherever trouble broke out. At the same time he quietly trained a secret security squad that became the scourge of leftists and other dissidents. He struck many Iranians as a larger-than-life figure, a fearsome avenger who carried the Shah's power into every corner of the country. In a remarkable quirk of history, his son, also General H. Norman Schwarzkopf, returned to the region as commander of Operation Desert Storm in 1990–1991 and also left a lasting imprint on its history.

□ □ □

Iranians in the mid-twentieth century were searching for new solutions to their old problems of poverty and underdevelopment, and like their counterparts in other countries, some embraced the emerging ideology of communism. During the 1930s, Reza Shah had imprisoned several dozen left-leaning professors and political organizers, and while they were behind bars together they spent much time discussing politics. When they were released after Reza's abdication, they constituted themselves as the Group of Fifty-Three and began searching for a new political platform. Some of them joined with a loose group of liberals, reformers, and social activists to form Iran's first real political party, called Tudeh (Masses). At its founding convention, held in 1942, Tudeh adopted a progressive program based on the principle that government should protect ordinary people from exploitation by the rich. It advocated sweeping reform, though not revolution or one-party rule. Young, patriotic, and idealistic, it seemed a promising movement. The British allowed it to function, and Soviet commissars, pleased by the presence of communists in its ranks, actively supported it.

For a time, Tudeh thrived as the party of modernity and European ideas. Its pro-Soviet faction, however, grew steadily stronger and finally, in 1944, seized control. Tudeh turned decisively toward Marxism and launched an intensive organizing campaign among the urban poor. It was so successful that on May Day 1946, it was able to fill the streets of Tehran and Abadan with tens of thousands of enthusiastic demonstrators. Several of its leaders won election to the Majlis that year and went on to help pass laws limiting child labor, establishing a forty-eight-hour workweek, guaranteeing maternity leaves, and setting a minimum wage.

Tudeh's growing power tempted the Soviet Union to make a daring strike against Iran. During World War II, the three Allied powers had agreed that they would withdraw their occupation forces from Iran six months after the end of hostilities, but when that deadline came in early 1946, Stalin ignored it. Citing vague threats to Soviet security, he declared that the Red Army would remain in Iran's northern province of Azerbaijan. When Tudeh activists there proclaimed a People's Republic of Azerbaijan, he ordered his troops to prevent Iranian soldiers from entering the province to reestablish their authority. Soon a local militia emerged, flush with weapons from Moscow. For a time it seemed that Azerbaijan might secede entirely, perhaps to join the Soviet Union or serve as a jumping-off point for a Soviet move against Turkey. But Azerbaijanis remembered Reza Shah and rebelled at the prospect of another dictatorship. Prime Minister Ahmad Qavam, an exceptionally talented statesman, traveled to Moscow and managed to persuade Stalin to step back from the brink of confrontation. He withdrew his soldiers as General Schwarzkopf's gendarmes marched into Tabriz, the provincial capital. The People's Republic of Azerbaijan passed into history. Jubilant Azerbaijanis celebrated by summarily executing all the Tudeh leaders they could find.

Mohammad Reza Shah rightly feared Tudeh, which was strongly antimonarchist, but for several years after the Azerbaijan episode he could find no way to act against it. After the assassination attempt of 1949 he came up with one. All evidence suggested that the failed assassin was a religious fanatic, but the Shah ignored it and accused Tudeh of organizing the attempt. He banned it and imprisoned dozens of its leaders.

Seizing on the public sympathy that the shooting had generated, the Shah also took several other steps to increase his power. He ordered the creation of a second legislative chamber, the Senate, which had been authorized by the 1906 constitution but never established; he liked the provision that gave him the right to appoint half the senators. Then he persuaded the Majlis to pass a bill allowing him to dissolve both chambers and call new elections at his pleasure. Finally and perhaps most important, he won from the Majlis a change in the way prime ministers were appointed. Under the constitution, the Majlis chose them and the Shah gave his assent. Now the system would work the other way, with the Shah choosing and the Majlis voting afterward to confirm or reject his nominee.

Mohammad Reza Shah took all of these steps with the discreet advice and support of the British. For many years, British officials had taken it as a matter of simple logic that since they had such a vital commercial stake in Iran, they must keep it stable and friendly. Without their assent, Mohammad Reza would not have been able to ascend the throne, and he fully understood the debt he owed them. When violent protests broke out at their refinery in 1946, they came to collect.

The riots that shook Abadan led many Iranians to rally to the workers' cause, partly out of instinctive sympathy but also because of the grossly unequal terms under which the Anglo-Iranian Oil Company operated. In 1947, for example, the company reported an after-tax profit of £40 million—the equivalent of $112 million dollars—and gave Iran just £7 million. To make matters worse, it never complied with its commitment under the 1933 agreement with Reza Shah to give laborers better pay and more chance for advancement, nor had it built the schools, hospitals, roads, or telephone system it promised. Manucher Farmanfarmaian, who in 1949 became director of Iran's petroleum institute, was appalled by what he found at Abadan:

Wages were fifty cents a day. There was no vacation pay, no sick leave, no disability compensation. The workers lived in a shantytown called Kaghazabad, or Paper City, without running water or electricity, let alone such luxuries as iceboxes or fans. In winter the earth flooded and became a flat, perspiring lake. The mud in town was knee-deep, and canoes ran alongside the roadways for transport. When the rains subsided, clouds of nipping, small-winged flies rose from the stagnant waters to fill the nostrils, collecting in black mounds along the rims of cooking pots and jamming the fans at the refinery with an unctuous glue.

Summer was worse. It descended suddenly without a hint of spring. The heat was torrid, the worst I've ever known—sticky and unrelenting—while the wind and sandstorms whipped off the desert hot as a blower. The dwellings of Kaghazabad, cobbled from rusted oil drums hammered flat, turned into sweltering ovens. . . . In every crevice hung the foul, sulfurous stench of burning oil—a pungent reminder that every day twenty thousand barrels, or one million tons a year, were being consumed indiscriminately for the functioning of the refinery, and AIOC never paid the government a cent for it.

To the management of AIOC in their pressed ecru shirts and air-conditioned offices, the workers were faceless drones. . . . In the British section of Abadan there were lawns, rose beds, tennis courts, swimming pools and clubs; in Kaghazabad there was nothing—not a tea shop, not a bath, not a single tree. The tiled reflecting pool and shaded central square that were part of every Iranian town, no matter how poor or dry, were missing here. The unpaved alleyways were emporiums for rats. The man in the grocery store sold his wares while sitting in a barrel of water to avoid the heat. Only the shriveled, mud-brick mosque in the old quarter offered hope in the form of divine redemption.

Under the leadership of Sir William Fraser, a famously obstinate Scotsman who hated the idea of compromise, Anglo-Iranian rejected every appeal to reform. Fraser's militancy and that of the British government were easy to understand. Britain had risen to world power largely because of its success in exploiting the natural resources of subject nations. More than half of Anglo-Iranian's profits went directly to the British government, which owned 51 percent of the shares. It paid millions of additional pounds each year in taxes and also supplied the Royal Navy with all the oil it needed at a fraction of the market price. Foreign Secretary Ernest Bevin was not exaggerating when he observed that without oil from Iran, there would be "no hope of our being able to achieve the standard of living at which we are aiming in Great Britain."

Iranians, of course, found it difficult to generate much sympathy for the British. Members of the Majlis began demanding that the oil company offer Iran a better deal, and in 1949 ten of them went so far as to submit a bill that would revoke its concession. Their pressure and the evident threat of continued violence at Abadan became too intense for the British to ignore. They needed a new framework to relegitimize their position in Iran.

Three months after the attempt on the Shah's life, Fraser arrived in Tehran to make his offer. The contract he proposed became known as the Supplemental Agreement, since it was intended to supplement the one Reza Shah signed in 1933. It offered Iran several improvements: a guarantee that Anglo-Iranian's annual royalty payments would not drop below £4 million, a reduction of the area in which it would be allowed to drill, and a promise that more Iranians would be trained for administrative positions. It did not, however, offer Iranians any greater voice in the company's management or give them the right to audit the company's books. The Iranian prime minister took this proposal as a basis for discussion and invited Fraser to negotiate their differences. Fraser dismissed him, declared that his offer was final, and flew back to London aboard his private plane.

"The British want the whole world," Finance Minister Abbasgholi

Golshayan lamented after Fraser stormed out of Tehran. But Mohammad Reza Shah, who knew he must do what Britain wanted, ordered the cabinet to accept the Supplemental Agreement, and on July 17, 1949, it did so. To take effect, however, it had to be approved by the Majlis, which was beyond the Shah's control.

Many members of the Majlis publicly denounced the Supplemental Agreement even before the cabinet accepted it. Others turned against it when Finance Minister Golshayan, whose position should have made him a faithful servant of the British, presented a fifty-page report he had commissioned from Gilbert Gidel, a renowned professor of international law at the University of Paris, that documented the accounting tricks by which Anglo-Iranian was cheating Iran out of huge sums of money. One outraged deputy, Abbas Iskandari, gave an impassioned speech denouncing the agreement that finished with a warning so far-reaching that even he may not have grasped its implications. Iskandari demanded that Anglo-Iranian begin splitting its profits with Iran on a fifty-fifty basis, as American oil companies were doing in several countries. If it refused, he warned, Iran would "nationalize the oil industry and extract the crude itself."

The Majlis's term was expiring and elections were approaching. Many deputies did not want to anger the Shah by voting against the Supplemental Agreement, but given the highly agitated state of public opinion they could hardly vote in favor. They chose to filibuster. For four days the Majlis chamber echoed with long denunciations of both the agreement and the generalized perfidy of Albion. Finally the clock wound down. The Supplemental Agreement was left to the next Majlis.

Mohammad Reza Shah was not amused by this turn of events, and he resolved to do whatever necessary to assure that the next Majlis would heed him. Using a variety of techniques ranging from the recruitment of royalist candidates to bribery and blatant electoral fraud, he managed to secure the election of many pliable deputies. His presumption that he could cheat voters as his father had, however, proved quite mistaken. Iranians were thirsty for democracy and could no longer be terrorized into silence. Several cities exploded in protest. Outrage was strongest in Tehran, where nationalist candidates led by the hugely popular Mohammad Mossadegh were declared losers.

Mossadegh issued a statement inviting all who believed in fair elections to gather in front of his home on October 13. Thousands turned up, and he led them through the streets to the royal palace. When they reached the gate, he turned to face them, delivered a fiery speech, and declared that he would not move until the Shah agreed to hold new and fair elections. He kept his word. For three days and nights he and several dozen other democrats sat on the palace lawn. Finally the Shah, who was about to embark on a tour of the United States and was anxious to avoid embarrassment, gave in.

By choosing to travel to the United States, the Shah was recognizing the emergence of a new world power, one whose will would shape Iranian history more decisively than anyone could have then imagined. President Truman hoped to use the visit, which stretched over several weeks in November and December of 1949, to persuade the young monarch that he must devote himself above all to improving the daily lives of his people. He was convinced that only social reform, not military power, would keep Iran safe from communism.

Truman sent his personal plane, the *Independence,* to bring the Shah to Washington and put him up at Blair House. Later the Shah went on to New York, where he was feted at the Metropolitan Museum of Art, and to a variety of destinations not usually on the itinerary of foreign dignitaries, among them Idaho, Kentucky, Arizona, and Ohio. Companies like Lockheed and General Motors held lavish dinner parties for him. The State Department arranged for him to be honored at Princeton and the University of Michigan. He attended a football game between Georgetown and George Washington, and before the game he was made an honorary captain of the George Washington team. At West Point and Annapolis he was welcomed with twenty-one-gun salutes.

Behind the scenes, however, the Shah's visit did not go well. In meetings with Truman, Secretary of State Dean Acheson, and General Omar Bradley, the chairman of the Joint Chiefs of Staff, he insisted repeatedly that what Iran needed most was a bigger army and more weapons. He asked for tanks, antitank weapons, trucks, and large stores of ammunition, as well as money to pay for tens of thousands of more soldiers and advanced training for a greatly expanded officer corps. His single-mindedness was understandable.

Under the Iranian constitution he controlled the military but nothing else, so a strong army was the key to his personal power. When his hosts tried to steer their conversations to the subject of Iran's social needs, he lost interest. Acheson warned him to pay attention to what had happened in China, where the Nationalist leader Chiang Kai-shek had enjoyed vast military superiority but lost power to ragtag Communists because he had sought "a purely military solution." The two sides could not come to an understanding. In the end, Truman sent his guest home without the military aid he had sought. The joint communiqué issued as the Shah departed said only that the United States would "bear in mind" his request for military aid.

After failing to persuade the Americans to pay for the military buildup that was his most fervent desire, the Shah returned to Iran to find his adversaries better organized than ever. His agreement to cancel the results of his rigged election had shown the limits of his power. It also had another, more far-reaching effect. After leaving the palace grounds following their successful sit-in, twenty of the triumphant protesters had met at Mossadegh's house and made a historic decision. They resolved to build on their victory by forming a new coalition of political parties, trade unions, civic groups, and other organizations devoted to strengthening democracy and limiting the power of foreigners in Iran. They christened it the National Front and by unanimous vote chose Mossadegh as its leader. With a formal organization behind him for the first time and aroused public opinion at his side, the sixty-seven-year-old patriarch now had all the tools he needed to launch his shattering challenge to the political order.

Mossadegh and six other founders of the National Front were elected to the Majlis in the new election they had forced the Shah to call. Their victories marked the arrival of something new in Iranian politics: an organized, sophisticated opposition bloc fired with nationalist zeal and confident of broad public support. Its emergence posed a considerable obstacle both to the Shah's immediate goal, which was to secure approval of the Supplemental Agreement, and to his longer-term project of reestablishing royal power. Two opposing visions of Iran's future were now in sharper conflict than ever before.

The Shah preferred weak prime ministers because he could bend them to his will, but at the beginning of 1950 he and the

British needed one strong enough to force the Majlis to approve the Supplemental Agreement. His first choice, Mohammad Saed, was decidedly unenthusiastic about the agreement and refused even to present it for a vote. After two months the Shah replaced him with a more strongly pro-British figure, Ali Mansur, but Mansur also proved unwilling to fight for the agreement. The British became impatient. In April they sent a new ambassador to Tehran, Sir Francis Shepherd, whose diplomatic experience had been in countries run by tyrants or foreign powers: El Salvador, Haiti, Peru, the Belgian Congo, and the Dutch East Indies. In one of his first cables back to the Foreign Office, Shepherd reported that although the Shah had ordered Mansur "to secure as soon as possible the passage of Supplemental Oil Agreement," Mansur seemed to have "no intention of carrying out his master's orders."

It did not take long for both the Foreign Office and Anglo-Iranian to conclude that Mansur was not their man. They needed a tougher prime minister. Their candidate was not a civilian, as was traditional in Iran, but General Ali Razmara, who had been one of General Schwarzkopf's most trusted officers and had then become chief of staff of the army. Only a man with his fierce determination, they believed, would be strong enough to face down Mossadegh and the National Front.

On June 20 the Majlis voted to create an eighteen-member committee to study the Supplemental Agreement. The British took this as an act of defiance and advised the Shah that he must respond by sacking Prime Minister Mansur and naming General Razmara to succeed him. Such advice could not be ignored.

Razmara's slight stature and ingratiating smile belied his energy, intelligence, and relentless ambition. He was a career soldier, forty-seven years old, known as ruthless and cold-blooded. Like most Iranian officers he had taken advantage of many corrupt opportunities, but he was also a man of unmistakable talent. His hero was the late Reza Shah, with whom he shared the belief that Iran could rise to greatness only under the rule of a harsh, unforgiving tyrant. Unlike Reza, however, he was a sophisticated cosmopolitan, educated at the French military academy and intimately aware of how important it was for Iranian leaders to placate foreign powers. He rose to power by winning their support. To the British, he promised quick passage of the Supplemental Agreement; to the Russians, freedom for Tudeh leaders imprisoned by Mohammad Reza Shah after the attempt on his life; and to the Americans, who were becoming more interested in the Middle East, a sympathetic ear and support in their anticommunist crusade.

The Majlis met at the end of June to debate Razmara's nomination. No one was surprised when Mossadegh delivered a blistering speech denouncing him as a tool of foreign powers and a dictator in the making. Nor was there any surprise when, after the speeches were over, Razmara was confirmed by a comfortable margin. He had used his power to help the campaigns of more than half the deputies, and they were repaying their debts.

Razmara took office convinced that destiny had chosen him to lead Iran back to greatness. Mossadegh believed the same about himself. So did the Shah. Only one of the three could emerge victorious from the coming confrontation.

Razmara's first days in office during that summer of 1950 would have discouraged a less formidable man. The arrival of a new American ambassador, Henry Grady, sparked an outbreak of rioting in which several people were killed; no one had anything against Grady personally, but politicized Iranians had become so angry at foreign interference in their country's affairs that the mere appearance of what seemed to be a new proconsul was enough to send thousands onto the streets. Prime Minister Razmara had to take this rising nationalism into account as he planned his political strategy. He told his British patrons that he could win approval of their Supplemental Agreement, but only if they revised it. Let Anglo-Iranian sweeten its offer, he suggested, by agreeing to open its books to Iranian auditors, train Iranians for managerial jobs, and make some of its royalty payments in advance as a sign of support for national development.

This was a shrewd proposal. By accepting it, Anglo-Iranian might well have undercut the National Front and stabilized its own position for years to come. Much to Razmara's dismay, however, the British rejected it out of hand. Ambassador Shepherd told him the company's offer was final and that the only sweetener it would accept "was perhaps free medical treatment of certain hysterical deputies who continued to denounce the Supplemental Agreement." By failing to recognize that the colonial era was ending and that they could maintain their world power only by working with the rising forces of nationalism, the British passed up a historic opportunity.

Razmara had no choice but to reconcile himself to the will of the Shah, the Foreign Office, and Anglo-Iranian. He named a finance minister known for pro-British views and resumed his campaign for ratification of the Supplemental Agreement. One of his key allies was a radio celebrity named Bahram Sharogh, who had risen to fame as a Nazi propagandist. During the early 1940s, Sharogh had been chief of Radio Berlin's Persian service, and his was the enthusiastic voice that brought Iranians their daily diet of news about Axis victories and the glorious future of German–Iranian relations. His broadcasts were filled with anti-British vitriol, and they fueled the hatred of British imperialism that spread through Iran. When the tide of the war turned, he mysteriously lost his job; some Nazi security officers suspected him of being a British agent. Not long afterward, to the astonishment of his listeners, he turned up at Radio Tehran and began broadcasting lavishly pro-British commentaries. Razmara named him director of "radio and propaganda," and he embraced Anglo-Iranian's cause with a fervor every bit as intense as that he had shown for the Nazis a decade earlier. Besides broadcasting streams of passionate reports himself, he helped Anglo-Iranian single out and bribe pliable newspaper columnists and editors.

By this time the Majlis had named the members of its oil committee. Mossadegh was of course among them, and at the committee's first meeting he was elected chairman. The committee met twice a week. Many of its members were no more interested in finding a compromise than Anglo-Iranian was. Manucher Farmanfarmaian, the director of Iran's petroleum institute, attended many of the sessions and later wrote about them:

> The committee was ostensibly set up to investigate the Supplemental Agreement and find grounds for settlement, but the technical and economic aspects of the agreement were rarely raised. The deputies were not well versed in oil and were interested in it only insofar as it related to politics. Instead, they fixated on the human costs. . . . Mossadegh dominated the proceedings. He criticized everything with great sarcasm, a technique he'd mastered

in the twenty-five years in which he'd done nothing but carp and bestow blame.... Mossadegh did not care about dollars and cents or numbers of barrels per day. He saw the basic issue as one of national sovereignty. Iran's sovereignty was being undercut by a company that sacrificed Iranian lives for British interests. This is what infuriated him about the government's willingness to compromise—and it was what made him decide unequivocally that AIOC had to go.

As the weather cooled in Tehran that autumn, the temperature of public opinion rose steadily. The British, by their refusal to compromise, had managed to unite a broad cross-section of the politically active population against them. They even pushed religious groups committed to Islamic law into a coalition with Mossadegh and other secular liberals. A few mullahs, including the young Ruhollah Khomeini, who thirty years later would emerge as the country's supreme leader, refused to join this coalition because they believed that Mossadegh and his allies had forsaken Islam. Most of the important ones, however, entered into a tactical alliance with the National Front. The most influential among them was the flamboyant and impassioned Ayatollah Abolqasem Kashani, who had never been considered a great religious scholar but who became a central figure in Iran's anti-imperialist movement. Kashani's father had been killed fighting the British in Mesopotamia during World War I, and he himself was held in a British prison camp during the Allied occupation of Iran in World War II. After his release, he quickly emerged as an incendiary popular leader. Mohammad Reza Shah tried to silence him by sending him into exile after the 1949 assassination attempt, but from Beirut he ran for a seat in the Majlis and won. Popular pressure forced the Shah to allow him to return, and hundreds of thousands turned out to welcome him. In his speech to the multitude, he hailed Mossadegh and the National Front as Iran's truest patriots.

Kashani was fiercely anti-Western, hated liberal ideas, and believed that Muslims should obey secular laws only if they were in harmony with the Islamic legal tradition known as *sharia*. If he was a nationalist, it was only in a limited sense; he wanted Iranians to control their own affairs but also imagined that once the infidels were pushed out, Iran would become part of a pan-Islamic commonwealth that would challenge both the Western and communist blocs. Yet like mullahs who had supported the Constitutional Revolution nearly half a century before, he saw the anti-British campaign as a sacred duty. In pursuit of that duty he plunged into politics, building his own faction in the Majlis and working tirelessly to mobilize the masses to Mossadegh's cause. "Islam warns its adherents not to submit to a foreign yoke!" he thundered at one rally.

With the bearded holy man Kashani and the Swiss-educated aristocrat Mossadegh stoking the anti-British fire, opinion in the Majlis turned ever more strongly against the Supplemental Agreement. Prime Minister Razmara tried to make a speech there in October appealing for its ratification but was drowned out by a stream of invective. After he took his seat, more than a dozen deputies rose to reply. All condemned Anglo-Iranian as a rapacious monster and Razmara as its lackey. Mossadegh was the most passionate. He denounced the Supplemental Agreement as an instrument of bondage and then, in an inspired coda, turned dramatically to Razmara and told him: "If you endorse this Agreement, you leave yourself with a disgrace which you will never be able to wash away."

On November 25 Mossadegh brought the Supplemental Agreement to a vote in his parliamentary committee. The committee assembled as usual in an anteroom at the Majlis. Bright sun shone on a light snow cover outside. Mossadegh and the four other committee members who belonged to the National Front proposed the radical option of nationalizing Anglo-Iranian, but the rest of the committee was not ready to go that far. On the question at hand, though, there was no dissent. The committee voted unanimously to recommend rejection of the Agreement.

Events now began to take on a momentum of their own. Iranian politics was moving into uncharted territory, and there was no steady hand at the tiller of state. Every day positions grew more polarized. No faction believed in the goodwill of any other. Discourse was conducted by insult and tirade.

At the end of December, news reached Tehran that the Arabian-American Oil Company, known as Aramco, had reached a new deal with Saudi Arabia under which it would share its profits with the Saudis on a fifty-fifty basis. Ambassador Shepherd immediately dispatched a cable to London urging that Anglo-Iranian make a similar offer to Iran. Both the Foreign Office and the oil company rejected the idea. By doing so, they lost another chance to resolve the looming crisis before disaster struck. Anglo-Iranian's manager in Tehran, E. G. D. Northcroft, advised the home office not to "attach much importance" to the nationalist movement.

The British position was so far removed from reality that Northrop's assistant, Mostafa Fateh, the company's highest-ranking Iranian employee and for decades its faithful servant, felt compelled to protest. He wrote an impassioned twenty-three-page letter to a member of Anglo-Iranian's board of directors, Edward Elkington, whom he had known when Elkington was posted in Iran. The letter was an eloquent warning that the company needed to recognize the "awakening nationalism and political consciousness of the people of Asia" and show "breadth of vision, tolerance for other people's views and clear thinking to avoid disaster." It described Anglo-Iranian's alliance with "corrupt ruling classes" and "leech-like bureaucracies" as "disastrous, outdated and impractical." Fateh said there was still enough support in the Majlis to ratify the Supplemental Agreement if the company would revise it to include a fifty-fifty profit share and shorten its term; otherwise the Agreement was doomed, since the company's policies had "alienated the liberal and progressive classes from Britain." His eloquent cri de coeur went unheeded. Fateh "is not to be trusted far," sniffed one British diplomat to whom Elkington showed it.

Confrontation now seemed inevitable. The prospect thrilled Iranian nationalists, who believed that history was finally giving them a chance to pull their country out from under the rule of British imperialists. In January 1951 they called a rally to launch a mass-based campaign aimed at forcing the nationalization of Anglo-Iranian. A huge crowd turned out. The first speakers were from the National Front, and they were duly cheered as they laid out their case. That was just the beginning. After the politicians were finished, a succession of mullahs came to the podium to proclaim that every good Muslim had a sacred duty to support nationalization. The last of them read a *fatwa* asserting that from his place in paradise, the Prophet Mohammad himself had condemned the Razmara government for selling Iran's birthright to infidel foreigners. Neither the secularists of the National Front nor the religious fundamentalists who followed Ayatollah Kashani were comfortable in alliance with each other, but they put aside their very deep differences in the interests of the great cause.

Poor Razmara was now in an impossible position. The masses had long since decided that he was at best a pawn of the British and at worst a traitor. He replied by insisting time and again that protesters, both inside the Majlis and outside, were pursuing a mad dream, and that the country's interest required it to make a deal with the British. But although he worked feverishly to salvage the British position, neither Anglo-Iranian nor the Foreign Office gave him a shred of support. Ambassador Shepherd went so far as to send him a letter advising that he take "a strong line" against ingrates who did not appreciate "the immense service to mankind of the British people in recent times."

Razmara soldiered bravely on. On March 3 he appeared before Mossadegh's oil committee and once again explained his opposition to the idea of nationalization. He said it would be illegal, would drive the British to unpredictable retaliation, and would devastate Iran's economy. That night Ambassador Shepherd cabled home that he himself had written "the gist" of Razmara's speech.

Iranians suspected as much and reacted with another outburst of protest. At a mass rally on March 7, calls for nationalization were replaced with chants of "Death to the British!" Razmara was out of time. Even the Shah knew it. Quietly, he had begun asking politicians of various stripes whom they would suggest as a new prime minister. Each gave the same answer: Mossadegh.

Everyone recognized that Razmara's days were numbered, but few anticipated how violently his career would end. On the same day that thousands of demonstrators gathered in Tehran to shout their hatred for Britain, Razmara and a friend of the Shah named Assadollah Alam drove to a Tehran mosque for the funeral of a religious leader. A young man with a pistol stepped from the crowd and fired. Razmara fell dead. Police officers seized the gunman, a carpenter named Khalil Tahmasibi who was a member of a religious terror group called Fedayeen-i-Islam.

"If I have rendered a humble service," he told interrogators, "it was for the Almighty in order to deliver the deprived Muslim people of Iran from foreign serfdom."

The circumstances of Razmara's assassination were never clarified. Evidence emerged to suggest that the fatal shot had been fired not by Tahmasibi but by a soldier acting on behalf of the Shah or members of his inner circle, and that Assadollah Alam had knowingly driven him to his fatal rendezvous. Years later a retired Iranian colonel wrote in his memoir that the fatal shot had come from a Colt revolver, available only to soldiers.

"An army sergeant, in civilian clothes, was chosen for the deed," he asserted. "He had been told to shoot and kill Razmara with a Colt, the moment Tahmasibi began to shoot. . . . Those who had examined the wounds in Razmara's body were in no doubt that he had been killed by a Colt bullet, not by the bullet of a weak gun."

Razmara had represented the last hope for conciliation. His cause was all but lost even before his assassination, and the day after the fatal shots were fired, Mossadegh's oil committee took the fateful step toward which it had been marching. By unanimous vote, it recommended that the Majlis nationalize the Anglo-Iranian Oil Company.

The next day, thousands of people gathered at a festive rally to hear Ayatollah Kashani applaud the committee vote and demand that the Majlis act quickly. No public figure could now oppose nationalization without fear of provoking the ire of the masses or worse. Even the newly named prime minister, Hussein Ala, a British-educated diplomat who understood the difficulties that nationalization was sure to bring, dared not speak against it.

At the British embassy, Ambassador Shepherd still believed that he had a chance to hold back the flood. He launched a campaign to persuade Majlis members to stay home on the day of the nationalization vote, thereby preventing a quorum. First he sent a message to the Shah urging him to "use all his influence" with monarchist and conservative deputies. Then he met with Prime Minister Ala and informed him curtly that "the company's operations cannot be legally terminated by an action such as nationalization." He suggested for the first time, though, that Anglo-Iranian might now be ready to consider the idea of a fifty-fifty profit split.

"A fifty-fifty arrangement might have been accepted a little while ago," Ala replied, "but now something more would be required."

The Majlis met on March 15 to cast its historic vote. Ninety-six deputies turned up, including several who had promised the Shah they would stay away. Every one voted in favor of nationalization.

Five days later the largely ceremonial Senate, which had come into existence only a few years earlier and half of whose members were appointed by the Shah, also voted its unanimous approval.

Mossadegh was now a hero of epic proportions, unable even to step onto the streets without being mobbed by admirers. Tribal leaders in the hinterlands celebrated his triumph, Ayatollah Kashani lionized him as a liberator on the scale of Cyrus and Darius, and even the communists of Tudeh embraced him. Over the next few weeks the Majlis voted overwhelmingly for every bill he presented. He was so clearly the man of the moment that Prime Minister Ala found no reason to remain in office, and in mid-April he resigned.

The British government, however, had no intention of surrendering. Its resolve was stiffened when Foreign Secretary Bevin, who had shown some sympathy for the Iranian position, resigned for health reasons and was replaced by the colossally unprepared Herbert Morrison. Morrison had spent thirty years working his way up through Labor Party ranks and had never claimed expertise in world affairs. His proudest achievements were building a new Waterloo Bridge and reorganizing London's transit system. He considered the challenge from Iran a simple matter of ignorant natives rebelling against the forces of civilization. In one of his first public statements as foreign secretary, he urged that British troops be moved toward Iran and stand "ready if necessary to intervene in Persian oil fields."

At Morrison's urging, top-level policymakers from the Foreign Office, the Admiralty, the Bank of England, and the Ministry of Fuel and Power joined to form a "Working Party on Persia." It commissioned several studies to use as background in dealing with the crisis, including one on the psychology of Iranians. The author, a British diplomat, asserted that the typical Iranian was motivated by

> an unabashed dishonesty, fatalistic outlook, [and] indifference to suffering. . . . The ordinary Persian is vain, unprincipled, eager to promise what he knows he is incapable or has no intention of performing, wedded to procrastination, lacking in perseverance and energy, but amenable to discipline. Above all he enjoys intrigue and readily turns to prevarication and dishonesty when-

ever there is a possibility of personal gain. Although an accomplished liar, he does not expect to be believed. They easily acquire a superficial knowledge of technical subjects, deluding themselves into the belief that it is profound.

To deal with such people on an equal or respectful basis would, of course, be absurd. Instead, the Foreign Office devised a three-pronged strategy to bring them back under control. First, Mohammad Reza Shah should be persuaded to dissolve the Majlis. Second, he should appoint Sayyed Zia, the aging British favorite who had helped Reza Shah come to power thirty years earlier, as prime minister. Third, the Truman administration in Washington should be urged "at least not to indicate any disagreement or divergence from our point of view." As this policy was being formulated, Anglo-Iranian decided to prove its resolve by reducing the living allowances it paid to Iranian workers. Thousands walked off the job in protest.

Soon afterward, the British began sending warships to the waters off Abadan. By mid-April three frigates and two cruisers were lurking within sight of the refinery. This raised tensions even higher. Oil workers poured defiantly onto the dusty streets, and a series of brawls left six Iranians, two British oil workers, and a British sailor dead. Some Iranians concluded that the British had embarked on a deliberate campaign of provocation in order to provide a pretext for military intervention.

Ambassador Shepherd believed he could bring the situation back under control if Iran had a new and more decisively pro-British prime minister. He insisted that the Shah nominate Sayyed Zia, and the Shah dutifully agreed. The Majlis scheduled a vote on his nomination for April 28. That morning, Shepherd issued a statement asserting that His Majesty's government would not negotiate anything under the threat of nationalization. With this show of strength and his friend Sayyed Zia at the head of government, he calculated, events would begin moving in a different direction. It was a highly unrealistic scenario and showed once again how completely the British had misjudged Iran's mood.

Not even the most fervent nationalist, however, could have predicted what happened when the Majlis assembled to debate Sayyed Zia's nomination. All eyes were, of course, on Mossadegh, the hero of the hour. Everyone expected him to lead the opposition with one of his withering tirades against the British and their traitorous errand-boys. But when the speaker asked who wished to begin the debate, Mossadegh sat quietly and expressionless. A prominent right-wing deputy named Jamal Emami, who was on the British payroll, took the floor instead. Emami did not even mention Sayyed Zia. Instead he launched into a bitter attack on Mossadegh, pillorying him for having plunged the Majlis into immobility and paralyzed the country with his constant carping. If the old man wanted a real challenge, Emami said scornfully, he should try being prime minister himself and see how difficult the job was. Mossadegh had several times turned aside suggestions that he take over the government, and Emami said he knew the reason why: Mossadegh was one of those irresponsible windbags who delight in making speeches about how wrong everyone else is, but never offer anything positive.

The chamber fell silent as Emami finished. Mossadegh waited for a long moment and then rose to his feet. Speaking slowly and deliberately, he said that he was honored and grateful for the suggestion that he become prime minister and would in all humility accept. Everyone was stunned, Emami most of all. Soon the shock turned to pandemonium. A formal motion was made that Mossadegh be named prime minister, and the speaker called for an immediate vote. It passed by a margin of seventy-nine to twelve.

Sensing the power he held at that moment, Mossadegh said that he would serve as prime minister only if the Majlis also voted to approve an act he had drawn up to implement the nationalization of Anglo-Iranian. Under its provisions, a parliamentary committee would audit Anglo-Iranian's books, weigh the claims of both sides for compensation, begin sending Iranians abroad to learn the skills of running an oil industry, and draw up articles of incorporation for a new National Iranian Oil Company. The Majlis approved it unanimously that very afternoon.

The unthinkable had now happened. Mossadegh, the symbol of Iranian nationalism and resistance to royal power, had suddenly arrived at the pinnacle of power. It was a moment of exhilaration but also of profound uncertainty. Everyone understood that a clash of titans was approaching. No one dared to guess what it might mean for Iran and the rest of the world.

CHAPTER 6

Unseen Enemies Everywhere

O n the morning of June 26, 1950, millions of Iranians and millions of Americans gathered appre-
hensively around their radios. All knew they
would hear news that might reshape their lives forever. Most were
grave and fearful. The crisis that was gathering in Iran, however, had
nothing to do with the one suddenly gripping the United States.

That day in Iran, the Shah announced that he would nominate
General Ali Razmara, the ill-fated army commander, as prime minister. In shops, factories, and tea houses across the country, people
huddled to ask one another what this might mean. Would Razmara
be able to strike a last-minute deal with the British? If not, what
would happen? Might British troops invade Iran? Would there
be a revolution? Was the nation headed toward redemption or
catastrophe?

Americans were preoccupied with very different news. Communist soldiers had just poured across the thirty-eighth parallel in
Korea and were racing southward. The United Nations Security
Council met in emergency session and warned the invaders that if
they did not withdraw, war would follow. Since both of the world's
superpowers had nuclear arsenals, many Americans feared that
Armageddon was at hand.

The huge gap between what preoccupied Iranians and what preoccupied Americans on that June day reflected the obsessions that gripped their countries as the second half of the twentieth century began. Iranians were marching toward a thrilling but also terrifying confrontation with Great Britain and its Anglo-Iranian Oil Company. Americans faced a prospect no less sobering. The war in Korea was final proof that their country was now locked in a worldwide struggle against a fearsome adversary.

In ways that neither nation yet understood, these two crises would ultimately become one. The United States, challenged by what most Americans saw as a relentless communist advance, slowly ceased to view Iran as a country with a unique history that faced a unique political challenge. Its duel with Britain became subsumed in the East–West conflict.

A great sense of fear, particularly the fear of encirclement, shaped American consciousness during this period. Allied leaders who met at Potsdam two months after the end of World War II pledged to cooperate "on a democratic and peaceful basis," but behind their generous words lay deep mistrust. Soviet power had already subdued Latvia, Lithuania, and Estonia. Communist governments were imposed on Bulgaria and Romania in 1946, Hungary and Poland in 1947, and Czechoslovakia in 1948. Albania and Yugoslavia also turned to communism. Greek communists made a violent bid for power. Soviet soldiers blocked land routes to Berlin for sixteen months. In 1949 the Soviet Union successfully tested a nuclear weapon. That same year, pro-Western forces in China lost their civil war to communists led by Mao Zedong. From Washington, it seemed that enemies were on the march everywhere.

In response to this changing international climate, President Truman approved the creation of the Central Intelligence Agency in 1947. Its vague original mandate, which was to carry out "functions and duties related to intelligence affecting the national security," was expanded a year later to include "sabotage, anti-sabotage, demolition and evacuation measures . . . subversion [and] assistance to underground resistance movements, guerrillas and refugee liberation movements, and support of indigenous anti-communist elements in threatened countries of the free world." In January 1950 the National Security Council prepared a seminal document, known as NSC-68, that asserted the need for the United States to confront communist movements not only in regions of vital security interest but wherever they appeared.

"The assault on free institutions is worldwide now," it concluded, "and in the context of the present polarization of power, a defeat of free institutions anywhere is a defeat everywhere."

The Cold War drove the United States to recognize not only the power of its enemies but also the vital importance of its friends. In 1949 it brought eleven of them together into a potent military alliance, the North Atlantic Treaty Organization (NATO). Solidarity between the United States and Britain was the bedrock of this new alliance. Differences over how to deal with countries like Iran could not be allowed to weaken it.

President Truman was among many who believed that the Soviets wished to draw Iran into their orbit. The day after North Koreans invaded South Korea, he told one of his aides that Korea was not the only country worrying him. He walked to a globe near his desk in the Oval Office, placed his index finger on Iran, and said, "Here is where they will start trouble if we aren't careful."

Britain and Russia had trampled on Iranian sovereignty for more than a century, and many Iranians naturally came to detest them both. For the United States, however, most felt only admiration. The few Americans they had come to know were generous and self-sacrificing, interested not in wealth or power but in helping Iran.

The American best-known to ordinary Iranians was an earnest young schoolteacher named Howard Baskerville, who was killed in 1909 while fighting alongside his Iranian friends in the Constitutional Revolution. He was revered as a martyr and called "the American Lafayette." Many took his sacrifice as proof of how much more admirable Americans were than other foreigners.

At the time Baskerville was shot down by royalist soldiers, a visionary American educator, Samuel Jordan, was beginning a forty-three-year stay in Tehran. His Alborz College was among the first modern secondary schools in the country, and thousands of its graduates went on to shape Iranian life. The Presbyterian mission for which Jordan worked also ran a hospital and one of the country's only schools for girls.

"Americans were regarded with nearly universal admiration and affection," one of its graduates wrote years later. "The American contribution to the improvement and, it was felt, the dignity of our impoverished, strife-torn country had gone far beyond their small numbers. . . . Without attempting to force their way of life on people or convert us to their religion, they had learned Persian and started schools, hospitals and medical dispensaries all over Iran."

The dedication of these exemplary men and women was not the only reason many Iranians admired the United States. American officials had spoken out to defend Iran's rights. The United States sharply criticized the 1919 Anglo-Persian Agreement through which Britain acquired colonial powers in Iran. That same year at Versailles, President Woodrow Wilson was the only world leader who supported Iran's unsuccessful claim for monetary compensation from Britain and Russia for the effects of their occupation during World War I. In the mid-1920s an American envoy in Tehran was able to report that "Persians of all classes still have unbounded confidence in America."

Until the outbreak of World War II, the United States had no active policy toward Iran. After the war, however, American power began reaching every corner of the world. The crucial role that oil played in the Allied victory led policymakers in Washington to focus especially on the Middle East. They sharpened their interest as the Cold War intensified.

A giant figure in American diplomatic history, Dean Acheson, directed United States policy toward Iran during this period. Acheson sympathized with the forces of Third World nationalism. With his gaunt frame, pin-striped suits, homburg, and jaunty mustache, he looked every inch the patrician, although in fact he had not been born into wealth. In his youth a Republican who admired Theodore Roosevelt, he later became a Democrat and served in Franklin Roosevelt's administration. Truman recognized him as a kindred spirit and, after winning the 1948 election, named him secretary of state. Both men were determined to show people in poor countries that the United States, not the Soviet Union, was their true friend.

Soon after taking office, Acheson named an energetic and liberal-minded Texan, George McGhee, as his assistant secretary for Near Eastern, South Asian and African affairs. McGhee was just thirty-eight years old when he assumed the influential post. He had studied geology at the University of Oklahoma and had gone on to win a Rhodes scholarship to Oxford. When he finished his studies, the Anglo-Iranian Oil Company offered him a job as a geophysicist in Iran, but he declined, returned to the United States, and started his own oil company. Its success made him wealthy enough to work for the State Department without pay. His background in the oil industry, however, led some in the British Foreign Office to mistrust him. They suspected him of trying to weaken Anglo-Iranian so that American oil companies, perhaps some in which he had a hidden interest, could take its place in Iran.

McGhee attended many of the meetings that Mohammad Reza Shah held with American officials during his visit to Washington at the end of 1949 and was put off by the young monarch's "grandiose and unrealistic" military ambitions. Soon afterward, he invited officials of Anglo-Iranian to a meeting. He told them that he had read their company's most recent annual report and was impressed with how much profit they were making. Perhaps it was time, he suggested, for the company to begin sharing its wealth more equitably with Iran. His guests scorned the idea. One of them went so far as to say that if Anglo-Iranian began giving in to Iran's demands, it would soon be left with "nothing in the till."

This debate sharpened over the next months. McGhee repeatedly warned directors of Anglo-Iranian that if they hoped to save Prime Minister Razmara and persuade the Majlis to approve their Supplemental Agreement, they must make concessions. At one point, angered by the company's insistence that it could not afford to pay Iran more, he asked the State Department's petroleum expert, Richard Funkhouser, to prepare a report on its operations. The report concluded that Anglo-Iranian was an "exceptionally profitable" company, that it sold its oil for between ten and thirty times the cost of producing it, and that its arrogance had made it "genuinely hated in Iran."

McGhee, deeply worried about what he saw as a looming disaster, decided to travel to London to press his case in person. He arrived there in September of 1950 to a frosty welcome. Senior officials of both the British government and Anglo-Iranian resolutely rejected his pleas for compromise. They told him that the company would not train more Iranians for supervisory positions, would not open its books to Iranian auditors, and would not offer Iran more money for its oil. "One penny more and the company goes broke," said the chairman, Sir William Fraser. That astonishing piece of mendacity made clear to McGhee that more talks were fruitless. He packed up and returned home.

British officials, steeped in the world's most fully developed colonial tradition, were baffled by what they saw as the Truman administration's refusal to agree that Britain should benefit from the work it had done in foreign countries. What seemed like rapacious imperialism to the Americans—and even more so to the Iranians—seemed only common sense to the British. They insisted that they were doing the world a great service by their work in Iran, as Sir Donald Fergusson, the permanent undersecretary at the Ministry of Fuel and Power, wrote in one memorandum:

> It was British enterprise, skill and effort which discovered oil under the soil of Persia, which has got the oil out, which has built the refinery, which has developed markets for Persian oil in thirty or forty countries, with wharves, storage tanks and pumps, road and rail tanks and other distribution facilities, and also an immense fleet of tankers. This was done at a time when there was no easy outlet for Persian oil in competition with the vastly greater American industry. None of these things would or could have been done by the Persian government or the Persian people.

The chasm between American and British perceptions of the gathering crisis in Iran was vividly symbolized by the new ambassadors both countries sent to Tehran in 1950. Henry Grady, the American, was an economist with firsthand experience in Greece and India, two countries where politics was being reshaped by nationalism. Grady believed that if the United States did not align itself with nationalist forces in the developing world, those forces would turn toward Marxism and the Soviet Union. He was a fervent anticommunist but an equally fervent anti-imperialist.

In both temperament and politics, Grady was the polar opposite of his British counterpart in Tehran, the fire-breathing Sir Francis Shepherd. The reports these two ambassadors sent back to their respective capitals were so different that they hardly seemed to be portraying the same country. Grady saw an impoverished land long exploited by the British, who sucked the country's lifeblood and treated the pitiful Shah like a servant. Shepherd, however, considered Anglo-Iranian a wise and paternal company that had brought

Iran nothing but good. He had no use for ungrateful Iranians—or meddling American diplomats—who believed otherwise.

In February 1951 George McGhee summoned all American ambassadors in the Middle East to a meeting in Istanbul. One of the main agenda items was the friction that had developed between the United States and Britain over the question of Iran. The gathered diplomats concluded that Anglo-Iranian's militancy was "one of the greatest political liabilities affecting the United States/United Kingdom interests in the Middle East." The company's "reactionary and outmoded policies," they declared in a secret memorandum, were not only creating a dangerously explosive situation but constituted "a handicap in the control of Communism in Iran." This consensus guided American policy through the Truman administration.

The Iranian crisis deepened over the next few weeks. Prime Minister Razmara was assassinated on March 7, and on March 15 the Majlis took its historic vote, "accepting the principle that oil should be nationalized throughout Iran." Some deputies may have believed that the British would find a way to live with this vote because the British Parliament itself had recently nationalized key British industries. As it did so, Foreign Secretary Ernest Bevin had mused, "What argument can I advance against anyone claiming the right to nationalize the resources of their country? We are doing the same thing here with our power in the shape of coal, electricity, railways, transport and steel." Bevin was out of office by the time the Iranian crisis exploded, however, and those he left behind in government agreed unanimously that although nationalization might be a wise path at home, it could not be abided abroad.

Immediately after the Majlis voted to nationalize Anglo-Iranian, McGhee flew to Tehran. He arrived on March 17 to find Ambassador Shepherd in a foul mood. Shepherd blamed the vote on Americans, specifically on Aramco, the Arabian-American Oil Company. Aramco's announcement that it would begin splitting its profits with the Saudi Arabian government on a fifty-fifty basis, Shepherd complained, had "thrown a wrench" into Britain's negotiating position. McGhee replied that he had warned Anglo-Iranian months earlier that the fifty-fifty deal was forthcoming. The company, he told Shepherd, had brought its troubles on itself by being "too rigid and too slow to recognize that a new situation had been created in Iran which required a new approach."

That evening McGhee called on the Shah. Their meeting was most disconcerting, as McGhee wrote afterward:

> I had been with the Shah about a year and a half earlier during his much-publicized official visit to Washington. He had then been a proud, erect young man, insistent that his requests be taken seriously. As I saw him in the darkened audience chamber in which he received me, lounging on a sofa, he was a dejected, almost broken man. I sensed that he feared he too might be assassinated. . . . Did he think with our support he could avert nationalization?
>
> The Shah said he couldn't do it. He pleaded that we not ask him to do it. He couldn't even form a government. Everyone was afraid. There were unseen enemies everywhere. . . . He looked lost, as if he thought the whole affair hopeless. I left him alone in his darkened room. I will always remember his sad, brooding face. . . . The specter of death and impending chaos hung gloomily over Tehran like a dark cloud. I was sad when I said goodbye.

On his way home, McGhee stopped in London and met there with Sir William Fraser, the Anglo-Iranian chairman, and Foreign Secretary Morrison. The meetings were so stormy that Morrison decided to send a delegation to Washington to present Britain's case. He named Sir Oliver Franks, the British ambassador in Washington, who had been McGhee's tutor in morals at Oxford, as its chairman.

The meetings stretched over nine days. British emissaries argued that allowing Iran to nationalize the oil company "would be widely regarded as a victory for the Russians" and would also "cause a loss of one hundred million pounds per annum in the United Kingdom's balance of payments, thus seriously affecting our rearmament program and our cost of living." Franks insisted that Iran had "no solid grievances" against either Britain or the oil company, whereas Britain was vitally concerned about losing "a prime strategic necessity." He described Anglo-Iranian as a crucial asset to the West "not only because of its magnitude as an element of our balance of payments . . . but also because of the power it gave us to control the movement of raw materials." Iranian oil was vital "to our common defense," and losing it would cripple "our ability to rearm."

McGhee listened for several days in quiet frustration. When he finally spoke, it was to warn once again that the British must compromise with Iran or face disaster. He urged them to start splitting their profits with Iran on a fifty-fifty basis, "which had an aura of fairness understandable to the ordinary man." The British would not be persuaded. "In the end," he wrote later, "I was, with great regret, forced to advise Franks in our final meeting on April 18 that their proposals did not, in the case of accommodation to nationalization, meet the requirements we saw for success."

Soon after the talks in Washington ended, Iran set out on its brave new course. On May 1, 1951, Mohammad Reza Shah signed the momentous law revoking Anglo-Iranian's concession and establishing the National Iranian Oil Company to take its place. The next day Britain demanded that the law be suspended. On May 6 Mohammad Mossadegh submitted his cabinet to the Majlis. It was immediately approved, and on that same day Mossadegh took office as prime minister.

Historic as Mossadegh's rise to power was for Iranians, it was at least as stunning for the British. They were used to manipulating Iranian prime ministers like chess pieces, and now, suddenly, they faced one who seemed to hate them. "All of Iran's misery, wretchedness, lawlessness and corruption during the last fifty years," the state-controlled Radio Tehran declared in a broadcast soon after Mossadegh took office, "has been caused by oil and the extortions of the oil company."

For a brief moment, Prime Minister Attlee seemed disposed to compromise. Attlee was a socialist who had helped draft the plans under which Britain had nationalized some of its own basic industries. At one cabinet meeting he suggested that Britain might make a public statement accepting nationalization of Anglo-Iranian, thereby giving Mossadegh "an opportunity of saving face," and then arrange some sort of complicated deal under which the company would retain most of its privileges. Herbert Morrison vigorously objected. He warned Attlee that any concessions to Iran would set an intolerable precedent and encourage nationalists everywhere. Attlee allowed himself to be persuaded and signed off on a cable to Ambassador Franks in Washington. It directed him to tell Acheson that "Persian oil is of vital importance to our economy, and that we regard it as essential to do everything possible to prevent the Persians from getting away with a breach of their contractual obligations."

Acheson, however, believed that Mossadegh represented "a very deep revolution, nationalist in character, which was sweeping not only Iran but the whole Middle East." He and others in the Truman administration never stopped urging their British counterparts to turn away from their policy of confrontation and to offer Mossadegh a legitimate compromise. They did this despite realizing that Mossadegh would not be easy to deal with, as a profile in the *New York Times* made clear:

> The tidal wave of nationalistic fervor that engulfed the Anglo-Iranian Oil Company in the space of a few weeks has now unexpectedly cast one of Iran's most redoubtable demagogues, the aged Mohammad Mossadegh, upon the pinnacle of power. In the popular view, the new Premier represents a figure of retributive justice who galvanized the impressionable Parliament and led it to victory over the dragon, Anglo-Iranian, which, in the eyes of many, had for years been feeding upon the vitals of the country. . . .
>
> A foreign diplomat, admitted recently to the new Premier's presence, asked Dr. Mossadegh to explain exactly how he intended to proceed with the expropriation of Anglo-Iranian. For half an hour Dr. Mossadegh described the misdeeds of British imperialism over the past 100 years. When he had finished, the diplomat repeated the question. Again the Premier denounced British imperialism. The interview ended there.
>
> What will Dr. Mossadegh do next? The question remains open and the answer is anybody's guess.

Messages that flew between Washington and London during mid-1951 did nothing to narrow differences between the two allies over how to deal with Mossadegh. On May 18 the State Department issued a public statement declaring that Americans "fully recognize the sovereign rights of Iran and sympathize with Iran's desire that increased benefits accrue to that country from the development of its petroleum." Morrison read it with dismay and in a cable to Ambassador Franks that afternoon said that he was "really rather annoyed at the American attitude of relative indifference to a situation which may be most grave to us all."

Soon afterward, Morrison sent a message to Acheson in which he sought to lay out the British position in the clearest possible terms. The issue Britain faced in Iran, he wrote, "concerns *the* major asset which we hold in the field of raw materials. Control of that asset is of supreme importance.... Parliamentary and public feeling in England would not readily accept a position where we surrender effective control of an asset of such magnitude."

The Americans were unmoved. On May 31 Truman sent a note to Attlee urging that negotiations "be entered into at once" to prevent a worsening of the "explosive situation" in Iran. Attlee replied that allowing Iran to get away with nationalization would have "the most serious repercussions in the whole free world." He realized, however, that given Truman's insistence, the British would have to make at least a show of engaging Mossadegh.

At Attlee's suggestion, Anglo-Iranian sent a delegation of officials led by the company's deputy chairman, Basil Jackson, to Tehran for negotiations. Mossadegh welcomed them by arranging for Iranian gendarmes to take over the Anglo-Iranian office at the western town of Kermanshah on the day they arrived. As if that were not enough to set the tone, Ambassador Grady restated the American position in an interview with the *Wall Street Journal.*

"Since nationalization is an accomplished fact, it would be wise for Britain to adopt a conciliatory attitude," Grady asserted. "Mossadegh's National Front party is the closest thing to a moderate and stable political element in the national parliament."

Iranians at the negotiating table said that they were willing to talk, but only after the visitors from London accepted nationalization of the "former company" as a fait accompli. Jackson refused, insisting that Iran was bound by the 1933 accord and could not renounce it until its sixty-year term expired. He had a counteroffer. Anglo-Iranian would pay Iran £10 million and another £3 million monthly while negotiations proceeded; it was also willing to transfer its assets to the newly created National Iranian Oil Company, but only if it could establish a new company that would have "exclusive use of those assets." This was a not-so-subtle declaration that Britain still did not accept the fact of nationalization. It reflected the Foreign Office's unaltered position, which was that the British "can be flexible in profits, administration or partnership, but not in the issue of control." To no one's surprise, Iranian negotiators rejected the offer.

On June 20 Mossadegh named a French-educated engineer, Mehdi Bazargan, as the managing director of the National Iranian

Oil Company. Bazargan flew immediately to Abadan, where British administrators were still running the refinery, and declared himself their new boss. His first order was that captains of British tankers must henceforth provide him with receipts before they sailed, listing the amount of oil they were carrying so he could keep track of how much was being exported.

The British considered this intolerable. They believed, as their United Nations ambassador asserted, that the oil was "clearly the legal property of the Anglo-Iranian Oil Company." When tanker captains refused to provide receipts, Bazargan threatened to have Anglo-Iranian's general manager, Eric Drake, arrested for sabotage. As that crime would carry the death penalty under a bill pending in the Majlis (it was later withdrawn), Ambassador Shepherd advised Drake to leave Iran. He did so and began running the company from an office in Basra, across the Shatt-al-Arab in Iraq. From there, he continued to refuse the demand for receipts. When the Iranians insisted, Sir William Fraser issued an order of his own from London. Tanker captains were to pump back all the oil in their holds and leave Abadan empty.

Iran had until that moment been the world's fourth largest oil exporter, supplying 90 percent of Europe's petroleum. Now, since it owned not a single tanker, it could not export a drop. That was fine with Fraser, who still believed he could bend the Iranians to his will. "When they need money," he predicted, "they will come crawling to us on their bellies."

For Fraser and his colleagues at Anglo-Iranian, as well as for officials of the British government, the very idea that Iran would nationalize its oil industry seemed absurd and impossible, even as it was happening. They had trouble taking it seriously. In their view the entire campaign was most likely a monumental bluff, a ploy to squeeze more money out of London, or, if not that, then simply a petulant outburst that would end when the consequences became clear.

"At no time before a year or two before 1951 did anyone contemplate that we would not stay there forever," Eric Drake recalled afterward. "We were there by an international agreement between the government of Iran and the Anglo-Iranian Oil Company, so there was no reason it should ever come to an end as far as we could see."

Britain's press enthusiastically jumped aboard the anti-Mossadegh bandwagon. The London *Times* blamed "irresponsible Persian politicians" for stirring up the country's uneducated masses. The *Economist* declared that Anglo-Iranian had become a "monumental scapegoat" and asserted: "No Persian with any common sense really believes that the Anglo-Iranian Oil Company is responsible for the horrifying poverty of the masses." The *Observer* described Mossadegh as a "Robespierre fanatic" and a "tragic Frankenstein" who was "obsessed with one xenophobic idea."

Across the Atlantic, the tone was quite different. The *Washington Post* asserted that most Iranians saw the oil company as "a thriving state within a stricken state—as a symbol of their poverty." The *New York Times* said that many Middle East specialists considered Mossadegh a liberator comparable to Thomas Jefferson or Thomas Paine. The *Chicago Daily News* reported that even many Britons were disturbed by the way their government was handling the issue. "British critics do not think that McGhee was really responsible for the Iranian crisis," its London correspondent wrote. "They agreed that the whole affair was badly handled by the Anglo-Iranian Oil Company with the connivance, by default, of the Foreign Office."

There was indeed dissent in Britain. Anglo-Iranian's own labor adviser, Sir Frederick Leggett, wrote to a friend in the Foreign Office that the company was in its "deplorable position" because it had "failed to make a gesture of recognition of Persian national aspirations." Minister of State Kenneth Younger complained in a memo to Morrison about "the short-sightedness and the lack of political awareness shown by the Anglo-Iranian Oil Company" and asserted that it "never even seriously tried" to make a "proper estimate" of the situation. Earl Mountbatten told his superiors at the Admiralty that instead of listening to the "notoriously bellicose" Herbert Morrison's advice on how to "cow these insolent natives," Britain should realize that "economic and military threats could only make things worse."

Even some British diplomats were sending contrary reports to the Foreign Office. The labor attaché in Tehran filed a cable describing conditions at Abadan as deplorable, saying that workers there lived in "cottages made of mud bricks, with no electricity, without outside water supply and sanitary arrangements . . . in other words, in veritable slums." And from Tel Aviv, the British minister forwarded a *Jerusalem Post* report that he said convinced him that Anglo-Iranian "deserved what happened." It was written by an Israeli who had spent several years working at Abadan alongside Iranians he described as "the poorest creatures on earth."

> They lived during the seven hot months of the year under the trees. . . . In winter times these masses moved into big halls, built by the company, housing up to 3,000–4,000 people without walls of partition between them. Each family occupied the space of a blanket. There were no lavatories. . . . In debates with British colleagues we often tried to show them the mistake they were making in treating the Persians the way they did. The answer was usually: "We English have had hundreds of years of experience on how to treat the Natives. Socialism is all right back home, but out here you have to be the master."

On June 28 Mossadegh issued an appeal to British technicians and managers at Abadan. He told them that Iran was "anxious to benefit" from their expertise and promised that if they stayed at their jobs, "our country will welcome you warmly." Fraser, determined that Iran not be able to run the refinery by itself, responded by ordering most of the company's British employees to leave Iran.

With Iranians already in control of the Anglo-Iranian office in Kermanshah, the next step was for them to take over the Abadan and Tehran offices. They did so during the last days of June. The head of the Abadan office had wisely moved his sensitive papers to the local British consulate, which Iranians could not enter. Richard Seddon, head of the Tehran office, was not as quick. When a delegation of Iranians arrived to search his home, they found many files still there, including some burning in the fireplace. An official of Iran's foreign ministry who was present that night summarized what they found:

> Although compromising documents had allegedly been removed, enough papers were left behind to make it easy for Mossadegh to prove that AIOC had interfered in all aspects of Iranian political life. The documents revealed that the company had influenced senators, Majlis deputies and former cabinet ministers, and that those who had opposed it had been subtly forced out of office. Newspapers had been paid to publish articles alleging that many

of the National Front's leaders were actually paid stooges of AIOC. . . .

Among the documents was evidence that former Prime Minister Ali Mansur had begged AIOC to allow him to remain in office, promising in return to appoint a new finance minister more agreeable to the company. Another set of letters revealed that AIOC had helped Bahram Sharogh to become director of Iran's Radio and Propaganda Department, and that on a trip to London he had been recruited to serve the company. There were also directives and reports on influencing guilds, through the Mayor of Tehran, to rise against those in the bazaar who supported the National Front.

The government quickly made these documents public, and many Iranians took them as further proof of the oil company's perfidy. Mossadegh said they proved that Anglo-Iranian had engaged in a "sinister and inadmissible" campaign to subvert Iranian democracy. Majlis deputies were driven to new levels of anticolonial outrage. So were news commentators, one of whom wrote in a Tehran paper: "Now that the curtain is lifted and the real identity of traitors posing as newspaper men, Majlis deputies, governors and even prime ministers is laid bare, these men should be riddled with bullets and their carcasses thrown to the dogs."

President Truman, still hoping to find a solution to the crisis, called a meeting of his National Security Council at the end of June. The facts laid before him were alarming. George McGhee's attempts to sway the Foreign Office and the Anglo-Iranian Oil Company had failed utterly. Anglo-Iranian had begun evacuating its employees from Abadan, and a complete shutdown of the refinery there was a real possibility. British warships were patrolling ominously offshore. Middle East experts on the National Security Council staff warned in a report that if the oil conflict could not be resolved, "the loss of Iran to the free world is a distinct possibility." Their report asserted that the British were seriously considering invading Iran and warned that such an invasion "might split the free world, would produce a chaotic situation in Iran, and might cause the Iranian Government to turn to the Soviet Union for help."

This left Truman more worried than ever. His fears were heightened by two messages he received in the next few days. The first, from Mossadegh, made clear that Iran and Britain remained on a collision course. Mossadegh complained about Britain's efforts to sabotage his nationalization project and added ominously, "There is no danger whatever to the security of life and property of the British nationals in Iran. Any spreading of false rumors on the part of the agents of the former oil company might, however, cause anxieties and disturbances."

Mossadegh's warnings arrived in blunter terms on July 1 from Ambassador Grady. In an anguished cable he warned Truman that Iran was in "a most explosive situation" and reported for the first time that Britain was looking for ways to overthrow Mossadegh. "The British, led by Mr. Morrison, seem to be determined to follow the old tactics of getting the government out with which it has difficulties," he wrote. "Mossadegh has the backing of 95 to 98 percent of the people of this country. It is utter folly to try to push him out."

What Grady considered "utter folly" was indeed what the British were planning. They had abandoned all hope of bringing Mossadegh around to their way of thinking and were not prepared to make the concessions he wanted. Ambassador Shepherd wrote in a cable to London that "the moment has come for us to try and get him out," so that Iran would once again have a prime minister who was "reasonable and friendly" rather than "rigid and impractical."

News from The Hague on July 5 further complicated matters. The International Court of Justice, acting at Britain's request, issued an "indication" recommending that Iran allow the oil company to continue functioning as before while negotiations proceeded. Iran had refused to participate in the case. The Court was empowered to adjudicate only disputes between nations, and Iranian officials asserted that since the 1933 oil accord was a deal between Iran and a private company, it had no right to intervene. The Iranian minister at The Hague dismissed its recommendation as "null and void" and "an intervention in our internal affairs."

That steeled Foreign Secretary Morrison's resolve. He marched to the House of Commons and took the floor to declare that the situation in Iran was "becoming intolerable." To assure that Mossadegh understood the intensity of his indignation, he added that the Royal Navy was "lying close to Abadan" and would be ordered into action "should the Persians fail to discharge their responsibilities."

Truman now saw greater peril than ever. To him, the question of who would control Iranian oil was only secondary. He was more worried that the argument between the United States and Britain over how to deal with Mossadegh might spiral out of control and split the Atlantic alliance. Determined to make a last effort at compromise, he wrote to Mossadegh suggesting direct American mediation:

> This matter is so full of dangers to the welfare of your own country, of Great Britain and of all the free world, that I have been giving the most earnest thought to the problems involved. . . . I have watched with concern the breakdown of your discussions and the drift toward a collapse of oil operations with all the attendant losses to Iran and the world. Surely this is a disaster which statesmanship can find a way to avoid. . . .
>
> I lay great stress on the action of the [World] Court. . . . Therefore, I earnestly commend to you a most careful consideration of its suggestion. I suggest that its utterance be thought of not as a decision which is or is not binding depending on technical legal considerations, but as a suggestion of an impartial body dedicated to justice and equity and to a peaceful world. . . .
>
> I have a very sincere desire, Mr. Prime Minister, to be as helpful to you as possible in this circumstance. I have discussed this matter at length with Mr. W. Averell Harriman, who as you know is one of my closest advisors and one of our most eminent citizens. Should you be willing to receive him, I should be happy to have him go to Tehran as my personal representative to talk over with you this immediate and pressing situation.

Averell Harriman was an accomplished diplomat who had served as ambassador to Britain, ambassador to the Soviet Union, and director of the Marshall Plan in Europe. He also knew Mohammad Reza Shah and was thought to have some expertise in matters Iranian. Immediately after Truman told him of his new mission, Harriman received an illustrious delegation at his Washington home: Secretary of State Acheson, Assistant Secretary George McGhee, two other State Department officials, and the British ambassador, Sir Oliver Franks. All agreed that the situation in Iran had become exceedingly dangerous. A small incident at Abadan, they feared, could lead the British to intervene militarily, which might in turn lead Mossadegh to seek Soviet help. Even if that did not happen, closing the refinery was sure to set off a wave of social and political turmoil.

Harriman's mission faced challenges even before it began. The British disapproved of the whole idea. In an impatient note to Acheson, Foreign Secretary Morrison said that Britain was "in grave difficulties" and needed not more negotiations but "whole-hearted support" from the United States. "I must tell you that one of our main difficulties in dealing with this intractable problem has arisen from a belief persistently held by many Persians that there is a difference of opinion between the American and British over the oil question," he wrote. "An approach by a representative of the President would, I fear, merely encourage Dr. Mossadegh in this belief."

This message confirmed Acheson's view that Morrison, as he wrote later, "knew nothing of foreign affairs and had no feel for the situation." He had even less use for Britain's hard-line ambassador in Tehran, Sir Francis Shepherd, whom he considered an "unimaginative disciple of the 'whiff of grapeshot' school of diplomacy." Their dislike was mutual. As soon as Shepherd learned that Acheson was sending an emissary to Tehran to interfere in what he considered his business, he called a news conference to express his "astonishment and chagrin" at the temerity of the Americans.

"What is the use of Harriman flying here?" he asked. "We are not inviting mediation in this matter." This was a highly undiplomatic outburst, and under instructions from the Foreign Office, Shepherd retracted it the next day.

It was in this climate that Ambassador Grady visited Mossadegh to deliver Truman's letter. He wore a white suit and a jaunty tropical hat and waved happily to photographers as he arrived. The bedside meeting, however, did not go well. At Mossadegh's request Grady read the letter aloud, and when he reached the passage in which Truman urged him to accept the Court's advice, Mossadegh broke out into a thirty-second fit of convulsive laughter. When he finally stopped, there was a long moment of silence. Mossadegh finally told Grady that Iran believed the World Court had no jurisdiction in this case. Then he launched into a long and increasingly angry denunciation of the United States, which he said had once upheld moral principles but was wilting in the face of British pressure. His tirade was so vitriolic that Grady did not even see the point of pressing Harriman's possible visit.

Acheson was much irritated when he received news of this encounter. He sent Grady a sharp note telling him that the Harriman mission was

> the one new positive element contained in the President's proposal and is the step to which the President and I attach greatest significance. I cannot believe that Mossadegh's initial reaction will, upon reflection, be his final one. Considerations of courtesy will lead him, I am convinced, to give President's message full consideration, and to receive President's personal rep who can give both you and Mossadegh the benefit of great thought which President has put to this matter and receive any suggestions which Mossadegh may have. Therefore request that you see Mossadegh again as speedily as possible and in tactful way, which I know you will employ, urge these considerations upon him.

Grady did as he was told, and Acheson's faith in his persuasive powers turned out to have been justified. He convinced Mossadegh that the Harriman mission was in everyone's interest. Harriman arrived in Tehran on July 15, 1951. His welcoming committee consisted of ten thousand enraged Iranians shouting, "Death to Harriman!"

CHAPTER 7

You Do Not Know How Evil They Are

Averell Harriman's first hours in Tehran were not auspicious. His limousine had to take a round-about route from the airport in order to avoid angry mobs. He made it safely to the guest palace that had been prepared for him but had to dine while the sound of gunfire echoed through the air. Mounted police and soldiers in armored cars were firing at protesters. By midnight the city was awash in blood and tear gas. More than twenty people lay dead and another two hundred were wounded.

Why did the protest end with such awful carnage? The next day's newspapers blamed Mohammad Reza Shah and General Fazlollah Zahedi, the hard-line interior minister, who, they said, had intentionally provoked violence in order to give Harriman the impression that Iran was in chaos. Prime Minister Mossadegh was furious and fired Zahedi before the day was out.

That afternoon, Harriman paid his first call on Mossadegh. It was a meeting different from any in Harriman's long diplomatic career. He was ushered into an upstairs bedroom in Mossadegh's modest home. There Mossadegh was reclining in bed, dressed in a camel-hair cloak. He welcomed Harriman weakly and said that he hoped during their talks to learn whether the United States was truly a friend of the oppressed or merely a puppet of the vile British. Harriman replied that he had lived in London and knew that there were good Britons as well as bad ones. Mossadegh demurred. "You do not know them," he mumbled. "You do not know them."

Mossadegh never saw any contradiction between his boundless respect for Britain's constitutional tradition and his contempt for its government and imperial history. During one of his meetings with Harriman, he mentioned a grandson on whom he doted. Harriman asked where the grandson was studying. "Why, in England, of course," Mossadegh replied. "Where else?"

In his cables back to Washington, Harriman described Mossadegh as "completely rigid" and "obsessed with the idea of eliminating completely British oil company operations and influence within Iran." His impression of the old man, as related by a biographer, reflected his frustrations:

> Caught in deception, as he often was, [Mossadegh] would respond with disconcerting, childlike laughter or a heart-rending confession, often followed by a repeat of the devious tactic with an ill-concealed new twist. He projected helplessness; and while he was obviously as much a captive as a leader of the nationalist fanatics, he relented on nothing. Under pressure, he would take to his bed, seeming at times to have only a tenuous hold on life itself as he lay in his pink pajamas, his hands folded on his chest, eyes fluttering and breath shallow.
>
> At the appropriate moment, though, he could transform himself from a frail, decrepit shell of a man into a wily, vigorous adversary. He would arrive at the entrance of Harriman's guest palace shuffling slowly along while leaning heavily on his cane; but once inside, he would throw the cane aside and sometimes forget where it was. The first time he was presented to Marie Harriman, he took hold of her hand and didn't stop kissing until he was halfway to her elbow. Later, he could be caught stealing glances at her, sometimes losing his train of thought altogether.

Harriman had brought a petroleum expert, Walter J. Levy, with him to Iran, and Levy accompanied him to several of his meetings with Mossadegh. Again and again, Levy enumerated the obstacles that Mossadegh's government would face if it tried to run the Abadan refinery by itself. There were almost no Iranians trained for senior administrative and technical positions, and even if by some miracle a way could be found to keep the oil flowing, Iran had no tankers to bring it to market. Loss of Anglo-Iranian's royalty payments, which in 1950 had reached nearly £10 million, would destabilize Iran and possibly lead to Mossadegh's overthrow and replacement by a Tudeh government controlled from Moscow. That in turn might provoke Western military intervention.

None of these arguments moved Mossadegh in the slightest. Foreign intervention, he insisted, was the root of all Iran's troubles, and "it all started with that Greek Alexander," who had burned Persepolis twenty-four centuries before. Whenever Levy paused after making what he thought was an especially trenchant point about how much Iran would suffer if it failed to reach an accord with the British, Mossadegh would roll his eyes and reply simply, "Tant pis pour nous." Too bad for us.

Harriman and his aides, accustomed to the give-and-take of traditional diplomacy, were driven to distraction by Mossadegh's maddening style of negotiation. "Dr. Mossadegh had learned to take one step forward in order to take two backward," the American interpreter, Vernon Walters, wrote afterward. "After a day's discussion, Mr. Harriman would bring Mossadegh to a certain position. The next day when we returned to renew the discussion, not only was Mossadegh not at the position where he was at the end of the previous day, he wasn't even at the position where he had been the day before that. He was somewhere back around the middle of the day before yesterday."

Walters was then a lieutenant colonel in the United States Army. His language skills had brought him to the attention of superiors and would help carry him through a stellar career that culminated with appointments as deputy CIA director and ambassador to Germany. He had an irreverent wit, once remarking that Mossadegh's nose "made Jimmy Durante look like an amputee." More important, he knew when to interpret literally and when to reshape indiscreet comments. On one occasion, for example, Ambassador Grady's wife greeted the Iranian leader by saying, "Dr. Mossadegh, you have a very expressive face. Every time you are thinking of nothing, I can tell by the blank stare on your face." Walters rendered this comment into French as: "Dr. Mossadegh, you have a very expressive face. Every time you are thinking deep thoughts, I can tell by the look of concentration on your face."

Mossadegh's talks with Harriman did not falter because of Mossadegh's negotiating style or his failure to grasp the intricacies of the oil industry. The real reason was the fundamental difference in the way the two men perceived the dispute. To Harriman, it was a matter of practicalities, a set of technical challenges that could be resolved by rational analysis, discussion, and compromise. Mossadegh saw it from an entirely different perspective. He believed that Iran was at the sublime moment of liberation. Imbued with the Shiite ideal, he was determined to pursue justice even to the point of martyrdom. Details about refinery management or tanker capacity seemed to him laughably irrelevant at such a transcendent moment.

When Harriman insisted that there must be a way for Mossadegh to build a new relationship with the British, the old man shook his head. "You do not know how crafty they are," he said. "You do not know how evil they are. You do not know how they sully everything they touch."

Most Iranians shared this view, as Walter Levy realized when he struck up a conversation with a group of people he met on a Tehran street. Their colloquy, as Levy later related it, went like this:

Levy: You realize that if the British technicians leave Abadan you will have to try to run the industry by yourselves?
Iranians: Yes.
Levy: You realize that you will fail to run the industry without the British?
Iranians: Yes.
Levy: So Iranian oil will no longer be produced for the world market?
Iranians: Yes.
Levy: And if Iranian oil is no longer produced, there will be no money in the Iranian treasury?
Iranians: Yes.
Levy: And if you have no money there will be a financial and economic collapse which will play into the hands of the Communists?
Iranians: Yes.

Levy: Well, what are you going to do about it?
Iranians: Nothing.

Unable to move Mossadegh through persuasion, Harriman decided to try influencing him indirectly. First he asked the Shah for help, but the Shah told him frankly that in the face of public opinion, there was no way he could say a word against nationalization. Then he called Iranian reporters to a news conference, and when they arrived, he began reading a statement that called on Iran to confront the crisis with "reason as well as enthusiasm." As soon as those words were out of his mouth, one journalist jumped to his feet and shouted, "We and the Iranian people all support Premier Mossadegh and oil nationalization!" The others began cheering and then marched out of the room. Harriman was left alone, shaking his head in dismay.

In pondering the question of who could influence Mossadegh and the masses, Harriman next came up with an outlandish idea: he would call on Ayatollah Kashani, the firebrand mullah who had become one of Iran's most powerful public figures. It is difficult to imagine two more different men. Harriman came from one of the world's richest families. He was a Skull-and-Bones man at Yale, a skier and a polo player who had spent his life in the highest society. Kashani had fought in the desert against the British, had been imprisoned by them, and was later sent into foreign exile at the Shah's order. He had a long black beard and wore a turban to match. His world was centered around a small, carpeted chamber where he sat for most of every day, meditating, praying, and plotting. Several times a week he emerged to visit a mosque or deliver a thunderous denunciation of imperialism to crowds of the faithful, who considered him a near-deity.

Harriman arrived at Kashani's door and was brought into a darkly curtained room where the holy man sat motionless. After removing his shoes, seating himself on a carpet, and expressing his respect, he said he hoped Kashani agreed that the oil crisis could be resolved only by some kind of agreement between Iran and Britain. Perhaps, he ventured, Kashani could help persuade Mossadegh to accept a British emissary. As soon as these first few sentences were translated, Kashani erupted with a stream of invective, the gist of which was that no self-respecting Iranian would ever meet with

British "dogs" and that the United States had turned itself into Iran's enemy by suggesting it. As for Iran's oil, it could remain in the ground for all he cared. "If Mossadegh yields," he concluded, "his blood will flow like Razmara's."

Not satisfied with that threat, the Ayatollah had another for Harriman himself. He asked if Harriman had heard of a Major Embry, and when Harriman said he had not, Kashani explained, "He was an American who came to Iran in 1911 or 1912. He dabbled in oil, which was none of his business, and aroused the hatred of the people. One day, walking in Tehran, he was shot down in the street, but he was not killed. They took him to the hospital. The enraged mob followed him to the hospital, burst into the hospital and butchered him on the operating table. Do you understand?"

With some effort Harriman managed to control his temper. "Your Eminence," he replied coldly, "you must understand that I have been in many dangerous situations in my life and I do not frighten easily." Kashani shrugged and said, "Well, there was no harm in trying."

Kashani's contempt for the idea of compromise, which was even more visceral than Mossadegh's, was not all that frustrated Harriman. The British disgusted him just as much, as he told Acheson in one cable:

In spite of the fact that the British consider oil interest in Iran their greatest overseas asset, no minister has visited Iran as far as I can find out, except Churchill and Eden on wartime business. Oil company directors have rarely come. Situation that has developed here is tragic example of absentee management combined with world-wide growth of nationalism in undeveloped countries. There is no doubt Iranians are ready to make sacrifices in oil income to be rid of what they consider to be British colonial practices. Large groups are in mood to face any consequences to achieve this objective. It is clear that British reporting and recommendations from here have not been realistic, and it seems essential that member of British government find out for himself what is going on here.

For a time it seemed that despite all the obstacles, some solution might be reached. Harriman finally managed to persuade Mossadegh to issue a statement saying that he would negotiate with a British envoy if "the British government on behalf of the former Anglo-Iranian Oil Company recognizes the principle of national-ization of the oil industry in Iran." To his immense irritation, how-ever, the Foreign Office rejected this overture. He decided to fly to London himself to plead for reason. There he met for three hours with the British cabinet. Its members were divided. Some argued for a continued hard line, but others agreed that it might be wise to send an emissary to Tehran. Prime Minister Attlee decided to dis-patch the Lord Privy Seal, Sir Richard Stokes, a wealthy member of the British elite with no experience in the Middle East.

Stokes was instructed to tell Mossadegh that the oil company would accept the principle that Iran's oil belonged to Iran, and also that it was now willing to share its profits on a fifty-fifty basis. The British must, however, remain in control of all drilling, refining, and export operations. This was in essence the same offer that Basil Jackson had brought to Tehran six weeks earlier, though Stokes was told not to admit this fact. He was to remain within the limits of Jackson's offer but could "dress it up and present its main points in different order, together with trimmings or sweetenings as might be required."

The first question Mossadegh asked Stokes when the two men met for the first time was whether he was Roman Catholic. When Stokes replied that he was, Mossadegh told him that he was unsuited for his mission because Catholics do not believe in divorce and Iran was in the process of divorcing the Anglo-Iranian Oil Company. Stokes was not amused. What Mossadegh was doing to Anglo-Iranian, he replied, was closer to murder than divorce.

That exchange set the talks off on a sour note. They were further complicated by Anglo-Iranian's decision on July 31 to shut the Abadan refinery. Company officials said they had no alternative. Storage tanks were full, and tankers could not sail since their cap-tains had been instructed not to sign the receipts Iran was demand-ing. It was a shattering step that reflected how deep the crisis had become.

Stokes knew full well that he was offering Mossadegh a deal that the prime minister had already rejected. In a cable home, Stokes said that the essence of his offer was to keep Anglo-Iranian operat-ing as before but "under a new name" and lamented that he had tried "a number of devices by which we could disguise this hard fact, but found nothing that was not either dangerous or too transparent for even the Persians to accept." For his part, Mossadegh declared himself willing to negotiate three points only: the continued sale of Iranian oil to Britain to meet its domestic needs, the transfer of British technicians to the service of the new National Iranian Oil Company, and the amount of money Iran should pay for Anglo-Iranian's nationalized assets.

As the talks ground on toward inevitable failure, Stokes and Harriman flew to Abadan for a look around. The different ways they occupied themselves reflected their vastly different approaches to the crisis. Stokes was quickly caught up in a diplomatic flap when the British consul first tried to expel Iranian officials from Abadan and then flew into a rage when an Iranian car drove ahead of his in the caravan escorting Stokes from the airport. The consul wrote an angry letter to the local governor demanding assurances that "in the future, the representative of His Majesty's Government is not subjected to such indignities." Iran's foreign ministry responded by expelling him from the country. Before departing, he cabled London to suggest that he wait in Basra so that he could be of assistance "in the event of a military action."

Harriman made better use of his time. He toured Abadan and sent a cable to Truman reporting that the slums he saw were "shocking for housing of employees of a large Western oil company." In later cables he complained that the British held "a completely nineteenth-century colonial attitude toward Iran." Instead of negotiating seriously, they issued only "rash statements" and "impulsive expressions of resentment" about what they considered the theft of their property in Iran. "I frankly feel that if the British government does not cooperate," he concluded, "it will make the success of my mission extremely doubtful if not impossible."

Harriman's nerves were further frayed by an attack of intestinal disorder and the sweltering midsummer heat. The palace where he was staying in Tehran was lavish but had only a few languid fans to stir the oppressive air. Desperate for relief, he began taking long flights to provincial capitals aboard his official plane, which was air conditioned. He ordered that the cabin be made as cold as possible, and he and his aides wrapped themselves in blankets while they enjoyed the chill. When Vernon Walters suggested that using a plane that burned eight hundred gallons of fuel per hour in order to cool off was a bit excessive, Harriman bristled in reply: "If you had seen my income taxes over a period of years, you would know that I have bought a number of these for the United States government."

Mossadegh met several more times with Stokes and at one point handed him a memorandum that seemed to offer a glimmer of hope. If the British would accept the right of Iranians to control their oil industry, he wrote, he would "fully and fairly" negotiate the oil company's "just claims" for compensation. Stokes was intrigued and cabled the Foreign Office, asking permission to explore what seemed to him a promising offer. The reply was stern, containing two brusque orders: there were to be "no further concessions," and Stokes was to break off the talks and return forthwith to London.

On August 22 the British cabinet imposed a series of economic sanctions on Iran. They prohibited the export of key British commodities, including sugar and steel, to Iran; directed the withdrawal of all British personnel from Iranian oil fields and of all but a "hard core" of about three hundred administrators from Abadan; and blocked Iran's access to its hard currency accounts in British banks. The next day Stokes left Tehran.

"The result is nothing," Mossadegh admitted at a news conference. "It is no good. Everything is finished."

As Stokes departed, Prime Minister Attlee sent a triumphant cable to Truman. "I think you'll agree breakdown in talks entirely due to Persian side," he wrote. "Only course now is, we hope, for complete U.S. public support of His Majesty's Government's position."

His appeal fell on deaf ears. Truman was mightily disappointed by the failure of Harriman's mission but placed much of the blame on Britain's intransigence. In a reply cable, he insisted that neither the British nor the Americans should take any steps that "would appear to be in opposition to the legitimate aspirations of the Iranian people."

Harriman paid a call on the Shah before leaving Tehran, and during their meeting he made a discreet suggestion. Since Mossadegh was making it impossible to resolve the crisis on a basis acceptable to the West, he said, Mossadegh might have to be removed. Harriman knew the Shah had no way of removing Mossadegh at that moment. By bringing up the subject, however, he foreshadowed American involvement in the coup two years later.

"It was a mission unlike any other," Vernon Walters wrote afterward. "There was an Alice in Wonderland quality to it which led me after three days to write back to Mr. Harriman's secretary in Washington to ask her to send me a copy of that book so I would know what was next on the program. It was in a sense a mission that failed, but it was a mission that cast a long shadow ahead on the great problems that the Western world was to have with oil two and a half decades later. These Dr. Mossadegh was not to live to see, yet in a way their true origin led back to him."

After the failure of these last attempts at negotiation, Foreign Secretary Morrison and Ambassador Shepherd intensified their efforts to depose Mossadegh. Shepherd broached the idea with his Iranian friends, and Mossadegh learned of these discussions almost immediately. On September 6 he made a speech to the Senate condemning them and warned that if the British did not cease their plotting, he would expel all remaining British citizens from Abadan in two weeks. Prime Minister Attlee responded by ordering the Royal Navy to strengthen the flotilla of warships hovering off Iran's coast.

For at least a year, the British had been considering the possibility of landing troops in Iran to secure what they considered to be their refinery and oil fields. In the autumn of 1950 Ambassador Franks had told American officials in Washington that his government believed that "the dispatch of a small U.K. force to southern Iran would have a steadying and not a provocative influence." The following April Sir George Bolton, the executive director of the Bank of England, passed to the Foreign Office a report from his Middle East adviser saying that the political tempo in Iran "is such that the possibility of direct intervention by taking over by force the fields and refinery must be considered." Minister of Defense Emanuel Shinwell told the cabinet that tolerating nationalization of Anglo-Iranian would set a terrible precedent and that "we must be prepared to show that our tail could not be twisted interminably." Anglo-Iranian officials predicted in a memorandum to the Foreign Office that if British troops landed at Abadan, "the Persians would probably climb down" and the company could import "thousands of colored men from East Africa to do labor that Iranians might refuse to perform."

In May 1951, two months before Harriman's arrival, the British drew up two detailed plans for the invasion and occupation of Iran. The first, code-named at different stages Buccaneer and Plan Y, contemplated the use of seventy thousand troops in a "seaborne assault combined with the arrival of the maximum possible forces by air" that would "seize and secure" the refinery and oil fields. A more limited alternative, Operation Midget, envisioned the seizure of only the refinery, either for a two-week period while tankers removed the oil in storage there or indefinitely, so that it could be used to refine oil from elsewhere in the Gulf. Advocates of these plans argued that they would not only keep oil flowing to Britain but would also send a patriotic thrill through the country. Lord Fraser, First Lord of the Admiralty, said that a bold military strike would dispel Britain's "dumps and doldrums" and prove that it would not tolerate "being pushed around by Persian pip-squeaks."

Some British officials doubted the wisdom of these plans, but sentiment for invasion was strong and might have carried the day had it not been for implacable opposition from the Truman administration. On May 16 the American ambassador to Britain, Walter Gifford, cabled Acheson that he was becoming "increasingly concerned" about the "belligerent atmosphere" in London. The Foreign Office, he warned, had come to believe that American objections to an invasion "are not very large and can probably be overcome."

"Against this background we fear that Brit, having made implied threat use of force, may eventually be faced with alternatives of either, against their better judgment, making good on this threat and risking unpredictable consequences or backing down and suffering resultant loss prestige and perhaps fatal weakening of their position," Gifford wrote. "It is our estimate that ultimate UK decision whether or not to use force will be in last analysis determined by extent to which US prepared support."

Acheson immediately understood the urgency of this message. He summoned Ambassador Franks and told him that the United States resolutely opposed "the use of force or the threat of the use of force" against Iran, and that Truman himself had "stressed most strongly that no situation should be allowed to develop into an armed conflict between a body of British troops and the Persian forces." His bluntness had the desired effect. Franks immediately sent a message home warning that if Britain went ahead with its invasion plans, Washington's "opposition to the British would probably become even more violent than it is at present."

Truman's position found much support in the American press. The *Wall Street Journal* lamented Britain's reliance on "nineteenth century threats." The *Philadelphia Inquirer* warned that a British invasion of Iran might bring "a quick outbreak of World War III." A popular CBS commentator, Howard K. Smith, asserted that many countries in the Middle East and beyond supported Iran, and that an invasion might "stir all the Southern Asians to a rebellion against the Western foreigner and cause serious trouble for both Britain and the United States."

Foreign Secretary Morrison, who led the war party in London, urged the Americans to change their position. He argued that it would be disastrous for the West if Britain were made to look "feeble and ineffective" at the hands of a man like Mossadegh, "whose fanaticism bordered on the mental." After the World Court issued its "indication," he asked Acheson whether the Americans would support an invasion if Iran refused to climb down. Absolutely not, Acheson replied; a British invasion of Iran under any circumstances would have "disastrous political consequences."

That was enough for Prime Minister Attlee, who had never been enthusiastic about the idea of occupying Iran. On July 19 his cabinet voted to defer the military option, balancing its decision by approving the dispatch of three army battalions to neighboring Iraq. Morrison, however, did not give up. After Mossadegh announced in September that the last Britons would soon be expelled from Abadan, Morrison told the cabinet that the time for invasion had come. Attlee agreed to a show of naval force in the Gulf, but definitively ruled out any more drastic military action.

"An occupation of Abadan Island would not necessarily bring about a change in the Persian Government and might well unite the Persian people against this country, and neither the oil wells nor the refinery could be worked without the assistance of Persian workers," Attlee told the cabinet. "If we attempted to find a solution by force we could not expect to find much support in the United Nations, where the South American governments would follow the lead of the United States and Asian governments would be hostile to us."

Having failed to persuade Attlee to order an invasion, Morrison decided to begin covert action. He turned first to two distinguished scholars who had spent years studying Iran and were sympathetic to the British position there. The first, Ann K. S. Lambton, had been press attaché at the British Embassy in Tehran during World War II and gone on to become one of Britain's leading scholars of Iran. At Morrison's request, she began suggesting "effective lines of propaganda" that the British might use to turn Iranian public opinion against Mossadegh.

Lambton's role was limited to giving advice in London. The other scholar Morrison recruited—at Lambton's suggestion—was a more flamboyant figure, and from him Morrison wanted much more than advice. He was Robin Zaehner, a veteran covert operative who had worked for the Secret Intelligence Service in Iran. Zaehner was fluent in Persian and well acquainted with the leading figures in Iranian politics. A Foreign Office memorandum described him as "a man of great subtlety," but with his squeaky voice and eccentric manner, he was hardly a conventional spy. An American who studied his career portrayed him as a colorful, multifaceted figure:

> Zaehner possessed extraordinary capacity to combine high thought with low living. He relished the lighter side of his duties. He held his own in gossip or discussion, whether about philosophy and religion or about human foibles. He drank heavily. Rather in the tradition of Aldous Huxley, Zaehner also experimented with drugs to increase his sensory perception of eternal verities. . . . To those who wished to learn about Iranian politics he recommended Lewis Carroll's *Through the Looking-Glass*. He tended to tell his superiors what he believed they wanted to hear. His temperament did not draw him to the more sinister side of intelligence operations, nor did he have the discipline for rigorous secrecy. Zaehner was an Oxford *bon vivant* transmogrified into a quasi–Secret Service agent.

In mid-1951 Morrison appointed Zaehner to a post as "acting counselor" at the British Embassy in Tehran. Although technically not an intelligence officer, Zaehner devoted most of his time to meeting with opposition figures and suggesting ways they could help undermine Mossadegh's government. His work greatly encouraged them, and his reports to the Foreign Office also had an important effect. He was the first outsider sent to Iran with the specific

Reza Shah was a harsh tyrant but also a visionary reformer. The British forced him from his throne in 1941. His eldest son, the future Mohammad Reza Shah, stands second from left.

The British built the world's largest oil refinery at Abadan on the Persian Gulf and made huge profits there. Their Anglo-Iranian Oil Company was supposed to be a partnership with Iran, but Iranians were not permitted to audit the books.

Abadan was a colonial outpost, with swimming pools and tennis courts for the British administrators and slum housing for tens of thousands of Iranian workers. Buses, cinemas, and other amenities were reserved for the British.

Prime Minister Mohammad Mossadegh thrilled Iranians when he nationalized the oil company in 1951. Here he is shown in the bed from which he often conducted business.

Mossadegh visited the United States in 1952. President Harry Truman tried to arrange a compromise between Iran and the British.

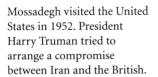

Henry Grady (above), the American ambassador to Iran, sought to prevent a clash between Mossadegh and the West. So did President Truman's special envoy, W. Averell Harriman (right).

On October 4, 1952, the unthinkable happened: the last Britons sailed away from Abadan. It was a triumph for Iranian nationalism and a humiliating defeat for the British. They set out to reverse it by overthrowing Mossadegh.

Mohammad Reza Shah wanted to guide Iran's future, but Prime Minister Mossadegh believed that monarchs should leave politics to elected leaders. The Shah bitterly resented Mossadegh's efforts to reduce his power.

Prime Minister Winston Churchill believed in covert operations and strongly encouraged the coup. He and Foreign Secretary Anthony Eden failed to win American support while President Truman was in office, but succeeded after Dwight Eisenhower assumed the presidency in 1953.

Soon after Eisenhower approved the coup, the CIA sent one of its most resourceful agents, Kermit Roosevelt, to Iran to carry it out.

The brothers who ran the overt and covert sides of American foreign policy during the Eisenhower administration were determined to overthrow Mossadegh: Secretary of State John Foster Dulles (above) and Director of Central Intelligence Allen Dulles.

The campaign against Mossadegh intensified after an anti-Mossadegh diplomat, Loy Henderson, arrived as American ambassador. Henderson (right) is shown talking to the ill-fated Foreign Minister Hussein Fatemi.

Sir Francis Shepherd, the British ambassador to Iran, worked tirelessly to undermine Mossadegh's government.

Asadollah Rashidian, one of Kermit Roosevelt's key Iranian agents, built support for the coup by bribing politicians, mullahs, newspaper editors, and gang leaders.

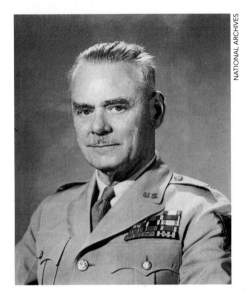

General H. Norman Schwarzkopf, father of the Gulf War commander, headed a crack police brigade in Iran during the 1940s and returned on a clandestine mission to help arrange the coup.

Ayatollah Abulqasim Kashani, a powerful fundamentalist cleric, supported Mossadegh at first but then turned against him. Kermit Roosevelt sent him $10,000 the day before the coup.

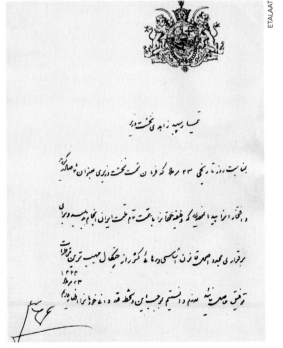

Princess Ashraf, the Shah's tough-minded twin sister, helped persuade her brother to support the coup. A British agent said he secured her cooperation by gifts of cash and a mink coat.

CIA agents persuaded the Shah to sign a decree dismissing Mossadegh from office and another (above) naming a disaffected officer, General Fazlollah Zahedi, to replace him. The decrees were of dubious legality, but they helped rally support for the coup.

The British and Americans chose General Zahedi (left) as the figurehead leader of their coup. Another key collaborator was Colonel Nematollah Nasiri (right), commander of the Shah's Imperial Guard.

On August 19, 1953, anti-Mossadegh crowds surged through the streets of Tehran. Some military units joined them, and by midnight they had succeeded in overthrowing the government.

The Shah, who had fled in panic when the coup seemed to be failing, flew home to reclaim his throne. Soon he began centralizing power in his own hands.

Mossadegh was arrested, tried by a military tribunal, and found guilty of treason. He spent three years in prison and the rest of his life under house arrest. He died in 1967.

Mohammad Reza Shah ruled harshly for twenty-five years and was finally overthrown in 1979. Revolutionaries like these carried portraits of Mossadegh, symbolizing their determination to take revenge for the 1953 coup. The new regime in Iran imposed fundamentalist rule, aided anti-Western terror groups, and inspired Islamic radicals in many countries.

assignment of trying to subvert Mossadegh. The progress he made strengthened the hand of those in London who believed that a covert action campaign against Mossadegh might succeed.

As British leaders ordered military steps to intimidate Iran and launched their covert campaign against its government, they also took a series of steps designed to cripple its economy. This might have seemed a logical strategy, since inflicting pain often breaks the will of nations just as it breaks the will of human beings. What the British failed or refused to realize, however, was that Mossadegh and the great majority of Iranians were ready to accept and even embrace much pain in their sacred cause. The Shiite religious tradition blended perfectly with the nationalist passion sweeping through Iran. Together they steeled the will of Iranians.

The British wished to make it impossible for the National Iranian Oil Company to function. The first tactic they used was discreet sabotage at the Abadan refinery. Eric Drake, the general manager at Abadan when it was nationalized, recalled years later that British managers did all they could to assure that machines didn't work and new managers couldn't find out how the place was run. "There was no question of violent resistance," he said, "but it's extraordinary how pieces of the plant would go wrong just when they were supposed to be doing something else."

These steps would not have kept the refinery from running if technicians had been available to run it. The National Iranian Oil Company placed advertisements in several European newspapers and specialized journals announcing that it wished to hire such technicians. British diplomats set out to assure that none would make it to Abadan. They persuaded Sweden, Austria, France, and Switzerland to deny exit visas to interested applicants. In Germany, which was still under Allied occupation, they asked the government to "refuse the grant of passports to German nationals intending to travel to Persia" unless they could prove they were not oil specialists; the Germans were in no position to resist. An American firm publicly offered the Iranian government help "to recruit 2,500 American technicians to run the oil industry," but withdrew the offer after being warned by the State Department that it was "contrary to British interests and embarrassing to the United States." An

American congressman, Owen Harris, introduced a bill authorizing the secretary of the interior to look for qualified experts and help them travel to Iran, but it died after British diplomats protested to the House Foreign Affairs Committee. And in Britain itself, twenty Anglo-Iranian employees who had left Iran but wanted to return were told that under the new sanctions regime, they would not be allowed to convert their salaries into British currency.

This well-coordinated campaign made it all but impossible for Iran to continue producing oil. The British, however, feared that Iran would find a way, either by using Iranian experts or by slipping some foreigners through the blockade. They resolved to assure that if that happened, Iran would find no customers.

Companies in Britain and the United States owned more than two-thirds of the world's oil tankers, but there remained the possibility that tankers from the Soviet Union or elsewhere might begin carrying Iranian oil. To prevent this, the Foreign Office first considered announcing that it would begin to "intercept foreign tankers on the high seas on the grounds that they were carrying stolen oil from Persia." After realizing that such a threat would violate international law, however, it decided on a different tactic. Anglo-Iranian placed advertisements in dozens of newspapers around the world warning that it would "take all such actions as may be necessary" against any country that bought oil from Iran. The company based its threat on the contention that Iranian oil was its lawful property under "the Convention of 29th April 1933." That was misleading language, since conventions are instruments between governments and the 1933 concession agreement was between a government and a company. Officials in several countries recognized that fact and made plans to buy oil that Iran had stockpiled or might produce.

During the summer of 1951, there were still more than three hundred Britons left at Abadan, and one of them, a deputy general manager named Alick Mason, had a way to intercept telegrams sent to the National Iranian Oil Company. In July he intercepted two from American oil companies offering to supply their own tankers if the NIOC would sell them ten million tons of crude over the next year. He informed his superiors in London. They in turn appealed to the State Department, which obligingly persuaded the companies to withdraw their offer. Similar appeals killed incipient deals between the NIOC and companies in Italy and Portugal. The Iranians then tried to arrange barter deals with India and Turkey, but British pressure aborted those deals, too.

As Britain tightened its noose, Iran fell into political turmoil. Bitter debates broke out in the Majlis, including one in which a deputy hurled his briefcase at a cabinet member. Moderates warned that Mossadegh had brought the country to the brink of disaster. Radicals argued with equal passion that he was not confronting the British strongly enough. The press, freer than at any time in Iranian history, was full of denunciations, accusations, and predictions of one form of doom or another. Ambassador Grady warned in interviews with Tehran newspapers that either war with the British or a communist takeover might be imminent.

Those were among Grady's last words as ambassador. His outspoken support for the cause of Iranian nationalism had greatly irritated the British, and, finally, Acheson decided that his "strong personality" had turned him into a liability. He removed Grady in September and replaced him with Loy Henderson, whose worldview was shaped by the East–West confrontation and who soon concluded that Mossadegh was "a madman who would ally himself with the Russians."

As the Americans changed ambassadors in Tehran, the British also adjusted their strategy. Having reluctantly ruled out the option of armed invasion, they decided to take their case to the United Nations Security Council. There they hoped to win approval for a resolution ordering Mossadegh not to expel their oil company from Iran. The debate would also give them a chance to present their case, which they believed was highly persuasive, to the court of world opinion.

Americans warned against this. Henry Grady, by then already a former ambassador, told a London newspaper that the British were foolishly giving Iranians "a great forum to tell the world how their oil company has oppressed the Iranian people, and to show that Western capitalism is tending to control, and possibly destroy, other countries in the underdeveloped part of the world." The State Department worried that the Soviet Union would veto any pro-British resolution, thereby strengthening its image as defender of the world's oppressed. In a note to Herbert Morrison, Acheson warned that forcing a United Nations debate might lead to "an irrevocable freezing of the Iranian situation."

The ever-obtuse Morrison, however, was determined to press ahead. When the American ambassador in London, Walter Gifford, called on him to deliver Acheson's note, he was met with a stern tongue-lashing:

> I had 45 minutes with Morrison this p.m. and found him in a petulant and angry mood. . . . He launched into a tirade about our attitude re Iranian problem. He was unhappy about [American suggestions for a watered-down Security Council resolution], reiterating a number of times "I will not be put in the dock with Mossadegh." . . . He said at one point "We have been the saints and Mossadegh has been the naughty boy." He emphasized he cld not understand US attitude. He expected 100 percent cooperation and was only getting 20 percent. . . . We had persistently inveighed against use of force and then when UK reverted to appeal to [the United Nations] to uphold rule of law, we not only had doubts re wisdom of action, but came up with res which failed to make any distinction between relative guilt and innocence of parties. . . . During all the forgoing conv, Morrison had kept [Acheson's note] folded in front of him. He finally picked it up and read it, shaking his head and muttering "This is defeatist—defeatist."

Morrison was sure that Britain's silver-tongued representative to the United Nations, Sir Gladwyn Jebb, would dominate the debate and run rhetorical rings around his Iranian counterpart. But if he thought that the prospect of confrontation in such august chambers would terrify Iranian leaders, he was quite mistaken. Mossadegh loved it—so much so that he resolved to come to New York and present his case in person.

This was a master stroke. The most eloquent figure Iran had produced in many centuries would now take to the world stage, and he would present not just the case of one small nation against one big company, but that of the wretched of the earth against the rich and powerful. Mossadegh was about to become the preeminent spokesman for the nationalist passion that was surging through the colonial world.

CHAPTER 8

An Immensely Shrewd Old Man

Throngs of admirers jammed the Tehran airport to cheer Mossadegh as he set out on his historic trip to New York. When he landed in Rome, his first stop, his plane was surrounded by news photographers while police officers struggled to control the crush of exuberant Iranian expatriates and other supporters who had waited half the day for a glimpse of him. The same frenzied scene was repeated at his next stop in Amsterdam.

New York, long accustomed to receiving world-famous figures, awaited Mossadegh with much curiosity. He was not just the "symbol of Iran's surging nationalism," as the *New York Times* called him, but a world leader with a great story to tell and a famously theatrical way of telling it. Everyone, with the possible exception of Britain's delegate to the United Nations, was eagerly awaiting his performance. "Whether Mossy is a phony or a genuine tear-jerker," warned the *Daily News,* "he better put everything he's got into his show if he goes on television here."

Mossadegh stepped gingerly from his plane on the afternoon of October 8, 1951. His son and personal physician, Gholam-Hussein, helped him down the steps. He did not speak, but issued a written statement to waiting reporters. It promised that the world would soon hear the story of a "cruel and imperialistic company" that had stolen what belonged to a "needy and naked people" and now sought to use the United Nations to justify its crime.

From the airport Mossadegh was taken to New York Hospital for a medical examination. Doctors pronounced him fit, and he decamped to the Ritz Tower Hotel at the corner of Park Avenue and Fifty-seventh Street. There he spent most of his time preparing the speech he would deliver to the Security Council. This was an era before Castro, before Sukarno, before Nkrumah and Lumumba. The voice of poor countries had seldom been raised in such rarefied chambers. Mossadegh's would be the first that most Westerners had ever heard.

As he waited for his moment, he devoured everything the American press was writing about his forthcoming performance. Typical of these previews was an edition of *Newsweek* that carried the cover line "Mossadegh: Fainting Fanatic." *Newsweek* praised Mossadegh's personal integrity, mentioning that he had turned down both his official limousine and his salary as prime minister; recounted his career as "incorruptible provincial governor, anti-British agitator, enemy of the tough old Shah Reza Khan, red-baiter and founder of the terrorist National Front"; asserted that although many Westerners had at first dismissed him as "feeble, senile, and probably a lunatic," they now saw him as "an immensely shrewd old man with an iron will and a flair for self-dramatization"; and wondered, along with much of the rest of the world, what this "fabulous invalid" would say and do in the days ahead.

"The stage was set for one of the strangest contests in the strange history of the United Nations—the tremulous, crotchety Premier versus Britain's super-suave representative, Sir Gladwyn Jebb," *Newsweek* reported. "And this might be the decisive act in the dramatic, tragic and sometimes ridiculous drama that began when Iran nationalized the Anglo-Iranian Oil Co. five months ago."

The confrontation for which Mossadegh had come to New York began even before he arrived. Gladwyn Jebb, the British delegate, had already given the Security Council a long summation of his government's position. Mossadegh read it carefully. It was a contemptuous dismissal of Iran's position and a ringing declaration that the oil beneath Iran's soil was "clearly the property of the Anglo-Iranian Oil Company."

> The plain fact is that, by a series of insensate actions, the Iranian Government is causing a great enterprise, the proper functioning of which is of immense benefit not only to the United Kingdom and Iran but to the whole free world, to grind to a stop. Unless this is promptly checked, the whole of the free world will be much poorer and weaker, including the deluded Iranian people themselves. . . .
>
> The Iranian Government, for obvious reasons of its own, perpetually represents the Anglo-Iranian Oil Company as a gang of unscrupulous blood-suckers whose one idea is to drain the Iranian nation of any wealth it may possess. . . . These wild accusations are simply not true. . . . Quite apart from its financial contributions to the Iranian economy, the record of the company in Iran has been one which must arouse the greatest admiration from the social point of view and should be taken as a model of the form of development which would bring benefits to the economically less-developed areas of the world. Far from trying to keep down the Iranian people, as has been alleged, the company has strained every effort to improve the standard of living and education of its employees so that they might be able to play a more useful part in the great work which remains to be done in Iran. . . . To ignore entirely these activities and to put forth the company as responsible for oppression, corruption and treachery could be described as base ingratitude if it were not simply ridiculous.

Jebb asked the Security Council to act before October 4, the date by which Mossadegh had vowed to expel the last Britons from Abadan. When he finished, however, the Iranian delegate rose to ask for a ten-day postponement to allow Mossadegh to travel from Tehran to New York. The Council president agreed, and by the time Mossadegh arrived, the situation at Abadan had indeed changed. On October 4 the last British nationals had assembled at the Gymkhana Club, one of their favorite retreats, and were ferried in groups out to the HMS *Mauritius,* which was standing by to take them across the Shatt-al-Arab to Basra. With that step, one of the mightiest commercial enterprises in imperial history closed its doors.

A reporter from the *New York Times* visited the ghostly expanse a few days later. "When seen from a distance across the plain, the fifty-odd steel chimneys of the refinery bear a striking resemblance to the still-standing remains of King Xerxes's Apadana and Hall of a Hundred Columns at Persepolis," he wrote. "But as a traveler draws nearer, the gleaming metal soon identifies the silent towers of idle Abadan as the colossus of the industrial age, not of the fifth century B.C. . . . The cars and buses of the nationalized oil company—all of them British-made—go by. There are people in the streets. But the visitor may scrutinize every passing face in this English town set in southern Iran without finding the features of a single Englishman. Indeed any European is stared at as a curiosity."

Excitement filled the air as the Security Council assembled on October 15 to hear from Mossadegh. Delegates fell silent when he entered the chamber. All gazed at the tall, elegant-looking statesman who had riveted the world's attention since coming to power six months before. Mossadegh seemed completely at ease, and with good reason. He was, after all, a trained lawyer from a distinguished family who had been educated in Europe and honed his persuasive talents in countless trials and parliamentary speeches. More important, he was utterly convinced not only that his case was just but also that Providence had brought him to this moment. He had come to New York to carry out the mission to which he had devoted his life.

A Brazilian diplomat, João Carlos Muniz, was presiding over the Security Council that Monday, and he gaveled it to order punctually at three o'clock. His first act was to invite Mossadegh and Allahyar Saleh, Iran's ambassador to the United Nations, to sit at the table normally reserved for council members. Then he recognized Jebb, who told his fellow delegates that Britain was no longer insisting "purely and simply on the return to the status quo," but only for negotiated relief from "the great damage inflicted not only on it but on the free world as a whole by the actions of the Iranian government." Jebb concluded by turning to face "the representative of Iran, who has come so far, and at such inconvenience to himself, to this meeting." He urged Mossadegh "not to take up an aggressively nationalistic and indeed, I might say, almost isolationist attitude, not to brood unduly on old imagined wrongs, but to concentrate on the broader aspects and to show by his attitude that he too welcomes a constructive solution."

Then it was Mossadegh's turn. He spoke in eloquent French. By way of introduction, he declared that Britain's complaint was baseless and that the Security Council had no jurisdiction over the matter in any case, since Iran was entitled to dispose of its natural resources as it saw fit. But since the United Nations was "the ultimate refuge of weak and oppressed nations," he had decided to appear nevertheless, "after a long journey and in failing health, to express my country's respect for this illustrious institution." His statement was long, detailed, and passionate. Begging the council to indulge him on account of his delicate condition, he said that he would ask Saleh to read most of it. First, however, he spoke himself, giving a concise but highly evocative summary of the case he was laying before the world:

My countrymen lack the bare necessities of existence. Their standard of living is probably one of the lowest in the world. Our greatest natural asset is oil. This should be the source of work and food for the population of Iran. Its exploitation should properly be our national industry, and the revenue from it should go to improve our conditions of life. As now organized, however, the petroleum industry has contributed practically nothing to the well-being of the people or to the technical progress or industrial development of my country. The evidence for that statement is that after fifty years of exploitation by a foreign company, we still do not have enough Iranian technicians and must call in foreign experts.

Although Iran plays a considerable role in the world's petroleum supply and has produced a total of three hundred fifteen million tons over a period of fifty years, its entire gain, according to accounts of the former company, has been only one hundred ten million pounds sterling. To give you an idea of Iran's profits from this enormous industry, I may say that in 1948, according to accounts of the former Anglo-Iranian Oil Company, its net revenue amounted to sixty-one million pounds; but from those profits Iran received only nine million pounds, although twenty-eight million pounds went into the United Kingdom treasury in income tax alone. . . .

I must add here that the population living in the oil region of southern Iran and around Abadan, where there is the largest oil refinery in the world, is suffering in conditions of absolute misery without even the barest necessities of life. If the exploitation of our oil industry continues in the future as it has in the past, if we are to tolerate a situation in which the Iranian plays the part of a mere manual worker in the oil fields of Masjid-i-Suleiman, Agha Jari and Kermanshah and in the Abadan refinery, and if foreign exploiters continue to appropriate practically all of the income, then our people will remain forever in a state of poverty and misery. These are the reasons that have prompted the Iranian parliament—the Majlis and the Senate—to vote unanimously in favor of nationalizing the oil industry.

With this, Mossadegh took his seat and handed the text of his statement to Saleh. He began by reading what Mossadegh had singled out as Iran's essential legal argument: "The oil resources of Iran, like its soil, its rivers and mountains, are the property of the people of Iran. They alone have the authority to decide what shall be done with it, by whom and how." Saleh took two hours to read the rest of Mossadegh's statement. It was a history of foreign intervention in Iran, with special attention to the steps Britain had taken "to reduce us to economic servitude."

"The record of British economic exploitation of Iran has been a sorry one," it concluded. "No one should be surprised that its consequence has been the nationalization of our oil industry."

After the reading of Mossadegh's statement was completed, the council voted to meet again the following day to continue its debate. News photographers waiting outside the chamber asked the two adversaries to shake hands for the cameras, and they did. As flashbulbs popped, they had a brief exchange.

"If God wills it, we will be friends again," Jebb told Mossadegh.

"We have always been friends with England," Mossadegh replied. "The former company dragged your country needlessly into this dispute."

The next day, pictures of the two men appeared in newspapers around the world. Mossadegh was the taller, and wore a broad smile. Jebb looked quizzical and bemused.

Tuesday's session began with tributes to Liaquat Ali Khan, the prime minister of Pakistan, who had just been assassinated. Liaquat was a figure much like Mossadegh. He had been a leader of the movement to end British colonialism in India and had worked closely with Pakistan's founding father, Mohammad Ali Jinnah, to build a democratic Muslim republic in what had been India's northern provinces. Following Jinnah's death, he had become what George McGhee, who met him several times, called "the unchallenged leader of his country." Like Mossadegh, he was a visionary statesman, highly educated and erudite. He was committed to secular Islam and sympathetic to Western values but at the same time frustrated by what he saw as crippling vestiges of imperialism that prevented poor countries from achieving true independence. Pakistan never again had a leader of his caliber, just as Iran never had another like Mossadegh.

Liaquat had personified the spirit of the young United Nations, and news of his murder shocked many delegates. They already had much on their minds. Mossadegh's epochal challenge to the British was unfolding at a time of unusual turbulence in the world. The Soviet Union had just conducted its second atomic bomb test, making clear that the threat of annihilation would shape history for generations to come. War was raging in Korea. Kashmir, claimed by both India and Pakistan, was also aflame. A state of emergency was declared in Egypt after an outbreak of anti-British rioting.

An election campaign in Britain was also on the world's agenda that autumn. Winston Churchill was running to reclaim his old job, and in several speeches he denounced Prime Minister Attlee for failing to confront Mossadegh firmly enough. He told a crowd in Liverpool that Attlee had betrayed "solemn undertakings" never to abandon Abadan. "I don't remember a case," he thundered, "when public men have broken their word so abruptly and without even an attempt at explanation." As the campaign progressed, Churchill became so belligerent on the Iran issue that Foreign Secretary Morrison asked him pointedly during one House of Commons debate whether he was urging war. He did not reply, but never denied that he liked the idea of invading Iran.

Despite all that was happening around the world, however, Mossadegh remained the man of the hour. In his sweeping indictment before the Security Council, he found words that stung his adversary and delighted his countless admirers. He began his second day at the microphone by ridiculing the British for trying "to persuade world opinion that the lamb has devoured the wolf."

"The government of the United Kingdom has made abundantly clear that it has no interest in negotiating, and has instead used every illegitimate means of economic, psychological and military pressure that it could lay its hands on to break our will," Mossadegh declared. "Having first concentrated its warships along our coasts and paratroopers at nearby bases, it makes a great parade of its love for peace."

Then it was Jebb's turn. How disappointing it was, he lamented, that Mossadegh's speech had been "so entirely negative, an attitude of mind which I regret to say has characterized the Iranian approach in all our long negotiations hitherto." Mossadegh faced a "distressing situation which has arisen entirely owing to his own folly." Since taking office, he had done nothing but belittle the achievements of the "prudent and far-sighted" Anglo-Iranian Oil Company, urge the appointment of "unqualified Iranians" to technical jobs, and trample on international law by ordering "the expropriation of foreign property." The crisis had grown out of Iran's "persistent refusal to recognize the sanctity of contracts."

On Wednesday, the session's third day, delegates from several countries spoke briefly and then Mossadegh asked to be recognized. He said only that he was "very tired" and handed his text to Mohammad Saleh, sitting beside him. It was a long and impassioned speech on which he had worked for most of the previous twenty-four hours:

> I have not made actual count of the pejorative words used by Sir Gladwyn Jebb in has various statements, but as you leaf through the pages of the record, defamatory word after defamatory word springs to the eye. Our actions are described as "insensate" and our people as "deluded." We have been "precipitate," "arbitrary," and have made life "intolerable." Our legislative process is described as one of "hustling." We are damned as "intransigent" and accused of presenting ultimatums. Our grievances are dismissed as "wild accusations." We are "ridiculous" and exhibit "base ingratitude." We are "intemperate," "exploiters" of our own people, and save our own necks by inflaming our people against foreigners. Our aims are "illusory" and our means of achieving them "suicidal." Our case is presented as one of the lame leading the blind in pursuit of a phantom. . . .
>
> We have long realized that our hopes for developing our country, improving the condition of our people and expanding the opportunities available to them were dependent to a great extent on this extraordinarily important national resource. The

record of the contribution that oil has made to our national prosperity is as pitiable as that of the crumbs which we have been allowed to pick up from the former company's table. . . . I respond readily to the United Kingdom representative's appeal to face the practical facts of the situation, and I am no less eager than he is to negotiate. Wherever the former company may operate in the future, however, it will never again operate in Iran. Neither by trusteeship nor by contract will we turn over to foreigners the right to exploit our oil resources.

The resolution Britain had brought to the Security Council, already diluted at the insistence of the United States, was weakened further by amendments from India and Yugoslavia. Ultimately it become nothing more than a call for goodwill on both sides. Even that was too much for Mossadegh. He insisted that the council had no right to pass any resolution at all. So profound was the impression he had made that most other governments felt they had no choice but to agree. On October 19 the council voted "to postpone the discussion of the question to a certain day or indefinitely." Britain and the United States abstained. It was a humiliating diplomatic defeat for the British.

"The Iranian oil dispute has done something that no other dispute in the history of the United Nations has been able to do," James Reston wrote in the next day's *New York Times*. "It has established the principle of total loss. It has proved what has heretofore been in doubt, namely that it is possible to have an argument in the United Nations in which everybody loses, including the large powers, the small powers, and the United Nations itself."

A solution to the oil dispute was now less likely than ever. Mossadegh remained fiercely determined to press ahead with his nationalization project, and the British remained equally determined to thwart it. President Truman decided to make a last effort at compromise and invited the Iranian leader to Washington.

Mossadegh had already proven himself adept at reaching the American public. He appeared several times on television, and the seeming logic of his case, which he always compared to the struggle for American independence, won him considerable sympathy. His personal quirks—the long, aristocratic face that would suddenly explode into laughter, the way he rested his seemingly weary head on his cane, the grand sweeps of his long arms—added to his appeal. They gave him the endearing aspect of a favorite, perhaps slightly eccentric, uncle or grandfather. Cameras followed him wherever he went in New York.

Before leaving for Washington, Mossadegh addressed Iranian students at Columbia University and told them that if they wanted to help their country, they should concentrate on learning how to run an oil industry. The next morning he set off by train, but instead of traveling directly to Washington, he made a brilliantly conceived stop in Philadelphia. There he visited Independence Hall, which he said symbolized the aspirations that united Americans and Iranians. Hundreds of onlookers cheered as he was photographed beside the Liberty Bell.

Truman had received a confidential profile of Mossadegh that reflected the American view of him. It said that he was "supported by the majority of the population" and described him as "witty," "affable," "honest," and "well informed." This could not have been more different from the British view, in which, according to various diplomatic cables and memoranda, Mossadegh was a "wild," "erratic," "eccentric," "crazy," "gangster-like," "fanatical," "absurd," "dictatorial," "demagogic," "inflammatory," "cunning," "slippery," "completely unscrupulous," and "clearly imbalanced" "wily Oriental" who "looks like a cab horse" and "diffuses a slight reek of opium."

Mossadegh's arrival at Union Station in Washington on October 23, 1951, was unforgettable. He stepped off the train with great difficulty, supported on one side by his cane and on the other by his son's steadying grasp. To all appearances, he was ready to collapse on the spot. Suddenly he saw Secretary of State Acheson, whom he had admired from afar but had never met. His face lit up and he seemed instantly rejuvenated. He dropped his cane, brusquely pushed his son aside, and skipped down the concourse to embrace his host.

The next day, President Truman walked across the street from the White House to meet Mossadegh at Blair House. Once again Mossadegh was the fading invalid who, with his dying breaths, wished to defend his oppressed people against evil. He leaned toward Truman and began feebly, "Mr. President, I am speaking for a very poor country, a country all desert—just sand, a few camels, a few sheep. . . ."

"Yes, and with your oil, just like Texas!" Acheson interjected. Mossadegh loved it. He snapped back in his chair and broke out into one of the laughing fits that were almost as famous as the ones in which he wept.

Truman began by telling Mossadegh that he felt great sympathy for Iran's cause. He was deeply afraid, however, that if the oil crisis spun out of control, Iran might fall into the hands of the Soviets, who were "sitting like a vulture on the fence waiting to pounce." If the Soviets took Iran, he warned, "they would be in a position to wage a world war." Mossadegh said he saw the same danger, but insisted that British intransigence was the factor most likely to throw Iran into chaos.

Recognizing that no compromise would be possible that day, Truman invited Mossadegh to stay in Washington for a while and spend some time with Acheson and George McGhee. To sweeten the invitation, he had arranged for Mossadegh to be installed at Walter Reed Hospital, where he could rest and be given a full battery of tests. To a man who had many ailments and believed he had many more, who felt comfortable in bed and never declined medical attention, this was an irresistible offer. Mossadegh was driven to the hospital that afternoon, and was thrilled to find that the presidential suite had been made ready for him.

Acheson and McGhee visited him the next day to lay out terms of what they believed would be a fair compromise with the British. Their formula, as the *New York Times* described it, was to "assure Iran the owner's control over her oil resource, but provide a so-called 'neutral' company with full authority to operate and manage the vast refineries and distribution facilities, and enable Britain to market the oil." Mossadegh rejected it out of hand.

The same offer had been transmitted to the British, and before they even knew of Mossadegh's reaction, they, too, rejected it. A senior diplomat at the Foreign Office, Sir William Strang, called it "expropriation at the expense of British interests." Chancellor of the Exchequer R. A. Butler said it failed to recognize the essential fact that "our own economic viability was at stake, which was much more important than Persia's."

There were more meetings and discussions, including an

extended debate over how much Iran would charge for its oil, when and if it ever began to flow again. No progress was made. "The general feeling here," James Reston wrote after Mossadegh had been in Washington for a week, "is that the United States intervened in the problem too late and cannot now be expected to find any compromise that will satisfy the United States, Britain and Iran."

Americans were indeed latecomers to the Middle East. The British scorned them as inexperienced and naïve. To a degree they were. They were instinctively repelled by Britain's colonial arrogance, especially in Iran, but did not have enough self-confidence to act decisively on their own.

The American failure to reach a deal with Mossadegh during his visit to the United States was not due to any lack of effort by George McGhee. He visited Mossadegh day after day, first at the hospital and then, after Mossadegh was released with a clean bill of health, at his suite in the Shoreham Hotel. "Despite great efforts I was unable to get him to understand the facts of life about the international oil business," he wrote afterward. "In the end he would always smile and say 'I don't care about that' when I would talk with him about oil prices, discounts or technicians. 'You don't understand,' he would say. 'It is a political problem.'"

In mid-November, after meetings with Mossadegh that lasted a total of seventy hours, McGhee finally gave up. When he came to tell Mossadegh, the old man already knew what was coming. "You've come to send me home," he told McGhee.

"Yes," McGhee replied. "I'm sorry to have to tell you that we can't bridge the gap between you and the British. It's a great disappointment to us, as it must be to you."

Mossadegh accepted the news quietly. He decided that before leaving Washington, he would accept an invitation to address the National Press Club. His speech was a denunciation of Britain, skillfully combined with praise for the United States and an appeal for financial aid. A State Department spokesman said that the appeal would be given "every consideration," but privately Mossadegh was told that a loan was impossible because the British would object too strenuously.

The most telling comment Mossadegh made before leaving Washington on November 18 was to Vernon Walters, who at Averell Harriman's request visited him alone just to be sure that he had not had a last-minute change of heart. "I know what you're here for, and the answer is still no," Mossadegh said when Walters appeared at his door.

"Dr. Mossadegh," Walters replied, "you have been here for a long time. High hopes have been raised that your visit would bring about some fruitful results, and now you are returning to Iran empty-handed."

At this, Mossadegh stared at his friend and asked, "Don't you realize that in returning to Iran empty-handed, I return in a much stronger position than if I returned with an agreement which I would have to sell to my fanatics?"

On his way home, Mossadegh stopped in Egypt. He was given an ecstatic welcome. Egyptians were already in the anti-imperialist frenzy that would produce the Suez crisis a few years later, and whenever Mossadegh appeared in public, they cheered him wildly. Newspapers hailed him as a hero who had "conquered history" and "won freedom and dignity for his country." He stayed for several days, was embraced by King Farouk, and signed a friendship treaty with Prime Minister Nahas Pasha. "A united Iran and Egypt," it pledged, "will together demolish British imperialism."

In Britain, a momentous political change had occurred. While Mossadegh was in the United States, Conservatives led by Winston Churchill had been elected to replace Prime Minister Attlee's Labor government. Like many British leaders of his generation, the seventy-seven-year-old Churchill had great trouble giving up the idea of Britain as an imperial power. As a young soldier in 1898, he had charged the Dervish lines at the decisive Battle of Omdurman that secured Sudan as a British colony. During World War I, he helped conceive the ill-fated Gallipoli campaign in Turkey. Later he directed British efforts to maintain control over Palestine and Mesopotamia and fervently opposed granting independence to India. He saw in Iran what he had seen for decades: a reliable source of oil at bargain prices. Iran was also one of Britain's last great foreign outposts, and Churchill knew that if it were lost, there would be little hope of saving Suez or the others that remained. Holding the line against Third World nationalism was one of his lifelong crusades, and in the sunset of his career he was determined to make a last stand.

Churchill had built his election campaign in part on the charge that Attlee "had scuttled and run from Abadan when a splutter of musketry would have ended the matter." In one of his first acts after taking office, he sent his new foreign secretary, Anthony Eden, to meet Acheson. He directed Eden to press the Iran matter and "be stubborn even if the temperature rises."

The change in Britain's government would prove decisive for Iran. Attlee had done whatever he thought possible on behalf of Anglo-Iranian, stopping only at the use of force. Churchill, who considered Mossadegh "an elderly lunatic bent on wrecking his country and handing it over to the Communists," was willing and even eager to cross that line. The fervor with which Mossadegh was welcomed in Egypt proved to Churchill that he was not only a danger to Britain's oil supply but also an intolerable symbol of anti-British sentiment around the world.

Britain's policy toward Mossadegh toughened immediately. Foreign Secretary Eden told Acheson that the Americans had spent too much time appeasing him, and that inviting him to Washington had been a mistake. From now on, he declared, Britain would be interested only in deposing him.

Among the Americans most devastated by Britain's decision to turn toward force was George McGhee. To him, it was the final blow in a campaign of mutual suicide, "almost the end of the world." His friend Henry Grady had been removed a few weeks earlier as ambassador to Iran, and around the time Mossadegh left Washington, McGhee himself accepted a new post as ambassador to Turkey. Both men had devoted untold amounts of energy to the idea of compromise in Iran, and that idea was now dead.

During that year of 1951, Mossadegh vaulted onto the world stage and came to dominate it. He had become a defining figure whose ideas, for better or worse, were reshaping history. No one was surprised when *Time* magazine chose him—not Harry Truman, Dwight Eisenhower, or Winston Churchill—as its Man of the Year.

Mossadegh looked stately and dignified on the cover of *Time.* The long article inside was full of dismissive insults about this "weeping, fainting leader of a helpless country" who was an "obstinate opportunist" and threw tantrums like "a willful little boy." But it also called him "the Iranian George Washington" and "the most world-renowned man his ancient race had produced for centuries."

Reflecting the ambivalence with which the United States regarded him, *Time* portrayed him as an exasperating and immature figure who nonetheless had a legitimate case to make:

> Once upon a time, in a mountainous land between Baghdad and the Sea of Caviar, there lived a nobleman. This nobleman, after a lifetime of carping at the way the kingdom was run, became Chief Minister of the realm. In a few months he had the whole world hanging on his words and deeds, his jokes, his tears, his tantrums. Behind his grotesque antics lay great issues of peace or war, which would affect many lands far beyond his mountains. . . .
>
> He was Mohammad Mossadegh, Premier of Iran in the year 1951. He was the Man of the Year. He put Scheherazade in the petroleum business and oiled the wheels of chaos. His acid tears dissolved one of the remaining pillars of a great empire. In his plaintive, singsong voice he gabbled a defiant challenge that sprang out of a hatred and envy almost incomprehensible to the West. . . .
>
> The British position in the whole [Middle East] is hopeless. They are hated and distrusted almost everywhere. The old colonial relationship is finished, and no other power can replace Britain. . . . The U.S., which will have to make the West's policy in the Middle East, whether it wants to or not, as yet has no policy there. . . . In its leadership of the non-Communist world, the U.S. has some dire responsibilities to shoulder. One of them is to meet the fundamental moral challenge posed by the strange old wizard who lives in a mountainous land and who is, sad to relate, the Man of 1951.

CHAPTER 9

Block Headed British

On a sunny July day in 1952, eight months after his return from Washington, Prime Minister Mossadegh was driven along an elm-shaded lane to the Saad Abad Palace for a showdown with Mohammad Reza Shah. Iran was no longer big enough for both of them. Behind closed doors at the palace, they faced off in a duel of wits and power. It ended with Mossadegh lying unconscious at the Shah's feet.

This meeting was supposed to be no more than ceremonial. Mossadegh had just been chosen by the Majlis to serve a full two-year term as prime minister, and according to custom, he was presenting the Shah with a list of his cabinet ministers. He took the occasion, however, to make a demand that no Iranian prime minister had ever dared to make. Mossadegh wanted the Shah to recognize the supremacy of the elected government by surrendering control of the war ministry. The Shah was outraged. Without the war ministry he would lose control of the army, the bulwark of his power, and be reduced to the status of a figurehead. Rather than lose his army, he told Mossadegh, he would "pack my suitcase and leave."

Mossadegh, who had mastered the art of political theater before the Shah was born, said not a word. He paused for a few moments to reflect, then rose to walk out. The Shah was struck with fear that

134

the old man would take to the streets and rouse the masses against him. He jumped up, ran to the door, and threw his body across it. Mossadegh insisted that he step aside. Impossible, the Shah replied; their discussion must continue. The standoff lasted for a minute or two. Mossadegh began breathing harder. Then he gasped, took a few steps back, and fainted.

An annex to the 1906 constitution made the Shah supreme commander of the Iranian army but also required him to cooperate with the elected government on political matters. Prime ministers had traditionally interpreted this as allowing the Shah to appoint the minister of war. By breaking with this tradition, Mossadegh provoked a crisis. As he lay in bed recovering from his collapse, he decided to resolve it in a way that shocked the country. The next morning, July 17, he resigned from office.

"Under the present circumstances it is impossible to conclude the final phase of the national struggle," he wrote to the Shah. "I cannot continue in office without having responsibility for the Ministry of War, and since Your Majesty did not concede this, I feel I do not enjoy the confidence of the Sovereign and, therefore, offer my resignation to pave the way for another government which might be able to carry out Your Majesty's wishes."

Did Mossadegh really wish to leave power, or was he just maneuvering for political advantage? At several crucial moments in his career, he had chosen to retire from public life rather than sully himself. He was so mortified by the Anglo-Persian Agreement of 1919 that he applied for residence in Switzerland and told his family he would live the rest of his life in exile. During the long reign of Reza Shah, he remained absolutely aloof from politics. In 1947, after an election-reform bill he had proposed in the Majlis was defeated, he retired to his estate at Ahmad Abad and announced the definitive end of his political life. These episodes reflected a martyr's streak in Mossadegh, perhaps reinforced by Shiite theology, that disposed him to choose stoic suffering over compromise with iniquity.

By the middle of 1952 Mossadegh was facing many troubles. Britain's boycott of Iranian oil had been devastatingly effective, and he knew that British agents in Tehran were working to subvert his government. For a time he hoped to ride out the crisis with American aid, but President Truman, who was under heavy pressure from

London, would not give him any. He sought help from the World Bank, but that effort also failed. Iranians were becoming poorer and unhappier by the day. Mossadegh's political coalition was fraying, and in his new term he could look forward to fighting a swarm of enemies.

It would be naïve, however, to believe that Mossadegh was truly eager to leave the exalted position he had reached in the eyes of Iranians and millions of others around the world. He wanted not to quit but to force Iranians to decide whether they really wanted him as their leader. Resigning was an inspired gamble.

For most of that spring, Mossadegh had been preoccupied with parliamentary elections. He had little to fear from a free vote, since despite the country's problems he was widely admired as a hero. A free vote, however, was not what others were planning. British agents had fanned out across the country, bribing candidates and the regional bosses who controlled them. They hoped to fill the Majlis with deputies who would vote to depose Mossadegh. It would be a coup carried out by seemingly legal means.

Iranian elections took several weeks to complete because of difficulties in transportation and communication. The first results came from big cities, and they were encouraging to Mossadegh. In Tehran all twelve National Front candidates were elected. Results in other parts of the country, where there was no one to monitor the voting, were quite different. These results did not in themselves disturb Mossadegh, whose faith in the popular will was boundless, but he became worried after violence broke out in Abadan and several other parts of the country where elections were being hotly contested. Aides told him that some of the candidates being elected were under the direct control of British agents. He was about to leave for The Hague to defend Iran against another British lawsuit at the World Court and feared that his absence might remove the last checks on his enemies' electoral chicanery. In June, after 80 candidates had been certified as winners of seats in the 136-seat Majlis, his cabinet voted to halt the elections. In a statement he asserted that since "foreign agents" were exploiting the election campaign to destabilize Iran, "the supreme national interests of the country necessitate the suspension of elections pending the return of the Iranian delegation from The Hague."

Mossadegh was legally entitled to take this step as long as the eighty seated members did not veto it, which they did not. He could also claim a measure of moral legitimacy, since he was defending Iran against subversion by outsiders. Nonetheless, the episode cast him in an unflattering light. It allowed his critics to portray him as undemocratic and grasping for personal power.

While Mossadegh dealt with this challenge, he also had to face another that most Iranians considered far more urgent. Their country was spiraling into bankruptcy. Tens of thousands had lost their jobs at the Abadan refinery, and although most understood and passionately supported the idea of nationalization, they naturally hoped that Mossadegh would find a way to put them back to work. The only way he could do that was to sell oil.

During the first half of 1952, tankers from Argentina and Japan managed to make their way into and out of Iranian ports despite Britain's proclaimed embargo. Another brought four thousand tons of Abadan oil to Venice, and after an Italian court rejected Britain's protest, Winston Churchill complained about "what paltry friends and allies the Italians are." Churchill realized that if he did not enforce the embargo more effectively, it would collapse.

In mid-June dock workers at the Persian Gulf port of Bandar Mashur welcomed the tanker *Rose Mary,* which had been chartered by a private Italian oil company that wanted to buy twenty million tons of Iranian crude over the next decade. The company had organized this "experimental voyage" to challenge Britain's embargo. If the *Rose Mary* could make her way safely back to Italy, the embargo would be broken and Iran would be on the road to economic recovery.

As Britain and Iran prepared for confrontation on the high seas, they also clashed at the World Court. The British were seeking an order declaring that the Abadan refinery and surrounding oil fields rightfully belonged to them. Their lawyers argued eloquently, but any hope they had of dominating the proceedings vanished when Mossadegh arrived. A crowd welcomed him at the Peace Palace, cheering wildly and rhythmically chanting his name. Inside, he gave a brief speech asking the judges to consider the moral and political aspects of the case as well as the strictly legal ones. Nationalizing Anglo-Iranian, he said, had been the only possible response to an intolerable situation in which the company had for years treated its Iranian employees "like animals" and manipulated Iranian governments to assure that it could continue plundering the country's most precious natural resource.

After his speech, Mossadegh retired to his hotel and did not appear again in court. Iran's case was presented over the course of three days by a team of Iranian lawyers and an eminent Belgian, Henri Rolin, a professor of international law and former president of the Belgian Senate. Over and over, Rolin returned to his central argument. The Court had no authority in the case, he asserted, because it concerned not two nations but a nation and a private company.

Mossadegh was at his hotel when news came that British warships had intercepted the *Rose Mary* and forced her to port at the British protectorate of Aden. In a court there, British lawyers argued that Anglo-Iranian was the legal owner of all Iranian oil and that therefore the *Rose Mary* was carrying stolen property. The verdict, which to no one's surprise was in Britain's favor, did not come for several months, but news that the Royal Navy was now intercepting tankers carrying Iranian oil was enough to scare off other customers. Mossadegh called a news conference to denounce the seizure, which he called "a vivid example of the way Britain is attempting to strangle us." Many Europeans were sympathetic. "I fear Dr. Mossadegh has managed to leave behind him in The Hague a generally favorable impression," the British ambassador cabled home to London.

Britain's seizure of the *Rose Mary* was a devastating blow to Mossadegh and his government. No oil company would now do business with Iran, so the country's main source of income was gone. Iran had earned $45 million from oil exports in 1950, more than 70 percent of its total export earnings. That sum dropped by half in 1951 and then to almost zero in 1952.

Mossadegh told Iranians that their campaign for national dignity required "deprivation, self-sacrifice and loyalty," and although most agreed, they suffered nonetheless. He eased their pain by promoting the export of products other than oil, especially textiles and foodstuffs, and by negotiating barter agreements with several countries. These and other steps kept Iran from collapsing, but they were no substitute for the income that oil exports would have earned.

The divisive election, the tightening British oil embargo, and the World Court case all weighed on Mossadegh's mind as he returned home from The Hague at the end of June. Two weeks later, he had his fainting fit in the Shah's salon and, the next day, resigned his office. His resignation was a godsend for his British enemies and for the Shah. They had hoped to manipulate the Majlis into blocking his reelection. Now he had done them the unimaginable favor of leaving on his own accord.

British officials had chosen the man they wished to succeed Mossadegh. He was the wily seventy-two-year-old politician Ahmad Qavam, who had served as prime minister in the mid-1940s. The British scholar/agent Robin Zaehner reported from his post in Tehran that "it was Qavam's desire to work closely with the British and to preserve their legitimate interests in Persia. . . . [He] greatly preferred that British influence should be exercised in Persia rather than that of the Americans (who were foolish and without experience) or that of the Russians, who were Persia's enemies."

At first the Shah was reluctant to support Qavam. His experience with Mossadegh had soured him on strong prime ministers, and he wanted one who was weak and pliable. Qavam was neither. The British, however, insisted on him. In the hours after Mossadegh submitted his resignation on July 17, the Shah mused inconclusively about how to proceed. That night a group of forty pro-British Majlis members met and nominated Qavam. Twenty-seven others gathered nearby to declare their undying loyalty to Mossadegh, the only figure capable of ruling Iran "at this momentous time in our history."

In the end the Shah succumbed to British pressure, as he was wont to do, and accepted Qavam. Foolishly believing that he had won a firm mandate, Qavam immediately began issuing harsh proclamations declaring that the day of retribution had come. He denounced Mossadegh for failing to resolve the oil crisis and for launching "a widespread campaign against a foreign state." Iran, he declared, was about to change. "This helmsman is on a different course," he declared in his first statement as prime minister. Anyone who objected to his new policies would be arrested and delivered into "the heartless and pitiless hands of the law."

Many Iranians did not realize that Mossadegh was really out of power until they heard Qavam deliver this proclamation over the radio. It triggered an explosion of protest. Crowds poured onto the streets of Tehran and other cities, chanting, "Ya Marg Ya

Mossadegh!" (Death or Mossadegh!). Qavam ordered the police to attack and suppress them, but many officers refused. Some joined the protesters and were joyfully embraced.

This spontaneous outburst was, above all, an expression of support for Mossadegh's decision to confront the Anglo-Iranian Oil Company. Many Iranians, however, were also drawn to him because of his commitment to social reform. Mossadegh had freed peasants from forced labor on their landlords' estates, ordered factory owners to pay benefits to sick and injured workers, established a system of unemployment compensation, and taken 20 percent of the money landlords received in rent and placed it in a fund to pay for development projects like pest control, rural housing, and public baths. He supported women's rights, defended religious freedom, and allowed courts and universities to function freely. Above all, he was known even by his enemies as scrupulously honest and impervious to the corruption that pervaded Iranian politics. The prospect of losing him so suddenly, and of having him replaced by a regime evidently sponsored from abroad, was more than his aroused people would accept.

On July 21 National Front leaders called for a general strike to show the nation's opposition to Qavam and support for Mossadegh, "the only popular choice to lead the national struggle." Within hours, much of the country was paralyzed. Ayatollah Kashani, who had learned that Qavam planned to arrest him, issued a *fatwa* ordering soldiers to join the rebellion, which he called a "holy war against the imperialists." Tudeh militants, still angry at Qavam for engineering the withdrawal of Soviet troops from Azerbaijan in 1947, eagerly joined the fray with cries of "Down With the Shah! We Want a People's Republic!"

Qavam and the Shah were shocked by this rebellion and responded by calling out elite military units. Soldiers opened fire on protesters in several parts of Tehran. Dozens fell dead. Young military officers, appalled by the carnage, began talking of mutiny. The Shah had completely lost control of the situation. His only choice was to ask for Qavam's resignation. Qavam submitted it at four o'clock that afternoon. Upon receiving it, the Shah sent for Mossadegh.

Their meeting was unexpectedly cordial. The Shah said he was now prepared to accept Mossadegh as prime minister and give him control of the war ministry. He asked if Mossadegh still wished to maintain the monarchy. Mossadegh assured him that he did, presuming of course that kings would accept the supremacy of elected leaders.

"You could go down in history as an immensely popular monarch if you cooperated with democratic and nationalist forces," he told the Shah.

The next day the Majlis voted overwhelmingly to reelect Mossadegh as prime minister. Qavam's term had lasted just four days. His fall on "Bloody Monday" was a huge, almost unimaginable victory for Iranian nationalists. It was an even greater personal triumph for Mossadegh. Without having given a single speech or even stirred from his home, he had been returned to power by a grateful nation.

The next day brought another piece of electrifying news. The World Court had turned down Britain's appeal, refusing to be drawn into the oil dispute. In London, the *Daily Express* carried the banner headline "Mossadegh's Victory Day." It was that and much, much more.

Mossadegh's support was now so broad and fervent that he could probably have dismissed the Shah, proclaimed the end of the Pahlavi dynasty, and established a republic with himself as president if he had wished. Instead he sent the Shah a peace offering. It was a copy of the Koran with a handwritten inscription: "Consider me an enemy of the Koran if I take any action against the constitution, or if I accept the presidency in case others nullify the constitution and change the form of our country's government."

For the British, this turn of events was a most disappointing setback. In the course of a single week they had gone from vague plotting to spectacular victory to utter defeat. With all that was at stake, however, they were hardly ready to give up. Instead they began carefully reviewing what they had done wrong. They concluded that they had made several mistakes. British intelligence officers had left too much of the planning and execution to Iranians. They had placed their faith in a civilian, Qavam, rather than in a military officer. Perhaps most important, they had acted alone, without American help. Next time—they were determined that there would be a next time—they would not repeat these errors.

□ □ □

The next round of British plotting was shaped by a series of insightful cables that George Middleton, the British chargé d'affaires in Tehran, wrote in the days following the July uprising. Middleton considered the uprising to have been "a turning point in Persian history" because it marked the emergence of a new political force, the mob. Britain's plan to replace Mossadegh had failed because a mob intervened. Next time, he wrote, the British must have the mob on their side.

Middleton also observed that during the uprising, a fair number of army officers had shown themselves less than loyal to Mossadegh. Under the right circumstances, they might join a future rebellion, but they would have to be rallied to the cause by an officer they trusted and admired. Middleton had an idea who that officer might be. He suggested Mossadegh's former interior minister, General Fazlollah Zahedi.

This was a fine choice. Zahedi was far from an ideal candidate—the *New York Times* described him as "a boulevardier with a penchant for gambling and beautiful women"—but was better than anyone else available. He had spent most of his life in uniform and was personally acquainted with almost every Iranian officer.

At the age of twenty-three, as a company commander, Zahedi had led troops into battle against rebel tribesmen in the northern provinces. Two years later Reza Shah promoted him to the rank of brigadier general. Impressed with his loyalty and his firm hand, the Shah made him governor of Khuzistan, the province where the Abadan refinery was located, in 1926; chief of the Tehran police in 1932; and commander of the important Isfahan garrison in 1941.

Zahedi shared Reza Shah's view of what Iran needed. Both men were soldiers at heart, strong, harsh, and ambitious. When World War II broke out, both sought to help the Germans. After the British deposed Reza Shah and forced him into exile, they focused on Zahedi. They identified him as a profiteer who was making huge sums from grain hoarding, but would have left him to his devices had it not been for his close connections to Nazi agents. When they discovered that he was organizing a tribal uprising to coincide with a possible German thrust into Iran, they decided to act.

In September 1942 senior officers of the Secret Intelligence Service summoned the legendary agent Fitzroy MacLean, whose exploits had taken him to clandestine battlegrounds from Tripoli to Tashkent, to a meeting in London. They told him that they wanted Zahedi gone. "How it was to be done they left me to work out by myself," MacLean wrote afterward. "Only two conditions were made: I was to take him alive and I was to do it without creating a disturbance."

The simplest approach would be to kidnap Zahedi from his home, but when MacLean arrived in Isfahan, he discovered that the home was too well guarded. His next idea was to snatch the general from his car, but that also proved impractical because military security was too tight. MacLean decided that he would have to find a ruse by which he could be introduced into Zahedi's presence.

His plan, which he laid out in a cipher telegram to London, was to masquerade as a Baghdad-based brigadier in the British army; send a message telling Zahedi that he was passing through Isfahan and wanted to pay his respects; arrive with one or two "resourceful characters"; and then, when he was alone with the general, pull a pistol and force him into their waiting car. Nearby, a platoon of infantrymen would be waiting "to lend a hand in case anything went wrong." MacLean's superiors granted him everything he asked, including permission to kill Zahedi if that became necessary, but on one point they would not yield. No one under any circumstances could be allowed to pretend he was a British brigadier. A real one would be supplied if necessary.

MacLean traveled to Qom, 150 miles north of Isfahan, where the local British commander had been instructed to give him whatever he needed. He needed a platoon of soldiers and rounded one up without difficulty after letting it be known that he was recruiting for a commando mission. At a ruined fort in the nearby desert, he and his men rehearsed for several days. Then, on the day before the planned abduction, he set out for Isfahan. With him was a genuine brigadier, supplied by the British consulate in Qom, "a distinguished officer whose well-developed sense of humor caused him to enter completely into the spirit of the somewhat equivocal role that had been allotted to him."

The arrangement to meet General Zahedi went perfectly. MacLean arrived in a car flying a large Union Jack. The guard at the gate was deep in conversation with a British agent who was part of MacLean's team and looked up only briefly as he passed. Two nondescript trucks, their cargo space covered with tarpaulins, were parked nearby. Inside were the soldiers MacLean had spent the last week training. They waited while he entered the brigade head-quarters:

> When, a couple of minutes later, General Zahedi, a dapper figure in a tight-fitting gray uniform and highly polished boots, entered the room, he found himself looking down the barrel of my Colt automatic. There was no advantage in prolonging a scene which might easily have become embarrassing. Without further ado, I invited the general to put his hands up and informed him that I had instructions to arrest him and that, if he made any noise or attempt at resistance, he would be shot. Then I took away his pistol and hustled him through the window into the car which was waiting outside with the engine running. . . . Soon we reached the point in the desert where we had spent the night, and here I handed over my captive to an officer and six men who were standing by to take him by car to the nearest landing-ground, where an airplane was waiting to fly him to Palestine. . . . In the general's bedroom I found a collection of automatic weapons of German manufacture, a good deal of silk underwear, some opium, [and] an illustrated register of the prostitutes of Isfahan.

Zahedi spent the rest of the war in a British internment camp. After his release, he resumed his career as if nothing had happened, serving as military commander in Fars province and then returning to his old job as police chief in Tehran. Mohammed Reza Shah named him to the Senate in 1950 and the next year persuaded Mossadegh to choose him as interior minister. Mossadegh dis-missed him a few months later, after he ordered the massacre of rioters who were protesting Averell Harriman's visit. Although Zahedi was no longer in the army, he was the president of the Retired Officers Association, which was made up mostly of men whom Mossadegh had cashiered and who were anxious for revenge. This constituency, coupled with his own boldness and well-known ruthlessness, led the British to choose him as the figurehead leader of their coup. They were willing to forget the unpleasantness of the past, and so was he.

The combination that George Middleton recommended in his cables—a mob plus Zahedi—became the core of the plot against

Mossadegh, and it never changed. Before serious planning could begin, however, the British had to win American cooperation. Prime Minister Churchill, who in the words of one of his foreign spies "enjoyed dramatic operations and had no high regard for timid diplomatists," spent the second half of 1952 trying to enlist President Truman.

In August Mossadegh invited an American oil executive named Alton Jones to visit Iran. Truman thought this was a fine idea and gave it his blessing, but when Churchill learned of it, he was mightily upset. He protested that any friendly overtures from the United States would undermine his campaign to isolate Mossadegh. Britain was supporting the Americans in Korea, he reminded Truman, and had a right to expect "Anglo-American unity" on Iran.

Nothing substantial came out of the Jones mission, but that did not shake Truman or his senior advisers from their desire to seek compromise with Mossadegh. They had concluded, in Acheson's words, "that the British were so obstructive and determined on a rule-or-ruin policy in Iran that we must strike out on an independent policy or run the risk of having Iran disappear behind the Iron Curtain." Truman urged Churchill to accept the fact of nationalization, which he said "seems to have become as sacred in Iran's eyes as [the] Koran." To continue resisting it, he warned, could provoke upheaval that would send Iran "down the Communist drain" and be "a disaster to the free world."

Churchill replied by proposing that he and Truman "send a joint telegram personal and confidential to Mossadegh." He wrote a draft. It was couched in friendly language but offered only a rehash of old British proposals. Truman would not sign. Doggedly Churchill pressed his argument that Britain and the United States must "gallop together" against Mossadegh. "I do not myself see," he told Truman, "why two good men asking only what is right and just should not gang up against a third who is doing wrong."

Finally Truman agreed to sign a watered-down version of Churchill's letter. It asked Mossadegh to do two things he had sworn never to do: allow the return of Anglo-Iranian to its old position in Iran and accept arbitration by the World Court based on the company's position before it was nationalized. If he complied, Britain would lift its economic embargo and the United States would give Iran $10 million in aid.

A few days after receiving the letter, Mossedegh read it scornfully to the Majlis. It was an affront, he said, because it failed to recognize that the "former company" had been finally and irrevocably nationalized. As for the aid offer, it "smacked of charity," which Iran did not want. To rising applause he declared that Britain "for centuries has been used to plundering poor nations," and that Iran would no longer accept its "oppressive terms." He concluded with a telling moral observation: "Abiding by law and respecting the rights of the weak not only would not diminish, but would greatly enhance the position and prestige of the strong."

Mossadegh then asked for and won Majlis support for a counterproposal. Iran would accept mediation by the World Court, but on two conditions. First, the Court would have to decide the case according to either Iranian law or "any law in any country nationalizing its industries in similar circumstances." Second, if the British were going to demand compensation, Iran must be allowed to make a counterclaim for its lost revenues.

These terms were reasonable enough to worry Churchill. Over the next few weeks he sent a series of cables to Truman urging him not to succumb to the temptation to negotiate. "We cannot I am sure go further at this critical time in our struggle," he insisted in one of them. "Mossadegh will come to reasonable terms on being confronted with a continued Truman-Churchill accord."

As these cables were flashing across the Atlantic, Churchill's foreign secretary, Anthony Eden, was hearing good news from his embassy in Tehran. General Zahedi had proven highly responsive to British overtures. He was ready to join a coup against Mossadegh, naturally with himself as the designated successor. Encouraged by this development, Eden sent Mossadegh a cold note rejecting his terms.

Unlike some of the other outsiders who shaped the Western intervention in Iran, Eden was familiar with the region. At Oxford he had studied Persian, which he considered "the Italian of the East." He read the epic *Shahnameh*, early Persian poetry, and inscriptions written by Darius. After graduating, he joined the Foreign Office. He was an undersecretary when Britain negotiated the 1933 accord that outraged Mossadegh and other Iranian nationalists. Later he made several extended visits to Iran. They did not leave him with a high opinion of the natives.

Eden, like Churchill, was a fervent defender of the colonial system. His contempt for the political and intellectual capacity of people in poor countries, which he did not hide, startled some foreigners. One of them was Dean Acheson, who was taken aback by Eden's view of Iranians. "They were rug dealers and that's all they were," Acheson lamented about Eden's attitude. "You should never give in, and they would always come around and make a deal if you stayed firm."

Eden's dismissive note confirmed Mossadegh's belief that Britain would never offer him anything but hostility. His belief turned to certainty when he learned of General Zahedi's meetings with British agents. Zahedi had also begun meeting with Ayatollah Kashani, who had been elected speaker of the Majlis and increasingly saw Mossadegh as a political rival. Tehran was alive with rumors that a coup was imminent. There was only one way for Mossadegh to rid himself of the British agents who were plotting it. On October 16 he announced that Iran was breaking diplomatic relations with Britain.

By the end of that month all British diplomats, and with them all British intelligence agents, were gone from Iran. It was a heavy and fateful blow. With it, Mossadegh dashed Britain's hopes of organizing a coup. If there was to be one, the Americans would have to stage it.

Having expelled the British before they could strike against him, Mossadegh and his allies moved to arrest General Zahedi and place him on trial for treason. They were stymied at first because, as a senator, Zahedi enjoyed parliamentary immunity. The Senate's two-year term had recently expired, however, and although senators had voted to remain in office for another four years, their action was plainly illegal. On October 23 the Majlis declared the Senate dissolved. The moment this act became law, Zahedi was subject to arrest. To avoid it, he went into hiding.

Britain now had no intelligence agents in Iran, Zahedi was out of circulation, and the Truman administration remained implacably against the idea of intervention. Plans for a coup were at a standstill. That was fine with Truman, who believed that the British were at least as much to blame for the "awful situation" as was Mossadegh. "We tried," he lamented in a handwritten letter to Henry Grady, his former ambassador in Tehran, "to get the block headed British to have their oil company make a fair deal with Iran. No, no, they could not do that. They knew all about how to handle it—we didn't according to them."

British leaders might have despaired at this point, but they saw a bright glimmer of hope on the horizon. A presidential election was forthcoming in the United States, and Truman was not running for reelection. The Republican candidate to replace him, Dwight Eisenhower, was running on a vigorously anticommunist platform. Eisenhower's rhetoric greatly encouraged Churchill and Eden. The moment he was elected, they called off their effort to influence Truman and shifted their focus to the incoming team.

Election day found Kermit Roosevelt in Tehran. His job running CIA operations in the Middle East gave him professional interests there and he visited from time to time, but this was no routine stop. The abrupt departure of British intelligence officers from Iran was a major event in Roosevelt's world. The British had spent decades building a covert network there, and now it was leaderless. This was an extraordinary opportunity for the United States. Roosevelt was determined to exploit it as best he could.

Born in Buenos Aires, where his father had business interests, brought up near grandfather Theodore's estate on Long Island, and educated at Harvard, Roosevelt was the prototype of the gentleman spy. He was in his twenties when World War II broke out, a junior faculty member in the Harvard history department. Eager for adventure, he joined the Office of Strategic Services, which was so clandestine that even many of the people who knew it existed did not know what its initials stood for; they called it Oh So Secret or, because its ranks were filled with well-connected Ivy Leaguers, Oh So Social. What Roosevelt did as an OSS agent is unknown, although he apparently spent time in Egypt and Italy. Not even his family ever found out. "That was spook talk," his wife said years later. "He didn't talk spooks to me."

Photos of Roosevelt taken around the time he went to Iran show him wiry and boyishly handsome, with dark-rimmed glasses and a winning smile. His family knew him as a bumbler who could barely change a light bulb, but at work he conveyed a very different impression. Associates described him as supremely self-confident without being overbearing. One writer later called him "insouciant coolness personified." During his reconnaissance mission in

November 1952, he did not meet any Iranians whom he knew to be British agents, but he was perceptive enough to sense that there were plenty of them around.

On his way home, Roosevelt stopped in London. He had friends in the upper ranks of the Secret Intelligence Service and had been musing with them for more than a year about ways of dealing with Mossadegh. Now, for the first time, these musings began to seem realistic. His friends told him that they were more determined than ever to carry out a coup and that both Eden and Churchill were pushing them, the latter "with special vehemence." Roosevelt was most intrigued:

> What they had in mind was nothing less than the overthrow of Mossadegh. Furthermore, they saw no point in wasting time by delay. They wanted to start immediately. I had to explain that the project would require considerable clearance from my government and that I was not entirely sure what the results would be. As I told my British colleagues, we had, I felt sure, no chance to win approval from the outgoing administration of Truman and Acheson. The new Republicans, however, might be quite different.

CHAPTER 10

Pull Up Your Socks and Get Going

E xcitement surged through the corridors of power in London when news came that Dwight Eisenhower had been elected president of the United States. British leaders had spent many frustrating months trying to persuade Harry Truman to join their campaign against the Iranian government. His steadfast refusals deeply discouraged them, but now the climate in Washington was radically changed. What had come to seem impossible was suddenly very possible indeed.

Over the years, Britain had assembled a formidable network of clandestine agents in Iran. Under the direction of "Monty" Woodhouse, the chief of the British intelligence station in Tehran during the early 1950s, these agents became proficient at everything from bribing politicians to organizing riots. Woodhouse and all other British spies, however, had to leave Iran when Prime Minister Mossadegh shut the embassy from which they worked. They left behind a fine band of subversives.

The principal figures in this underground network were the three extraordinary Rashidian brothers. Their father had made a fortune in shipping, banking, and real estate, and he bequeathed to them not just his wealth but his boundless admiration for all things

British. Beginning in the early 1950s the Secret Intelligence Service paid them £10,000 each month, the equivalent of $28,000, a staggering sum by Iranian standards, to suborn Iranians in what the CIA called "such fields as the armed forces, the Majlis (Iranian parliament), religious leaders, the press, street gangs, politicians and other influential figures."

"Seyfollah, the eldest and a musician and philosopher, was the brains of the triumvirate and a superb conversationalist and host," one historian wrote about the brothers. "He was a student of history and liked to quote Machiavelli. Asadollah was the organizer, political activist and confidante of the Shah, while Qodratollah was the businessman and entrepreneur."

Directors of the Secret Intelligence Service were pained to think that such outstanding agents were going to waste in Iran when there was such urgent business to be done there. Eisenhower's election gave them hope that the Americans would pick up where they had been forced to leave off. Kermit Roosevelt encouraged them further during his visit to London. So eager were they to resume their plotting that they could not even wait for Eisenhower to take office. In mid-November of 1952, less than two weeks after the election, they sent Woodhouse to Washington.

Woodhouse met with his CIA counterparts and with men who would take important posts in the Eisenhower administration. Since he had no love for the Anglo-Iranian Oil Company—he considered its directors "stupid, boring, pigheaded and tiresome"—and since he knew that American officials didn't care much about its troubles anyway, he shaped his appeal around the rhetoric of anticommunism:

> I argued that even if a settlement of the oil dispute could be negotiated with Mossadegh, which was doubtful, he was still incapable of resisting a coup by the Tudeh party, if it were backed by Soviet support. Therefore he must be removed. I had with me a draft plan for the purpose. . . .
>
> Two separate components were dovetailed into the plan, because we had two distinct kinds of resources: an urban organization run by the [Rashidian] brothers, and a number of tribal leaders to the south. We intended to activate both simultaneously. The urban organization included senior officers of the army and

police, deputies and senators, mullahs, merchants, newspaper editors and elder statesmen, as well as mob leaders. These forces, directed by the brothers, were to seize control of Tehran, preferably with the support of the Shah but if necessary without it, to arrest Mossadegh and his ministers. At the same time, tribal leaders were to make a show of force in the direction of major cities in the south. . . .

I had obtained the Foreign Office's agreement to a list of fifteen politicians, any one of whom would be acceptable to us as prime minister if he were equally acceptable to the Americans. The list was in three categories, crudely labeled "Old Gang," "New Gang," and "Intermediate." The third category included General Fazlollah Zahedi, who soon emerged in discussion as the figure most likely to be acceptable to both British and American policymakers. I had been in touch with him before we were expelled from Tehran, and it was clear that the Americans were also in touch with him since we had left. He was an ironic choice, for during World War II he had been regarded as a German agent. An operation to kidnap him and put him out of circulation had then been organized by Fitzroy MacLean. Now we were all turning to him as the potential savior of Iran.

Over the course of his meetings in Washington, Woodhouse detected "steadily increasing interest" in his proposal for what the British called "Operation Boot." Frank Wisner, a New York lawyer who had become the CIA's director of operations, was strongly positive. So was Wisner's newly named boss, Allen Dulles. State Department officials were markedly less enthusiastic, but John Foster Dulles would overrule their reluctance as soon as he was sworn in as secretary of state.

By the time Woodhouse flew home, the incoming administration had committed itself, albeit informally, to a covert operation aimed at removing Mossadegh. It had also accepted Britain's nominees to play the two key roles: General Zahedi as Iran's designated savior and Kermit Roosevelt as the CIA field commander who would place him in office. A plan would be ready soon after Eisenhower took office. John Foster Dulles and Allen Dulles would win his approval and then do the deed.

The Dulles brothers, whose work was vital to the success of Operation Ajax, were unique in American history. Never before or since have siblings run the overt and covert sides of United States foreign policy simultaneously. During their terms as secretary of state and director of central intelligence, they worked in near-perfect harmony to achieve their common goals. Among the first and most urgent was Mossadegh's overthrow.

Foster and Allie, as the brothers were known, were born into privilege. Their grandfather, John Watson Foster, was secretary of state when they were children, and he often allowed them to meet his guests and eavesdrop on their meetings. During the era of McKinley and Theodore Roosevelt, they spent many formative hours in Washington salons and acquired an easy familiarity with the ways of power. Allie, who from childhood displayed what his biographer called "an insatiable curiosity about the people around him," took secret notes on what he heard.

Both brothers attended Princeton and did well, with Foster, the elder by five years, graduating first in his class. Although they were always close, they had quite different personalities. Allie was affable and easygoing. He enjoyed tennis, wine, and elegant parties, and at one point had a mistress who was undergoing analysis by Carl Gustav Jung. Foster was stern and gruff, known for opening and closing meetings with grunts instead of expressions of welcome or thanks. It was said that even his friends didn't like him much.

By the time the brothers had both graduated from Princeton, one of their uncles, Robert Lansing, was Woodrow Wilson's secretary of state. Partly as a result of his influence, they both pursued interests in world affairs. Allie joined the State Department when World War I broke out. He was sent to Bern, which as the capital of neutral Switzerland was a center of émigré life, and then to Berlin and Istanbul, also hotbeds of intrigue. At each post he plunged eagerly into intelligence work. He proved himself highly adept at recruiting informers, debriefing travelers, observing military movements, and assessing the strengths and weaknesses of foreign governments.

While Allie was learning the espionage business, Foster launched his legal career in New York. After he graduated from law school, his grandfather arranged an interview for him at the legendary firm of Sullivan & Cromwell. He was hired as a junior clerk and soon found himself working with one of the most quietly influential groups of men in the world. Sullivan & Cromwell was no ordinary law firm but a center of international business and finance. Its lawyers were brokers among kings, presidents, and plutocrats, and its clients included many of the world's most important banks and business cartels. Foster dealt directly with many of them, including J. P. Morgan & Company, the International Nickel Company, and the Cuban Sugar Cane Corporation. He distinguished himself as a maker of high-level deals and an expert in international finance. When the firm's managing partner died in 1926, Foster was given the job. One of his first decisions was to recruit his brother.

Allen Dulles was fresh out of law school and had not even been admitted to the bar, but his unusual skills and wide range of contacts made him a great asset to Sullivan & Cromwell, which advertised itself as having "unusual and diversified means of obtaining information." In effect he was an intelligence officer for hire. He enjoyed his work but longed for more excitement. When World War II broke out, he, like Kermit Roosevelt, joined the OSS. He was posted in Europe, where he studied the Nazi intelligence system and worked to penetrate and undermine it.

Foster spent the war years at home, making speeches and publishing articles warning of the threat that Soviet expansionism posed to "the accumulated civilization of these centuries." He became a leading figure in Republican politics. In 1948 he served as the foreign policy adviser to the Republican presidential candidate, Governor Thomas Dewey of New York. Many assumed that he would become secretary of state when Dewey won, but after Dewey's surprising loss to Truman he had to return to his law practice and bide his time. Allen, who rejoined the firm after the war, had dreamed of becoming Dewey's ambassador to France, but that plan, too, was spoiled by the election result.

The Dulles brothers developed a special interest in Iran. Foster always mentioned Iran when he spoke or wrote about countries he believed might soon fall to communism. Allen visited Tehran in 1949 on behalf of a Sullivan & Cromwell client, an engineering firm looking for construction contracts. His trip gave him a chance to observe both the twenty-nine-year-old Shah, whom his wife called "the gloomy prince," and the fiery opposition leader, Mohammad Mossadegh. Later that year, when the Shah visited New York, Allen arranged a "small private dinner" for him and one hundred members of the Council on Foreign Relations.

In 1947 the wartime OSS was transformed into the Central Intelligence Agency. Allen Dulles had many friends in the new agency, and at their request, he wrote a series of secret reports urging it to launch a worldwide program of "covert psychological warfare, clandestine political activity, sabotage and guerrilla activity." Soon after Truman chose General Walter Bedell Smith as the director of central intelligence, Smith brought Dulles into the agency, first as a consultant and then as deputy director.

Allen Dulles was one of the country's most ambitious intelligence experts. John Foster Dulles had become widely known as a world-class international lawyer who moved easily in elite Republican circles. Both reached the pinnacle of power when Eisenhower took office.

"Beedle" Smith stayed with them, moving from the CIA to become undersecretary of state. Smith had been Eisenhower's chief of staff during the war and remained one of his most trusted friends. In his new position, he was ideally placed to assure that the CIA, the State Department, and the White House would work seamlessly on sensitive projects like the coup against Mossadegh.

On a cold day shortly before Eisenhower's inauguration, Smith summoned Kermit Roosevelt for a gruff conversation about Iran. Smith had supported the idea of a coup during the Truman administration, but his superiors overruled him. Now he was eager to proceed. It had been two months since Woodhouse's visit to Washington, and Smith was losing patience.

"When are those ——ing British coming to talk to us?" Smith demanded. "And when is our goddamn operation going to get underway?" Roosevelt assured him that everyone was ready, but it would be unseemly to move before Eisenhower was inaugurated.

"Pull up your socks and get going," Smith told him. "You won't have any trouble in London. They'll jump at anything we propose. And I'm sure you can come up with something sensible enough for Foster to OK. Ike will agree."

Eisenhower was inaugurated on January 20, 1953. Days later, the American ambassador in Tehran, Loy Henderson, began contacting Iranians he thought might be interested in working to overthrow Mossadegh. Like his new bosses in Washington, Henderson had given up hope for a compromise. In one cable to Washington, he described Mossadegh as "lacking in stability," "clearly dominated by emotions and prejudices," and "not quite sane." In another, he asserted that the National Front was composed of "the street rabble, the extreme left ... extreme Iranian nationalists, some but not all of the more fanatical religious leaders, [and] intellectual leftists, including many who had been educated abroad and did not realize that Iran was not ready for democracy." He and George Middleton, his British counterpart, took the extraordinary step of composing a joint message to their home offices expressing their shared conclusion that the longer Mossadegh remained in power, the likelier it was that Iran would fall to communism.

Through an emissary, Henderson even opened a channel to General Zahedi, who, he told Dulles in a cable, was "not ideal" but had "more chance of piloting Iran through the turbulent days following Mossadegh's resignation than any other candidate now on the horizon." Zahedi had assured Henderson that if he reached power, he would "take a strong stand toward the Communists." He added, however, that it would be "impossible for Iranians to remove the present government by their own efforts."

Henderson sent a cable to Washington endorsing this view. It was received with great enthusiasm, so much so that Beedle Smith gave it to Eisenhower with a cover note calling it "very accurate." Smith also sent a reply to Henderson telling him that the United States had decided it could "no longer approve of the Mossadegh government and would prefer a successor government." He sent copies of his cable to CIA headquarters in Washington and to the CIA station in Iran. It amounted to a formal, though secret, declaration of war on Mossadegh.

Only one important figure in the Eisenhower administration still hoped for compromise with Mossadegh: President Eisenhower himself. Two weeks before his inauguration, he met with Churchill in New York and did not seem at all interested when Churchill mentioned Iran. In fact, he complained that Britain's efforts to involve the United States in its Iranian troubles had done nothing but "get Mossadegh to accuse us of being a partner in browbeating a weak nation."

Churchill was wise enough not to press his case at that moment. He knew that planning for a coup was already well underway, and that the Dulles brothers were on his side. In February he dispatched "C," the chief of British intelligence, Sir John Sinclair, to Washington to convey the intensity of his interest.

While Sinclair was in Washington, Iranian tribal leaders who were on the British payroll, working with General Zahedi, launched a short-lived uprising in the southern provinces. Mossadegh suspected the Shah was involved and suggested that he consider leaving Iran until passions cooled. By all accounts including his own, the Shah was more than willing to go. Minister of Court Hussein Ala described him as being in an "almost hysterical state" and on the brink of a "complete nervous breakdown and irrational action."

Mossadegh's foreign-sponsored enemies, however, cleverly turned news of the Shah's planned trip to their advantage. In sermons, street-corner speeches, and newspaper articles, they charged that Mossadegh was forcing the Shah to leave against his will and that his next step would certainly be to abolish the monarchy. They organized a mob to converge on Mossadegh's house on the night of February 28, and as the crowd swelled in size, a jeep carrying an army colonel and one of the most colorful gang leaders in Tehran, Shaban "The Brainless" Jafari, smashed through the front gate. Mossadegh, in his pajamas, was forced to flee over his back garden wall. A British diplomat cabled home that the mob "was certainly organized by Kashani, and was not a spontaneous expression of a loyalty deep-seated or significant enough to stiffen the Shah."

By the next afternoon Tehran was quiet again, partly because the Shah had announced that he was canceling his travel plans. The sudden appearance of a paid mob and its willingness to attack the prime minister, however, contributed to an atmosphere of growing instability. It also gave coup planners more ammunition for their campaign to persuade Eisenhower that Iran was sliding dangerously toward chaos.

Neither Eisenhower nor anyone in his inner circle ever wrote an account of how he came to support the idea of a coup. Evidence suggests, however, that he did so during March, two months after his inauguration. The Dulles brothers seized on the violence that erupted in Tehran on February 28. Even Ambassador Henderson acknowledged that the protest had been organized rather than genuine, but evidently no one told that to Eisenhower. Instead, Allen Dulles sent him an intelligence estimate warning that "the

Iran situation has been slowly disintegrating" and "a Communist takeover is becoming more and more of a possibility."

It was not an easy sell. At a meeting of the National Security Council on March 4, Eisenhower wondered aloud why it wasn't possible "to get some of the people in these down-trodden countries to like us instead of hating us." Secretary of State Dulles did not reply directly, but he delivered a sobering analysis of the situation in Iran. His words, as reported by the official note-taker, suggested that the United States could no longer stand by without acting:

> The probable consequences of the events of the last few days, concluded Mr. Dulles, would be a dictatorship in Iran under Mossadegh. As long as the latter lives there was little danger, but if he were to be assassinated or removed from power, a political vacuum would occur in Iran and the Communists might easily take over. The consequences of such a takeover were then outlined in all their seriousness by Mr. Dulles. Not only would the free world be deprived of the enormous assets represented by Iranian oil production and reserves, but the Russians would secure these assets and thus henceforth be free of any anxiety about their petroleum situation. Worse still, Mr. Dulles pointed out, if Iran succumbed to the Communists there was little doubt that in short order the other areas of the Middle East, with some sixty percent of the world's oil reserves, would fall into Communist control.

Later that week, Foreign Secretary Eden visited Washington. At several of his top-level meetings, Eden broached the subject of Iran and the proposed coup. He found everyone except Eisenhower sympathetic. Alton Jones, the oil executive who had traveled to Iran the year before, was a personal friend of Eisenhower's, and Eisenhower told Eden that he wanted to send Jones back "to make the best arrangement he could to get the oil flowing again." He said he considered Mossadegh "the only hope for the West in Iran," precisely the view Truman had held.

"I would like to give the guy ten million bucks," Eisenhower told the surprised Eden.

Eden tried gently to change Eisenhower's mind, telling him at one point that "we would be better occupied looking for alternatives to Mossadegh, rather than trying to buy him off." In the best diplomatic tradition, however, he left the real work to the intelligence officers he had brought with him. While he spoke softly at the White House, they were honing their plot with comrades at the CIA and the State Department.

The Dulles brothers had developed an excellent sense of how to bring their boss around to their way of thinking. On March 7 John Foster Dulles and Eden issued a joint communiqué saying they had agreed on a new offer that would allow Iran to "retain control of its own oil industry and of its own oil policies." That sounded fine to Eisenhower, but it did not honestly reflect the offer itself, which, like every other one the British had made over the past two years, was based on the premise that they would return to run the Iranian oil industry. Mossadegh rejected it and told Ambassador Henderson that he was disappointed that the Eisenhower administration had "allowed the United Kingdom to formulate United States policies concerning Iran." He made several counterproposals, even offering at one point to submit to mediation by Switzerland or Germany, but the British and their new friends in Washington ignored them.

While Eden was in Washington, the Rashidian brothers were doing their best to stir up trouble in Iran. Partly through their efforts, prominent figures who had been part of Mossadegh's coalition began to turn against him. Ayatollah Kashani, the most outspoken defector, damned Mossadegh with the vitriol he had once reserved for the British. He began using thugs to intimidate his rivals and even pushed a bill through the Majlis pardoning Khalil Tahmasibi, the convicted assassin of Prime Minister Razmara. Other former Mossadegh allies who broke with him to pursue their own agendas included Muzzaffar Baqai, head of the worker-based Toilers party, and Hussein Makki, who had helped lead the takeover of the Abadan refinery and was at one point considered Mossadegh's heir apparent. Robin Zaehner wrote in a report to London that the successful effort to pull Kashani, Baqai, and Makki away from the National Front was "created and directed by the brothers Rashidian."

These defections greatly weakened the National Front and left Mossadegh isolated and vulnerable. They also immeasurably strengthened the Dulles brothers in their effort to persuade President Eisenhower that the time had come for the United States to act. At a National Security Council meeting on March 11, Secretary of State Dulles asserted that Americans must become "senior

partners with the British in this area." Eisenhower expressed no disagreement.

"The President said that he had very real doubts whether, even if
we tried unilaterally, we could make a successful deal with
Mossadegh," the note-taker at that meeting reported. "He felt that it
might not be worth the paper it was written on, and the example
might have grave effects on United States oil concessions in other
parts of the world."

Eisenhower had come to the conclusion that Iran was collapsing,
and that the collapse could not be prevented as long as Mossadegh
was in power. He stopped inquiring about the prospects for compromise. Those around him took his change in tone as a sign that
he would not resist the idea of a coup. On March 18 Frank Wisner
sent a message to his British counterparts saying that the CIA was
now prepared to discuss the details of a plot against Mossadegh.
Two weeks later, Allen Dulles approved the dispatch of $1 million to
the CIA station in Tehran, for use "in any way that would bring
about the fall of Mossadegh."

These developments greatly encouraged the British. During
April, the Foreign Office formally embraced Operation Ajax. Then,
in what amounted to explicit recognition that command was passing from their hands to the Americans, British agents sent word to
the Rashidian brothers that they should now work with the CIA.

Iranians connected to the Rashidian network decided that they
could push Iran further toward chaos by kidnapping high government officials. Their preferred targets, Foreign Minister Fatemi and
General Riahi, the newly appointed chief of staff, traveled with too
many bodyguards, so they settled on the Tehran police chief,
General Mahmoud Afshartus. Some of the plotters had personal ties
to Afshartus, and one invited the chief to his home on April 19. There
he was seized, blindfolded, and spirited to a cave outside of town.
Police officers identified the kidnappers almost immediately, but as
the officers closed in, one of Afshartus's captors shot and killed him.

This murder had the desired effect. It shocked the country and
also eliminated a popular officer who might have been a formidable
obstacle to the success of the forthcoming coup. General Zahedi,
who had resurfaced after treason charges against him were dropped,
was implicated in the killing. He took refuge in the Majlis, under
Ayatollah Kashani's protection.

Unaware of how decisively the Americans had turned against him, Mossadegh next decided to appeal directly to Eisenhower. In a letter dated May 28 he said that Iranians were "suffering financial hardships and struggling with political intrigues carried on by the former oil company and the British government." They would be deeply grateful for "prompt and effective aid" from the United States, or for American support for a stalled $25-million loan that Mossadegh was seeking from the Export-Import Bank, or at least for permission to sell oil to American companies. Eisenhower took a month to reply. When he did, it was to suggest that Mossadegh could best repair Iran's economy by resolving his dispute with the British:

> The failure of Iran and the United Kingdom to reach an agreement with regard to compensation has handicapped the Government of the United States in its efforts to help Iran. There is a strong feeling in the United States, even among American citizens most sympathetic to Iran and friendly to the Iranian people, that it would not be fair to the American taxpayers for the United States Government to extend any considerable amount of economic aid to Iran so long as Iran could have access to funds derived from the sale of its oil. . . . I note the concern reflected in your letter at the present dangerous situation in Iran, and sincerely hope that before it is too late, the Government of Iran will take such steps as are in its power to prevent a further deterioration in that situation.

This letter told Mossadegh what Eisenhower's intimates already knew: that the new administration had reversed American policy toward Iran. No longer would there be efforts to make the best of the situation, as under Truman, and no longer would there be criticism of the British for favoring a coup. In fact, by the time Eisenhower sent his reply to Mossadegh, both men knew what was afoot.

Eisenhower had already given tacit approval to the coup plot, but because of its momentous scope, tacit approval was not enough. On June 14 Allen Dulles went to the White House to brief him. Sensing the president's desire not to know too much, Dulles gave him only what Kermit Roosevelt called "the most 'broad brush' outline of what was proposed." That was all Eisenhower needed, and he gave his blessing. Around the same time Churchill gave his own secret—and much more enthusiastic—approval.

Planning for the plot was already quite advanced by the time Eisenhower and Churchill formally endorsed it. Two veteran intelligence officers, one American and one British, had met in Cyprus to draw up a detailed blueprint. Both were old Iran hands. The CIA man was Donald Wilber, who had worked for years as an archaeologist and an architect in the Middle East, served in Iran during World War II as an OSS agent, and then divided his time between advanced studies at Princeton and work as a consultant to the CIA specializing in psychological warfare. In 1952 Wilber had spent six months running the CIA's "political action" office in Tehran, an assignment that gave him a firsthand view of political and military factions favoring and opposing Mossadegh. His British counterpart, Norman Darbyshire, had served extended tours of duty in Iran and worked closely with Robin Zaehner. When the British intelligence station in Tehran was forced to close, it was moved to Cyprus and Darbyshire was named to head it.

These two agents, now working for governments that shared the same goal in Iran, struck up a close working relationship, as a CIA history of the coup—written by Wilber himself—later reported:

> It soon became apparent that Dr. Wilber and Mr. Darbyshire held quite similar views of Iranian personalities and had made very similar estimates of the factors involved in the Iranian political scene. There was no friction or marked difference of opinion during the discussions. It also quickly became apparent that the SIS was perfectly content to follow whatever lead was taken by the Agency. It seemed obvious to Wilber that the British were very pleased at having obtained the active cooperation of the Agency and were determined to do nothing which might jeopardize US participation. At the same time there was faint envy expressed over the fact that the Agency was better equipped in the way of funds, personnel and facilities than was SIS.

Wilber and Darbyshire agreed that although General Zahedi had his weaknesses, he was the only Iranian with enough "vigor and courage" to rally opposition forces. Their plan to place him in power, which would be altered several times before the blow was struck, was carefully considered and straightforward:

☐ Through a variety of means, covert agents would manipulate public opinion and turn as many Iranians as possible against Mossadegh. This effort, for which $150,000 was budgeted, would "create, extend and enhance public hostility and distrust and fear of Mossadegh and his government." It would portray Mossadegh as corrupt, pro-communist, hostile to Islam, and bent on destroying the morale and readiness of the armed forces.

☐   While Iranian agents spread these lies, thugs would be paid to launch "staged attacks" on religious leaders and make it appear that they were ordered by Mossadegh or his supporters.

☐   Meanwhile, General Zahedi would persuade and bribe as many of his fellow officers as possible to stand ready for whatever military action was necessary to carry out the coup. He was to be given $60,000, later increased to $135,000, to "win additional friends" and "influence key people."

☐   A similar effort, for which $11,000 per week was budgeted, would be launched to suborn members of the Majlis.

☐   On the morning of "coup day," thousands of paid demonstrators would stage a massive antigovernment rally. The well-prepared Majlis would respond with a "quasi-legal" vote to dismiss Mossadegh. If he resisted, army units under Zahedi's control would arrest him and his key supporters, and then seize military command posts, police stations, telephone and telegraph offices, radio stations, and the national bank.

Working closely with comrades in Washington and Tehran, with whom they were in constant contact over a Cyprus-based radio network, Wilber and Darbyshire finished this blueprint at the end of May. On June 3 Ambassador Henderson arrived in Washington to be briefed on its contents. He stayed to attend a crucial meeting on June 25, at which plans for the coup were laid out in detail.

President Eisenhower did not wish to hear details of covert operations and so did not attend this meeting. His closest foreign policy advisers, however, were all there. The meeting was held in John Foster Dulles's office at the State Department. When the plotters had assembled, Dulles picked up the report Wilber and Darbyshire had written and said, "So this is how we get rid of that madman Mossadegh!"

Kermit Roosevelt explained how he proposed to carry out the

coup, and when he was finished, Dulles asked the others what they thought. Allen Dulles and Beedle Smith endorsed the plan without reservation. So did Secretary of Defense Charles Wilson. Two senior State Department officials—Henry Byroade, the assistant secretary for Middle East affairs, and Robert Bowie, the director of the policy planning staff—went along with slightly less enthusiasm, certainly realizing that they would not remain in their jobs long if they dissented. When it was Henderson's turn to speak, he said he had no love for "this kind of business," but that in this case "we have no choice."

"That's that, then," Secretary of State Dulles said with an uncharacteristic grin. "Let's get going."

With this unanimous vote, the United States gave its final go-ahead for Operation Ajax, or Operation Boot, as the British continued to call it. The governments in London and Washington were finally united in their enthusiasm. One looked forward to recovering its oil concession. The other saw a chance to deliver a devastating blow against communism.

There was dissent from this new unity. Some of it came from career diplomats like Charles Bohlen, a former ambassador to the Soviet Union, who subjected one British diplomat in Washington to what the diplomat called "an emotional tirade" against the planned coup. Several CIA officers also opposed the idea. One of them was Roger Goiran, the chief of the CIA station in Tehran.

Goiran had built a formidable intelligence network, known by the code name Bedamn, that was engaged in propaganda activities aimed at blackening the image of the Soviet Union in Iran. It also stood ready to launch a nationwide campaign of subversion and sabotage in case of a communist coup. The Bedamn network consisted of more than one hundred agents and had an annual budget of $1 million—quite considerable, in light of the fact that the CIA's total worldwide budget for covert operations was just $82 million. Now Goiran was being asked to use his network in a coup against Mossadegh. He believed that this would be a great mistake and warned that if the coup was carried out, Iranians would forever view the United States as a supporter of what he called "Anglo-French colonialism." His opposition was so resolute that Allen Dulles had to remove him from his post.

While Allen Dulles marshaled resources for Operation Ajax,

John Foster Dulles became its most enthusiastic cheerleader. He followed the preparations with delight and also great impatience. At one point he became alarmed when Iran was discussed at a high-level meeting but no mention was made of the planned coup. The next morning he telephoned his brother at the CIA to ask anxiously whether something had gone wrong. According to a memo of their conversation: "The Secy called and said in your talk about Iran yesterday at the meeting you did not mention the other matter, is it off? AWD said he doesn't talk about it, it was cleared directly with the President, and is still active. . . . AWD said it is moving along reasonably well."

Thus reassured that the plot was afoot, Secretary of State Dulles confined his public statements to generalized laments about the course of events in Iran. His comment at a news conference in July might have been read as a warning couched in highly diplomatic language. "Recent developments in Iran, especially the growing activity of the illegal Communist party, which appears to be tolerated by the Iranian government, have caused us concern," he said. "These developments make it more difficult for the United States to give assistance to Iran so long as the government tolerates this sort of activity."

By the time Kermit Roosevelt entered Iran on July 19, the country was aflame. Mossadegh's supporters in the Majlis had voted to remove Ayatollah Kashani from his position as speaker, and the resulting clash led more than half the deputies to resign. Demonstrations demanding dissolution of the Majlis shook Tehran. Mossadegh announced that he would hold a referendum on the question and pledged to resign if voters did not vote to oust the existing Majlis. The referendum, hurriedly convened at the beginning of August, was a disastrous parody of democracy. There were separate ballot boxes for yes and no votes, and the announced result was over 99 percent in favor of throwing out the Majlis. The transparent unfairness of this referendum was more grist for the anti-Mossadegh mill.

Mid-August found Roosevelt and his team of Iranian agents in place and ready to strike. They had pushed Iran to the brink of chaos. Newspapers and religious leaders were screaming for Mossadegh's head. Protests and riots organized by the CIA had turned the streets into battlegrounds. Antigovernment propaganda,

CHAPTER 11

I Knew It!
They Love Me!

A sharp knock on the door of an apartment in one of Tehran's northern suburbs brought two audacious co-conspirators together for the first time. One was the most wanted man in Iran. The other would have been even more wanted if the police knew he existed.

Kermit Roosevelt had much to worry about as he knocked. The night before, he and his men had failed in an attempt to overthrow Prime Minister Mossadegh. His superiors at the CIA in Washington were urging him to flee. Roosevelt, however, had resolved to risk a second attempt.

Extra police officers were on the street that Sunday morning, August 16, 1953. Sirens wailed as security agents swooped down on conspirators implicated in the abortive coup. Roosevelt drove carefully, stopped at red lights, and arrived at General Zahedi's apartment without incident.

By this hour Zahedi had hoped to be prime minister. Instead, he was a hunted fugitive. If he had any hope of success now or even of saving his skin, it lay with Roosevelt. Zahedi knew who must be knocking and opened the door himself.

Roosevelt skipped the pleasantries. He had come to ask just one question: Was Zahedi prepared to try again? Without hesitation, Zahedi said that he was. That was the answer Roosevelt needed.

Both men then agreed that it was too dangerous for Zahedi to remain where he was. Roosevelt had arranged to hide him at the villa of a fellow agent, three blocks from the American embassy. They walked down the apartment stairs and slipped into Roosevelt's car. The putative leader of Iran lay on the floor in back, covered with a blanket, as he was driven to his new hideout.

After stashing Zahedi, Roosevelt drove back to what he had begun calling his "battle station" at the embassy compound. There he met two American diplomats who had been assigned to monitor the plot. Both told him frankly that they thought the game was up. The handful of officials in Washington who knew about Operation Ajax were also ready to surrender. Beedle Smith, the undersecretary of state who had been one of the coup's most fervent promoters, sent a gloomy note to President Eisenhower saying that the United States would now "probably have to snuggle up to Mossadegh."

Roosevelt, however, still had considerable assets. One was General Zahedi, who had many friends in the officer corps and was willing to do whatever necessary to reach power. Equally formidable was a far-flung network of Iranian agents and subagents. This network had been assembled at great cost and had shown its ability to spread inflammatory rumors, place provocative articles in newspapers, manipulate politicians, influence mullahs, and produce hired crowds on short notice. It had not yet been fully tested.

Roosevelt also had the two treasured *firmans,* decrees that the Shah had signed dismissing Prime Minister Mossadegh and naming Zahedi to replace him. They gave the planned coup an air of legitimacy. Few Iranians would stop to debate whether the Shah had the legal right to issue such decrees. For them, respecting royal power was an ancient tradition. The *firmans* gave the plotters of Operation Ajax a way to wrap themselves in that tradition.

At their hurried meeting that morning, General Zahedi had urged Roosevelt to make copies of the *firman* naming Zahedi prime minister and to distribute them throughout the city, especially in the tough southern neighborhoods where mobs were recruited. This was a brilliant idea, and Roosevelt immediately embraced it. By midday he had commandeered one of the few copying machines to be found in Tehran. He not only sent copies of the *firman* out with every agent he could find but also arranged for facsimiles to appear on the front pages of the next day's newspapers. Later he dispatched trusted couriers, including two Iranian officers armed with false identity papers, to carry copies to military commanders in outlying cities.

To assure that the *firman* reached as wide an audience as possible, Roosevelt sent a message to the two American news correspondents in Tehran, who represented the Associated Press and the *New York Times*. It was an invitation to a secret meeting with General Zahedi. Both eagerly accepted, and a car was dispatched to pick them up. When they got to the safe house, however, they were brought not to Zahedi but to his sharp-minded son Ardeshir. He presented them with copies of the *firman* and, in perfect English, delivered an impassioned speech about its importance.

Even given the circumstances, it was a very odd meeting. The man on whose behalf it was called never appeared. Security was provided by the host's young wife, who sat in a rocking chair close to Ardeshir Zahedi with a pistol under her knitting. Most curious to the reporters, however, was a large and unfamiliar machine that was clattering loudly nearby.

"Lo and behold, there was a huge copying machine," Kennett Love of the *New York Times* recalled later. "Now this was 1953, and a copying machine is about the size of two refrigerators. But at that time neither I nor most American journalists or most American people would have been able to tell you what the initials CIA stood for."

By Sunday afternoon Roosevelt had conceived his new plan. On Monday and Tuesday his agents would spread across Tehran to bribe politicians, mullahs, and anyone else who might be able to turn out crowds at a crucial moment. During those same two days he would send mobs into the street to commit mayhem in Mossadegh's name. Then on Wednesday he would pull his mobs off the street, use military and police units to storm government buildings, and strike the final blow by capturing Mossadegh.

To accomplish all this, Roosevelt relied on a handful of proven Iranian agents. Most important were the three Rashidian brothers. Roosevelt had known them for several years, had arranged for them to be flown to CIA headquarters in Washington for what he called "thorough tests of their veracity," and had developed great admiration for their tradecraft. Besides the Rashidians, who were originally British assets, Roosevelt also used several Iranians who had been trained by the CIA. The two best, Ali Jalili and Farouk Keyvani, began working for the CIA in early 1951 as organizers of the propaganda and sabotage network known as Bedamn. They had organized riots and carried out other clandestine tasks so successfully that the CIA came to consider them "vitally important principal agents of the Tehran station." Like the Rashidians, they had been brought to Washington, debriefed at length by Kermit Roosevelt and other CIA operatives, given code names (sometimes "Nossey" and "Cafron," other times "Nerren" and "Cilley"), and chosen as key operatives in the plot against Mossadegh. They and the Rashidians, however, never met. Roosevelt kept the identities of his main Iranian operatives secret even from each other.

As Roosevelt prepared his second attempt against Mossadegh, he ordered these and other agents to begin circulating a false version of the first one. The story they were to give out was that Mossadegh had tried to seize the Shah's throne but was thwarted by patriotic officers. Corrupt newspaper editors gave this lie front-page coverage. Only a few reported the truth, which was that Mossadegh had been the coup's intended victim, not its instigator.

Mossadegh and his aides, however, paid little attention to the newspapers. They believed that the Shah had been behind Saturday's rebellion. If that was true, then his flight into exile meant that there would be no more attempts at what Foreign Minister Fatemi called "royal robbery of the rights of the people." They never imagined that the plotters who launched the Saturday coup would soon try again.

When a reporter asked Fatemi how his government would deal with captured plotters, he replied offhandedly that officials were "considering what to do" but had "not yet reached the stage of decisions." Other cabinet ministers, including Mossadegh himself, also let their guard down. They withdrew loyal troops from the streets and spent crucial hours asking one another questions raised by the Shah's flight into exile. Had he abdicated? Must a regency council be appointed? Was there to be a new dynasty? Should the monarchy be abolished?

While government officials airily debated their country's long-term future, Kermit Roosevelt was hard at work trying to shape its next few days. He knew he would need military units to help carry out his coup and asked the military attaché at the American embassy, General Robert McClure, to find some. McClure, who was well acquainted with Iranian officers, decided to start at the top, with the chief of staff, General Riahi.

He could not have had high hopes, because Riahi was known for his loyalty. Even if Riahi would not switch sides and join the plotters, however, McClure hoped that at least he would remain neutral. His first gambit was to suggest that Riahi leave town. Perhaps, he ventured, the two of them could head out to the countryside for a few days of fishing. Riahi coldly declined. Then McClure, who was not known for subtlety, abruptly changed his tone. He told Riahi that his military mission was accredited to the Shah, and therefore he would always recognize the Shah's legitimacy. Iranian commanders, he added bluntly, should do the same. Riahi became indignant and showed him the door.

Later that Sunday, McClure had a second failure. Roosevelt sent him by plane to Isfahan, with instructions to try to enlist the garrison commander there, but once again McClure's imperious style worked against him. He waved a copy of the *firman* and brusquely told the commander that he must send troops to fight Mossadegh. The commander replied that he took orders only from Iranians, not Americans. Two rebuffs in the space of a few hours cost McClure his temper. As he left the Isfahan garrison, he turned back to the commander and angrily vowed, "I will kick Mossadegh out of office!"

By the time McClure's plane landed back in Tehran, he had calmed down and decided what to do next. Accompanied by a couple of aides, he set out on a tour of small military outposts in the capital itself. At each post he offered the commander money and a promise of promotion if the coup succeeded. This time he had better luck. Several officers accepted his emoluments, including two who commanded infantry regiments and one who commanded a tank battalion. They promised to be ready when called.

Roosevelt now had military units standing by to crush street disorders. His next task was to arrange the disorders. For this, he called on his energetic and well-connected agents Jalili and Keyvani. First, he told them, he wanted "black" crowds that would rampage through the streets shouting their allegiance to communism and Mossadegh. They were to break windows, beat innocent bystanders, shoot at mosques, and generally arouse the outrage of citizens. Then there had to be "patriotic" mobs that would suppress these rowdies, preferably with the help of friendly police officers.

Jalili and Keyvani were worried. They had provided services like this before, but what Roosevelt was now proposing would be by far their biggest operation. It could also place them in great danger, especially if the operation failed. At one point they went so far as to suggest that they would like to pull out of the plot altogether. Roosevelt persuaded them to stay by offering them a simple choice. If they stayed, they would receive $50,000 for their rowdies and themselves. If not, he would kill them. They decided to take the cash. Roosevelt handed it to them on the spot.

That Sunday had begun in abject defeat. By the time evening fell, Roosevelt could feel his confidence returning. Before retiring for the night, he sent a cable to Washington saying that there might still be a "slight remaining chance for success."

No one in Washington shared Roosevelt's optimism. Soon after he awoke on Monday morning, he was handed a cable from headquarters urging him to leave Iran as soon as possible. It was the second time in thirty-six hours that his superiors had advised him to flee. This time he obliged by preparing an escape plan—it involved him, Zahedi, and a handful of others fleeing on a plane owned by the American air attaché—but thought no more of it.

At midmorning news from the street began to trickle in. It was all good. Gangs of thugs pretending pro-Mossadegh sympathies were making their way from the slums of Tehran's south side toward the center of town. Some true nationalists and communists innocently joined them. By the time they reached Parliament Square, which was dominated by a towering equestrian statue of Reza Shah, they numbered in the tens of thousands. How many were true militants and how many provocateurs is uncertain, but there were plenty of both.

Cheers went up when several men began climbing up to the monument. One carried a heavy chain coiled around his neck. He wrapped one end of it around the bronze horse's neck and tossed the other end down to the ground, where it was hooked to the bumper of what Kennett Love called "a sort of military-looking command car." Then the men began sawing and chiseling away at the horse's feet. Finally, with a great crash, the statue fell to the ground. It was another victory in Roosevelt's campaign to polarize Iran.

"This was the best thing we could have hoped for," he wrote later. "The more they shouted against the Shah, the more the army and the people recognized them as the enemy. If *they* hated the Shah, the army and people hated them. And the more they ravaged the city, the more they angered the great bulk of its inhabitants. Nothing could have dramatized the guts of the conflict more effectively or more rapidly. On Sunday there had been some rioting and pillaging, but Monday put the frosting on the cake."

Mossadegh had naively ordered police officers not to interfere with people's right to demonstrate, so the mob was able to rampage more or less at will. This was a great boon to Roosevelt, since any riots at all, even ones that he did not control, served to persuade Iranians that their country was sinking into chaos and needed a rescuer. Still, Roosevelt worried that Mossadegh might change his mind and order the police to crack down. The police might even prove bold enough to fight against rebellious soldiers when the coup reached its climax. Roosevelt cast about for a way to blunt their power.

He found his instrument that afternoon, when Ambassador Loy Henderson unexpectedly turned up. After attending the meeting in Washington at which the coup was given final approval, Henderson had thought it wise not to return to his post until Mossadegh was overthrown. He traveled to a resort in the Austrian Alps and waited for news. On August 14, unable to sit still so far away from the action, he flew to Beirut. When he heard radio reports that the coup had failed, he commandeered a Navy plane from the local American embassy and flew to Tehran. Upon arriving at the embassy, he went straight to Roosevelt, who briefed him on the state of affairs.

Roosevelt confessed with considerable understatement that he had "run into some small complications." Henderson asked if there was anything he could do to help. After a moment of reflection, Roosevelt came up with an outlandish idea. He would make Henderson his tool in an attempt to unnerve Mossadegh.

Roosevelt knew that Mossadegh was a deeply compassionate man who could be moved to tears by the plight of a single widow or orphan. Not a conspirator by nature, Mossadegh had an almost childlike faith in the sincerity of most other people. He was also a very decent, even chivalrous man who appreciated form, ceremony, and diplomacy. Despite the troubles of recent months, he had a soft spot for Americans. If Roosevelt could find a way to exploit these traits in his adversary's character, he might throw "the old bugger" off balance or force him to make a false move. It was a classic challenge of psychological warfare, and it would produce the most surreal encounter of Operation Ajax.

"What in heaven's name do I do?" Henderson asked when Roosevelt proposed sending him to Mossadegh.

"My suggestion," Roosevelt replied, "would be to complain about the way Americans here are being harassed. Anonymous telephone calls saying, 'Yankee go home!' or calling them obscene names. Even if a child picks up the phone, the caller just shouts dirty words at him."

Henderson agreed to do as Roosevelt wished. He added that if Mossadegh asked him about American support for subversion in Iran, he would "make it quite plain that we have no intention of interfering in the internal affairs of a friendly country." Roosevelt considered this a noble sentiment but said nothing.

Monday evening was "a most active and trying time for the station," according to the CIA's postmortem. Roosevelt spent four hours in an intensive planning session with his key operatives, among them the Rashidian brothers, General Zahedi and his son Ardeshir, and General Hedayatollah Guilanshah, a former air force commander who had committed himself to the plot. All were smuggled into and out of the embassy compound under blankets or in car trunks.

Roosevelt was now acting entirely on his own. There had been no backup plan in case the first coup failed, so he simply improvised as he went along. He was in constant motion and had neither the time nor the desire to clear his decisions with superiors. Even if he had wanted to do so, communications technology was cumbersome and unreliable. So during those crucial days, no one in Washington or London had any idea what he was doing.

From the beginning, Roosevelt had realized that the fate of Mossadegh's government would ultimately be decided on the streets. His Iranian agents were able to produce crowds almost instantly. He devised a plan to use both pro- and antigovernment riots, but in the end the nature of the mob's demands was almost irrelevant. A mob crying for Mossadegh's ouster was, of course, ideal, but one that supported him was also helpful because it would help polarize opinion and perhaps even provoke royalist soldiers into repressive reaction. All that really mattered was that Tehran be in turmoil.

The riots that shook Tehran on Monday intensified on Tuesday. Thousands of demonstrators, unwittingly under CIA control, surged through the streets, looting shops, destroying pictures of the Shah, and ransacking the offices of royalist groups. Exuberant nationalists and communists joined in the mayhem. The police were still under orders from Mossadegh not to interfere. That allowed rioters to do their job, which was to give the impression that Iran was sliding toward anarchy. Roosevelt caught glimpses of them during his furtive trips around the city and said that they "scared the hell out of me."

The crucial event of that day, however, took place not on the streets but behind closed doors. At midafternoon Ambassador Henderson came to call on Mossadegh. The old man was at a distinct disadvantage. He had no idea that clandestine agents based at the American embassy were working day and night to overthrow his government. And since he did not imagine that there existed such a person as Kermit Roosevelt, he could not guess that Roosevelt was using Ambassador Henderson to lay a trap for him. Still, he knew that outside powers had been involved in Saturday's failed coup. He should have been on guard.

Mossadegh received the ambassador in formal attire, signaling the importance of their meeting. He was distinctly cool, with what Henderson called "smoldering resentment" palpable behind his courtesy. The United States had taken the official position that the Shah was still Iran's leader, and Mossadegh protested this American support for "a man who is now no more than a rebel." Henderson replied that although the Shah had indeed fled, the Prophet Mohammad had also fled from Mecca in his time, and from that moment his influence had only grown. This comment surprised Mossadegh, and he paused to consider it. Henderson decided that it was time to deliver the speech Roosevelt had devised for him. He spoke sternly, his voice rising to a crescendo of staged indignation.

"I must tell you that my fellow citizens are being harassed most unpleasantly," he began. "Not only do they get threatening phone calls, often answered by their children, who are then subjected to rude words children should not even hear; not only are they insulted in the streets when going peacefully about their business. In addition to all the verbal aggression they are exposed to, their automobiles are damaged whenever they are left exposed. Parts are stolen, headlights are smashed, tires are deflated, and if the cars are left unlocked, their upholstery is cut to pieces. Unless this kind of harassment is stopped, Your Excellency, I am going to ask my government to recall all dependents and also all men whose presence here is not required in our own national interest."

Mossadegh might well have laughed at this mendacious monologue. Americans had organized the upheaval in Iran, but Henderson was portraying them as its victims. As proof, he offered highly exaggerated accounts of supposed outrages. But amazingly, Mossadegh seemed genuinely pained by these fanciful stories and alarmed at the prospect of Americans leaving Iran. Henderson reported that he was "visibly shaken" and quickly "became confused, almost apologetic."

Roosevelt had perfectly analyzed his adversary's psyche. Mossadegh, steeped in a culture of courtliness and hospitality, found it shocking that guests in Iran were being mistreated. That shock overwhelmed his good judgment, and with Henderson still in the room, he picked up a telephone and called his police chief. Trouble in the streets had become intolerable, he said, and it was time for the police to put an end to it.

With this order, Mossadegh sent the police out to attack a mob that included many of his own most fervent supporters. Then, to assure that his partisans would not return to the streets the next day, he issued a decree banning all public demonstrations. He even telephoned leaders of pro-government parties and ordered them to keep their people at home. He disarmed himself. It was his "fatal mistake," according to an account published in *Time* magazine a week later.

Over the next couple of hours, Mossadegh made several other missteps. Determined to show how serious he was about cracking down on street protests, he mobilized soldiers commanded by General Mohammad Daftary, an officer known for his zeal in repressing civil strife. But Daftary, who had been Tehran's police chief under the assassinated Prime Minister Razmara several years before, was also an outspoken royalist and close to Zahedi. There was every reason to suspect that if ordered into action, he would lead his men directly to the side of the conspirators. That is precisely what he did. The next day they fought not to defend but to depose the government.

Soon after Mossadegh issued his fateful order, the crackdown began. "Policemen and soldiers swung into action last night against rioting Tudeh (Communist) partisans and Nationalist extremists," Kennett Love reported in the *New York Times.* "The troops appeared to be in a frenzy as they smashed into rioters with clubs, rifles and night sticks, and hurled tear gas bombs."

Among those who had no idea of the turning tide in Tehran was His Imperial Majesty, Mohammad Reza Shah. After arriving in Baghdad, he had insisted that he was not involved in an attempted coup but had dismissed Mossadegh for "gross violations of the constitution." Like almost everyone else involved in the plot, he assumed that Saturday's failure meant the end of Operation Ajax. On Tuesday morning he and Empress Soraya boarded a British Overseas Airways Corporation jet and flew to Rome. "Both looked worn, gloomy and anxious as they left the aircraft," the *London Times* reported.

The Shah seemed resigned to a long absence from Iran. When an American reporter asked him if he expected ever to return, he replied, "Probably, but not in the immediate future." A British correspondent predicted that he would "probably join the small colony of exiled monarchs already in Rome."

As the Shah was checking into the Excelsior Hotel in Rome, however, Roosevelt was working hard to bring him home. The next day would be the climactic one. If everything went as planned, by midday the streets would be full of boisterous pro-Shah demonstrators. Citizens would see them as decent people fed up with the chaos of recent days, and a sympathetic constabulary would not interfere.

With the help of his invaluable Iranian agents, Roosevelt had organized a most extraordinary mob. Along with street thugs and other unsavories, it included many members of Tehran's traditional athletic societies. These athletes prided themselves not just on their strength but on acquired skills like juggling and acrobatics. On festive occasions they would join parades or give shows. These were not wealthy men. Some earned their livings with enterprises like protection rackets at the vegetable market. They expected the leaders of their societies to help sustain them. When the CIA came looking for rioters, they were ready and eager.

"In Iran you can get a crowd that's fearsome," John Waller, the head of the CIA's Iran desk, mused afterward. "Or you can get a friendly crowd. Or you can get something in between. Or one can turn into the other."

Roosevelt had already assured himself of support from the police force, which had fallen largely under General Daftary's sway, and from several military units. Now he also had the makings of a fine mob. The indispensable Assadollah Rashidian, however, was worried that the mob would not be big enough. He urged Roosevelt to strengthen his hand by making a last-minute deal with Muslim religious leaders, many of whom had large followings and could produce crowds on short notice. The most important of them, Ayatollah Kashani, had already turned against Mossadegh and would certainly be sympathetic. To encourage him, Rashidian suggested a quick application of cash. Roosevelt agreed. Early Wednesday morning he sent $10,000 to Ahmad Aramash, a confidant of Kashani's, with instructions that it be passed along to the holy man.

Wednesday was August 19, the 28th of Mordad by the Iranian calendar. On this day Roosevelt hoped to change the course of a nation's history. After he packed up the $10,000 for Kashani and sent his couriers on their way, though, he found himself with little to do. The time had come for others to act. Roosevelt could only wait and watch.

The news that his agents brought during the morning hours was all encouraging. People by the thousands were gathering at mosques and public squares. In their vanguard, giving the whole event a carnival air, were the outlandish athletes. Some waved barbells over their heads. Others juggled heavy pins. Many bared their barrel chests and wore little more than extravagant mustaches and loincloths. More than a few carried knives or homemade clubs. It was as exotic a tribe as ever marched to overthrow a government:

> They started with the Zurkaneh giants, weight lifters who developed their physiques through an ancient set of Iranian exercises which included lifting progressively heavier weights. The Zurkanehs had built up tremendous shoulders and huge biceps. Shuffling down the street together, they were a frightening spectacle. Two hundred or so of these weightlifters began the day by marching through the bazaar, shouting "Long Live the Shah!" and dancing and twirling like dervishes. Along the edges of the crowd, men were passing out ten-rial notes. . . . The mob swelled; the chant "Long Live the Shah!" was deafening. As the throng passed the offices of a pro-Mossadegh newspaper, men smashed the windows and sacked the place.

No one tried to stop the insurgents as they marched toward the city center. Police officers at first encouraged them and then, as the afternoon wore on, began leading them. There was no counter-demonstration. Mossadegh's supporters, respecting his wish and the message of the previous night's beatings, had stayed home.

The only other group that could have mobilized to defend the government was Tudeh, but its leaders spent the day in meetings, unable to decide whether to act. Mossadegh did not trust them anyway and did not want their help. One Tudeh leader had called him the day before and volunteered Tudeh shock troops if Mossadegh would arm them. "If ever I agree to arm a political party," he swore in reply, "may God sever my right arm!"

Mossadegh's hostility was not, however, the real reason Tudeh leaders did not call out their street fighters on that crucial day. Like most of the world's communist parties, Tudeh was controlled by the Soviet Union, and in times of crisis it followed orders from Moscow. On this day, however, no orders came. Stalin had died a few months earlier and the Kremlin was in turmoil. Soviet intelligence officers who would normally be concentrating on Iran were preoccupied with the more urgent challenge of staying alive. Whether any of them even considered trying to defend Mossadegh is among the remaining mysteries of Operation Ajax. Scholars have sought access to records in Moscow that might resolve it, but their requests have been denied.

As the morning wore on, crowds surging out of Tehran's southern slums filled the air with chants of "Death to Mossadegh!" and "Long live the Shah!" Hundreds of soldiers joined in, some of them in trucks or atop tanks. So did tribesmen from outside the city, mobilized by chiefs who had been paid by Kermit Roosevelt's agents. Groups of rioters attacked and burned eight government buildings and the offices of three pro-government newspapers, including one, *Bahktar-e-Emruz,* that was owned by Foreign Minister Fatemi. Others attacked the foreign ministry, the general staff headquarters, and the central police station. They raked all three buildings with gunfire and were met with withering volleys in return. Men fell by the dozen.

Roosevelt's agents kept bringing him good news. Late in the morning, one of them reported that the "huge mob" had occupied every one of the city's main squares. Another told him that the garrison commander in Kermanshah, four hundred miles to the west, had joined the cause and was leading his men toward the capital. A squad led by Ali Jalili captured the military police headquarters and freed plotters who had been arrested after Saturday's coup attempt. Among them was Colonel Nasiri, who immediately began marshaling his Imperial Guard to help the insurgents.

Some of the tens of thousands of people who took over the streets that day had always opposed Mossadegh for one reason or another. Others were former supporters who had turned against him during the political conflict of recent months. Many were what the *New York Times* called "bazaar thugs and bully-boys" who had no political convictions at all and marched because they had been paid a good day's wage to do so.

"That mob that came into north Tehran and was decisive in the overthrow was a mercenary mob," asserted Richard Cottam, who was on the Operation Ajax staff in Washington. "It had no ideology, and that mob was paid with American dollars."

Mobs, however, need leadership to be effective, and while gang leaders like Shaban the Brainless were big and strong, they were by no means clever. Most of the leaders who emerged over the course of that Wednesday were midranking military officers. Like their civilian counterparts, they were a mixture of the committed and the suborned. A goodly number had been persuaded to join the coup by the authority of the *firman* naming Zahedi as prime minister. If the Shah had spoken, they reasoned, the army was bound to obey.

These soldiers lent the uprising an air of legality. They also brought considerable firepower, including tanks and artillery, and they led the attacks on many government buildings. Without their moral authority and combat skills, the coup might well have failed.

Everything seemed to be going according to plan when, just before midday, the door to Roosevelt's command post burst open. He looked up, in hope of seeing another agent with reports from the front line, but instead saw his radio operator, distraught and on the verge of tears. In his hand he held an urgent message from Beedle Smith in Washington. Smith had sent it twenty-four hours earlier, but there had been a delay passing it through the relay station in Cyprus. It was another order, in stronger language than the two previous ones, for Roosevelt to flee immediately.

This message could not have arrived at a more absurdly inappropriate moment. Roosevelt, who could sense that victory was at hand, broke out laughing when he read it. "Never mind, chum," he told the confused radio man. "Buried underground as you are, you have no way of knowing. But the tide has turned! Things are going our way! Right will triumph! All for the best, in the best of all possible worlds!"

Roosevelt sent the radio man back to his burrow with a reply for General Smith. It said: "Yours of 18 August received. Happy to report R. N. Ziegler [Zahedi] safely installed and KGSAVOY [the Shah] will be returning to Tehran in triumph shortly. Love and kisses from all the team."

That was, of course, premature, but it reflected the supreme confidence that Roosevelt now felt. By his own account, he was "grinning from ear to ear." He had not eaten a proper meal in days and suddenly he felt hungry. An acquaintance of his who was a counselor to Ambassador Henderson maintained a home in the embassy compound, and he strolled over for lunch and a drink.

Outside, Tehran was in upheaval. Cheers and rhythmic chants echoed through the air, punctuated by the sound of gunfire and exploding mortar shells. Squads of soldiers and police surged past the embassy gate every few minutes. Yet Roosevelt's host and his wife were paragons of discretion, asking not a single question about what was happening.

A radio was on. Although the announcer was reading nothing

more interesting than grain prices, Roosevelt listened carefully. He had sent one of his Iranian teams to storm the station. If things went well, the programming would soon change.

As the three Americans ate in silence, the radio announcer started speaking ever more slowly, as if he were falling asleep. After a time, he stopped altogether. Obviously something unusual was happening at the station. Roosevelt smiled knowingly at his baffled luncheon partners. There were several minutes of dead air, followed by the sounds of men arguing. "It doesn't matter who reads it, the important thing is that it be read!" one finally shouted with an air of authority. Then, in loudly emotional tones, he began shouting what Roosevelt called "well-intended lies, or pre-truths."

"The government of Mossadegh has been defeated!" the man cried. "The new prime minister, Fazlollah Zahedi, is now in office. And His Imperial Majesty is on his way home!"

Roosevelt did not recognize the voice—an army officer had beaten his agent to the microphone—but the message was just as he had wished: "The government of Mossadegh was a government of rebellion, and it has fallen." Roosevelt rose from the table, thanked his hosts for their hospitality, and withdrew.

It was shortly after two o'clock as Roosevelt made his way back to the command post. His comrades, who had also been listening to Radio Tehran, were in ecstasy. When Roosevelt appeared, they looked up, and for a silent moment all shared the delicious realization that the day was theirs. A moment later they were dancing around the narrow room. Roosevelt remembered them "literally bubbling over with joy."

What should they do next? One agent, surmising that the mob was now at its peak of enthusiasm, suggested that it was time to produce Zahedi. Roosevelt said no, it was still too soon.

"There is nothing to be gained by rushing," he said. "Let's wait till the crowd gets to Mossadegh's house. That should be a good moment for our hero to make his appearance."

Military units led by anti-Mossadegh officers had already begun converging on the house. Inside, loyal soldiers built fortifications and prepared for battle. They were armed with rifles, machine guns, and Sherman tanks mounted with 75-millimeter cannons. Late in the afternoon the assault began. Defenders beat back wave after wave, leaving the sidewalks littered with bodies. Then, after an hour of one-sided combat, the assailants gave a great cheer. Friendly army units had arrived with tanks of their own. A close-quarters artillery duel soon broke out. Operation Ajax was approaching its climax.

Once Roosevelt learned that the assault had begun, he decided to fetch General Zahedi from the hideout where he had been closeted for two days. Before leaving, he summoned General Guilanshah, who, like Zahedi, was at a CIA safe house impatiently awaiting instructions. Roosevelt asked the general to find a tank and bring it to Zahedi's hideout. He scribbled the address on a scrap of paper and then drove there himself.

When Roosevelt arrived, Zahedi was sitting in a basement room wearing only underwear. He was thrilled to hear that his moment had finally come. As he was buttoning the tunic of his dress uniform, there was a rumble outside. General Guilanshah had arrived with two tanks and a cheering throng.

In later years, perhaps inevitably given his grandfather's fame as a swashbuckler, a story took hold that Roosevelt had ridden triumphantly atop the lead tank as it crashed through the streets of Tehran toward Mossadegh's house. In fact, Roosevelt realized as soon as he heard the crowd accompanying General Guilanshah that he should not even be seen in Zahedi's presence. As the door to the basement burst open, he jumped into a small cavity behind the furnace. From there, he watched the jubilant crowd embrace Zahedi, lift him high, and carry him out.

After the column departed, Roosevelt crept out of his hiding place, walked back to his car, and drove through the tumultuous streets toward the embassy. There he and his aides toasted impending victory. "Actually, to all intents and purposes it was no longer impending but won," he wrote afterward. "Our colonel from the west [Kermanshah] would not reach Tehran until evening, but the rumor of his movement had given us all we needed. The actual arrival of his troops simply added more enthusiasm to a town already drunk with victory."

The tank on which Zahedi was riding turned first toward Radio Tehran. There, surrounded by delirious admirers, he made his way toward the upstairs studio. It had been decided that martial music should be played before Zahedi spoke to the nation, and one of Roosevelt's agents had brought along a likely-looking record from the embassy library. As Zahedi approached, a technician played the first song. To everyone's embarrassment, it turned out to be "The Star-Spangled Banner."

Another, more anonymous tune was quickly chosen and played. Zahedi then stepped to the microphone. He declared himself "the lawful prime minister by the Shah's order" and promised that his new regime would do everything good: build roads, provide free health care, raise wages, and guarantee both freedom and security. About oil he said nothing at all.

Military and police units loyal to Zahedi were taking control of Tehran. One seized the telegraph office and sent messages across the country declaring that Mossadegh had been deposed. Another found and captured General Riahi, the army chief of staff. Several joined the battle outside Mossadegh's home.

At this moment, completely unaware of these events, the dejected Mohammad Reza Shah was dining at his Rome hotel, accompanied by his wife and two aides. Suddenly, a handful of news correspondents burst into the dining room, pushed their way to the Shah's table, and thrust wire service reports from Tehran into his hands. At first he was incredulous. "Can it be true?" he blurted. The color drained from his face. His hands began shaking violently. Finally he jumped to his feet.

"I knew it!" he cried out. "I knew it! They love me!"

Empress Soraya, less moved, rose and placed her hand on her husband's arm to steady him. "How exciting," she murmured.

After the shock passed, the Shah regained his composure. He turned to the correspondents and told them, "This is not an insurrection. Now we have a legal government. General Zahedi is premier. I appointed him." After a pause he added, "Ninety-nine percent of the population is for me. I knew it all the time."

Still in something of a daze, the young monarch made his way to the hotel lounge, where a throng of reporters and curious tourists was gathering. His first desire, he told them, was to return home. "It is a cause of grief to me that I did not play an important part in my people's and my army's struggle for freedom and, on the contrary, was away and safe," he said. "But if I left my country, it was solely because of my anxiety to avoid bloodshed."

Although the coup was now on the brink of success, Mossadegh still resisted. As fighting raged around his house, he sat with remarkable calm in his bedroom. Bodyguards had covered most of the window with a steel plate, so he could hear but not see what was happening outside. When his personal aide, Ali Reza Saheb, urged him to flee, he shook his head and replied, "If it's going to happen, if it's going to be a coup d'etat, I think it is better that I stay in this room and I die in this room."

The attackers outside felt momentum on their side. They had heard Zahedi proclaim his victory over the radio, and they knew that a friendly column of soldiers from Kermanshah was approaching. As ammunition supplies inside the house began to dwindle, they tightened their circle.

Loyal military officers might have rushed to defend Mossadegh if they had known what was happening. They did not, largely because General Riahi, who would have called them into action, was under arrest. Before being arrested, however, Riahi managed to call his deputy, General Ataollah Kiani, who commanded the Ishrat Abad barracks in what was then an outlying Tehran neighborhood. Kiani immediately ordered an infantry battalion and a tank battalion to assemble and follow him toward the city center. Before he had gone far, he ran into a rebel column commanded by General Daftary. Of the two men, Daftary was by far the more sophisticated and persuasive.

"We are colleagues and brothers, all faithful to the Shah," he told Kiani. "We should not fire at each other."

After a few more minutes of honeyed words, Kiani was won over. The two generals and their aides embraced in what Iranians call a "kissing party." Kiani's men, who might have saved Mossadegh, returned to their barracks.

Fighting at Mossadegh's house raged for two hours. After the firing from inside stopped, a platoon of soldiers stormed in. They found the house empty. Mossadegh had escaped at the last moment, pushed over a back garden wall by fleeing aides. Officers poked around the house for an hour or so, packed the best pieces of Mossadegh's furniture onto waiting trucks, and drove off. They had chased the old man away, and even though they did not have him, they knew they had done well.

As the victorious soldiers melted into the night, rioters who had cheered them on swarmed into the house to loot and destroy. Some set fires. Others pulled doors, windows, and appliances onto the sidewalk and began selling them, haggling over prices as flames lit up the night behind them. Mossadegh's refrigerator went for the equivalent of thirty-six dollars.

Back at the embassy compound, the handful of covert agents who had planned the coup were, in Roosevelt's words, "full of jubilation, celebration, and occasional totally unpredictable whacks on the back as one or the other of us was suddenly overcome with enthusiasm." Diplomats on the embassy staff looked on curiously. They asked nothing and Roosevelt told them nothing.

Around the time that Mossadegh's house was being set afire, a car pulled up at the gate of the American embassy. The driver honked wildly, and Roosevelt hurried out to see who it might be. It was Ardeshir Zahedi. He jumped from the car, and the two men hugged each other fervently.

"You must come now to my father, to pay your respects to the new prime minister!" Ardeshir said.

"Let's have a brief word with Ambassador Henderson before we go," Roosevelt replied. "I think he deserves to be told officially, and you are the proper person to do it."

Arm in arm, the two co-conspirators half-danced their way along a path that led to the ambassador's residence. Henderson was sitting beside his swimming pool. He had put a bottle of champagne on ice, and when his visitors arrived, he popped the cork. They told him the glorious news, including the fact that the new prime minister had named two of Roosevelt's Iranian agents as cabinet ministers. First they drank to the new government, then to the Shah, then to Eisenhower and Churchill, and finally to one another. When the bottle was empty, Ardeshir said that it was time for him to take Roosevelt to meet the country's new leader. He took his leave from Henderson with a warm embrace.

General Zahedi had established temporary headquarters at the Officers Club near the center of town. The mood there was ecstatic, and when Roosevelt arrived, he was swamped by well-wishers. He didn't recognize most of them, but many seemed to know him. Everyone, even people he had never seen, wanted to hug him and kiss both his cheeks. Zahedi finally rescued him and called for order. He made a brief speech and then called on Roosevelt.

Wild cheers erupted as Roosevelt stepped forward. A few people in the club knew that he had organized the coup, and others no doubt suspected it. This, however, was no time for gloating.

Roosevelt spoke only a few disingenuous sentences, with Ardeshir translating.

"Friends, Persians, countrymen, lend me your ears!" he began, and the din subsided. "I thank you for your warmth, your exuberance, your kindness. One thing must be clearly understood by all of us. That is that you owe me, the United States, the British, *nothing at all*. We will not, cannot, should not ask anything from you—except, if you would like to give them, brief thanks. Those I will accept on behalf of myself, my country and our ally most gratefully."

There was another round of hugging and kissing, and then, as quickly as he could, Roosevelt withdrew. For days he had been working without a break, the fate of a nation in his hands. Now exhaustion began to overwhelm him. He commandeered a car and driver, made his way back to the embassy compound, walked through the darkness to the home where he had been given lunch, and knocked on the door. Minutes later he was sound asleep.

About three hundred people died in Wednesday's fighting, half of them in the final battle at Mossadegh's house. Some of the civilian victims were found with 500-rial notes still in their pockets. Roosevelt's men had distributed the notes that morning to dozens of their subagents.

The next day, newspapers around the world reported Mossadegh's fall. Most of their accounts were as perceptive as could have been expected, given the fact that the true story was a closely guarded secret and would remain so for decades.

"The sudden reversal was nothing more than a mutiny by the lower ranks against pro-Mossadegh officers," Kennett Love wrote in the *New York Times*. "Wednesday morning at about nine, a group of weightlifters, tumblers and wrestlers armed with iron bars and knives began marching toward the center of the city shouting pro-Shah slogans. That was all the troops needed. Ordered to break up the demonstration, they turned their weapons against their officers. Spontaneously the mobs shifted from Mossadegh's to the Shah's bandwagon."

Don Schwind of the Associated Press, who like Love had been on the streets watching the coup unfold, filed a chronology of the day's events. He reported that the coup "started rolling" at nine o'clock in the morning, as "mobs armed with sticks and stones," together with soldiers and police officers, began marching toward the city center. "By 7:00 P.M. local time, the last nest of resistance in the capital, Mossadegh's home and the compound surrounding it, was in the hands of Zahedi's forces," he concluded. "The first Zahedi men to break into Mossadegh's room found only the body of his personal bodyguard. Mossadegh and his cabinet colleagues are still missing."

For Roosevelt and his co-conspirators, this was, as the CIA post-mortem put it, "a day that should never have ended, for it carried with it such a sense of excitement, of satisfaction, and of jubilation that it is doubtful any other can come up to it." Festivities at the Officers Club continued through much of the night. Zahedi, realizing instinctively that he must take quick and decisive steps to consolidate his new power, slipped out for a quick tour of police stations, accompanied by Hamid Reza, the crown prince, who symbolized Zahedi's ties to the royal family. The tour convinced him that police commanders were loyal to his new regime. Thus assured, he returned to the Officers Club and slept for a few hours.

Immediately after rising on Thursday, Zahedi summoned General Nader Batmanqelich, a veteran officer who had provided valuable military help the night before in exchange for a promise that he would be named chief of staff if the coup succeeded. When Batmanqelich arrived, Zahedi quickly swore him in and then gave him his first orders. He was to suppress all demonstrations, close all borders, and purge pro-Mossadegh officers from the army and the police.

There was much more for Zahedi to do in his first hours as prime minister. First he convened a quick meeting of his newly named cabinet. Then he drafted an order replacing several governors suspected of pro-Mossadegh sympathies. He ordered the release of many prisoners, including twenty who had been charged in the murder of the police chief Mahmoud Afshartus earlier that year. His only trip outside the Officers Club was to Radio Tehran, where he broadcast a brief speech giving Mossadegh twenty-four hours to surrender.

It was a quick role reversal. Just four days before, Zahedi had been the fugitive and Mossadegh the prime minister who demanded, in a broadcast over the same radio station, that he turn himself in within twenty-four hours. Mossadegh had offered a reward of 100,000 rials, the equivalent of $1,200, for information about Zahedi's whereabouts. Now Zahedi offered the same sum for information about Mossadegh.

At midmorning the new prime minister dispatched a telegram to Mohammad Reza Shah, telling him that Iranians were "counting the minutes" until his arrival. The Shah's departure from Rome, however, had hit some minor snags. Empress Soraya had not borne up well under the pressure of recent months, and at the last moment it was decided that she should stay in Rome for treatment of "nervous strain." Then someone pointed out that although the British had placed a chartered airliner at the Shah's disposal, his already battered nationalist credentials might be further weakened if he returned to Tehran in a plane with British markings. It was decided that he should wait for another one.

Mossadegh could not have hidden for long even if he wanted to, so Zahedi was not surprised when he telephoned the Officers Club at six o'clock that evening to arrange his surrender. Zahedi asked him where he was hiding, which turned out to be a private home downtown, and sent General Batmanqelich to pick him up. As a precaution against an assassination attempt by Mossadegh's enemies—or a rescue attempt by his friends—Zahedi ordered tanks onto the street and machine-gunners onto rooftops along the route.

An hour later the car carrying Mossadegh pulled into the courtyard of the Officers Club. The prisoner, haggard and dressed in pajamas, leaned heavily on a yellow Malacca cane as he emerged. Guards saluted him, and he saluted them back. Inside, he was helped to an elevator and taken to Zahedi's office on the third floor.

"Peace be with you," Mossadegh told the man who had defeated him.

"And also with you," Zahedi replied.

The two men spent twenty minutes behind closed doors. From all indications they spoke without rancor. When they emerged, Zahedi ordered that Mossadegh and the three aides who had surrendered with him be brought to comfortable suites upstairs. He then directed Tehran Radio to stop calling them insulting names and to refer to them instead as "their excellencies."

The Shah was less generous. As Mossadegh was surrendering in Tehran, he was touching down in Baghdad aboard a Dutch airliner that had been chartered at a reported cost of $12,000. Eight Iraqi air force fighters escorted his plane to the airport, and as he stepped off, a military band played the Iranian national anthem. When reporters asked him what he had planned for the deposed prime minister, he turned serious.

"The crimes of Mossadegh are the most serious a person can be responsible for," the Shah said solemnly. "Mossadegh is an evil man who wanted only one thing out of life: power at all costs. To accomplish this end he was willing to sacrifice the Iranian people, and he almost succeeded. Thank God my people finally understood him."

What a difference six days had made! On Sunday the Shah had passed through Baghdad as a ragged exile. Now he was on his way home as a triumphant monarch. The Beechcraft in which he had fled was still on the tarmac. He flew it home himself.

The Shah's plane touched down in Tehran at seventeen minutes after eleven o'clock on that Saturday morning and taxied to a stop in front of a stiff formation of soldiers from the Imperial Guard. He emerged resplendent in an air force uniform that had been flown to him in Baghdad for the occasion. Prime Minister Zahedi was the first to pay his respects, falling to his knees and pressing his lips to the monarch's proffered hand. Hundreds of other admirers had turned out, and when Zahedi stepped back, they surged forward. Several of them, including Colonel Nasiri, General Batmanqelich, Ayatollah Kashani, Shaban the Brainless, and Ambassador Loy Henderson, had given crucial help to Operation Ajax. The Shah greeted each of them and then turned to survey the delirious crowd. "His eyes were moist," one correspondent reported, "and his mouth was set in an effort to control his emotions."

In a radio address that evening, the Shah promised to "repair the damage done to the country." He left no doubt that he blamed Mossadegh for most of it. "I nurse no grudge in my heart, and extend clemency," he said. "But when it comes to violations of the constitution which we are under oath to preserve—an oath that was forgotten by some—and to dissolution of the Majlis, disintegration of the army and the dissipation of treasury funds, the law must be carried out, as desired by the people."

Prime Minister Zahedi, who was with the Shah as he spoke, embraced this tough line. Reporters asked him why Mossadegh, now accused of such high crimes, was being held in relative luxury at the Officers Club. "That bad man has been treated too well so far," he replied. "Tomorrow I will send him to the city jail."

Zahedi was emboldened not just by his victory but by concrete, though secret, expressions of support from the United States. The CIA had decided in advance to give his new government $5 million immediately after he took power, and it was provided as planned. There was also an extra million for Zahedi himself.

With the new regime now firmly in control, it was time for Kermit Roosevelt to leave Iran as quietly as he had arrived four weeks earlier. Before departing, however, he wished to see the Shah one last time. Discretion dictated that their meeting should be as secret as their previous ones, since Roosevelt's presence in Tehran, not to mention the nature of his activities, was still unknown to all but a very few Iranians. He sent word that he would like to stick to the midnight schedule of past weeks and suggested Sunday evening.

That final meeting was unlike any of their previous ones. The car that brought Roosevelt through the gates of the Saad Abad Palace was officially marked as property of the United States. Roosevelt sat tall inside instead of lying under a blanket. Royal guards who had looked away when he arrived for past visits saluted him crisply.

A courtier met Roosevelt, escorted him up the palace's twenty-nine wide steps, and brought him to the Shah's lavishly appointed sitting room. The monarch motioned him to be seated. Vodka was served, and each man took a glass. The Shah raised his and told Roosevelt, "I owe my throne to God, my people, my army—and to you!" They drank quietly, savoring their triumph.

"It is good to see you here, rather than in an anonymous car on the street outside," the Shah told Roosevelt after that first toast.

"It *is* good, Your Majesty."

"The new prime minister, who is now your good friend, as you know, will be coming shortly. Is there anything you would like to discuss before he arrives?"

"Well, sir," Roosevelt ventured after a moment's hesitation, "I wonder if you have had a chance to make up your mind on what you will do with Mossadegh, Riahi and the others who plotted against you?"

"I have thought much about that. Mossadegh as you know surrendered himself just before my return. He will be sentenced, if the court follows my suggestion, to three years of house arrest in his village. After that he will be free to move about in, but not outside, that village. Riahi will spend three years in jail and will then be released to do as he pleases—*if* what he pleases is not objectionable. A few others will get similar punishment. There is one exception. Hussein Fatemi cannot be found yet, but he will be. He was the most vituperative of them all. He urged on the Tudeh gangs that pulled down statues of me and my father. When we find him, he will be executed."

Roosevelt said nothing in reply. A few moments later Prime Minister Zahedi was escorted in. He bowed to the Shah and smiled broadly at Roosevelt, who repeated that the new regime owed nothing to the United States since "the outcome is full repayment."

"We understand," Zahedi answered. "We thank you and will always be grateful."

The three people in that palace room were among the few who had any idea how Operation Ajax was engineered. They took a silent moment to share their satisfaction. "We were all smiles now," Roosevelt wrote afterward. "Warmth and friendship filled the room."

After a few minutes, the Shah rose to escort Roosevelt back to his car. On the way out he reached into his jacket, pulled out a gold cigarette case, and presented it to his guest "as a souvenir of our recent adventure." Then, unexpectedly, a barrel-chested military officer appeared. It was Colonel Nasiri, who had played key roles in both the failed coup on Saturday and the successful one four days later.

"I have made only one promotion," the Shah said. "I present you now to *General* Nasiri."

It was after one o'clock in the morning when Roosevelt returned to the embassy compound. Ambassador Henderson was waiting for him. Henderson had arranged for Roosevelt's departure later that morning, aboard the naval attaché's plane to Bahrain.

Roosevelt barely slept. Soon after dawn he was driven to a remote hangar at the Tehran airport. Several of the men with whom he had carried out the coup were there to send him off. "I stumbled onto the plane," he wrote later, "with tears in my eyes."

CHAPTER 12

Purring Like a Giant Cat

A few days after Mossadegh surrendered to the new regime, a platoon of soldiers appeared at his suite in the Officers Club. The new prime minister, Fazlollah Zahedi, had ordered him transferred to a military prison. There he remained for ten weeks while an indictment was drawn up. When it was ready, Mossadegh was brought before a military tribunal and charged with treason for having resisted the Shah's dismissal order and for "inciting the people to armed insurrection." He defended himself vigorously, asserting that the *firman* had been delivered as part of a midnight coup d'etat and was in any case illegal, since Iranian prime ministers could not be dismissed without a no-confidence vote in the Majlis.

"My only crime," Mossadegh told his judges, "is that I nationalized the Iranian oil industry and removed from this land the network of colonialism and the political and economic influence of the greatest empire on earth."

The guilty verdict was a foregone conclusion. Along with it came the sentence: three years in prison, followed by house arrest for life. Mossadegh served the full prison term and upon his release in the summer of 1956 was brought to his home in Ahmad Abad.

One morning soon after his arrival, the new secret police, called Savak, organized a crude maneuver to impress upon him the terms of his incarceration. A gang of thugs turned up in front of his home, and they began shouting violent anti-Mossadegh slogans. At their head was none other than the gang leader Shaban the Brainless, who had become one of the regime's favorite enforcers. For a time the mob seemed ready to storm the house. It retreated after one of Mossadegh's grandsons fired several rifle shots into the air from inside. Several minutes later two Savak officers arrived and asked to see the prisoner. They carried a letter for him to sign. It was a request that Savak agents be assigned to protect him. Mossadegh, who understood the realities of power, signed it without protest. Within an hour Savak agents took up posts outside and inside the walled complex where he lived. Their standing orders, which did not change for the rest of Mossadegh's life, were to allow no one other than relatives and a few close friends to visit him.

In the weeks following the coup, most of Mossadegh's cabinet ministers and prominent supporters were arrested. Some were later released without charge. Others served prison terms after being convicted of various offenses. Six hundred military officers loyal to Mossadegh were also arrested, and about sixty of them were shot. So were several student leaders at Tehran University. Tudeh and the National Front were banned, and their most prominent supporters were either imprisoned or killed.

Hussein Fatemi, who had been Mossadegh's foreign minister, was the most prominent figure singled out for exemplary punishment. Fatemi was a zealous antimonarchist, and during the turbulent days of August 1953 he had attacked the Shah, whom he called "the Baghdad fugitive," with special venom. Iran had fallen into its misery, Fatemi asserted at one point, because "for the last ten years a dirty, hateful and shameful royal court has been the servant of the British embassy." In one speech he addressed the absent monarch: "O traitor Shah, you shameless person, you have completed the criminal history of the Pahlavi regime! The people want revenge. They want to drag you from behind your desk to the gallows." Now that the tables were turned, the Shah had his chance, and he did not miss it. Just as he had promised Kermit Roosevelt, he arranged for Fatemi to be summarily tried, convicted of treason, and executed.

Fatemi had once compared the Shah to a snake "who bites mortally when the opportunity presents itself." In the end he was among those who suffered the deadly bite. Because of his fate, and also because he was the only member of Mossadegh's inner circle who was a descendant of the Prophet Mohammad, his memory is honored in Iran today. One of the main boulevards in Tehran is Dr. Hussein Fatemi Avenue.

In the years after Mossadegh fell from power, Mohammad Reza Shah made him a nonperson about whom it was considered unseemly to speak. Little could be published about him, and nothing at all that was positive. In 1962, having consolidated his increasingly repressive regime, the Shah allowed the National Front to emerge from its illegality and hold a rally, on the condition that each speaker mention Mossadegh's name just once. One hundred thousand people turned out. They knew the stipulation the Shah had placed on speakers, and when each mentioned Mossadegh the allotted one time, they let out a thunderous cheer. That was the last time the Shah allowed the National Front to gather in public.

Mossadegh's wife died in 1965, and although she had stayed in Tehran during the years he was at Ahmad Abad, they remained very close and her death severely affected him. In a letter to a friend he wrote that he was "deeply in pain from this tragedy . . . and now I pray God to take me soon, too, and relieve me of this pathetic existence." Several months later he developed an ailment that was diagnosed as throat cancer. Mohammad Reza Shah sent him a message suggesting that he seek treatment abroad, but Mossadegh refused and chose an Iranian medical team instead. He traveled to Tehran with a police escort and spent several months there under medical treatment. Doctors succeeded in removing his tumor but then subjected him to heavy doses of cobalt. That may have done more harm than good. His health continued to decline. On March 5, 1967, at the age of eighty-five, he died. No public funeral or other expression of mourning was permitted.

The Anglo-Iranian Oil Company, which later changed its name to British Petroleum, tried to return to its old position in Iran, but public opinion was so opposed that the new government could not permit it. Besides, the logic of power dictated that since the United States had done the dirty work of overthrowing Mossadegh, American companies should share the spoils. Ultimately, an international consortium was organized to assume the rich concession. Anglo-

Iranian held 40 percent of the shares, five American companies together held another 40, and the remainder was distributed to Royal Dutch/Shell and Compagnie Française de Pétroles. The non-British companies paid Anglo-Iranian $1 billion for their 60 percent of the concession. Although the consortium was run by foreigners, it retained the name Mossadegh gave it—National Iranian Oil Company—to preserve the façade of nationalization. It agreed to share its profits with Iran on a fifty-fifty basis but not to open its books to Iranian auditors or to allow Iranians onto its board of directors.

In the years that followed, Mohammad Reza Shah became increasingly isolated and dictatorial. He crushed dissent by whatever means necessary and spent huge amounts of money on weaponry—$10 billion in the United States alone between 1972 and 1976. He had that amount of free cash because of the sharp increase in oil prices during those years. The $4 billion that Iran received from the consortium in 1973 reached $19 billion just two years later.

On the rare occasions when he mentioned Mossadegh, the Shah was contemptuous of his "infantile xenophobia" and "strident nationalism." He told one friend: "The worst years of my reign, indeed of my entire life, came when Mossadegh was prime minister. The bastard was out for blood, and every morning I awoke with the sensation that today might be my last on the throne."

When Iranians' anger began boiling over in the late 1970s, the Shah found that since he had crushed all legitimate political parties and other opposition groups, there was no one with whom he could negotiate a compromise. In desperation, he named a prime minister, Shapour Bakhtiar, who had been deputy minister of labor in Mossadegh's government. The Shah must have felt history's breath on his neck when Bakhtiar visited Mossadegh's grave in Ahmad Abad immediately after taking office, made a speech there pledging fidelity to "Mossadegh's ideals", named a government made up largely of National Front sympathizers, and placed a photo of Mossadegh behind him whenever he addressed the press. At that point, however, doom was so close that the Shah had no choice but to accept such effrontery.

Ayatollah Ruhollah Khomeini, who as a young mullah had strongly opposed Mossadegh, emerged in the late 1970s as Mohammad Reza Shah's most potent enemy. The Shah had sent him into exile in 1964, but from Turkey, Iraq, and finally Paris, he continued preaching his fundamentalist message. When Bakhtiar became prime minister, Khomeini scorned and denounced him. "Why do you talk of the Shah, Mossadegh, money?" he demanded in one radio speech. "These have already passed. Islam is all that remains."

In one of the most stunning political collapses of the twentieth century, the Shah was forced to flee his homeland in January 1979. This time the CIA was not able to return him to his throne. The next year he died in Egypt, reviled by almost everyone. Ayatollah Khomeini replaced him as the arbiter of Iran's destiny.

Men associated with Mossadegh and his ideals dominated Khomeini's first government. The prime minister was Mehdi Bazargan, whom Mossadegh had dispatched to Abadan in 1951 to run the refinery there after the British departed. Ibrahim Yazdi, the head of a small political party dedicated to preserving Mossadegh's legacy, became deputy prime minister and then foreign minister. In the first postrevolutionary election, Khomeini permitted another Mossadegh admirer, Abolhassan Bani-Sadr, to run for and win the presidency.

For a brief period after the revolution, it seemed that from the grave, Mossadegh was returning to power. The high school in Ahmad Abad was named after him. So was the main street in Tehran, which had formerly been Pahlavi Avenue. A commemorative stamp was issued in his honor. On March 5, 1979, the twelfth anniversary of his death, an enormous crowd flooded into Ahmad Abad. It was one of the largest gatherings in modern Iranian history. People had to park their cars miles away and walk the rest of the distance. President Bani-Sadr led the tributes and announced plans to move Mossadegh's body to a mausoleum in Tehran. The family demurred, wisely suspecting that if political tides changed, the mausoleum might be desecrated.

These tributes to Mossadegh were in part an effort by Iranians to give him the homage they had not been permitted to give while the Shah was in power. They were also intended as a message to Ayatollah Khomeini and his mullahs. By celebrating Mossadegh, Iranians were expressing their wish for a regime like his: nationalist, democratic, and based on the rule of law. It soon became clear that Khomeini had not the slightest intention of establishing such a

regime. He had broadened his mass appeal by embracing supporters of the National Front, but as soon as he consolidated power, he
pushed them out. Before long, he began arresting them. Among
those who had to flee the country to save their lives was Hedayat
Matine-Daftary, the only one of Mossadegh's grandchildren who
had been bold enough to venture into politics.

The window that had been opened for Mossadegh's admirers
was now closed. Tehran's main street was renamed again, this time
in honor of the Twelfth Imam. Mossadegh's secularism was as
abhorrent to the new regime as his democratic vision had been to
the old one. The mullahs, like Mohammad Reza Shah before them,
came to realize that allowing Iranians to honor Mossadegh would
inevitably lead to calls for a government based on his principles.
That they could not tolerate, and so they did all they could to suppress his memory.

The men who organized and carried out the 1953 coup soon scattered. General Zahedi, the prime minister who replaced Mossadegh,
pleased the Shah with his repressive campaign against nationalists
and leftists. Before long, however, the two men had a falling out.
Zahedi, like Mossadegh, was a strong figure who believed that
prime ministers should be free to run their own governments. The
ambitious Shah could not abide that. Just two years after the coup,
he forced Zahedi from office and later sent him abroad as ambassador to the United Nations office in Geneva. He died there in
1963.

Zahedi's son Ardeshir, whose quick wits and perfect English
made him a valuable asset to the coup plotters, went on to a long
and successful career. Although he was still in his midtwenties when
his father became prime minister, he quickly emerged as a highly
influential figure, serving simultaneously as his father's closest
adviser and as a chamberlain to the Shah. His influence did not
diminish after his father's fall, and in 1957 he married the Shah's
eldest daughter, Princess Shahnaz. Wary of his growing power, the
Shah sent him off to golden exile as ambassador to Great Britain,
where those who knew of his role in the coup embraced him. Later
he returned to Tehran for a term as foreign minister and then
became the ambassador to the United States. In that post he

defended the Shah to the bitter end. After the Islamic Revolution of 1979, he moved to a villa in Switzerland. He never admitted his role in the coup and even published a rambling article asserting that the CIA was not involved either.

"Mossadegh's fall was not due to any dirty tricks the CIA might have played," he wrote. "My father never had any meetings with CIA agents."

Asadollah Rashidian, whose subversive network of journalists, politicians, mullahs, and gang leaders was crucial to the success of Operation Ajax, prospered in the years that followed. He and his brothers remained in Tehran, and his business ventures flourished under the Shah's patronage. His home became a salon at which politicians and other influential figures spent many evenings discussing the nation's future. Several times the Shah used him as a secret emissary to foreign governments. In the mid-1960s, however, the Shah became uncomfortable with the presence in Tehran of such a sophisticated and well-connected figure, especially one who knew so many secrets. Rashidian sensed this and moved to his beloved England to live out his remaining years in comfort.

Not everyone who helped stage the coup was lucky enough to live into retirement. One to whom the Shah was especially ungrateful was General Nasiri, the officer who led the first, unsuccessful coup against Mossadegh and who also played an important role in the one that succeeded. For years after Mossadegh's defeat, Nasiri served faithfully as commander of the Imperial Guard. He did the Shah's bidding so willingly and discreetly that in 1965 he was placed in charge of the brutally repressive Savak. In that post he did the Shah's dirtiest work without complaint for more than a decade. Enemies of the Shah accused him of horrific crimes. When they began their final drive to power in the late 1970s, the Shah sought to placate them by removing Nasiri from office. Later, claiming to be shocked at reports that Savak had employed torturers, the Shah threw his old friend into prison. Soon after the 1979 revolution, mullahs dispatched Nasiri to a firing squad. Tehran newspapers published photos of his bloody corpse.

Mossadegh's loyal chief of staff, General Riahi, spent a year in prison after the coup and then returned to his original profession, engineering. After the 1979 revolution, he became minister of defense. He served for a few months, until the tide of radicalism overwhelmed Mehdi Bazargan's government, and then returned to private life until his death several years later in Tehran.

The Shah gave Shaban the Brainless, the most famous leader of the mob that rampaged through Tehran during the fateful days of August 1953, a yellow Cadillac convertible. He became a familiar figure on the streets of Tehran, driving slowly around town with a pistol on each hip, ready to jump out and attack anyone who seemed pro-Mossadegh or anti-Shah. Savak agents called on him from time to time when they wanted someone beaten or otherwise intimidated. After the Islamic Revolution, Shaban moved to Los Angeles and published a memoir denying that he had done much of what Iranians had seen him do.

Princess Ashraf, the Shah's strong-willed twin sister, became something of an international celebrity in the years after her brother was returned to his throne. For a time she served as chairman of the United Nations Human Rights Commission, where she defended his regime against what she called "unsubstantiated allegations of widespread tortures and killings by Savak." By her own account, her life was unhappy, marked by three failed marriages and the shock of her son's murder in Paris after the Islamic Revolution, evidently at the hands of killers dispatched from Tehran. After the revolution, comforted by her share of the billions of dollars her family had spirited out of Iran over the years, she took up residence in New York. In a memoir she admitted that there had been such a thing as Operation Ajax and even put its cost at $1 million, but denied what other participants reported about her role.

Monty Woodhouse, the British agent whose clandestine mission to Washington in January 1952 laid the groundwork for what was then called Operation Boot, returned after its success and had a friendly chat with Allen Dulles. "That was a nice little egg you laid when you were here last time," Dulles told him. Woodhouse was later elevated to the peerage as Lord Terrington. He became a Conservative member of Parliament and the chief editor of Penguin Books. His great passion in later life was the history of Greece and Byzantium, about which he wrote extensively. He also wrote a memoir in which he spoke frankly about both his role in the Iran coup and the coup's aftermath.

"It is easy to see Operation Boot as the first step towards the Iranian catastrophe of 1979," Woodhouse conceded. "What we did not foresee was that the Shah would gather new strength and use it so tyrannically, nor that the US government and the Foreign Office would fail so abjectly to keep him on a reasonable course. At the time we were simply relieved that a threat to British interests had been removed."

Herbert Morrison, the British foreign secretary whose belligerence helped set his country on a collision course with Iran, retired from politics in 1959 at the age of seventy-one and was named to a life peerage. In his later years he seemed scarcely to remember the passion with which he had denounced Mossadegh and defended the Anglo-Iranian Oil Company. His autobiography includes detailed accounts of his role creating the National Fire Service and passing the Road Traffic Act of 1930, but he devoted less than a page to Iran. He asserted that he had favored "sharp and forceful action" against Mossadegh, but that Prime Minister Attlee refused to approve an invasion because it "would take a lot of time and might therefore be a failure."

Attlee wrote in his memoir that choosing Morrison as foreign secretary was "the worst appointment I ever made." He never regretted his decision not to go to war in Iran. "Such action would no doubt have been taken in former times, but would, in the modern world, have outraged opinion at home and abroad," he wrote. "In my view, the day is past when commercial undertakings from industrialized countries, having obtained some concession, can carry on their business without regard to the feelings of the people of the country in which they are operating. . . . The Anglo-Iranian Oil Company showed a lack of sensitivity in not realizing this."

Winston Churchill's biographers have paid almost no attention to his central role in the coup against Mossadegh. Most books about him do not even mention it. Churchill once said privately that he considered the coup to have been "the finest operation since the end of the war," but he never considered it more than an obscure footnote to his career.

The chief hero or villain of the piece, Kermit Roosevelt, went on to an oddly undistinguished career. On his way home from Tehran after the coup, he stopped in London and gave Churchill a private briefing. "Young man," Churchill told him when he finished, "if I had been but a few years younger, I would have loved nothing better than to have served under your command in this great venture." A few days later Roosevelt repeated his briefing at the White House for President Eisenhower, John Foster Dulles, Allen Dulles, and a small group of other senior officials. Soon afterward, at a secret ceremony, Eisenhower awarded him the National Security Medal.

Roosevelt concluded his White House briefing by warning that the CIA should not take his success in Iran to mean that it could now overthrow governments at will. The Dulles brothers, however, took it to mean exactly that. They were already plotting to strike against the left-leaning regime in Guatemala and asked Roosevelt to lead their coup. He declined. In 1958 he left the CIA. After spending six years with Gulf Oil, he struck out on a series of moderately successful consulting and lobbying ventures. He died in 2000, still considering August 1953 to have been the highlight of his life. Until his dying day, he believed fervently that the coup he had engineered was right and necessary.

Was it? There can, of course, be no final answer to this crucial question. A host of factors influence the course of history, and drawing conclusions about causes and effects is always dangerous. Nonetheless, few would deny that the 1953 coup in Iran set off a series of unintended consequences. Its most direct result was to give Mohammad Reza Shah the chance to become dictator. He received enormous amounts of aid from the United States—more than $1 billion in the decade following the coup—but his oppressive rule turned Iranians against him. In 1979 their anger exploded in a shattering revolution led by Islamic fundamentalists.

Soon after the Shah was overthrown, President Jimmy Carter allowed him to enter the United States. That sent Iranian radicals into a frenzy of rage. With the blessing of their new leaders, they stormed the American embassy in Tehran and held fifty-two American diplomats hostage for more than fourteen months. Westerners, and especially Americans, found this crime not only barbaric but inexplicable. That was because almost none of them had any idea of the responsibility the United States bore for imposing the royalist regime that Iranians came to hate so passionately. The hostage-takers remembered that when the Shah fled into exile in 1953, CIA agents working at the American embassy had returned him to his throne. Iranians feared that history was about to repeat itself.

"In the back of everybody's mind hung the suspicion that, with the admission of the Shah to the United States, the countdown for another coup d'etat had begun," one of the hostage-takers explained years later. "Such was to be our fate again, we were convinced, and it would be irreversible. We now had to reverse the irreversible."

The hostage episode changed the course of American political history and poisoned relations between Iran and the United States. It led the United States to support Iraq in its long and horrific war with Iran, in the process consolidating the Iraqi dictatorship of Saddam Hussein. Within Iran, it strengthened the most militant elements in the revolutionary coalition. One of Ayatollah Khomeini's closest advisers, Ayatollah Ali Khamenei, who later succeeded him as the country's supreme leader, justified the regime's radicalism by declaring, "We are not liberals like Allende and Mossadegh, whom the CIA can snuff out."

Fundamentalist clerics who consolidated power in Iran during the early 1980s not only imposed a form of religious fascism at home but turned their country into a center for the propagation of terror abroad. Their support for the hostage-takers who seized American diplomats in Tehran was only the beginning of their fierce anti-Western campaign. Soon afterward, they began financing and arming Hamas, Hezbollah, and other Middle Eastern factions known for their involvement in political kidnapping and assassination. They sent agents around the world to kill scores of Iranian dissidents and other perceived enemies, among them former prime minister Shapour Bakhtiar. American investigators implicated them in both the 1983 suicide bombing that killed 214 American marines in Beirut and the 1996 attack that killed another 19 marines in Saudi Arabia. Prosecutors in Argentina asserted that they ordered one of the most heinous anti-Semitic crimes of the post-Holocaust era, the 1994 bombing of the Jewish community center in Buenos Aires, which took ninety-three lives.

With their devotion to radical Islam and their eagerness to embrace even the most horrific kinds of violence, Iran's revolutionary leaders became heroes to fanatics in many countries. Among those who were inspired by their example were Afghans who founded the Taliban, led it to power in Kabul, and gave Osama bin-Laden the base from which he launched devastating terror attacks. It is not far-fetched to draw a line from Operation Ajax through the

Shah's repressive regime and the Islamic Revolution to the fireballs that engulfed the World Trade Center in New York.

The world has paid a heavy price for the lack of democracy in most of the Middle East. Operation Ajax taught tyrants and aspiring tyrants there that the world's most powerful governments were willing to tolerate limitless oppression as long as oppressive regimes were friendly to the West and to Western oil companies. That helped tilt the political balance in a vast region away from freedom and toward dictatorship.

As a postrevolutionary generation came of age in Iran, Iranian intellectuals began assessing the long-term effects of the 1953 coup. Several published thoughtful essays that raised intriguing questions. One appeared in an American foreign-policy journal:

> It is a reasonable argument that but for the coup, Iran would be a mature democracy. So traumatic was the coup's legacy that when the Shah finally departed in 1979, many Iranians feared a repetition of 1953, which was one of the motivations for the student seizure of the U.S. embassy. The hostage crisis, in turn, precipitated the Iraqi invasion of Iran, while the [Islamic] revolution itself played a part in the Soviet decision to invade Afghanistan. A lot of history, in short, flowed from a single week in Tehran. . . .
>
> The 1953 coup and its consequences [were] the starting point for the political alignments in today's Middle East and inner Asia. With hindsight, can anybody say the Islamic Revolution of 1979 was inevitable? Or did it only become so once the aspirations of the Iranian people were temporarily expunged in 1953?

From the vantage point of history, it is easy to see the catastrophic effects of Operation Ajax. They will continue to plague the world for many years. But what would have been the effect of *not* launching the coup? President Truman insisted until his last day in office that the United States must not intervene in Iran. What if President Eisenhower had also held this view?

Those who defend the coup argue that the Soviet Union was waiting for a chance to strike against Iran. They say that a preemptive coup was necessary because rolling back a Soviet takeover would have been very difficult and perhaps impossible. In their view, the gamble that the Soviets would not act, or that their action could be reversed, was too risky.

"It was a question of much bigger policy than Iran," John Waller, one of the last surviving veterans of Operation Ajax, asserted decades later. "It was about what the Soviets had done and what we knew about their future plans. It's interesting to see what Russia put on its priority list, what it wanted. Iran was very high on it. If anybody wasn't worried about the Soviet menace, I don't know what they could have been believing in. It was a real thing."

Sam Falle, who as a young British diplomat accompanied Monty Woodhouse on his mission to Washington and was later posted in Tehran, held to the same conclusion. In his memoir he wrote that the coup "was of course immoral" because it constituted interference in the internal affairs of a foreign country. But he added, "1952 was a very dangerous time. The Cold War was hot in Korea. The Soviet Union had tried to take all Berlin in 1948. Stalin was still alive. On no account could the Western powers risk a Soviet takeover of Iran, which would almost certainly have led to World War III."

History casts some doubt on these fears. Stalin had tried during the late 1940s to subvert Iran through a combination of military and political means, and for a time his soldiers actually controlled a large swath of northern Iran. Diplomatic pressure from Washington and Tehran forced him to withdraw. This suggests that the Soviets might have been reluctant to try again.

After Stalin's death in early 1953, a regime emerged in the Kremlin that adopted a less aggressive foreign policy. It was not clear at the time, however, that this would be the case. A reckless brute like Beria might have come to power rather than the relatively moderate Khrushchev, and he might have been ready to launch even the most provocative expansionist adventures. This was a danger the CIA believed it could not ignore.

Another open question is the strength of the pro-Soviet Tudeh party during the early 1950s. The Dulles brothers claimed that Tudeh had assembled a vast network that was ready to seize power as soon as Mossadegh fell or was pushed from office. Scholars who have studied Tudeh and its allied organizations doubt this. Tudeh was divided between intellectuals who opposed Mossadegh because they saw him as an obstacle to communism and a mass base made up largely of people who admired him. It had cells in the army and civil service, but they may not have been as large or influential as they were made to seem. Long after the coup, a scholar interviewed the American diplomat who specialized in monitoring Tudeh during the early 1950s, along with two CIA agents who were posted with him at the United States embassy in Tehran. They admitted "that the Tudeh was really not very powerful, and that higher-level U.S. officials routinely exaggerated its strength and Mossadegh's reliance on it."

The crucial question of whether the American coup was necessary to prevent the Soviets from staging a coup of their own cannot be conclusively answered. No one will ever know how the Soviets might have acted or how successful they would have been. The coup certainly had disastrous aftereffects. What might have been the effects of not carrying it out must remain forever in the realm of speculation.

How did Iran reach the tragic crossroads of August 1953? The main responsibility lies with the obtuse neocolonialism that guided the Anglo-Iranian Oil Company and with the British government's willingness to accept it. If the company had shown even a modicum of good sense, it could have reached a compromise with the Iranian authorities. If it had cooperated with Prime Minister Razmara, who wanted the British to remain in Iran, Mossadegh might never even have come to power. But the men who ran the company, and the government officials who coddled them, were frozen in their imperial mindset and contemptuous of Iranians and their aspirations. Dean Acheson had it exactly right when he wrote: "Never had so few lost so much so stupidly and so fast."

Acheson also, however, laid blame on Mossadegh himself, whom he described as "inspired by a fanatical hatred of the British and a desire to expel them and all their works from the country regardless of the cost." Certainly, Mossadegh was almost as resistant to compromise as were the British. At several points he might have declared victory and made a deal. In the summer of 1952, for example, he was an unassailable national hero. He had been returned to power by a spontaneous mass uprising and had won a great victory over the British at the World Court. President Truman was on his side. A more pragmatic leader might have seized on this moment, but Mossadegh was not a pragmatist. He was a visionary, a utopian, a millenarian. The single-mindedness with which he pursued his campaign against Anglo-Iranian made it impossible for him to compromise when he could and should have.

Another great failure in Mossadegh's judgment was his inability or refusal to understand how the world looked to Western leaders. They were in a state of near-panic about the spread of communist power. Mossadegh believed that his conflict with Anglo-Iranian had nothing to do with the global confrontation between East and West. This was highly unrealistic. The men who made decisions in Washington and Moscow viewed everything that happened in the world as part of the war they were waging for control of the world's destiny. It was foolish of Mossadegh to believe that he could separate Iran's grievance, justified though it was, from this all-encompassing conflict.

Mossadegh was also naïve in his assessment of the communists who controlled Tudeh and were working assiduously to penetrate Iran's government, army, and civil society. He detested autocracy and believed that all Iranians should be allowed to say and do what they wished. The fact that communists had taken advantage of democratic systems in Eastern Europe to seize power and destroy democracy seemed not to affect him. His refusal to crack down on communist movements in Iran put him on Washington's death list. This may have been unjust, but it was the harsh reality of the age. By failing to recognize it, Mossadegh strengthened his enemies.

Never during his twenty-six months in power did Mossadegh attempt to forge the National Front into a cohesive political movement. It remained a loose coalition without central leadership or an organized political base. In the Majlis election of 1952 Mossadegh made no effort to assemble a slate of candidates committed to its program. This made it highly vulnerable to outsiders who sought to break it apart, and prevented it from developing a following that might have been mobilized to defend the government at crucial moments.

Despite his historic misjudgments, however, Mossadegh can hardly be considered to have been a failure as prime minister. His achievements were profound and even earth-shattering. He set his people off on what would be a long and difficult voyage toward democracy and self-sufficiency, forever altering not only their history but the way they viewed themselves and the world around them. He dealt a devastating blow to the imperial system and hastened its final collapse. He inspired people around the world who believe that nations can and must struggle for the right to govern themselves in freedom. He towers over Iranian history, Middle Eastern history, and the history of anticolonialism. No account of the twentieth century is complete without a chapter about him.

Mossadegh and the Anglo-Iranian Oil Company brought disaster on themselves by refusing repeated efforts at compromise. Their final crack-up, however, would not have happened if British and American voters had not cooperated. They did so quite unwittingly. Iran was a visible but not overwhelming issue in the political campaign that brought the aging Winston Churchill back to power in London. It was hardly an issue at all in Dwight Eisenhower's campaign, although fear of a worldwide communist advance certainly shaped the perceptions of many voters. The outcome of both elections was determined as much by a simple desire for change as by anything else. In faraway Iran these outcomes shaped the course of all future history. If Churchill and Eisenhower had not won, there would have been no Operation Ajax.

The election in the United States was especially significant because it brought John Foster Dulles and Allen Dulles to power. They were driven men, intensely focused on the worldwide communist threat. Their decision to make Iran the first battleground of their crusade may or may not have been wise, but they deserve to be judged harshly for the way they made it. Even before taking their oaths of office, both brothers had convinced themselves beyond all doubt that Mossadegh must go. They never even considered the possibility that a coup might be a bad idea or that it might have negative consequences. History might view their action more favorably if it had been the result of serious, open-minded reflection and debate. Instead, it sprang from petulant impatience, from a burning desire to do something, anything, that would seem like a victory over communism. Ideology, not reason, drove the Dulles brothers. Iran was the place they chose to start showing the world that the United States was no longer part of what Vice President Richard Nixon called "Dean Acheson's college of cowardly Communist containment."

There was no substantial difference in the way Truman and Eisenhower assessed the communist threat. Both believed that

Moscow was directing a relentless campaign of subversion aimed at world domination, that Iran was one of this campaign's likeliest targets, and that the United States had no higher national priority than to resist and defeat it. They differed profoundly, however, in their views of how to shape America's resistance. Truman accepted and even welcomed the rise of nationalism in the developing world. He believed that by placing itself alongside nationalist movements, the United States could show the world that it was the truest friend of Asia, Africa, and Latin America. The idea of overthrowing foreign governments was abhorrent to him, in part because he recognized that the long-term consequences were entirely unpredictable and might well be catastrophic.

Truman spent many hours thinking and talking about Iran, but Eisenhower was far less engaged. He allowed the Dulles brothers to shape his administration's policy toward the restive Third World. They were anxious for quick and visible successes in their anticommunist crusade and saw covert action as a way to achieve them. Preemptive coups, actions against threats that had not yet materialized, seemed to them not only wise but imperative. They did not worry about the future consequences of such coups because they believed that if the United States did not sponsor them, its own future would be endangered.

The success of Operation Ajax had an immediate and far-reaching effect in Washington. Overnight, the CIA became a central part of the American foreign policy apparatus, and covert action came to be regarded as a cheap and effective way to shape the course of world events. Kermit Roosevelt could sense this view taking hold even before he had finished delivering his White House briefing on September 4, 1953.

"One of my audience seemed almost alarmingly enthusiastic," he wrote afterward. "John Foster Dulles was leaning back in his chair. Despite his posture, he was anything but sleepy. His eyes were gleaming; he seemed to be purring like a giant cat. Clearly he was not only enjoying what he was hearing, but my instincts told me that he was planning as well."

Dulles was indeed planning. The next year he and his brother organized the CIA's second coup d'etat, which led to the fall of President Jacobo Arbenz of Guatemala and set off a sequence of events in that country that led to civil war and hundreds of thousands of violent deaths. Later the CIA set out to kill or depose foreign leaders from Cuba and Chile to the Congo and Vietnam. Each of these operations had profound effects that reverberate to this day. Some produced immense misery and suffering and turned whole regions of the world bitterly against the United States.

The final question to be answered is why Operation Ajax succeeded. The answer has a great deal to do with luck and happenstance. Had key participants made different decisions at any one of a half-dozen different points, the coup would have failed.

Kermit Roosevelt might have decided to give up and go home after the failed attempt of August 15. More plausibly, Mossadegh and his advisers might have dealt more sternly with the plotters. "Mossadegh should have reacted immediately and had them all shot," Shapour Bakhtiar said in an interview years later. That would almost certainly have saved the day, but it was not Mossadegh's nature.

The coup might also have failed if Mossadegh had been quicker to order his police to crack down on the hostile crowds that Roosevelt and his agents sent into the streets; if, when Mossadegh finally did order a crackdown, he had chosen a loyal officer rather than the outspokenly conservative General Daftary to carry it out; if Daftary had not intercepted and managed to turn back the loyalist column headed by General Kiani that was on its way to defend the government; if the loyal chief of staff, General Riahi, had managed to escape capture and mobilize more loyal units; if Mossadegh had called his supporters onto the streets instead of ordering them to stay home in the twenty-four hours before the final blow was struck; or if communists from the well-organized Tudeh party had decided to swing into action on Mossadegh's behalf.

Undoubtedly, there would have been no coup in August 1953 if it had not been for the CIA. The CIA devised Operation Ajax, paid a large sum to carry it out—estimates of the final cost range from $100,000 to $20 million, depending on which expenses are counted—and assigned one of its most imaginative agents to direct it. Yet Kermit Roosevelt and his comrades could not have succeeded without help from Iranians. Two groups provided invaluable help.

First were the Rashidian brothers and other covert agents who had spent years building the subversive network that Roosevelt found waiting for him when he arrived. Second were the military officers who provided decisive firepower on the climactic day.

Iran was falling toward chaos during Mossadegh's last weeks. British and American agents had worked relentlessly to split the National Front and the rest of Iranian society, and their efforts proved how vulnerable an undeveloped society can be to a sustained campaign of bribery and destabilization. Yet Mossadegh himself helped bring Iran to the dead end it reached in mid-1953. It may be an exaggeration to assert, as some have done, that at some level he actually wished to be overthrown. Nonetheless, he had run out of options. Many Iranians sensed this and were ready for a new beginning.

Foreign intelligence agents set the stage for the coup and unleashed the forces that carried it out. At a certain point, however, the operation took on a momentum of its own. The great mob that surged through the streets of Tehran on August 18 was partly mercenary and partly a genuine expression of people's loss of faith in Mossadegh. The CIA laid the groundwork for that day's events but even in its own postmortem admitted: "To what extent the resulting activity stemmed from the specific efforts of all our agents will never be known."

Iranians understood very soon after the coup that foreigners had played a central role in organizing it. In the United States, however, that realization was very slow in coming. Only when anti-American hatred exploded in Iran after the Islamic Revolution of 1979 did Americans even realize that their country was unloved there. Slowly, they were able to discover the reason why.

Just four months after Mossadegh's overthrow, Richard Nixon traveled to Iran and pronounced himself much impressed with both Prime Minister Zahedi and Mohammad Reza Shah. President Eisenhower was more circumspect. He did not visit Iran until 1959 and stayed for just six hours. The Shah gave him a festive welcome and presented him with a silver peacock inlaid with sapphires and rubies. In private, however, the two leaders had a disagreement that foreshadowed trouble to come. Eisenhower warned the Shah that military strength alone could not make any country secure, and urged him to pay attention to his people's "basic aspirations." The

Shah replied that security in the Middle East could be achieved "only by building Iran's military strength."

Eisenhower never admitted the American role in Operation Ajax. In his memoir, he recalled receiving a briefing about it but said it was written, rather than oral, and described Roosevelt as "an American in Iran, unidentified to me." He was a bit more candid in his diary. There he wrote: "The things we did were 'covert.'" He admitted, as he did not in his memoir, that Roosevelt had given him a personal briefing about the coup. "I listened to his detailed report," he wrote, "and it seemed more like a dime novel than historical facts."

Forty-seven years after the coup, the United States officially acknowledged its involvement. President Bill Clinton, who had embarked on what proved to be an unsuccessful effort to improve American relations with Iran, approved a carefully worded statement that could be read as an apology. Secretary of State Madeleine Albright delivered it during a speech in Washington.

"In 1953 the United States played a significant role in orchestrating the overthrow of Iran's popular prime minister, Mohammad Mossadegh," she said. "The Eisenhower administration believed its actions were justified for strategic reasons. But the coup was clearly a setback for Iran's political development. And it is easy to see now why many Iranians continue to resent this intervention by America in their internal affairs."

A handful of American historians have devoted themselves to studying the 1953 coup and its effects. They agree, to different degrees and with different emphases, that the coup defined all of subsequent Iranian history and reshaped the world in ways that are only now becoming clear. Here are some of their observations:

James A. Bill: American policy in Iran during the early 1950s succeeded in ensuring that there would be no Communist takeover in the country at the time, and that Iranian oil reserves would be available to the Western world at advantageous terms for two decades afterwards. It also deeply alienated Iranian patriots of all social classes and weakened the moderate, liberal nationalists represented by organizations like the National Front. This paved the way for the incubation of extremism, both of the left and of the right. This extremism became unalterably anti-American. . . . The fall of Mossadegh marked the end of a century of friendship between the two countries, and began a new era of U. S. intervention and growing hostility against the United States among the weakened forces of Iranian nationalism.

Richard W. Cottam: The decision to overturn Mossadegh was a truly historic one. Iran was at the point of change at which the percentage of the population entering the political process, or disposed to do so, was increasing in geometric progression. These awakening individuals would look to leaders whom they recognized and trusted for the norms, values and institutions they could support. Had Mossadegh, the National Front and the religious leaders who interpreted the Koran more liberally remained in control of the Iranian government, they could have served as the socializing agents for this awakening mass. Instead, they were replaced by a royal dictatorship that stood aloof from the people. . . . U. S. policy did change Iran's history in fundamental ways. It helped oust a nationalist elite which had looked to the United States as its ideological ally and its one reliable external supporter. In helping eliminate a government that symbolized Iran's search for national integrity and dignity, it helped deny the successor regime nationalist legitimacy.

Mark J. Gasiorowski: In retrospect, the United States–sponsored coup d'etat in Iran of August 19, 1953, has emerged as a critical event in postwar world history. . . . Had the coup not occurred, Iran's future would undoubtedly have been vastly different. Similarly, the U. S. role in the coup and in the subsequent consolidation of the Shah's dictatorship were decisive for the future of U. S. relations with Iran. U. S. complicity in these events figured prominently in the terrorist attacks on American citizens and installations that occurred in Iran in the early 1970s, in the anti-American character of the 1978–79 revolution, and in the many anti-American incidents that emanated from Iran after the revolution, including, most notably, the embassy hostage crisis. Latter-day supporters of the coup frequently argue that it purchased twenty-five years of stability in Iran under a pro-American regime. As the dire consequences of the revolution for U. S. interests continue to unfold, one can wonder whether this has been worth the long-term cost.

James F. Goode: Mossadegh was no saint, as even his advisors recognized. He could be stubborn and narrow-minded. Yet he was the most popular leader in modern times, at least prior to the [Islamic] revolution. . . . If Mossadegh was a prisoner of the past—opposed to dictatorial rule, supportive of constitutional government, hating foreign influence—the Americans were no less prisoners of the Cold War mindset that would not tolerate neutralism in the struggle against godless Communism.

Mary Ann Heiss: In the long term it may well be true that the inability of the British and the United States to deal with Mossadegh, whose policies seem moderate in hindsight, cleared the path not so much for the Shah and his agents over the next several decades but for the far more radical, dangerous and anti-Western regimes that would follow after 1979. . . . U. S. involvement in the [1953] coup and the 1954 consortium agreement convinced the Iranian people that the United States cared little for their interests, that it was more concerned with propping up British imperialism than with assisting their national self-determination and independence. These convictions led Iranian nationalists to dub the United States the Great Satan and to blame it for all their nation's ills during the next twenty-five years. . . . By subverting Iranian nationalism, the oil dispute of the 1950s laid the seeds for the Islamic Revolution that would come twenty-five years later and that would usher in even more anti-Western regimes in Tehran than Mossadegh's. As a result, its consequences continue even now to cast a shadow over the Persian Gulf and beyond.

Nikki R. Keddie: The 1953 coup, which culminated a year later in an oil agreement leaving effective control of oil production and marketing and fifty percent of the profits in the hands of the world oil cartel companies, had an understandably traumatic effect on Iranian public opinion, which has continued down to the present. . . . Feelings against the United States government became far stronger when it became known that the United States was heavily involved in the 1953 overthrow of Mossadegh. American support over twenty-five years for the Shah's dictatorship and nearly all its ways added to this anti-American feeling. Hence, in both the British and American cases, however exaggerated and paranoid some charges by Iranians may be, suspiciousness and hostility have their roots in real and important occurrences;

chiefly, participation in the overthrow of popular revolutionary movements and support of unpopular governments.

William Roger Louis: Nations, like individuals, cannot be manipulated without a sense on the part of the aggrieved that old scores must eventually be settled. . . . In the short term, the intervention of 1953 appeared to be effective. Over the longer term, the older advice not to interfere would seem to be the better part of political wisdom.

These views come close to a consensus. They eerily vindicate those who opposed the use of force against Mossadegh. President Truman predicted that mishandling the Iran crisis would produce "a disaster to the free world." Henry Grady, his ambassador in Tehran, warned that a coup would be "utter folly" and would push Iran into "a status of disintegration with all that implies." Anyone reading those words in the quarter-century after 1953 would have thought them wildly mistaken. Later history, however, redeems them and the men who spoke them. The results of Operation Ajax were just as dire as they predicted, although the backlash—or "blowback," as intelligence agents call it—took longer to materialize than anyone expected.

A fair case can be made that Iran was not ready for democracy in 1953. It might well have fallen into disarray if the United States had not intervened, although if American and British intelligence officers had not meddled so shamelessly in its domestic politics, it might also have returned to relative calm. It is difficult to imagine, however, an outcome that would have produced as much pain and horror over the next half-century as that produced by Operation Ajax. Only a Soviet takeover followed by war between the superpowers would have been worse.

The coup bought the United States and the West a reliable Iran for twenty-five years. That was an undoubted triumph. But in view of what came later, and of the culture of covert action that seized hold of the American body politic in the coup's wake, the triumph seems much tarnished. From the seething streets of Tehran and other Islamic capitals to the scenes of terror attacks around the world, Operation Ajax has left a haunting and terrible legacy.

Epilogue

My Iranian tour guide looked tired but happy when we met in the faded lobby of the Laleh Hotel in Tehran. A conspiratorial grin spread across his face. "I have worked a miracle for you," he told me triumphantly. "We are going to Ahmad Abad!"

I had come to Iran looking for traces of Mohammad Mossadegh. The trip had not been easy to arrange. When I met with an Iranian diplomat in New York to apply for a visa, he told me that my project sounded intriguing, but that it would have to be fully reviewed by the Islamic authorities in Tehran. Over the next few months I called him almost every day, but there was never any hint of progress. Finally I concluded that this path was leading nowhere. I wanted to be in Iran for the forty-ninth anniversary of the 1953 coup, and he admitted that there seemed little prospect of that.

"Maybe I should apply for a tourist visa," I suggested.

"You could try," he replied.

His tone sounded less than encouraging, but I took him at his word. I found a travel agent who specializes in sending people to exotic countries. Two weeks later, with her help, I had a visa in hand.

On the long Turkish Airlines flight across the Atlantic and then

on to Tehran, I wondered what awaited me. My first hint that I was
not entirely welcome came when I checked into the Laleh, which is
one of the city's largest hotels. Less than a year had passed since the
9/11 terror attacks in New York, and the desk clerk gave me the key
to Room 911. To my protests, he could only shrug and reply that
this was the room to which I had been assigned.

A few hours later the telephone rang. I had asked an Iranian
friend to try to find people who might have known Mossadegh or
been loyal to the National Front, and she now insisted that I come
to see her immediately. When I arrived, she told me that a government official had called her with a stern warning. She was not to
telephone anyone on my behalf and should also tell me that if I met
with anyone at all, I would be summarily deported. What, then,
about our plans to travel to Ahmad Abad on the anniversary of the
August 19 coup?

"I can't go with you," she said. "They don't want me to do any
work for you at all."

The anniversary was still a few days away. Tehran offers little in
the way of diversion, and on my visa application I had expressed a
desire to return to Isfahan, which I had visited on an earlier trip. I
spent several days there and found the spectacular tiled palaces and
mosques as dazzling as I had the first time. On my flight back to
Tehran I sat next to a middle-aged businessman who, like everyone
I met in Iran, detested the Islamic regime and thought well of
Americans. Naturally I asked him about my favorite subject.

"You're too young to remember Mossadegh," I ventured, "but
you must have heard about him. What did you hear? What did you
learn?"

He paused for a moment to reflect. To speak of Mossadegh is
not forbidden in Iran, nor would Iranians obey any such prohibi-
tion. But for five decades, excepting only a brief couple of years after
the Islamic Revolution of 1979, he has been cast as a dubious figure
at best, more likely a traitor.

"I don't know that much about him," my new acquaintance told
me. "I know he nationalized our oil industry. But the main thing
about Mossadegh is that he represents freedom. In his time there
was free speech, there were free elections, people could do what they
wanted. He reminds us that there was a time in Iran when we had
democracy. That's why our government is afraid of him."

When I arrived back at the Laleh, I was assigned once again to Room 911. My guide—American tourists in Iran must travel with a guide—was not happy to learn that I wished to visit Mossadegh's home at Ahmad Abad. I had planned simply to hire a taxi and go there, but the guide told me that was quite impossible. This struck me as odd, since Ahmad Abad is a farm village far from any military base or secret installation. Still, it is inextricably linked with the man who for eleven years was its sole prisoner and most famous citizen.

It was August 18, the night before the anniversary of the coup, when my guide appeared with good news about the miracle he had worked. I asked him why arranging such a seemingly innocuous trip should be so difficult. By his expression he seemed to tell me that if I understood Iran better, I would not have asked such a foolish question.

"For three reasons it is difficult," he explained. "First of all, this is not a routine site. It's not on the tourist program. The ministry of culture has a list of places that tourists can visit, and you're supposed to stick to those places. No tourist ever goes to Ahmad Abad! Second, you did not list Ahmad Abad as a place you wanted to visit when you requested your tourist visa. We made a program for you based on your requests, and that program has been approved by the ministry. You're supposed to stick to the program. And third, you don't have the right visa to visit a place like that. If you had a journalist's visa, you could travel anywhere, but not on a tourist visa. It was all very difficult and very complicated. A whole machinery had to be set in motion."

The guide must have noticed my scowl, because after this litany he hastened to add, "You don't have to feel specially obligated to me. I would have done it for any of my tourists."

Ahmad Abad lies an hour's drive west of Tehran. A highway runs most of the distance, and after leaving it, visitors wind their way past small factories and through barley and sugar beet fields. No sign points the way, nor does any mark the entrance to the village. There is only a small kiosk where sweets are sold. On the day I arrived, two small boys were sitting in the shade in front of it.

"Ask them who Mossadegh was," I said to my guide. He did, and the boys broke into smiles, shaking their heads as if we must be dunces.

"He nationalized the oil industry!" one of them replied. The other one laughed. I was impressed.

The road into Ahmad Abad stops at the gate of a compound surrounded by a high brick wall. There is no name on the gate, but a quick look around made clear that there is no place in town nearly as imposing as this. It had to be Mossadegh's home. I rang the bell and waited.

After a minute or two, a young woman opened the gate. Before us stretched a footpath about eighty yards long, lined on both sides by tall elm trees. Through the trees we could see a handsome two-story brick home with green frames around the doors and the windows.

For more than a decade Mossadegh never left this compound. He could have, because his sentence confined him only to the village, not strictly to the compound. Police agents, however, were under orders to follow and observe him if he stepped beyond the gates. He preferred solitude to their company.

The compound is quite a pleasant place, with paths through gardens and arbors, and the manor house is comfortable though hardly luxurious. Mossadegh was not idle here during his long imprisonment. He supervised the work of about two hundred peasants who worked in nearby fields, training them in the use of modern farm equipment and even winning an agricultural prize for a scheme that increased sugar beet production. His family had traditionally produced lawyers and doctors, and since he had already learned most of what there was to know about law, he devoted himself to studying medicine. He read medical texts and boiled local roots to make antimalaria medicine. When villagers became sick, he treated them. For those who fell seriously ill, he wrote notes that gained them admission to the Najmieh Hospital in Tehran, which his mother had founded. Many brought him their small problems and found him unfailingly attentive and generous.

During his long hours of solitude, Mossadegh spent much time in his upstairs library. He immersed himself in old interests, reading Islamic philosophy and the works of political theorists like Montesquieu and Rousseau, and developed new ones like cooking. He eliminated fried foods from his diet and ate only those that had been steamed or boiled. One of his favorite books, which is still in his study, was the *Larousse Gastronomique.*

Still, for one who lived within the walls of this compound for so long, it must have taken on something of the air of a prison. During his years there, Mossadegh was often unwell, suffering from periodic bouts of bleeding ulcers and other ailments. Relatives who visited him say that he was depressed, discouraged, and demoralized. He mourned not for the loss of his own power but for the collapse of his dreams for Iran. Nothing he did in Ahmad Abad was able to raise his spirits.

"I am effectively in jail," he wrote in his memoir. "I am imprisoned in this village, deprived of all personal freedoms, and wishful that my time would be up soon and I would be relieved of this existence."

The caretaker who escorted my guide and me into Mossadegh's compound said that visitors appear there regularly, especially on weekends. On this day, however, the forty-ninth anniversary of the coup that brought down his government on August 19, 1953, we were the only ones. I had come halfway around the world to be here.

In his will Mossadegh expressed a desire to be buried at the Ebne Babooyeh cemetery in Tehran, alongside the graves of those killed defending his government during the clashes of July 1952. Mohammad Reza Shah, fearing that Mossadegh's grave might become a focus of opposition, would not permit that. Relatives then decided to bury his remains without ceremony in Ahmad Abad. He had instructed them to construct no memorial, not even a gravestone, to mark the place. Those wishes were carried out. He now lies beneath the floor of what was once his dining room.

The carpeted room is small but pleasant, with windows that admit streams of sunlight. Over the years it has taken on the air of a shrine. A low wooden table covered with woven cloth stands over the spot where Mossadegh's body is buried. On it there are two candles and a Koran. Most Iranian visitors follow tradition by laying a hand lightly on the cloth and reciting a verse that acknowledges God's mercy and compassion.

Walls of this room are covered with images of Mossadegh. Some are painted in oil, others sketched in pen or pencil. One is an embroidery that shows him against the background of an Iranian flag. A silk-screen print carries a quote from one of his speeches: "As I am an Iranian and a Muslim, I oppose anything that is against Iran or Islam." There is a photo of him vigorously defending himself at his trial and another, more plaintive one of him sitting alone and lost in thought during his house arrest. The one I liked best shows him at the Liberty Bell in Philadelphia, laying his finger on the famous crack.

This was the room where Mossadegh ate his daily meals and often received visitors. I spent a long time there, allowing my imagination to take me back to those days. Finally I thanked the caretaker and asked if I could walk around the grounds. She had no objection. I wandered among the shade trees and peered into a garage where a pale green 1948 Pontiac that belonged to Mossadegh's wife sits unused.

After a few minutes, another, more intriguing object caught my attention. Leaning against the back wall were the tall double doors of a sturdy iron gate. It was the only object salvaged from the house in Tehran where Mossadegh lived most of his life, including his tumultuous years as prime minister.

What history this gate has seen! Through it, the American and British ambassadors to Iran, along with special emissaries like Averell Harriman, passed countless times as they sought to persuade Mossadegh to give up or modify his plan to nationalize his country's oil industry. Crowds of thugs banged on it as they shouted "Death to Mossadegh!" during the aborted 1952 uprising. During that same uprising, a jeep carrying Shaban the Brainless crashed through the gate as Mossadegh scurried to safety over a back wall. There is still a large dent near the bottom that is probably a result of that crash.

The house before which this gate once stood was wrecked and burned on the night of August 19, 1953, and later the debris was bulldozed to make way for an apartment building. All that remains is the gate. This gives it great historical importance and, for those who knew Mossadegh or have tried to learn about him in the years since his death, an almost spiritual aura. I placed my hand on it and held it there for a long time.

Only a few people in Ahmad Abad could remember Mossadegh.

I found one of them, Abolfathi Takrousta, working on his car in the dusty street outside his home. He is a truck driver and a farmer who worked as a cook in the Mossadegh complex when he was a teenager. When I told him why I had come, he brightened instantly and invited me onto his patio for tea and pistachio nuts. Birds sang as we sat under a grape arbor and talked about bygone days.

Although many accounts describe Mossadegh as having suffered from various ailments, especially in his later years, and although his three years in solitary confinement cannot have been healthy for a man his age, Mr. Takrousta remembered him as strong and vigorous. Once Mr. Takrousta began talking, stories flowed out. Mossadegh had opened a pharmacy where medicine was distributed free to villagers, loaned money to those in need, built an insulated shed to keep ice in summertime, and distributed free bags of grain to each of his laborers at Ramadan and on New Year's Day.

"Mossadegh was not like a normal landlord," Mr. Takrousta told me. "He ran his estate like a charity. Most of what he grew, he gave back to the workers. Everyone here loved him. Any kind of a problem that you had, you would go to him and he would take care of it. From the highest official to the poorest worker, he treated everyone the same."

One day, my new friend told me, a peasant came to Mossadegh to complain that he had been detained by some of the local Savak agents, taken to their headquarters, and beaten while they shouted questions about Mossadegh's habits and conversations.

"It was the only time I ever saw him get angry. He called the police chief and shouted at him to come to the house immediately. When he got to the house, Mossadegh pushed him against a wall, held his cane against the guy's throat and shouted: 'You are here to watch me, and you have no right to abuse anyone else. If you have a problem, you come to me and only me! Don't ever, ever lay a finger on one of my people again!' This was a Savak officer and not a nice man at all, but when this happened he started apologizing and begging forgiveness. After that, the police never went near us. The jailer was afraid of the prisoner!"

I asked if Mr. Takrousta and his neighbors felt different from people in other villages, and he assured me that they did.

"We not only *feel* different, we *are* different," he told me. "We're different because of the effect Mossadegh had on us. Visitors come here from far away. They don't come to any other village. People here are proud that we had the privilege of having such a great man here. We try to behave according to the example he gave us. We have a sense of charity, cooperation, unity, solidarity. We take the hands of people in need. People from other villages know we're like this, and when they have problems, they come to us and we help them. You can't think of Ahmad Abad without thinking of Mossadegh. He's the father of our nation but also the father of this village. It's really a shame that they destroyed his government."

I asked who "they" were. Mr. Takrousta paused, unsure of himself. He stared up at the sky for a long moment and then spoke slowly.

"I'm a simple, uneducated villager," he said. "I don't know who 'they' are. But whoever they are, they don't want our people to be free and raise ourselves up."

We had spent more than an hour talking, and my host followed Iranian tradition by inviting me to stay for lunch. I declined as politely as I could, shook his hand, and thanked him profusely. For a while afterward I wandered aimlessly through the village. Later I checked back at the manse to see whether any other guests had appeared to mark this anniversary. None had. A group of Mossadegh's admirers had considered holding a rally that day, but several were facing prosecution for various political offenses and did not want to provoke the authorities.

Beginning in the 1990s, and especially after the reform-minded Mohammad Khatami was elected president in 1997, Iranians used Mossadegh as a symbol in their political debates. Anyone who paid tribute to him or waved his portrait was implicitly challenging the principles of Islamic rule. Laws forbade calling for a democratic republic to replace the Islamic regime, but praising Mossadegh's legacy was another way of doing the same thing. I found that many Iranians still associated his name with the idea of freedom.

"Oh, he was a good leader," one young man told me. "When he was in power, you could say what you wanted. Not like today. Shah killed him, right?" Not exactly, I replied. But in a sense perhaps yes.

Islamic leaders do not know quite what to make of Mossadegh.

They take his defeat as proof of their view that Iran is the eternal victim of cruel foreigners. Because he was a secular liberal, however, they cannot embrace him as a hero.

The Iranian press reflected this ambivalence in the way it covered the forty-ninth anniversary of the 1953 coup. One television station broadcast a damning documentary about it, but there was hardly a mention that Mossadegh was the victim. A small group of pro-government students rallied outside what was once the American embassy, but they, too, limited themselves to condemning "the crimes of the Great Satan against the Iranian nation" and did not refer to Mossadegh.

Only two of Tehran's fourteen daily newspapers ran stories to mark the anniversary. One of them, *Entekhab*, which is a mouthpiece for hard-liners, described the coup as having been launched "against Mossadegh and also Kashani," a bizarre rewriting of history that portrays Ayatollah Kashani as a victim of foreign intervention rather than as one of its agents. The lesson of the coup, this article said, was that Iranians must support their leaders because dissent only served the interests of "warmongers in the White House."

The other article, in the moderate paper *Fereydoon Shayesteh*, was quite different. It described August 19, 1953, as "the day despotism returned," and although carefully avoiding any praise of Mossadegh, it summarized the episode quite well: "The coup was carried out by professionals from both inside and outside Iran, and it cost millions of dollars. It is not at all true that, as some people have said and written, the coup happened because of internal opposition and mistrust of Mossadegh. It became possible when various well-known politicians, many of whom owed their careers to Mossadegh, broke with him and used all their means to ruin his reputation. These accusations have had no lasting effect, and in the years after the coup, those who made them never managed to win back the people's respect."

During my stay in Tehran, I tried to find some of the buildings associated with the coup, but without much success. Tehran has grown enormously since then, and as in many big cities, growth has meant the destruction of many old neighborhoods. I did drive slowly past the now-empty American embassy compound from which Kermit Roosevelt worked and where American hostages were imprisoned years later. Slogans were painted in large letters on the outside walls, conveniently translated into English. "We Will Make America Face a Severe Defeat," one says. Another proclaims: "The Day the US Praises Us, We Should Mourn."

The only other landmark I could find that Mossadegh would have recognized was the Saad Abad Palace. On the lawn outside, he sat for three days in 1949, demanding that the Shah annul that year's fraudulent election. Inside are rooms where he met often with the Shah, including on the day in 1952 when he had his dramatic fainting fit. The palace is now open to visitors. As I approached, I asked my driver to pull to the side of the long driveway before we reached the entrance. He was mystified, but I had calculated that this must have been where the car carrying Kermit Roosevelt stopped on the nights when he had his clandestine meetings with the Shah. I could easily visualize the Shah walking down the steps ahead, coming through the darkness, and sliding into the car beside him.

Inside, the palace is opulent to the point of excess. Marble, fine woods, old paintings, and richly woven carpets define its décor. I spent much time looking around the Shah's private reception room, which I guessed was where he received Roosevelt on the night they celebrated their victory and bid each other farewell. A large salon upstairs might have been the place where the Shah sat on a table during his meeting with General Schwarzkopf, but of course there was no one who could tell me for sure.

Even though I had been forbidden to interview Iranians about Mossadegh and his regime, the casual conversations I had with ordinary people made it abundantly clear that most held him in high regard. Someday his house in Ahmad Abad will be a museum and will draw streams of pilgrims from across Iran and beyond. I mentioned this to the caretaker while I was there, and she told me that creating such a museum was exactly what the Mossadegh family wished.

"The Mossadegh family?" I asked. During a visit to London, I had met Hedayat Matine-Daftary, the grandson who had fled Iran one step ahead of a vigilante mob. Now I learned that another grandson, Mahmoud Mossadegh, had stayed behind and become a prominent physician in Tehran. It was he who paid to maintain the house at Ahmad Abad, including building the caretaker's cottage and paying her salary. She did not have his telephone number, but with the help of my guide I located him in Tehran. Mahmoud Mossadegh agreed to come to my hotel for dinner that night.

I came down from Room 911 a few minutes before the appointed time. For the better part of an hour I sat waiting near the hotel's main entrance. Just as I began wondering if I had somehow missed my guest, he appeared. I had no idea what he would look like but recognized him immediately. He was tall and fair-skinned, with a strong, self-confident air about him. Most striking of all were his clothes. He wore a business suit and tie, a fashion I had never seen in Iran. As I approached him, I saw that the tie was from Harvard. It turned out that he had just returned from celebrating his forty-fifth class reunion.

"Actually, the whole thing was Averell Harriman's idea," he told me. "I translated for a few of Harriman's meetings with my grandfather. One day he asked me where I wanted to go to college. I told him I assumed I would go somewhere in England, but he said the United States would be better. I asked him where in the United States. He was a Yale man, but for whatever reason he suggested Harvard. So when the time came I applied, and that was that!"

Even before we reached the elevator, Doctor Mossadegh had taken me back to the days when his grandfather was in power. His father was none other than Gholan-Hussein Mossadegh, who had been the prime minister's physician and had accompanied him on his trips to the United Nations in New York and the World Court in The Hague. Gholan-Hussein Mossadegh had passed away years earlier, as had all of the prime minister's five children except one, his daughter Majid, who had spent most of her life at a mental hospital in Switzerland. Grandchildren and great-grandchildren had scattered and, for the most part, avoided politics. Doctor Mossadegh told me that he had never been involved in anything other than medicine. The only public position he ever held was general secretary of the Iranian Society of Fertility and Sterility.

Doctor Mossadegh did not turn up alone that night. With him, dressed in jeans and a white T-shirt, was his son Ali, who was in his mid-twenties. Most of our conversation centered on Prime Minister Mossadegh. The doctor was full of stories and memories. Some were sad, particularly those about how morose Mossadegh became during his decade of enforced isolation. Even the trivial stories were insightful. Mossadegh, for example, used to peel Kleenex tissues apart because he thought that using them at full two-ply strength was a wasteful extravagance.

A few of the doctor's recollections were of true historic interest. He told me that a few weeks before the 1953 coup, he attended a reception at the home of an Iranian diplomat in Washington and overheard the wife of Colonel Abbas Farzanegan, a military attaché who was on the CIA's secret payroll, boast that her husband was involved in a plot that would soon make him a cabinet minister. The next morning Mahmoud Mossadegh cabled this intelligence home to his grandfather.

"Later on, after the coup, I asked him if he had received my cable. He said, 'Of course I did.' When I asked him why he hadn't done something about it, he told me there was nothing he could have done. He said he knew full well that this coup was coming. His choice was to surrender or arm his supporters and call them out to civil war. He hated to think about giving up everything he believed in, but the other alternative was out of the question."

As we spoke, Ali Mossadegh, the late prime minister's great-grandson, listened intently but said little. As dessert was served, I tried to draw him out. In fluent English, he told me that he was studying international relations. Nothing, I thought, could be more appropriate for an intelligent young man with such a pedigree. So did he dream of a career in public life?

The two Mossadeghs, father and son, looked at each other after I asked this question. Obviously they had discussed it between themselves, probably many times. The doctor remained silent as we both waited for the answer.

"No, I won't go into politics," Ali Mossadegh told me. "I'm afraid of the risk. Not the risk to me, but to our family name. We have a very family-oriented society in this country. Wherever you go, even before people ask who you are, they ask whose son you are. Everything you do reflects on your family. If any of us commits even the slightest error, it tarnishes the name of our family and of Prime Minister Mossadegh. I'm just an ordinary human being. I make mistakes like everyone else. That's fine as long as I'm just a private person, but if I become a politician, my mistakes will be held against the family, even against family members who are dead. My life is going to be like my father's life. All we want to do is preserve the heritage of our family. I want to practice honesty, generosity, and the other qualities that people associate with the name Mossadegh. Public life is not for me. I doubt it will be for anyone else in our family. It's too great a responsibility."

NOTES

Chapter 1: Good Evening, Mr. Roosevelt

Firsthand accounts of the events of August 15–19, 1953, appeared in the *New York Times* and in newspapers served by the Associated Press, among them the *Chicago Tribune*. An official account is included in the CIA's clandestine service history, *Overthrow of Premier Mossadeq of Iran, November 1952–August 1953*, written by Donald M. Wilber and referred to here as "Service History." A summary of this history was published in the *New York Times* on April 16, 2000, and the full document is available at www.nytimes.com. Kermit Roosevelt's memoir is *Countercoup: The Struggle for Control of Iran* (New York: McGraw-Hill, 1979). Other accounts of the coup appear in Ambrose, Stephen, with Immerman, Richard H., *Ike's Spies: Eisenhower and the Intelligence Establishment* (Garden City, N.Y.: 1981); Diba, Farhad, *Mohammad Mossadegh: A Political Biography* (London: Croom Helm, 1986); Dorril, Stephen, *MI6: Inside the Covert World of Her Majesty's Secret Intelligence Service* (New York: Free Press, 2000); Elm, Mostafa, *Oil, Power and Principle: Iran's Oil Nationalization and Its Aftermath* (Syracuse, N.Y.: Syracuse University Press, 1992); Gasiorowski, Mark J., *U.S. Foreign Policy and the Shah: Building a Client State in Iran* (Ithaca, N.Y.: Cornell University, 1991); Goode, James F., *The United States and Iran: In the Shadow of Mussadiq* (New York: St. Martin's, 1997); Katouzian, Homa, *Mussadiq and the Struggle for Power in Iran* (London: I. B. Tauris, 1999); Mosley, Leonard, *Power Play* (Baltimore: Penguin, 1974); Prados, John, *Presidents' Secret Wars: CIA and Pentagon Covert Operations Since World War II* (New York: William Morrow, 1986); Woodhouse, C. M., *Something Ventured* (London: Granada, 1982); and Zabih, Sepehr, *The Mossadegh Era: Roots of the Iranian Revolution* (Chicago: Lake View Press, 1982); in articles, including Abrahamian, Ervand, "The 1953 Coup in Iran," in *Science & Society*, vol. 65, no. 2 (Summer 2001); Gasiorowski, Mark J., "The 1953 Coup d'Etat in Iran," in *International Journal of Middle East Studies*, no. 19 (1987); Louis, William Roger, "Britain and the Overthrow of the Mossadeq Government," in Gasiorowski, Mark J., and Byrne, Malcolm (eds.), *Mohammad Mossadeq and the 1953 Coup in Iran* (Syracuse, N.Y.: Syracuse University Press, forthcoming 2003); Gasiorowski, Mark J., "The 1953 Coup d'Etat Against Mossadegh" in that same volume; and Love, Kennett, *The American Role in the Pahlavi Restoration on August 19, 1953* (unpublished), the Allen Dulles Papers, Princeton University (1960); and in two videos, History Channel, *Anatomy of a Coup: The CIA in Iran*, Catalogue No. AAE-43021; and *Mossadegh*, Iranian Movies (www.IranianMovies.com), Tape No. 3313.

Mossadegh fried in Persian oil: *Frankfurter Neue Presse,* October 17, 1952.

Woodhouse emphasizes communist threat: Woodhouse, C. M., op. cit., p. 117.

Philby on Roosevelt: Roosevelt, op. cit., p. 110.

Roosevelt's feeling at border crossing: Roosevelt, ibid., pp. 138–40.

Roosevelt at tennis: Roosevelt, ibid., p. 154.

Zahedi receives over $100,000: Service History, p. B2; and Gasiorowski, Mark J., "The 1953 Coup d'Etat Against Mossadegh," in Gasiorowski and Byrne, op. cit.

Groups CIA wished to influence, Service History, ibid., p. 7.

Cottam on Iranian press: *Anatomy of a Coup* (video), op. cit.

Shah hates taking decisions: Falle, Sam, *My Lucky Life in War, Revolution, Peace and Diplomacy* (Lewes, Sussex: Book Guild, 1996), p. 80.

Shah sent Ashraf away: *Foreign Relations of the United States 1952–1954, Volume X, Iran 1951–1954,* (Washington, D.C.: Government Printing Office, 1989), p. 675.

Ashraf's eyes lit up: Dorril, op. cit., p. 586.

Ashraf's meeting with Shah: Service History, op. cit., p. 24.

Schwarzkopf brings bags of money: Mosley, op. cit., pp. 216–219; and Roosevelt, op. cit., p. 147.

CIA gave Shah cover mission: Service History, op. cit., p. 25; and Katouzian, op. cit., pp. 39–40.

Schwarzkopf meets Shah: Service History, op. cit., p. 29.

Roosevelt presumed meeting Shah would be necessary: Roosevelt, op. cit., p. 149.

Roosevelt authorized to speak: Roosevelt, ibid., p. 154.

Roosevelt's costume: Roosevelt, ibid., p. 155.

Roosevelt's first meeting with Shah: Roosevelt, ibid., pp. 156–157.

Roosevelt tells Shah United States will not accept second Korea: Service History, op. cit., pp. 33–34.

Roosevelt meets agents in cars: Roosevelt, op. cit., p. 162.

Roosevelt's later meetings with Shah: Roosevelt, ibid., pp. 163–166.

Shah feels stubborn irresolution: Service History, op. cit., p. 35.

Shah will fly to Baghdad: Roosevelt, op. cit., p. 161.

Fake message from Eisenhower: Roosevelt, ibid., p. 168.

Firmans arrive: Roosevelt, ibid., pp. 170–171.

Time moved slowly: Roosevelt, ibid., p. 171.

CIA report on coup preparations: Service History, op. cit., pp. 36–38.

Nothing to do but wait: Service History, ibid., p. 38.

"Luck Be a Lady": Roosevelt, op. cit., p. 172.

Roosevelt drives past Riahi's home: Roosevelt, ibid., p. 172.

Shah will look for work: *Foreign Relations of the United States 1952–1954, Volume X,* op. cit., p. 747.

Roosevelt close to despair: Roosevelt, op. cit., p. 173.

Waller telegram: Waller's remarks at conference in Oxford, England, June 10, 2002.

Fatemi speech: *New York Times,* August 17, 1953.

Chapter 2: Curse This Fate

Ferdowsi lament: Mackey, Sandra, *The Iranians: Persia, Islam and the Soul of a Nation* (New York: Plume, 1996), p. 62.

Hidden Imam: Tabatabai, Allamah Sayyid Muhammad Husayn, *Shi'ite Islam* (Albany: State University of New York, 1977), p. 214.

Fischer on Shiites: Fischer, Michael M. J., *Iran: From Religious Dispute to Revolution* (Cambridge, Mass.: Harvard University Press, 1980) pp. 24–27.

Battle cry of Ismail: Mottadeh, Roy, *The Mantle of the Prophet: Religion and Politics in Iran* (New York: Pantheon, 1985), p. 173.

Ismail adopts Shiism: Arjomand, Said Amir, *The Shadow of God and the Hidden Imam* (Chicago: University of Chicago Press, 1984), p. 109.

Modern author on Isfahan: *Nagel Encyclopedia Guide*, quoted in Arab, Gholam Hossein, *Isfahan* (Tehran: Farhangsara, 1996), p. 1.

Curzon on Qajars: Ghods, M. Reza, *Iran in the Twentieth Century: A Political History* (Boulder, Colo.: Lynne Rienner, 1989), p. 2.

Chapter 3: The Last Drop of the Nation's Blood

Curzon on Reuter concession: Curzon, George Nathaniel, *Persia and the Persian Question, Vol. 1* (London: Longmans, Green and Co., 1892), p. 480.

Tobacco revolt and *fatwa:* Afary, Janet, *The Iranian Constitutional Revolution, 1906–1911: Grassroots Democracy, Social Democracy, and the Origins of Feminism* (New York: Columbia University Press, 1996), pp. 29–33.

Shah borrows half a million pounds: Keddie, Nikki, *Roots of Revolution: An Interpretive History of Modern Iran* (New Haven, Conn.: Yale University Press, 1981), p. 67.

D'Arcy concession: Ferrier, R. W., *The History of the British Petroleum Company, Vol. 1: The Developing Years 1901–1932* (London: Cambridge University Press, 1982), p. 42.

Demand for national assembly: Martin, Vanessa, *Islam and Modernism: The Iranian Revolution of 1906* (Syracuse, N.Y.: Syracuse University Press, 1989), p. 74.

British secretary accepts *bast:* Afary, op. cit., p. 55.

Majlis must decide: Martin, ibid., p. 99.

British diplomat: Martin, ibid., p. 199.

Thrown out law of the Prophet: Martin, ibid., p. 125.

Constitutional government not advisable: Martin, ibid., p. 114.

Overthrow of Islam: Martin, ibid., p. 62.

Two enticing words: Martin, ibid., p. 128.

Openness against insularity: Mackey, op. cit., p. 136.

We want the Koran: Mackey, ibid., p. 152.

Lying between life and death: Bayat, Mangol, *Iran's First Revolution: Shi'ism and the Constitutional Revolution of 1905–6* (New York: Oxford University Press, 1991), p. 244.

Prize from fairyland: Churchill, Winston, *The World Crisis 1911–1914* (New York: Charles Scribner's Sons, 1923), p. 134.

Curzon on Persia's importance: *Documents on British Foreign Policy 1919–1939,* First Series, Vol. IV (London: Government Printing Press), pp. 1119–1121.

Reza Khan in disturbances: Farmanfarmaian, Manucher, and Farmanfarmaian, Roxane, *Blood and Oil: Inside the Shah's Iran* (New York: Modern Library, 1999), p. 115.

Reza's speech: Elwell-Sutton, L. P., "Reza Shah the Great: Founder of the Pahlavi Dynasty," in Lenczowski, George, *Iran Under the Pahlavis* (Stanford, Calif.: Hoover Institute, 1978), p. 18.

Involvement of British officers: Katouzian, Homa, op. cit., pp. 16–17.

Nicholson on Persia: Ferrier, op. cit., p. 589.

Khorasan massacre: Mackey, op. cit., p. 182.

Hamedan baker: Author's interviews in Iran, 2002.

Reza orders mail returned: Mackey, op. cit., p. 178.

Reza largest landowner in Iran: Mackey, ibid., p. 173.

Only one thief in Iran: Ghods, op. cit., p. 93.

Newspaper on common goals in Iran and Germany: Ghods, ibid., p. 166.

Allied leaflet: Goode, James F., *The United States and Iran: In the Shadow of Mussadiq* (New York: St. Martin's, 1997), pp. 9–10.

Chapter 4: A Wave of Oil

Helpless crew: Longhurst, Henry, *Adventure in Oil: The Story of British Petroleum* (London: Sidgwick and Jackson, 1959), p. 21.

Petroliferous territory: Longhurst, ibid., p. 17.

Ahmad Shah as elderly child: Yergin, Daniel, *The Prize: The Epic Quest for Oil, Money and Power* (New York: Simon and Schuster, 1991), p. 136.

Telegram to Reynolds: Longhurst, op. cit., p. 31.

Mastery itself was the prize: Churchill, op. cit., p. 136.

Sunshine, mud, and flies: Longhurst, op. cit., p. 45.

Curzon on wave of oil: *London Times*, November 22, 1918.

Production increases at Abadan: Heiss, Mary Ann, *Empire and Nationhood: The United States, Great Britain, and Iranian Oil, 1950–1954* (New York: Columbia University Press, 1997), p. 6.

Royalty payment in 1920: Heiss, ibid., p. 6.

Reza burns file: Elm, op. cit., p. 31.

Cadman had attended Reza's coronation: Bill, James A., *The Eagle and the Lion: The Tragedy of American-Iranian Relations* (New Haven, Conn.: Yale University Press, 1988), p. 59.

Terms of 1933 oil accord: Heiss, op. cit., p. 13.

Cadman cable: Longhurst, op. cit., p. 78.

Strike at Abadan: Farmanfarmaian, op. cit., p. 186.

Increase in oil production during 1940s: Bamberg, J. H., *The History of the British Petroleum Company: Vol. II: The Anglo-Iranian Years, 1928–1954* (Cambridge, U.K.: Cambridge University Press, 1994), p. 242.

Assessment of young Mossadegh: Katouzian, op. cit., p. 1.

Mossadegh's reaction to Anglo-Persian Agreement: Katouzian, ibid., p. 13.

Cousin's view of Mossadegh: Farmanfarmaian, op. cit., pp. 166–170.

If subjugation were beneficial: Azimi, Fakhreddin, "The Reconciliation of Politics and Ethics, Nationalism and Democracy: An Overview of the Political Career of Dr. Mohammad Musaddiq," in Bill, James A., and Louis, William Roger (eds.), *Mussadiq, Iranian Nationalism, and Oil* (London: I. B. Tauris, 1988), p. 50.

Cut off my head: Katouzian, op. cit., p. 25.

Mossadegh taken prisoner: Katouzian, ibid., p. 33.

Chapter 5: His Master's Orders

(The notation FO refers to numbered documents of the British Foreign Office.)

Shah's affairs: Forbis, William H., *Fall of the Peacock Throne: The Story of Iran* (New York: Harper and Row, 1980), p. 53.

Chauffeur in one-way street: Arfa, Hassan, *Under Five Shahs* (New York: William Morrow, 1965), p. 305.

Succession to Reza Shah: Farmanfarmaian, op. cit., pp. 141–142; and Katouzian, pp. 39–40.

General Schwarzkopf's background: Schwarzkopf, H. Norman, *It Doesn't Take a Hero* (New York: Bantam, 1992), pp. 3–4.

Anglo-Iranian's 1947 profits and Iran's share: Farmanfarmaian, op. cit., p. 212.

Conditions at Abadan: Farmanfarmaian, ibid., pp. 184–185.

Bevin on British standard of living: Yergin, op. cit., p. 427.

Fraser proposes Supplemental Agreement: Heiss, op. cit., p. 7.

British want the whole world: Elm, op. cit., p. 55.

Iskandari threat to nationalize oil: Katouzian, op. cit., pp. 67–68.

Shah's visit to United States: Bill, op. cit., p. 40.

Visit did not go well: McGhee, George, *Envoy to the Middle World: Adventures in Diplomacy* (New York: Harper and Row, 1983), pp. 66–71.

Joint communiqué: Alexander, Yonah, and Nanes, Allen (eds.), *The United States and Iran: A Documentary History* (Frederick, Md.: Alethia Books, 1980), p. 208.

No intention of carrying out orders: FO 371/91448, quoted in Elm, op. cit., p. 63.

British will treat hysterical deputies: FO 371/91512.

Sharogh role: Elm, op. cit., p. 70.

Work of oil committee: Farmanfarmaian, op. cit., pp. 241–242.

Kashani on foreign yoke: Cottam, Richard W., *Nationalism in Iran* (Pittsburgh: University of Pittsburgh Press, 1979), p. 152.

Mossadegh warns Razmara of disgrace: Elm, op. cit., p. 71.

Northcroft says nationalists unimportant: FO 371/91524, quoted in Elm, op. cit., p. 74.

Fateh letter to Elkington: Elm, ibid., pp. 75–76.

Britain's immense service to mankind: Elm, ibid., p. 79.

Shepherd wrote the gist: Elm, op. cit., p. 80.

Statement of Razmara's assassin: Cottam, op. cit., p. 151.

Mossadegh doubts effectiveness of bodyguards: Katouzian, op. cit., p. 83.

Colonel on Colt bullet: Katouzian, ibid., p. 84.

Shepherd messages to Shah and Ala, and Ala's response: Elm, op. cit., pp. 81–82.

Morrison urges troops toward Iran: Elm, op. cit., p. 83.

Qualities of typical Persian: Goode, op. cit., p. 24.

Foreign Office strategy: Elm, op. cit., p. 84.

Emami on British payroll: Dorril, op. cit., p. 573.

Chapter 6: Unseen Enemies Everywhere

CIA mandate: NSC 10/2, "National Security Council Directive on Office of Special Projects," quoted in Etzold, Thomas H., and Gaddis, John Lewis, *Containment: Documents on American Policy and Strategy, 1945–1950* (New York: Columbia University Press, 1978), pp. 125–128.

NSC-68: *Foreign Relations of the United States, 1950, Vol. I*, pp. 237–292.

Truman points to Iran: Truman conversation with George M. Elsey, June 26, 1950, quoted in Byrne, Malcolm, "The Evolution of U.S. Policy Toward Iran After World War II," in Gasiorowski and Byrne, op. cit.

Baskerville as American Lafayette: Bill, James A., op. cit., p. 17.

American contribution: Farman Farmaian, Sattareh, *Daughter of Persia: A Woman's Journey From Her Father's Harem Through the Islamic Revolution* (New York: Anchor, 1992), pp. 56–57.

Unbounded confidence in America: Cottam, Richard W., *Iran and the United States: A Cold War Case Study* (Pittsburgh: University of Pittsburgh Press, 1988), p. 39.

McGhee finds Shah's plans grandiose: McGhee, op. cit., p. 69.

Nothing in the till: McGhee, ibid., p. 320.

Funkhouser report: *Foreign Relations of the United States, 1950, Vol. V,* pp. 76–96.

One penny more: Bill, op. cit., p. 72.

Fergusson report: Louis, William Roger, "Britain and the Overthrow of the Mossadeq Government," in Gasiorowski and Byrne, op. cit.

McGhee meeting in Istanbul: *Foreign Relations of the United States, 1951, Vol. V,* pp. 60–71.

Bevin on nationalization: Bill and Louis, op. cit., p. 6.

McGhee meets Shah: McGhee, ibid., pp. 326–328.

McGhee meets Shepherd: McGhee, op. cit., p. 326.

Meetings in Washington: *Foreign Relations of the United States 1952–1954, Vol. X,* op. cit., pp. 37–42; also McGhee, op. cit., p. 335.

Radio Tehran's broadcast: Goode, op. cit., p. 31.

Morrison cable to Franks: FO 371/91535, quoted in Elm, op. cit., p. 112.

Acheson on Mossadegh: Chase, James, *Acheson: The Secretary of State Who Created the American World* (New York: Simon and Schuster, 1998), p. 353.

New York Times profile of Mossadegh: May 7, 1951.

State Department recognizes sovereign rights of Iran: Alexander and Nanes, op. cit., p. 216.

Morrison annoyed: FO 371/91535, quoted in Elm, op. cit., p. 17.

Morrison message to Acheson: FO 371/91471, quoted in Abrahamian article in *Science and Society,* op. cit.

Truman exchange with Attlee: *Foreign Relations of the United States 1952–1954, Vol. X,* op. cit., pp. 59–63.

Grady on nationalization: *Wall Street Journal,* June 9, 1951.

Jackson proposal: Elm, op. cit., pp. 115–116.

Iranian oil clearly British property: *Security Council Official Records,* 559th Meeting, October 1, 1951, p. 11.

They will come crawling: *New York Herald Tribune,* July 15, 1951.

Drake on staying forever: Interview in *Mossadegh* (video), op. cit.

Morrison in House of Commons: Elm, op. cit., p. 89.

Patrick Hurley testimony: *Baltimore Sun,* June 21, 1951.

British press on Mossadegh: Abrahamian article in *Science and Society,* op. cit.

Washington Post sees stricken state: April 7, 1951.

New York Times on comparisons of Mossadegh to American patriots: November 8, 1951.

Chicago Daily News on McGhee: June 30, 1951.

Leggett on Anglo-Iranian: FO 371/91522, quoted in Elm, op. cit., p. 90.

Younger on Anglo-Iranian: Sampson, Anthony, *The Seven Sisters: The Great Oil Companies and the World They Made* (New York: Viking, 1975), p. 120.

Mountbatten on Morrison: Elm, op. cit., pp. 90–91.

Labor attaché on Abadan: FO 371/91628, quoted in Elm, ibid., p. 103.

Jerusalem Post: FO 371/91628, citing *Post* article of July 6, 1951, quoted in Elm, ibid., pp. 103–104.

Mossadegh appeal to British technicians: Elm, op. cit., p. 118.

Secret British documents: Elm, op. cit., p. 120.

Throw them to the dogs: Elm, ibid., p. 121.

National Security Council report: NSC 107/2, in *Foreign Relations of the United States 1952–1954, Vol. X,* op. cit., pp. 71–76.

Mossadegh letter to Truman: *Foreign Relations of the United States 1952–1954, Vol. X,* ibid., pp. 77–79.

Grady cable: *Foreign Relations of the United States 1952–1954, Vol. X,* ibid., pp. 79–81.

Shepherd wants to get Mossadegh out: FO 371/91582, quoted in Heiss, op. cit., p. 94.

Iranian minister at The Hague: *New York Times,* July 6, 1951.

Truman letter to Mossadegh: Alexander and Nanes, op. cit., pp. 218–219.

Morrison opposes Harriman mission: *Foreign Relations of the United States 1952–1954, Vol. X,* op. cit., pp. 82–84.

Acheson view of Morrison and Shepherd: Abrams, Rudy, *Spanning the Century: The Life of W. Averell Harriman, 1891–1986* (New York: Morrow, 1992), p. 470.

Shepherd opposes Harriman mission: *New York Herald Tribune,* July 13, 1951.

Foreign Office directs Shepherd to apologize: FO 371/91562, cited in Elm, op. cit., pp. 126–127.

Grady should urge Mossadegh to accept Harriman mission: *Foreign Relations of the United States 1952–1954, Vol. X,* op. cit., p. 88.

Chapter 7: You Do Not Know How Evil They Are

Mossadegh tells Harriman he doesn't know British: Walters, Vernon A., *Silent Missions* (New York: Doubleday, 1978), p. 242.

Mossadegh sends grandson to English school: Walters, ibid., p. 253.

Harriman finds Mossadegh rigid and obsessed: *Foreign Relations of the United States 1952–1954, Vol. X,* op. cit., p. 94.

Harriman's impression of Mossadegh: Abramson, Rudy, op. cit., p. 472.

Mossadegh on foreign influence, and "Tant pis pour nous": Walters, op. cit., pp. 251–252.

Walters on Mossadegh's negotiating style: Walters, ibid., p. 250.

Walters compares Mossadegh to Jimmy Durante: Walters, ibid., p. 248.

Walters's translations: Walters, ibid., pp. 253–254.

Mossadegh on crafty and evil British: Walters, ibid., p. 247.

Levy colloquy: *New York Times,* October 7, 1951.

Harriman's failed news conference: Abramson, op. cit., p. 473.

Harriman meets Kashani: Abramson, op. cit., pp. 474–475; and Walters, ibid., p. 255.

Harriman cable on Anglo-Iranian's absentee management: Abramson, op. cit., p. 476.

Mossadegh agrees to negotiate if British accept nationalization: Abramson, op. cit., p. 476.

Instructions to Stokes: FO 371/91575, quoted in Elm, op. cit., p. 134.

Mossadegh and Stokes on divorce: FO 371/91577, quoted in Elm, op. cit., p. 135.

Stokes finds proposals too transparent: FO 371/91578, quoted in Elm, ibid., p. 137.

Stokes visit to Abadan: FO 371/91580, quoted in Elm, ibid., p. 136.

Harriman shocked by conditions at Abadan: Abramson, op. cit., p. 479.

Harriman says lack of British cooperation endangers his mission: *Foreign Relations of the United States 1952–1954, Vol. X*, op. cit., p. 103.

Harriman's trips to cool off: Walters, op. cit., p. 257.

Stokes told to offer no further concessions: FO 371/91579, quoted in Elm, op. cit., p. 141.

The result is nothing: *Newsweek*, September 3, 1951.

Attlee-Truman exchange: Goode, op. cit., p. 43.

Walters recalls a mission unlike any other: Walters, op. cit., p. 263.

Franks says British troops would have a steadying influence: *Foreign Relations of the United States 1950, Vol. V*, op. cit., pp. 233–237.

Bolton suggests direct intervention: FO 371/91525, quoted in Elm, op. cit., p. 156.

Shinwell doesn't want tail twisted: Elm, ibid., p. 157.

British could bring Africans to Abadan: Elm, op. cit., p. 160.

Plans to invade Abadan: Elm, op. cit., pp. 155–168; and Goode, op. cit., p. 33.

Lord Fraser on dumps and doldrums: Elm, op. cit., p. 162.

Gifford tells Acheson of invasion plans: *Foreign Relations of the United States 1952–1954, Vol. X*, op. cit., pp. 54–55.

Acheson warns Franks against invasion: FO 371/91534, quoted in Elm, op. cit., p. 158.

Wall Street Journal laments threats: April 7, 1951.

Philadelphia Inquirer warns of World War III: August 28, 1951.

Howard K. Smith commentary: May 20, 1951, reported in FO 371/91538, quoted in Elm, op. cit., p. 159.

Morrison on Mossadegh's fanaticism: Morrison, Herbert, *An Autobiography* (London: Odhams, 1960), p. 281.

Acheson warns of disastrous consequences: Elm, op. cit., p. 165.

Attlee tells cabinet there will be no invasion: Elm, op. cit., pp. 166–167.

Lambton advises Foreign Office on propaganda lines: Louis article in Gasiorowski and Byrne, op. cit.

Zaehner combines high thought with low living: Louis article, ibid.

Drake on lack of cooperation with Iranians: Interview in *Mossadegh* (video), op. cit.

British prevent foreign oil experts from traveling to Iran: Elm, op. cit., pp. 148–150.

Foreign Office places advertisements: FO 371/91613, with text of ads, quoted in Elm, ibid., p. 146.

Mason intercepts telegrams: Elm, ibid., pp. 146–147.

Acheson on Grady's strong personality: Acheson, Dean, *Present at the Creation: My Years at the State Department* (New York: Norton, 1969), p. 224.

Henderson considers Mossadegh a madman: Heiss, op. cit., p. 180.

Grady warns against giving Iran a forum: *London Daily Standard*, October 15, 1951.

Acheson warns Morrison against U.N. debate: *Foreign Relations of the United States 1952–1954, Vol. X*, op. cit., p. 201.

Gifford on his meeting with Morrison: *Foreign Relations of the United States 1952–1954, Vol. X*, ibid., p. 205.

Chapter 8: An Immensely Shrewd Old Man

Mossadegh is symbol of surging nationalism: *New York Times,* October 9, 1951.

Daily News on Mossy: *Newsweek,* August 15, 1953.

Mossadegh statement upon arriving in New York: *New York Times,* October 9, 1951.

Newsweek on Mossadegh: August 15, 1953.

Jebb opening statement to Security Council: *Security Council Official Records,* 559th Meeting, October 1, 1951.

New York Times on idle Abadan: October 19, 1951.

Jebb urges Mossadegh not to brood: *Security Council Official Records,* 560th Meeting, October 15, 1951.

Mossadegh speech to Security Council: *Security Council Official Records,* ibid.

Mossadegh and Jebb on British-Iranian friendship: Goode, op. cit., p. 57.

McGhee on Liaquat: McGhee, op. cit., p. 93.

Churchill in Liverpool: *London Times,* October 3, 1951.

Second day of Security Council meeting: *Security Council Official Records,* 561st Meeting, October 16, 1951.

Third day: *Security Council Official Records,* 562nd Meeting, October 17, 1951.

Reston column: *New York Times,* October 18, 1951.

Truman received profile of Mossadegh: *White House Declassified Documents* (Washington: Government Printing Office, 1975), Doc. 780.

Adjectives British applied to Mossadegh: Abrahamian article in *Science & Society,* op. cit.

Mossadegh arrival at Union Station: Acheson, op. cit., pp. 503–504.

Mossadegh meets with Truman: Acheson, ibid., p. 504.

New York Times describes compromise proposal: October 25, 1951.

Strang rejects proposal: FO 371/91609, quoted in Elm, op. cit., p. 187.

Butler on Britain's viability: FO 371/91602, quoted in Elm, ibid., p. 188.

Reston says United States intervened too late: *New York Times,* October 18, 1951.

McGhee's efforts with Mossadegh: McGhee, op. cit., pp. 390–391.

McGhee bids farewell to Mossadegh: McGhee, op. cit., p. 403.

Walters pays final visit to Mossadegh: Walters, op. cit., p. 262.

Egyptian newspapers hail Mossadegh: Elm, p. 193.

Mossadegh and Nahas Pasha issue statement: McGhee, op. cit., p. 404.

Churchill says Attlee had scuttled and run: Dorril, p. 560.

Churchill directs Attlee to be stubborn: FO 371/91609, quoted in Elm, op. cit., p. 189.

Churchill describes Mossadegh as elderly lunatic: Goode, op. cit., pp. 34–35.

McGhee sees almost the end of the world: McGhee, op. cit., p. 403.

Mossadegh as man of the year: *Time,* January 7, 1952.

Chapter 9: Block Headed British

Shah will pack his suitcase: Katouzian, op. cit., p. 122.

Mossadegh argues and faints: Katouzian, op. cit., p. 123; and Musaddiq, Mohammad (edited by Homa Katouzian), *Musaddiq's Memoirs: Dr. Mohammad Musaddiq, Champion of the Popular Movement of Iran and Former Prime Minister* (London: Jebhe, 1988), p. 340.

Mossadegh's resignation letter: Zabih, Sepehr, *The Mossadegh Era: Roots of the Iranian Revolution* (Chicago: Lake View Press, 1982), p. 40.

Mossadegh statement on suspending election: Zabih, ibid., p. 38.

Churchill on Italians: FO 371/10465, quoted in Elm, op. cit., p. 268.

Mossadegh at World Court: Elm, ibid., pp. 208–214; and Heiss, op. cit., p. 129.

Voyage of *Rose Mary:* Heiss, ibid., p. 130.

Mossadegh leaves favorable impression: Elm, op. cit., p. 213.

Drop in oil revenue and Mossadegh reaction: Elm, ibid., pp. 271–272.

Zaehner on Qavam: Katouzian, op. cit., pp. 121–122.

Majlis members split between Mossadegh and Qavam: Zabih, op. cit., pp. 41–41.

Qavam statements as prime minister: Zabih, ibid., p. 44; and Katouzian, op. cit., p. 124.

Kashani denounces Qavam: Elm, op. cit., p. 242.

Tudeh protests against Qavam: Zabih, op. cit., p. 63.

Mossadegh presents Koran to Shah: Elm, op. cit., p. 247.

Mossadegh tells Shah he could go down in history: Zabih, op. cit., p. 66.

Middleton cables: Louis article in Gasiorowski and Byrne, op. cit.

New York Times on Zahedi: August 20, 1953.

MacLean on Zahedi's arrest: MacLean, Fitzroy, *Eastern Approaches* (London: Penguin, 1991), pp. 266–274.

Churchill has no regard for timid diplomatists: Woodhouse, op. cit., p. 125.

Churchill concerned about Jones trip, and exchange with Truman: Elm, op. cit., pp. 250–252; and Goode, op. cit., p. 87.

Acheson says British want rule or ruin: Elm, op. cit., p. 257.

Truman says nationalization has become as sacred as the Koran: Heiss, op. cit., p. 140.

Joint letter to Mossadegh: Elm, op. cit., pp. 250–252.

Mossadegh says Britain has plundered poor nations: Elm, ibid., p. 253.

Churchill urges Truman not to go further: Elm, ibid., p. 254.

Eden on Persian language: Eden, Anthony, *Full Circle: The Memoirs of Sir Anthony Eden* (Boston: Houghton Mifflin, 1960), p. 211.

Acheson on Eden's view of Iranians: Chase, op. cit., p. 353.

Truman letter to Grady: Henry Grady Papers, Box 2, 1952, at Harry Truman Library.

Roosevelt didn't talk spook: *New York Times,* June 11, 2000.

Roosevelt is coolness personified: *The Independent* (London), June 15, 2000.

Roosevelt thinks Republicans might be different: Roosevelt, op. cit., p. 107.

Chapter 10: Pull Up Your Socks and Get Going

Rashidians receive £10,000 monthly: Dorril, op. cit., p. 564; and Woodhouse, op. cit., p. 118.

Recipients of foreign bribes: Service History, op. cit., p. 7.

Description of Rashidian brothers: Bill, op. cit., p. 91.

Woodhouse on Anglo-Iranian directors: Dorril, op. cit., p. 580.

Woodhouse on his Washington presentation: Woodhouse, op. cit, pp. 117–118.

Background of John Foster Dulles: Preussen, Ronald W., *John Foster Dulles: The Road to Power* (New York: Free Press, 1982).

Background of Allen Dulles: Grose, Peter, *Gentleman Spy: The Life of Allen Dulles* (Boston: Houghton Mifflin, 1994).

Allen Dulles urges CIA to launch worldwide covert action program: Grose, ibid., p. 292.

Smith tells Roosevelt to get going: Roosevelt, op. cit., pp. 115–116.

Henderson says Mossadegh lacks stability: Goode, op. cit., p. 82.

Henderson on National Front: Ambrose, op. cit., p. 109.

Joint cable from Henderson and Middleton: Brands, op. cit., p. 272.

Henderson in touch with Zahedi: Brands, ibid., pp. 272–279.

United States can no longer approve of Mossadegh government: Service History, op. cit., p. 2.

Eisenhower complains about British efforts: Elm, op. cit., p. 277.

Sinclair visits Washington: Louis article in Gasiorowski and Byrne, ibid.

Shah in hysterical state: *Foreign Relations of the United States 1952–1954, Vol. X,* op. cit., pp. 681–683.

Shaban crashes through gate: Kennett Love article in Allen Dulles papers, op. cit.; and *New York Times,* August 23, 1953.

Mob organized by Kashani: FO 371/10562, quoted in Elm, op. cit., p. 295.

Allen Dulles warns of communist takeover: *Foreign Relations of the United States 1952–1954, Vol. X,* op. cit., p. 689.

March 4 meeting of National Security Council: *Foreign Relations of the United States 1952–1954, Vol. X,* op. cit., p. 693.

Eisenhower considers Mossadegh only hope for West and wants to give him $10 million: FO 371/104614, quoted in Elm, op. cit., pp. 282–283.

Dulles and Eden issue communiqué: Elm, op. cit., pp. 277–283.

Pardon for Tahmasibi: Azimi, Fakhreddin, *Iran: The Crisis of Democracy 1941–53* (London: I. B. Tauris, 1989), p. 298.

Zaehner report on splitting National Front: Abrahamian article in *Science & Society,* op. cit.

Eisenhower has real doubts: *Foreign Relations of the United States 1952–1954, Vol. X,* op. cit., p. 713.

Wisner says CIA ready to discuss plot: Louis article in Gasiorowski and Byrne, op. cit.

Allen Dulles approves $1 million: Service History, op. cit., p. 3.

Afshartus kidnapping: Louis article in Gasiorowski and Byrne, op. cit., note 170; and Dorril, op. cit., p. 585.

Eisenhower letter to Mossadegh: *New York Times,* July 10, 1953.

Eisenhower and Churchill approve plot: Service History, op. cit., p. vi; Prados, John, *Presidents' Secret Wars: CIA and Pentagon Covert Operations Since World War II* (New York: William Morrow, 1986), p. 95; Dorril, op. cit., p. 587; Woodhouse, op. cit., p. 125; and Louis article in Gasiorowski and Byrne, op. cit.

Wilber and Darbyshire begin work in Cyprus: Service History, op. cit., pp. 5–6.

Initial plan for coup: Service History, pp. B1–B10 and 16–18; and Gasiorowski article in Gasiorowski and Byrne, op. cit.

Dulles on getting rid of this madman: Roosevelt, op. cit., p. 8.

Dulles polls advisers and then decides to get going: Roosevelt, ibid., p. 18; Elm, op. cit., p. 299; and Bill and Louis, op. cit., p. 283.

Bohlen opposes coup: FO371/98603.

Goiran opposes coup: Dorril, op. cit., p. 584.

Bedamn budget compared to worldwide covert action budget: Gasiorowski article in Gasiorowski and Byrne, op. cit.

John Foster Dulles asks Allen Dulles if plot is still on: *Foreign Relations of the United States 1952–1954, Vol. X,* op. cit., p. 737.

John Foster Dulles makes public statement: *Foreign Relations of the United States 1952–1954, Vol. X,* op. cit., p. 338.

Wilber on anti-government propaganda: Wilber, Donald N., *Adventures in the Middle East: Excursions and Incursions* (Princeton, N.J.: Darwin, 1986), pp. 188–189.

Chapter 11: I Knew It! They Love Me!

For sources of information about the events of mid-August 1953 in Tehran, see notes for Chapter 1.

Roosevelt meets Zahedi: Roosevelt, op. cit., pp. 166–167; and Service History, p. 45.

Smith on snuggling up to Mossadegh: *Foreign Relations of the United States 1952–1954, Vol. X,* op. cit., p. 748.

Ardeshir Zahedi receives journalists: Kennett Love article, op. cit.; and Dorril, op. cit., p. 592.

Love on copying machine: *Anatomy of a Coup* (video), op. cit.

Roosevelt had sent Rashidians to Washington: Roosevelt, op. cit., p. 80.

Jalili and Keyvani vitally important: *Service History,* op. cit., p. 7.

Fatemi on royal robbery: *London Times,* August 17, 1953.

McClure mission: Elm, op. cit., p. 306; and Service History, op. cit., p. 46.

Jalili and Keyvani prefer money to execution: Dorril, op. cit., p. 595; and Gasiorowski article in Gasiorowski and Byrne, op. cit.

Roosevelt sees slight chance of success: Service History, op. cit., p. 51.

Roosevelt prepares escape plan: Gasiorowski article in *International Journal,* op. cit.

Love on military-looking car: *Mossadegh* (video), op. cit.

Roosevelt on anti-Shah protesters: Roosevelt, op. cit., p. 180.

Roosevelt admits small complications, gives Henderson assignment: Roosevelt, ibid., pp. 183–184.

Roosevelt describes Mossadegh as old bugger: Roosevelt, op. cit., p. 163.

Monday was active and trying time: Service History, op. cit., p. 56.

Riots scare Roosevelt: Roosevelt, op. cit., p. 179.

Henderson meets Mossadegh: Roosevelt, op. cit., p. 185; and *Foreign Relations of the United States 1952–1954, Vol. X,* op. cit., p. 750.

Mossadegh's fatal mistake: *Time,* August 31, 1953.

Daftary leads troops to royalist side: Dorril, op. cit., p. 593; and Katouzian, op. cit., p. 191.

New York Times on policemen swinging into action: August 19, 1953.

Shah arrives in Rome: *London Times,* August 19, 1953.

Shah doesn't expect to return home in immediate future: *New York Times,* August 19, 1953.

Shah likely to join colony of exiled monarchs: *London Daily Telegraph,* August 19, 1953.

Waller on crowds in Iran: *Anatomy of a Coup* (video), op. cit.

Ten thousand dollars sent to Kashani: Dorril, op. cit., p. 593; and Gasiorowski article in *International Journal,* op. cit.

Zirkaneh giants: Ambrose, *Ike's Spies,* op. cit., p. 210.

Mossadegh refuses to arm Tudeh: Author's interview with former Tehran mayor, Nosratollah Amini, June 23, 2002; and Lapping, op. cit., p. 215.

Tribal chiefs paid by Roosevelt's agents: Gasiorowski article in Gasiorowski and Byrne, op. cit.

New York Times on bully-boys: August 23, 1953.

Cottam on mob: *Mossadegh* (video), op. cit.

Smith exchanges cables with Roosevelt: Roosevelt, op. cit., p. 190.

Roosevelt hears radio broadcast: Roosevelt, ibid., pp. 187–191.

Roosevelt fetches Zahedi: Roosevelt, op. cit., pp. 193–194.

Roosevelt toasts impending victory: Roosevelt, ibid., p. 194.

Radio plays "Star-Spangled Banner": Interview with Malcolm Byrne in *Anatomy of a Coup* (video), op. cit.

Shah and Empress react to news of coup: *London Times,* August 20, 1953.

Shah regrets not playing important part: *New York Times,* August 19, 1953.

Mossadegh says he prefers to die: Saheb interview in *Mossadegh* (video), op. cit.

Kissing party: Elm, op. cit., pp. 307–308; and Katouzian, op. cit., p. 192.

Roosevelt and comrades full of jubilation: Roosevelt, op. cit., p. 195.

Meeting of Roosevelt, Henderson, and Ardeshir Zahedi: Roosevelt, ibid., pp. 195–196.

Roosevelt speaks at victory party: Roosevelt, ibid., pp. 195–197.

Some victims had banknotes in their pockets: Elm, op. cit., p. 308.

Three hundred killed: *New York Times,* August 20, 1953; and *Time,* August 31, 1953.

New York Times on sudden reversal: August 23, 1953.

Associated Press on Zahedi's coup: *Chicago Tribune,* August 20, 1953.

A day that should never have ended: Secret History, op. cit., p. 77.

Zahedi sends Batmanqelich to pick up Mossadegh: Diba, op. cit., p. 186.

Mossadegh arrives and greets Zahedi: *Chicago Tribune,* August 21, 1953.

Zahedi orders that Mossadegh be addressed respectfully: *Chicago Tribune,* August 21, 1953.

British airliner unsuitable: London *Times,* August 21, 1953.

Dutch airline charter: *New York Times,* August 23, 1953.

Shah on Mossadegh's crimes: *New York Times,* August 23, 1953.

Shah's airport reception: *New York Times,* August 23, 1953.

Shah's radio speech: London *Times,* August 24, 1953.

Zahedi will send Mossadegh to city jail: London *Times,* August 24, 1953.

Zahedi's government receives millions from CIA: Service History, op. cit., p. xiii.

Zahedi receives $1 million for himself: Gasiorowski, *US Foreign Policy and the Shah,* op. cit., p. 90.

Roosevelt's final meeting with Shah: Roosevelt, pp. 199–202.

Roosevelt leaves with tears in his eyes: Roosevelt, ibid., p. 203.

Chapter 12: Purring Like a Giant Cat

Mossadegh on his only crime: Musaddiq, op. cit., p. 74.

Riot outside Mossadegh's home: Author's interview with Mahmoud Mossadegh, August 19, 2002.

Officers arrested and executed: Diba, op. cit., p. 191.

Tudeh activists executed: Abrahamian, Ervand, *Iran between Two Revolutions* (Princeton, N.J.: Princeton University Press, 1982), p. 280.

Fatemi on traitor Shah, and snake who bites: Goode, op. cit., p. 123.

1962 rally: Diba, op. cit., p. 193.

Mossadegh wants God to take him: Musaddiq, op. cit., p. 80.

Consortium agreement: Elm, op. cit, pp. 310–331; Heiss, op. cit., pp. 187–220; and Goode, op. cit., pp. 138–153.

Shah on Mossadegh's xenophobia: Pahlavi, Mohammad Reza, *Mission for My Country* (New York, McGraw-Hill, 1960), pp. 302, 127.

Shah on Mossadegh's nationalism: Pahlavi, Mohammad Reza, *Answer to History* (New York: Stein and Day, 1980), p. 84.

Shah on worst years of his life: Goode, op. cit., p. 155.

Bakhtiar visits Mossadegh's grave: Goode, ibid., p. xiii.

Khomeini rants at Bakhtiar: Farmanfarmaian, op. cit., p. 452.

Ardeshir Zahedi denies CIA involvement: Zahedi, Ardeshir, "What Really Happened," www.ardeshirzahedi.com.

Shaban receives Cadillac: Diba, op. cit., p. 190.

Ashraf on unsubstantiated allegations: Pahlavi, Ashraf, *Faces in a Mirror* (Englewood Cliffs, N.J.: Prentice-Hall, 1980), p. xiv.

Dulles on Woodhouse's nice little egg: Dorril, op. cit., p. 596.

Woodhouse on first step toward catastrophe: Woodhouse, op. cit., p. 131.

Morrison recalls little about Iran: Morrison, op. cit., pp. 281–282.

Eden defends decision not to wage war: Eden, op. cit., pp. 246–247.

Eden on Morrison: Harris, Kenneth, *Attlee* (London: Weidenfeld and Nicholson, 1982), p. 472.

Churchill considers Ajax finest operation: Service History, op. cit., p. 81.

Roosevelt meets Churchill: Roosevelt, op. cit., p. 207.

Eisenhower awards medal to Roosevelt: Prados, op. cit., pp. 91–92.

Hostage-taker fears another coup: Zahrani, Mostafa T., "The Coup That Changed the Middle East: Mossadeq v. the CIA in Retrospect," in *World Policy Journal* (Summer 2002).

Khamenei says his movement not like Mossadegh's: Abrahamian article, op. cit.

Iranian intellectual on legacy of coup: Zahrani article in *World Policy Journal*, op. cit.

Waller defends coup: Statement to conference in Oxford, England, June 10, 2002.

Falle on legacy: Falle, op. cit., p. 81.

Tudeh strength exaggerated: Gasiorowski article in Gasiorowski and Byrne, op. cit.; Behrooz, "The 1953 Coup in Iran and the Legacy of the Tudeh," in Gasiorowski and Byrne, ibid.; and Abrahamian article in *Science & Society*, op. cit.

Acheson on losing so much so stupidly: Acheson, op. cit., p. 503.

Acheson on Mossadegh's responsibility: Acheson, ibid., p. 504.

Nixon on Acheson's cowardly college: *New York Times*, November 2, 1952.

Dulles purrs: Roosevelt, op. cit., p. 209.

Bakhtiar says Mossadegh should have shot plotters: *Mossadegh* (video), op. cit.

CIA says some facts will never be known: Service History, op. cit., p. 67.

Eisenhower meets Shah: *New York Times*, December 15, 1959.

Eisenhower refers obliquely to coup: Eisenhower, Dwight, *Mandate for Change: The White House Years, 1953–1956* (Garden City, N.Y.: Doubleday, 1963), p. 164;

and Ambrose, Stephen, *Eisenhower: The President* (New York: Simon and Schuster, 1984), p. 129.

Albright acknowledges American responsibility: *New York Times,* March 18, 2000.

Bill on legacy: Bill, op. cit., pp. 288–289.

Cottam on legacy: Cottam, *Iran and the United States,* op. cit., pp. 261–263.

Gasiorowski on legacy: Gasiorowski article in *International Journal,* op. cit.

Goode on legacy: Goode, op. cit., p. 124.

Heiss on legacy: Heiss, op. cit., pp. 234–238.

Keddie on legacy: Keddie, op. cit., pp. 142, 275–276.

Louis on legacy: Bill and Louis, op. cit., pp. 255–256.

BIBLIOGRAPHY

Abrahamian, Ervand. *Iran Between Two Revolutions* (Princeton, N.J.: Princeton University Press, 1982).

——. "The 1953 Coup in Iran" (article), in *Science & Society*, vol. 65, no. 2 (Summer 2001).

Abramson, Rudy. *Spanning the Century: The Life of W. Averell Harriman, 1891–1986* (New York: William Morrow, 1992).

Acheson, Dean. *Present at the Creation: My Years at the State Department* (New York: Norton, 1969).

Afary, Janet. *The Iranian Constitutional Revolution, 1906–1911: Grassroots Democracy, Social Democracy, and the Origins of Feminism* (New York: Columbia University Press, 1996).

Akhavi, Sharough. *Religion and Politics in Contemporary Iran: Clergy State Relations in the Pahlavi Period* (Albany: State University of New York Press, 1980).

Alexander, Yonah, and Nanes, Allen (editors). *The United States and Iran: A Documentary History* (Frederick, Md.: Alethia Books, 1980).

Ambrose, Stephen. *Eisenhower: The President* (New York: Simon and Schuster, 1984).

——, with Immerman, Richard H. *Ike's Spies: Eisenhower and the Intelligence Establishment* (Garden City, N.Y.: Doubleday, 1981).

Amirsadeghi, Hossein (editor). *Twentieth-Century Iran* (London: Heinemann, 1977).

Andrew, Christopher. *Secret Service: The Making of the British Intelligence Community* (London: Heinemann, 1985).

Arab, Gholam Hossein. *Isfahan* (Tehran: Farhangsara, 1996).

Arfa, Hassan. *Under Five Shahs* (New York: William Morrow, 1965).

Arjomand, Said Amir. *The Shadow of God and the Hidden Imam* (Chicago: University of Chicago Press, 1984).

——. *The Turban for the Crown: The Islamic Revolution in Iran* (New York: Oxford, 1988).

Attlee, Clement R. *As It Happened: The Autobiography of Clement R. Attlee* (New York: Viking, 1954).

Avery, Peter. *Modern Iran* (New York: Praeger, 1965).

——, et al. (editors). *The Cambridge History of Iran* (7 vols.) (Cambridge, U.K.: Cambridge University Press, 1968–1991).

Azimi, Fakhreddin. *Iran: The Crisis of Democracy 1941–53* (London: I. B. Tauris, 1989).

Bamberg, J. H. *The History of the British Petroleum Company: Volume II: The Anglo-Iranian Years, 1928–1954* (Cambridge, U.K.: Cambridge University Press, 1994).

Banani, Amin. *The Modernization of Iran 1924–41* (Stanford, Calif.: Stanford University Press, 1966).

Bayat, Mangol. *Iran's First Revolution: Shi'ism and the Constitutional Revolution of 1905–6* (New York: Oxford University Press, 1991).

Bill, James A. *The Eagle and the Lion: The Tragedy of American-Iranian Relations* (New Haven, Conn.: Yale University Press, 1988).

—— and Louis, William Roger (editors). *Mussadiq, Iranian Nationalism, and Oil* (London: I. B. Tauris, 1988).

Blair, John M. *The Control of Oil* (New York: Pantheon, 1976).

Brands, H. W. *Inside the Cold War: Loy Henderson and the Rise of the American Empire 1918–1961* (New York: Oxford University Press, 1991).

Brock, Ray. *Blood, Oil and Sand* (Cleveland: World, 1952).

Butler, D. E. *The British General Election of 1951* (London: Macmillan, 1952).

Central Intelligence Agency (written by Donald N. Wilber). *Overthrow of Premier Mossadeq of Iran, November 1952–August 1953* (Clandestine Service History, 1954, unpublished); summary published in *New York Times,* April 16, 2000, text available at www.nytimes.com.

Chace, James. *Acheson: The Secretary of State Who Created the American World* (New York: Simon and Schuster, 1998).

Churchill, Winston S. *The World Crisis, Volume I* (New York: Scribners, 1928).

Cottam, Richard W. *Nationalism in Iran* (Pittsburgh: University of Pittsburgh Press, 1979).

——. *Iran and the United States: A Cold War Case Study* (Pittsburgh: University of Pittsburgh Press, 1988).

Curzon, George Nathaniel. *Persia and the Persian Question* (London: Longmans, Green and Co., 1892).

Department of State. *Foreign Relations of the United States 1952–1954, Volume X: Iran 1952–1954* (Washington, D.C.: Government Printing Office, 1989).

Diba, Farhad. *Mohammad Mossadegh: A Political Biography* (London: Croom Helm, 1986).

Donoughue, Bernard, and Jones, G. W. *Herbert Morrison: Portrait of a Politician* (London: Weidenfeld and Nicholson, 1973).

Donovan, John C. *The Cold Warriors: A Policy-Making Elite* (Lexington, Mass.: Heath, 1974).

Donovan, Robert A. *Conflict and Crisis: The Presidency of Harry S Truman 1948–1953* (New York: Norton, 1982).

Dorril, Stephen. *MI6: Inside the Covert World of Her Majesty's Secret Intelligence Service* (New York: Free Press, 2000).

Dulles, Allen. *The Craft of Intelligence* (New York: Harper and Row, 1963).

Durraj, Manocher. *From Zarathustra to Khomeini: Popular Dissent in Iran* (Boulder, Colo.: Lynne Rienner, 1990).

Eden, Anthony. *Full Circle: The Memoirs of Sir Anthony Eden* (Boston: Houghton Mifflin, 1960).

Eisenhower, Dwight. *Mandate for Change: The White House Years, 1953–1956* (Garden City, N.Y.: Doubleday, 1963).

Elm, Mostafa. *Oil, Power and Principle: Iran's Oil Nationalization and Its Aftermath* (Syracuse, N.Y.: Syracuse University Press, 1992).

Elwell-Sutton, L. P. *Persian Oil: A Study in Power Politics* (London: Lawrence and Wishart, 1955).

Etzold, Thomas H., and Gaddis, John Lewis. *Containment: Documents on American Policy and Strategy, 1945–1950* (New York: Columbia University Press, 1978).

Eveland, Wilbur C. *Ropes of Sand: America's Failure in the Middle East* (New York: Norton, 1980).

Falle, Sam. *My Lucky Life in War, Revolution, Peace and Diplomacy* (Lewes, Sussex: Book Guild, 1996).

Farman Farmaian, Sattareh. *Daughter of Persia: A Woman's Journey From Her Father's Harem Through the Islamic Revolution* (New York: Anchor, 1992).

Farmanfarmaian, Manucher, and Farmanfarmaian, Roxane. *Blood and Oil: Inside the Shah's Iran* (New York: Modern Library, 1999).

Fatemi, Faramarz S. *The U.S.S.R. in Iran: The Background History of Russian and Anglo-American Conflict in Iran and Its Effect on Iranian Nationalism and the Fall of the Shah* (South Brunswick, N.J.: Barnes, 1980).

Fatemi, Nasrollah Saifpour. *Oil Diplomacy: Powderkeg in Iran* (New York: Whittier Books, 1954).

Ferrier, R. W. *The History of the British Petroleum Company: Volume I: The Developing Years, 1901–1932* (London: Cambridge University Press, 1982).

Foran, John (editor). *A Century of Revolution: Social Movements in Iran* (Minneapolis: University of Minnesota Press, 1994).

Forbis, William H. *Fall of the Peacock Throne: The Story of Iran* (New York: Harper and Row, 1980).

Ford, Alan W. *The Anglo-Iranian Oil Dispute of 1951–1952* (Berkeley: University of California Press, 1954).

Gasiorowski, Mark J. *U.S. Foreign Policy and the Shah: Building a Client State in Iran* (Ithaca, N.Y.: Cornell University Press, 1991).

——. "The 1953 Coup d'Etat in Iran" (article), *International Journal of Middle East Studies,* no. 19 (1987).

——, and Byrne, Malcolm (editors). *Mohammad Mossadeq and the 1953 Coup in Iran* (Syracuse, N.Y.: Syracuse University Press, forthcoming 2003).

Ghani, Cyrus. *Iran and the Rise of Reza Shah: From Qajar Collapse to Pahlavi Power* (London: I. B. Tauris, 2000).

Ghods, M. Reza. *Iran in the Twentieth Century: A Political History* (Boulder, Colo.: Lynne Rienner, 1989).

Gilbert, Martin. *Winston S. Churchill: Volume VIII: Never Despair, 1945–1965* (Boston: Houghton Mifflin, 1988).

Goode, James F. *The United States and Iran: In the Shadow of Mussadiq* (New York: St. Martin's, 1997).

Graham, Robert. *Iran: The Illusion of Power* (New York: St. Martin's, 1980).

Grose, Peter. *Gentleman Spy: The Life of Allen Dulles* (Boston: Houghton Mifflin, 1994).

Hairi, Abdul-Hadi. *Shi'ism and Constitutionalism in Iran* (Leiden, The Netherlands: E. J. Brill, 1977).

Halliday, Fred. *Iran: Dictatorship and Development* (London: Penguin, 1980).

Hamilton, Charles W. *Americans and Oil in the Middle East* (Houston: Gulf Publishing, 1962).

Harris, Kenneth. *Attlee* (London: Weidenfeld and Nicholson, 1982).

Heikal, Mohamed. *Iran, the Untold Story: An Insider's Account of America's Iranian Adventure and Its Consequences for the Future* (New York: Pantheon, 1982).

Heiss, Mary Ann. *Empire and Nationhood: The United States, Great Britain, and Iranian Oil, 1950–1954* (New York: Columbia University Press, 1997).

History Channel. *Anatomy of a Coup: The CIA in Iran* (video), Catalogue No. AAE-43021.

Iranian Movies. *Mossadegh and the 1953 Coup by CIA* (video), Tape No. 3313, IranianMovies.com.

Irving, Clyde. *Crossroads of Civilization: 3,000 Years of Persian History* (New York: Barnes & Noble, 1979).

Jeffreys-Jones, Rhodri. *The CIA and American Democracy* (New Haven, Conn.: Yale University Press, 1989).

Katouzian, Homa. *The Political Economy of Modern Iran: Despotism and Pseudo-Modernism 1926–79* (New York: New York University Press, 1981).

——. *Mussadiq and the Struggle for Power in Iran* (London: I. B. Tauris, 1999).

Keddie, Nikki R. *Religion and Rebellion in Iran: The Tobacco Protest of 1891–1892* (London: Frank Cass, 1966).

——. *Roots of Revolution: An Interpretive History of Modern Iran* (New Haven, Conn.: Yale University Press, 1981).

——, and Gasiorowski, Mark J. (editors). *Neither East nor West: Iran, the Soviet Union, and the United States* (New Haven, Conn.: Yale University Press, 1990).

Krause, Walter W. *Soraya, Queen of Persia* (London: Macdonald, 1956).

Lapping, Brian. *End of Empire* (London: Granada, 1985).

Ledeen, Michael, and Lewis, William. *Debacle: American Failure in Iran* (New York: Alfred A. Knopf, 1981).

Lenczowski, George. *Iran Under the Pahlavis* (Stanford: Hoover Institute, 1978).

Levy, Walter J. *Oil Strategy and Politics, 1941–1981* (Boulder, Colo.: Westview, 1982).

Limbert, John W. *Iran: At War with History* (Boulder, Colo.: Westview, 1987).

Longhurst, Henry. *Adventure in Oil: The Story of British Petroleum* (London: Sidgwick and Jackson, 1959).

Longrigg, Stephen H. *Oil in the Middle East: Its Discovery and Development* (Oxford: Oxford University Press, 1968).

Louis, William Roger. *The British Empire in the Middle East 1945–1951* (Oxford: Oxford University Press, 1984).

Love, Kennett. *The American Role in the Pahlavi Restoration on August 19, 1953* (unpublished), the Allen Dulles Papers, Princeton University (1960).

Lytle, Mark Hamilton. *The Origins of the Iranian-American Alliance 1941–1953* (New York: Holmes and Meier, 1987).

Mackey, Sandra. *The Iranians: Persia, Islam and the Soul of a Nation* (New York: Plume, 1998).

MacLean, Fitzroy. *Eastern Approaches* (London: Penguin, 1991).

Martin, Vanessa. *Islam and Modernism: The Iranian Revolution of 1906* (Syracuse, N.Y.: Syracuse University Press, 1989).

McGhee, George. *Envoy to the Middle World: Adventures in Diplomacy* (New York: Harper and Row, 1983).

McLellan, David S. *Dean Acheson: The State Department Years* (New York: Dodd, Mead, 1976).

Milani, Mohsen M. *The Making of Iran's Islamic Revolution: From Monarchy to Islamic Republic* (Boulder, Colo.: Westview, 1994).

Millspaugh, Arthur C. *American in Persia* (Washington, D.C.: Brookings Institution, 1946).

Monroe, Elizabeth. *Britain's Moment in the Middle East, 1914–1971* (Baltimore: Johns Hopkins University Press, 1981).

Morrison, Herbert. *An Autobiography* (London: Odhams, 1960).

Mosley, Leonard. *Power Play: The Tumultuous World of Middle East Oil, 1890–1973* (London: Weidenfeld and Nicholson, 1973).

Mottahedeh, Roy. *The Mantle of the Prophet: Religion and Politics in Iran* (New York: Pantheon, 1985).

Musaddiq, Mohammad (edited by Homa Katouzian). *Musaddiq's Memoirs: Dr. Mohammad Musaddiq, Champion of the Popular Movement of Iran and Former Prime Minister* (London: Jebhe, 1988).

Nicholson, Harold. *Curzon: The Last Phase, 1919–1925* (London: Constable, 1934).

Pahlavi, Ashraf. *Faces in a Mirror* (Englewood Cliffs, N.J.: Prentice-Hall, 1980).

Pahlavi, Mohammad Reza. *Mission for My Country* (New York, McGraw-Hill, 1960).

———. *Answer to History* (New York: Stein and Day, 1980).

Prados, John. *Presidents' Secret Wars: CIA and Pentagon Covert Operations Since World War II* (New York: William Morrow, 1986).

Preussen, Ronald W. *John Foster Dulles: The Road to Power* (New York: Free Press, 1982).

Ramazani, Rouhullah K. *Iran's Foreign Policy 1941–1973* (Charlottesville: University Press of Virginia, 1975).

———. *The United States and Iran: Patterns of Influence* (New York: Praeger, 1982).

Rand, Christopher T. *Making Democracy Safe for Oil: Oilmen and the Islamic East* (Boston: Little Brown, 1975).

Roosevelt, Kermit. *Countercoup: The Struggle for Control of Iran* (New York: McGraw-Hill, 1979).

Rose, Kenneth. *Superior Person: A Portrait of Curzon and His Circle in Late Victorian England* (New York: Weybright and Talley, 1969).

Rubin, Barry. *Paved with Good Intentions: The American Experience and Iran* (New York: Oxford University Press, 1980).

Saikal, Amin. *The Rise and Fall of the Shah* (Princeton, N.J.: Princeton University Press, 1980).

Sampson, Anthony. *The Seven Sisters: The Great Oil Companies and the World They Made* (New York: Viking, 1975).

Schwarzkopf, H. Norman. *It Doesn't Take a Hero* (New York: Bantam, 1992).

Seldon, Anthony. *Churchill's Indian Summer: The Conservative Government 1951–1955* (London: Hodder and Stoughton, 1981).

Shawcross, William. *The Shah's Last Ride: The Fate of an Ally* (New York: Simon and Schuster, 1988).

Shuster, William Morgan. *The Strangling of Persia* (New York: Century, 1912).

Sick, Gary. *All Fall Down: America's Tragic Encounter with Iran* (New York: Random House, 1985).

Stassen, Harold, and Houts, Marshall. *Eisenhower: Turning the World Toward Peace* (St. Paul, Minn.: Merrill Magnus, 1990).

Tabataba'i, Allamah Sayyid Muhammad Husayn. *Shi'ite Islam* (Albany: State University of New York Press, 1977).

Truman, Harry S. *Years of Trial and Hope, 1946–53* (Garden City, N.Y.: Doubleday, 1978).

Vicker, Ray. *Kingdom of Oil: The Middle East, Its People and Its Power* (New York: Charles Scribner's Sons, 1974).

Walters, Vernon A. *Silent Missions* (New York: Doubleday, 1978).

Warne, William E. *Mission for Peace: Point Four in Iran* (New York: Bobbs-Merrill, 1956).

Wilber, Donald N. *Adventures in the Middle East: Excursions and Incursions* (Princeton, N. J.: Darwin, 1986).

——. *Contemporary Iran* (New York: Praeger, 1963).

——. *Iran: Past and Present* (Princeton, N. J.: Princeton University Press, 1976).

Woodhouse, C. M. *Something Ventured* (London: Granada, 1982).

Wright, Denis. *The Persians Amongst the English: Episodes in Anglo-Persian History* (London: I. B. Tauris, 1985).

Yergin, Daniel. *The Prize: The Epic Quest for Oil, Money and Power* (New York: Simon and Schuster, 1991).

Zabih, Sepehr. *The Mossadegh Era: Roots of the Iranian Revolution* (Chicago: Lake View Press, 1982).

INDEX

Adolescents after Divorce

Adolescents
after Divorce

Christy M. Buchanan

Eleanor E. Maccoby

Sanford M. Dornbusch

HARVARD UNIVERSITY PRESS

Cambridge, Massachusetts · London, England · 1996

12-00

#34410069

Library of Congress Cataloging-in-Publication Data

Buchanan, Christy M.
  Adolescents after divorce / Christy M. Buchanan, Eleanor E.
Maccoby, Sanford M. Dornbusch.
    p. cm.
  Includes bibliographical references and index.
  ISBN 0-674-00517-1 (alk. paper)
  1. Children of divorced parents—United States—Attitudes.
2. Teenagers—United States—Attitudes. 3. Divorce—United States.
4. Divorce—Psychological aspects. I. Maccoby, Eleanor E., 1917– .
II. Dornbusch, Sanford M. III. Title.
HQ777.5.B796 1996
306.874—dc20   96-11882

To the adolescents who trusted us
with their feelings and
experiences,
and who responded so thoughtfully
and candidly to our questions

CONTENTS

PREFACE

The decision to divorce is grueling for most parents, who often worry heavily about the impact of divorce on their children. Like other parents, those who divorce want to provide their children with the opportunities to develop into well-functioning, happy, responsible, independent adults. And despite doomsayers' predictions concerning the impact of divorce and "broken families" on children and society, research clearly shows that many children adapt quite well after their parents' divorce. Perhaps even more children would thrive if more information and more support were provided for divorcing parents and the professionals who work with them.

This book was written in an effort to help those parents whose best or only option is divorce. Our research was conducted under the assumption that, for good or ill, divorces will continue to happen. Our aim was never to argue for or against divorce. Rather, we wanted to find out what circumstances of family life after divorce were associated with good adjustment on the part of children, so that both parents and professionals could enhance children's development. With the indispensable help of over five hundred adolescents, we discovered much about what matters—and what does not matter—with respect to adolescents' well-being after divorce. Our hope is that making this information available will aid and encourage parents in this difficult situation, and ultimately improve the lives of their children.

Some of the findings reported in Chapters 4, 5, and 6 were previously reported in Buchanan, Maccoby, and Dornbusch (1992). Certain findings in Chapter 11 previously appeared in Buchanan, Maccoby, and Dornbusch (1991).

We are tremendously grateful for the generous support of the W. T. Grant Foundation (grant no. 88119688 to Eleanor E. Maccoby and Sanford M. Dornbusch) and of the Center for the Study of Families, Children, and Youth at Stanford University. Our thanks also go to Wake Forest University, whose summer support for faculty and other resources contributed in important ways to the completion of this book. We are indebted to Sue Dimicelli and Patricia Weaver, who demonstrated extraordinary commitment to this project, helping with a wide variety of tasks ranging from endless typing to data analysis. Their hard work, as well as their support and encouragement, made our lives less stressful throughout every phase of this endeavor. We are also grateful for the good work of the interviewers, for the research assistance of Sue Monahan, and for the advice and comments of our colleagues Lee Cronbach and Kate Funder and two reviewers. Finally, this project would not have been possible without the patience and enduring support of our families. We especially want to thank Jeff, Kelly, Riley, Brady, Mac, and Red.

February 1996

Concepts and Methods

1

Introduction

Each year, a large new group of children joins the growing number of those whose parents have divorced. For at least some period of time, these children must adapt to life in a single-parent family. From the child's standpoint, the loss of the familiar everyday presence of the parent who has left the household is often a major event that initiates a cascade of consequences. Although many families attempt to make up for this loss by arranging visitation with the "outside" parent, it is a very different situation for the child to spend time with the two parents in two different households than it was to see them together in the same setting. In addition, the child's new life may involve a change in neighborhood or school, new caretakers while the custodial parent works longer hours, and a substantial drop in standard of living.

Much has been written concerning the adjustment of children whose parents have divorced. These children have been compared with children in nondivorced families to see what kinds of adjustment problems, if any, occur when parents have separated. There is evidence that parental divorce does, indeed, increase the risk of several forms of maladaptation in children. But popular articles on the subject (for example, Whitehead, 1993) not only exaggerate the risks but oversimplify the issues. For example, we now know that many of the problems seen in children from divorced families were evident before the parents separated (Block, Block, and Gjerde, 1986; Cherlin et al., 1991), so that the problems cannot be attributed simply to the divorce itself. Furthermore, the dictum "Two parents are better than one," while generally true, needs to be qualified to read "Two *allied* parents are better than one" (Amato and Keith, 1991; Emery, 1982; Peterson and Zill, 1986). And popular writings tend to lose sight of the fact that many children with divorced parents

3

function adequately or even exceptionally well, especially after the initial disrupted period following parental separation has passed (Amato and Keith, 1991; Chase-Lansdale, Cherlin, and Kiernan, 1995).

The first central fact that needs to be understood is the enormous diversity in postdivorce family life (Amato, 1993; Barber and Eccles, 1992; Furstenberg, 1990). The second is the dynamic quality of the post-divorce period—the fact that divorce is not just one event, but part of a set of changes that unfold over time. Some children adapt well to these changes, and get on with their developmental agendas. Others falter or even regress. Our purpose in this book is not to pursue the question of whether divorce is good or bad for children. We take seriously the fact that there is a great deal of variability in how children adjust to divorce. Thus we seek to understand the conditions that make divorce more or less difficult for children—that enable some to cope with their new and changing life situation in positive ways and that interfere with positive adaptation for others. We have no wish to downplay the grief, the sense of betrayal, the disorientation, that children experience when their parents separate. We believe that the optimal situation for children's development is, in most cases, living in a single household with two parents, both of whom are committed to the children's welfare and who are able to cooperate with each other—when such a family setting is a real possibility. But the main question we are asking is not how marriages might be made more stable—important though that issue is—but how to optimize the life chances of children whose parents do divorce.

Factors That May Affect Children's Postdivorce Functioning

Analysts of family structure have pointed to a number of conditions that may account for the tendency for children of divorce to exhibit more problems, on average, than children whose parents have not divorced. The variability in these factors among divorced families may help us to understand the variability we see in children's adjustment. Some of the conditions most commonly thought to be important can be classified as follows (see also Amato, 1993).

1. *Loss of a parent.* Children's parents are their anchors. Parents provide the structure for children's daily lives, and even when parents are not functioning very well, children depend on them for a sense of security that enables them to cope with their developmental tasks. When one parent leaves the home, the child realizes a shattering possibility: parents are not always there. If one leaves, the other might too. But at the time

of divorce, families differ greatly in the degree to which a parent disappears from the child's life. In a few cases, both parents remain completely accessible, in others partly accessible, and in other cases only one continues to be part of the child's life. The hypothesis is that children's powerful anxiety over losing one or both parents will be considerably mitigated by ensuring continuing contact and a continuing emotional bond with both.

2. *Interparental conflict.* Previous research has indicated that conflict between parents can be seriously harmful to children, particularly if they are directly exposed to the conflict (Camara and Resnick, 1988; Cummings and Davies, 1994; Emery, 1982; Johnston and Campbell, 1988). Presumably there is a build-up of conflict between parents before the decision to divorce is made. Moving into separate residences ought to mean that episodes of conflict occur less frequently, and by virtue of the separation of the warring parties, all family members may experience some relief from the intense levels of conflict surrounding the divorce itself. Still, in many families, conflict between the parents continues at some level (Maccoby and Mnookin, 1992). It is reasonable to expect that children's adjustment in the postdivorce period will depend, at least to some extent, on the level of conflict that is maintained between their parents or, alternatively, on the extent to which parents can moderate their conflict or shield the children from exposure to it. In an extensive review of the literature on children's adjustment to divorce, Amato (1993) concluded that the level of continuing interparental conflict was the most well-documented predictor of outcomes following divorce.

3. *Diminished parenting.* Many believe that when children from divorced families exhibit problems, this happens primarily because the divorce has brought about a deterioration in the quality of parenting provided by the custodial parent (with the custodial parent typically being the mother). Indeed, considerable evidence exists that a period of "diminished parenting," at least during the first two years following divorce, does occur. Studying single divorced mothers in the first two postdivorce years, Hetherington and colleagues reported that the emotional distress being experienced by these mothers was in many cases translated into a lowered level of responsiveness to their preschool-aged children, lessened vigilance for their safety and emotional states, less patience, and a more peremptory style of discipline and control (Hetherington, Cox, and Cox, 1982). The mothers were also less able to maintain organized household routines: to provide meals on time, monitor bedtimes, and the like. This diminished quality of parenting seemed to be directly responsible for some of the children's behavior problems, and

when the quality of parenting recovered—as it did in many cases within two years—the children's behavior also improved. Others have noted that single mothers are less likely to have a participatory parenting style than are mothers who have not been divorced or mothers who have remarried—in other words, single mothers are more likely to let their adolescent children make decisions without parental input (Dornbusch et al., 1985).

More recent work by Hetherington and colleagues (Hetherington and Clingempeel, 1992) with early adolescent children (average age: eleven years) whose parents had been divorced for a longer time than had parents in Hetherington's earlier studies did not implicate diminished parenting as a major reason for poorer adjustment in divorced compared with nondivorced families, but did point to the importance of quality of parenting in children's adjustment within each type of family structure (nondivorced, divorced, remarried). We expect, then, that children's success or failure in coping with the postdivorce situation depends at least in part on the quality of parenting maintained by the primary custodial parent.

Widespread recognition of these factors[1] as potentially affecting the post-divorce lives of families has led to (or been accompanied by) changes in the statutes governing divorce and the legal processes that surround it. Certain of these changes appear to be designed to mitigate some of the risks just listed. We believe that research on conditions that may soften or exacerbate the effects of divorce on children must continue to focus on these factors, but that the new legal context must now be taken into account as well, as changing arrangements for custody and visitation may interact with the interpersonal factors that have proved to be important to date.

The Changing Legal Context for Divorce

The past two decades have seen great changes in the legal context of divorce. In the United States and most other industrialized nations, "fault-based" statutes have all but disappeared. There has also been a change in presumptions about which parent will get custody. Although the custody of children almost automatically went to mothers earlier this century (unless the mother was proved "unfit"), divorce statutes are now carefully couched in gender-neutral terms. Neither fathers nor mothers are to be given preference in custody awards; rather, custody decisions are to be made individually, case by case, in accordance with what appears to be the best interests of the child. And the courts, more and more, have been withdrawing from the decision process, leaving custody decisions to the two parents whenever possible and turning to mandatory mediation when parents cannot agree.[2] Presumably these changes are intended to make divorce procedures less adversarial, and to minimize postdivorce conflict by helping parents to formulate agreed-upon plans for the children's lives.

In practice, it has proved difficult to determine what custodial arrangements are in the best interests of children. There is no clear consensus among family-law attorneys, judges, or mediators concerning how children's time should be divided between the two parents. Still, a basic premise of the new legal context for divorce is that children should have access to both parents—presumably to soften the child's sense of being abandoned by a parent. Although there were early claims that the custodial parent ought to have veto power over whether and under what conditions children would see the "outside" parent (Goldstein, Freud, and Solnit, 1979), this point of view has not prevailed. Current laws generally embody provisions that encourage visitation with noncustodial parents and impose costs on custodial parents who attempt to impede visitation. Furthermore, joint custody arrangements have been recognized or even given preference. These changes have been justified in terms of the presumed benefits to children of maintaining relationships with both parents, but they also reflect strong pressure from fathers' rights groups, who have claimed that fathers and mothers should have equal rights of access to their children.

Whether because of the current legal climate or because of changes in the climate of public attitudes or both, there is evidence that children now maintain contact with noncustodial parents at higher rates than was formerly the case. For example, quite high rates of "father dropout" were reported by Furstenberg and colleagues (1983), who studied children for whom parental divorce occurred mainly in the early 1970s. Higher rates of contact between children and their noncustodial fathers, however, have been reported for more recent divorces (Braver et al., 1991; Bray and Berger, 1990; Maccoby and Mnookin, 1992; Seltzer, 1991), and the little information available on noncustodial mothers indicates that they maintain even higher rates of contact with their children than do noncustodial fathers (Furstenberg et al., 1983; Maccoby and Mnookin, 1992). The more recent data thus indicate that large numbers of children are now spending time in two different parental households. We may speculate about what this means for their lives. It seems obvious that they must face greater exposure to conflicting parental standards and expectations than they would if they lived in only one household. Their divided lives may also involve greater exposure to interparental conflict, along with the loyalty conflicts that can stem from maintaining relationships with two parents who continue to harbor hostility toward each other. These negative factors might, of course, be offset by the presumed value of receiving support and guidance from two parents rather than one. The fact is, though, that we know next to nothing concerning how children integrate—or fail to integrate—their experiences in two households. It is a major purpose of this book to explore this question.

The state of California was among the first to reform its divorce laws, and following the changes, there was an increase in the number of families awarded joint physical custody. California was, therefore, a promising locale in which to study the postdivorce lives of parents and children in the context of the new legal climate.

The Stanford Custody Project

The Stanford Custody Project has followed a diverse group of divorcing families in two northern California counties. Families were initially enrolled in the study approximately five years after the major revisions of California divorce law went into effect (the intake period for the study was from September 1984 to April 1985). Approximately 1,100 families, all having at least one child under sixteen years of age, were enrolled. Although the mothers were awarded physical custody of the children in a substantial majority of these families, there were nevertheless sizable subgroups in which the fathers had primary custody or in which parents were sharing custody. The sample thus presents an opportunity to contrast three different custodial arrangements.

The research has been conducted in two phases: in the first (Study 1), parents were interviewed on three successive occasions, covering a period of approximately three and a half years from the time of parental separation. That phase of the study dealt focally with the residential and visitation arrangements for the children—how these arrangements were arrived at, whether they were stable over time, and if not, how and why they changed. Both legal and physical custody (or "residence")[3] were considered. A second major focus was on co-parenting: how the parental responsibilities were divided between the two parents, how (and whether) parents communicated, whether they were able to cooperate in matters concerning the children, and how much interparental conflict existed. The findings of the first phase of the research have been reported in *Dividing the Child: Social and Legal Dilemmas of Custody* (Maccoby and Mnookin, 1992).

All of the information in that book represents the parents' perspectives, and it told us little about how the children were weathering the many changes and stresses in their lives. We felt it important to get the perspective of the children themselves, and therefore undertook the second phase of the research (Study 2): a follow-up study of the adolescent children in the families included in phase l. Although it would have been interesting to learn about the children of all ages, we limited ourselves to interviews with children aged ten to eighteen, who had been six years old or older at the time their parents separated. Many of the children in the families included in the parent study—indeed, the majority of children in those families—were toddlers or preschoolers at the time of their parents' divorce, and we recognize that our findings in the present study may not apply in some respects to these younger children. The advantage of focusing as we did on the older children is that, by the age of ten and older, children were able to describe their lives in detail, and they were capable of reflecting on their own perceptions and reactions to the events in their families. Telephone interviews with these children produced a wealth of data on life inside diverse households. The adolescents' experiences and the quality of their adjustment are the subject of the chapters that follow.

The fact that the families of our adolescents were studied longitudinally during the first three and a half years following the parents' separation provided us with a unique opportunity. We were able to link information obtained from the adolescents to information obtained from their parents during the preceding several years. In particular, we could contrast the adjustment of adolescents whose parents maintained a cooperative co-parental relationship with those whose parents were conflicted. And we could see whether adolescent adjustment was related to the history of an adolescent's residential arrangements. In the earlier study, we found that residential arrangements were often unstable and in a number of cases did not correspond to the form of physical custody specified in the divorce decree. Substantial numbers of children moved from one parental household to another, or into or out of joint custody. We could ask not only about the impact of each of the three residential arrangements on a child's adjustment, but also about the impact of a history of residential instability.

The Focus of the Adolescent Study

As we noted earlier, previous research on the adjustment of children whose parents have divorced has pointed to the processes within the primary residential home as being especially important. In particular, the closeness of the emotional relationship between the residential parent and the child, the amount of conflict between them, and the presence of firmly established standards of behavior—along with careful monitoring by the parent of the child's performance in meeting these standards—have emerged as significant factors for children's adjustment.[4] We assessed the kind of parent-child interactions that occurred within our adolescents' primary residence (as seen from the adolescents' perspective), and then examined how these processes were related to adolescent adjustment.

Although parent-child interactions in the nonresidential household have seldom been examined, we believed that they might matter too, at least for children who spent substantial amounts of time with the other parent. We therefore examined a variety of processes in both parental households, as reported by the adolescents experiencing them.

Given the changing views and practices about who should have custody of children after divorce, we were also interested in how processes and interactions in each home varied as a function of residential arrangement. In families that have not divorced, fathers and mothers often assume somewhat different parental roles and display somewhat different parenting styles (Maccoby, 1995). Little is known concerning whether this differentiation survives when mothers or fathers become single parents. Do single parents become "both father and mother" to the children, adding to their own accustomed roles the functions and styles formerly characterizing the ex-spouse? Or do they continue to function primarily in their accustomed ways? If the latter, then the family processes prevailing in father-headed households might be somewhat different from those in mother-headed households, and these differences might have consequences for children's adjustment.

Specific Objectives

As noted, a central concern of this book is to compare and contrast the three major residential arrangements: primary mother residence, primary father residence, and dual residence (an arrangement in which the child's residential time is fairly equally shared between the two parental households). We compared these three residential arrangements with respect to the experiences and adjustment of the adolescents in each. Our first set of questions was as follows:

1. Does the adjustment of adolescents depend in any degree on their current residential arrangement? And is adjustment related to how stable this arrangement has been since the parents separated?
2. Do processes such as rule-setting, emotional support, or parent-child conflict differ between mothers' and fathers' households? Is it more difficult for a parent to monitor children, maintain predictable household routines, or achieve emotional closeness when children are in joint custody (dual residence) rather than living primarily in one parental household?
3. What factors are linked to adjustment of adolescents within each residential arrangement? Can differences in within-household processes between residential arrangements explain any differences in adolescent adjustment that occur?

Of course, the situation an adolescent faces in a parent's household may be affected by whether the parent has a new partner and how serious that relationship is. As just one possible example, we know that the advent of new partners may affect the amount of conflict between the two divorced parents (Maccoby and Mnookin, 1992), which may in turn redound upon the relationship between the parents and the adolescent. We also know relatively little about the conditions under which adolescents are willing to accept the authority of a new parental figure in their lives. These considerations led to an additional set of questions:

1. Is adolescent adjustment related to whether the residential parent has a new partner? Does it matter whether the new partner merely lives with the parent and adolescent, or whether a remarriage has occurred?
2. Is the impact of a residential father's new partner similar to that of a residential mother's new partner?
3. Does the existence of a new partner for the residential parent affect adolescents' relationships with nonresidential parents?
4. What factors are related to adolescents' acceptance of their parents' new partners?

Another major objective of our study was to examine what it means to adolescents to spend time in two different parental households. Although dual-resident adolescents are faced with this experience most intensively, it is also faced by young people who live primarily with one parent and visit the other. For adolescents who had their primary residence with one parent, several questions were pertinent:

1. What patterns of visitation are maintained between adolescents and nonresidential parents? How is visitation experienced by adolescents, and how much voice do they feel they have in visitation schedules?
2. To what extent does the quality of the relationship with a nonresidential parent depend on the frequency of contact? What other factors predict the quality of that relationship?
3. Do large amounts of visitation with the nonresidential parent interfere in any way with processes in the residential home? with the relationship between child and residential parent?
4. Is adolescent adjustment related to how much contact the adolescent has with the nonresidential parent? to the quality of the relationship with the nonresidential parent?

For both the adolescents in dual residence and those who lived primarily with one parent and visited the other, two major questions were posed:

1. Does having a close relationship with one parent make it more or less difficult to maintain a close relationship with the other? Is it beneficial for adolescents to maintain a close relationship with both parents after divorce, or is a close relationship with one parent "enough" to facilitate good adjustment?
2. In terms of the adolescent's adjustment following divorce, does it matter how consistent the rules and standards of the two households are?

As we noted earlier, there is every reason to believe that adolescent adjustment will be related to whether the two parents continue to be in conflict with each other. The fact that the parents must maintain some sort of contact if the children are to go back and forth between households must mean that there are continuing opportunities for interparental conflict to occur. At the same time, we know that there are some parents who manage to do business together in a reasonably cooperative fashion, and others who are neither cooperative nor conflicted in their co-parental relationship but, rather, simply stay disengaged from each other even though the children are members of both parental households (Maccoby and Mnookin, 1992). We were concerned with how the levels of co-parental conflict or cooperation that had prevailed since the divorce were related to adolescent adjustment. In addition, there are many references in the divorce literature to the potential problem of loyalty conflicts for children of divorce. According to Emery (1988), "most children . . . feel the pressures created by torn loyalties even when parents cooperate relatively well" (p. 13). We wanted to examine the extent to which adolescents reported torn loyalties or feelings of being "caught" between their parents, the conditions under which these feelings were likely to occur, and the relation of such feelings to adolescent adjustment.

We recognized that the answers to some or all of our questions would not be the same for adolescents of the two sexes. Some studies have indicated that children adjust better when living with the same-sex parent, but several of these studies have utilized very small samples, and the hypothesis needs examining with a larger and more diverse group of divorcing families. Also, it was quite possible that the younger adolescents in our sample would react differently than the older ones to their parents' breakup and the events that have followed it. Many changes occur over the adolescent years: children become more and more independent, less concerned and more comfortable with the physical changes of puberty, and more susceptible to risky behaviors and several kinds of adjustment problems (for example, depression and deviance). Thus for most of the questions we examined, we looked at whether the answers differed depending on whether we were talking about boys versus girls, or younger versus older adolescents.

Overview of the Book

The book is divided into three parts. Part I (Chapters 1–3) sets out the goals and methods of the study and discusses the assessment of family processes, interparental relationships, and adolescent adjustment. In addition, the contexts of our adolescents' lives are described: their residential history, the characteristics of their households, and major events that have occurred recently in their lives. We also provide a general picture of the adjustment and well-being of our adolescents as a group.

In Part II (Chapters 4–7), the three residential arrangements are compared with respect to the adjustment of the adolescents living in them, as well as the contextual factors, interpersonal relationships, and forms of parental control and management that prevail in each. Subsequently, within each residential group, the connections between characteristics of the family and adolescent adjustment are examined. A comparison of the predictors of adjustment in each residential group allows us to consider whether adjustment is linked to the same or different family processes within each. We are also able to address whether differences in adjustment among residential groups have to do with differences among arrangements in the family environment. Finally, the impact of parents' new partners on adolescents' experience and adaptation is explored, as is the adolescent's acceptance of a new partner.

In Part III (Chapters 8–12), we explicitly examine the experience of participating in two different parental households. Visitation and the nature of the adolescent's relationship with the nonresidential parent are explored, focusing on the way in which they relate to characteristics of household and family functioning, and to adjustment. Adolescents' feelings of being caught between their parents are studied, as are the effects of inconsistency between the two households in patterns of control and management.

In Chapter 13, we summarize our main findings and consider their implications.

2

Methods

This book is about the way adolescents were adjusting to their post-divorce lives approximately four and a half years after their parents separated. All of the adolescents in our study were members of families who had experienced a divorce, and whose parents had participated in a previous phase of this research (Study 1). Study 1 began at the time the parents filed for divorce, during 1984–1985. Our interviews with the adolescents took place between November 1988 and June 1989. For Study 1, during the period between the divorce filing and the adolescent interview, we talked to at least one of the adolescent's parents—and often both—on several (up to three) occasions.[1] The first parent interview (Time 1, or T1) took place at six months after the separation, the second (T2) at one and a half years after the separation, and the third (T3) at three and a half years after the separation. Thus we had a good deal of information about recent family history—the amount of conflict that had been involved in the divorce process, where the adolescent had lived, parental remarriage, residential moves, the relationship between the parents—before we talked to the adolescents themselves in Study 2 (or T4). The research reported in this book thus concerns the adolescent children in the Study 1 families, and it links the children's adjustment to the conditions of their parents' divorce and custody arrangements as well as to concurrent family functioning and circumstances.

The Sample

There were 1,500 children whose parents remained in Study 1 throughout the three-year postdivorce period. Ideally, we would have conducted in-depth assessments (including, for example, behavioral observations and reports by teachers or parents) on at least a random subset of these children. Such in-depth assessments are expensive and time-consuming, however, and to undertake them would have meant severely restricting our sample size. Using a small subsample would have kept us from achieving some of the most important objectives of our work, for example, comparisons of children living in different residential arrangements, or comparisons of children from high-conflict versus low-conflict divorces. The limitations of taking a small random sample would have been especially great given the large age range of the children from Study 1 (0–16 at parental separation) and the fact that predictors of adjustment to divorce vary for children of different ages.

As noted in Chapter 1, our main objective in Study 2 was to go beyond the information and viewpoints provided by parents in Study 1 by exploring the perspective of the children themselves. We wanted a sample of substantial size, sufficient to represent the diversity of family circumstances that was evident in Study 1. We decided, therefore, to rely on interviews rather than on in-depth clinical assessments, and to focus on the older children among our Study 1 families—those old enough to take part in a telephone interview. Some pilot work, and our reading of the research literature, led us to choose the age range from ten to eighteen (inclusive). We believed (rightly, as it turned out) that it would be possible for children in this age range to talk to us cogently about their current life situations and their experiences in their maternal and paternal households. Hoping to obtain a sample large enough for the needed comparisons of subgroups, we elected to interview all of the children in our Study 1 families who met the age criterion.

The target sample for the adolescent study thus consisted of children at or between the ages of ten and eighteen. Ten-year-olds were interviewed if they were in fifth grade and would be eleven by June 1, 1989. In cases where adolescents were already eighteen years old when we began interviewing in the fall of 1988, we tried to recruit that family as early in the data collection period as possible. This was done for two reasons: to reach these older children before they turned nineteen, and to catch those children who had moved after high school before they had been out of the home for very long. By interviewing these adolescents early in the data collection period, we were able to obtain information about their recent past—when they were still living with one or both parents—and to classify them according to their prior residential arrangement.

There were 647 children within our target age range in the Study 1 families. Ultimately we interviewed 522 adolescents from 365 families, or

81 percent of our intended group. In 12 percent of the target cases, a parent or child refused to participate. Five percent of the cases were not locatable, and 2 percent were not eligible for the study owing to the parents' reconciliation, the death of a parent or the child, or a mental handicap that precluded participation. In 229 of the families that agreed to participate (63 percent), only one adolescent was interviewed; in 118 families (32 percent), two adolescents were interviewed; in 18 families (5 percent), three or four children were interviewed.

How Representative Is Our Sample?

The adolescents in our study were all members of families who lived in two counties in Northern California at the time the parents divorced. The children's residences had fanned out geographically somewhat since the beginning of Study 1 because of residential moves on the part of the parents, but the large majority of our adolescents still lived within or close to the original two counties. We do not know in what respects they are representative of young people who live in other parts of the country. We know that teenage cultures do vary by geographical region. Analysis of population statistics indicated that the parents in our Study 1 families were better educated and had higher incomes than the national average (Maccoby and Mnookin, 1992), although the sample was diverse, ranging from people on public assistance to people of some wealth. Similarly, although the adolescents in our sample were living in somewhat more affluent circumstances on the average than might be true of a sample taken elsewhere in the country, conditions in the neighborhoods in which our adolescents lived varied from comfortable suburbia to inner-city crowding and shabbiness. As might be expected from a California sample, fewer of our adolescents were African-American, and more were ethnically Hispanic, than would be found in a national sample. In addition, because of California laws in the early 1980s that favored joint custody and liberal visitation rights, our sample may not be fully representative of other geographic regions with respect to the families' custody and visitation arrangements. Our adolescents were probably more likely than those in states not favoring joint custody or liberal visitation to maintain relatively high levels of contact with both parents (see Chapters 3 and 9).

How representative were our sample families of all families from the two California counties that filed for divorce during this time? The families in Study 1 were originally selected from the court records of divorce filings over a specified intake period. Although not all the families whose names appeared in the court records could be reached and interviewed, both recruitment and maintenance rates were high in Study 1. The attrition that did occur in recruitment and maintenance over the three-year span of Study 1 did not change the composition of the sample materially, with the exception that families retained in the study included a higher proportion of people with joint custody than was the case for the families not successfully recruited. Study 1 families (and their children) were thus reasonably representative of the families in which divorce occurred during the specific time period when sample selection occurred (Maccoby and Mnookin, 1992).

Finally, how well do the adolescents we interviewed in Study 2 represent all adolescents we could have recruited? Very well, it appears. Analyses comparing the families of adolescents we interviewed with the families in which either the parent or the adolescent refused to participate, or who were not located, indicated that we were somewhat more successful in recruiting families in which parents had more education. The two groups of families did not differ with respect to income, ethnicity, the amount of conflict or cooperation between parents, parents' hostility, or parents' satisfaction with the residential arrangement as measured in the three parental interviews. At the level of the individual child, there were no differences between adolescents we interviewed and adolescents we did not in parents' reports of child unhappiness (measured at T2), irritability, independence, or being difficult to manage (measured at T2 and T3). There were also no differences in age or sex of adolescents between the interviewed and noninterviewed groups. We were slightly less successful in recruiting adolescents who had been living with their fathers at the time of the last parent interview than adolescents who had been living with their mothers or with both parents. On the whole, then, our sample of adolescents was not distorted by the loss of 19 percent of our original target group: the adolescents not recruited were very similar to those who participated in the study. More detailed information on the participants in Study 2 can be found in Chapter 3.

Interviewing More than One Adolescent per Household

A crucial issue we faced was how to handle families in which more than one child fell within our target age range. In the past, many researchers have limited their samples to one sibling per family. They have reasoned that siblings, in some respects, are not independent cases, so that the usual statistical tests of significance would not be valid if more than one sibling were included in a sample. We knew that we would face this problem if we gathered data from more than one child per family: siblings in a given family obviously always have the same score on family-level variables such as parental income or education; they almost always live in the same residence, and almost always share the same schedule of visits to the nonresidential parent; and they share the same divorce history, as reflected in the data obtained from parental interviews during the first three years after the divorce.

We were reluctant, however, to limit our sample to only one sibling per family. For one thing, this would seriously underrepresent children who had siblings within our age range. That is, children with no such siblings would have a 100 percent chance of being in the sample, those with one target sibling would have a 50 percent chance, children with two target siblings would have a 33 percent chance, and so forth. For any outcome on which children with siblings might differ from those without them, such a sampling strategy introduces distortion.

An additional problem with the strategy of selecting one adolescent per family involved choosing the adolescent to be included. To follow the strategy of taking only the oldest child would overrepresent older children and restrict the age range. Even choosing a child at random—a popular solution—raises the question of which random choice to use (since different random samples will, by chance, sometimes produce different results).

Another, perhaps more important, reason for our reluctance was that correlations between siblings on most of our outcome variables were expected to be (and were) low. Current research on siblings (for example, Dunn, 1990) makes it clear that siblings often respond quite differently to the antecedent conditions we used as predictors. Siblings also differ in a number of ways that were pertinent to our analyses: on sex and age, and on the relationship with each parent (for example, closeness to parents or feelings of being caught between parents). In these respects, siblings are, in fact, independent cases.

For these reasons, we chose to interview all eligible adolescents in a family. In our analyses, we considered two solutions that would allow us to use all of the data we had gathered: (1) using data from all children but using the number of families as our degrees of freedom in statistical analyses, and (2) weighting each individual's scores by the inverse of the number of siblings in the sample. Both of these solutions had the potential to become unwieldy, however, as we carried out the complex analytic tasks planned for the study. Furthermore, we were not convinced that either of them actually solved the problem of correlated error among our cases.

In the end, we took the following approach in the vast majority of our analyses. We conducted each analysis at least twice: once using all cases and once using a subsample consisting of all adolescents in families where only one was interviewed, but only one adolescent per family, chosen on a random basis, in families where more than one adolescent was interviewed. When the results of these two analyses agreed with regard to direction and statistical significance, we have reported the statistics from the full sample. When results differed, we repeated the analyses on at least one, possibly two, additional random subsamples. On the basis of these analyses, we identified those relations that seemed to be robust versus those that appeared borderline through examination of both the magnitude of differences between means and tests of statistical significance. Our discussion of results in such cases reflects our subsequent judgment.

There were two instances where this strategy was not used. First, if an analysis used only or primarily "family-level" factors (for example, interparental conflict at any point during Study 1 or parental remarriage status in Study 2) as either the predictor (independent) variables or the predicted (dependent) variable, analyses were almost always conducted using random subsamples (in other words, only one adolescent per family) rather than all cases (see Chapter 7 for an exception). In such instances, as we have noted, siblings are clearly nonindependent cases because their scores on these measures are exactly the same. Second, in Chapter 6, where a series of quite complicated analyses involving large numbers of factors was conducted, each analysis building on the results of a previous analysis, it was virtually impossible to follow the usual strategy. The results of the Chapter 6 analyses are therefore based on all cases. Our experience using both the full sample and the random samples in the many analyses reported in other chapters leads us to believe, however, that the results of analyses using all cases are almost always supported using random subsamples. Especially because we emphasize the strongest and most consistent results throughout Chapter 6, we feel confident that the results reported are trustworthy.

The Telephone Interview

We initially planned to conduct face-to-face interviews with our adolescent subjects, but we quickly encountered several impediments to such a plan. First, the adolescents were geographically scattered, and some had moved away from the Bay Area. Second, even those who lived near enough for us to visit proved difficult to catch at home. This problem was especially common for adolescents who were spending time in both parental households, but even those who were not were involved in a variety of extracurricular activities that meant inconsistent schedules from one day to another. We were forced to consider telephone interviews, which could be more easily done in the evening, and which would permit repeated call-backs to locate adolescents at home. Existing evidence on the reliability and validity of telephone interviews was encouraging. Among adults, the amount and type of information disclosed over the telephone is comparable to that obtained in face-to-face interviewing when good interviewing techniques are employed (Groves and Kahn, 1979; McCormick et al., 1993). In addition, investigators who have used this method with adolescent populations find that adolescents are comfortable with the telephone as a mode of communication, and that information obtained in this manner is reliable and valid (Furstenberg et al., 1983; Montemayor and Brownlee, 1987).

Although establishing rapport may be somewhat more difficult than in face-to-face interviews, using telephone interviews with our adolescent subjects had potential advantages. First, recruitment and scheduling were easier and less costly, allowing us to achieve our goal of recruiting larger numbers of adolescents in the less common residential arrangements. Second, adolescents may feel less inhibited about discussing sensitive issues over the phone; in particular, the telephone makes it possible to reduce the salience of talking with an older person.

In order to recruit participants into the study, a packet of information was mailed to one parent in each family with eligible adolescents. The parent chosen to receive the initial mailing was the person who had participated in Study 1. If both parents had participated in the earlier study, the mailing, with rare exceptions, was sent to the parent with whom the child was living.

In order to maximize the reliability and validity of the information we collected, interviewers went through a minimum of thirty-five hours of training, much of which focused on developing and maintaining rapport with the adolescents. Interviews averaged one hour in length. At the conclusion of the interview, adolescents were sent a check for ten dollars and a letter thanking them for participating.

Measures

Our objectives called for devising questions that would assess two major areas: adolescent adjustment and the factors that might lead an adolescent to adjust well or poorly following parental divorce. Here we summarize the measures under their major categories.[2] More detailed information about the questions asked and scales constructed is provided in subsequent chapters, where findings concerning specific scales are discussed. In addition, statistics for each scale, including average scores, range of scores, and scale reliability can be found in Appendix Table B.1.

Adolescent Adjustment

"Problem behaviors." In previous research on adolescent adjustment, investigators have often distinguished between two forms of adjustment difficulties: the "externalizing" forms—including aggression, substance use, truancy, and a variety of delinquent or antisocial acts—and the "internalizing" forms, including depression, anxiety, withdrawal, and suicidal impulses. These two kinds of problem behavior are not mutually exclusive, of course, and in cases of severe maladjustment individuals are likely to display both. In our battery of adjustment measures, we included a measure of depression/anxiety and measures of several aspects of deviance (for example, substance use; antisocial acts such as destroying property or carrying a weapon; and various kinds of rule-breaking at school, including truancy, copying others' work, and cutting classes).

School adjustment. We asked the adolescents about the grades they were getting in school and about the amount of effort they were putting into their schoolwork, as indexed by the time they spent on homework and their level of attention to schoolwork in class.

"Worst problem." Although scores on the outcomes of depression, deviance, and school adjustment were moderately correlated (correlations among depression, deviance, and either grades or school effort ranged from .14 to .38 in absolute value), the correlations were not so high as to rule out the possibility that individual adolescents exhibit adjustment problems in different ways. For example, one adolescent might become depressed while another acts out, while yet another slacks off in school. For this reason, we also constructed a score that represented an adolescent's worst problem—his or her worst score on depression/anxiety, deviance, or school effort.

Personal resources. Adjustment is not only a matter of the presence or absence of problems. Also pertinent are the positive skills and resources adolescents can bring to bear on solving the problems they face. We assessed several such personal resources. These included conflict resolution styles, close relationships with peers, and interests in a range of recreational and other extracurricular activities.

Factors That May Affect Adjustment

Demographic factors. We assessed the usual battery of demographic factors—parental income and education, family size, and age and sex of child—and we added information on the out-of-home working hours of both parents. In addition, we inquired about the composition of both parental households: the presence of parents' new partners, stepsiblings, and half-siblings.

Arrangements for residence and visitation. It was central to our objectives to consider adolescents' adjustment in relation to the amount of contact they had with each of the two parents. We therefore asked in detail about residence and visitation: which parent the adolescent lived with most of the time, how often overnight or daytime visits to the nonresidential parent occurred during regular portions of the school year, and how much contact there was with each parent during vacations. In Study 1, we had learned that there was substantial shifting in these arrangements as time passed; given the data on residence obtained from T1–T4, therefore, we created an index of the stability of each adolescent's residential arrangement over the span of time since the parents had separated.

Life stresses. A substantial literature indicates that adjustment is affected by the incidence of a variety of life changes, such as residential moves, loss of a pet, or illness of a family member. When many changes happen at the same time, stress factors cumulate, and stressors with which an adolescent might cope successfully if taken one at a time may be much more difficult to handle. Although we knew that all of our adolescents had had to cope with the stress of their parents' divorce, we needed to consider the context of other stressors—related and unrelated to the divorce—in our adolescents' lives. We therefore included a "life stress" inventory in our measures.

Interparental relationships. Especially for adolescents who continue to spend some time with each parent, the relationship between the two divorced parents can be crucial. We wanted to know whether the parents had developed a modus operandi that enabled them to do necessary business together and whether they were able to cooperate in matters concerning the children. We relied in part on measures of interparental hostility, and co-parental discord or cooperation, that had already been derived from Study 1 data. In addition, we asked the adolescents in Study 2 for their perceptions of parental discord and cooperation, both generally and on matters that specifically concerned the adolescents' lives.

Parent-child relationships. We assessed the quality of the adolescents' relationships with each parent, including feelings of closeness and trust, desire to be like the parent (what we call "identification with" a parent), and how many joint activities adolescents engaged in with each parent. Negative aspects of the relationship, such as the amount of conflict between parent and child, and children's feelings of disengagement from the home (feelings of not wanting to be there, or not feeling at home there) were also measured. In addition, we asked about "role reversal"—the extent to which adolescents felt they needed to take care of a parent and the frequency of parents' confiding in their children and relying on them for emotional support.

Parental control and management. Households differ with respect to the amount of structure they provide for their adolescent children. In some households, there are regular routines for activities like meals, chores, bedtimes, or television watching, and adolescents are expected to conform to—and participate in—the family routines. In other households, adolescents have much more autonomy and can function fairly independently of the activities of other household members. In addition, some parents insist on being involved in decisions concerning their children's lives (how they spend their money, where they can go after school, when they must be home); other parents leave such decisions up to the child. To assess these dimensions of management and control, we asked about decision-making practices between parents and adolescents, about the presence or absence of predictable household routines, about rules concerning the adolescent's activities inside and outside the home, and about the chores adolescents were expected to do in each household. In addition, we asked how successfully each parent monitored the adolescent, that is, the extent to which parents knew of the adolescent's whereabouts and activities.

Feelings of being caught between one's parents. Previous researchers have noted the problem of loyalty conflicts for children of divorce. We asked our adolescents about how often they felt caught between their parents, about specific instances of being used as a messenger or spy, and about how often they felt hesitant to talk to one parent about the other parent or household.

Analyses

We used a wide range of statistical analyses to address the questions of interest to us. Because of this variety, it is impossible to summarize our "analytic strategy" beyond what we have already described concerning how we handled the inclusion of more than one adolescent in our sample. Information about analyses appears in each chapter, as we address each specific question or set of questions.

3

The Adolescents

All the young people selected for our study were interviewed four to four and a half years after their parents filed for divorce. There was variation in the time it took for the legal divorce to become final, but in most cases, the divorce decree had been issued several years before we interviewed the adolescents. Our sample was therefore uniform with respect to the amount of time that had passed between the parental separation and divorce and our interview with the adolescent. In most other respects, however, the sample was heterogeneous.

In this chapter, we describe the adolescents who participated in our study: their age, sex, grade in school, and birth order within the family. Then we discuss some of the characteristics of their families: their parents' socioeconomic level, ethnic identity, and employment status, and the composition of each parental household. We outline the adolescents' residential history, noting which parent or parents they had lived with and whether they had changed their residence during the four and a half years since their parents' separation. In addition, the reasons for such changes are examined. We also briefly describe the level of visitation by our adolescents with their nonresidential parents. Finally, we consider some of the important and often stressful events that had recently taken place in the lives of the young people in our sample, as an aid to understanding something about the context of their behavior and adaptation.

The Sample

The sample of adolescents was equally split on gender; it was 50.8 percent male and 49.2 percent female. Our respondents were also fairly equally distributed across the eligible age range (see Appendix Table B.2). For the most part, their grade in school matched their ages, but a small group (about 2 percent) had dropped out of school before graduating from high school. The sample also includes a small group of older adolescents who had finished high school; about 2 percent were no longer in school, and about 6 percent were taking college courses. These young people were still within our ten-to-eighteen-year age range, and some were still living at home. Those who had gone away to college had lived at home until very recently, so that it was possible to get a picture from them of their living situation and their relationships with their parents prior to leaving home.

The majority of the young people in our sample had at least one natural sibling, although 15 percent were the only children of their parents' marriage. When there were siblings, the adolescents in our sample were more likely to be the eldest (41 percent), rather than either a middle child (12 percent) or the youngest of the children (30 percent). Two percent of the adolescents were members of twin pairs. Of course not all of our respondents' siblings were within the eligible age range for inclusion in our study, but in 37 percent of the sample families, more than one sibling was interviewed (see also Chapter 2).

Characteristics of the Adolescents' Parents

The diversity of the sample is apparent in the characteristics of the parents (see Appendix Table B.3). One-third of the mothers and almost as many fathers (30 percent) had only a high school education or less. At the upper end of the scale of educational attainment, fathers outnumbered mothers: 27 percent of the mothers and 42 percent of the fathers had graduated from college, and more than twice as many fathers (18 percent) as mothers had completed an advanced degree.

The employment status of the two parents also differed. Although most mothers and fathers were employed full time (defining full time as working forty or more hours per week), nearly three times as many mothers (17 percent) as fathers (6 percent) were not employed outside the home. Seventeen percent of mothers and only 3 percent of fathers were working less than full time, and twice as many fathers (55 percent) as mothers were working long hours—forty-five or more hours per week.

The employed fathers of the children in our sample had much higher annual earnings than the employed mothers. Although 50 percent of the employed fathers were earning $40,000 per year or more, only 7 percent of the employed mothers were earning that much. And although the majority of fathers paid child support when the children were living with the mothers, the amounts paid made up only a small fraction of the income differential (Maccoby and Mnookin, 1992). Because the large majority of the adolescents in our sample lived with their mothers, most were spending a great deal of time in poor or lower-middle-income households. It is important to note, however, that the sample covers a wide range of households, from the very poor to the wealthy.

We did not obtain information about ethnicity directly from the adolescents, but we did have information about the ethnicity of both parents. In 73 percent of the families, both parents were non-Hispanic White; in 7 percent both were Hispanic; in 4 percent both were Asian; and in 2 percent both were African-American. In 14 percent of the families, the two parents were from different ethnic groups.

Composition of the Parental Households

Adolescents were asked who lived in each parental household, and Appendix Table B.4 displays the information they gave us. A new spouse was sharing the parent's household in about a third of the cases, with 37 percent of the fathers remarried and 32 percent of the mothers. A substantial minority of the parents' households (15 percent of the mothers' and 19 percent of the fathers') included a new live-in partner to whom the parent was not (as yet) married. Thus about half the parental households either already formally contained a stepparent or were less formally using or testing such an arrangement, while approximately half were still single-parent households.

A father's new wife was more likely to have brought children from a previous marriage into the household than was a mother's new husband; there were thus stepsiblings present more often in fathers' homes. This discrepancy reflects the general tendency for children to live with their mothers following divorce. And a small proportion of the remarried couples (just under 10 percent) had had new children of their own by Time 4, adding half-siblings to the household. As already noted, the majority of the adolescents in our sample had full siblings as well. Father-resident adolescents were less likely to be sharing a household with natural siblings, in part because a higher percentage of father-residence adolescents had one or more siblings who were living with their mother (custody of multiple siblings having been "split" between mother and father).

In some cases (7 percent), the household was shared with an adult relative—a grandparent, aunt, or uncle of the adolescent. A few parents

(9 percent) shared households with unrelated "roommates" or "roomers," presumably to make housing costs more manageable. On the whole, however, the parental households contained only nuclear family members—either single parents with children, or repartnered parents with children.

Adolescents' Residential History

The parent interviews conducted during Study 1 provided information concerning the residence of each of our adolescents at three points in time after the parents separated. At Time 4, the adolescents themselves reported the amount of time they were spending with each parent. For all four time periods, we defined "dual" residence as meaning that a child usually spent at least four overnights per two-week period with each parent during the school year. If children usually spent eleven or more overnights with their mother, they were considered to be living primarily with her. Similarly, children who spent eleven or more overnights with their fathers during usual two-week periods in the school year were classified as father-resident.

Figure 3.1 shows that over two-thirds of the adolescents were living with their mothers at each of the four time periods, and the proportion changed very slightly over time—dropping off by 1.5 percentage points at Times 3 and 4. The proportion living primarily with their fathers increased somewhat, while the proportion living in dual residence dropped off slightly. In general, the adolescents who participated in Study 2 had been somewhat more likely to live with their fathers after the divorce than to live in dual residence. At Time 4, our sample consisted of 366 mother-resident adolescents, 100 father-resident adolescents, and 51 dual-resident adolescents. One percent of the adolescents were living primarily with someone other than their mother or father; these adolescents are excluded from the analyses about residence and visitation.

These proportions contrast with our earlier findings in Study 1 from the full sample of divorcing families (Maccoby and Mnookin, 1992). When families with children of all ages were included, more had adopted dual residence than father residence at Times 1, 2, and 3. The incidence of father residence was higher for older children than for younger children, and the authors suggested that this probably reflected an assumption on the part of many parents that father residence was more feasible for children who were no longer "of tender years." By contrast, the propor-

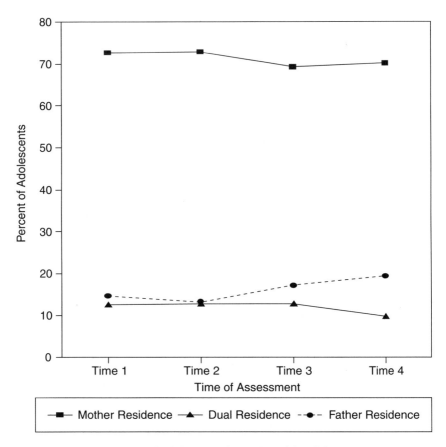

Figure 3.1 Percentage of adolescents in each residential arrangement at
the four times of assessment following parents' separation.

tion living in dual residence was lower for older children than for
younger. This fact may stem from older children having more "say" in
where they will live, with a number of adolescents preferring to avoid the
complexity and inconvenience of dual residence (Maccoby and Mnookin,
1992). Given these age trends documented in Study 1, it is not surprising
to find that father residence is slightly more common than dual residence
among the adolescents in Study 2.

Among our adolescents, more boys than girls lived with their fathers
or in dual residence, and more girls than boys lived with their mothers
(see Figure 3.2), indicating a same-sex-parent bias in children's de facto
residence.

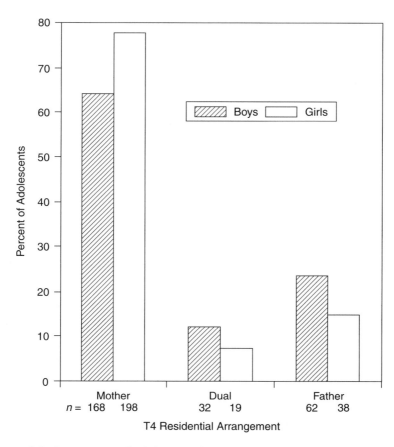

Figure 3.2 Percentage of adolescents in each residential arrangement at Time 4, by sex of adolescent. Excluded are five adolescents not living with either natural parent.

How many of our adolescents had been in the same residential arrangements over the four and a half years following their parents' separation? Figure 3.1 presents a misleading picture of great residential stability. In fact, these overall residence rates mask various compensating residential shifts. Nearly one-third of our adolescents had moved from one residential arrangement to another during the four-year period since their parents separated, and 13 percent had moved between households more than once.

When adolescents shifted residence, they were more likely to move out of dual residence than into it, and adolescents dropping out of dual residence most commonly moved into the mother's household rather than the father's (see Table 3.1). The number of adolescents who moved from the mother's household to the father's (10 percent of the total sample) was greater than the number who moved from the father's house to the mother's (6 percent). However, the *proportion* of adolescents initially in mother residence who moved in with their fathers (about one-sixth) was smaller than the proportion of adolescents who made the reverse move (over two-fifths of those initially living with fathers).

When adolescents had changed residences, they were asked the reasons for the change (see Table 3.2). The most common reason given was a move to a new location on the part of one or both parents, and this was mentioned more often by adolescents who had moved in with their mother than those who had moved into dual or father residence. Geographical moves on the part of parents brought a number of factors into play. For some adolescents the strongest motive was to remain near their friends. As one boy put it: "My mother moved from all my friends, so I wanted to live with Dad." An issue that was particularly important to older adolescents was the opportunity to finish school at the school they had been attending. A boy who had just finished high school said, "Mom moved . . . I decided for my senior year that I wanted to be at my old school. My dad lives closer to it." As is evident from these examples,

Table 3.1 The direction of residential moves[a]

Residential status		Percentage of entire sample
Now living with mother		70.3
Have lived with her continuously	(57.0)	
Moved in from father residence	(5.5)	
Moved in from dual residence	(7.8)	
Now living in dual residence		9.9
Have lived in dual continuously	(5.9)	
Moved in from mother residence	(2.4)	
Moved in from father residence	(1.6)	
Now living in father residence		19.8
Have lived with him continuously	(6.9)	
Moved in from mother residence	(10.1)	
Moved in from dual residence	(2.8)	

a. This table excludes fifteen cases of adolescents who were living with someone other than their mother or father at one of the four interview periods. For those adolescents who had moved more than once, the most recent move is counted here.

Table 3.2 Reasons given for change in residence by adolescents whose residential arrangement changed between Time 1 and Time 4, by T4 residential arrangement, in percent[a]

Reason[b]	T4 residential arrangement		
	Mother ($n = 62$)	Dual ($n = 13$)	Father ($n = 61$)
A parent moved	45	23	21
Family conflict	15	0	30
Adolescent missed nonresidential parent	5	38	10
Other home provided better environment	10	0	16

a. For those adolescents who had moved more than once, the most recent move is counted here.

b. The reasons listed here are the four most frequently given. Percentages in each column do not sum to 100 because a variety of reasons were given less commonly and are not listed here. Also, more than one reason was coded for some adolescents.

when the residential parent moved and the adolescent switched to the other parent's residence, the switch usually represented the adolescent's own choice, reflecting the priority given by young people to stability in their out-of-home environments. In these cases, the parents appear to have gone along with the adolescent's choice, sometimes willingly, sometimes reluctantly.

The next most common reason for a change in an adolescent's residential arrangement was conflict among family members. This reason was given more often by adolescents who moved into either mother or father residence than by those who moved into dual residence; in addition, it was given more often as a reason for moving into father residence than into mother residence. Commonly, the conflict was between the adolescent and the residential parent:

(Adolescent who moved from mother's to father's household): "I got that role which you call 'teenager' and sometimes when I would sass back at my mother [her response] made me mad. So I didn't want to live with her anymore."

(Adolescent who moved from father to mother): "My dad wasn't treating me right. I didn't like living with him . . . I decided to move in with my mom."

(Adolescent who moved from mother to father): "I couldn't stand living with my mom . . . She said if I wanted to leave, leave. So I did."

In some cases, the familial conflict was between the adolescent and a parent's new partner:

(Adolescent who moved from dual residence to mother): "There was a lot of conflicts [*sic*] over the years. There was a big blow-up . . . and it sort of had to do with my stepmom. We didn't get along too well."

(Adolescent who had moved several times and was currently living alone): "I moved in with my dad 'cause I missed him. Then . . . I went back with my mother because I had disagreements with my father's partner. [Interviewer: How about getting your own place?] Well, I just had disagreements with my mother's boyfriend."

(Adolescent who had moved from father to mother): "Well, my step-mom moved in. I just didn't like her. That's when I moved in with my mom."

(Adolescent who moved from father to mother): "It was lack of communication between me and my dad . . . My stepmom and stepbrother are a problem . . . The rules are different . . . He didn't ask me about remarrying."

Although a variety of family conflicts were given as a reason for moving from one parental household to another, family conflicts were never given as the reason for moving into dual residence. Why did adolescents move into dual residence? Quite a few adolescents said that they had missed their nonresidential parent and wanted to spend more time with him or her. The parents responded by arranging a more equal division of the child's time between the two parents.

In contrast to the interpersonal conflict we have described, some adolescents moved because they felt that the parent with whom they resided was away too much or not attentive enough to their needs. As examples, adolescents cited moving in with parents who would have family meals, get home from work earlier, take the time to sign them up for special classes or sports teams, or simply have rules and discipline.

In some cases, moves were dictated by the desire (on the part of the adolescent, the parents, or both) to have the child live in the environment that would be most supportive for the child's schoolwork. A child who was doing poorly in school might be shifted to the other household in the hope that the other parent could provide better supervision of homework or school attendance:

(Adolescent who had moved in with her father): "I moved in with my father because of my school attendance record . . . He's more strict with me cutting."

(Adolescent who moved from mother to father): "I think one of the major reasons was basically I got a lot of educational support from my dad . . . And, he gets paid more, so I really didn't have to worry about financial support. I felt that perhaps my dad would be, uh, in a better position . . ."

Unfortunately the tape of this interview becomes inaudible at this point. Although we cannot be sure, we suspect this adolescent had future college expenses in mind.

Although these interview excerpts suggest a fairly high level of conflict between adolescents and their parents, we should remember that the remarks came from the minority of adolescents, about a third, who had moved from one parental household to the other, or in or out of dual residence. Adolescents who changed households reported higher levels of familial conflict than did the two-thirds who remained in their initial residential arrangement. In addition, those who moved for positive reasons usually gave few details about their situations, while those with negative reasons—like most of the cases cited above—tended to report at length. These negative cases are not typical of our sample as a whole, but they do represent an important subgroup of troubled families.

Siblings: Living Together or Apart?

So far, we have been describing the Time 4 residence situation—and residence history—for individual adolescents, without regard to where their siblings lived. For those adolescents who had siblings, most (65 percent) had the same residential arrangement as their siblings. In a substantial minority of families, however, the children did not have the same residential arrangement; one child might be sharing residential time fairly equally between the two parents (dual residence) while other children in the same family were living primarily with the mother or the father. More commonly, one or more of the children lived with the mother while one or more lived with the father. We have labeled families in which the children do not all share the same residential arrangement as having "split" residence. This pattern was relatively rare over the whole sample at the time of the third parent interview (10 percent of children aged three to eighteen had a sibling living in a different residential arrangement at that time), but in the present sample of children aged ten to eighteen it was more common (35 percent of adolescents with siblings). Young people living with their fathers were especially likely to have a sibling living in a different residential arrangement: 42 percent of these adolescents lived apart from a sibling, as opposed to 11 percent of mother-resident adolescents and 8 percent of dual-resident adolescents.

Visitation

Children who are in dual residence of course spend substantial amounts of time with each of their parents, but most children who live primarily with one parent are by no means cut off from the other parent. Among adolescents who lived primarily with their mother or their father, the amount of contact with the nonresidential parent varied from never seeing this parent to staying overnight at the other parent's household two or three times in a typical two-week period during the school year. When a divorce decree specifies that one parent shall have "reasonable visitation" with the children, a common arrangement is for the children to spend every other weekend with the nonresidential parent.

Visitation will be discussed in detail in Chapter 9. For the present, we simply note that levels of contact with the nonresidential parent were quite high. Only 7 percent of our adolescents had not seen a nonresidential parent (mother or father) within the past year. The numbers of adolescents who had very little or no contact with their nonresidential parent are similar to those derived from recent national studies. For example, Seltzer (1991) reported that for children under eighteen whose parents had been separated five years or less, 11 percent had not seen their nonresidential father in the past year. The rate of noncontact specifically for adolescents was not given, but visitation was generally higher the older the child,[1] so the rate of noncontact was likely quite similar to our own.

At the other extreme, 70 percent of our sole-resident adolescents reported having seen the nonresidential parent within the past month. And approximately half of sole-resident adolescents had regular visits with the nonresidential parent that involved an overnight stay during nonvacation portions of the school year. The number of adolescents that sustained high contact with nonresidential parents may be somewhat higher in our sample than in the country as a whole, although the comparison is harder to make than the comparison concerning no contact because the time units measured across studies are not identical. For example, Seltzer (1991) found that 58 percent of children under eighteen saw their nonresidential fathers at least once a month, and 33 percent saw him at least once a week, and as noted above, these rates would be somewhat higher if the sample were restricted to children in the adolescent age range. These numbers are lower than the ones we have cited, but the level of contact is also somewhat more restricted (for example, of the 70 percent of adolescents in our sample who had seen their nonresidential parent in the last month, at least some did not see that parent every month). On the whole, our assessment is that the levels of contact represented in our sample are fairly close to national norms; however, the possibility exists that visitation rates were somewhat higher in California at the end of the 1980s than was true for adolescents elsewhere in the country.

Life Stresses

In later chapters we will examine the adjustment of the adolescents in our sample. In doing so, it will be important to understand the situations to which they had to adapt. We asked our subjects a series of questions about events that had occurred in the past year—illnesses or deaths of people close to them, changes in schools or residence, changes in relationships with boyfriends or girlfriends, changes in parental jobs and family financial circumstances, and so forth. A complete list of life events about which we inquired appears in Table 3.3. Illness of close persons was a common occurrence. For a substantial minority, instability of the home and family situation also was reported: residential moves were common, sometimes accompanied by a change of schools, changes in parental jobs, or a new person (often the new partner of a parent) moving into the household. Changing relations with peers also figured strongly in our adolescents' reports of life events: a large number had had a fight with a close friend, and many had broken up with a boyfriend or girlfriend, or had begun to date or go steady—intensely important events in the eyes of teenagers.

Adolescent Adjustment

How well adjusted was this group of adolescents nearly five years after their parents' separation? There can be no general answer: young people differ enormously in how well they cope with any major life stress, including the divorce of their parents. Nevertheless, we would like to

Table 3.3 Life events occurring in the past year, from most
to least common

Event	Percentage of adolescents reporting "yes"
A close person was seriously ill or hospitalized	49.8
Adolescent had serious fight with a close friend	47.9
Adolescent began to date or go steady with someone	40.8
Parent changed jobs	38.4
Adolescent changed schools	37.5
Adolescent broke up with boyfriend or girlfriend	32.6
Family moved to new house	30.7
New person joined the household	30.5
Favorite pet died or disappeared	29.7
Close person died	28.2
Family had serious financial troubles	23.1
Mother or father spent more time away from home (because of job change or for other reason)	21.3
A new baby was born in the family	20.7
Adolescent started wearing braces or glasses	19.2
Parent lost job	15.0
Someone in family was assaulted, or was victim of other violent crime	15.0
Adolescent was seriously ill or hospitalized	9.4

know whether most of our adolescents had managed to weather this enormous stress reasonably well, so that they were functioning within a "normal" range, or whether a substantial number carried deep and lasting scars.

Our study was not designed to answer this question. There are no national or regional norms on the measures we have used, so that we cannot say how a cross-section sample of all adolescents (including those with never-divorced parents) would have answered our questions. Furthermore, we did not interview a comparison group of adolescents from nondivorced families in our catchment area.[2] Our primary purpose was to compare the postdivorce adjustment of adolescents in different living situations. Furthermore, relying on the absolute level of self-reports is always risky, because people often see themselves in a rosier light than others see them. And identifying a cut-off point that separates "normal" from problematic functioning is, of course, an arbitrary decision. Keeping these caveats in mind, we still may learn something of value simply by taking the adolescents' answers at face value, to see how often these answers reflect what appears to be satisfactory functioning. We give only a rough sketch of these self-reports, however, because of the limitations on what can be gleaned from overall mean scores.[3]

Depression/Anxiety

The average score on this scale fell just at the midpoint of the range of possible scores (mean = 15.2, range 0–30), and approximately a quarter of the cases scored in the upper third of the range. This means that a sizable minority of our adolescents were reporting fairly frequent symptoms of depression or anxiety. Another quarter of the sample were in the lower third of the range, meaning that they reported that in the last month they had seldom or never experienced most of the fairly moderate symptoms (feeling tired, irritable, worried) included in the scale. We must remember that adolescence is a time when such symptoms usually increase among unselected groups of adolescents (Buchanan, Eccles, and Becker, 1992), so although we most likely have a higher proportion of depressed adolescents reporting substantial symptoms of depression than would be the case among adolescents overall,[4] the difference is probably not drastic.

Deviance

Our adolescents reported very low levels of all forms of deviant behavior. Nearly two-thirds reported not a single instance of using drugs or alcohol, stealing someone else's property, vandalizing property, or getting into any sort of trouble with the police during the past year. Only 15 percent reported more than one such event. Breaking school rules (cutting classes, arriving late, cheating on tests) was reported somewhat more often, but the mean score on these items was still only 7.2 out of a possible range of 4–16. Our measure of overall deviance, for which we combined breaking school rules, antisocial acts, and substance use, had a possible range of 15–60, and the median score was only 20, with no cases above 46. We recognize that even though we promised our subjects anonymity, they knew that we knew their identity. Delinquent activities were therefore undoubtedly somewhat underreported. Nevertheless, the reported levels are quite low.

School Performance and Effort

On the whole, the adolescents reported fairly good grades. The mean was 5.8 on a scale in which 5 means "about half B's and half C's" and 6 means "mostly B's." Only a little over 10 percent of the adolescents had grades at the low end of the scale ("mostly D's" or "about half C's and half D's"); over two-fifths said they were getting "mostly A's" or "about half A's and half B's." The meaning of these reports depends, of course, on the grading standards of the schools these adolescents attended, but it seems clear that many more adolescents were doing at least moderately well in school than were close to failure. With respect to the amount of effort put into schoolwork, scores clustered at the middle of the possible range.

Personal Resources

Our scores for adolescents' personal resources present a reasonably positive picture: most adolescents said they were more likely to try to resolve interpersonal conflicts through compromise and discussion than through aggressive tactics. But quite a few also said that they used avoidance (withdrawal). Most reported a variety of extracurricular activities that they enjoyed doing (such as sports, dancing, computer games, playing a musical instrument or singing, reading, collecting something), and very few presented a picture of aimless drifting in their use of out-of-school time. Most also reported having at least one close same-sex friend on whom they relied.

Relationships with Parents

Levels of conflict with parents were low. Adolescents were asked whether they had discussed with either parent during the past two weeks a variety of issues (for example, chores around the house, whether they could bring a friend to the house when no adult was home, how late they could stay out). If a discussion had occurred, they were asked how angry the discussion had become. Even for the issue that produced the most parent-child conflict, only two-fifths of the adolescents said that any significant amount of anger had been involved,[5] and most said that the discussion had not been heated. We suspect that this situation is comparable to that which prevails between most teenagers and their parents (see, for example, Montemayor, 1983).

Our adolescents were asked a series of questions concerning the closeness and openness of their relationship with each parent. For each item, the adolescent rated closeness on a five-point scale, for example, from "not at all open" to "very open." The mean scores (across items) fell at the level of 4 on the five-point scale for closeness to mothers, with a quarter of the sample answering "5" on a majority of the questions. Scores for fathers were somewhat lower. Most important, only a small proportion of adolescents described their relationships with 1's and 2's on the closeness items—5 percent did so for relationships with mothers, and 10 percent for relationships with fathers. On the whole, these adolescents described a close, trusting relationship with both parents.

Satisfaction with the Living Situation

The adolescents were asked to rate on a ten-point scale how satisfied they were with the way their time was divided between the two parental homes. The mean score of 6.9 indicates that the majority of adolescents rated themselves well above the midpoint of the satisfaction scale. One-third rated themselves at the upper end—at 8, 9, or 10—while only 13 percent rated themselves at the low end—at 1, 2, or 3. Although there was a considerable range in satisfaction, the majority of adolescents appeared to have adapted fairly well to the special conditions that arose when their parents formed two different households.

Summary

Although it is possible that there are somewhat more adolescents in our sample who are showing signs of significant depression than would be true of a sample of adolescents from nondivorced families, it is our judgment that the majority of our adolescents fall within a "normal" range of adjustment. This conclusion is consistent with other current assessments of adolescents whose families have experienced divorce (Amato and Keith, 1991; Barber and Lyons, 1994; Kelly, 1993). In terms of deviance, school performance, personal resources, relationships with parents, and adaptation to their residential and visitation arrangements, adolescent self-reports were typically positive. It is even more important to note, however, that variation was great on all our measures. There were many who were doing very well, living well-organized, goal-oriented, reasonably happy lives. A smaller group manifested problems of several kinds. The chapters that follow will attempt to uncover the conditions that affect whether an adolescent will adapt well or poorly to the circumstances following parental divorce.

Comparing Residential Arrangements

4

Adolescent Adjustment

Although most adolescents live with their mothers after their parents have divorced, some do not. Two alternative arrangements—father or joint physical custody—have become more common, and their benefits and drawbacks are actively debated. It has become important to learn as much as we can concerning these different custodial arrangements—how well they work as time passes, and what kind of conditions they provide for the young people living in them.

At the outset, we need to distinguish between the divorce decree's specifications for physical custody of the children and the children's actual residence. They are often not the same. As Maccoby and Mnookin (1992) reported for the sample of California families from which our adolescent sample was drawn, fewer than half of the families who had been awarded joint physical custody were actually maintaining a joint arrangement three years after filing for divorce. We saw in Chapter 3 that a substantial proportion of adolescents in these families had moved from one parental household to another since their parents had separated, although such moves usually meant that they would be living in an arrangement different from the one specified in the divorce decree. In this book, we are concerned with the actual residence of the adolescent, rather than with the physical custody specified in the legal divorce agreement.

Our goal in the next few chapters is to compare mother residence, father residence, and dual residence. We begin by examining how well the adolescents in each arrangement are adapting to their life situation—in other words, how they score on various measures of adjustment. We are aware, of course, that different residential arrangements can emerge under widely varying circumstances, so that a simple comparison of adolescent adjustment by type of arrangement can be misleading. Certain types of families or children may select certain arrangements, and these preexisting characteristics may, in turn, affect the way in which the arrangements work out for the adolescents. In order to clarify the source of any residence differences in adolescent adjustment, we have taken the following steps:

1. In this chapter, we first compare the different residential arrangements on their economic and "human capital" resources ("demographic factors"), and then statistically control for differences in resources related to residence in our comparisons of adolescent adjustment by type of residence.
2. In Chapter 5 we compare the different arrangements on a variety of aspects of home life, including residential stability over time, number of life stresses, past and present family relationships, and current parental styles of control and household management. By including indicators of earlier family functioning, in addition to information about the family's current status, we are able to gain insight into whether certain residential arrangements are associated with a more or less difficult history.
3. In Chapter 6, we examine the links between adolescent adjustment and multiple characteristics of the family or home, separately for each residential group. These analyses tell us which of the many indicators of family functioning—past or present—are most predictive of adolescents' adjustment four and a half years after their parents' divorce.

Residence Differences in Demographic Factors

Table 4.1 summarizes the residence differences in the demographic and "human capital" characteristics of families. Adolescents in dual residence were, on average, younger by about one year than adolescents in mother or father residence. Although others have found children in father residence to be older than children in mother residence (Maccoby and Mnookin, 1992; Sweet and Bumpass, 1987; Wallerstein and Blakeslee, 1989), within the limited age range of our sample, the adolescents in father and mother residence were almost identical in age.

There were proportionally more boys than girls in dual and father residence, and proportionally more girls in mother residence. These sex differences concur with those reported by Maccoby and Mnookin (1992) for the entire Stanford Custody Study sample, where it was found that boys were more likely to live initially in dual and father residence. Yet

Table 4.1 Demographic characteristics by residential arrangement

	Residence			
	Mother	Dual	Father	
Max. N (all cases)	366	51	100	
Max. N (random sample)	241	41	81	
Measure				Residence effect
Mean age of adolescent	14.2	13.2	14.3	$F(2,514) = 3.99*$ (D < M, F)
Percentage male	46	63	62	$\chi^2 (2, N = 517) = 11.44**$
Mother's education[a]	5.1	5.7	4.7	$F(2,358) = 10.26****$ (D > M > F)
Father's education[a]	5.4	6.0	5.2	$F(2,359) = 3.14*$ (D > M, F)
Mother's average earnings, T1–T3[a,b]	20.4	20.7	16.6	$F(2,350) = 3.11*$ (M > F)
Father's average earnings, T1–T3[a,b]	42.1	54.9	44.5	$F(2,340) = 3.28*$ (D > M)
Mother's household income[a,b]	36.1	34.3	25.7	$F(2,301) = 5.36**$ (M > F)
Father's household income[a,b]	45.8	54.4	49.8	$F(2,243) = 1.08$

a. Analyses done using a random sample.
b. In tens of thousands.
*$p < .05$.   **$p \leq .01$.   ****$p \leq .0001$.

for that larger sample, a child's sex was not related to whether a child would shift into or out of dual or father residence, which indicates that the residence differences in sex composition that were established during the initial custody decision largely remain four years later.

Because dual residence has the potential to be somewhat more complicated and require more resources than other arrangements (for example, places for children to sleep and keep belongings are needed in both homes), we anticipated that families who maintained this arrangement four and a half years after separation would be advantaged in some respects. Several previous studies have found higher socioeconomic levels among families with joint custody arrangements than among those with some form of sole custody (Kline et al., 1989; Pearson and Thoennes, 1990). And in the larger sample of parents from the Stanford Custody Study, families initially adopting dual residence had higher levels of education and income than did families adopting sole-residence arrangements (Maccoby and Mnookin, 1992). Table 4.1 shows that, in families with adolescent children, the educational advantage of dual-resident families remains. Both mothers and fathers in families that were maintaining dual residence at Time 4 had higher levels of education than did their sole-resident counterparts. Mothers' education was higher in dual-resident families than in mother-resident ones, and lowest of all among families in which the children lived with their fathers. The education of fathers in dual residence was higher than that of fathers in either sole-resident arrangement. The education of sole-resident mothers did not differ from that of sole-resident fathers.

In terms of economic resources, however, dual-resident families did not have so clear an advantage. Whether we consider personal average earnings over the postseparation period or total household income at Time 3 (which includes support payments from nonresident parents and contributions from remarried new partners), mothers' income was similar in dual and mother residence. As was true for education, mothers in families in which the adolescent was living with the father had the lowest incomes. Fathers in dual residence had higher personal earnings, but not significantly higher household income, than did fathers in other residential arrangements.[1]

More striking than the differences in resources between dual-resident families and sole-resident families was the difference between the earnings of mothers and fathers. Over all residential arrangements, fathers' earnings were more than twice as high as mothers', and fathers' household incomes were substantially higher even after the effects of new spouses' incomes and child-support payments were taken into account. In terms of the income in the residential household, adolescents living primarily with their fathers were economically better off in comparison with mother-resident adolescents.

As we considered which statistical controls to employ for comparisons of adolescent adjustment in the three types of residences, it was clear that we needed to control for age and sex of the adolescent. (In addition, in all of our analyses we look at whether residence differences vary for boys and girls.) We wondered, however, whether it was necessary to control for both parental education and parental income. The two were, of course, correlated ($r = .42$ for mothers, $.41$ for fathers). Somewhat surprisingly, associations between parental education or income and our adjustment measures were quite weak, with most close to zero. One exception was the link between higher parental education and higher school grades, higher school effort, and a lower likelihood of problems as measured by our "worst problem" scale. In another exception, higher income of the residential parent was associated with *higher* levels of overall deviance and substance use ($r = .11, p < .05$ and $r = .12, p < .01$, respectively). Thus parental education appeared to have a stronger positive relation to adjustment than did parental income, although neither set of relations was impressive.

When parental education and income were considered jointly in their relation to residence, parental education was more strongly related. Not surprisingly, given the similarities in income between parents in dual residence and other parents, education had considerably more weight than the income of either parent in determining whether an adolescent would be in dual residence. A mother's earnings were also unrelated to her adolescents' residence type once education was controlled, but a low level of education remained significantly associated with the adolescent's being in father residence. For fathers, a high level of education meant that a father was less likely to have primary custody of his adolescent children, but as with mothers, fathers' incomes bore no relation to the probability of their children living with them after education was controlled. Given these findings, we controlled for parental education, not income, in the comparisons that follow. In order to simplify the analyses, we controlled for average parental education, which was at least as highly correlated with adjustment as was the education of the residential parent.[2]

Residence and Psychosocial Adjustment

Several previous studies have provided information on children's adjustment in different custodial arrangements. Most of these studies, however, have methodological limitations that constrain our ability to generalize from them. Some investigators have stated that children benefit from joint custody, but base these claims on small, primarily clinical, samples (Abarbanel, 1979; Glover and Steele, 1989; Neugebauer, 1989; Steinman, 1981), often lacking a sole-residence control group (Abarbanel, 1979; Irving, Benjamin, and Trocme, 1984; Steinman, 1981). Others assume that because fathers are happier and feel more involved in joint custody arrangements than in other arrangements, this must mean that children do better in joint custody; outcomes for the children, however, are not examined (Grief, 1979; Simring, 1984). Larger studies that have used comparison groups and have controlled for confounding background factors suggest that when families are relatively cooperative and low in conflict, joint-residential arrangements are, indeed, associated with positive child outcomes (Luepnitz, 1986; Shiller, 1986a, 1986b), but that when families remain in conflict, joint custody leads to poor child outcomes (Johnston, Kline, and Tschann, 1989; Nelson, 1989).

The rare studies that have included a group of families in which the children live with their fathers after divorce have, for the most part, focused on the question of whether children fare better when living with a same-sex parent. It has been argued that each parent is more effective when dealing with a same-sex child, and that the loss of a same-sex parent after divorce is more damaging for children than the loss of an opposite-sex parent—presumably because children need an adult same-sex role model. Several small-sample studies of elementary school–aged children support this view. Among their conclusions, they find that children living with a same-sex parent have greater social competence, more appropriate sex-role development, higher self-esteem, lower levels of behavioral problems, better understanding of the divorce, and greater satisfaction with visitation and living arrangements than do children living with an opposite-sex parent (Camara and Resnick, 1988; Santrock, 1970; Santrock and Warshak, 1979; Santrock, Warshak, and Elliott, 1982; Warshak and Santrock, 1983). One study also reported on adolescents, again finding better outcomes among those living with their same-sex parents (Peterson and Zill, 1986). In a review of the literature, Zaslow (1988, 1989) concluded that sex differences in children's response to divorce—with boys adjusting more poorly—arise primarily from this phenomenon. Not all studies, however, have found adjustment to be related to residence with a same-sex parent (Kurdek, Blisk, and Siesky, 1981), and therefore we examine this issue with our data.

As noted in Chapter 2, our investigation of the links between residential arrangement and adolescent adaptive characteristics and adjustment focused on the following aspects of adjustment: personal resources (conflict resolution styles, breadth of activities enjoyed, closeness of peer relationships), internalizing problems (depression/anxiety), externalizing problems (overall deviance and subtypes of deviant behavior), and school adjustment (grades, school effort).

Personal Resources

Means, by residence, for the "personal resources" scales are in Appendix Table B.5.

Conflict resolution styles. Among children of divorce aged six to seventeen years, Kurdek (1987) found that the best-adjusted children were good at conflict resolution. The ability to resolve conflict in constructive ways may be an indicator of psychosocial maturity; it may also be an asset that leads to positive adjustment through optimal resolution of difficult situations. We asked adolescents how they ordinarily dealt with interpersonal conflict, specifically when they had a disagreement with a friend. As noted in Chapter 2, three major modes of resolution emerged: compromise, avoidance or withdrawal, and confrontation or attack. Considerable variation among adolescents in self-reported styles of conflict resolution was evident, and adolescents—especially girls—in all three residential groups were more likely to say that they used a compromising approach than an attacking or avoidant one. There were no residence differences, however, in the mode of resolution used.

Enjoyment of activities. The importance of academic and social competence has been cited as a factor in children's resilience to stress (see, for example, Garmezy, Masten, and Tellegen, 1984; Rutter, 1979). In a broader sense, involvement in a variety of activities that one finds enjoyable may be considered a sign of positive adaptation. Furthermore, having enjoyable activities to absorb one's time and attention under stressful circumstances may buffer the stressors and promote positive adjustment more generally. Thus we asked the adolescents about activities—including, for example, sports, using a computer, playing a musical instrument, or singing—that they engaged in *and* enjoyed. Although some adolescents had many activities they enjoyed and others had few, variation in enjoyable activities was not related to residential arrangements.

Friendships. A close relationship with a same-sex friend provides an important source of social support for adolescents (Kurdek, 1987; Werner and Smith, 1982), so we examined adolescents' ability to have and keep a close friend. We found, as have other studies, that girls reported greater closeness in their same-sex friendships than did boys, but for neither sex was there any difference in this closeness by residential arrangement. In a similar vein, we asked our respondents how they usually spent their after-school time, and the girls were more likely than the boys to mention talking on the phone, hanging out with friends, or partying—forms of time use that imply involvement in a social network. Once again, however, these kinds of after-school activities did not differ by residence.

Internalizing and Externalizing Problems

Means, by residence, for internalizing problems, externalizing problems, and school adjustment are in Appendix Table B.6.

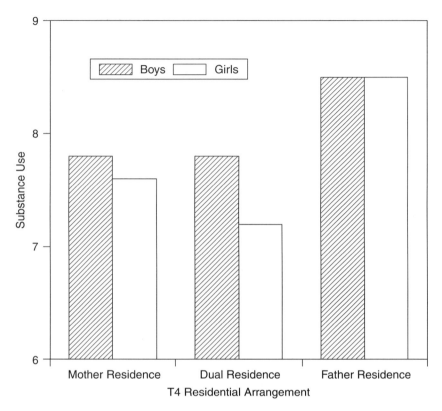

Figure 4.1a Substance use by adolescents in each residence and gender group. Means are adjusted for age of adolescent and the average education of the two parents.

Depression/anxiety. Adolescence is a time when sex differences in depression become substantial (Buchanan, Eccles, and Becker, 1992; Nolen-Hoeksema and Girgus, 1994). Our findings are consistent with the existing literature in showing higher levels of depression/anxiety among girls than among boys. However, levels of depression/anxiety did not depend on the adolescent's residential arrangement.

Deviance. As noted in Chapter 2, we approached the question of "externalizing" (deviant) behavior with questions about three subareas: substance use, school deviance, and antisocial behavior. Our measure of overall deviance was the sum of the items from these three subscales. The boys in our sample were somewhat more likely to report deviant behavior in general than were the girls; in particular, they were more likely to report

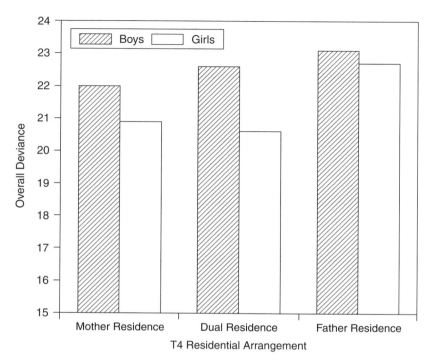

Figure 4.1b Overall deviance of adolescents in each residence and gender group. Means are adjusted for age of adolescent and the average education of the two parents.

antisocial forms of deviant behavior (for example, damaging property or carrying a weapon). This sex difference is consistent with a considerable body of evidence that boys are more likely than girls to display a variety of antisocial behaviors during adolescence as well as at younger and older ages (Eagly and Steffen, 1986; Hyde, 1984; Maccoby and Jacklin, 1974).

There were also small differences in the level of deviance by residence. Adolescents who were living with their fathers reported more substance use (use of tobacco, alcohol, and other illicit substances) than did other adolescents, and in this residential group, girls' scores were as high as boys' (see Figure 4.1a). The incidence of school deviance and other forms of antisocial behavior did not differ among the residential groups, but when the three subscales were combined into the overall deviance scale, the level of deviance was somewhat (and significantly) higher among adolescents living with their fathers than among adolescents living with their mothers (see Figure 4.1b). Deviance was as low among adolescents in dual residence as it was among adolescents in mother residence, but lower among dual-resident adolescents than among those in father residence. Given the lower number of cases in dual residence, the difference between dual and father residence was statistically significant only for substance use, but the order of magnitude of the difference on overall deviance was as great as for the mother-father comparison.

Because of the relation between higher parental income and higher deviance reported earlier, we repeated these analyses controlling for residential parent's income instead of average parental education. Using income as a control eliminated the differences in deviance between residential groups. Thus the father's higher income appears to be a *disadvantage* with regard to involvement in deviant activities among the adolescents in his care. In Chapters 5 and 6 we investigate whether this is because fathers, in working at more lucrative jobs, work longer hours and consequently have less time to supervise or monitor the activities of their adolescents.

School Adjustment

Grades. We have only the reports of the adolescents themselves concerning their school grades, but self-reports are reasonably good indicators of actual grade levels (Dornbusch et al., 1987). A score of 6 reflects grades of "mostly B's," and this is the average level for the girls in our sample. The boys' average was at the "about half B's and half C's" level, although the sex difference was not significant. The adolescents in dual residence reported the highest grades, but this residence difference was of borderline significance.[3]

School effort. The degree of effort adolescents put forth in school was not related to residence for boys, but was lower for father-resident girls than for mother-resident girls. Even so, the sex difference in the impact of residence was weak, and dropped out when analyses were conducted on subsamples using one adolescent per family rather than the entire adolescent sample. If dual-resident adolescents were dropped from the analysis, and the comparison was done only with mother- and father-resident adolescents, the difference for girls was stronger, although it was still only of borderline ($p \leq .10$) significance in random samples.

Worst Problem

When an adolescent is troubled, this may express itself in different ways: some individuals may become depressed or anxious, some may "act out"

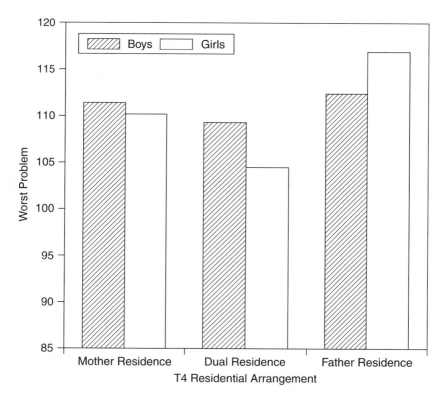

Figure 4.2 "Worst problem" score of adolescents in each residence and gender group. Means are adjusted for age of adolescent and the average education of the two parents.

in deviant ways, and some may lose motivation to do well in school. As noted in Chapter 2, we created a "worst problem" score to account for this diversity of ways to express maladjustment. The "worst problem" score reflects the worst score an adolescent received in any of three domains—depression/anxiety, overall deviance, or school effort.[4] Thus this score indicates how troubled adolescents were in the domain for which they showed the most problematic behavior. Using the "worst problem" score, we find that adolescents living with their fathers ($M = 114.6$) had a higher incidence of troubled behaviors than those in either maternal ($M = 110.8$) or dual ($M = 106.9$) residence (see Figure 4.2). Although, statistically speaking, the difference applied equally to both sexes, examination of Figure 4.2 suggests that the difference between father residence and the other residence groups is larger for girls than it is for boys. For both boys and girls, dual-resident adolescents were slightly better off than those in mother residence on this measure.[5]

Summary

As noted in Chapter 3, our adolescents' reports about their behavior and feelings indicated that their adjustment was, on average, satisfactory. Still, we have identified considerable variation within our sample, and some of our adolescents were considerably better adjusted than others. How much of this variation was associated with residential arrangements? Our answer is: not a great deal. Variation within each of the groups was large, and the three groups had similar group averages on both personal resources and adjustment. Nevertheless, some small group differences did emerge, especially when we considered each adolescent's most severe problem. On our "worst problem" measure, an adolescent was considered to be functioning suboptimally if she or he was "acting out," depressed, or doing poorly in school. Young people in father residence were, on average, functioning less well in at least one area than were young people in the other residential groups. The group who appeared to be functioning best were those in dual residence, and the mother-resident group was intermediate. These findings are made more striking by the fact that father residence might be considered advantaged in that residential fathers typically had considerably higher incomes than residential mothers. Yet, in our sample, household income did not appear to have an important direct link with adjustment, and where it did, it was linked to worse adjustment (a higher level of deviance).

It is, of course, possible that the advantages of father residence with regard to household income are offset by other disadvantages that co-occur with father residence. Despite recent increases in the incidence of father residence, it is still a relatively uncommon arrangement. Fathers get custody more often when the mother has been relatively uninvolved with the children before the separation (see Maccoby and Mnookin, 1992). They may also be more likely to get custody when the mother has personal problems or when the children are difficult to handle. In Chapters 5 and 6, we further examine the question of whether father residence at Time 4 is associated with a more difficult family history, to investigate whether the slightly higher level of difficulties among adolescents living with their fathers is a result of fathers' having gained custody in particularly disadvantageous situations.

As we saw earlier, a number of researchers have claimed that children of divorce fare better when in the custody of the same-sex parent. In general, we did not find support for this hypothesis. The boys in our sample were generally doing as well when living with their mothers as when living with their fathers, and sometimes slightly better. When we found significant differences among residential groups, they generally applied to adolescents of both sexes. That is, statistically speaking, there were no grounds for concluding that residence differences applied only to girls or only to boys. A more informal inspection of the means for the two sexes, however, indicates that difficulties in father residence are sometimes limited to, or more pronounced for, girls. So it may be true that, on average, girls are better off when living with their mothers. But it may also be the case that boys are better off in their mothers' care—they certainly are no worse off.

In attempting to understand what might underlie these small residence differences in adjustment, we need to consider the environments of different residences in more detail. In the next chapter, we turn to an exploration of life in each residential arrangement: Who lives in the home? How much do parents work? How many major life stresses have been experienced? What are family relationships like? What styles of parental control and management are used? We look at whether and how these aspects of life in one's home differ by residential arrangement. After considering such factors in Chapter 5, in Chapter 6 we examine the links between the characteristics of these environments and the adaptation of the adolescents in them.

5

Life in the
Residential Home

In this chapter we examine what life is like for adolescents in the different residential arrangements. First, we compare the arrangements with respect to several past and current contextual factors likely to influence the kind of life an adolescent experiences in the home: (a) How stable has the residential arrangement been over the time since the parental separation? In other words, how likely is it that an adolescent has been in his or her current arrangement ever since the separation, and how likely is it that he or she has changed residences at least once? (b) How stressful has life been for the adolescent in the past year? Are some arrangements linked with more life stress than others? (c) How many children are in the original family? Do parents' decisions about where their children are to live depend on how many children they have? (d) How many people are currently living in the residential home, and who are they? For example, what is the likelihood that stepparents, stepsiblings, or half-siblings are present in each arrangement? and (e) How many hours does the residential parent work per week?

Second, we examine the quality of relationships within the family, including the nature of the ongoing relationship between the parents as well as the nature of the relationship between the residential parent and the adolescent. Third, we compare the extent to which parents exert control in the household, and the ways in which households are managed.[1] The quality of family relationships and the styles of parental control and management have been consistently linked to psychosocial adjustment among children and adolescents in both divorced and nondivorced families.

Contextual Factors

Stability of the Residential Arrangement

There were large residential differences in the stability of residence over time (see Figure 5.1).[2] Adolescents in mother residence at Time 4 were much more likely than adolescents in father or dual residence to have remained in their initial residential arrangement since the separation. Adolescents in father residence were the most likely to have shifted residence at some point since the separation. There was a trend for these differences in stability of residence to be somewhat stronger for girls than for boys; in other words, girls in mother residence were especially likely to have been there ever since the parental separation, and girls in father residence were especially likely to have moved in with their fathers after initially living elsewhere (for most, with mothers).

The differences in stability of residence most likely have to do with the reasons different residential arrangements are adopted. As we have noted

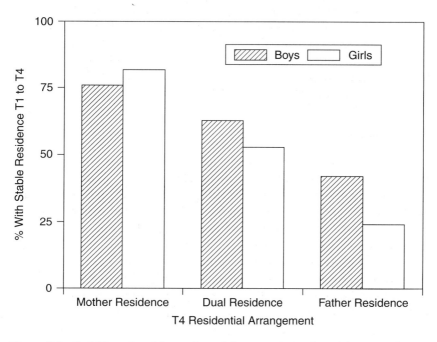

Figure 5.1 Stability of residence for adolescents in each residence and gender group.

in previous chapters, despite recent shifts toward gender-neutrality in divorce law, a strong preference for maternal custody remains in both legal decrees and actual practice (Maccoby and Mnookin, 1992). When parents arrive at their own decision about custodial arrangements with little dis-agreement—as most do—they usually opt for maternal physical custody. Furthermore, legal processes probably embody some de facto presump-tion for mother custody, and most mothers are strongly determined to retain custody of their children after divorce. Those mothers who might not otherwise insist on mother custody often feel social pressure to do so. Among families who do elect sole-father residence, therefore, there may often be special family circumstances that make it difficult for the mother to retain some form of custody. Alternatively, the children themselves may have chosen to live with their fathers, often after spending some time living with their mothers. Adolescents who switch to father residence at some point after the separation do so because of complications in the mother's ability to maintain a household, conflict between the mother and child, the inability of the mother to "control" a difficult child, or simply because of the adolescent's desire to live with her or his father after a time away from him (see Chapter 3). The fact that father residence is more likely to be chosen in situations of maternal or familial difficulties, or at the adoles-cents' initiative, may help to explain why this residential arrangement is more unstable than other arrangements and also why it carries a higher likelihood of life stress, as we see next.

Life Stresses

As Figure 5.2 shows, adolescents living with their fathers reported more total stresses within the past year than did adolescents in other arrange-ments. We examined each individual stress in order to see which specific life stresses were experienced more often by father-resident adoles-cents. We found that a new baby was more likely to be born into the father's household than the mother's, and that father-resident adoles-cents were slightly more likely to say that they had moved in the past year than were mother-resident adolescents. Boys in father residence were more likely than boys in mother residence to report that someone close to them had died. Adolescents who lived primarily with their fathers were also more likely than other adolescents to have broken up with a boy-friend or girlfriend. This difference remained even if we took into ac-count the differences in age between the groups. Adolescents in dual

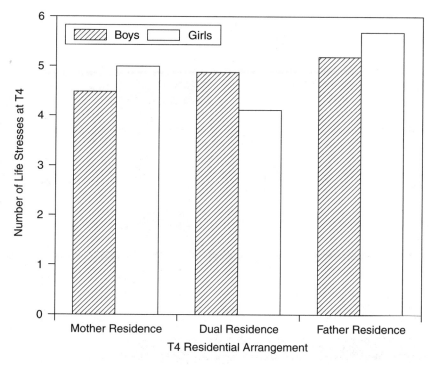

Figure 5.2 Number of life stresses in the last twelve months for adolescents in each residence and gender group.

residence were least likely to say that their families had experienced serious financial difficulties.

Family Size and Household Composition

Dual-resident families had slightly fewer natural children than those using father residence. Given the complexities of dual residence, it is not surprising to find evidence that such an arrangement is somewhat more likely to be maintained when fewer children are involved; even so, the difference is very small. Residential fathers and residential mothers had similar numbers of children living in their homes, but there *was* a difference in who those children were: girls living primarily with fathers were more likely to live with stepsiblings than girls living primarily with mothers, and both boys and girls were more likely to live with half-siblings in father residence than in mother residence (see Figure 5.3). The greater

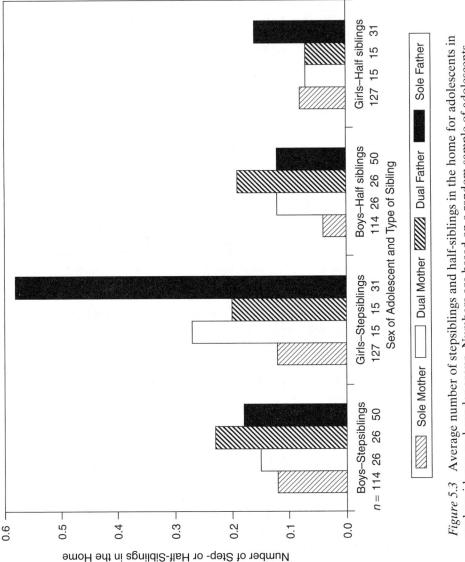

Figure 5.3 Average number of stepsiblings and half-siblings in the home for adolescents in each residence and gender group. Numbers are based on a random sample of adolescents using only one adolescent per family.

number of half-siblings in father residence than mother residence is consistent with adolescents' reports that father-resident households were more likely to have experienced a new birth within the past twelve months. There were no differences by residential arrangement in the likelihood that the mother or father was remarried, or had a new unmarried partner living in the home. Although fathers were no more likely to be remarried than mothers, the greater number of new births in the fathers' households is most likely due to the fact that fathers' new wives were often younger than their former spouses (Maccoby and Mnookin, 1992).

Parents' Working Hours

Fathers worked more hours per week, on average, than mothers (see Figure 5.4). In addition, girls in mother residence had mothers who worked more hours per week, on average, than did girls in dual residence.

Interparental Relationships

Joint physical custody is sometimes awarded by the courts to parents who cannot agree on a residential arrangement. Not surprisingly, some researchers have found higher levels of conflict and hostility between parents implementing joint physical custody than among other parents (Nelson, 1989). Among the full sample of parents in the Stanford Custody Study, parents who had been awarded joint physical custody were more likely to have experienced high legal conflict during the settlement process. Nonetheless, we expected that parents still maintaining dual-residence arrangements four and a half years after their separation would be less conflictual and more cooperative than other parents, in part because a number of the more highly conflictual families who had been awarded joint custody had shifted to a sole-residence arrangement (Maccoby and Mnookin, 1992). In addition, there are some parents who voluntarily implement joint physical custody—either initially or at some point after the initial separation—because they are more cooperative and agreeable than other parents (Pearson and Thoennes, 1990). Because of these trends, we expected that parents using dual residence several years after separation would be those who had been able to cooperate well over time. We also expected that interparental conflict might be higher in father residence than in other arrangements, because a higher proportion of father-residence arrangements come about because of family difficulties.

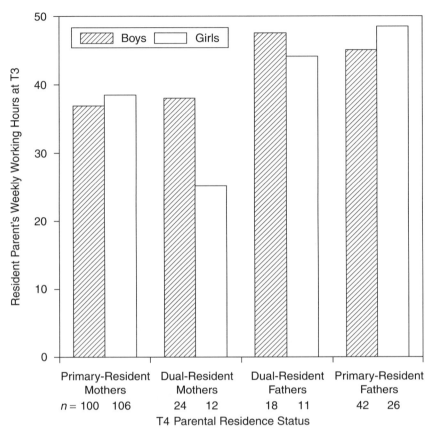

Figure 5.4 Average number of hours worked per week at T3 by parents of adolescents in each residence and gender group. Numbers are based on a random sample of adolescents using only one adolescent per family.

To our surprise, we found that Time 4 residence was generally unrelated to past or present conflict or cooperation in co-parenting as reported by parents or adolescents. Adolescents in dual residence did report parents as more cooperative at Time 4 than did adolescents in other residential arrangements, and at Time 2, a similar finding emerged for boys only. These differences indicate some tendency for the relatively small group of families who were maintaining a dual-resident arrangement at T4 to be more cooperative than other divorced parents, although the differences are generally small and not pervasive across all measures or subgroups.

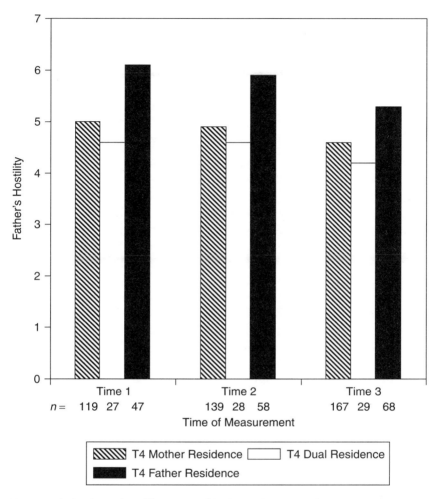

Figure 5.5 Father's hostility as rated by interviewer at Times 1 through 3, by adolescent's residential arrangement. Numbers are based on a random sample of adolescents using only one adolescent per family, and means are adjusted for age of adolescent and the average education of the two parents.

More consistent differences emerged on interviewers' ratings of parental hostility made during the interviews with the parents (Times 1–3). With only one exception (ratings of mother's hostility at T1), the hostility of parents toward each other was rated as having been higher in families that were maintaining father residence at T4 than in other families.[3] Figure 5.5 illustrates these differences using ratings of fathers' hostility.

The level of hostility between parents in mother residence as compared with dual residence was not significantly different. Similar residence differences, showing higher levels of hostility in the homes of adolescents in father residence, emerged if we compared measures of "residential parent's hostility" and "maximum parental hostility."

Parent-Adolescent Relationships

We anticipated possible differences between adolescents in the primary care of their mothers and those in the care of their fathers in terms of the quality of their relationships with the residential parent. Youniss and Smollar (1983) documented rather extensively the ways in which relationships between adolescents and mothers differ from relationships between adolescents and fathers in two-parent families. In families in which parents remain married, adolescents tend to have multidimensional relationships with their mothers. Mother-adolescent relationships are usually close and intimate, with the mother playing the role of confidante and friend at the same time that she functions as an authority figure and disciplinarian. Relationships between children and mothers also tend to have higher levels of conflict, however. Fathers usually have a less intimate or expressive relationship with their children, serving primarily as authority figures, advisors, and models. Relationships tend to be respectful but more distant than those between an adolescent and mother. Collins and Russell (1991) have noted that fathers may withdraw, especially from daughters, after the start of puberty.

With younger children, fathers also tend to have a more playful relationship than do mothers (Maccoby, 1995; Parke and Tinsley, 1981; Russell and Russell, 1987). The playful aspect of father-child relationships likely extends into adolescence, although this has been less well documented. In one relevant study, Montemayor and Brownlee (1987) did find that although adolescents spent less time with their fathers than with their mothers, their time with their fathers was more playful and more likely to center around leisure activities than time with their mothers. In fact, in these researchers' sample, 69 percent of the time adolescents spent with their fathers was spent in leisure activities.

If these qualitative differences between parents hold up in single-parent families, one might expect adolescents in our sample to feel closer to residential mothers than to residential fathers. It is possible, however, that such differences are reduced or eliminated in situations of divorce for several reasons. For example, single mothers may not have the same time to be emotionally available that mothers in two-parent families have (Stolberg and Cullen, 1983). In one study, relationships with both parents were more subdued and guarded among adolescents in divorced families than among adolescents in two-parent families (Smollar and Youniss, 1985). Furthermore, fathers who obtain sole custody of their children may be the very fathers who have developed or are able to develop warm relationships with their children.[4] Or fathers may develop more intimate relationships with their children over time in a situation where the mother is not present (see Gjerde, 1986).

It is also possible that adolescents maintain closer relationships with the residential parent of the same sex. In other words, we might expect girls to be closer to residential mothers than residential fathers, while expecting the reverse to be true for boys. Santrock and Warshak (1979, p. 115) hypothesized that parents may "know how to interact more effectively and feel more comfortable" with a child of the same sex. If this is true, closer relationships between same-sex parents and children than between opposite-sex parents and children would be expected.

How might relationships between adolescents and their parents in dual residence compare with parent-adolescent relationships in sole residence? Because adolescents in dual residence continue to see both parents on a regular basis, we might expect that these adolescents would maintain relationships with both parents that are at least as close as relationships between adolescents and their sole-resident parents. It may even be the case that relationships between dual-resident parents and adolescents are closer than those between sole-resident parents and adolescents if, by giving parents a regular "break" from parenting, dual-resident arrangements allow parents to focus more fully on parenting during times when their children are with them. Some have argued, however, that children who have high levels of contact with parents who are or have been in conflict may have trouble maintaining attachments to both parents, owing to a higher likelihood of divided loyalties (Goldstein, Freud, and Solnit, 1979). If this latter speculation is correct, adolescents in dual residence may in fact report lower levels of closeness to both parents than adolescents in sole-resident arrangements report for their sole-resident parent.

As Table 5.1 shows and as we noted in Chapter 3, our adolescents generally reported feeling close to their parents. The range of possible scores on our closeness scale was from 9 to 45, and the average of each residential group was well above the midpoint on this scale. This indicates that most of our adolescents felt "quite" or "very" close to each par-

Table 5.1 Parent-adolescent relationships in three residential arrangements, by sex of adolescent[a]

Measure of parent-adolescent relationship	Mother-resident mothers		Dual-resident mothers		Dual-resident fathers		Father-resident fathers		Significant differences[b]
	M	(n)	M	(n)	M	(n)	M	(n)	
Closeness to (range: 9–45)[c]									
Boys	37.3	(168)	37.3	(31)	35.9	(32)	35.7	(62)	PM > PF
Girls	35.9	(197)	39.3	(18)	37.8	(19)	32.7	(38)	Girls: DF > PF
Trust of (range: 2–12)									
Boys	9.8	(168)	10.0	(31)	9.8	(32)	9.9	(61)	
Girls	9.4	(197)	10.1	(18)	9.5	(19)	9.5	(38)	
Identification with (range: 2–10)									
Boys	7.6	(168)	8.3	(31)	7.8	(32)	7.1	(62)	PM > PF
Girls	7.0	(196)	7.8	(18)	7.5	(19)	6.8	(38)	DF > PF
Activities with (range: 0–11)									
Boys	4.1	(162)	4.9	(31)	5.3	(32)	5.0	(62)	Boys: PF > PM, DM > PM
Girls	4.3	(184)	3.9	(16)	4.6	(17)	4.0	(36)	
Average conflict with (range: 0–5)									
Boys	1.9	(162)	1.6	(31)	1.7	(32)	1.8	(62)	
Girls	1.9	(184)	1.8	(16)	1.8	(17)	1.8	(36)	
Maximum conflict with (range: 0–5)									
Boys	2.5	(162)	2.1	(31)	2.1	(32)	2.3	(62)	
Girls	2.6	(184)	2.4	(16)	2.4	(17)	2.5	(36)	

Disengagement from household (range: 3–14)								
Boys	7.2	(168)	6.9	(31)	7.2	(32)	7.2	(62)	PM > DM
Girls	7.4	(197)	5.9	(18)	6.1	(19)	7.7	(38)	*PF > DF*
Remembers special days (range: 1–3)								
Boys	2.93	(168)	2.92	(31)	2.82	(32)	2.85	(61)	PM > PF
Girls	2.91	(195)	2.99	(18)	2.98	(19)	2.81	(38)	
Eagerness to see (range: 1–5)								
Boys	3.5	(146)	3.7	(31)	3.3	(32)	3.4	(58)	
Girls	3.7	(173)	3.5	(16)	3.3	(17)	3.6	(36)	
Parent confides in adolescent (standardized; actual range: 0–7)								
Boys	3.7	(168)	4.0	(31)	3.3	(32)	2.9	(62)	PM > PF (esp. for girls)
Girls	3.8	(197)	3.8	(18)	3.2	(19)	2.1	(38)	DF > PF
Adolescent nurtures parent (standardized; actual range: 0–6)								
Boys	3.4	(168)	2.7	(31)	2.4	(32)	2.8	(62)	PM > PF
Girls	3.3	(197)	3.2	(18)	2.9	(19)	2.7	(38)	PM > DM

a. Means and standard deviations are adjusted for age of adolescent and the appropriate form of parental education (that is, mother's education when comparing relationships with mothers; father's education when comparing relationships with fathers) by entering these variables as covariates in the analysis. Means presented for sole-mother and sole-father residence are from analyses comparing each with their counterparts in dual residence; these means differ only slightly from the adjusted means that emerge from analyses comparing sole-residence mothers to sole-residence fathers. Significant differences in italics indicate borderline (weak) effects.

b. PM = primary-mother residence; PF = primary-father residence; DM = dual-mother residence; DF = dual-father residence.

c. Unless otherwise noted, ranges are possible, not actual, ranges.

ent—they felt, for example, that they could talk openly with the parent, that the parent was genuinely interested in the adolescent's problems, could be relied on for needed help, often expressed affection, and so forth. In a similar vein, the majority of adolescents said they would like to resemble their parents, and reported low levels of conflict with them. Variation existed within each residential group, of course, and some adolescents reported feeling very close to both parents, some to only one, and a few to neither (in Chapter 10, we look more specifically at these different patterns of closeness). Similarly, some adolescents reported frequent conflict with their parents, although most did not.

Within the general pattern of close relationships, there were some differences in the quality of the parent-adolescent relationship depending on the adolescent's residential situation.

Primary Mother versus Primary Father Residence

Did the quality of the relationship adolescents had with their primary residential parent depend on whether the adolescent was living with the mother or the father? The answer to this question can be found by comparing the means for relationships with "mother-resident mothers" with the means for relationships with "father-resident fathers" in Table 5.1. For both boys and girls, relationships with the residential parent were closer if that parent was the mother, rather than the father. Identification with the residential parent was also somewhat greater for mother-resident than for father-resident adolescents, and residential mothers were more likely to remember special days than residential fathers. It is important to note that there were no differences between sole-resident mothers and sole-resident fathers on several other indices of the affective relationship, including trust, conflict, and disengagement from the home. The findings provide some general evidence, however, for closer emotional and affective relationships with mothers than with fathers. We did not find that adolescents were closer to the same-sex parent, because boys as well as girls showed the tendency toward greater closeness to their mothers.

Fathers' tendency to "play" more with children (at least with their sons) was also noted: boys in the custody of their father had more joint activities with him over a month's time than boys in the custody of their mother had with her.

Given a tendency for adolescents to report greater emotional closeness to mothers than to fathers, it was not surprising to find that residential mothers were much more likely to confide in and lean on their children than were residential fathers. This was especially true if the adolescent was a girl, but it was true for boys as well. Adolescents also felt more need to take care of, and worried more about, residential mothers than residential fathers.

Dual versus Sole Residence

In several respects the relationships between an adolescent and a given dual-resident parent resembled the relationship an adolescent would have with that parent were he or she in the primary care of that parent (see Table 5.1: compare mother-resident mothers with dual-resident mothers and father-resident fathers with dual-resident fathers). In this sense, dual-resident adolescents appear to spend enough time with each parent to sustain relationships at the level that one could expect from a sole-residence arrangement with each parent. In fact, in some cases, the parent-child relationship was even better for adolescents in dual residence than for adolescents in sole residence. Boys in dual residence had more activities with their mothers than boys in sole-mother residence, and both boys and girls felt less disengaged from the mother's home when they were in dual residence than when in sole-mother residence. This difference in disengagement may reflect the fact that there are more opportunities to disengage the more total time one spends in a home. The fact that adolescents spent less time with their mothers when in dual residence than when in primary maternal residence, however, did not impair their ability to remain close to their mothers, as already noted. In addition, adolescents in dual residence were slightly less likely to find themselves in a "nurturing" role for their mothers (that is, to worry about their mothers and to feel that mothers needed to be taken care of) than were adolescents in primary mother residence.

Adolescents also had somewhat better relationships with their father when they lived with him only part of the time (in dual residence) than when they lived in his primary care. Girls felt closer to fathers in dual residence than to fathers in sole residence, and identification with their father was slightly higher among dual-resident adolescents (both boys and girls) than among father-resident adolescents. Dual-resident fathers also confided in their adolescents slightly more than did primary-resident fathers.

All of the evidence presented thus far indicates that relationships with each parent individually are at least as good for adolescents in dual residence as they are for adolescents in the primary care of a particular parent. As such, these results discount the hypothesis that adolescent children of divorce are not able to maintain positive relationships with both parents after divorce. In confirmation of this, when we examined residence differences on measures that captured closeness to *both* parents, or comfort in *both* homes, dual-resident adolescents were equally happy, if not happier, with their relationships than were adolescents in sole residence (see Chapter 8). In addition, as we will show in Chapter 11, dual-resident adolescents were not more likely, in general, to feel caught between their parents than other adolescents.

Parental Control and Management

Goldstein and colleagues (1979) argued that splitting time between parents—and thereby splitting authority for a child between the parents—would be dangerous. Presumably, it was thought to be difficult under such circumstances for either parent to exert authority and maintain control. For example, the mere fact that one's child is not present in the household for a significant part of every week, month, or year may make it difficult for dual-resident parents to monitor their children's activities and behavior adequately. The frequent transitions usually involved in dual-residence arrangements may also make it more difficult to maintain established patterns such as a consistent dinner time or a routine for cleaning the house. Thus, on the one hand, families in dual residence may exhibit lower levels of parental control and household organization than other families. On the other hand, if parents in dual residence can cooperate (back each other up, keep each other informed), monitoring and control might be better than in families where only one parent is integrally involved and vigilant. In this case, dual residence may be the closest one can come to the two-parent, nondivorced situation.

Parental control and organization may also differ in households run by fathers and those run by mothers. There is some evidence that adolescents have less parental supervision in single-mother homes than they do in nondivorced families or reconstituted families (Dornbusch et al., 1985). Yet in two-parent families, mothers are as likely to be disciplinarians and authority figures as fathers (Youniss and Smollar, 1983). Perhaps single mothers do no worse than single fathers. Fathers often have had less experience in household management than mothers (Lamb et al., 1987) and may, therefore, be less effective at establishing and maintaining organization and routines. No study to date has examined these aspects of parenting among single-parent fathers in comparison with single-parent mothers.

We turn to this comparison now, utilizing the reports of adolescents concerning the nature of control and management experienced in mothers' and fathers' households. As noted in Chapter 2, we assessed several aspects of control and management. We asked adolescents how much they thought each parent really knew about a variety of things: their whereabouts and activities during their free time, how they spent their money, and who their friends were. We also asked what rules there were (if any) about how late they could stay out on weeknights and weekend nights. Building on previous work by Dornbusch and colleagues (for example, Dornbusch et al., 1985), we asked about the locus of decision making concerning issues affecting the adolescent's daily life (for example, who decides how late he or she may stay out, what classes to take in school, what clothes to buy or wear, or how to spend money). A "Household Organization" scale reflected the regularity and predictability of household routines. Adolescents were also questioned about their perception of the fairness and consistency of household rules, about how frequently they did a number of household chores in each home, and about whether an adult was present when they came home after school.

Primary Mother versus Primary Father Residence

As can be seen in Table 5.2, styles of parental control and management were remarkably similar in maternal and paternal households. We found no notable differences in decision-making practices, school night or weekend curfews, how well household routines were organized and maintained, chores, or whether an adult was home after school. The single consistent difference had to do with monitoring, and this was found only for girls, not boys: father-resident girls were more likely to say that their fathers did not "really know" as much about their activities, in comparison with the level of parental knowledge attributed to mothers by mother-resident girls. Adolescents living primarily with their mothers were also somewhat more likely to think that rules were fair and to accept those rules than were adolescents living primarily with their fathers.

Dual versus Sole Residence

To our surprise, we found that dual-resident households appeared to function somewhat differently for adolescents of the two sexes. Boys in

Table 5.2 Parental control and management in three residential arrangements, by sex of adolescent[a]

Measure of parental control/management	Mother-resident mothers		Dual-resident mothers		Dual-resident fathers		Father-resident fathers		Significant differences[b]
	M	(n)	M	(n)	M	(n)	M	(n)	
Monitoring (range: 5–15)[c]									
Boys	11.7	(162)	11.6	(31)	11.4	(32)	11.8	(61)	Girls: PM > PF
Girls	12.1	(184)	12.6	(16)	12.1	(17)	10.9	(36)	Girls: DF > PF
Youth-alone decision making (range: 0–1)									
Boys	.46	(162)	.51	(31)	.51	(32)	.44	(62)	
Girls	.41	(184)	.37	(16)	.39	(17)	.42	(36)	
Youth-decides decision making (range: 0–1)									
Boys	.62	(162)	.70	(31)	.71	(32)	.62	(62)	*Boys: DM > PM*
Girls	.59	(184)	.52	(16)	.51	(17)	.57	(36)	
Joint decision making (range: 0–1)									
Boys	.68	(162)	.58	(31)	.58	(32)	.69	(62)	
Girls	.76	(184)	.79	(16)	.82	(17)	.72	(36)	
School night curfew (range: 0–6)									
Boys	2.1	(162)	2.4	(30)	2.6	(28)	1.9	(62)	
Girls	2.2	(184)	2.2	(16)	1.9	(12)	2.0	(35)	
Weekend night curfew (range: 0–8)									
Boys	3.5	(162)	3.8	(28)	4.5	(31)	3.3	(62)	Girls: PM > DM
Girls	3.6	(184)	2.8	(15)	3.1	(17)	3.4	(35)	Boys: DF > PF

	Mean	(N)	Mean	(N)	Mean	(N)	Mean	(N)	
Household organization (range: 9–63)									
Boys	38.6	(168)	40.2	(31)	40.1	(32)	39.3	(62)	PM > PF
Girls	36.9	(197)	40.7	(18)	40.0	(19)	37.4	(38)	
Acceptance of rules (range: 5–25)									
Boys	19.2	(168)	19.0	(31)	19.0	(32)	18.8	(62)	
Girls	18.9	(197)	19.6	(18)	19.1	(19)	17.7	(38)	
Chores (range: 11–44)									
Boys	27.6	(168)	25.6	(31)	25.4	(32)	27.3	(62)	
Girls	26.5	(197)	25.8	(18)	23.9	(19)	25.8	(38)	
Adult home after school (range: 0–1)									
Boys	.46	(145)	.41	(30)	.53	(27)	.42	(57)	
Girls	.50	(168)	.46	(14)	.44	(11)	.35	(31)	

a. Means and standard deviations are adjusted for age of adolescent and the appropriate form of parental education (that is, mother's education when comparing control by mothers; father's education when comparing control by fathers) by entering these variables as covariates in the analysis. Means presented for sole-mother and sole-father residence are from analyses comparing each with their counterparts in dual residence; these means differ only slightly from the adjusted means that emerge from analyses comparing sole-residence mothers with sole-residence fathers. Significant differences in italics indicate borderline (weak) effects.

b. PM = primary-mother residence; PF = primary-father residence; DM = dual-mother residence; DF = dual-father residence.

c. Ranges are possible, not actual, ranges.

dual residence reported making more decisions on their own—with or without discussion with parents—than did boys living with either their mothers or their fathers.[5] Weekend curfews set in fathers' homes were also later for dual-resident than for single-resident boys. These findings suggest that controls are relaxed or attenuated somewhat for boys if they are living in dual residence. The opposite appears to be the case, however, for dual-resident girls. Dual-resident fathers knew more about what their adolescent daughters were doing than did sole-resident fathers, and dual-resident girls had earlier weekend curfews than girls living with their mothers.

Putting our findings another way, we found evidence of a slight double standard in parental dealings with adolescents of the two sexes when they were in dual residence. With regard to decision making and weekend curfews, boys in dual residence were granted more freedom than were girls, and these sex differences did not exist or were not as large for adolescents living with either their mothers or their fathers.

Summary

The expectation that adolescents might adjust differently when living in mother, father, or dual residence is based on the assumption that these arrangements might differ with respect to processes we know to influence developmental outcomes. Of primary interest is the question of whether these arrangements differ with respect to the interpersonal dynamics prevailing among family members and whether there are differences in the degree to which parents maintain optimal levels of control and organization in the home. Therefore, in this chapter, we have compared the three groups with respect to (a) contextual factors, including who lives in the home and whether the adolescent has lived in this home ever since the divorce; (b) the quality of the relationship between the two parents; (c) the quality of the relationship between the adolescents and their residential parent(s); and (d) the degree of parental control and management in the household.

Having compared our three residential groups with respect to this variety of contextual and interpersonal factors, we can now identify the factors that have the potential to explain the modest differences in adjustment among adolescents living in the different residential arrangements. Identifying differences among residential groups in such areas as the amount of interparental hostility or the stability of residence over time is only the first step, of course, in discovering whether such differences are indeed related to the fact that adolescents in one residential group are doing better or worse than adolescents in another residential group. The complex interrelationships among multiple potential causal factors, and between the potential causal factors and adolescent adjustment, will be taken up in the next chapter. For the present, we simply summarize what we have found about the differences among our residential groups, and discuss briefly how these *might* be related to the differences in adolescent adjustment.

In Chapter 4, we reported that there were somewhat more well-functioning adolescents among our dual-resident adolescents, and somewhat fewer among those living with their fathers. Why might this be? Let us first consider why there might be a higher incidence of problems among adolescents living with their fathers. An obvious possibility is the residential instability of this group. Only about one-third of the adolescents who were living with their father at the time we interviewed them had been living with him all along. This proportion stands in contrast to the other two groups: 79 percent of the adolescents in mother residence and 60 percent of those in dual residence had lived in these arrangements continuously over the four and a half years since their parents separated. The simple fact that most of the adolescents in father residence had moved in after initially living with their mothers (or in dual residence) presents the following question: to what extent is the higher incidence of poor functioning among adolescents living with their fathers explained by a drift of especially troubled children into father residence, and to what extent is it the case that father residence is in some way more difficult to adjust to, at least for a subgroup of the adolescents in this arrangement?

Apart from residential instability, there are other aspects of the father-residence situation that might help to account for difficulties experienced by the adolescents living there. Adolescents in this group had experienced certain life stresses somewhat more often in the past year than other adolescents, and they were more likely to have had to adapt to living with stepsiblings (if the adolescent was a girl) and half-siblings. In addition, as already noted, the father-residence group was the one with the highest average level of prior hostility between the parents. To the extent that ongoing conflict is a central factor in children's adjustment to divorce, this may explain the higher number of problems among father-resident adolescents.

Adolescents (especially the girls) living with their father also reported feeling somewhat less close to him than young people living in other arrangements felt toward their residential parents. In fact, girls felt closer to their father when they were in dual residence than they did when they were living with him most of the time. We asked the adolescents how much they would like to be like each parent, and for children of both sexes, the wish to emulate the father was greater in the dual-resident group than it was among those who lived primarily with their fathers. We see, then, that at least in a subgroup of father-resident cases, there is tension or emotional distance in the father-child relationship when the two live together most of the time.

Finally, fathers also appeared to have some difficulty monitoring the whereabouts and activities of adolescent daughters who lived primarily with them. This finding is consistent with what the parents themselves reported at earlier times: although most residential fathers did not report great difficulty in monitoring their children, their average level of self-reported difficulty in this respect was significantly greater than that of residential mothers (Maccoby and Mnookin, 1992).

We also need to consider the somewhat better functioning of the dual-resident adolescents. The favorable status of dual-resident youth is somewhat surprising, in view of the stresses that surely must be involved in going back and forth between parental households and trying to maintain school-related activities, friendships with peers, extracurricular activities, and family relationships while living in two different places. Such stresses must be outweighed by advantages inherent in the arrangement. In Chapter 4 we saw that the dual-resident families included more parents from the upper end of the socioeconomic spectrum. The adolescents were also younger, on the average, than those in the other groups, and our younger adolescents had lower scores on deviance and depression. Yet these factors cannot account for the differences that emerged on our measures of adolescent functioning, because we controlled for age of adolescents and education of parents in our analyses.

Our dual-resident children had other advantages, however. To begin with, their parents had somewhat more harmonious relationships with each other. According to ratings of each parent's hostility toward the former spouse made by interviewers at Times 1, 2, and 3, levels of hostility were lower between parents whose adolescents were in dual residence than between parents whose adolescents were in father residence. And according to the reports of the adolescents, there was somewhat more active cooperation between parents in dual residence than between parents in either mother or father residence. A further possible advantage for dual-resident adolescents is the fact that they maintained close positive bonds (of trust, affection, and identification) with both their mother and their father, remaining as close or closer to each parent as adolescents in sole-resident arrangements were with their residential parent. As we shall see in Chapter 10, adolescents in sole-resident arrangements (especially mother-resident arrangements) were not as close to their nonresidential parent as they were to their residential parent, meaning that close relationships with both parents were in fact more common among dual-resident adolescents.

Finally, we must consider the possibility that the relatively favorable status of dual-resident adolescents is due, at least in part, to self-selection. A substantial portion (40 percent) of our small group of dual-resident adolescents had moved into this arrangement after initially living primarily with either their mother (in the typical case) or their father. Generally speaking, the reasons children move into dual residence were more child-centered than those underlying other residential moves (see Chapter 3; Maccoby and Mnookin, 1992). Furthermore, families who try dual residence and find it unworkable for some reason select themselves out, leaving in our dual-residence group those who were willing to expend the extra effort entailed in the dual arrangement.

When legal policymakers pressed for changes in divorce statutes in the late 1970s and early 1980s—changes that would permit wider adoption of joint physical custody and liberal visitation—they believed that children would benefit from frequent and continuing contact with both parents. Our results so far are consistent with the view that de facto joint physical custody (in other words, dual residence) can indeed be supportive to adolescent children of divorced parents: these children do stay emotionally close to both parents, and in terms of adjustment we certainly have not found dual residence to be harmful, in comparison with the alternatives. Clearly, however, considering the variation in functioning among the adolescents in dual residence, it is important to examine further the conditions under which a dual arrangement does and does not work well for the children involved (see Chapters 6 and 11).

In the next chapter, we will address the question of whether residence differences in adjustment can be explained by residence differences in any of the household characteristics we have examined here. Given the rather small differences in adjustment between residences, however, we first take up the additional question of how the aspects of the residential household that we have considered in this chapter are related to various aspects of adolescent functioning *within* each residence and gender group, regardless of whether absolute levels of a characteristic differed among the residential groups.

6

Linking Home Life and Adjustment

Our goal in this chapter is to examine the connections between the quality of adolescents' adjustment and the characteristics of the environment in their residential homes (also referred to as "family processes" or "household processes"). In Chapter 4, we compared adolescents in the three major residential arrangements with respect to their adjustment and found small differences, with adolescents in father residence functioning somewhat less well than other adolescents. In Chapter 5, we documented various differences in the family relationships and in parental control and management that existed in each arrangement, but as with adjustment, most differences were small, and the similarities between residential arrangements outnumbered the differences. Given such findings, our major interest became determining which processes were linked to adjustment within each residential group.

In particular, we wanted to see whether family environments in each kind of household were linked in similar ways to adjustment. Although certain basic processes (for example, parent-child closeness, parental supervision) are important in all homes, adolescents living with their mothers may benefit from somewhat different aspects of parenting than do adolescents whose primary parent is the father. As we have noted, the parenting styles of mothers and fathers tend to differ on the average, leading some experts to speculate that each parent contributes something unique to children's development. In a similar vein, boys and girls may need different things from mothers and from fathers; thus there may be differences in the relations between family environments and adjustment depending on the sex of the adolescent. Finally, differences in the temperament or background of those youngsters who end up living in different residence arrangements may cause them to benefit from different aspects of parenting.

There are several reasons, then, to expect that the conditions that promote positive adjustment after divorce may differ by residence, by sex, or both. Consequently, we explored extensively which processes were most important for the adjustment for boys and girls in each residential arrangement. In what follows, we first report predictors of adjustment for adolescents in the two sole-resident arrangements (in other words, father residence versus mother residence); at the end of the chapter we look at predictors of adjustment for dual-resident adolescents.

Simplification of Measures and Method of Analysis

Even with our relatively large sample, we could not simultaneously include in our analyses all the detailed measures of the family and household environment that we considered in Chapter 5. In that chapter, the processes we considered were grouped into four sets of characteristics that we believed were potentially important:

1. The family context (for example, the number and kind of individuals living in the home, the stability of the residential arrangement, the number of life stresses);
2. The quality of the interparental relationship;
3. The quality of the parent-adolescent relationship; and
4. The degree and kinds of parental control and management in the home.

We thus approached the question of "What best predicts adjustment?" with these sets of processes in mind. For ease of reference, we will call them "context" (set 1), "interparental relationship" (set 2), "parent-child relationship" (set 3), and "parental control and management" (set 4).

For each of these sets except the first, we combined several of the more detailed measures into an overall score representing that set.[1] To measure the closeness and warmth of the adolescent's relationship with the residential parent, we combined our earlier measures of closeness, trust, identification, and amount of joint activity (henceforth called "overall closeness"). We also combined our measures of parental monitoring, school night curfew, weekend night curfew, youth-alone decision making, household organization, and acceptance of rules into a composite we call

Table 6.1 Variables entered into analyses predicting adolescent adjustment for each residence and gender group

Context
  Age of adolescent
  Residential parent's education
  Stability of residence (T1–T4)
  Life stress (T4)
  Original family size
  Stepparent in home (T4)
  Nonremarried new partner in home (T4)
  Number of stepsiblings in home (T4)
  Number of half-siblings in home (T4)
  Residential parent's working hours (T3)

Interparental Relationship
  Maximum parental hostility or parental conflict composite (T3)
  Frequency of parental arguing (T4)
  Parental agreement (T4)

Parent-Child Relationship
  Parent-child "overall closeness" (T4)
  Disengagement from home (T4)
  Parent-child conflict (T4)
  Parent confides in child (T4)
  Child nurtures parent (T4)

Parental Control and Management
  Household management (T4)
  Chores (T4)

"household management." Other aspects of the parent-child relationship and of parental control and management that were not highly related to "overall closeness" or "household management" were kept separate in the analyses.

To measure the interparental relationship, we considered using a composite score based on parental discord at T2 and T3, lack of parental cooperative communication at T2 and T3, and both mother's and father's hostility at T1 and T3. Exploratory work with this composite, however, revealed that maximum parental hostility at T3 (a score taking either the mother's or father's hostility score, whichever was higher) was at least as powerful as the composite, and sometimes more so, in predicting adjustment. The information we provide below concerning the relations be-

Table 6.2 Correlations of selected measures of context, family relationships, and household processes with "worst problem," by sex and residence, for sole-resident adolescents[a]

	Mother residence		Father residence	
Maximum *n*	Boys (167)	Girls (196)	Boys (61)	Girls (37)
Set 1: Context				
Stability of residence	−.01	−.01	−.29*	−.32+
Life stress	.27***	.23**	.34**	.16
Residential parent remarried[b]	−.10	−.12	−.10	−.19
Residential parent has cohabiting new partner[b]	.06	−.02	.25+	.08
Set 2: Interparental Relations				
Maximum hostility (T3)[b]	.15	−.16+	.16	.24
Parents agree (T4)	−.17*	−.13+	−.09	−.03
Parents often argue (T4)	.26***	.07	.41**	.22
Set 3: Parent-Child Relationship (Residential Parent)				
Overall closeness	−.31****	−.34****	−.06	.09
Child disengaged from res. parent's household	.20*	.40****	.43***	.14
Parent-child conflict	.23**	.17*	.27*	.12
Parent confides in child	−.15+	−.14+	−.18	.26
Child nurtures parent	−.00	.12+	.10	.23
Set 4: Parental Control and Management (Residential Parent)				
Household management	−.41****	−.40****	−.34**	.18

a. Correlations are controlled for adolescent's age and residential parent's education.
b. Based on a sample of only one adolescent per family, selected randomly.
+$p \leq .10$.   *$p \leq .05$.   **$p \leq .01$.   ***$p \leq .001$.   ****$p \leq .0001$.

tween interparental conflict on adolescent adjustment will therefore be based primarily on our score for maximum parental hostility at T3.

Table 6.1 lists the variables in each set that were used to predict adjustment.

Table 6.2 shows the correlations of our major predictor variables with the "worst problem" score (as an illustrative index of adjustment) by sex and residence group, for adolescents living primarily with either their mother or their father. Although these correlations give basic information about the relation between family processes and adolescent adjustment in each group, and in most cases will serve to demonstrate the points we want to make, they represented only a starting point for our purposes. Because the predictor variables were related to one another in complex ways—sometimes in ways that differed by residence or sex—we needed to consider the sets of variables jointly and successively, to try to identify the factors that had the strongest impact, overall, on adjustment. For three of the four residence-by-sex groups (all except father-resident girls), we used multiple regression to do this.[2] Our procedure for exploring process-adjustment links for father-resident girls and for dual-resident adolescents of the two sexes was necessarily more limited, because there were not enough cases in these three smaller groups to carry out analyses with more than four or five predictors at a time. Thus our analysis for father-resident girls and dual-resident boys and girls is more qualitative in nature, based on examination of correlations and simple regressions using each individual predictor (controlling for age) and comparing the relations with those that emerged for the other three groups.

Although we rely, in the discussion that follows, on the correlations in Table 6.2 to demonstrate many of our findings, we will note instances where results of our more complex analyses differed from those indicated by the correlations in Table 6.2. We turn now to a consideration of the specific aspects of context and family process that proved to be important in predicting adolescents' adjustment in sole-resident families.

Predictors of Adjustment for Sole-Resident Adolescents

Stability of Residence

We reported in Chapter 3 that approximately one-third of the young people in our sample had moved between parental households—or into or out of dual residence—at least once during the four and a half years since their parents had separated. The rate of residential instability was particularly high among adolescents who ended up living with their fathers. Although the *proportion* of adolescents living with their mother at Time 4 who had not lived with her continuously was low, the *number* of adolescents who moved in with their mothers at some time after parental separation was comparable to the number who moved in with their fathers.

Moving from one parental household to another can be a stressful event in itself, especially if accompanied by parental disputes. At the same time, it can be a symptom of other problems if it occurs because of conflict between the child and the parent whose house the child is leaving. In such situations, adolescents who move from one parental household to another might include a substantial group of difficult children. We expected, therefore, that children who moved would have higher levels of adjustment problems than children who were residentially stable, and this turned out to be true—but only (to our surprise) for the adolescents currently in father residence. Adolescents in father residence who had moved one or more times since their initial residential arrangement were doing worse in several respects than adolescents who had been with their father all along. Instability of residence was linked to lower levels of school effort and to poorer adjustment on the "worst problem" scale for both boys and girls in father residence, and to higher levels of substance use for boys in father residence. None of these negative findings was present for the adolescents who had moved in with their mothers at some point after the initial residential arrangements were established.

Why was instability linked with the expected negative outcomes only among father-resident adolescents? Is it because the adolescents who chose to move in with their fathers over time were more troubled to begin with? Data reported in Chapter 3 indicated that negative family circumstances were more likely to precipitate moves into father residence than mother residence. For example, our adolescents cited family conflict more often as a reason for moving in with their father than for moving in with their mother, whereas a parent's relocation was more often given as a reason for moving in with their mother. This provides some evidence that problems in family relationships—and possibly problems in children's adjustment as well—are more likely to predate moves into father residence than moves into mother residence.

Unfortunately, data on children's adjustment prior to shifts in residence that would be comparable to the data we obtained at T4 did not exist. In the earlier parent interviews, however, parents reported briefly on their children's unhappiness, irritability, and problems in school, and the adolescents who had moved in with their fathers by T4 were not different on these measures than the adolescents who had shifted to mother residence. Thus the meager evidence we have on adjustment over time does not indicate that fathers' households were accumulating more troubled adolescents. We recognize, however, that these earlier measures of adjustment are limited and may not be sensitive enough to capture early problems among these children.

Our data also do not indicate that the relation between residential stability and poor adjustment among father-resident adolescents is completely attributable to poor family relationships that might predict both instability and poor adjustment. Although the relation between stability and adjustment weakened somewhat when interparental hostility and current household processes were controlled, it never dropped out entirely. Thus the fact that father-resident adolescents who have not lived with their father continuously since the divorce were less well adjusted is not completely explained by a drift of children from homes with poorer family relationships or other household conditions. It is possible again, however, that we have not captured the essential components of those relational or personal problems that might contribute to less optimal outcomes among those adolescents who later move in with their fathers.

One further possible explanation for the link between residential instability and poor adjustment only in father residence may have to do with the ability of this particular group of adolescents to adapt to stressful circumstances. A change in residence can be stressful, no matter what the reason for the change. Perhaps the adolescents in father residence were less able to cope with this particular stress, either because they were more likely to be experiencing other simultaneous stresses (see Chapter 5) or because they had fewer personal or family resources available to rely on.

Life Stress

The amount of life stress that an adolescent reported experiencing in the preceding twelve months turned out to be a strong and pervasive predictor of a number of problems in adjustment. Higher life stress was linked to a greater tendency to use attacking conflict-resolution strategies in conflict with peers, especially among father-resident adolescents. It was also predictive of higher depression, higher substance use, higher school deviance, higher antisocial behavior, and—not surprisingly given these links—was associated with higher overall deviance and more extreme "worst problem" scores. For almost every aspect of adjustment, the association between life stress and negative adjustment was present for both boys and girls, and mother- and father-resident adolescents alike.

Furthermore, life stress had a direct association with poor adjustment. We considered the possibility that stress might have negative consequences mainly by undermining the quality of parent-child relationships or by weakening parental management and control. We found, however, that even after taking these factors into account, life stress retained its predictive power.

Parents' New Partners

With few exceptions, previous research on parental repartnering after divorce, and its effects on children, focuses on situations where a remarriage has taken place. We know a fair amount about the relationships between children and their stepparents, and about the challenges stepparents face with stepchildren (see, for example, Bray and Berger, 1993a; Hetherington and Clingempeel, 1992; Lutz, 1983; Pasley and Ihinger-Tallman, 1987). In our study, we looked not only at whether a parent had remarried but also at whether a parent had a new partner living in the home to whom he or she was not married. We examined each of these repartnering conditions separately. We consistently found that having a stepparent was associated with positive adjustment. For both boys and girls, having a stepparent in the home was linked with higher levels of compromise as a conflict-resolution strategy used with peers, and father-resident boys with a stepmother also reported less use of attack as a strategy during peer conflicts. For all adolescents, having a stepparent in the home was also linked with lower levels of school deviance and with better adjustment on the "worst problem" scale.[3] Boys with stepparents also had lower levels of substance use, antisocial behavior, and overall deviance, and higher grades in school.

The presence of an unmarried new partner in the home, by contrast, was associated for boys with higher levels of almost every problem we measured: higher use of attack and lower use of compromise in peer conflict-resolution, higher substance use, higher school deviance, higher antisocial behavior, higher overall deviance (see Figure 6.1), lower grades, lower school effort, and poorer adjustment on the "worst problem" scale.[4] Father-resident girls were also less likely to use compromise in resolving peer conflicts and more likely to use substances when there was an unmarried new partner living in the father's home.

Why is the presence of a parent's new partner in the home more problematic if remarriage has not occurred? We will consider this question further in Chapter 7, but here we simply note some possibilities. First, unmarried new partners may not have legitimated their presence in the eyes of an adolescent, and adolescents may respond to that presence

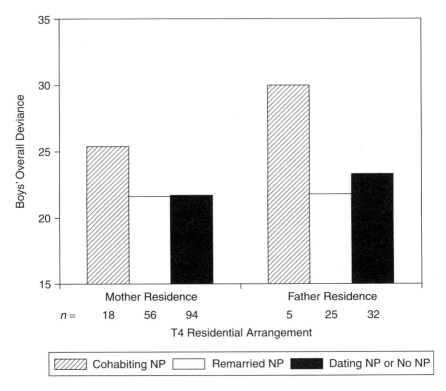

Figure 6.1 Overall deviance by residential parent's new-partner (NP) status for boys in mother and father residence. Means are adjusted for age of adolescent and residential parent's education.

with a lack of acceptance and respect that has subsequent repercussions in terms of adolescent "rebellion" or acting out. Adolescents may interpret a parent's relationship with an unmarried partner as primarily sexual; marriage, on the other hand, may be seen as a commitment by the new partner to care for the family.

It is also possible that relationships and processes in the home are less optimal for child rearing when an unmarried new partner is present in the home. For example, the presence of an unmarried new partner in the home may absorb the attention of the residential parent in an exclusive way, thus disrupting the relationship between the resident parent and the adolescent or weakening the residential parent's control. Our results suggest that these hypotheses may partly explain the association between the presence of an unmarried new partner and adolescent adjustment.

When the quality of the parent-child relationship and the level of parental management are considered, the association between having an unmarried new partner present and adolescent adjustment is reduced in magnitude.[5] The positive effects of parental remarriage are also attenuated (although they do not disappear) when the affective quality of the parent-child relationship and household management are considered. Thus it would appear that the presence of a new spouse tends to strengthen a resident parent's parenting, while the presence of an unmarried new partner tends to weaken it.

These are not the only possible routes by which parents' new partners could be related to adolescent adjustment. An alternative possibility is that new partners may be more reluctant to marry into a family with children when those children are less well adjusted. The number of adolescents in our sample whose parents had a cohabiting partner was small relative to the other new-partner groups, but the association between having an unmarried new partner in the home and poor adjustment was surprisingly strong and consistent, especially for boys. Future research clearly needs to pay attention to the role of unmarried new partners and to household processes associated with the presence of unmarried new partners in the home.

Interparental Relationships

When interparental relationships were assessed from the reports of the adolescents at T4, we found that, in general, the more conflictual the interparental relationship, the more problems the adolescent exhibited. Adolescent-reported parental arguing was associated with higher levels of depression and lower school effort among adolescents, particularly boys. Similarly, every group except mother-resident girls reported higher levels of overall deviance and a more severe "worst problem" in situations when parents argued frequently. And in all groups of sole-resident adolescents, school deviance was higher under conditions of frequent parental arguing. Consistent with these findings, adolescent-reported parental agreement on issues concerning the child was generally modestly associated with positive adjustment.

Although these findings fit with our hypotheses and the reports from many other studies that interparental conflict is injurious to children, it is possible that when we use adolescents' reports of their parents' relationship, we get a reporting bias: unhappy or poorly functioning adolescents may also tend to see their parents negatively. When we use our independent measures of the interparental relationship, derived from the parents themselves at earlier points in time, we get a mixed picture, with negative associations sometimes emerging for boys only, or for father-resident adolescents only. Specifically, the higher the maximum level of hostility between parents at T3, the more substance use among father-resident adolescents and the more overall deviance among father-resident adolescents and mother-resident boys (in other words, only for mother-resident girls was overall deviance *not* linked to higher levels of hostility). Higher levels of hostility were also linked with more use of attacking conflict-resolution strategies among father-resident boys. Counterintuitively, hostility was associated with better adjustment on the "worst problem" scale for girls in mother residence. Given that we have no theoretical backing for this result, and that it does not fit with the general pattern of results concerning interparental conflict, we believe that it is a chance occurrence.

This package of results indicates that ongoing parental conflict is associated with minor negative outcomes, such as school deviance, for all adolescents. In addition, parental conflict is associated with more extreme negative outcomes for boys in particular, and sometimes for father-resident girls as well. In general, these associations do not change when we add measures of parent-child closeness and/or parental management to the prediction of adjustment, so the link between parental conflict and adolescent adjustment does not appear to be accounted for by these factors.

Parent-Child Relationships

The overall closeness of the relationship between residential parent and child was positively associated with adjustment, but primarily for adolescents living with their mothers. For example, higher levels of overall closeness predicted less depression and less school deviance only for adolescents in mother residence. There were, however, a couple of positive associations for father-resident girls as well: among these girls, a warm father-daughter relationship was associated with more compromise in conflicts with peers, as well as with lower levels of substance use. Although Table 6.2 indicates that parent-child closeness also predicted an adolescent's "worst problem" for adolescents in mother residence, this association disappeared in analyses in which parental management was included. The link between parent-child closeness and parental management, and their combined impact on adjustment, is considered separately below.

What did we find with regard to negative aspects of the parent-adolescent relationship? For all sole-resident adolescents, disengagement from the residential home was strongly related to depression. Clearly, disengagement from the home might be a symptom of depression as much as a cause. We cannot pin down the causal direction with our data. Even if disengagement were primarily a symptom of depression, however, it is a symptom with worrisome implications. When adolescents stay away from home and avoid contact with the adults in the household when they are at home, it implies that there are a number of difficulties in the home environment, at least from the adolescent's point of view. Emotional withdrawal from the home may also make a child more prone to act out and more vulnerable to negative peer influences. Our data suggest that this occurs mainly among boys, who are, in general, more likely than girls to engage in deviant or antisocial activities: for boys in our sample, disengagement from the residential home was linked to several aspects of problematic behavior, including antisocial behavior, low grades, and weak school effort. Disengagement from the residential home also presumably means that there are more out-of-school hours in which an adolescent not only has no place to study but has fewer opportunities to receive adult encouragement, support, or supervision for homework, which may contribute to a weaker school performance.

A small number of negative outcomes were also more likely when there were higher levels of parent-child conflict.[6] Adolescents reporting higher levels of conflict with their parents were more likely to use attack strategies and less likely to use compromise in conflictual interactions with their peers. Conflict with father for adolescents in father residence was also associated with higher levels of substance use and higher levels of overall deviance, although the relations were weaker (and insignificant) for girls than they were for boys. Girls in father residence were especially likely to report lower school effort when they had higher levels of conflict with their fathers. In all of these cases it is possible that conflict not only provokes these kinds of behaviors, but that the reverse process may be at work: conflict may occur as a result of the problematic behavior on the part of the adolescents. In all likelihood, the process is a circular one.

A parent's tendency to confide in an adolescent, reflecting some degree of role reversal, may be seen as a danger sign. With only one exception, however, we did not identify any negative outcomes of such confiding.

For girls living with their fathers, the more a father confided in that daughter, the more school deviance she reported. With regard to an adolescent's "worst problem," there was, initially, a modest association between parental confiding and *positive* adjustment. When other aspects of context and family relationships were accounted for, however, this relationship disappeared. Confiding by the parent was most likely part of a pattern of parent-child closeness, and had little independent importance.

Feelings of having to nurture, or take care of, a parent had more consistent and pervasive negative consequences. (These associations emerged only after taking into account other aspects of family context, interparental relationships, and the parent-child relationship, and are not apparent in the correlations presented in Table 6.2.) More feelings of care-taking responsibilities toward the residential parent were linked with higher levels of depression and a more severe "worst problem" score for girls in both mother and father residence.[7] Boys who felt the need to care for a residential parent showed the effects in their school effort and performance: they had lower grades and lower school effort.

Parental Control and Management

The extent to which the residential parent was aware of the adolescent's activities, and maintained an organized home where there were consistent and predictable rules and expectations, was a strong predictor of adjustment. For all groups except father-resident girls, higher levels of household management were linked to lower substance use, lower school deviance, less antisocial behavior, less overall deviance, higher school effort,[8] and lower "worst problem" scores.

The relation between household management and positive adolescent adjustment remained strong and significant even after the context (set 1), the interparental relationship (set 2), and the parent-child relationship (set 3) were controlled. Thus the importance of management and control does not simply reflect other aspects of an adolescent's home environment, but stands independently as a powerful element in adolescent well-being.

Why were father-resident girls an exception? Why, for them, did correlations indicate that higher levels of management might be linked to poorer overall adjustment, as indexed by "worst problem"? Although the correlation was not significant, it went counter in direction to our hypotheses and to the results for other sole-residence adolescents. To investigate this anomaly, we looked at the relations between "worst problem" and each component of "household management" individually, and separately for younger (fourteen years old or younger) and older adolescent girls.[9] We found, first of all, that for the younger daughters, the more the father knew about their activities, the more organized the household was, and the more consistent and fair the rules were, the less severe the worst problem score was.[10] For these young girls in the care of their fathers, however, adjustment was better the more these girls made their own decisions (apart from the father) and the later their curfews. The correlation between youth-alone decision making and "worst problem" for father-resident girls fourteen years and under was particularly strong ($r = -.52, p \leq .05$). We hesitate to attach too much importance to these counterintuitive findings, given the small number of girls on which they are based. On the one hand, it is possible that if girls who live with their fathers following divorce are more independent, or have "grown up" especially fast, they can handle higher levels of autonomy at earlier ages. If fathers attempt to impose too much control on these girls, already experienced in making their own decisions, the girls may in fact react negatively. On the other hand, the results suggest that it is still beneficial for these fathers to monitor their daughters' activities, run an organized and predictable home, and set rules that are consistently enforced and well explained.

Parent-Child Closeness and Parental Management Considered Jointly

Parent-child closeness and parental control and management are not independent of each other; in our sample, overall closeness and household management were correlated at .62. And as we reported above, the overall closeness of the parent-child relationship was more frequently and more strongly related to adjustment (particularly for mother-resident adolescents) when parental management was not simultaneously considered. When "overall closeness" and "household management" were considered jointly, however, management was a more important direct predictor of most aspects of adjustment, especially of what we might consider "externalizing" behaviors (for example, deviance). In an earlier publication, we reported the same finding with regard to parent-child closeness and parental monitoring (a major component of "household management") (Buchanan, Maccoby, and Dornbusch, 1991). Our conclusion in that earlier report was that parent-child closeness enabled parents to monitor their adolescents more effectively, which in turn promoted better adjustment. Our current results support that conclusion using the broader constructs of parent-child "overall closeness" and the parent's "household management."[11]

The high correlation between parent-child closeness and parental management in our sample, however, also led to some counterintuitive results. For example, although mother-daughter overall closeness—when considered alone—was associated with less substance use for mother-resident girls, it was associated with *more* substance use when household management was included in the analysis. Thus when both constructs were used to predict substance use, the positive effects of closeness were captured in the degree to which mothers maintained an organized home in which the daughter's activities were monitored. Closeness in excess of that related to good supervision and management in the home appeared to be related to more substance use, and may reflect a more permissive parenting style.

To test this possibility, we looked explicitly at different patterns of closeness and management as they related to substance use among mother-resident girls. Results indicated that when high overall closeness was accompanied by high management (an "authoritative" parenting style; see Baumrind, 1991b, and Lamborn et al., 1991), substance use was, in fact, low—as we would expect—but not significantly lower than when high management was accompanied by low mother-daughter closeness (see Figure 6.2). When overall closeness was high but management was low—a more "permissive" parental style—mother-resident girls tended to use alcohol and other substances more frequently, indeed at about the same level as for girls whose mothers were low in both closeness and control. Substance use among mother-resident girls was thus much more strongly influenced by household management than by mother-child closeness—when management was high, whether closeness was high or low, substance use was low.

Another counterintuitive result that emerged concerning parent-child closeness occurred for daughters in father residence: father-daughter closeness was associated with more school deviance among these girls. We therefore investigated patterns of parent-child closeness and parental management in relation to school deviance for father-resident girls. In this case, low levels of father-daughter closeness when coupled with high levels of management (akin to "authoritarian" parenting) were associated with the lowest levels of school deviance. High levels of management coupled with close relationships, however, were unaccountably

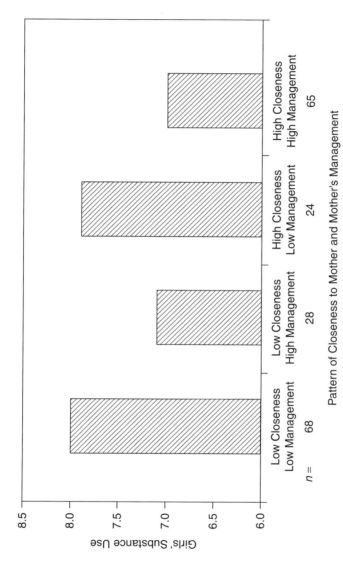

Figure 6.2 Substance use in mother-resident girls, by patterns of mother-daughter closeness and maternal household management. Means are adjusted for age of adolescent.

associated with high levels of school deviance. This finding goes sharply against the vast literature on the benefits of authoritative styles of parenting.

Thus we find that an authoritarian style of parenting may in fact discourage minor forms of deviant behavior among father-resident girls, although there is no indication in the rest of the data that such a style of parenting was otherwise particularly beneficial (with the exception noted above that an "authoritarian" style of parenting was as "good" as an "authoritative" style with respect to substance use in mother-resident girls). Furthermore, although we have argued that girls and boys may need or benefit from somewhat different kinds of parenting from mothers and fathers, we have no reason to believe that an authoritative parenting style by fathers, in and of itself, should be detrimental to girls' development. We are therefore inclined to believe that the relation between father-daughter closeness and school deviance, though significant, represents a chance occurrence among this relatively small group of father-resident girls. In other words, despite this one counterintuitive finding, we do not believe that girls living with their fathers are exempt from the overall benefits of authoritative parenting. As we noted earlier, affective closeness in the father-child relationship did have benefits with respect to daughters' substance use and use of compromise. Otherwise, father-daughter closeness was simply not a strong direct predictor of adjustment. We do not want to underestimate its indirect importance, however; as we reported in Buchanan, Maccoby and Dornbusch (1991) and emphasized above, parent-child closeness has indirect benefits for adjustment, because close relationships appear to facilitate successful parental monitoring of a child's activities.

Less Important Aspects of Family and Household

We have summarized those aspects of the family and home that had the most powerful and consistent links with adolescent adjustment. What aspects of family and home did we investigate that did not turn out to be important, at least with any consistency? First, family size. The number of children in the original family had only sporadic relations with adjustment; the relations that did emerge indicated a possible benefit to adolescents of having at least one sibling, perhaps especially for boys living with their mothers. Although research by Hetherington and colleagues (for example, Hetherington and Clingempeel, 1992) indicates that siblings are not altogether supportive of one another after their parents divorce, it is possible that simply having a sibling who is also going through the family transition is ultimately helpful. Given the sporadic nature of our results on this point, however, further investigation of this hypothesis is needed.

A second factor that did not turn out to be important with respect to adjustment was the number of hours the residential parent worked outside the home. This "nonfinding" may be important, as parents may wonder whether working outside of the home is detrimental to adolescent adjustment, especially in situations where there may not be a second parent at home. Our data suggest that the number of hours worked outside of the home by the residential parent is not directly related to adjustment problems among adolescents.

We were interested, however, in whether working hours had an indirect link to problems such as adolescent deviance, through interference with a parent's control and management of the household. We were especially interested in this question because of the finding, reported in Chapter 4, that higher levels of income were related to higher levels of deviance. We thought that higher income might be related to longer working hours, which would interfere with parenting control and management, giving adolescents more opportunities to participate in deviant activities. We found a very modest relation between more working hours and less adequate parental monitoring, but the strength of the relation varied by residence and sex of the adolescent. It was strongest for girls living with mothers in sole ($r = -.16, p \le .05$) or dual ($r = -.68, p \le .05$) residence, and boys living in father residence ($r = -.18$, not significant). Shorter working hours thus enhance parents' knowledge of their adolescents' activities only modestly and sporadically. Furthermore, because controlling for the number of working hours did not eliminate the link between parental income and deviance, a greater number of hours worked does not explain why adolescents of high-earning parents are more likely to be involved in deviant activities. Overall, then, our data do not indicate that the number of parental working hours, in and of itself, is important to an adolescent's well-being. Other research (for example, Galambos et al., 1995) suggests that when employment is stressful for a parent, it affects adolescent adjustment by interfering with the quality of the parent-adolescent relationship. Although one would expect working many hours per week to increase the odds of a parent feeling stressed and the resulting "spillover" effects, our data indicate that absolute number of hours worked is not the only, nor even the most important, factor to consider.

Finally, the amount of responsibility adolescents had for chores in the home, in contrast to household management more generally, had very little to do with adjustment. The only consistent finding with respect to "chores" was that adolescents who had more chores assigned were also more likely to compromise when in conflict with peers. Other research has documented that having chores and responsibility in the home contributes to prosocial behavior (Mussen and Eisenberg-Berg, 1977; Whiting and Whiting, 1975); perhaps we are seeing some small evidence of this link in our sample. We do not want to overinterpret either our scanty significant finding or our more pervasive absence of effects, however. Chores may have benefits in areas of adjustment other than those we have focused on in this study.

Dual-Resident Adolescents

Up until now, we have been considering the relation between conditions in the major residential home and adolescent adjustment. Adolescents in dual residence, by definition, spend substantial amounts of time in both parental homes, and the conditions that prevail in each home ought to have a noticeable impact on the adolescent's functioning. Perhaps the two homes have an equal impact, or perhaps one is more salient in the adolescent's life than the other. A possible approach to exploring the role of the two households would be to examine them jointly: for example, to put closeness to mother and closeness to father together into an analysis predicting adjustment. We encountered a major problem with this approach, however. The conditions in the two homes—at least as reported by the dual-resident youth—were surprisingly similar. For example, adolescents who reported high levels of conflict with one parent usually also reported high levels of conflict with the other ($r = .72$).[12] We do not know to what extent these high correlations reflect a real similarity between the two households, or to what extent they simply mean that the adolescents perceived the two households to be similar. Whichever is the case, it was not legitimate to use such highly correlated variables as independent predictors. We therefore averaged the scores of the two parents and used the average scores in examining the links between processes and adjustment. Our averaged scores tell us whether, taken together, the two households are characterized by high or low positive affect, high or low management, and so on.

Before we summarize the findings for the dual-resident adolescents, two factors are important to keep in mind: to begin with, the group is the smallest of our residential groups, having only 32 boys and 19 girls (together, approximately 10 percent of our sample). These small numbers do not allow us to consider as many household characteristics simultaneously as was possible for the other residential groups, especially when considering the two sexes separately. But the small numbers mean something else, too. Many of the families maintaining dual residence four and a half years after parental separation were "survivors," people who had managed to sustain the arrangement against the odds. Dual residence has proved to be an arrangement that is especially difficult to sustain when either parent moves (Maccoby and Mnookin, 1992), and it calls for a higher level of communication between the parents than some divorced couples are able to manage. As we saw in Chapter 3, although 4 percent of the sample had moved into dual residence during the life of the study, over 10 percent had moved out. Thus the 10 percent of the sample sustaining dual residence at Time 4 are matched by another 10 percent of adolescents who had tried it and dropped out for a variety of reasons. The "survivors" must be seen as a highly selected group of families, although we do not know all the conditions that help some families to stick with the arrangement while others leave.

The small number of adolescents who moved into dual residence after having initially lived with only one parent are also, very likely, a select group. As we reported in Chapter 3, when people adopted dual residence after initially having a sole-residence arrangement, they generally did so for positive and "child-centered" reasons. So the "choosers" as well as the "survivors" are select groups in which both parents and children may be closer and better functioning, and in which parents may be more highly motivated than other parents to have children maintain good relationships with both parents.

Having said this, we begin by considering some of the contextual factors that we examined above for sole-resident families. Table 6.3 displays the correlations between an adolescent's "worst problem" and characteristics of the context, family relationships, and household processes for dual-resident adolescents; as with the sole-resident adolescents, these correlations serve to illustrate some of the major findings we will discuss.

With regard to the adjustment of father-resident adolescents—but not mother-resident adolescents—it mattered whether they had lived in the same arrangement since their parents had separated or instead had moved at least once from one parental household to the other. The meaning of residential instability is somewhat different for dual-resident youth than it is for sole-resident youth, however. It means that an adolescent has moved from primary residence in one of the parental households into an arrangement where substantial time is spent in both households. In such cases the adolescent has not "moved out" of either parent's

Table 6.3 Correlations of selected measures of context, family relationships, and household processes with "worst problem," by sex, for dual-resident adolescents[a]

	Boys (32)	Girls (19)
Maximum *n*		
Set 1: Context		
Stability of residence	−.18	−.37
Life stress	.23	−.14
Mother's working hours (T3)[b]	.55**	−.08
Father's working hours (T3)[b]	.07	−.07
Set 2: Interparental Relations		
Maximum hostility (T3)[b]	.33	−.01
Set 3: Parent-Child Relationship (Average of Two Parents)		
Overall closeness	−.24	−.15
Child disengaged from household	−.11	.40
Parent-child conflict	.53**	.72**
Parent confides in child	.05	−.02
Child nurtures parent	.16	−.14
Set 4: Parental Control and Management (Average of Two Parents)		
Household management	−.49**	−.13

a. Correlations are controlled for adolescent's age and average parent's education.
b. Based on a sample of only one adolescent per family, selected randomly.
**$p \leq .01$.

household, but has simply begun spending more time with the parent who was formerly only visited. Thus the change may, overall, be more positive in the sense that it strengthens or renews ties to a less-seen parent. Still, any residential change may be stressful in some sense. We found, however, that residential instability had few connections with adolescent adjustment among dual-resident youth. It was not related to performance in school, or to deviance. Only in the small group of girls was there any indication of a link; for them, instability was associated with an attacking style of conflict resolution and with depression, and although not significant, the link with a higher "worst problem" score was equal in magnitude to the link among sole-resident adolescents.

Life stress, too, was less strongly associated with adjustment in the dual-resident group than it was for sole-resident adolescents. Does maintenance of a close association with both parents mean that when stresses occur in one household—the loss of a pet, illness of a family member—the impact of these events is buffered because the adolescent can rely on the resources of the other household? We do not know, but it is a plausible explanation.

It would be desirable to know about the impact of stepparents and cohabiting new partners in the two parental households where dual-resident adolescents spend their time. We have too few cases in this residential arrangement, however, to permit subdividing them according to the repartnering status of each parent and sex of the adolescent. For example, only nine dual-resident mothers and six fathers had cohabiting new partners, and only eleven and fourteen, respectively, were remarried. Combining boys and girls, it appears that the presence of a stepfather in the mother's home may have beneficial effects similar to those documented for adolescents whose sole-resident parent had a remarried new partner. But given the low numbers we hesitate to speculate further; a good understanding of the impact of repartnering by dual-resident parents must await larger samples.

Number of parental working hours was perhaps somewhat more important among dual-resident adolescents than it was among sole-resident adolescents. There were no relations between fathers' working hours and the adjustment of their dual-resident children. Mothers' working hours were more strongly related, although the linkages were sporadic. For boys, mothers' long hours were associated with higher substance use, worse grades, and a higher "worst problem" score; for girls, they were associated with an attacking conflict-resolution style.

With regard to family relationships and processes, the adjustment of the adolescents in dual residence was generally linked to the same factors that proved important for sole-resident adolescents. A high level of household management once again emerged as a predictor of several aspects of adolescent adjustment: for boys, it predicted a compromising, rather than an attacking, mode of conflict resolution, as well as high school effort and low scores on "worst problem." For girls, it predicted avoidance in conflict situations and also low levels of deviance. A close positive affective tie between the child and parents appeared from the first-order correlations to be a strong predictor of good adjustment in boys, but when it was combined in analysis with household management, it was management, not closeness, that turned out to be most important for adolescents of both sexes. Thus, as was the case for sole-resident adolescents, the closeness of the relationship between the child and parents, in and of itself, proved not to be as strong a factor as we had expected. But management of the home was important, and, at least for boys, a close relationship enabled the parent to engage in more effective management and control.[13]

The amount of conflict the dual-resident adolescents reported having with their parents was a significant predictor of adjustment, although the specific aspects of adjustment it predicted differed somewhat for the two sexes. For boys, conflict with parents predicted deviance and an attacking rather than a compromising style of conflict resolution; in other words, it predicted "acting out" behaviors. For girls, although the same associations were present, they were weaker, and the stronger associations were with higher depression and lower school effort.

When dual-resident adolescents reported that they were "disengaged" from the parental households, they were also more likely to report symptoms of depression, as were sole-resident adolescents. We noted earlier that this correlation may simply reflect the fact that disengagement is another symptom of depression. It is, perhaps, more meaningful that, for girls, disengagement was related to lowered grades.

What we thought of as role reversal—parent confiding in the child, or the child feeling the need to take care of the parent—appeared to have little or no relation to adolescent adjustment for the dual-resident group. Although an adolescent's feeling the need to "nurture" a parent was associated with some negative adjustment indices among sole-resident youth, this did not occur in the dual-resident group. Indeed, among the small group of girls, there were tendencies in the other direction—toward an association with favorable adjustment.

Interparental hostility, as reported by parents one year before the adolescent interview, was associated with higher levels of depression among dual-resident adolescents, and for the girls, with lower school grades. In general, however, the effects of interparental hostility were not as pervasive as they were for adolescents in sole residence. It is possible that a number of the parents who have managed to sustain a dual-resident arrangement have found ways of insulating the children from their interpersonal conflict (see Chapter 11).

Understanding Residence Differences in Adjustment

In Chapter 5, we reported that different residence groups differed moderately on some of the very characteristics that we now have found to be most important in predicting adolescent adjustment: the number of life stressors, residential instability, parent-child closeness, and household management (in particular, parental monitoring). Is it because father-resident adolescents have less favorable environments on these dimensions that they also report somewhat more problems in adjustment (see Chapter 4)? In general, yes. The residence differences in adjustment drop out when these aspects of the family and home context are controlled, with the exception that father residence remains associated with poorer adjustment for two subgroups of adolescents: those that have moved in with their father after initially living with their mother or in dual residence, and those from families with high levels of hostility between parents (see Buchanan, Maccoby, and Dornbusch, 1991). Otherwise, the association of father residence with a somewhat higher "worst problem" score appears to reflect somewhat lower levels of closeness and, consequently, monitoring by the residential parent, although the issue is more complex than it may appear. As we have already discussed at length, we cannot completely rule out the possibility that more difficult children (especially girls) select themselves into father custody to begin with, and are subsequently more difficult to monitor and be close to. Furthermore, as we have noted, although emotional closeness appears to facilitate monitoring and subsequently adjustment among all groups of adolescents, the associations among other components of "overall closeness" and "household management" have some peculiarities among father- and dual-resident (see note 13) girls. These peculiarities may be an artifact of the small size of these groups, or they may have to do with characteristics of the kinds of girls that select themselves into father or dual residence.

In many respects, the adjustment of adolescents in dual residence was similar to that of adolescents in mother residence (see Chapter 4). There was, however, a tendency for dual-resident adolescents to have the best scores on some adjustment measures (depression, grades, worst problem), even if the differences were not statistically significant. We reported in Buchanan, Maccoby, and Dornbusch (1991) that this advantage is not completely accounted for by lower levels of interparental conflict in these families. The question of whether the small advantage of being in dual residence has to do with the fact that dual-resident adolescents were more likely to maintain close relationships with not just one, but two, parents will be taken up in Chapter 10.

Summary

In terms of understanding adolescent adjustment after divorce, we find that contextual factors as well as interpersonal family factors are important. Several facets of family context were strongly and consistently related to adjustment. For adolescents as a group, the more life stresses they experienced, the worse they did on a variety of indices. This is in line with other research pointing to the cumulative effects of multiple stresses for adolescents (see, for example, Rutter, 1979; Simmons et al., 1987), and points to the toll taken by a variety of emotional and physical events such as moving, financial stress, and illness. A related finding is that changing residences one or more times since the parental separation had fairly strong links to negative adjustment, although only for father-resident adolescents. Moving is a stressful event. Instability of residence may itself have negative repercussions because it necessitates adaptation on the part of the adolescent and the family, and some adolescents and families will not be able to adapt easily or well. The fact that instability of residence was linked to poor adjustment only for father-resident adolescents may indicate that these families have fewer resources available to help them cope with the stresses of this transition. It may also indicate, however, that instability is a symptom of problems as well as a potential cause. As we have noted, shifts into father residence are likely to occur under more difficult circumstances more often than shifts into mother or dual residence.

Among adolescents living primarily with either the mother or the father, we found that when the residential parent had remarried, this was generally a positive factor for adolescent adjustment. When the residential parent had an unmarried cohabiting new partner, however, the implications were different: in these households, adolescent adjustment (for boys, primarily) appeared to suffer. We will explore these matters further in Chapter 7, where we take up the issue of parents' new partners in detail. We had too few cases to determine whether similar patterns prevailed for adolescents in dual residence.

What about the quality of the relationship between parents? On the basis of a solid body of literature pointing to the harmful effects of interparental conflict on children (see Amato, 1993; Cummings and Davies, 1994; Depner, Leino, and Chun, 1992), we expected that higher parental conflict would be related to negative adjustment in our adolescents. And indeed, there were some indications of such a relation, especially if we used adolescents' reports of T4 parental conflict. Our earlier measures of parental conflict derived from the reports of parents themselves did not have a great deal of predictive power. The stronger associations between interparental conflict and adolescent adjustment when using adolescents' reports of interparental conflict indicate that a reporting bias may be at work: adolescents who are not doing well see the world in more negative terms and therefore report more conflict between their parents as well as a number of other negative perceptions. However, adolescent reports may measure the conflict to which the adolescent is exposed better than reports from parents. Furthermore, the level of conflict reported by the adolescents was occurring at the same time that adjustment was being measured. Although having experienced conflict in the family in the past is expected to be a negative factor in children's adjustment, we also know that children's adjustment can benefit from reductions in conflict over time. It may be that some parents have become less conflictual between the T3 and T4 interviews (and that a small number may have become more conflictual), and that T4 adolescent adjustment is thus most closely related to the level of conflict that persists at T4.

The connections we did find between interparental conflict and adolescent adjustment were stronger for boys than for girls, and stronger for father-resident adolescents than for other residential groups. Other research has indicated that boys and girls do not differ so much in whether they react to interparental conflict, but in how they react. In line with sex-role expectations, investigators have found that boys are more likely to show externalizing problems (acting out, expressing hostility) and girls are more likely to show internalizing problems (withdrawal, emotional distress). We did not find this distinction, however. Although we did find associations between interparental conflict and deviance for boys, we also found boys reporting higher depression in situations of high conflict. And there were very few instances of association between interparental conflict and depression or any other problem among mother-resident girls. Cummings and Davies (1994) suggest that the diversity of findings concerning sex differences in response to parental conflict indicates considerable variability in response within each sex, and that no conclusions can be drawn about typical patterns. Our results appear to support this assessment.

Why should conflict be more detrimental for father-resident adolescents? Perhaps because, in father residence, the more hostile parent was usually the father, while in mother and dual residence, the more hostile parent was usually the mother. It may be more stressful for children to deal with anger and hostility exhibited by fathers than by mothers.

A close, intimate relationship between the residential parent and adolescent was generally associated with positive adjustment. However, when the overall closeness of the parent-child relationship and the residential parent's level of management and control were considered jointly, it was management and control that remained important, and parent-child closeness was no longer substantially related to adolescent adjustment (with the exception of depression among mother-resident adolescents). This implies that when the parent and adolescent have a close, intimate relationship marked by warmth, trust, and joint activities, the parent is able to stay in touch with the details of the adolescent's life and feelings. In turn, being informed about the child's interests, temptations, and relationships with friends enables a parent to be effective in averting negative outcomes by providing appropriate help, guidance, and discipline (see also Buchanan, Maccoby, and Dornbusch, 1991). The importance of "management/control," however, goes beyond successful monitoring. It also involves providing a structured milieu for the child, a milieu in which daily household events are predictable and family members can adapt readily to one another's routines. Such a structured environment reduces stress and permits other aspects of daily life to unfold more smoothly. Close affective relationships between parents and adolescents may also facilitate such a milieu by enhancing mutual respect and cooperation among family members.

Disengagement from the residential home (feelings of not wanting to be there, or not feeling at home there) was one of the strongest predictors of depression. Quite likely, withdrawal from the home is a symptom of an adolescent's depressed state. There were also links between disengagement and deviant behavior, and for these relations, disengagement might facilitate deviance as well as result from it. These findings are in line with a body of evidence indicating that disengagement or detachment from the family during adolescence is not associated with healthy developmental outcomes (Hill and Holmbeck, 1986; Noller, 1994; Rutter et al., 1976). We also found conflict between parents and children to be associated with some negative outcomes, but these associations were few in number.

Finally, we found little evidence that parents' confiding in their adolescents, at least to the extent that parents in our sample engaged in this kind of behavior, is associated with negative adjustment of any kind. Extreme cases of confiding in children may be detrimental, but within the range reported here, confiding appears harmless. However, when adolescent children—for whatever reason—feel that they need to take care of a parent or feel excessively worried about a parent's well-being, there are negative consequences, at least for sole-resident adolescents. When we speak of potential detrimental results of "role reversal" among children of divorce, therefore, it appears important to differentiate between two types of situations. In one type, the parent reveals personal feelings and needs to the child, but conveys a sense of competence in coping with those feelings and needs. In the other type of situation, conversations and other behavior take place in such a way that the adolescent feels insecure about the parent's own adjustment and feels responsible for making things better.

As is evident, many of the predictors of adjustment turned out to be similar for adolescents from different residential arrangements, and for boys and girls. With a few exceptions (for example, stability of residence over time, interparental conflict, disengagement from the home), what adolescents "need" to promote healthy adjustment, or what interferes with healthy adjustment, does not vary substantially depending on the sex of the adolescent or depending on whether the primary caretaker is the mother, the father, or both parents. There were indications, however, that the benefits of what would be considered "good parenting" (high parent-child closeness and high household management) were somewhat more tenuous in father residence—particularly for girls—than they were in mother residence. For example, father-adolescent closeness did not have direct links to positive adjustment for either sex (although closeness did facilitate father's monitoring and household management), and certain aspects of low management (high levels of youth-alone decision making and late curfews) were linked with better adjustment of girls. These anomalies suggest that although sole-resident fathers—like sole-resident mothers—can enhance their adolescents' chances for positive adjustment by engaging in effective parenting practices, these practices alone are not as effective as they are in mother residence. The difference in effectiveness, of course, may be due to the different characteristics of families and adolescents that select themselves into father residence. Another possibility, indicated in Chapter 10, is that father-resident adolescents need to maintain a relatively good relationship with their nonresidential mothers as well as with their fathers in order to benefit from a good relationship with their fathers.

In summary, in this chapter we have described the major characteristics of the residential home and relationships that appear to promote adjustment of adolescents after divorce. In the next chapter, we consider in more detail the impact of a new partner in the residential home.

7

Adaptation to
New Partners

We saw in Chapter 6 that the presence of a parent's new partner was related to adolescent adjustment. Over the sample as a whole, but especially for boys, a residential parent's remarriage was associated with positive outcomes, while the presence of an unmarried new partner in the household was associated with adjustment problems. Now we look in more detail at what happens in a family when a new partner enters the scene. We proceed from the assumption that when a new partner enters the household, family processes may change in ways that range from minimal to substantial. Some changes may be conducive to positive developmental outcomes for adolescents; others may present special difficulties for them. We want to examine in detail how new partners influence family dynamics.

There is a body of research on stepfamilies, focusing on the adjustment of children in remarried as compared with single-parent or nondivorced families (Bray and Berger, 1993a; Ganong and Coleman, 1984; Hetherington and Clingempeel, 1992; Zill, 1988). These studies have not examined the possible impact of new relationships in which men and women do not remarry but date or live with new partners. Most parents who have divorced do eventually remarry. However, there is usually an extended period during which one or both parents begin to date, focusing more and more on one person as a new partner. Some of these parents choose to live with a new partner for a period of time before remarrying. This series of events unfolds more rapidly for some individuals than others, of course, and some go through several intimate new relationships before settling down. We believe the different stages of parental repartnering may have different implications for children in the family. For example, when a biological parent regularly dates someone who is not living in the home, the parent may invest a great deal of time in the dating relationship while the family derives little benefit from the relationship in terms of help with parenting or management of the household. At the same time, a dating relationship may be less disruptive to family routines than the presence of a new person living in the household whose needs and participation in family processes must be accommodated.

In this chapter we contrast three types of new-partner relationships: (1) steady dating (the parent was seeing a new partner on a regular and usually exclusive basis, and the adolescent identified this person as the boyfriend or girlfriend of the parent in question); (2) cohabiting (there was a new partner living in the same household with, but not married to, the parent); and (3) remarriage. We also compare these three new-partner situations with situations in which the parent was not dating any one person on a regular basis. Because we studied a variety of relationships that did not involve marriage, we primarily use the term "new partner" (NP) rather than "stepparent," "stepfather," or "stepmother." When we refer to "new mothers" and "new fathers," we mean any new partner, whether married or not. Although there were a few cases in our sample in which a parent was living with a same-sex roommate, we have no way of knowing whether any of these arrangements involved homosexual relationships. When we speak of repartnering, our discussion will be concerned exclusively with the formation of heterosexual couples.

We first describe the repartnering status of the two parents of adolescents in our sample. We then examine what relation the presence of a new partner has, if any, to the characteristics of the family context and processes (the quality of relationships between the residential parent and the adolescent, and the nature of parental management and control). Next we look more specifically at the relationships between adolescents and their parents' new partners and at the conditions that affect the quality of the adolescent–new partner relationship, including how accepting the adolescent is of this new partner. Finally, we look at the relation between an adolescent's acceptance of the parent's new partner and the adolescent's adjustment.

Stages of Repartnering

Our adolescents' parents, having typically been separated from their former spouses for about four and a half years, were in various stages of the repartnering process (see Table 7.1).

Table 7.1 Mothers' and fathers' repartnering status by
residential arrangement[a]

Repartnering status	Adolescents' residence		
	Mother	Dual	Father
Mother's NP status	(*n* = 241)	(*n* = 41)	(*n* = 81)
No new partner	37%	46%	27%
Dating regularly	18	12	17
Cohabiting	12	17	25
Remarried	33	25	31
	100%	100%	100%
Father's NP status	(*n* = 237)	(*n* = 41)	(*n* = 81)
No new partner	25%	32%	31%
Dating regularly	16	24	15
Cohabiting	21	12	15
Remarried	38	32	39
	100%	100%	100%

a. Percentages are based on a sample of only one adolescent per family, selected randomly.

The parents who were maintaining dual residence for their children were somewhat less likely to be remarried. This is not surprising, for when parents do remarry, joint physical custody becomes harder to maintain. In part this is true because remarriage often involves residential moves that place the two parental households farther apart (Maccoby and Mnookin, 1992). Among all residential parents—that is, those who had either primary or dual physical custody of their adolescent children—about one-third had remarried, about one-third had a "steady" new partner, and about one-third were either not dating at all or dating casually.

Repartnering and Family Context and Processes

In comparing families in different stages of parental repartnering with respect to family context and processes, we had to consider that a mother's repartnering might have a different impact on the family than a father's repartnering; furthermore, the repartnering of either parent might have a different impact on boys than on girls. Being most interested in the impact of a *residential* parent's new partner, we examined the impact of the mother's new partner in households where the adolescents lived with their mothers (in primary or dual residence) separately from impact of a father's new partner in households where the adolescents lived with their fathers (in primary or dual residence),[1] and we examined whether the impact of a new partner in each of these situations was different for boys than for girls.

We also recognized that some new partners had children of their own; these children may or may not have been brought into the adolescent's household. As reported in Chapter 3, stepsiblings were present in about 7 percent of mothers' households, and about 21 percent of fathers' households (these percentages include children of cohabiting new partners as well as remarried new partners). Although our analyses in Chapter 6 of the presence of step- or half-siblings in the home indicated that there were few overall relations with adolescent adjustment, it is possible that the impact of a new partner's children varies depending on the status of the new partner or other family factors. Unfortunately, however, to subdivide our four repartnering groups according to whether stepsiblings were present would have created subgroups too small for analysis. Therefore we have not included this factor in the analyses reported below.

Family Context and Demographics

Appendix Table B.7 shows the differences between new-partner groups on selected context variables. Adolescents living in the households of remarried parents tended to be somewhat younger than those in the households of unremarried parents. Mothers who were remarried also had somewhat lower levels of education, on the average, than did those with no new partner. There was a tendency for fathers who were cohabiting to have lower levels of education than other fathers, although the differences were not statistically significant. Because of these modest differences in adolescents' age and parents' educational attainment by parents' new-partner status, we controlled statistically for adolescent age and for residential parent's education in subsequent analyses.[2]

When a new partner had taken up residence in the mother's home, she worked fewer hours than did mothers still living singly, an average of nearly ten hours per week less. Mothers' average earnings were somewhat lower too, though not significantly so. It seems likely that the economic support provided by resident new partners enables many mothers to cut back on their working hours when they wish or need to do so. Alternatively, mothers who work only part time may have more time and inclination to develop new-partner relationships.

Having a live-in new partner (whether married or cohabiting) had quite a different meaning for fathers. Their working hours were higher, and to a modest extent, their personal earnings were higher as well, when they lived with a new partner. These data indicate that the burden of providing economic support for the household shifts toward men upon remarriage (and probably upon cohabitation as well), a process that is in line with other findings concerning employment and income changes of men and women after divorce and remarriage (Duncan and Hoffman, 1985; Espenshade, 1979).

Relationships between the Two Biological Parents

It is important to know whether, when parents acquire new partners, this affects their ability to cooperate with their ex-spouses as they deal with the children of the former marriage. At Time 3, a year before our study was done, cooperation was highest between ex-spouses who had not yet begun to date (or in the case of mothers, who were only dating casually). When a parent had remarried, disengagement between the parents, as well as a conflicted co-parental relationship, was more common than when parents had either not begun to date or were in the early stages of repartnering (Maccoby and Mnookin, 1992). At Time 4, we asked the adolescents how frequently their parents talked to each other, how often they argued, how much they cooperated, and how much they agreed about rules, discipline, and privileges for the adolescent. The reports of adolescents living with their mothers (in sole or dual residence) about these matters were not related to the mother's stage of repartnering. Father-resident adolescents, however, reported that their parents argued less if their father was remarried. The amount of parental agreement over the children's regimen was not seen by these adolescents as differing according to the father's repartnering status.

There were some indications that among fathers who had remarried by T4, hostility toward the ex-spouse and interparental conflict had been high in the past. We noted in Chapter 5 that there was a history of greater interparental hostility among the families in which the adolescent children lived primarily with the father. This problem appears to be found most commonly among the father-resident families in which the father had remarried. At the time we interviewed the adolescents, however, the remarried fathers did not appear to be in either an especially conflicted or especially cooperative relationship with the children's mothers. In general, at least as far as adolescent perceptions are concerned, the presence of a parent's new partner had very little impact on the relationship between the two parents.

Mothers' Repartnering and Parent-Adolescent Relationships

Literature on preadolescents' adjustment to remarriage has suggested that girls may have particular trouble with a mother's remarriage because it threatens an especially close relationship formed between mothers and daughters during the postdivorce period. Did we find evidence of particularly close mother-daughter relationships when a mother was not remarried, or disrupted relationships after remarriage? Yes and no, respectively (see Figure 7.1). Adolescents—particularly girls—appeared to have better relationships with resident mothers when the mother did

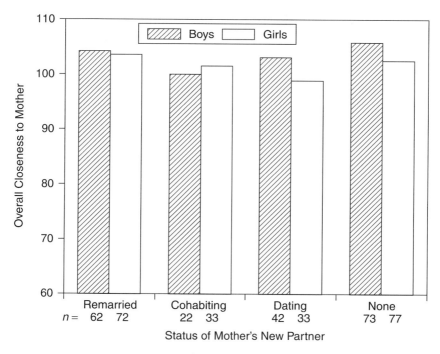

Figure 7.1 Overall closeness to mother among mother- and dual-resident adolescents, by status of mother's new partner and sex of adolescent. Means are adjusted for age of adolescent and mother's education.

not have a new partner or when she was remarried, and poorer relationships with her if she was just dating (especially for girls) or cohabiting (especially for boys). We also found that, for adolescents of both sexes, closeness to remarried mothers was greater the longer she had been remarried.

As further evidence of good mother-child relationships when the mother was remarried, disengagement from the mother's home was lowest in the remarried group, especially in contrast to the "dating only" group and, again, especially for girls. Average conflict between adolescents (both boys and girls) and their mothers was also lowest when the mother was remarried—lower than when she was either dating or cohabiting.

Remarriage *was* related to a certain level of distancing in the mother-adolescent relationship, as indicated by measures of role reversal (see Figure 7.2). For example, when a mother had a new partner living in the home, she was less likely to confide in her adolescent children. This effect was found primarily among boys.[3] It appears that a mother's new live-in partner takes the place of her children as a confidant, although daughters are less likely to lose that role than sons. Both daughters and sons were less likely to worry about their mother, or feel the need to take care of her, when the mother's new partner had moved into the household. The distancing indicated by these measures is likely to represent a move toward more healthy family functioning, although it is possible that the change is perceived negatively by the adolescents who are being "replaced."

In sum, our findings among adolescents indicate that relationships between children of both sexes and their resident mothers are as good when the mother is remarried as they are when she has no new partner. We do find, however, indications of more troubled relationships when the mother is involved in new relationships that do not involve remarriage. Relationships in families where the mother is dating seem to be especially strained; that is, these adolescents report feeling less close to their mothers, and they report higher levels of conflict and disengagement. Hetherington (1987) reported that mother-daughter conflict was elevated in families in which the mother had only been remarried for a short time (less than two years), but that the relationship improved over time. Our findings appear to fit this pattern, and extend it to show that the early stages of parental repartnering, even before remarriage, may be the most difficult for mothers and their children.

Does a mother's new partner influence adolescents' relationships with their fathers? For adolescents living with their mothers, the mother's

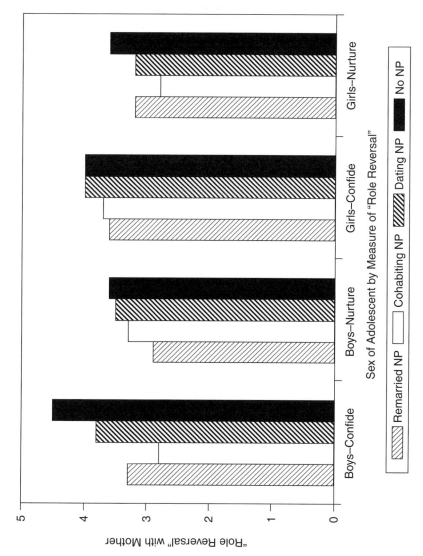

Figure 7.2 Mothers' confiding in adolescents and adolescents' feelings of nurturing mother among mother- and dual-resident adolescents, by status of mother's new partner (NP) and sex of adolescent. Means are adjusted for age of adolescent and mother's education.

remarriage did not appear to interfere with the adolescent-father bond. If anything, closeness was somewhat enhanced, at least for girls.[4] These findings are consistent with the report by Furstenberg, Morgan, and Allison (1987) that the presence of a stepfather did not hurt a child's relationship with an outside father. Our data suggest, in fact, that the father-child relationship may actually be better if the mother has remarried. Several factors may account for this finding. For example, when mothers remarry, nonresident fathers may make increased efforts to stay close to their children, in order not to be replaced. Alternatively, adolescents may idealize their nonresident fathers in contrast to their stepfathers. A further possibility is that remarriage may lessen the mother's emotional involvement with her former spouse, so that she less often undermines or derogates him in the children's presence.

Fathers' Repartnering and Parent-Adolescent Relationships

In contrast to the situation between residential mothers and their children, adolescents living with their fathers or in dual residence appeared to have the best relationships with "dating only" fathers (see Figure 7.3). Both boys and girls felt somewhat closer to fathers who were dating as compared with fathers who were remarried, cohabiting, or had no new partner.[5] Girls identified more with fathers who either had no new partner or were only dating, by comparison with those whose new partner had moved into the father's household. Fathers and adolescents also participated in more activities together when the father was only dating than in any of the other groups. The better quality of father-child relationships when the father was dating regularly was partially, but not completely, a reflection of the fact that these fathers worked fewer hours per week. Number of working hours was only modestly related to the quality of the father-adolescent relationship among father- and dual-resident adolescents. When we took the number of working hours into account, the differences between dating fathers and other fathers (in their relationships with their adolescents) were reduced slightly (and sometimes became nonsignificant), but relationships with dating fathers consistently had the highest means. So it seems that the enhanced father-child relationships between adolescents and fathers who are only dating may have other roots as well.[6] Perhaps when fathers begin to date, they make special efforts to prove to themselves and their children that their commitment to the children can continue unimpeded despite the new ties. Also, new partners who are women may be more inclined

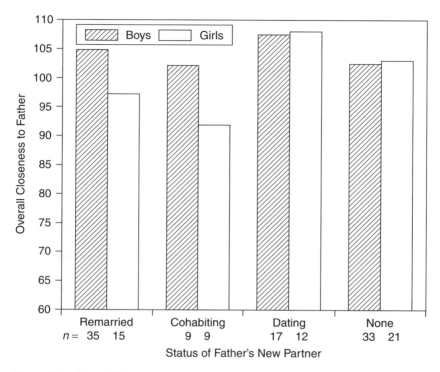

Figure 7.3 Overall closeness to father among father- and dual-resident adolescents, by status of father's new partner and sex of adolescent. Means are adjusted for age of adolescent and father's education.

than new partners who are men to become involved with the entire family even in the early stages of the relationship, and they may make greater efforts right off the bat to get to know the children. New partners who are men might require more time to become involved with the children of a new romantic interest. If this is true, a father's dating new partner would be less likely to distract the father from the children than a mother's dating new partner, and might even enhance the father's relationship with his children, at least initially. But this is speculation. We can only state that while a residential mother's dating is something of a negative factor for her children's relationship with her, a residential father's appears positive.

Fathers, like mothers, when remarried or living with someone, were less likely to confide in their adolescents (see Figure 7.4). In this case, the difference was especially apparent for daughters.[7] Stepmothers and fa-

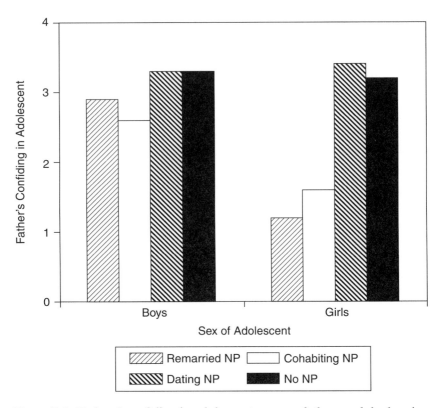

Figure 7.4 Fathers' confiding in adolescents among father- and dual-resident adolescents, by status of father's new partner and sex of adolescent. Means are adjusted for age of adolescent and father's education.

thers' new live-in girlfriends tended to take the daughter's place as the father's confidante, more than was the case for sons. This parallels the finding reported for mothers' households, where a stepfather or live-in boyfriend also tended to replace the opposite-sex adolescent as confidant.

When fathers either dated or remarried, this seemed to draw father- and dual-resident adolescents closer to their mothers. Underscoring this increased closeness, the father- or dual-resident adolescents whose fathers had remarried expressed more eagerness to see their mothers than did the adolescents in the other groups combined. The father's remarriage clearly did not weaken the relationship that father-resident children have with their mothers. If anything, the relationship with the mother was enhanced. As with mothers who remarried, this stronger connection may be the result of increased efforts by the nonresident mother not to be replaced, the adolescent's idealization of the nonresident mother in contrast to the stepmother, or a softened attitude toward the ex-spouse on the part of remarried fathers.

Parental Control and Management

In line with the hypothesis that dating a new partner may be more time consuming and present more of a distraction from the home, we found that adolescents reported lower overall household management in mother-resident homes when the mother was dating a new partner than when she was not dating at all or had remarried (see Figure 7.5a). The mother-resident households in which the mother was dating were also the least likely to have an adult home after school.

In fathers' households, the highest levels of parental control were found when the father was remarried. Remarried fathers were reported to have the highest levels of overall household management, significantly higher than fathers with no new partner or a cohabiting new partner (see Figure 7.5b).[8] Adolescents also had somewhat earlier weekend curfews and were more likely to report having an adult home after school when their father was remarried.[9] Neither the mother's nor the father's repartnering status was related to the locus of decision making with respect to issues affecting the adolescent's life. That is, parents were neither more nor less likely to be involved in joint decision making with their adolescents if they were remarried.

Other investigators have found that an additional adult in the home leads to increased supervision and better control and management of adolescents (Dornbusch et al., 1985; Hetherington, 1987). In some respects, we found this as well. The advantage, however, was limited to a remarried new partner. Cohabiting new partners did not appear to enhance household management or supervision of the adolescent for either mothers or fathers. Furthermore, a remarried new partner in the home for the mother was an advantage only in comparison with situations in which she was dating a new partner who lived elsewhere, and not in comparison with having no new partner at all. Single mothers who were not dating anyone more than casually appeared to monitor their adolescents and manage their homes as successfully as did remarried mothers. In contrast, a residential father's monitoring and management did benefit

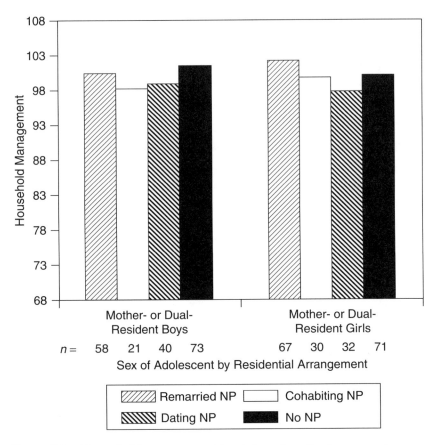

Figure 7.5a Household management by status of mother's new partner (NP) and sex of adolescent, for mother- and dual-resident adolescents. Means are adjusted for age of adolescent and mother's education.

from the presence of a remarried new partner in comparison with having no new partner.

Adolescents' Acceptance of Parents' New Partners

We focus now on the kind of relationships that adolescents developed with their residential parent's new partner. We assessed these relationships in several ways. First, the adolescents were asked a battery of questions about closeness to, and joint activities with, their parent's new partner; these questions were the same as those asked about the adoles-

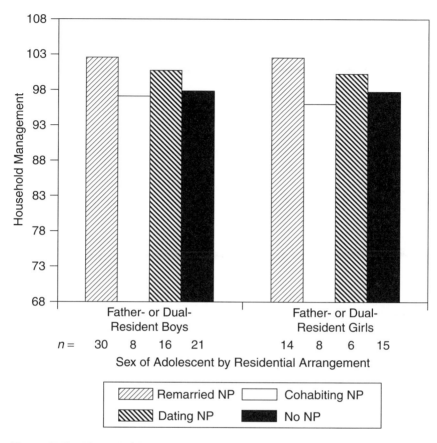

Figure 7.5b Household management by status of father's new partner (NP) and sex of adolescent, for father- and dual-resident adolescents. Means are adjusted for age of adolescent and father's education. Numbers are based on a sample of only one adolescent per family, selected randomly. See note 8.

cents' relationships with their biological parents. For both fathers' and mothers' new partners, the average level of closeness or activities reported by the adolescents was close to the mid-range of the scale (see Table 7.2). But more important, there was variability in the scores: some adolescents reported being very close to their parents' new partners; others reported hardly any intimacy at all. Similarly, some shared no joint activities with the new person, while some shared as many activities with the new partner as they did with the residential parent.

Table 7.2 Average closeness to, and joint activities with, parents' new partners[a]

Relationship measure	Mother's new partner	Father's new partner
Closeness to (range: 9–45)[b]	28.6	28.1
Number of joint activities with (range: 0–8)	3.3	3.4
Maximum *n*	(259)	(95)

a. These reports include only the adolescents' reports concerning their *residential* parent's new partners (in other words, the partners of primary- or dual-resident parents). Subjects whose residential parents did not have a new partner are excluded.

b. Ranges are possible, not actual, ranges.

In addition to the questions concerning closeness and joint activities, we asked two questions specifically focused on relationships with parents' new partners. The first was meant to examine the role of the new partner in the adolescent's life: "Is your (parent's new partner) mostly like a father (mother) to you? Like a friend? Just another person? Or someone you wish weren't part of your life?" The second inquired about the adolescent's willingness to accord authority to the parent's new partner: "In general, do you think your (parent's new partner) has the right to set up rules or tell you what you can or can't do?" Figure 7.6 displays the distribution of responses to each of these questions.

As Figure 7.6 shows, only about one-fourth of the adolescents accorded the parent's new partner full parental status. But at the other extreme, few adolescents appeared hostile or resentful toward their parent's new partner. Most commonly, the new partner was seen as a kind of friend. With regard to adolescents' willingness to accept the authority of a residential parent's new partner, a little less than half of the adolescents unequivocally rejected the idea of a parent's new partner exercising authority, answering our question about whether the new partner had the right to make rules or tell them what to do by saying simply, "No way!" or "Definitely not." Or as one late-adolescent boy elaborated more fully: "I don't think so, because . . . he's not really my father. I don't know, he's around a lot, but I think he just feels like kind of a friend. Usually I just ignore him . . . I would rather not have him set up things for me to do. My parents could pretty much take care of that."

But about as many adolescents as denied the new partner parental authority willingly accorded authority to the new partner. Willingness to accept the new partner's authority appeared to be somewhat more com-

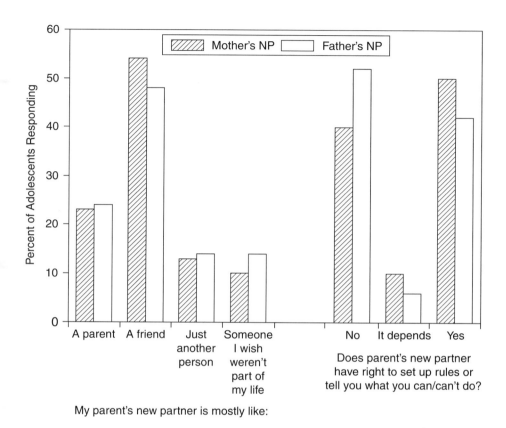

Figure 7.6 Percentage of adolescents indicating different levels of acceptance of residential (sole or dual) parent's new partner (NP). Adolescents whose parents did not have a new partner are excluded from this graph.

mon in cases where a parent and child had moved into a new partner's already-established home, as opposed to cases where the new partner had moved into the adolescent and parent's existing household. Here are some comments illustrating the bases on which adolescents accepted the new partner's authority:

(Early-adolescent[10] boy in mother residence): "When we bought our house it was pretty crappy; now it's really nice. He does a lot around the house, and he helped me fix up the house, so I guess he can tell me what to do."

(Late-adolescent boy in mother residence): "He doesn't do it that often, but yeah, because it's for my own good."

(Early-adolescent boy in mother residence): "I like him a lot and he's a friend and if he told me not to do this, no problem. I'd decide not to 'cause he knows more about it than I would."

(Mid-adolescent girl in father residence): "Well kinda, yeah, 'cause . . . she's an adult, and she's older, and I gotta, you know, respect what she says."

(Mid-adolescent girl in father residence): "Yeah, I think [new mother is] . . . a caring person . . . I know she cares about me."

(Early-adolescent boy in father residence): "Yeah, 'cause it's her home."

A small number of adolescents found our question difficult to answer, and expressed ambivalence or reservations concerning a new partner's right to authority. Less than 10 percent said that the new partner's rights depended on other factors, such as the type of rule or the extent to which that new partner contributed to the home financially. For example, one boy said explicitly that he would obey his stepfather on a family trip provided that the stepfather financed the outing. The following quotes further illustrate some of the ambivalence that was expressed:

(Late-adolescent girl): "No, but yes, because he pays for everything. I would like to say no, but in my mind I know 'yes.' I don't agree, no, that he should be able to give me rules on my life, but yes, to give me rules of the house and stuff like that." (Interviewer: "Would you say yes or no?") "I'm going to go for *no*."

(Late-adolescent girl): "I think she has the right because this is her house—her and my father's house. If she has to help pay the bills and if she does most of the work around the house, but other than that, she really, I don't think she has any business at all. I mean I know she cares about me." (Interviewer: "So you're saying you don't think she should set up rules?") "It really depends on what situation. If it's something that I really don't care about, then fine; she can say whatever she wants. Usually she'll say it, and I'll just do whatever I'm going to do anyway."

Certain rights were accorded to a stepparent or cohabiting new partner simply because he or she was a member of the household and therefore deserved consideration in matters such as noise or clean-up. For example, one boy said: "Well, I say he has a right to say what time I come in at night, because, you know, he lives in the same house and he has to get up in the morning to go to work, and he doesn't want me coming in at one in the morning. I can see that. But that's about it: just curfew." Another boy said he refrained from practicing on his trumpet when his mother's new partner was home because the partner did not like the noise.

But a right to set rules of the household often did not extend to rights to control the adolescent's personal life and decisions. Certain areas of decision making were set aside as areas over which only the natural parents had rights, areas that were "not the new partner's place" to be involved. And adolescents often voiced acceptance of a new partner's authority if it was derived from or in line with the natural parent's authority ("It's okay if he checks with my mom first"), or voiced problems with authority that differed from that of a biological parent ("If my dad lets me do it, [my stepfather] should let me do it too").

As Figure 7.6 indicates, there were few differences in relationships with stepfathers (or mothers' boyfriends) compared with stepmothers (or fathers' girlfriends), a finding that is somewhat at odds with previous findings that relationships between children and stepmothers are more troubled than those between stepfathers and children (Furstenberg, 1987; Ihinger-Tallman, 1988). Adolescents in our sample were somewhat more willing to accept rule-making from the mother's new partner than the father's, but on the whole it made little difference whether the new partner was in the mother's or the father's household. More striking is the variation within each residential group, with some adolescents readily accepting their parents' new partners and forming close relationships with them, while other adolescents remained distant or even hostile.

Factors Related to Acceptance of New Partners

In this section we treat all measures of the relationship with and acceptance of the new partner as continuous measures. In other words, adolescents who said "Yes," they would accept a new partner's authority, were considered high in acceptance, and adolescents who answered "No" were considered low in acceptance. Those adolescents who said "It depends" were considered moderate in acceptance. With regard to the question about the new partner's role, answering that the new partner was "like a parent" indicated high acceptance and, at the other end, answering that the new partner was "someone I wish weren't a part of my life" indicated low acceptance.

Table 7.3 Correlations of new-partner acceptance with age of adolescent[a]

Measure of acceptance	Mother's new partner	Father's new partner
Closeness to NP	−.26****	−.23*
Joint activities with NP	−.34****	−.18+
Acceptance of NP's authority	−.34****	−.25*
NP's perceived role	−.25	−.18+
Maximum *n*	(260)	(95)

a. These reports include only the adolescents' reports concerning *residential* parent's new partners (in other words, the partners of primary- or dual-resident parents). Subjects whose residential parents did not have a new partner are excluded.
$^+p \le .10$ $^*p \le .05$. $^{****}p \le .0001$.

Age and Sex of the Adolescent

Age was a major factor in the adolescent's acceptance of a parent's new partner. Younger adolescents accepted a parent's new partner more readily than did older ones, and this was true of both new fathers and new mothers (see Table 7.3).

Although we did not assess how willing our adolescents were to accept the authority of their natural parents, it is reasonable to expect that this, too, would decline with increasing age. We did assess closeness to both residential mothers and residential fathers, and there were similar age differences in closeness to parents and parents' new partners. The age differences in acceptance of a new partner reflect, no doubt, a general developmental trend of decreasing involvement with and increasing independence from adults in general, and are not necessarily specific to parents' new partners.

There has been some speculation, however, that early adolescence is the time of greatest resistance to new partners, on the grounds that the issues of adolescent sexuality and autonomy are emerging strongly at this time, and that these new developments create resistance that is moderated as the adolescent becomes more mature. Evidence from other research suggests that the entry of a new partner is, in fact, more difficult during early adolescence than at younger ages (Hetherington, 1993). In contrast, our findings suggest that new partners entering a family may have an advantage in forming positive relationships if the children are in early, rather than later, adolescence. There are limitations in our ability to draw this conclusion, however. First, although all new partners in our sample had entered the family less than four years before the time we talked with the adolescents, there was variability concerning when in that four-year period the new partner "arrived." Our results simply suggest that early adolescents are more accepting than are older adolescents of new partners, and do not speak directly to when it might be most difficult for a new partner to establish a relationship with the adolescent. Second, we assessed only limited aspects of the adolescent–new partner relationship; for example, we do not know how much active conflict took place between the adolescent and the new partner. It may be that early adolescents experience more conflict with parents' new partners than do older adolescents, whereas older adolescents experience less conflict but are more emotionally distant from the new partner. These possible relations need more explicit attention in future research.

With regard to the sex of the adolescent, we expected girls to be less accepting of both new fathers and new mothers. With regard to mother-resident children, a growing body of research suggests that girls put up more resistance than boys to the entry of their mothers' new partners into the family (see, for example, Bray and Berger, 1993a; Clingempeel, Brand, and Ievoli, 1984; Hetherington, 1993; Hetherington and Clingempeel, 1992; Hetherington, Cox, and Cox, 1982; Santrock et al., 1982). Hetherington has suggested that, at least among preadolescents, girls become closer than boys to their mothers during the postdivorce period, and therefore find the appearance of a stepfather or mother's boyfriend more threatening and more disruptive. Furthermore, boys are believed to be more welcoming of a new male role model or male companion in the family. Girls in turn are believed to be less accepting of their father's new partner, although for somewhat different reasons. Girls are thought to have stronger feelings of loyalty toward their biological mothers, thus being more likely to resent a stepmother for trying to "take the place" of the biological mother. It is also possible that, when fathers are not dating or married to a new partner, some girls fill a traditional female role in their fathers' households—cooking, shopping, cleaning, or entertaining. Even though household chores can be something teenagers would rather avoid, managing a household is nevertheless an adultlike role that conveys a certain status, so these girls may feel displaced when a father's new partner takes over these duties. We have also seen that the entrance of a new partner into the father's home takes the daughter's place as a confidante to some extent. Adolescent daughters who have enjoyed this status with their fathers may begrudge losing it.

Table 7.4 Acceptance of parents' new partners, by sex of adolescent[a]

Measure of acceptance	Mother's new partner			Father's new partner		
	Boys	Girls	*t*	Boys	Girls	*t*
Closeness to NP	29.7	27.6	+	29.6	25.6	*
Joint activities with NP	3.7	3.0	*	3.7	2.7	*
Acceptance of NP's authority	1.2	.97	*	.93	.86	n.s.
NP's perceived role	3.0	2.8	n.s.	3.0	2.6	+

a. These reports include only the adolescents' reports concerning *residential* parent's new partners (in other words, the partners of primary- or dual-resident parents). Subjects whose residential parents did not have a new partner are excluded.
$+p \leq .10$. $*p \leq .05$.   n.s. = not significant.

In line with our expectations, boys accepted new partners somewhat more readily than did girls (see Table 7.4), although the differences were strongest for emotional closeness and shared activities, and less strong or consistent for acceptance of authority. In fact, with respect to accepting the authority of the mother's new partner, the sex difference was limited to early adolescents (see Figure 7.7),[11] suggesting that the age decline in acceptance of authority noted earlier occurs earlier for girls than for boys. Thus our results confirm previous findings comparing boys' and girls' relationships with new partners, although the mechanisms accounting for the differences are still in need of illumination. After all, mother-resident girls in our sample were not closer to their mothers than were mother-resident boys; why, then, would they view a new father more negatively? And if boys are eager to have a male companion in mother-resident homes, why do girls in father-resident homes not feel the same way about new mothers? Such questions are not answered by our study.

New-Partner Status

Did an adolescent's acceptance of a new partner depend on whether the new couple was remarried, cohabiting, or merely dating regularly? We have not been able to locate previous studies that examine this question, and we can imagine scenarios that would predict different outcomes. Re-marriage may confer legitimacy on a parent's new partner; however, it also makes that partner's presence more permanent, more intrusive, and hence possibly more unwelcome to the adolescent. And it is not obvious whether

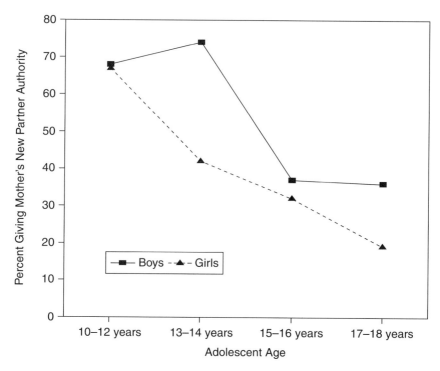

Figure 7.7 Acceptance of the authority of mother's new partner among mother- and dual-resident adolescents by age and sex of adolescent.

a cohabiting new partner would be more or less acceptable to an adolescent than someone the parent is merely dating. Regular dating partners are presumably less threatening in terms of their potential to "replace" a nonresident parent, but they may take a lot of the residential parent's time. The adolescent also has fewer opportunities to interact with and become attached to someone who is not living in the household.

We found that, especially in mothers' homes, remarried new partners gained the most acceptance from adolescents (see Table 7.5). The advantage of remarriage was especially apparent when it came to acceptance of authority. When asked about her mother's new boyfriend's right to exercise authority, an early-adolescent girl put it succinctly: "When he gets married to Mom, yes. [Interviewer: Now?] No." Furthermore, adolescents living with their mothers accorded somewhat more acceptance to a mother's boyfriend if he was living in the household than if he and the mother were merely dating.

Table 7.5 New-partner status and adolescents' acceptance[a]

Measure of acceptance	A. Acceptance of mother's new partner				
	Dating (D)	Cohabiting (C)	Remarried (R)	F	Significant differences
Closeness to NP	25.2	27.2	30.9	10.69****	R > C, D
Joint activities with NP	2.6	3.5	3.7	6.65***	R, C > D
Acceptance of NP's authority	.57	.94	1.4	26.48****	R > C > D
NP's perceived role	2.8	2.9	3.0	1.87	
Maximum *n*	(71)	(55)	(133)		

Measure of acceptance	B. Acceptance of father's new partner				
	Dating (D)	Cohabiting (C)	Remarried (R)	F	Significant differences
Closeness to NP	27.8	25.9	29.1	.86	
Joint activities with NP	3.3	2.6	3.7	1.81	
Acceptance of NP's authority	.38	.68	1.27	9.21***	R > C, D
NP's perceived role	2.9	2.5	2.9	1.37	
Maximum *n*	(27)	(18)	(50)		

a. Means are adjusted for age and sex of adolescent. These reports include only the adolescents' reports concerning *residential* parent's new partners (in other words, the partners of primary- or dual-resident parents). Subjects whose residential parents did not have a new partner are excluded.

***$p \leq .001$.   ****$p \leq .0001$.

Acceptance of a father's new partner was less strongly related to marital status than was acceptance of a mother's new partner, and there were indications that adolescents' closeness to and activities with a father's new partner might be lowest for cohabiting girlfriends. But the major finding is that acceptance and positive feelings were consistently highest when a remarriage had occurred.

Was the greater acceptance of remarried new partners explained by the fact that the adolescents had known them longer? Not entirely. The differences associated with remarriage remained even if we controlled for the length of time the parent and new partner had been living together or dating. From the adolescents' standpoint, it appears that marriage confers legitimacy on a parent's relationship, giving the new partner a right to greater consideration and respect. Remarriage also probably gives the adolescent some confidence that the parent's new partnership will last, so that the adolescent can feel free to form an attachment with less fear of the loss often associated with more temporary liaisons. At the same time, we should not ignore the possibility that parents may be more likely to remarry if the new partner is someone the children can readily accept.

Closeness to the Residential Parent

Preadolescent children who have a close and involved relationship with a custodial parent are thought to have more difficulty accepting a stepparent (Furstenberg and Spanier, 1984; Hetherington, 1993). It would be understandable if children, including adolescents, who were closely bonded with a parent were jealous of his or her new partner and fearful that the adults' new love life would interfere with the close parent-child relationship. Yet it seems that adolescents, who typically want more independence from parents than do younger children, would be less likely to resent a new partner's intrusion in terms of its effect on the amount of time their parent spends with them. Thus, although previous work suggested that we might find that greater closeness between the adolescent and the resident parent would be related to less closeness to or acceptance of the new partner, we were not sure that those predictions would apply to our adolescent sample.

In contrast, there were many reasons to expect a positive correlation between adolescents' closeness to their residential parents and closeness to and acceptance of parents' new partners. For one thing, certain children—by virtue of temperament or training—are easier for everyone to get along with, and both natural parents and stepparents undoubtedly respond more positively to a pleasant and cooperative child than to a difficult and resistant one. Some adolescents are also undoubtedly more open than others are to the formation of positive relations with new adults, depending perhaps on their attachment history or other interpersonal experiences that have made them more or less wary of attachments. A strong bond with the residential parent may signify a positive interpersonal history that presumably could foster a child's readiness for new relationships. Furthermore, a parent who has a close relationship with a child also has a better chance of providing direct, concurrent support for the budding relationship between the child and the new partner.

Table 7.6 Correlations between closeness to parent and acceptance of parent's new partner[a]

Measure of acceptance	Closeness to mother		Closeness to father	
	Boys	Girls	Boys	Girls
Closeness to NP	.58****	.62****	.47***	.62****
Joint activities with NP	.26**	.36****	.11	.26
Acceptance of NP's authority	.05	.35****	.18	.39*
NP's perceived role	.24**	.28***	.26*	.41*
Maximum *n*	(122)	(138)	(59)	(36)

a. These reports include only the adolescents' reports concerning *residential* parents and their new partners (in other words, primary- or dual-resident parents and their new partners). Subjects whose residential parents did not have a new partner are excluded. Correlations are adjusted for age of adolescent.

$*p \le .05.$ $**p \le .01.$ $***p \le .001.$ $****p \le .0001.$

Our findings primarily support these latter hypotheses (see Table 7.6). The overall pattern of results suggests that the closer the relationship between an adolescent and a residential parent, the more likely the adolescent was to have a close relationship with the parent's new partner and the more likely the adolescent was to accept that person's authority. Our evidence certainly did not suggest that the two relationships were at odds with each other. The relation between closeness to the residential parent and acceptance of his or her new partner's authority was greater for girls than for boys in some instances, especially among children in father residence (the correlation between closeness to a father and acceptance of the authority of a new mother was .69 for father-resident girls and .16 for father-resident boys).[12]

Closeness to the Nonresidential Parent

The entry of a residential parent's new partner into an adolescent's life may affect the adolescent's relationship with the nonresidential parent. In turn, the kind of relationship the adolescent has with the nonresidential parent may influence that adolescent's acceptance of the residential parent's new partner. For example, children who are very close to the nonresidential parent may experience more loyalty conflicts and more resistance to having the residential parent's new partner "take the place" of the nonresidential parent. Presumably, too, the more time an adolescent spends with the nonresidential parent, the more opportunities there would be for loyalty conflicts to be activated. In addition, children who develop close relationships with the residential parent's new partner may become less dependent on their relationship with the nonresidential parent; indeed, the new partner may in some ways begin to take the place of the nonresidential biological parent (Bray and Berger, 1990, 1993b). Alternatively, as we argued above, some children—by virtue of temperament, social maturity, or family contexts that are more conducive to positive interaction—may have good relationships with most of the significant adults in their life, while others may have good relationships with few. Given these different predictions, we were not sure what to expect with regard to the relation between closeness to the nonresidential parent and closeness to and acceptance of the residential parent's new partner.

Contrary to speculation that greater amounts of time spent with a non-residential parent would interfere with a good relationship with the residential parent's new partner, and contrary to evidence from work by others (Cherlin and Furstenberg, 1994), we found that the amount of visitation an adolescent had with the nonresidential parent had no association with the nature of the relationship between an adolescent and the residential parent's new partner. This was true whether we were considering the effect of contact with a nonresidential father or a nonresidential mother.

Similarly, the various measures of adolescents' acceptance of their parents' new partners were almost entirely unrelated to the adolescent's closeness to the nonresidential parent (see Table 7.7). For girls living with their mothers, there was a small tendency for those who were close to the mother's new partner to be close to their nonresidential fathers as well (a relation in the opposite direction from what might have been predicted from considerations of loyalty conflicts), but other indicators showed no impact of closeness with nonresidential fathers on relationships with mothers' new partners.

In fathers' households, there were no statistically significant relations between closeness to the nonresidential mother and an adolescent's acceptance of the father's new partner. We should note, however, that three out of the four correlations for father-resident girls have a negative sign, and two of these are moderate in magnitude.[13] These data hint, then, that strong ties between a girl and her nonresidential mother may interfere somewhat with accepting a stepmother or father's girlfriend. This observation is speculative, of course, given the small number of father-resident girls who have new mothers; however, other authors have hypothesized just such a link (Clingempeel and Segal, 1986).

Table 7.7 Correlations between closeness to nonresidential parents and acceptance of residential parent's new partner for sole-resident adolescents[a]

Measure of acceptance	Closeness to nonresidential father		Closeness to nonresidential mother	
	Boys	Girls	Boys	Girls
Closeness to NP	.08	.29**	.07	−.05
Joint activities with NP	−.04	.03	−.17	.01
Acceptance of NP's authority	−.13	.13	−.09	−.20
NP's perceived role	−.06	.04	.08	−.32
Maximum n	(96)	(119)	(39)	(22)

a. Subjects whose residential parents did not have a new partner are excluded. Correlations are adjusted for age of adolescent.

**$p \leq .01$.

Does the fact that we generally find adolescents' relationships with their nonresidential parents and residential "new parents" to be independent mean that we must abandon our hypothesis that "nice" children tend to have good relationships with everyone? Yes—or at least, the hypothesis must be modified. It now seems more reasonable to say that an adolescent's relationships with adults may be similar within a household. Each household may elicit different attitudes and behaviors on the part of the adolescent, that then influence all relationships within that home. As one example, consider an adolescent who strongly resists the presence of her mother's new partner. If that adolescent is rude, defiant, or cold toward the new partner, it will become difficult for the mother to maintain a good relationship with that adolescent. Thus low acceptance of the mother's new partner could very well weaken the child's closeness to her mother. The nonresidential father, in contrast, is not involved in the child's interactions with the mother or her new partner. Nor must he deal with the child's day-to-day behavior in the other household. Thus the adolescent's relationship with the nonresidential father can apparently continue, independent of the relationships in the other home.

Conflict between Biological Parents

In studies of divorce, little attention has been paid to the impact of discord between the biological parents on the kind of relationship a child develops with a parent's new partner. The possible nature of such a connection seems obvious enough: the left-over hostility between formerly married couples is often heavily tinged with jealousy and anger concerning the former spouse's new sexual relationships. If these feelings are conveyed to the child in the form of disparagement of the former spouse's new partner, it ought to become more difficult for the child to accept this new partner. We did not have information concerning the extent to which the conflict between former spouses centered on new partners, although certainly in some cases it was a fundamental problem. We found, however, no relations between interparental hostility, discord, or cooperation and the quality of adolescents' relationships with their parents' new partners.

Acceptance of New Partners and Adolescent Adjustment

Given that closeness to or acceptance of the new partner was strongly and positively related to an adolescent's closeness to the residential parent, we controlled for adolescents' closeness to their residential parent when we examined the associations between adolescents' acceptance of new partners and adolescents' adjustment. We wanted to know what impact a good relationship with the new partner might have above and beyond the impact of a good relationship with the residential parent.

Overall, we found sporadic relations between acceptance of the new partner and adolescent adjustment. Among the more promising relations, more acceptance was related to less depression/anxiety, less overall deviance, less school deviance, less severe "worst problem" scores, and more compromise in conflict resolution. It was also related to a measure of adjustment that we have not introduced yet: unstructured time use. Adolescents who were close to and accepting of parent's new partners were less likely to spend time just "hanging out" (as opposed to engaging in planned, organized activities). "Unstructured time use" has not emerged in our other analyses as a uniquely interesting aspect of adolescent adjustment, above and beyond the level of deviance. It did, however, emerge as particularly interesting in some of the subsequent analyses involving acceptance of the new partner, which is why we mention it here.

We reported in Chapter 6 that the presence of a parent's new partner in the adolescent's household was one of the stronger predictors of adolescent adjustment, at least among sole-resident adolescents. The presence of a stepparent was a positive factor for both sexes and in both parental households, although the relations were somewhat stronger and more numerous for boys than for girls. The presence of an unmarried parental partner, in contrast, was often a negative factor, again, especially for boys. In this chapter, we have seen that remarried new partners were also more accepted by adolescents than were unmarried ones. Thus we were interested in the extent to which the greater acceptance of remarried new partners explained the better adolescent adjustment in situations of remarriage.

To explore this question, we chose a subset of our adjustment measures to focus on: compromise in conflict resolution, school deviance, overall deviance, "worst problem," and unstructured time use. We chose this particular set of adjustment indices because each was related to the presence of a stepparent for all or most adolescents (as reported in Chapter 6), and each was related to acceptance of the authority of either the mother's or the father's new partner.

For each of these adjustment measures, we conducted a regression analysis in three steps. In the first step, the adjustment measure was predicted with the adolescent's closeness to his or her residential parent and the adolescent's age and sex. We needed to control for these three variables because each was related both to acceptance of the new partner and to adolescent adjustment. In the second step, we added a variable reflecting whether the residential parent (sole or dual) had remarried. Finally, in the third step, we added the adolescent's acceptance of the authority of residential parents' new partners.[14] What we wanted to see was whether adding the "acceptance of authority" measure would reduce or eliminate the relation between remarriage and adolescent adjustment. If so, we would have evidence that the level of acceptance of the new partner "mediated" or explained the link between marital status and adolescent adjustment. In other words, we would know that one primary reason that adolescents were doing better in situations of remarriage was because they were more likely to accept the new partner under such circumstances.

Was the association between remarriage and adjustment due to remarried new partners' having greater acceptance? In most instances, yes.[15] The results reported in Table 7.8 indicate that, for children living with their mothers or in dual residence, the greater acceptance of the mother's new partner's authority that occurs with remarriage accounts for at least some of the improved adolescent adjustment in situations of remarriage. Remarriage in and of itself, apart from its association with greater acceptance of the new partner, has a weaker (and in most cases, nonsignificant) relation to adjustment.

Table 7.8 Stepwise analyses of remarriage and new-partner acceptance in relation to selected aspects of adolescent adjustment[a]

Variables entered at each step	Mother as residential parent (mother and dual residence) (Maximum $n = 260$)	Father as residential parent (father and dual residence) (Maximum $n = 95$)
Compromise		
Step 1. Closeness to residential parent	.19**	.03
Step 2. Closeness to residential parent	.16**	.04
Residential parent remarried	.16**	.18+
Step 3. Closeness to residential parent	.14*	−.01
Residential parent remarried	.11+	.12
Acceptance of NP's authority	.13+	.14
School Deviance		
Step 1. Closeness to residential parent	−.15**	.13
Step 2. Closeness to residential parent	−.14*	.13
Residential parent remarried	−.05	−.12
Step 3. Closeness to residential parent	−.12*	.18+
Residential parent remarried	−.01	−.05
Acceptance of NP's authority	−.12+	−.16+
Deviance		
Step 1. Closeness to residential parent	−.17***	−.12
Step 2. Closeness to residential parent	−.16**	−.12
Residential parent remarried	−.10+	−.10
Step 3. Closeness to residential parent	−.13*	−.08
Residential parent remarried	−.04	−.03
Acceptance of NP's authority	−.17**	−.15+
Worst Problem		
Step 1. Closeness to residential parent	−.22***	−.11
Step 2. Closeness to residential parent	−.20***	−.12
Residential parent remarried	−.11+	−.14
Step 3. Closeness to residential parent	−.18**	−.10
Residential parent remarried	−.06	−.12
Acceptance of NP's authority	−.14*	−.04
Unstructured Time		
Step 1. Closeness to residential parent	−.01	.10
Step 2. Closeness to residential parent	.01	.10
Residential parent remarried	−.12*	−.07
Step 3. Closeness to residential parent	.04	.21+
Residential parent remarried	−.05	.08
Acceptance of NP's authority	−.21**	−.33**

a. The entries in this table are standardized regression coefficients (betas). Age and sex of adolescents were entered in each step of the analyses, although their betas are not shown here.
+$p \leq .10$.   *$p \leq .05$.   **$p \leq .01$.   ***$p \leq .001$.   ****$p \leq .0001$.

For adolescents living with their fathers, the evidence is weaker. There is some evidence for the mediation hypothesis with respect to school deviance, overall deviance, and unstructured time use: the relations between remarriage and these aspects of adjustment, though not significant to begin with, were reduced when acceptance of the new mother's authority was controlled, and acceptance of the new mother predicted lower levels of these problems. In the case of compromising as a means of conflict resolution, we could also make a case for mediation, although the evidence is even less strong.[16] There is no evidence that the beneficial effects of a father's remarriage on adolescents' "worst problem" result from the greater acceptance of the authority of that remarried partner. In sum, evidence that the beneficial effects of remarriage were due to adolescents' greater acceptance of a remarried new mother was less strong than it was for new fathers, but there were still hints of this effect.

The fact that adolescents spent less time simply "hanging out" when they accepted the authority of a residential parent's new partner was not predicted, but it is interesting. We originally had thought of unstructured time as a kind of way station to deviance. And indeed, more unstructured time use was significantly related to higher levels of deviance. Spending a lot of time "hanging out" might reflect either boredom or a lack of goals, either of which could increase vulnerability to the influence of deviant peers. As popular wisdom has it, the devil finds work for idle hands.

With regard to the reasons that acceptance of a new partner should protect against unstructured use of time, our first hypothesis was that children must be spending more time in joint activities with a new partner whom they accept, and so would have less time to spend in unplanned drifting. We found, however, that, although adolescents who accepted a new partner did spend more time in joint activities with that partner, the amount of such joint activity was not related to the amount of unstructured time (nor to the adolescent's level of deviance). Something else about the acceptance of the new partner is important, over and above the time spent with that new partner. Another possibility is that adolescents who accept the authority of this new adult are respectful of authority in general, and are therefore more likely to use their time in productive ways—ways that are encouraged and esteemed by parents, teachers, and other adults—and less likely to get into trouble. At present, all we can say is that having an accepted new adult partner is related to enhanced family bonds, and it may help to build barriers against deviance.

Summary

One of our most important findings is that the impact of a new partner on family functioning depends on whether that partner is married to the residential parent or is simply cohabiting or regularly dating that parent. In addition, the various forms of repartnering had somewhat different relations with family processes depending on whether we were talking about mother's homes or father's homes.

In homes in which the mother had sole or dual physical custody, remarriage was generally associated with positive family functioning. For example, when the mother was remarried, adolescents were closer to her, and there were higher levels of household management and control, in comparison with other forms of repartnering. On these aspects of family functioning, however, remarriage was no better or worse than having no new partner. The benefits of remarriage over not dating at all came primarily in the domain of "role reversal." Mothers who were remarried—in addition to those who had a cohabiting new partner—were less likely to confide in their adolescents (especially sons), and adolescents of these mothers were less likely to feel worried about their mother. Adolescents did not perceive a mother's remarriage to have any impact on the relationship between the biological parents. Furthermore, her remarriage did not appear to interfere in any way with the adolescent's relationship with the nonresidential biological father.

A father's remarriage also brought about some advantages in terms of family processes. In particular, the level of management and control in his home was highest when he was remarried. And remarried fathers, like remarried mothers, were less likely to confide in their adolescent children, especially their daughters. But adolescents were less close to remarried fathers than they were to fathers who were only dating or who did not yet have a regular new partner. Although we do not fully understand the reason, adolescents had the best quality of relationship with fathers who were regularly dating someone. This finding needs replication and more in-depth study and analysis in order to uncover what in these situations is beneficial for the adolescent.

Like mother-resident adolescents, father-resident adolescents did not become more distant from their nonresidential parent when the residential parent remarried. On the contrary, father-resident adolescents whose fathers were remarried were even closer to their mothers than were other adolescents. This finding, together with the slight evidence that father-resident girls were less likely to accept a new mother when their relationship with their own mother was close, provides some potential support for the view that a new mother is more threatening to adolescents than is a new father. In other words, adolescents—perhaps especially adolescent girls—may be particularly protective of their mother (even when they do not live with her) and particularly reluctant to have anyone take her place in their lives.

Our data also point to conditions under which acceptance of a parent's new partner is most likely. Early adolescents and boys were closer to and more accepting of parents' new partners than were older adolescents and girls. New partners who were married to the biological parent also received more acceptance than cohabiting new partners, or new partners who were dating the biological parent regularly but not living in the home. These results persisted after we controlled for the amount of time that the relationship had existed. In addition, adolescents who had close relationships with their residential biological parent were more likely to also be close to and accepting of that parent's new partner. Maintaining a relationship with the nonresidential parent did not appear to help or hinder adolescents' relationships with residential new partners, with the possible exception noted above of girls in father residence, who were somewhat less accepting of a new mother when they were close to their own mothers. Crosbie-Burnett (1991) also found that continuing involvement with a nonresidential parent did not interfere with relationships in stepfamilies, even in cases of high contact between former spouses.

When mothers or fathers acquire a new partner, they surely hope to win acceptance of that person by their children. Whether or not such acceptance has any concrete advantages for the adolescent in terms of adjustment, it surely makes home life more peaceful and happy than it would be in situations where the new partner is resented. Our results indicate, however, that the benefits may go beyond having more peace in the home. Adolescents who had better relationships with their parents' new partners were also somewhat better adjusted than were other adolescents (they had lower depression and lower deviance, and were more likely to work out compromises when faced with conflict). Of course, we cannot determine to what extent good relationships are the cause of better adjustment or a result of it, but the link is there, and worth further examination. Our results also indicate that the greater acceptance received by remarried new partners at least partially accounts for the better adjustment of adolescents who have stepparents.

Living in
Two Homes

8

Living in Two Homes: Introduction

In Part II we described what life was like for adolescents and their families in different residential arrangements, and examined how different family experiences and processes were related to differential adjustment among the adolescents in those arrangements. We focused on the family life and background of the *residential* home. Because dual-resident adolescents really have two "residential homes," these earlier chapters touched on issues, and potential advantages and disadvantages, of going back and forth between two homes on a relatively frequent basis. For the most part, however, our concern was with what individual postdivorce homes (the home in which the adolescent spent the majority of his or her time) were like, and for dual-resident adolescents this was defined as the average of the two "residential" homes. What we have ignored to this point is that children in sole-resident arrangements often spend substantial time in both parental homes, and even when little time is spent with a nonresidential parent, the child remains, in some sense, a part of two families. In Part III, therefore, we explicitly consider issues of membership in two homes and two families.

When a divorce involves children, the now separated homes and families of the ex-spouses remain linked by those children. Although from an objective viewpoint—and even from the viewpoint of the divorcing spouses—divorce may split one family system into two separate family systems, the child remains a part of each of those new families (see Maccoby and Mnookin, 1992). In addition, the child may still view the original nuclear family as one family, a family that is now divided (Funder, 1991). Consider, for example, the following comments from adolescents in our study, when telling us what they did not like about their living or visitation arrangement. Even four and a half years after the divorce,

143

these children viewed the original family as the complete and whole family, and the postdivorce family as split, separated, "not together."

(Mid-adolescent male): "I don't like being a partial family. I like being the 'great American 4' family: Mom, Dad, two kids, you know."

(Early-adolescent female): "[I don't like that] the family is not together."

(Early-adolescent male): "[I don't like that] I don't get to see both of [my parents] all the time."

Children's views of the postdivorce family—as one split family or as two separate families—may influence the ease with which they negotiate interactions or transitions between homes and, ultimately, adjust to the divorce. Regardless of the child's perception of the entire family unit, however, after divorce the child does remain a member of a subsystem with each parent, and each of these subsystems continues to be influenced by the nature of the other and by the nature of the postdivorce interparental relationship. Emotional ties between parents, and between a non-residential parent and child, may endure in very real ways even when a child spends little or no time in one of the two homes. For example, if a child lives with a mother who maintains a high level of hostility toward her ex-spouse, and if that mother expresses her hostility openly in front of the child, the child's emotional—if not physical—membership in a subsystem that involves the father may be quite salient to both mother and child. Furthermore, the quality and intensity of the child's emotional ties to the nonresidential parent may have much to do with how adjustment to the divorce proceeds.

To the extent that a child does maintain contact with both parents, the child must negotiate not only the changes that take place within one home when a parent moves out and the lingering feelings of one sort or another about each parent, but the reality of life with each parent in two separate homes. Although we know something about the effects of varying amounts of time spent with a noncustodial parent in terms of a child's adaptation to divorce (see Chapter 9; Hess and Camara, 1979; Hetherington, Cox, and Cox, 1978, 1982; Kurdek, Blisk, and Siesky, 1981), we know little about the more intimate emotional and practical experiences of being an active member of two families. What are the specific challenges faced by adolescents who continue to see both parents, how prevalent and how difficult are those challenges, and how do adolescents handle them? On a practical level, how do they negotiate transitions between homes, and what is the extent of their input into the quantity and nature of their continuing involvement in both homes? What is the effect of an adolescent's ongoing relationship with one parent on the relationship with the other? How is the adolescent's experience of integrating and negotiating relationships with each parent influenced by the amount of time spent in each home, or by the nature of the interparental relationship? And how does the need to split time with one's parents influence or interact with other typical needs and desires of adolescence (for example, being available to peers, holding a part-time job)?

One of the central organizing questions in Chapters 8–12 has to do with the nature of family subsystems, and the boundaries between subsystems, after divorce. Family systems theorists and others have emphasized the importance for healthy family and child functioning of warm, child-focused parent-child bonds within the context of a strong parental alliance. What are the consequences of parents' maintaining—or not maintaining—an alliance when they are now part of new, separate, family systems? Under what conditions can the child maintain close relationships with both parents? And is this characterization of a healthy family system still important with regard to child adjustment when parents are no longer living together?

We investigated these questions concerning the experience of membership in two families mainly among those adolescents who actually spent time in two homes, although for some issues (for example, reasons for visiting a nonresidential parent), the time in the nonresidential home could be very slight and the issue still relevant. For other issues (for example, whether rules and expectations for behavior were different in the two homes), time spent in each home had to be more substantial for the issue to apply. We also considered, however, issues of continuing membership in two families that were relevant even to adolescents who no longer saw one parent. These issues were, of course, emotional rather than practical in nature, and our discussion of them is based on the premise articulated earlier that even an absent parent remains a child's parent and thus part of a family system for the child.

Plan for Part III

In this introductory chapter, we describe general levels of satisfaction with the way time is split between parents, and adolescents' feelings about their acceptance and comfort in two homes. Given this context, we then discuss some of what adolescents like and dislike about being part of two homes, and aspects of the situation that make membership in two homes more or less difficult.

In Chapter 9, we look at how the amount of time spent in the nonresidential household is related to the postdivorce experience. Our earlier discussions of how residential arrangements compared with respect to family processes and adolescent adjustment bear on the issue of how much time the adolescent spends with each parent; by definition, residential arrangements differ in this respect. Our previous discussion is extended, however, by examining the variety of visitation patterns adolescents have with the nonresidential parent. We look at how the amount of visitation is related to characteristics of relationships within the family: the interparental relationship and the adolescent's relationship with both the residential and the nonresidential parent. We also take up the question of how visitation may affect life in the residential home. Finally, we consider the relation between visitation and the adolescent's adjustment.

In Chapter 10, we move away from the amount of visitation, per se, to look in more detail at what goes on in nonresidential homes and at relationships between adolescents and their nonresidential parents. We begin by describing the nonresidential parent and home in comparison with relationships and processes in residential homes. Having set this context, we then address the question of how the nonresidential parent-child relationship is related to adolescents' adjustment. Does this relationship contribute anything to the adolescent's well-being, above and beyond the relationship between the adolescent and the residential parent? Central to questions concerning the effects of one home on the other is the question of how relationships with the two parents are linked. Does a close relationship with the nonresidential parent interfere with an adolescent's relationship with the residential parent? Can an adolescent maintain close relationships with two parents? If so, does closeness to both parents have positive consequences, or does it interfere with adjustment because it leads to feelings of tension and conflicts of loyalties for the adolescent (a question also addressed in Chapter 11)? We extend this inquiry by examining the broader question of whether the "effects" of being close to one parent vary depending upon how close an adolescent is to the other parent. For example, is it more beneficial, in terms of adjustment, to be close to a residential parent when one is not also close to a nonresidential parent? We also examine the effect of the co-parenting relationship on the parent-child relationships. Of most interest is whether ongoing conflict between parents after divorce interferes with the adolescent's relationships with one or both parents, and whether the impact of being close to a nonresidential parent depends on the nature of the relationship between the parents.

In Chapter 11 we examine adolescents' experience of feeling caught between their parents. The concept of feeling or being caught between parents may best typify how familial subsystems continue to interact after a family separates, even when a child spends little or no time with one parent. Regardless of whether the child sees the nonresidential parent, the residential parent can pressure a child to take sides in the conflict with the other parent, which may give rise to loyalty conflicts (Emery, 1988). Of course, when a child does see both parents, both may try to engage the child in alliances, or use the child to carry out what should be parental activities (for example, carrying messages to the ex-spouse or gaining information about the ex-spouse's home or activities). Family systems theory that has emerged from the study of nondivorced families suggests that such alliances and the erosion of boundaries between subsystems have potentially grave consequences for the child (Aponte and Van Deusen, 1981; Minuchin, 1974).

In Chapter 12 we examine discrepancies across households in parental rules and expectations for behavior. After divorce, opportunities and inclinations for parents to communicate about rules and expectations are greatly reduced, conceivably making inconsistent parenting quite common. We do not know, however, whether inconsistency is in fact common, or what the implications of inconsistency across homes are for the adolescent's experience.

Dividing Time between Households

In our study, most adolescents had spent at least some time in both homes within the year preceding their interview. Very few had not seen an outside parent in the previous year (twenty-six adolescents had not seen their fathers; four had not seen their mothers). Slightly fewer had not even talked to an outside parent over the telephone (twenty-five had not seen *or* talked to their fathers; only one had not seen or talked to mother). Thus continuing practical—as well as emotional—ties existed for the great majority of the adolescents whose parents had separated four and a half years earlier. In general, how satisfied were these adolescents with the amount of time they spent with each parent, and how comfortable were they in each home?

All 522 adolescents were asked to rate their satisfaction "with the time spent with each parent" on a scale where "1" meant "completely dissatisfied," and "10" meant "completely satisfied," and all but one adolescent responded. Mean satisfaction was almost 7, indicating that most adolescents felt fairly happy with their situation. Only 4 percent rated themselves as completely dissatisfied, and an additional 9 percent rated themselves as a "2" or "3" on this scale. Satisfaction had much to do with the amount of time adolescents spent with each parent. Adolescents in dual residence, who spent a great deal of time with both parents, had higher levels of satisfaction ($M = 7.8$) than did adolescents in sole-mother residence ($M = 6.9$) or sole-father residence ($M = 6.1$). Only one dual-resident adolescent gave a satisfaction score as low as "4"; all other dual-resident adolescents rated themselves at "5" or above. And although the absolute amount of visitation with a nonresidential parent (mother or father) for adolescents in sole-resident arrangements was not significantly related to degree of satisfaction, one of the most common complaints of adolescents who rated themselves as "completely dissatisfied" (a "1" or "2") with the division of time between parents—when asked what they did not like about their living or visitation arrangement—was that they missed their nonresidential parent, that they did not see him or her enough. Thus to a large extent, satisfaction had to do with getting to see both parents, and dissatisfaction was more likely to reflect wanting more—rather than less—contact with a parent.

The satisfaction of adolescents in mother residence was also higher than the satisfaction of adolescents in father residence, suggesting that it may have been harder for adolescents to be separated from their mothers than from their fathers. This finding is consistent with others (see Chapters 5 and 10) indicating that adolescents may have stronger emotional bonds with their mothers than with their fathers.

The greater the distance between parental homes, the lower was the satisfaction with the division of time, even after controlling for absolute amount of contact with the nonresidential parent. Perhaps because of the increased difficulty in making transitions, or because of the lessened flexibility with which an adolescent could go back and forth between homes, the distance between homes had an independent impact on adolescents' happiness with their arrangement.

We asked adolescents where they felt "at home"—at their mom's, dad's, both places, or neither place. About one-quarter (27 percent) of the adolescents living in one of the three major residential arrangements at the time of the interview (and who had at least seen both parents in the past year—$n = 463$), said they felt at home in both places. Adolescents in dual residence (43 percent) and father residence (35 percent) were more likely to say that both places felt like home than were adolescents in mother residence (22 percent). The majority of those living primarily with one parent said that their primary parent's residence felt most like home. For father-resident adolescents, however, this group (52 percent) was smaller than was the case for mother-resident adolescents, 71 percent of whom felt at home mainly in their primary residence.

A very small percentage of adolescents did not feel at home in either place (3 percent overall); slightly more father-resident adolescents (7 percent) than mother-resident (2 percent) or dual-resident (2 percent) adolescents chose this option. As with satisfaction, adolescents' comfort in each home appears related to having higher levels of contact with both parents, and additionally, to the gender of the nonresidential parent. When the mother was the nonresidential parent, adolescents were more likely to feel at home in the nonresidential home, but less likely to be satisfied with the division of time between parents, than when the father was the nonresidential parent. The differences between adolescents in mother and father residence were present even when controlling for the amount of contact with the nonresidential parent.

Several themes relevant to the experience of living in two homes and two families emerged when adolescents were asked what they liked and disliked about their living and visitation arrangements. Of course, for every theme, there is a "counter-theme." For example, although many adolescents felt that living in two homes made it difficult to do things with friends, there were others who said that having two sets of friends—one at each home—was a benefit of living in two homes. Obviously an individual's experience depends on many factors, including the temperament and personality of the adolescent and each of the parents, the family history before and after the divorce, and the communities in which each parent lives, among others. What we do here is to summarize some of the more prevalent responses that bear on adolescents' feelings about spending time in two homes or being a part of two families.

By far the most common type of remark that adolescents made about their living/visitation arrangements was a simple comment on their feelings about the amount of time they spent with both parents. Many adolescents who were in contact with both parents said that what they liked was that they could see both parents. Some of these adolescents went on to say that the time they now had with each parent was special, and that they currently spent more time with each parent than before their parents separated. They also liked being able to talk to each parent alone. For instance, one early-adolescent boy in dual residence said he liked "being able to see one parent at a time and talking to them without one or the other coming in . . . I like to be able to have private talks." A late-adolescent girl in mother residence said she got along better with her parents now that they were not living together, and an early-adolescent boy, also in mother residence, said, "I get to spend a lot more time with my mother than I used to because she's not with my father." These adolescents enjoyed the opportunity to receive attention from, and develop a relationship with, each parent individually.

Other adolescents, rather than enjoying special time alone with each parent, lamented the fact that they could not be with both parents together. When with one parent, they missed the other. One early-adolescent girl in dual residence said she didn't like the fact that "you miss the other one, and you don't really get to see them as much as if they both lived together." Another young adolescent, this time a boy in father residence, said, "I miss my mom when I'm over at Dad's and I miss my dad when I'm over at my mom's." An early-adolescent boy in dual residence said, "I wish they would be together still . . . I don't like having to see one parent one time and one parent the other time." Like the adolescents quoted earlier in the chapter, these adolescents still struggled with feelings that the family was not complete when they were not all together. Related to this, many adolescents also voiced real sadness over not having one or the other parent as a regular part of their lives. To these children, it did not seem right that they did not have ready access to both parents.

(Late-adolescent female in father residence): "[I don't like] not having [Mom] with me twenty-four hours a day—I don't like not being with her."

(Early-adolescent female in father residence): "[I don't like that] I can't see my mom whenever I want to."

(Mid-adolescent male in mother residence): "[I don't like that] he's not, like, always there. I can see him when I want to but, like, he's not in the house. It's not like walking distance to his house."

(Early-adolescent female in mother residence): "[I don't like] that I can't spend lots of time with my dad, . . . my dad used to play games with me."

(Mid-adolescent male in mother residence): "[I don't like that] I don't see my dad every single day. My dad can't be there every time I need him."

Feelings of enjoying time separately with each parent and of missing one parent when with the other are not mutually exclusive. Yet we infer that adolescents who generally feel one way or the other differ in the extent to which they have been able to accept the transformation of one family into two rather than still seeing the original family as their one true family. Parents' attempts to make access to each as easy as possible given the constraints of living in different homes undoubtedly help ease this transition for children.

Certainly, an adolescent's feelings about visitation and the experience of living in two homes reflect the quality of the adolescent's relationships and activities with each parent and in each household. For example, some adolescents said that their father slept a lot, or that their mother would go out with her boyfriend during their visit, and many commented on being bored at one house or the other. When parents spend their time predominantly in adult activities during times when they are responsible for their children, adolescents may be less likely to see the postdivorce situation as one that gives them positive access to both parents. Feelings also undoubtedly reflect the quality of family life before the separation. Among our adolescents were those who wished their parents had never divorced as well as adolescents who felt relieved that their parents were no longer living together. The latter adolescents, although they may have missed one parent or the other, clearly felt that their lives—including, for some, their own relationships with each parent—had improved since the divorce.

Another frequently voiced issue had to do with the flexibility (or lack thereof) of plans for spending time with each parent. Many of the older adolescents, and a few of the younger ones, mentioned flexibility as a plus:

(Early-adolescent male in dual residence): "[I like that] I can trade. If I don't want to go I can trade the next Wednesday or next Tuesday. And I don't have to go, and then the other parent gets that Tuesday or that next day."

(Mid-adolescent female in mother residence): "I like when it's not . . . scheduled for me to go visit [my father] at a set time every week 'cause it gives me a little more . . . freedom . . . I just have more of a choice."

(Mid-adolescent female in mother residence): "I like having the freedom to say yes or no if I want to see [Dad] or not. I like it better when it's not like every weekend or every other Saturday or something like that . . . It's nice that I can say, 'I'm busy this weekend. How about next week?'"

(Late-adolescent female in mother residence): "[I like that] I can do whatever I want. If I want to see my dad I can, but if I want to be at my mom's I can do that too."

(Late-adolescent female in father residence): "[I like that] if there's nothing else going on I can [see Mom]. There's no set appointment."

(Late-adolescent female in father residence): "[I like that] I have the freedom . . . my dad knows that I'm busy, and that I've got school and work . . . There's lots of flexibility."

(Late-adolescent male in father residence): "I like that I can go when I want and stay as long as I feel, and come back when I want."

(Late-adolescent female in mother residence): "I don't think it's fair that we can only have certain times when we can see our mother or father. I don't think it should be scheduled so strict."

Comments such as these point out the need to accommodate and adjust to older adolescents' increasingly busy lifestyle and extrafamilial interests. Younger children were more apt than older ones to like a set schedule, so as not to be put in the position of having to make decisions about when and when not to visit. Some adolescents felt that when it was up to them to decide, if they chose to spend time with one parent, the other would feel hurt. Even some of the older adolescents, who first mentioned flexibility as a positive, also pointed out its negative side, as did this older adolescent in father residence:

"Because I don't have set times sometimes my dad puts pressure on me to not go [to my mom's]. That's one thing about having set times. It wouldn't be up to me."

At least one young female, however, voiced concern over inflexibility, not because set visitation interfered with friends or other activities, but because she sometimes felt insecure about leaving her mother. This girl, who lived primarily with her mother, said:

"I like . . . seeing my father for the weekend, but . . . sometimes I feel sad, like the day before I leave, because . . . maybe I'd miss my mom a lot. You know, 'cause . . . I'm . . . attached to my mom a lot . . . Sometimes I don't want to go because, I guess, I'm scared or I just don't want to go."

The comments indicate that parents may have to strike a delicate balance between flexibility and scheduled visits. Having a set schedule not only promotes continued contact with both parents (Maccoby and Mnookin, 1992), but may relieve the child from having to make guilt-provoking choices between parents. Set schedules recognize and respect the ongoing relationship between the child and each parent. But especially as children get older and more involved with friends, work, and school, rigid adherence to a schedule may interfere with these other important aspects of adolescent development. Divorced parents face a special challenge in allowing their adolescents to invest time in developmentally appropriate extrafamilial activities without loosening the child's bonds with one or the other parent. Even when parents remain married, this particular challenge of adolescence may be difficult; when children must participate in two homes in order to maintain bonds with both parents, the challenge becomes even more difficult.

Not surprisingly, many adolescents talked of the difficulty in choosing between parents, and between parents and friends or other extracurricular activities. Many adolescents struggled with guilt over not spending "enough" time with one parent or the other. For instance, one mid-adolescent boy in mother residence said, "I feel like I should spend more time with my dad, but, you know, I'm at the age where I don't have to, so usually I don't. But . . . I've a pretty guilty conscience over it." Although adolescents in nondivorced families may also feel occasional guilt for choosing to spend time with peers or in other extrafamilial activities, the child of divorce may experience the tension between family ties and growing independence from family even more acutely, given the need to spend time with each parent separately. One boy in mother residence articulately voiced his frustration over being in a position that made him feel guilty:

"I know that I should at least go see [Dad] every once in a while. I don't like the guilt I feel when I don't go. And I don't like the fact that I'm at a total inconvenience just because they wanted to get a divorce. It's not like I didn't want to see them . . . I mean . . . you like your parents, you know, but it's not like you put out time to go visit them. . . . You think your parents are the people you are around, not people you have to go and visit. It kinda changes the relationship from being a parent almost to like going and seeing your grandma or something."

Many adolescents, without specifically mentioning guilt, simply commented on the difficulty in having to balance visitation with other activities. Even if parents allowed flexibility in scheduling visits around a child's activities, adolescents often found it hard to fit visitation in with everything else they wanted to do:

(Early-adolescent female in father residence): "Sometimes I have something I want to do, and the next weekend I might be going to [Mom's] house, and I might want to do that and when I do that, usually they switch weekends around, and sometimes things I want to do land on each weekend and I can't really do it because I have to spend the time with my mom."

(Mid-adolescent female in father residence): "I have friends, and if I go over to my mom's house, it's kinda hard to plan things with my friends and my mom."

(Late-adolescent male in mother residence): "[I don't like] trying to fit my dad in . . . I have my whole life here, and I have to take time out and drop everything to go there. It's kinda hard . . . Between work and my friends and everything like that . . . basically, it's just kind of hard to fit him into your schedule."

Conversely, other adolescents liked the fact that they did not feel guilty when they chose not to visit:

(Late-adolescent female in father residence): "With [an older adolescent] I don't think you can have any kind of a quality time unless I want it to be there. . . . I do like it because I don't feel like, when I go over to my mom's house, I'm pressured to stay two nights or one night or any amount of time . . . I know people who are supposed to spend every other weekend with their other parent. If you don't it's going to really hurt their feelings. I'm not in that position. You don't want to spend your weekend with your parents. You're going out with your friends."

Yet some adolescents who were allowed to choose friends over family still felt sad that they didn't have more time for their parents:

(Mid-adolescent female in mother residence): "Sometimes I wish it could be more. Maybe like four Saturdays or something, except that I have so many school things and I don't have enough time, but sometimes I wish it could be like a couple of more hours a week or something."

(Mid-adolescent female in mother residence): "I don't get over there much, because . . . I've got a lot of things going on, like friends and then activities, so actually, I don't get over there as much as I'd like to."

(Late-adolescent male in father residence): "I wish I . . . just wouldn't do some of the things . . . that I do now [so I could] just go over there and spend some time with [Mom]. It's kind of impossible."

Feelings of guilt over not spending enough time with one or the other parent were voiced less frequently by adolescents in dual residence than adolescents in sole-resident arrangements. In addition, dual-resident adolescents—regardless of age—were less likely to mention having to choose between parents and friends as something they disliked about their living arrangement. Perhaps because they typically saw both parents a great deal, it may have been easier for the dual-resident adolescent to choose to spend time with friends when a choice between the two arose.

Many adolescents enjoyed having "two different environments" in which to live. "I like being able to have a change . . . going from one house to another house" said one young female in dual residence. An early-adolescent male living primarily with his father liked having two different homes and two sets of friends; he summed it up with "I like change once in a while." For some, the availability of two homes provided an escape from unpleasant situations at one home or the other. Adolescents in all residential arrangements mentioned as a benefit of their living situation that when they were unhappy or bored at one house they could escape to the other house.

(Early adolescent in dual residence): "[I like that] I can get away from my dad's girlfriend. And that's about it. I get tired of one house and get to go to the other house."

(Middle adolescent in dual residence): "[I like that] you get a break from each parent . . . Sometimes one parent will be angry at you or something like that and you can go to the other parent's house . . . Basically, it's the fact . . . you can just trade off if one parent is getting on your nerves."

(Early adolescent in mother residence): "[Visiting] gives me a chance to get away from Mom 'cause if I'm with her alone too much of the time we get at each other's throats."

(Early adolescent in mother residence): "I don't have to deal with Mom if I don't want to. I can go to my dad's and I get to see him."

(Middle adolescent in father residence): "If you get sick of one parent, there's always the other one."

In some homes, where methods of dealing with conflict might otherwise be violent or abusive (emotionally or physically), having an avenue of escape might be adaptive. And being able to escape conflict or boredom by going to another parent's home may have better long-term consequences than escaping to friends or other nonfamilial establishments—an option that might be used by adolescents who are unhappy while living in a nondivorced family. There may be many instances, however, where the opportunity to escape cuts off more positive resolutions to conflict or more creative solutions to boredom before they can be reached. The frequency and destination of "escapes" from the parental home owing to conflict or boredom merits more detailed investigation among both divorced and nondivorced families.

The practical aspects of moving back and forth between homes were seen as a hassle by some of the adolescents, especially in dual-residence but also in sole-resident arrangements. Several adolescents told us of situations in which things they needed were at the other home; sometimes they could be retrieved and sometimes they could not. Remembering schedules was also difficult for some adolescents and their parents. The movement from one home to the other also contributed to feelings among some adolescents of always being on the go, of being unsettled.

(Early adolescent in dual residence): "[I don't like] moving. Just having to pack up every week."

(Early adolescent in dual residence): "It's kind of a hassle because sometimes you forget when you have to leave, and packing up all the time."

(Late adolescent in dual residence): "Things I don't like are when I don't know where my stuff is . . . or just remembering my parents' schedules . . . what they're doing, not knowing when they are going to be home. Like I go over there and I don't remember where they went."

(Middle adolescent in mother residence): "[I don't like that] my parents get . . . confused on which weekend I was over there."

(Early adolescent in mother residence): "Sometimes I get confused about where I'm going if they have to switch nights."

(Early adolescent in dual residence): "[I don't like that] I'm with one parent one day and then all of a sudden I go to the other parent's. It's all chopped up going back and forth."

(Middle adolescent in mother residence): "[I don't like] feeling like a package that's being stamped 'return to sender.' It's not that I feel unwanted. It's just that it makes me feel so awkward being sent back and forth."

(Late-adolescent in father residence): "It's hard to pin down a schedule, or create a livable lifestyle . . . I forget things at the wrong house. I don't feel like I have a patterned lifestyle."

(Early adolescent in dual residence): "Another thing that I don't like is going from one house to the other and . . . it seems to me I'm always hurried."

The fact that moving presented difficulties must be countered by the knowledge that most adolescents liked seeing both parents; the hassles of moving may be seen as "necessary evils." Yet the frequency with which these sentiments were voiced suggests that whatever parents can do to ease the burden of remembering schedules and transferring belongings could make the experience of living in two homes more positive. For example, a child might have a minimum set of clothing and everyday necessities at each home. Lists of things that must be taken back and forth, or a special bag where such items are kept, might reduce the possibility of forgetting homework, permission slips, and other essentials.

Two other themes voluntarily articulated by adolescents will be only briefly mentioned here because they are explored in more detail in later chapters. The first involves having different sets of rules in the two homes and the second, feelings of being torn between parents. Having two different sets of rules and expectations was a boon to some adolescents and a problem to others. Not surprisingly, some adolescents liked—and took advantage of—the fact that they could get away with things in one home that wouldn't be allowed in the other. Others found it frustrating and confusing. And adolescents often voiced with strong emotion their frustration with behaviors on the part of their parents that put them in the middle of ongoing parental battles. Because both of these themes are central to understanding the nature and consequences of ongoing inter-parental and parent-child bonds after divorce, and because they were areas in which we had more extensive quantitative as well as qualitative information, they are taken up in detail in Chapters 11 and 12.

9

Visitation

In the past two decades, a number of states have modified their divorce statutes in order to encourage decisions about custody and visitation that will allow children to sustain relationships with both parents. For example, the revised California custody code that became effective in 1980 included the following preamble:

> Section 4600 (a) The Legislature finds and declares that it is the public policy of this state to assure minor children of frequent and continuing contact with both parents after the parents have separated or dissolved their marriage.

The statute further included a "friendly parent" provision:

> Section 4600 (b) (1) In making an award of custody to either parent, the court shall consider which parent is more likely to allow the child or children frequent and continuing contact with the noncustodial parent.

The change represented an effort to be "fair" to both parents, and was part of the general trend toward making divorce laws more gender-neutral. But in addition, several then-current pieces of research indicated that children living with their mothers seemed to adjust better to the divorce if they had generous visitation with their nonresidential fathers (Hess and Camara, 1979; Wallerstein and Kelly, 1980). Hetherington, Cox, and Cox (1978, 1982) reported benefits from continued contact with fathers, except in cases where conflict between the parents was very high or the father was emotionally disturbed. But these studies were all based on relatively small and selective samples.

As we discussed earlier with regard to custody arrangements, children may derive several benefits from continued contact with both parents. First and foremost is the knowledge that they have not been abandoned by a parent. Continued contact with both parents should shield children from at least some of the grief or guilt over the loss of a parent that can occur when a parent simply disappears. In addition, a nonresidential parent with whom the child has a continuing relationship should be able to provide a variety of supports, such as emotional support when the residential parent is functioning poorly or when the residential parent and child are in serious conflict. A nonresidential parent who continues to be involved in the child's life may also be more willing to provide financial support, particularly in later years when college costs become an issue. And in the case of the illness, death, or institutionalization of the residential parent, the child who has continued to see the outside parent presumably has a viable alternative residence. The availability of the nonresidential parent for visitation may also provide support for the residential parent: much-needed time off from child care and, in the best case, a continuing united front between parents with respect to the rules and values by which the child is expected to live.

Continuing visitation has potential risks, however. One concern is that visitation for children necessarily involves some degree of continued contact between the divorced parents, and such contact may create opportunities for sustained, overt conflict—conflict that may well be harmful to the children. Furthermore, the more time the child spends in the nonresidential parent's household, the more the child may be exposed to two different sets of values, to conflicting demands, or possibly to weakened parental control because each parent is unable to monitor or supervise the child's activities in the other home. The continued involvement of the nonresidential parent in the child's life may also disrupt or intrude upon the functioning of the residential parent's family. The negative effects of these factors might neutralize, or even outweigh, the potential benefits to children of high levels of visitation.

After the original studies mentioned above were completed, several other studies assessed the functioning of children who had varying degrees of contact with the nonresidential parent. The findings of these studies have been mixed (see Amata and Rezac, 1994, for a review). Although many still indicated a positive link between visitation and child functioning, the links were often small. And in contrast to the earlier studies, several of the more recent—and larger—studies indicated no link at all between children's adjustment and how much contact they had with their father. For example, Furstenberg, Morgan, and Allison (1987) selected, as a subsample of the National Survey of Children (NSC) conducted in 1981, a group of 227 children aged eleven to sixteen who were living with their divorced mothers. The investigators found that the amount of contact children had with their fathers was not related, for either boys or girls, to any of the major adjustment dimensions studied (problem behavior, emotional distress, or academic difficulties). In another study of several hundred children from the National Longitudinal Survey of Youth (NLSY), contact with fathers was similarly unrelated to children's well-being (King, 1994); what was more important was a father's payment of child support.

Using yet another large national sample, Zill (1988) looked at the question of continued contact with a nonresidential parent among children of remarried divorced parents—that is, children living with one natural parent and a stepparent. This is one of the rare studies that includes children living with their fathers ($n = 216$) as well as a larger group of children living with their mothers ($n = 1084$). Still larger groups of single-parent and nondivorced families were available for comparison. The children ranged in age from three to seventeen years, although most were over age ten. Zill found that for children living with their mother and stepfather, the frequency of contact with their biological father was unrelated to the incidence of behavior problems in the children. By contrast, among children living with their father and a stepmother, problems were more frequent the less often the children saw their mothers. Indeed, the incidence of behavior problems was twice as high among children who never saw their mother as it was among children who saw her on a weekly basis.

In summary, recent studies are not as clear in establishing the importance of continuing contact with the nonresidential parent as were earlier studies, and the mixture of findings in the current literature suggests that the impact of visitation probably depends on additional factors such as the sex of the nonresidential parent, the level of conflict between the parents, or the quality of the relationship between the child and the nonresidential parent (Amato, 1993; Amato and Rezac, 1994; Bray, 1991; Kelly, 1993).

In the interviews with the parents of the adolescents in our study (Maccoby and Mnookin, 1992), some findings on visitation emerged that will help to set the stage for the present analyses of visitation among adolescents. Considering all the children from the earlier study—regardless of their age—it was found that the frequency of overnight visitation remained fairly stable over the three postseparation years for both mother-resident and father-resident children. Fathers who started out with only daytime visitation, however, tended to drop out over time. By

Time 3, a substantial proportion (42 percent) of nonresidential fathers were seeing their children seldom or not at all. For nonresidential mothers, however, daytime visitation increased with time, and the proportion having little or no contact with the children decreased (by T3, the proportion was 23 percent).

In the first year after parental separation, children between three and eleven years of age visited the nonresidential parent more frequently than did younger or older children. However, a child's age did not affect whether the amount of visitation increased or decreased thereafter (Maccoby and Mnookin, 1992). We expected, on the basis of these trends, that in the sample of adolescent children reported on here visitation should be somewhat lower than the levels reported for T3 from the parent sample as a whole, for two reasons. First, the adolescent follow-up sample did not include children who were under six years when their parents separated, and who were more frequent visitors with their nonresidential parents throughout the first three postseparation years than the oldest children (twelve to fourteen years old at parental separation). Second, the passage of an additional postseparation year was expected to bring additional decline in rates of visitation for children of all ages, at least for children living with their mothers.

We had information about the amount of current (T4) contact with the nonresidential parent for 347 mother-resident adolescents and 98 father-resident adolescents. Not included in these groups are the young people who had moved out of both parental homes by the time we interviewed them (and therefore current contact information did not reflect what it may have been when they were living at home), and those who were in dual residence. Within both mother and father residence, there was considerable variation in the amount and timing of visitation with the nonresidential parent. In the discussion that follows, we first compare mother-resident and father-resident adolescents with respect to the incidence of different patterns of visitation with the nonresidential parent, and examine whether visitation is related to demographic factors and the distance between the two parental households. We then turn to the following issues:

1. What visitation arrangements seemed most satisfactory to adolescents? How flexible were the arrangements, and how much voice did adolescents have in negotiations about visitation?
2. How is the amount of visitation related to the kind of interaction the two parents have with each other?

3. Is the amount of visitation related to the closeness of the relationship adolescents maintain with the nonresidential parent? Is visitation related to the closeness of the relationship with the residential parent?
4. Does the amount of visitation appear to have an impact on the functioning of the residential parent's household?
5. What is the relation between visitation and adolescent adjustment?
6. For each of the above questions, we consider whether the relation of interest depends on a variety of other factors. Where reasonable to do so, we consider modifying effects of: age or sex of the adolescent; parent's remarriage status; amount of conflict between parents; and adolescent's relationships with either the residential or the nonresidential parent.

Recognizing that the answers to these questions might not be the same for adolescents living with their fathers and visiting their mothers as for adolescents living with their mothers and visiting their fathers, we analyzed these two groups separately.

The Amount and Kind of Visitation

The adolescents in our sample were asked "When did you last see your (nonresident parent)?" The large majority of adolescents who lived primarily with one or the other parent had seen the nonresidential parent quite recently—about 70 percent had seen the nonresidential parent within the previous month for both residence groups (see Figure 9.1). For only a very few adolescents, 7.5 percent among mother-resident and 4.1 percent among father-resident, more than a year had elapsed since the last contact. It is especially interesting that the length of time since the nonresidential parent was last seen was very similar for father-resident and mother-resident adolescents.

For the adolescents who had seen the nonresidential parent within a year but not within the past month (approximately one-fourth of the sole-resident adolescents), the contact was sometimes brief. In a few cases, the nonresidential parent had come to Christmas or Thanksgiving dinner, or to the celebration of a child's birthday, but had not been in contact otherwise. In other cases, the child had spent some vacation time with the nonresidential parent but had not been in contact during the regular portions of the school year. More detail about visitation was thus

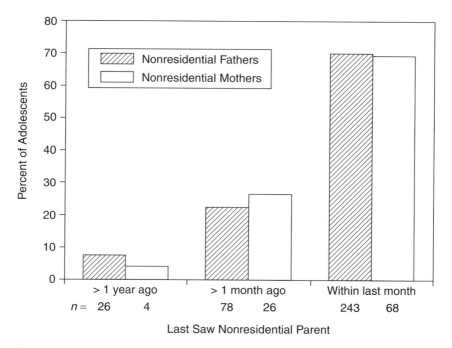

Figure 9.1 Time of most recent contact with the nonresidential parent for sole-resident adolescents, by residential arrangement.

obtained by asking separately about vacation time and visits during the regular school year.

In earlier parent reports, certain differences between overnight and daytime visiting had emerged. Overnight visits almost always occurred on a regular schedule; daytime visiting was frequently sporadic and less planned. Daytime visiting was also less stable from one year to the next than was overnight visiting. As we already noted, among mother-resident adolescents, overnight visits to the father were quite well maintained over time, while daytime visiting dropped off. So we also asked about overnight versus daytime visitation. For school-year visiting, adolescents were asked how many overnights they usually spent in a two-week period, not including vacations. If they said they never stayed overnight, they were asked about daytime visits: how many hours they spent in such visits during a usual two-week period during the school year. Then they were asked how many days (over and above the usual school-year pattern) they spent with the nonresident parent during their last summer's vacation, and the most recent spring and Christmas vacations.

In devising a scale for the amount of visitation, we gave vacation visits less weight than regular visitation every two weeks during the school year, and we gave overnight visits more weight than daytime visits. On the basis of their answers to the series of questions, adolescents were grouped into four visitation categories:

1. "Little or no visitation" ($n = 139$). No overnights, and less than eight hours of daytime visitation during typical two-week periods of the school year; less than two weeks of vacation time.
2. "Vacation only" ($n = 91$). Two or more weeks of vacation time, but no overnights and less than eight hours of daytime visitation during typical two-week periods of the school year.
3. "Moderate visitation" ($n = 97$). One overnight, or eight hours or more of daytime visitation, during typical two-week periods of the school year.
4. "Frequent visitation" ($n = 118$). Two or three overnights in typical two-week periods of the school year.

Adolescents who spent four or more overnights per two-week period with each of the parents were considered to be in dual residence (see Chapter 3) and, as noted, have not been included in the analysis of visitation that follows.

The "little or no visitation" group includes those few adolescents who had not seen the nonresidential parent in the past year. Nearly half of the adolescents in this group, however, had done some daytime visiting during the school year, ranging from one hour to six hours per two-week period. (The mean hours of daytime visiting per two weeks for the "little or no visitation" group was 1.2 for mother-resident adolescents, and .84 for father-resident adolescents.) About half of these adolescents also spent some of their vacation time with their nonresidential parent, with fourteen adolescents reporting a one-week stay. The average amount of vacation time spent by these adolescents was 2.8 days.

Some of the adolescents in the vacation-only group also did small amounts of daytime visiting during the school year: .65 hours per two weeks was the average for mother-resident adolescents, and .30 hours for father-resident adolescents. These adolescents did not typically spend overnights with the nonresidential parent.

We recognized that our four-step "scale" might not be linear. That is, there is no way of knowing how much importance to give to a two- to four-week stay with the nonresident parent during the summer, com-

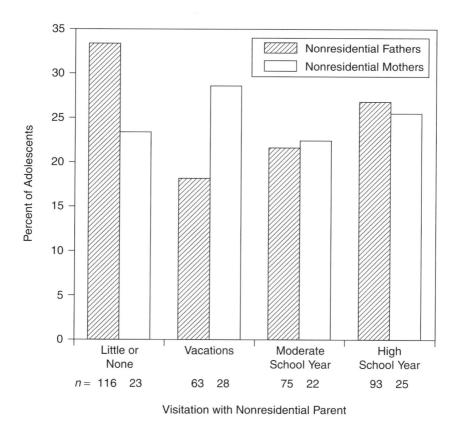

Figure 9.2 Level of contact with the nonresidential parent for sole-resident adolescents, by residential arrangement.

pared with spending every other weekend (Friday and Saturday nights) during the school year. Most of the analyses using visitation in this chapter and subsequent chapters, therefore, have been done in the form of analyses of variance, which do not assume linearity.[1]

With regard to the amount of visitation, there was somewhat less visitation with nonresident fathers than with nonresident mothers (see Figure 9.2). One-third of the adolescents living with their mothers seldom or never visited their fathers, while slightly under one-fourth of the father-resident adolescents were similarly out of touch with their mothers. In contrast, more father-resident adolescents (28.6 percent) than mother-resident adolescents (18.2 percent) were in the vacation-only group. The similarity between the two residential groups in terms of the two highest visitation categories, however, was striking: exactly 48 percent of the adolescents in each group visited with their nonresidential parents moderately or frequently during the school year.

Visitation and Demographic Characteristics

The amount of visitation with nonresidential parents was related to a number of characteristics of the adolescents and their families (see Appendix Table B.8 for details of visitation and demographics). Adolescents who had frequent overnight visitation with their nonresidential parents were younger, on the average, than adolescents with lower levels of visitation; adolescents who seldom or never saw their nonresidential parent were the oldest group, and this held true for both mother- and father-resident adolescents. Although the percentage of boys and girls in each visitation group was not significantly different, there was a somewhat higher concentration of boys in the highest visitation group (for both mother and father residence). We considered this association strong enough to make it wise to control for both age and sex of subjects in the analyses that follow. For both residential groups, father's education was significantly associated with the visitation patterns. For father-resident adolescents, it was the vacation-only group that had fathers with the highest levels of education. For mother-resident adolescents, both the vacation-only group and the frequent-visitation group had fathers with the highest levels of education. The average of mother's and father's education levels showed a similar pattern as that for father education; thus, mid-parent education was controlled in subsequent analyses as a way of taking into account the education levels of both parents. As we noted in Chapter 7, the frequency of visitation was not related to the remarriage status of either mother or father in either residential group.

When children started out living with their mother following the parental separation, they usually continued to do so over the next several years. Father residence was much less stable, however, and a majority of the adolescent children who were living with their fathers at the time of the adolescent interview had not lived with him continuously since the separation, having been in either mother or dual residence at some point in the interim (Maccoby and Mnookin, 1992; Chapters 3 and 5). Within each of the residential groups, however, the amount of visitation was not significantly related to whether the adolescent had continuously remained in the same residential arrangement.

Visitation and Travel Distance

As might be expected, adolescents reporting higher levels of visitation also reported living geographically closer to the nonresidential parent. Approximately two-thirds of the adolescents whose parents lived within an hour's driving time from each other's houses visited the nonresidential parent during typical two-week periods throughout the school year. These fairly high levels of school-year visitation were found in both mother-resident and father-resident families, so long as the two parents lived within what might be considered reasonable weekend driving range. This proportion dropped to 50 percent for those living between one and two hours apart. Differences between mother-resident and father-resident families emerged when the distance was even greater: nearly half the father-resident adolescents who lived from two to eight driving hours away from their mothers visited her (or were visited by her) on at least a biweekly basis during the school year, while only a fifth of the mother-resident adolescents visited their fathers this frequently when they lived so far apart. The vast majority of mother-resident adolescents who lived over two hours away from their fathers either visited primarily during vacations or visited hardly at all. Because most of the driving for visitation purposes tends to be done by the nonresidential parent (Maccoby and Mnookin, 1992), the difference in visitation between nonresidential mothers and nonresidential fathers when distances are great may reflect a greater willingness on the part of nonresidential mothers to drive longer distances to pick up and return children. Instead, or in addition, it may reflect a greater effort on the part of children to see nonresidential mothers over nonresidential fathers. The difference in contact with nonresidential mothers versus nonresidential fathers remains when the nonresidential parent's working hours are accounted for; thus the difference is not simply due to the fact that fathers work longer hours and therefore may have less time or less freedom to get away from work to travel longer distances.

Phone Calls to the Nonresidential Parent

Adolescents who visited their nonresidential parents most frequently also talked to them most frequently on the telephone. The average was four to five times a week for adolescents in the two highest visitation categories and one to two times a week for adolescents in the two lowest visitation categories. The difference was especially strong for mother-resident adolescents, but held for father-resident adolescents as well. Presumably the higher rate of telephone calls for adolescents with frequent visitations reflects in part the need for more contact to arrange visits and the lower likelihood that the phone call would be a long-distance one. It is likely, however, that adolescents and nonresidential parents who see one another more often also feel freer to call one another to talk about a variety of things other than visitations, especially when a regularly scheduled visit cannot take place.

Adolescents' Reports of Their Experiences in Visitation

Adolescents gave us their perceptions concerning the reasons they visited their nonresidential parents, how flexible their visitation arrangements were, whether they could exercise any influence over the visitation plans their parents made, how much they looked forward to visiting, and how satisfied they were with their visitation arrangement. The large majority of adolescents (87 percent), when offered a series of possible reasons for visiting (from which they could choose as many as applied), said they visited because they wanted to (see Figure 9.3). About one-third also said that they did not want to hurt the nonresidential parent's feelings by not going. Older adolescents were more likely to express this latter kind of sentiment, which may reflect the older adolescents' higher levels of involvement outside the home. A little over one-fifth of adolescents felt that they were required to go, and had no choice. Males were slightly more likely than females to say they visited because they had to, and less likely to say they visited because they wanted to. Adolescents living with their fathers were more likely than those living with their mothers to say that visitation provided a way to get away from the residential parent. Older adolescents also more often selected this reason for visitation than did younger adolescents.

We looked at whether boys and girls or older and younger adolescents had different reasons for visiting nonresidential mothers versus nonresidential fathers. In only one case did the proportion of individuals using a reason for visiting mother versus father differ by group: among older adolescents (aged fourteen years and older), fewer father-resident adolescents (78 percent) gave "because I want to" as a reason for visiting the nonresidential parent than did mother-resident adolescents (88 percent).[2]

Visitation schedules can become an arena of conflict between adolescents and their parents. Although in some families the distance between

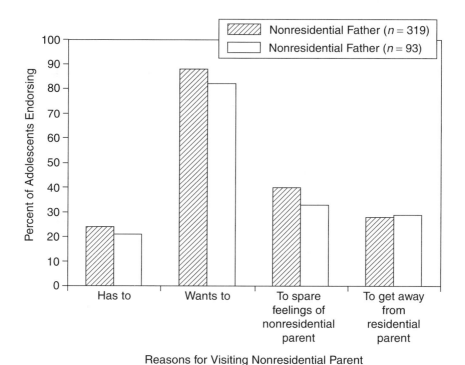

Figure 9.3 Percentage of adolescents in sole residence endorsing various reasons for visiting their nonresidential parent, by residential arrangement. Means are adjusted for age and sex of adolescent, the average education of the two parents, and amount of contact with the nonresidential parent. Excludes adolescents who had not seen their nonresidential parent in the past year.

parents places rather strict limits on visitation, especially during the school year, for families who live close enough for regular visits, situations may arise in which parents and children don't see eye to eye on visitation. In particular, such conflicts arise when either a parent or a child wants to change the visitation schedule. On the one hand, children sometimes resist visitation, even though nonresidential parents truly want to spend time with them and even though residential parents support that visitation. Especially among adolescents, conflicts arise between activities with friends or extracurricular activities in school and scheduled visitation times, and children may lobby with the residential parent to cancel a visit. On the other hand, children sometimes are eager to go for visits at times that are inconvenient for the parents, or when the residential parent wants to block visitation, feeling that the visits are not in the child's best interests (or the residential parent's own interests). The adolescents in our sample were asked about occasions when they were scheduled to visit the other parent but did not want to go, and about occasions when they wanted to visit the nonresidential parent but could not. A substantial number of adolescents in both residential arrangements had had such experiences. The links between residence or visitation and having had such experiences were the same for boys and girls. Overall, mother-resident adolescents were somewhat more likely to say they did not want to go on a scheduled visit than were father-resident adolescents (see Table 9.1); there was no difference in the desire to be with the nonresidential parent at unscheduled times between mother- and father-resident adolescents. This latter sentiment was more dependent on the level of visitation for mother-resident adolescents than for father-resident adolescents. Among mother-resident adolescents, frequent visitors and vacation visitors were more likely to say they wished they could be with their fathers at unscheduled times than were those who visited relatively seldom.

Feelings of not wanting to visit the nonresidential father when one was supposed to visit were reported more often by moderate and frequent visitors—a fact that probably reflects the greater frequency of scheduled visits, and hence more opportunities for conflicts to arise between visiting and other activities the child might want to participate in. Although father-resident adolescents with moderately high levels of visitation also reported feelings of not wanting to visit when they were supposed to, it is surprising to note that adolescents who had the highest levels of visitation with their mothers seldom reported such conflicted feelings—about as infrequently as adolescents with the two lowest levels of visitation.

Whether adolescents were actually able to go to a nonresidential parent's home when they wanted to differed more among the visitation groups than did simply having the desire: adolescents in the two low-visitation groups were usually not able to go. It is not surprising that the adolescents in the vacation-only group would not be able to make an unscheduled visit on short notice, considering that the nonresidential parent lived quite far away in many cases. In the two groups of more frequent visitors, about half went when they wanted to. When adolescents did not want to go on a scheduled visit, about two-thirds said that they had been able to cancel or reschedule on at least some occasions.

The ability to change plans did not differ depending on whether the adolescents were in mother or father residence. We also found no sex differences, either overall or within each residential arrangement, in the ability to change plans, although the numbers of cases in some of these analyses—especially when considering father residence—became too small for our tests to be meaningful.

Often the reasons given for not being able to change visitation plans had to do with parents' work schedules or other commitments that parents could not change. For example, one girl in mother residence said: "I can't just call up and say I want to come over 'cause [my father] . . . has a lot of work to do. I usually can't see him because he doesn't have time." Similarly, one boy in father residence told us: "My mom couldn't have me over . . . she had to work." Some adolescents couldn't visit a parent because he or she didn't have living accommodations big enough for them to stay over. Still others said that a residential parent worried that visits to a nonresidential parent would lead the adolescent to "run away" to that home.

Adolescents are not always aware of the considerations that determine their parents' decisions about visitation schedules, and situations may arise that seem arbitrary to the adolescents. One boy in mother residence told us that he couldn't visit his father when he wanted to, because "my mom made up some excuse. We were supposed to go visit my father . . . We didn't go." Although standing by an agreement made in the divorce proceedings may make a lot of sense to the parents, adhering rigidly to a schedule because "it's what we agreed on" may also seem arbitrary to adolescents. An early-adolescent female in mother residence told us, "I'm not allowed to see [Dad] during school . . . It wasn't his time to see me . . . it wasn't in the divorce papers." Another girl in mother custody said that she went to her father's even when she didn't want to, because "it's in the custody agreement so I have to . . . There was one week where I had tons of tests and everything and I didn't want to go there just to work and I really didn't want to go . . . but I had to . . . It's in the agreement and I have to go see him."

In response to a more general question about how much influence they felt they could have over changes in the visitation schedule, most adolescents placed themselves at about the midpoint of a five-point scale running from "not much say at all" to "a great deal." There were no sex differences in adolescents' answers to this question, but older adolescents felt they had more control over whether they would visit, and when, than did younger ones.

Table 9.1 Adolescents' reports of their experience with visitation, for adolescents in sole residence[a]

| Measure | Level of visitation | | | | F values |
	Little or none (1)	Vacation only (2)	Moderate (3)	High (4)	
"In the past year, has it happened that you were at your (residential parent's) house and wanted to be with your (nonresidential parent)?" Percentage responding "yes":					
Mother-resident adolescents (visit father)	42.9 (n = 115)	68.6 (n = 63)	52.2 (n = 75)	66.3 (n = 93)	Residence: 3.72[+,b] Visitation: 1.10 (n.s.) Residence × Visitation: 2.10[+]
Father-resident adolescents (visit mother)	67.6 (n = 23)	58.5 (n = 28)	74.2 (n = 22)	73.2 (n = 25)	(Mother res.: 1 < 2,4; 3 < 2) (Father res.: n.s.)

On the whole, most of the adolescents in our sample seemed to take the visitation arrangements in stride. They were asked: "When you are at your (residential parent's) house, and thinking about going to (or seeing) your (nonresidential parent), how do you usually feel?" The five-point scale from which they could choose an answer ran from "very reluctant" to "very eager." Overall, adolescents expressed more eagerness than reluctance. Adolescents living with their fathers were more eager to visit mothers ($M = 3.6$) than were adolescents living with their mothers to visit fathers ($M = 3.3$), and this difference did not vary by sex or age of adolescent. In both residential arrangements, younger adolescents were more eager to visit than were older adolescents: for mother-resident adolescents the correlation between age and eagerness was $-.23$, and for father-resident adolescents it was $-.22$.[3]

Eagerness to visit *was* related to the level of visitation: for both mother-resident and father-resident adolescents, those who seldom saw the nonresidential parent were the least eager to visit (see Figure 9.4). For mother-resident adolescents, only those adolescents who saw their fathers little or none of the time had lower levels of eagerness; those in the vacation-only group looked forward to their visits with their fathers as much as the more frequent visitors. For the father-resident adolescents, high-frequency visitors were more eager to visit mother than the adolescents who rarely visited. Although the relation between visitation and eagerness is statistically weaker for the father-resident adolescents, in part this is a result of the lower number of children in this arrangement. Of course, we don't know to what extent adolescents who initially had low levels of contact with a nonresidential parent became less eager to visit over time, or to what extent adolescents who were not eager to visit were subsequently less likely to do so.

After answering all the specific questions about their visitation situation, adolescents were asked a global question: "Think of a scale from 1 to 10, where 1 is completely dissatisfied and 10 is completely satisfied. How satisfied are you with the time you spend with each parent?" As noted in Chapter 8, adolescents living with their mothers were somewhat more satisfied than adolescents living with their fathers. We also noted there that satisfaction appeared to be linked to time spent with each parent, with satisfaction highest among adolescents who had high levels of contact with both parents (the dual-resident adolescents), and with adolescents who were very dissatisfied typically citing their failure to see one parent or the other as the reason for their dissatisfaction. To our surprise, then, within each sole-residence group, satisfaction was unrelated to the frequency of

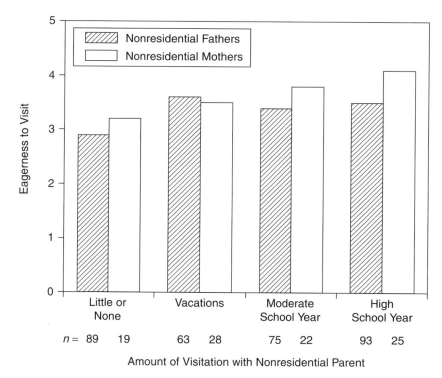

Figure 9.4 Sole-resident adolescents' eagerness to visit their nonresidential parent, by residential arrangement and level of contact with the nonresidential parent. Means are adjusted for age and sex of adolescent and the average education of the two parents. Excludes adolescents who had not seen their nonresidential parent in the past year.

visitation. Most adolescents appeared to have adapted themselves to whatever pattern of visitation the family had adopted.

Visitation and the Interparental Relationship

One might expect that visitation would covary with the amount of conflict or hostility between parents. On the one hand, after four and a half years, visitation might be lower for adolescents whose parents are not on good terms. On the other hand, as we noted earlier, some people believe that ongoing visitation can foster continued high levels of conflict between ex-spouses. Interestingly, what we found was that visitation with the nonresidential parent four and a half years after divorce—for both mother- and father-resident adolescents—was related only to the mother's earlier level of hostility, not to the father's (see Table 9.2). For mother-resident adolescents, mother's hostility was highest in the lowest visitation group and lowest in the highest visitation group. Mother's hostility was also high right after the divorce (T1) in the moderate visitation group, but by three and a half years after the separation, it had dropped to levels similar to the vacation-only and high-visitation groups. It appears, then, that residential mothers function as gatekeepers: if they remain hostile toward their ex-spouses, they can cut off (or minimize) their children's visitation. The father's level of hostility had little or no bearing on whether he received visits from mother-resident adolescents.

For father-resident adolescents, it was once again the mother's hostility, not the father's, that mattered. And here there was some evidence that visitation could maintain or exacerbate parental hostility. Mothers were especially hostile in the highest, as well as the lowest, visitation group, and cooperative communication between the parents at T2 had been especially low for these two groups. So for some families, maternal hostility either led to the termination of her visitation or resulted from being shut out, but for other families, frequent visitation may have kept the flames of maternal anger and hostility burning. Our data indicate that for both mother- and father-resident adolescents, it is the mother's feelings about her ex-spouse that are more closely linked to the nonresidential parent's continuing contact with the child.

Visitation and Adolescents' Relationships with Each Parent

Advocates of measures that foster continued contact between children and their nonresidential parents have emphasized that such contact fosters a close relationship with these parents, and that having a close relationship is beneficial to children in the long run. Skeptics have urged that it is mainly the residential parent that matters in children's development, and have raised the question of whether continued involvement by the nonresident parent may interfere with the major relationship. We compared adolescents who had different levels of visitation with their nonresidential parent on several measures of their relationship with each parent, and the patterns are very clear. On average, adolescents who visit have better relationships with their nonresidential parent than adolescents who do not visit (they feel closer to them—as shown in Figure 9.5—they trust them more, they identify more with them, and the two share more joint activities). Adolescents who rarely visit their nonresidential parent are also less

Table 9.2 Relation of visitation frequency to the interparental relationship[a]

Measure of interparental relationship	Level of visitation				$F_{visitation}$
	Little or none (1)	Vacation only (2)	Moderate (3)	High (4)	
Mother-Resident Adolescents (visit father)					
Maximum n	(67)	(31)	(44)	(57)	
Mother's hostility (T1)	6.5	5.0	6.5	4.7	7.27**** (1,3 > 2,4)
Father's hostility (T1)	5.4	4.2	4.7	5.3	1.75[b]
Mother's hostility (T2)	6.0	5.4	5.1	4.6	3.02* (1 > 4)[c]
Father's hostility (T2)	5.3	4.6	4.6	4.9	.46
Mother's hostility (T3)	5.6	5.0	4.8	4.4	2.83* (1 > 4)
Father's hostility (T3)	5.0	5.0	4.1	4.6	1.04
Father-Resident Adolescents (visit mother)					
Maximum n	(15)	(19)	(16)	(16)	
Cooperative communication (T2)	3.6	4.7	5.8	3.2	9.02**** (3 > 1,4) (2 > 4)
Mother's hostility (T1)	6.5	4.0	4.8	6.3	3.69* (2 > 1,4)
Father's hostility (T1)	6.0	6.5	5.4	5.9	.62
Mother's hostility (T2)	6.3	5.6	4.8	5.8	.78
Father's hostility (T2)	7.1	5.4	5.0	6.1	1.98
Mother's hostility (T3)	6.3	5.5	4.2	6.6	3.06* (3 < 1,4)
Father's hostility (T3)	5.8	4.5	5.3	6.2	1.88

a. Statistics are based on a random sample. Means are controlled for age and sex of adolescent and mid-parent education.

b. In two other random samples, $1,4 > 2$ (at $p \leq .10$ and $p \leq .05$).

c. Effect weakens to trend level ($p \leq .10$) in random samples.

$*p \leq .05.$ $****p \leq .0001.$

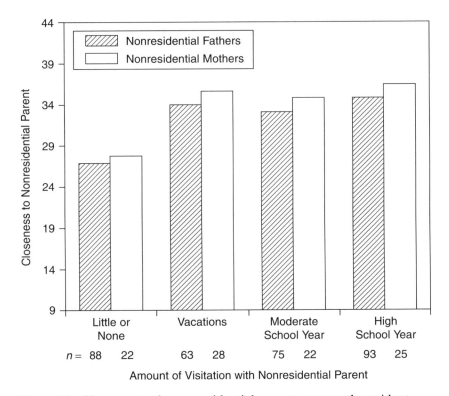

Figure 9.5 Closeness to the nonresidential parent among sole-resident adolescents, by level of contact with the nonresidential parent and residential arrangement. Means are adjusted for age and sex of adolescent and the average education of the two parents. Excludes adolescents who had not seen their nonresidential parent in the past year.

likely to have that parent confide in them and less likely to feel the need to nurture that parent (see Figure 9.6),[4] no doubt due to the lack of exposure to what is going on in the seldom-seen parent's life.

The link between more contact and a better relationship with the nonresidential parent is not at all surprising; very likely, the better relationship adolescents have with their nonresidential parent, the more they keep up visitation. Subsequently, the higher levels of visitation likely promote continued better relationships over time. What *is* surprising is that adolescents who see their nonresident parent as seldom as our lowest visitation group still report considerable closeness (above the midpoint of a scale that ranges from 10 to 45 points). And it is especially interesting

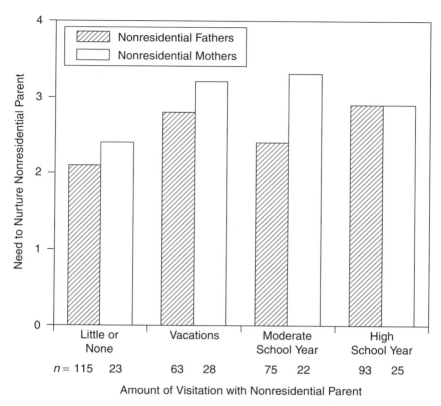

Figure 9.6 Sole-resident adolescents' reports of feeling the need to nurture their nonresidential parent, by level of contact with the nonresidential parent and residential arrangement. Means are adjusted for age and sex of adolescent and the average education of the two parents. Excludes adolescents who had not seen or talked to their nonresidential parent in the past year.

that even a small amount of visitation—only a two-week or longer vacation visit—appears sufficient to sustain a close relationship from the adolescents' perspective—nearly as close as that maintained by adolescents who spend two or three overnights with the nonresident parent every two weeks during the school year. This pattern is found among adolescents in both residential arrangements, and for boys as well as girls. In general, the relation between visitation and closeness is the same for older and younger adolescents as well, although for adolescents in mother residence the association is somewhat stronger for adolescents under age fourteen.

Our data also show that the gain in closeness to the nonresidential parent is *not* made at the expense of the relationship with the residential parent. Adolescents who visited their nonresidential parent frequently were extremely similar to adolescents who hardly ever visited the nonresidential parent in their relationships with their residential parent, and once again this was true regardless of whether the primary parent was the mother or the father, or whether the adolescent was male or female, old or young. We were particularly interested in whether adolescents would become more disengaged from the residential parent's household—in the sense of spending more time alone in their own rooms even when others were present in the house, or in spending more time away from the residential house—if they visited their nonresidential parent frequently. This did not turn out to be the case.

The only instance in which amount of visitation with the nonresidential parent was associated with the relationship between the residential parent and the child concerned the adolescents' felt need to nurture their mother. Adolescents who saw their nonresidential father rarely were more likely than other mother-resident adolescents to feel the need to nurture their mothers. Perhaps a lack of visitation itself leads to feelings of higher responsibility for one's mother because the mother-child relationship is more isolated, thus leading mother and child to depend on each other more than they would otherwise. Alternatively, this association may reflect some other aspect of families in which the fathers maintain little contact (for instance, lower levels of practical or financial aid) that may make life more difficult for mothers in this group, leading adolescents in this group to feel sorry for and worry about them.

Visitation and the Functioning of the Residential Parent's Household

Even though closeness to the residential parent may not be affected by the amount of visitation, it is still possible that residential parents may find it more difficult to manage households in which the children come and go frequently between the two parental households. Or, to the extent that the sharing of parenting has positive benefits (for example, a regular "break," support from the ex-spouse on parenting matters), high visitation might be linked with better household functioning. We examined whether the adolescents in our sample were reporting closer or looser monitoring by the residential parent, tighter or looser household organization, greater or less youth autonomy in decision making, or earlier or later curfews depending on the amount of visitation with the nonresidential parent.

We found no evidence that high levels of visitation interfered with or enhanced control and management in father-resident homes. Among mother-resident adolescents younger than age fourteen, regular school-year visitation was linked to somewhat more opportunities for the youth to make decisions alone—with or without discussion with parents—than was lower visitation (see Table 9.3). Among the older adolescents, however, high levels of visitation were associated with a lower likelihood that youths made final decisions concerning a range of issues, as well as a higher likelihood of earlier curfews on both school nights and weekends, than was less frequent visitation. Thus among older adolescents in mother residence, higher levels of visitation either allowed the parent to maintain a tighter rein at home or reflect a pattern of more controlled parenting (in other words, the very parents who maintain more control in the residential household may also be more likely to insist on regular and frequent visitation, even among older adolescents).

Visitation and Adolescent Adjustment

We noted earlier the questions that have been raised concerning the impact of visitation on the well-being of children in divorcing families, with the early research having indicated that mother-resident children were benefited by visits with their fathers and more recent work having called this finding into question. There has been very little work examining the effects of visits to mothers upon children who live with their fathers. We thus examined the relation between the level of visitation and adolescent adjustment.

As Table 9.4 shows, the amount of visitation with fathers had virtually no relation to the adjustment of mother-resident adolescents. A very modest exception initially was found in relation to grades—the group who saw their fathers primarily (or only) for a two-week or longer vacation period had the lowest grades—but this result weakened in random subsamples. It is puzzling that the vacation-only group should be different both from adolescents who see their fathers less often and from those who see them more often. As far as grades are concerned, it would be reasonable that fathers could only help with homework and otherwise support children's school effort if they see the children during the regular school year. But fathers' unavailability for help with schoolwork did not

Table 9.3   Relation of visitation frequency to mother's control and management in mother-residence homes, by age of adolescent[a]

Measure of control/management	Level of visitation				F_{visit}	F_{age}	$F_{interaction}$
	Little or none (1)	Vacation only (2)	Moderate (3)	High (4)			
Youth decides							
Adolescents under 14 years	.47	.43	.61	.51	5.95***	40.99****	6.89***
Adolescents 14 years and older	.77	.71	.71	.51		Older: 4 < 1,2,3 Younger: 3 > 1,2	
School night curfew							
Adolescents under 14 years	.75	.67	1.32	.79	3.49*	178.36****	4.12**,b
Adolescents 14 years and older	3.84	3.32	3.18	2.47		Older: 4 < 1,2,3; 3 < 1 Younger: n.s.	
Weekend night curfew							
Adolescents under 14 years	1.60	1.66	2.18	1.80	2.53+	223.50****	4.15**
Adolescents 14 years and older	5.65	5.53	4.99	4.07		Older: 4 < 1,2,3 Younger: n.s.	

a. Means are controlled for age and sex of adolescent and mid-parent education.

b. Effect weakens in random subsamples.

$+p \leq .10.$ $*p \leq .05.$ $**p \leq .01.$ $***p \leq .001.$ $****p \leq .0001.$ n.s. = not significant.

Table 9.4 Relation of visitation frequency to adolescent adjustment[a]

Measure of adjustment	Level of visitation				$F_{visitation}$
	Little or none (1)	Vacation only (2)	Moderate (3)	High (4)	
Mother-Resident Adolescents (visit father)					
Maximum n	(115)	(63)	(75)	(93)	
Depression/anxiety	15.9	15.8	15.2	14.4	.84
Deviance	21.3	22.3	21.3	20.3	2.28[+,b]
School grades	5.9	5.3	6.0	5.9	3.01*,c (2 < 1,3,4)
School effort	14.8	14.3	15.0	14.5	.74
Worst problem	110.9	112.8	109.4	110.3	.78
Father-Resident Adolescents (visit mother)					
Maximum n	(23)	(28)	(22)	(25)	
Depression/anxiety	17.2	13.7	17.6	13.6	2.59[+,b]
Deviance	24.8	22.1	22.4	23.0	1.00
School grades	5.2	5.5	5.4	5.5	.14
School effort	14.1	14.5	14.2	14.4	.05
Worst problem	119.2	111.9	116.8	111.2	1.17

a. Means are controlled for age and sex of adolescent and mid-parent education.

b. This result does not hold up in random samples.

c. This result weakens in random samples.

$+p \leq .10.$ $*p \leq .05.$

appear to affect the competence of adolescents who spent little or no time with their fathers. Overall, the differences in adjustment measures for adolescents with different amounts of visitation with fathers were remarkably small.

We examined whether the group averages might conceal countervailing trends in which visitation affected boys one way and girls another; or whether visitation might have different effects on adolescents of different ages. We found no interactions of visitation with age or sex of adolescent. We also did not find that the relation between visitation and adjustment differed by either parent's remarriage status, with one exception: if nonresidential fathers were remarried, adolescents were most depressed if they rarely saw him and least depressed if they saw him frequently. Perhaps when adolescents have the opportunity to spend time with fathers and their new wives, they can more easily feel a part of this new family; adolescents whose fathers remarry and also discontinue visitation may leave adolescents feeling abandoned or "left behind."

The relation between father visitation and adjustment did not differ depending on how close the adolescent felt to either parent. We also did not find that more visitation was linked to worse adjustment in situations of high parental conflict. There were only a small number of instances in which the relation between visitation and adjustment differed depending on the interparental relationship, and these instances generally pointed to a differential impact of vacation-only visitation. Vacation-only visitation was associated with poor adjustment if parental cooperation was low or hostility was high, but relatively good adjustment if parental cooperation was high or hostility was low. The low number of instances where such differential relations occurred leads us to view this particular set of findings somewhat skeptically, but it may indicate that infrequent (but regular) visitation is especially difficult for children when parents do not get along. Given that previous research concerning divorce and children's contact with the nonresidential parent has not looked in detail at the implications of visiting a parent infrequently but for substantial periods of time (such as summer vacations), this may be a form of visitation that deserves more focused attention.

The amount of visitation with mother also had very little relation to the adjustment of father-resident adolescents. And the effect of visiting mothers did not depend on the age or sex of the adolescents, on mother's or father's remarriage status, on adolescents' feelings of closeness to either parent, or on the degree of interparental conflict or cooperation.

Summary

In our sample of adolescents, few adolescents had "drop-out" nonresident parents; most had had at least some contact with their nonresidential parent within the past year. For many of the adolescents (a third of the mother-resident adolescents and a quarter of the father-resident adolescents), however, the contact was fairly minimal and not very regular. Adolescents were, not surprisingly, less likely to see parents who lived over two hours away (by car), but visitation was more often maintained despite long driving distances for father-resident adolescents visiting their mothers than for mother-resident adolescents visiting their fathers.

Whether visitation was being maintained at T4 was related to the amount of hostility the mother maintained toward her former spouse, but not to the father's hostility. It seems, then, that mothers function as gatekeepers who are able to exercise some control over the amount of visitation that will occur.

The amount of visitation, in and of itself, was related to very little about the adolescents or their primary residences. Visitation did not interfere with the residential parent's ability to monitor the adolescent or manage the household. If anything, older adolescents who visited their fathers frequently experienced more control by their residential mothers. And in line with some other studies (Furstenberg, Morgan, and Allison, 1987; Hess and Camara, 1979; King, 1991; Kurdek, Blisk, and Siesky, 1981; Luepnitz, 1982), there were few direct links between visitation and adolescent adjustment. But unlike some other studies (Amato and Rezac, 1994; Hetherington, Cox, and Cox, 1978, 1982; Zill, 1988), we did not find that the impact of visitation for sole-resident adolescents varied depending on the quality of the interparental relationship or the parents' remarriage status.

The primary finding with regard to visitation and its possible benefits is that when adolescents did visit the nonresidential parent—even if only for a couple of weeks in the summer—they were able to have a closer relation with the nonresidential parent than if visitation did not occur. Given that some visitation occurred, the amount of visitation mattered very little: vacation-only visitors were as close to their nonresidential parents as were more frequent visitors. The pattern of visiting only during vacations often occurred when the parent and adolescent lived a substantial distance apart. Thus even under circumstances of geographic distance and infrequent but regular and sustained contact, adolescents appear to be able to sustain a close relationship with the nonresidential parent. As we have already noted in detail, this is most likely due to a circular process. Adolescents and nonresidential parents who have close relationships are, no doubt, more likely to spend time together, but in addition, closer relationships can be maintained or enhanced when adolescents and parents continue to see each other. In the next chapter, we examine whether this enhanced closeness with the nonresidential parent provides benefits to the adolescent.

10

Life in the
Nonresidential Home

In this chapter we consider the impact of the nonresidential parent and home on the adolescent. First, however, we need to set a context for the nonresidential household. How do the relationship with the nonresidential parent and the kind of home that parent maintains compare to those of the residential parent? And does the answer to this question depend on which parent is residential and which is nonresidential, or whether the adolescent is a girl or boy? We address these questions before examining the relations between the quality of the nonresidential home and adolescent adjustment.

The Nature of the Nonresidential Home

Parent-Child Relationships

Two trends emerged concerning adolescents' relationships with their parents (see Appendix Table B.9 for means for both nonresidential and residential parents on the various constructs used to measure parent-child relationships). The first trend has to do with a comparison of relationships with a given parent (say, the mother), depending on whether that parent was a residential or a nonresidential parent. Not at all surprisingly, adolescents usually reported closer relationships with a parent of a given gender if they lived with that parent than if they just visited him or her. This was especially true of father-child relationships: both boys and girls who lived with their fathers—in sole or dual residence—reported better relationships with them on several indices (trust, identification, remembering special days, and to a lesser extent, closeness itself) than did adolescents who only visited their fathers. Living with one's mother was associated with

187

better relationships with her as well, but only for girls. Unexpectedly, boys reported feeling equally close to, and equally likely to share activities with, residential and nonresidential mothers. The lack of a difference for boys indicates a particularly good relationship with the nonresidential mother, and not a poor relationship with the residential mother.

Along with closeness, and living with a parent, often comes conflict (Flanagan, Schulenberg, and Fuligni, 1993; Furman and Buhrmester, 1985a, b; Hartup et al., 1993; Youniss and Smollar, 1983). Accordingly, adolescents who lived with their father not only felt closer to him, but also reported more conflict with him and more disengagement from his household than adolescents who only visited their father. Surprisingly, however, conflict between adolescents and mothers did not depend on whether the mother was residential or nonresidential. Especially for girls, the level of conflict with nonresidential mothers was equal to that experienced with residential mothers,[1] one of the first indications we had that father-resident girls had more negative relationships with their nonresidential parent than did other groups of adolescents.

The second trend we noted, which was in line with previous research comparing relationships with mothers and fathers in nondivorced families (see, for example, Youniss and Smollar, 1983), was that adolescents tended to have somewhat closer relationships with their mothers than with their fathers. In Chapter 5, for example, we reported that adolescents were somewhat closer to residential mothers than to residential fathers. A comparison of adolescents' relationships with nonresidential mothers and nonresidential fathers revealed that, in some respects, adolescents also enjoyed better relationships with a nonresidential parent if that parent was a mother than if that parent was a father (see Appendix Table B.9).[2] For example, nonresidential mothers were reported to be more likely to remember special days, and adolescents reported more eagerness to visit them, than was the case for nonresidential fathers. These differences held for both boys and girls. But for girls, this is where the differences favoring nonresidential mothers ended. Only boys trusted nonresidential mothers more[3] (see Figure 10.1), and only boys identified more with nonresidential mothers than with nonresidential fathers. Girls in father residence, in contrast, experienced higher conflict with their mother (see Figure 10.2) and more disengagement from their mother's home than girls in mother residence experienced with their father. For boys, then, we see a somewhat more positive relationship with nonresidential mothers than nonresidential fathers, a positive relationship not accompanied by higher conflict. In contrast, girls had very similar relationships with nonresidential mothers

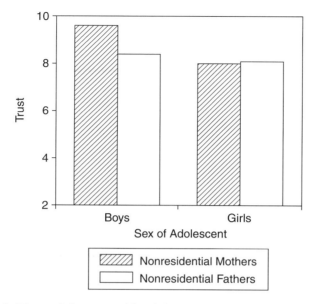

Figure 10.1 Trust of the nonresidential parent among sole-resident adolescents, by residential arrangement and sex of adolescent. Means are adjusted for age of adolescent and nonresidential parent's education.

and nonresidential fathers on most positive dimensions, but had more conflict with nonresidential mothers. Together with the finding reported earlier that the conflict between girls and nonresidential mothers is as high as that between girls and residential mothers, these results indicate that girls living with their fathers have more difficult relationships with their nonresidential mothers than other adolescents have with their nonresidential parents. Father-resident girls do not appear to be more distant, necessarily, from nonresidential mothers than one would expect on the basis of the mother's nonresidential status, but their emotional relationship appears to have a larger negative component. This is in line with previous speculations (see Chapters 3, 4, 5, and 6) that problems in the mother-child relationship represent one reason why children, especially girls, end up living with their fathers after divorce.

The two trends just described—greater closeness to residential parents than nonresidential parents and greater closeness to mothers than fathers—combined to create the following phenomenon with regard to a comparison of relationships between individual adolescents' residential and nonresidential parents (for the means for these comparisons, see

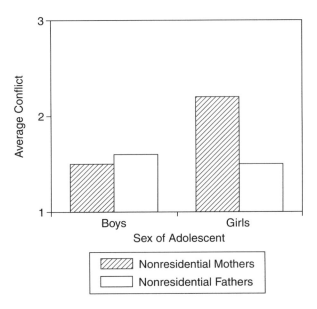

Figure 10.2 Average conflict with the nonresidential parent among sole-resident adolescents by residential arrangement and sex of adolescent. Means are adjusted for age of adolescent and nonresidential parent's education.

Appendix Table B.9): adolescents in mother residence were quite a bit closer (across several measures) to their residential parent (mother) than to their nonresidential parent (father); adolescents in father residence, particularly the boys, were about equally close to their residential parent (father) and their nonresidential parent (mother). The closer relationship with mothers for mother-resident adolescents emerged on every measure of parent-child relationships, and is demonstrated for closeness in Figure 10.3. Adolescents in mother residence also had higher levels of conflict with their mother and higher levels of disengagement from their mother's home than they had with their nonresident father.

For father-resident adolescents as a group, as already noted, relationships with mother and father were very similar. Adolescents in father residence, particularly boys,[4] felt equally close to their mothers and fathers and trusted them equally. Nonresidential mothers were as likely as residential fathers to remember special days, and adolescents were equally eager to see residential fathers and nonresidential mothers. The amount of conflict also did not differ by the parent's residential status for

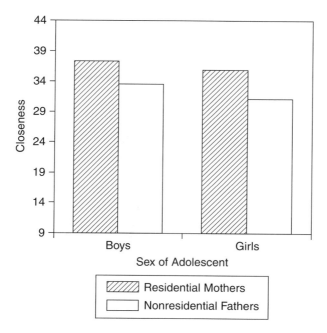

Figure 10.3 Closeness to mother versus father for mother-resident adolescents, by sex of adolescent.

father-resident adolescents.[5] And nonresidential mothers actually confided more in their children than did residential fathers. Only joint activities and disengagement were higher for residential fathers than for nonresidential mothers. Although identification with the residential father was higher than identification with the nonresidential mother among girls, father-resident boys identified with their mothers somewhat more than with their fathers (as did boys in the other residential arrangements). This sex difference in identification with each parent supports the earlier findings indicating a more troubled relationship between the nonresidential mother and girls, compared with boys, in father residence. The finding also points to a particularly positive relationship between boys and nonresidential mothers.

Parental Management and Control

There were few differences in the type and extent of parental management and control depending on residential status (see Appendix Table

B.10 for means). There were some small differences indicating more control on the part of a residential parent, as one might expect. For example, adolescents, especially in mother residence, were more closely monitored by the residential parent. And father-resident adolescents were less likely to have decision-making authority in their residential father's home than in the home of their nonresidential mother. There were no differences in decision-making practices between residential mothers and nonresidential fathers for mother-resident adolescents, however. Father-resident adolescents rated the rules in the nonresidential mother's home as more fair and consistent than those in the residential father's home, whereas mother-resident adolescents reported no difference in the fairness and consistency of rules between residential mothers and nonresidential fathers. Not surprisingly, adolescents spent more time doing chores in the residential home than in the nonresidential home, whether they were in mother or father residence, although this was slightly more true of mother-resident adolescents. The difference in chores between households was also greater among boys than among girls.

The Nonresidential Parent and Adolescent Adjustment

Of what importance are the nature of the nonresidential parent–child relationship and the processes within the nonresidential home? Does the nature of the relationship with or the home environment of the nonresidential parent have any impact on adolescent adjustment beyond the effect of the residential home? In the next section, we focus on the quality of the nonresidential parent–child relationship (how close it is, how conflictual) and its relation to adolescent adjustment after divorce. The impact of management and control practices in the nonresidential home is taken up in Chapter 12, in the context of consistency of parenting across households.

We have noted in earlier chapters that close, connected relationships between parent and child are important for healthy psychological and emotional adjustment of adolescents. But it is not clear from the available literature whether there are benefits from being close to two parents, or whether a strong, trustworthy relationship with one parent will suffice. If one parent is "enough," must the "good" relationship be with the residential parent, or can a close relationship with the nonresidential parent substitute for a more distant residential parent–child relationship? Can sustained closeness to the nonresidential parent after divorce ever be harmful? It is also not clear whether closeness to mother and closeness to father (or, conversely, the lack of closeness to one or the other) have different consequences. In situations of divorce, it is crucial to know whether the consequences of the nonresidential parent–child relationship depend on which parent is the nonresidential parent.

To examine these questions, we focused on five adjustment indices: depression/anxiety, overall deviance, school grades, school effort, and the adolescent's "worst problem." Aspects of the nonresidential parent–child relationship were used as predictors of adjustment: the overall closeness of the parent-adolescent relationship (the composite described in Chapter 5, made up of "emotional closeness," "trust," "identification," and "joint activities"), parent-child conflict, disengagement from the home, eagerness to see the parent, and whether the parent remembered special days such as holidays and birthdays.

First, we focused on whether the quality of the relationship between the nonresidential parent and adolescent was related in any way to the adolescent's adjustment, beyond the quality of the adolescent's relationship with the residential parent.[6] We examined the relation between various aspects of relationship quality and adjustment separately for male and female adolescents in each residential arrangement. In this way, we examined not only the general importance of the nonresidential parent but also whether the importance of that relationship varied as a function of who the nonresidential parent was—mother or father—and of the gender of the child.[7] Table 10.1 displays the relations that emerged.

Parent-Child Closeness

The closer the relationship between adolescents and their nonresidential parents, the less depression the adolescents experienced and the less severe was their "worst problem." In addition, adolescents who had closer relationships with their nonresidential parents tended to have higher grades. Although the strength of these associations varied among the different groups and depended on the measure of adjustment, the analyses indicated that the relation was basically the same for both boys and girls in both mother and father residence. The one exception is that for girls in father residence, but not boys, levels of deviance were lower if they maintained close relationships with their nonresidential mothers. Thus the overall closeness of the relationship with a nonresidential parent—whether mother or father—appears to be moderately linked with several aspects of better adjustment for both boys and girls.

Table 10.1 Associations between quality of nonresidential parent–adolescent relationship and adolescent adjustment for sole-resident adolescents[a]

Measures of relationship with nonresidential parent and adjustment	Mother-resident adolescents			Father-resident adolescents			Quality × Residence × Sex β	Quality × Residence β	Quality × Sex β	Quality main effect β
	Boys	Girls	All	Boys	Girls	All				
Parent-Child Overall Closeness										
Maximum n	(151)	(184)	(335)	(61)	(38)	(99)				
Depression	-.05	-.13+	-.11*	-.05	-.12	-.11	n.s.	n.s.	n.s.	-.12**
Deviance	-.02	-.04	-.02	-.00	-.45***	-.18*	-.08+	-.09*,b	n.s.	n.s.
School grades	.07	.07	.07	.23+	.12	.18+	n.s.	n.s.	n.s.	.09*,c
School effort	.16+	-.01	.06	.09	.08	.11	n.s.	n.s.	n.s.	n.s.
Worst problem	-.11	-.14*	-.13*	-.01	-.33*	-.13	n.s.	n.s.	n.s.	-.13***
Parent-Child Conflict										
Maximum n	(89)	(74)	(163)	(30)	(14)	(44)				
Depression	-.31*	.11	-.06	-.08	-.51	-.26	-.14*	n.s.	n.s.	n.s.
Deviance	.27*	.07	-.13	.09	-.02	.07	n.s.,d	n.s.	.12*	n.s.
School grades	-.04	-.02	-.01	-.26	.38	-.13	n.s.	n.s.	n.s.	n.s.

School effort	.09	.14	.14	−.11	−.21	−.19	n.s.	n.s.[e,g]	n.s.	n.s.
Worst problem	−.37**	.08	−.13	.17	.16	.16	−.11+	n.s.	.11+	n.s.
Disengagement from Home										
Maximum n	(106)	(101)	(207)	(44)	(21)	(65)				
Depression	−.05	.01	−.01	−.03	−.07	−.07	n.s.	n.s.	n.s.	n.s.
Deviance	.05	.13	.07	−.04	.25	.06	n.s.	n.s.	n.s.	n.s.
School grades	−.09	−.07	−.08	−.01	.01	−.01	n.s.	n.s.	n.s.	n.s.
School effort	−.10	−.10	−.10	−.04	−.55*	−.23+	n.s.	n.s.[d]	n.s.	−.14*[,b]
Worst problem	.00	.06	.02	−.03	.43*	.10	n.s.	n.s.	n.s.[d,g]	n.s.
Eagerness to See										
Maximum n	(146)	(174)	(320)	(58)	(36)	(94)				
Depression	−.02	−.01	−.03	−.11	.10	−.04	n.s.	n.s.	n.s.	n.s.
Deviance	.04	.03	.04	.05	−.36*	−.13	n.s.	−.11*[,f]	n.s.	n.s.
School grades	.09	−.07	−.00	−.04	.02	−.01	n.s.	n.s.	n.s.	n.s.
School effort	.16+	.01	.07	−.16	.09	.01	.09+	n.s.	n.s.	n.s.
Worst problem	−.05	−.02	−.03	.17	−.09	−.01	n.s.	n.s.	n.s.	n.s.

Table 10.1 (continued)

Measures of relationship with nonresidential parent and adjustment	Mother-resident adolescents			Father-resident adolescents			Quality × Residence × Sex	Quality × Residence	Quality × Sex	Quality main effect
	Boys	Girls	All	Boys	Girls	All	β	β	β	β
Remembers Special Days										
Maximum n	(167)	(196)	(363)	(61)	(38)	(99)				
Depression	−.18*	−.07	−.13*	−.22+	−.01	−.10	n.s.	n.s.	n.s.	−.13**
Deviance	−.12+	−.07	−.09+	−.11	−.16	−.11	n.s.	n.s.	n.s.	−.08+,f
School grades	.22**	.09	.15**	.28*	−.12	.08	−.10*	n.s.	−.08+,g	.12
School effort	.24**	−.07	.06	.28*	−.17	.06	−.09+	n.s.	−.15**	n.s.
Worst problem	−.25***	−.06+	−.15**	−.18	−.06	−.11	n.s.	n.s.	.09*,b,g	−.14**

a. Numbers are standardized beta weights from regressions predicting adjustment with quality of the relationship with the nonresidential parent, controlling for quality of the relationship with the residential parent and age of adolescent. Sex is controlled in analyses not broken down by sex.

b. Effect is not significant in random subsamples.

c. Effect weakens in random subsamples.

d. Effect becomes significant in random subsamples.

e. Effect becomes marginally significant ($p \leq .10$) in random subsamples.

f. Effect becomes more significant in random subsamples.

g. Although this particular two-way interaction was significant, the change in R^2 as a result of the three two-way interactions entered into the second step of the regression analyses was not significant. Because this particular two-way interaction was of interest in and of itself (and not just as part of the set of two-way interactions), we still note its individual significance.

$*p \leq .05.$ 　 $**p \leq .01.$ 　 $***p \leq .001.$ 　 $+p \leq .10.$ 　 n.s. = not significant.

Remembering Special Days

Besides parent-child closeness, remembering special days like birthdays and holidays was the only other aspect of the nonresidential parent–child relationship that was consistently related to adolescent adjustment. The more likely a nonresidential parent was to remember special days, the less depressed and less deviant the adolescent, and the less severe the "worst problem." In addition, for boys—those in father residence, particularly—having a nonresidential parent who remembered special days was linked to higher grades and higher effort in school. Thus the more the nonresidential parent remembered holidays and birthdays, the more the son was invested in school. Why was the ability of the nonresidential parent to remember special days one of the most important predictors of adolescent adjustment? Perhaps the symbolic value of remembering holidays and birthdays is particularly important to children of divorce. By remembering such days a parent is communicating that the child is important and not forgotten, even in situations where parent and child do not often see each other or where the relationship cannot be characterized as emotionally warm or close.

Other Aspects of the Relationship

The more negative aspects of the relationship with the nonresidential parent—disengagement from the nonresidential home and conflict with the nonresidential parent—mattered little with regard to adolescent adjustment. Disengagement from the nonresidential home was not associated with any index of adjustment.[8] There were also no associations between nonresidential parent–child conflict and adjustment that held for all subgroups of adolescents, and the associations that did emerge were counterintuitive. For example, higher levels of conflict with nonresidential fathers (but not nonresidential mothers) were sporadically linked to better, not worse, adjustment for boys. Although we envisioned high levels of conflict between parents and children as a negative factor in children's adjustment, perhaps within the range of conflict experienced by nonresidential fathers and their sons conflict was indicative of a higher level of engagement with the father that was positive for those boys.

Adolescents' eagerness to see the nonresidential parent was also virtually unrelated to their adjustment. Among girls, greater eagerness to see the nonresidential mother was linked to lower levels of deviance.[9] And there was a slight tendency for boys in mother residence to report more school effort when they also reported eagerness to see their nonresidential father. These associations, however, are probably too weak and too sporadic to be meaningful.

Summary

It is important to make it clear that we cannot establish whether a better relationship with the nonresidential parent leads to better adjustment in the adolescent, or whether adolescents who are better adjusted maintain better relationships with their nonresidential parent. There is reason to believe that both processes are at work. A conservative interpretation of our findings is that a continuing positive relationship with the nonresidential parent, in general, does not pose risks for the adolescent. And in fact positive effects may be felt from closeness in the nonresidential parent–child relationship and from having a nonresidential parent who remembers special days—even among father-resident girls, who, on average, have more negative relationships with their nonresidential mothers. The strength of the associations we have reported is small, indicating that any impact is weak to moderate; nonetheless, the associations were consistently positive and, in the cases we have noted, strong enough to reject the notion of chance associations. Of course, the small magnitude of the associations also suggests that any impact of the nonresidential parent–child relationship is moderated by other factors (for example, the quality of the relationship between the parents or between the residential parent and child), and we consider this possibility in subsequent sections. Before considering other aspects of the context in which the relationship with the nonresidential parent is embedded, however, we need to address several issues concerning the findings thus far.

Do these data provide any support for the notion that adolescents need most to retain a good relationship with their same-sex parent? It has been argued that children benefit from sustaining a relationship with the same-sex parent (Santrock and Warshak, 1979; Warshak and Santrock, 1983; Zaslow, 1989), and Gunnoe (1994) provides some support for the importance of a relationship between adolescents and a same-sex nonresidential parent. Our own data on the adjustment of adolescents living with same-sex versus opposite-sex parents (reported in Chapter 4), however, did not indicate that, in general, living with the same-sex parent promoted better adjustment than living with the opposite-sex parent. Our data on nonresidential parents also do not indicate a special need to maintain a close relationship with the same-sex parent, with the possible exception that girls benefit slightly more than boys do from a sustained relationship with their mother. Although for most of our adjustment indices, boys and girls appeared to benefit equally from the continued relationship with a nonresidential mother, a close relationship with and eagerness to see nonresidential mothers was linked to lower levels of deviant behavior for girls only. Although conflict with the nonresidential father was most strongly linked to various adjustment measures for boys in mother custody, it was linked in a counterintuitive way: more conflict with nonresident fathers was associated with better adjustment. These sporadic findings certainly do not point to any special value of maintaining a relationship with the same-sex parent. The more important message seems to be that nonresidential parents have a small but positive role to play in promoting positive adjustment in their adolescents. This is true even for nonresidential mothers and their daughters, whose relationships tend to be more negative, on average, than other nonresidential parent–child relationships.

This message raises another important question. If a good relationship with the nonresidential parent can promote positive outcomes in adolescents, and if visitation promotes a good relationship with the nonresidential parent (as we reported in Chapter 9), why did we not find that visitation with the nonresidential parent, per se, promoted positive adolescent adjustment? The answer to this question is complex, but has to do with the fact that the associations between visitation and the nonresidential parent–child relationship, and between this relationship and adolescent adjustment, are small, and vary in strength depending on other factors. For example, low visitation interferes with closeness mainly at the extreme. Children cannot be close to a nonresidential parent if they never or almost never see that parent. But even modest levels of contact appeared to allow relationships between nonresidential parents and adolescents that were as close as those that occurred when contact was high. Furthermore, although visitation opens the door to a close relationship, it certainly does not guarantee one. Closeness clearly depends on many factors, including how committed and involved the nonresidential parent is, his or her personality, or the supportiveness of other members of the nonresidential household. Similarly, closeness to the nonresidential parent is of some benefit to most adolescents, but is no guarantee of better adjustment. As will be seen shortly, closeness to a nonresidential parent may help with adjustment more under some circumstances, such as when there is not too much discord between the residential and nonresidential parent. In the end, we conclude from these data that sustained closeness to a nonresidential parent is more important to adolescent adjustment than is visitation per se; visitation levels are not precise enough indicators of what happens in the course of visitation to capture the changes in adjustment that may occur as a result of those happenings.

Patterns of Positive Affect with Each Parent and Adolescent Adjustment

We conclude from the results just reported that a good relationship with the nonresidential parent can sometimes be a positive factor in adolescent adjustment, beyond the relationship with the residential parent. In addition, however, we wished to know whether the effect of the relationship with the nonresidential parent varied as a function of the relationship with the residential parent. In other words, is there benefit to having a good relationship with two parents, or is a good relationship with one parent "enough"? Is a good relationship with a nonresidential parent of greater benefit when an adolescent is not close to the residential parent than when a good residential parent–child relationship already exists?

Before exploring the potential benefits of remaining close to both parents, we must ask whether children *can* remain close to both parents after divorce. Some argue that in situations of interparental conflict, it is very difficult for a child to maintain positive relationships with both parents; later in this chapter we will address the link between ongoing interparental conflict and closeness to each parent. Four and a half years after divorce, however, many parents are not actively in conflict; in fact, many parents shield their children from such active conflict throughout the divorce process. In general, what can one expect concerning the relationships a child of divorce can maintain with each parent? Some believe that the circumstance of divorce itself—the fact that parents are enough at odds to go through with a divorce—makes it difficult, if not impossible, for children to remain close to both parents. According to this controversial view, it is as if children's closeness to two people who are so different that they cannot remain married is a zero-sum game, in which increases in closeness to one of the opposing parties must be associated with decreases in closeness to the other (see Goldstein, Freud, and Solnit, 1979).

Other perspectives offer different predictions. For instance, an attachment perspective (for example, Bowlby, 1973) would predict that if children have a trusting and secure relationship with at least one parent they are more likely to be able to have close relationships with other adults, including the other parent. Or, from a personality perspective, the types of parents who develop and nurture truly positive relationships with their children are more likely to possess personality traits (sensitivity, warmth) or interpersonal orientations (maturely developed) that are conducive to allowing their children physical and emotional access to the other parent. These latter perspectives not only suggest that a child can be close to both parents, but that closeness to one parent will be predictive of closeness to the other.

Our data generally support the latter views. Overall, among our adolescents, having a close relationship with mother was positively, albeit moderately, related to having a close relationship with father ($r = .19$, $p < .0001$). The magnitude of this relation varied for different subgroups of adolescents, however. For example, the correlation between overall closeness with mother and overall closeness with father for adolescents in dual residence was .55 (as opposed to .20 in mother residence and .07 in father residence). Only among one group was the correlation between mother-child closeness and father-child closeness not positive: the correlation was $-.15$ (not statistically significant) for father-resident girls.[10] Thus a good relationship with one parent was generally predictive of a good relationship with the other, except for father-resident girls.

To begin to examine the relation between patterns of closeness with both parents and adjustment, we focused first on sole-resident adolescents. We examined whether the impact of a close relationship with the nonresidential parent differed depending on the level of closeness to the residential parent. We also investigated whether the answer to this question varied by residential arrangement (in other words, depending on the gender of the residential and nonresidential parent).[11]

For four out of the five adjustment measures (all except school grades), the relation of nonresidential parent–adolescent closeness to adjustment depended on the closeness of the residential parent–adolescent bond *for father-resident adolescents only*. In other words, the "effect" of a close relationship with a nonresidential mother depended on the degree of closeness to the residential father (see Figures 10.4 and 10.5). If adolescents reported being close to their residential father, a close relationship with their mother in addition was beneficial; the group of father-resident adolescents that were engaged in a close relationship with both parents were better adjusted than any of the other father-resident adolescents. In contrast, adolescents who had close relationships with their residential fathers and *not* their nonresidential mothers tended to have the lowest levels of adjustment. If adolescents were *not* engaged in a close relationship with their residential father, being close to their mother did not add consistent

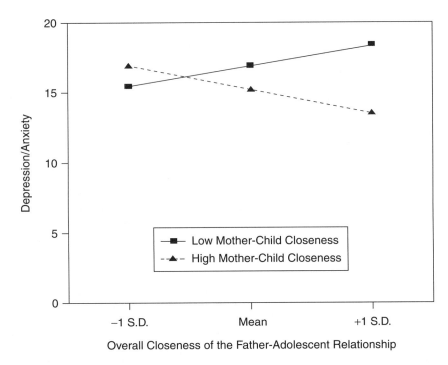

Figure 10.4 Depression/anxiety at different levels of father-child and mother-child closeness for father-resident adolescents.

benefits with regard to adjustment; adolescents who had a close relationship with their mother and those who did not were generally similar in their levels of depression, deviance, school effort, and "worst problem" in situations where the father-adolescent relationship was not close.[12]

In contrast, for mother-resident adolescents, the associations between closeness in the father-child relationship and adjustment did not vary depending on what the relationship with the mother was like. In general, closeness between an adolescent and the residential mother was the stronger predictor of several adjustment measures; the relationship with the father appeared to add modest additional benefits for selected measures of the relationship and selected measures of adjustment, sometimes for both genders and sometimes only for boys, but any relations were independent of the quality of the relationship between an adolescent and his or her mother. As a result, in instances where the relationship with the nonresidential father *was* related to better adjustment, adolescents who had good relationships with both parents were better off than ado-

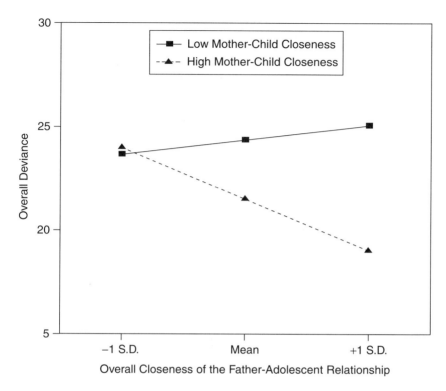

Figure 10.5 Overall deviance at different levels of father-child and mother-child closeness for father-resident adolescents.

lescents who had good relationships with only their father or with neither parent (see Figure 10.6). But the benefits of being close to both parents over being close to only the residential parent were not as great in mother residence as they were in father residence.[13] In addition, the relationship with the mother was clearly a stronger predictor of adolescent adjustment than was the relationship with the nonresidential father, and it predicted better adjustment regardless of the level of father-child closeness.

In sum, although having a close relationship with both parents was of some benefit to both mother-resident and father-resident adolescents, it was of more benefit to father-resident adolescents. For father-resident adolescents, in fact, a close relationship with their mother appeared to be necessary for adolescents to benefit from a close relationship with their father. Adolescents did not benefit, however, from being close only to the nonresidential parent in either mother or father residence.

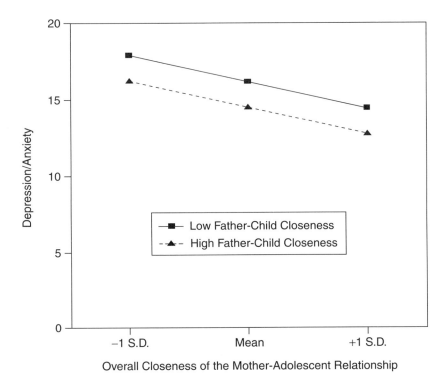

Figure 10.6 Depression/anxiety at different levels of mother-child and father-child closeness for mother-resident adolescents.

Thus far we have excluded dual-resident adolescents from analyses looking at the relations between closeness to the nonresidential parent and adjustment, because dual-resident adolescents do not have a nonresidential parent. In Chapter 5, however, we noted that adolescents in dual residence maintained close, positive affective bonds with both their mother and their father, remaining as close or closer to each parent as adolescents in sole-resident arrangements were with their residential parent. Is it the fact that adolescents in dual residence were more likely to have close relationships with two parents after a divorce than adolescents in sole residence that accounts for their somewhat better levels of adjustment (see Chapter 4)?

To test this, we looked at an adolescent's "total closeness" to both parents (to do this, we summed the reported closeness to two parents). We then examined whether any advantage of being in dual residence on the "worst problem" index remained when taking account of this total closeness.[14] When closeness to two parents was controlled, dual-resident adolescents no longer had better scores on "worst problem," indicating that their better adjustment was a reflection of their better relationships with both parents.

Interparental Conflict and the Parent-Child Relationship

Given that a continuing positive relationship with the nonresidential parent appears to carry some benefits for adolescents, it becomes important to know what factors enhance or interfere with that relationship. As we have already noted, continuing contact with the nonresidential parent—even at the level of summer visitation—is one such factor. Another that may be important for the quality of the nonresidential parent–child relationship is the amount of continuing conflict between the two parents. Earlier in this century, Fritz Heider (1958) proposed a balance theory of interpersonal relations that, applied to the social network of parent, parent, and child, predicts great difficulty for the child in remaining close to both parents when those parents are actively conflictual or hostile (see Johnston and Campbell, 1987, for such an application). In short, this theory predicts that instability in a social network (in this case the network of parent, parent, and child) will result if there exists an odd number of negative relations. If the bond between parents is negative, tension and instability in the network is expected to be resolved by the severing or souring of at least one parent-child bond.

In addition to Heider's formulation, several theoretical and empirical analyses suggest that an important mechanism by which parental conflict contributes to behavior problems and/or psychological distress in children is through the disruption of healthy parent-child relationships (Buchanan, Maccoby, and Dornbusch, 1991; Fauber et al., 1990; Patterson, 1982; Sessa and Steinberg, 1991). But what, exactly, is the impact of interparental conflict on the parent-adolescent relationship? Does it have an equally negative effect on the adolescent's relationship with each parent? Perhaps adolescents withdraw from both parents when those parents cannot get along, or perhaps neither parent has the energy to invest in the parent-child relationship under such circumstances. Alternatively, and more in line with Heider's prediction, interparental conflict may lead to alignment with a particular parent, an alignment that may be systematic in some fashion (for example, more often with mothers than with fathers; more often with a residential parent than with a nonresidential parent; more often with a same-sex parent than with an opposite-sex parent).

Given these unanswered questions, we looked at the relation of inter-parental conflict to adolescent-mother and adolescent-father closeness,[15] separately for each gender and residential arrangement, for sole-resident adolescents. The central question we sought to answer was whether interparental conflict was likely to interfere with the nonresidential parent–child relationship, and, if so, whether it was more likely to interfere with this relationship than with the relationship between the residential parent and child. We also wanted to know if the answers to these questions depended on the adolescent's sex or residential arrangement. In addition, we examined several indices of interparental conflict; in situations of divorce it might be important to distinguish between types and sources of conflict (for example, conflict specifically over co-parenting issues versus general parental hostility; or hostility toward the former spouse expressed by the residential versus nonresidential parent).

Table 10.2 displays the correlations between the various measures of interparental conflict and adolescents' closeness to their residential and nonresidential parents for all sole-resident adolescents combined, and for each sex by residence group.[16]

Interparental Conflict and Closeness to the Nonresidential Parent

In general, for adolescents living in either mother or father residence, a conflictual or noncooperative relationship between the parents was associated with a less close relationship between the adolescent and the nonresidential parent. Six of the seven measures of the interparental relationship (all except hostility of the nonresidential parent) were related to closeness to the nonresidential parent in the expected direction: higher conflict and hostility were linked to reduced closeness, and higher cooperation and agreement were linked with greater closeness. Hostility of the nonresidential parent was associated with less close relationships with the nonresidential parent only for girls in father residence.[17] Furthermore, the relation between several of the other conflict measures and closeness to the nonresidential parent was particularly strong for girls in father residence.[18] Thus girls' relationships with their nonresidential mothers appear especially vulnerable to interparental conflict. These findings also indicated that in father residence, girls' relationships with their mothers were more adversely affected by parental conflict than were boys' relationships with their mothers; in mother residence, any adverse impact of parental conflict on the relationship with father was similar for boys and girls.[19]

Table 10.2 Correlations between the interparental relationship and parent-adolescent closeness for adolescents in sole-residence arrangements at T4

Measure of the interparental relationship	All sole-resident adolescents[a]			Mother-resident boys[b]			Mother-resident girls[b]			Father-resident boys[b]			Father-resident girls[b]		
	n	NRP[c]	RP[d]	n	NRP	RP	n	NRP	RP	n	NRP	RP	n	NRP	RP
Parent Report															
Discord (T3)	287	−.16**	−.07	104	−.24*	−.11	122	−.14	−.02	38	.07	.07	23	−.26	−.27
Cooperative communication (T3)	286	.17**	.02	104	.14	−.07	121	.18+	.04	38	−.06	.09	23	.43*	.07
Residential parent's hostility (T3)	382	−.17**	−.02	137	−.25**	−.03	161	−.10	−.05	53	−.02	−.07	31	−.34+	.20
Nonresidential parent's hostility (T3)	317	−.09	−.08	108	.03	.02	136	−.10	−.16+	46	.11	.07	27	−.48*	.02
Adolescent Report															
Frequency of arguing (T4)	431	−.14**	−.00	148	−.06	.01	185	−.09	−.01	60	−.02	.08	38	−.57***	−.05
Parental agreement	437	.34***	.27***	151	.23***	.33***	187	.30***	.34***	61	.26*	.27*	38	.28+	.41*
Parental Cooperation (T4)	282	.24***	.29***	109	.10	.23*	106	.32***	.25*	45	.17	.56***	22	.39+	.17

a. Correlations partial the effects of age and sex of adolescent and residential arrangement.
b. Correlations partial the effects of age of adolescent.
c. NRP = nonresidential parent.
d. RP = residential parent.
+$p \leq .10$. *$p \leq .05$. **$p \leq .01$. ***$p \leq .001$.

We also looked at whether the relation between interparental conflict and adolescents' closeness to the nonresidential parent differed for older and younger adolescents, or for adolescents with different levels of contact with the nonresidential parent. There were only a couple of selective instances where age or level of contact mattered. Within the age range in our sample, older adolescents' relationships with their parents appeared slightly more susceptible to the negative influences of discord at T3. In addition, in some instances the relation between interparental conflict and a less close nonresidential parent–child relationship held primarily for adolescents who rarely saw their nonresidential parent. In these instances (the associations between T3 maternal hostility and closeness to nonresidential fathers, and between T4 parental arguing or agreement and closeness to nonresidential mothers), if the adolescent was spending regular time with the nonresidential parent—even if only for several weeks in the summer—the quality of the relationship with that parent appeared to be unaffected by the problems between the parents. This indicates that continued visitation with a nonresidential parent may help children to maintain positive ties with that parent even in the face of continued interparental disharmony.

Does the association between interparental conflict and lower levels of closeness to the nonresidential parent occur because, under conditions of interparental conflict, the residential parent is more likely to restrict access to the nonresidential parent? Our results suggest not. Accounting for nonresidential parent contact does not eliminate the relation between better interparental relationships and a closer nonresidential parent–child relationship. The associations between various measures of the interparental relationship and contact with the nonresidential parent were, overall, quite weak and seldom significant (see also Chapter 9). Only in the case of mother-resident boys was there some evidence of an indirect link between interparental conflict (mother's hostility in particular) and less close relationships with father because of reduced visitation. It thus appears that negative interparental relationships interfere with the parent-child relationship for reasons that are more emotional and psychological than a product of the amount of contact. Clearly, the negative emotions expressed by the residential parent may influence the child to view the nonresidential parent more negatively. Alternatively, characteristics of the nonresidential parent may stimulate interparental conflict or hostility as well as difficulty in developing or sustaining a close parent-child relationship.

Interparental Conflict and Closeness to the Residential Parent

In contrast to the findings regarding closeness to the nonresidential parent, closeness to the residential parent was not related to the level of conflict or cooperation between parents as reported by the parents themselves, to the degree of hostility between parents, or to adolescent-reported frequency of parental arguing. Only adolescents' reports of parental cooperation or agreement at T4 were consistently associated with closeness to the residential parent. And only for older adolescents was hostility on the part of either parent—but especially the residential parent—associated with lower levels of closeness to the residential parent.[20]

Summary

For four of the seven conflict measures we used (T3 cooperation, residential parent hostility, nonresidential parent hostility, and T4 frequency of arguing), interparental conflict was most likely to interfere with the nonresidential parent–child relationship.[21] This was true for boys and girls who were living with their mothers, but for adolescents living with their fathers, interparental conflict interfered with the relationship with nonresidential mothers primarily or only among girls (see Figure 10.7 for an illustration using residential parent's hostility).

Parental cooperation and agreement as reported by adolescents at T4, in contrast to the other parental relationship measures, were related as strongly to closeness to the residential parent as they were to the nonresidential parent. Perhaps when both parents—in the adolescents' eyes—were trying to cooperate at the time of the final interview both enhanced their relationships with that adolescent. It is also possible, however, that adolescents' own reports of parental cooperation or agreement were biased by the adolescents' feelings of closeness to both parents; in other words, when adolescents felt close to both parents, they might also have been more likely to view them as cooperative. Even with these caveats, most of our results suggest that ongoing interparental conflict is more likely to interfere with the nonresidential parent–child relationship.

In sum, the circumstances of high interparental conflict appear to make it difficult for adolescents to develop or sustain close relationships to the nonresidential parent. To some extent, the adolescent's relationships with both parents may be vulnerable to the effects of conflict, but the vulnerability appears greatest for the nonresidential parent, particularly the non-

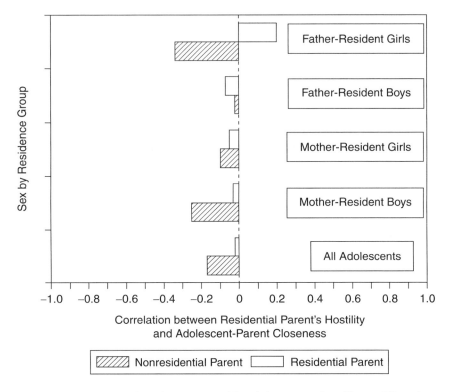

Figure 10.7 Correlations between residential parent's hostility at T3 and adolescents' closeness to both residential and nonresidential parents, by residence and sex of adolescent. Correlations are adjusted for age of adolescent.

residential mothers of girls who live primarily with their fathers. Is this evidence for alignment as a consequence of parental conflict? In a sense, yes, because adolescents may experience differential levels of closeness with the two parents, typically feeling closer to the residential parent under conditions of parental conflict. There is more evidence for alignment than there is for adolescent children's withdrawal from both parents.

Interparental Conflict, Closeness to the Nonresidential Parent, and Adolescent Adjustment

Earlier we reported generally positive findings regarding maintaining a close relationship with the nonresidential parent and adolescent adjustment. We wondered, however, if maintaining a close relationship with the nonresidential parent would be especially beneficial under conditions where parents got along with each other, and perhaps especially harmful when parents were still highly conflicted. Therefore we investigated how interparental conflict or cooperation interacted with parent-adolescent closeness in predicting adjustment. We also considered residential arrangement in order to see whether the effects of experiencing different patterns of interparental conflict and parent-child closeness depended on whether the adolescent's nonresidential parent was the mother or the father.[22]

We found little support for this interactive hypothesis. For example, using discord at T3 as the measure of interparental conflict, we found that depression was lowest among adolescents who reported both high closeness to the nonresidential parent and low interparental discord (see Figure 10.8). Under conditions of high interparental discord, the quality

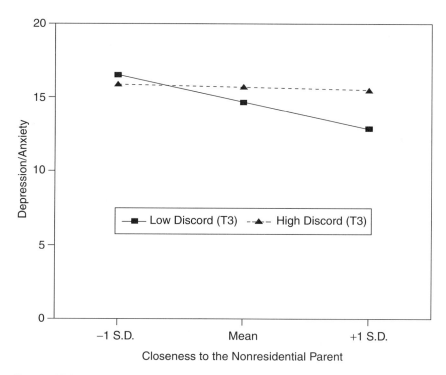

Figure 10.8 Depression/anxiety at different levels of interparental discord at T3, by level of adolescent's closeness to the nonresidential parent.

of the relationship with the nonresidential parent was of little consequence; being close to the nonresidential parent in conditions of high
conflict was neither detrimental nor beneficial. Thus in some cases adolescents may benefit from the combination of close relationships with the
nonresidential parent and positive interparental relationships even more
than they would from each factor independently. But there were many
instances in which no interactive effects of these two factors were found,
indicating that in most instances the two factors were independent.

Summary

The majority of the adolescents in our study continued to maintain some
kind of contact with their nonresidential parent after the divorce (see
Chapter 9). The quality of nonresidential father–child relationships was
lower on many indices than the quality of the relationship between those
children and their residential mothers. This is not surprising, because children—even in nondivorced families—are often closer to mothers
(Youniss and Smollar, 1983), and the greater contact with a residential
parent provides more opportunities to develop or sustain closeness, trust,
and intimacy. What is perhaps more surprising is the similarity in the
relationships with residential fathers and with nonresidential mothers
among boys. Even when boys were not living with their mothers, they
managed to stay almost as closely involved with them as they did with their
residential fathers. Girls in father residence, although similar on some
dimensions in their relationships with father and mother, were more likely
than boys to favor their relationships with their residential fathers.

In line with these observations, the quality of the relationship between
an adolescent boy and his nonresidential parent depended on whether
the nonresidential parent was a mother or a father. Father-resident boys
reported greater intimacy on a variety of measures with their nonresidential mothers than did mother-resident boys with their nonresidential
fathers. For girls, in comparison with boys, there was less evidence of
intimacy with the nonresidential mother; instead, these girls reported
higher levels of friction. Girls also reported more distance and somewhat
more conflict with nonresidential mothers than with residential mothers,
while boys' relationships with mothers were good regardless of their
residential status. Considered together, these results indicate a potentially troubled relationship between girls and nonresidential mothers
(particularly because of the higher levels of conflict) and a particularly
good relationship between boys and nonresidential mothers.

What is the role of the nonresidential parent in adolescent adjustment? Again, we have to begin by acknowledging that the causal direction of the associations that emerged is not clear. Our findings do, however, suggest that a continuing relationship with the nonresidential parent contributes positively to adolescent adjustment, although the magnitude of any general effect is modest. The aspects of the relationship that have this modest but positive relation with good adjustment are the overall closeness of the nonresidential parent–child relationship and the tendency of nonresidential parents to remember special days and holidays. Conflict with and disengagement from the nonresidential parent were less consistently related to adolescent adjustment. Furthermore, father-resident adolescents especially appeared to need a close relationship with both parents—having a close relationship with only one parent, father or mother, did not enhance adjustment. For adolescents in mother residence, in contrast, the relationship with their mother was clearly most strongly related to adjustment; adolescents were better off the closer they were to their mother,[23] regardless of their closeness to their father. The closeness of the father-adolescent relationship made an additional, though small, contribution to adjustment. As in father residence, however, closeness to the nonresidential parent alone was not especially helpful for adolescents.

We did not find that maintaining a close relationship with a nonresidential parent in situations of interparental conflict was especially harmful. We did find that ongoing conflict between parents can interfere with an adolescent's relationship with the nonresidential parent, however. Such conflict appears to have little or no bearing on the adolescent's relationship with the residential parent. These findings support the view that it is difficult for an adolescent to remain close to both parents when those parents are in conflict, and suggest that the most likely result of interparental conflict is a worsening of the relationship with the parent whom an adolescent sees least. Of course, it is also possible that adolescents have poor relationships with those same nonresidential parents with whom the residential parent finds it hardest to get along; only longitudinal data looking at the changes in the quality of the nonresidential parent–child relationship over time can distinguish between these possibilities.

11

Feeling Caught between
One's Parents

As we attempt to understand the experience of being part of two homes and two families, the issue of loyalty conflicts comes to the fore. It has been assumed by both popular and academic writers that feeling love and allegiance toward both parents after a divorce generates internal conflicts in children. Loyalty toward one parent is thought to preclude or interfere with the love for the other parent if the two parents do not love each other (Heider, 1958; Johnston and Campbell, 1987), so that when parents divorce, children are put in the position of having to choose between their parents and yet not being able to make such a heart-rending choice. Yet despite references to this concept in popular writing (for example, Rosemond, 1994) as well as in the scholarly divorce literature (for example, Clingempeel and Segal, 1986; Goldstein, Freud, and Solnit, 1979; Johnston and Campbell, 1987; Levy and Chambers, 1981; Shiller, 1986b; Wallerstein and Blakeslee, 1989; Wallerstein and Kelly, 1980), there has been little empirical research on loyalty conflicts. Detailed discussions tend to be clinical in nature (see, for example, Johnston and Campbell, 1987; Oppawsky, 1989; Wallerstein and Kelly, 1980) and based on clinical assessments or case studies. In our study, we attempted to study loyalty conflicts systematically in a broad sample of adolescent children of divorce, and examine both the predictors and the consequences of such conflicts.

It is a tenet of family systems theory that healthy family functioning requires the maintenance of clear boundaries between the parental subsystem and the children. These boundaries are obviously weakened when children are drawn into parental negotiations, tensions, or active conflicts; children can thereby feel pressure to take sides or form alliances with one parent or the other. Boundaries can be eroded in a number of

Table 11.1   Questions assessing adolescents' experience of feeling caught between their parents

How often do you feel caught in the middle between your mother and your father? (1 = never, to 4 = very often)

How often does your mother [father] ask you to carry messages to your father [mother]? (1 = never, to 4 = very often; maximum score between mother and father used)

Does your mother [father] ever ask questions about your father's [mother's] home that you wish she [he] wouldn't ask? (1 = yes, 2 = no; maximum score between mother and father used)

When your mother [father] is around, how often do you hesitate to talk about things concerning your father [mother]? (1 = never, to 4 = very often; maximum score between mother and father used)

ways, as for example when one or both parents use the child as a confidant or as a go-between. The consequences for children of playing such roles are expected to be stress, confusion, and anxiety (Aponte and Van Deusen, 1981; Emery, 1988; Minuchin, 1974).

We asked our adolescents several questions intended to capture the extent to which they felt caught between their parents (see Table 11.1). First, adolescents answered the direct question "How often do you feel caught in the middle between your mother and your father?," intended to assess subjective feelings of being caught. In addition, they were asked about aspects of parental behavior that might indicate potential triangulation or boundary diffusion (specifically, parents' attempts to use the adolescent as either a message carrier or an informer) as well as their feelings of needing to hide emotions or information regarding one parent from the other. Although all adolescents answered the first question ("how often do you feel caught"), the other questions were only asked of adolescents who had enough face-to-face or telephone contact with each parent to be able to answer the question. The answers to these questions were combined to create an overall index of the extent to which an adolescent felt caught between his or her parents (see Buchanan, Maccoby, and Dornbusch, 1991, for more details).

Adolescents' Comments

Almost two-thirds of the adolescents in our sample said that they felt caught between their parents at least sometimes. Ten percent said they felt caught "very often." For adolescents who said they felt caught at least sometimes, we then asked if they could give us an example of an instance in which they felt that way. Adolescents had little trouble answering these questions, and their responses helped us to understand the variety of situations that led to such feelings.

As anticipated, one commonly mentioned scenario involved parents asking their children to carry messages. Adolescents described a number of situations involving communication between their parents when asked to give an example of something that made them feel caught:

> (Early-adolescent female): "When one parent tells me to tell the other one something, tell them this and tell them that. Tell her that I don't want you to do that anymore or something. Things like that."

> (Early-adolescent female): "Like when they're arguing and my dad doesn't want to talk to my mom. I can't be all that specific, but . . . he's trying to yell at her through me, and I have to tell her these things, that, you know, kind of feel caught in the middle because . . . you're just telling her things you don't want to tell her."

> (Early-adolescent male): "Like when my parents disagree on paying for . . . something, usually I have to talk on the phone for them 'cause they don't want to talk to each other."

> (Mid-adolescent female): "Usually my father will say he doesn't have enough money to buy . . . something that [my sibling or I] need or that we want and he'll say, 'Tell your mother to get it,' and then we'll say, 'Mom, he said he can't 'cause he doesn't have enough money,' and she'll make that dissatisfied noise that all parents make."

Adolescents clearly had difficulty carrying messages that were angry, disparaged the other parent in some way, or touched on sensitive issues such as child support payments. It is easy to see why it would be hard to tell a parent, "Dad said to tell you you're money-hungry" or "Mom said to tell you you're just being stubborn." Yet comments from those we interviewed suggested that even being asked to carry seemingly harmless messages can be stressful. Adolescents do not feel comfortable with the responsibility of carrying adult messages, especially because they can then become the target of frustration for any confusion or misunderstanding in the messages relayed. For example, one boy said that he felt caught when he had to tell his mother about when he would visit her. If he got mixed up on the times, both parents would be angry with him. Because of this, he wished his father would make the arrangements directly with his mother.

We also had anticipated that children would feel caught between their parents if asked by either of them to report on the other home or parent. This expectation was supported by some of the responses to the question "Can you give me an example of what makes you feel caught?" One girl who lived with her mother expressed her frustration:

> "[I feel caught] every time I go visit [my father]. I come home and I'm bombarded with twenty questions . . . I always get it because [my mother] thinks, you know, [my father's new partner] is going to try and turn me around, put me against her or something, but that's not going to happen. That's why she's asking 20 million questions."

Another girl complained:

> "My father will tell my mom he's going to do something, and then she'll ask me if he's done it. I get caught in the middle."

One boy in mother residence did not mention the issue of parents asking questions in the context of feeling caught between one's parents, but he ended the interview by telling us:

> "After I finish getting back from visiting my father, I get interrogated by my mom. You know what I mean? Like 'What happened?' This and that. 'Where did you go?' You know, 'Did he say anything about me?' [Interviewer: How did you feel about that?] Real uncomfortable. I don't like it."

Another commonly mentioned cause of feeling caught between one's parents was the denigration of one parent by the other in the child's presence. Many such instances were reported. This kind of behavior put children in the uncomfortable position of feeling that they needed to defend the parent being criticized. Here are some examples:

> (Late-adolescent female): "My dad would cut down my mom for things she'd done, and I'd defend her. And my mom would cut down my dad for things he'd done and I'd defend him, and I was in the middle, and they both thought I was against them, and they'd always use me as an in-between instead of talking to each other. They'd tell me what they were upset at the other person for, and they'd expect me to tell them that, and then I was out of bounds."

> (Mid-adolescent female): "My dad kinda knows that I am, you know, I'm with my mom, and he talks about her sometimes, and he tries to tell me not to say anything to her. Or my mom will complain about how much money Dad gives us. [Interviewer: He knows you're closer (to your mom)?] Yeah, we're closer, and sometimes he tries to cut her down."

(Mid-adolescent female): "My mom says things about my dad, and I don't know what to say . . . Sometimes my dad will say things about Mom is like, taking all this money."

(Mid-adolescent female): "Just when, like, I guess one of them mentions, 'I can't believe what he did' or 'what she did.' Or 'He's not such and such' or 'She's not such and such' like mature enough to handle it or something like that."

A final common thread was adolescents' experience of explicitly being made to choose between their parents in some way. Sometimes parents went so far as to ask the child whom he or she loved most; in many other cases they did not demand such a direct choice, but they taxed the child with decisions about with whom to spend the holidays, with whom to live, or simply with whom to spend time on a particular occasion. These latter kinds of decisions can be extremely difficult for children to make, because the choice is seen as an indication of preference for one parent over the other:

(Late-adolescent male): "Well, sometimes they used to try to put me on the spot and ask me about which one I'd rather live with in front of the other."

(Early-adolescent female): "Sometimes when they ask me who would I rather be with or who do I like most."

(Early-adolescent male): "[When] they were going to split up . . . we had to choose who we were going to go with . . . I didn't want to leave my mom or dad."

(Mid-adolescent male): "My mom wants me, and my dad wants me at the same time that weekend, and he's making us choose."

These excerpts summarize some of the main themes in the adolescents' comments concerning feelings of being torn between their parents. Other issues were mentioned as well. Many adolescents simply said that they felt caught when parents fought, and some felt especially uncomfortable when parents fought over something that had to do with them. Other adolescents felt caught when parents compared homes, or when parents told them conflicting stories concerning the divorce or the interparental relationship. What kinds of family circumstances increase the likelihood of these events occurring? And what aspects of children make them more or less vulnerable to feeling caught in response to potentially difficult situations?

Predictors of Feeling Caught between One's Parents

Characteristics of the Adolescent

It is possible that factors within the child, as well as from the child's environment, affect the likelihood that any particular child will experience loyalty conflicts. For instance, as others have pointed out (Kalter and Rembar, 1981; Wallerstein and Kelly, 1980), children's level of cognitive and emotional maturity will influence how they react to interparental conflict and divorce. Children's capacity to reason about parental conflict, including the ability to understand multiple perspectives or to understand in realistic terms one's own responsibility (or lack thereof) for parental conflict and its resolution, will certainly be related to their tendency to experience loyalty conflicts. Thus the age of the child is one "child" factor that is likely to be a predictor of feeling or being caught between one's parents.

Similarly, sex differences in the desire or willingness to take on responsibility for keeping parents happy, or to attempt to remain loyal to two "warring" parties, are likely to lead to sex differences in the tendency to become caught between one's parents. There is some evidence that females are more often concerned with maintaining harmonious interpersonal relationships and with resolving conflict in mutually satisfying ways (Gilligan, 1982; Maccoby, 1990; Miller, Danaher, and Forbes, 1986), and that their higher interpersonal caring orientation leads to greater emotional distress (Gore, Aseltine, and Colten, 1993). If this is so, we might expect girls to be more likely than boys to be caught between their parents.

Among our interviewees (who ranged in age from ten to eighteen), older adolescents were somewhat more likely to report feelings of being caught between their parents than were younger adolescents. The correlation between age and feelings of being caught was small but significant ($r = .12$). Girls ($M = 5.1$) reported more feelings of being caught than did boys ($M = 4.4$). The sex difference was virtually the same for older as for younger adolescents.

Characteristics of the Family Environment

Factors external to the child that might predict the extent of loyalty conflicts include the degree of interparental conflict, the level of contact with each parent, the quality of the adolescent's relationships with each

Table 11.2 Relations between the interparental relationship and feelings of being caught between one's parents[a]

Measure of the interparental relationship	Relation to "feeling caught"	
	β	*t*
Discord (T3) (*n* = 339)	.27	5.14****
Cooperative communication (T3) (*n* = 338)	−.19	−3.56***
Maximum hostility (T3) (*n* = 513)	.19	4.40****
Frequency of arguing (T4) (*n* = 514)	.33	8.07****
Cooperation (T4) (*n* = 334)	−.19	−3.48***

a. Statistics are from regression equations that control for age and sex of adolescent.

***$p \leq .001$.   ****$p \leq .0001$.

parent, and the existence of new romantic partners for one or both parents.

We expected loyalty conflicts to be higher when interparental conflict was higher, due to increases in parental pressure to take sides as well as to increased fear of negative consequences of loyalty to one or the other parent (Aponte and Van Deusen, 1981; Emery, 1988), and this is what we found. Regardless of the measure of interparental relationships used—whether level of conflict, hostility, or cooperation between the parents, and whether reported by parent or adolescent—the quality of the interparental relationship was associated with the tendency to feel caught between one's parents (see Table 11.2).

Although the extent to which parents disagree or argue after divorce and the extent to which they talk to each other and attempt to work together are related, they also represent two separate dimensions of parenting. The intersection of these two dimensions is likely to be important when considering effects on children. For example, Maccoby, Depner, and Mnookin (1990) identified four co-parenting patterns based on the degree to which parents disagreed and tried to undermine each other in parenting and the degree to which they tried to communicate and work cooperatively in co-parenting. "Conflicted" parents were high in conflict and low in cooperation. "Cooperative" parents were high in cooperation and low in conflict. "Disengaged" parents were low in both conflict and cooperation. The fourth combination—high in both conflict and cooperation—was relatively rare and will not be considered here. When we examined feelings of being caught among adolescents whose parents

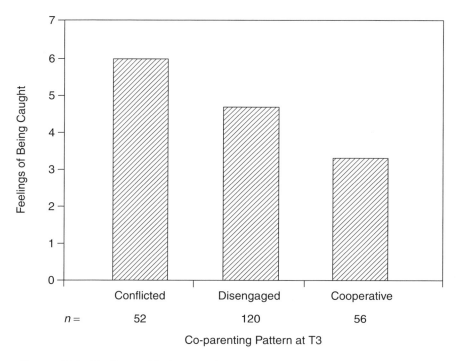

Figure 11.1 Feelings of being caught between one's parents by co-parenting pattern at T3. Means are adjusted for age and sex of adolescent and are based on a sample of only one adolescent per family, randomly selected.

displayed each of the three more common patterns, we found that adolescents from conflicted families were more likely to feel caught than adolescents from disengaged families, who were in turn more likely to feel caught than adolescents from cooperative families (see Figure 11.1).

The relation between interparental conflict and feelings of being caught was very similar for older and younger adolescents. There was some indication, however, that the relation was stronger for girls than for boys when using adolescents' own perceptions of the relationship between their parents as the index of parental interaction. Feelings of being caught were higher for both boys and girls under conditions of high arguing at T4 or low cooperation at T4, but the difference in feeling caught between those situations and more harmonious conditions was greater for girls (see Figure 11.2 for the findings for T4 parental arguing). Sex differences in the response to the quality of the interparental relationship did not emerge for any measures of relationship quality as re-

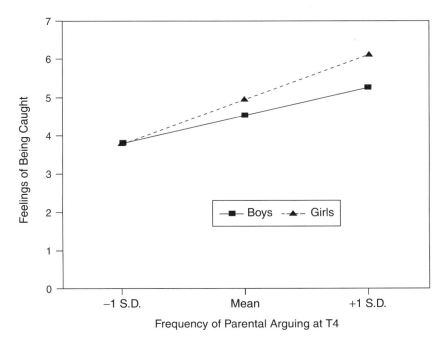

Figure 11.2 Feelings of being caught between one's parents by frequency of parental arguing at T4 and sex of adolescent. Means are adjusted for age of adolescent.

ported by parents. These results concerning adolescent-reported interparental cooperation and frequency of parental arguing also modify our interpretation of the sex difference reported earlier. Sex differences in feelings of being caught occurred mainly when parents were perceived as being very uncooperative or argumentative. There was virtually no difference in boys' and girls' reports of feeling caught at low levels of adolescent-reported conflict (or high cooperation); the sex difference emerged when parents were reported to get along poorly.

One of the fears professionals have had about joint custody is that high levels of contact with both parents after a divorce—especially when parents maintain high levels of conflict—will lead to situations in which children become caught between their parents, presumably because there is greater opportunity for parents to use children as mediators in their conflicts. To see whether feelings of being caught were related to the amount of time spent with each parent, we examined both residential arrangement (sole-mother, sole-father, and dual residence) and visitation arrangements (for those adolescents in sole-residence arrangements). The amount of visitation for sole-resident adolescents was not related to feelings of being caught. Residential arrangement was marginally related to being caught between one's parents, but contrary to some predictions it was adolescents in father residence—rather than those in dual residence—who were most likely to feel caught.[1] The mean levels of feeling caught for mother residence, dual residence, and father residence were 4.7, 4.1, and 5.4, respectively. Thus we do not find that spending substantial time with both parents, in and of itself, leads to more feelings of being caught between their parents for adolescent children of divorce.

We looked next at whether the effects of level of contact on feeling caught between one's parents were dependent on the co-parenting relationship. In other words, we wanted to know whether adolescents who spent considerable time in both households (for example, dual-resident adolescents) were more likely than other adolescents to feel caught between their parents if those parents were in high conflict.[2] We found that when parents were in high conflict (or low in cooperation), dual-resident adolescents were more likely than sole-resident adolescents to report feeling caught between their parents. When parents got along well (didn't fight, did cooperate, were not hostile), however, dual-resident adolescents were less likely than sole-resident adolescents to feel caught between their parents (see Figure 11.3). This interactive effect of dual residence and interparental conflict was the same for boys and girls.

The very definition of "loyalty conflict" implies that children who feel strong emotional ties to both parents will be more likely to feel torn between those parents, particularly when they cannot get along with each other. To examine this assumption, we divided adolescents (at the median) into "High" and "Low" groups on both closeness to mother and closeness to father. Adolescents at the median were included in the "Low" closeness group. We then combined "High/Low" closeness to mother with "High/Low" closeness to father to form the following categories: "close to two parents," "close to only one parent," and "close to neither parent." Contrary to our expectations, adolescents who were close to both parents reported fewer feelings of being caught between their parents ($M = 4.1$) than adolescents who were close to only one parent ($M = 5.2$) or who were not close to either parent ($M = 5.1$). This was true of older and younger adolescents, and of boys and girls.

Was being close to both parents conducive to loyalty conflicts in situations where those parents were in high conflict? No. Regardless of level of conflict, the adolescents least likely to feel caught were those who felt

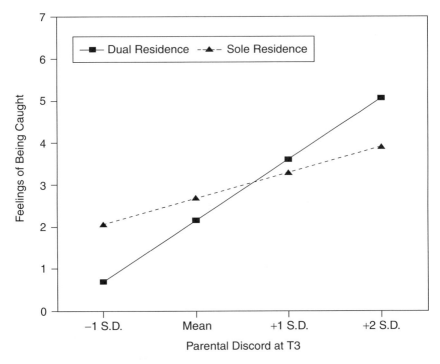

Figure 11.3 Feelings of being caught between one's parents by residential arrangement and level of parental discord at T3. Means are adjusted for age and sex of adolescent.

close to both parents. And the relation between parent-adolescent close-ness and feeling caught did not vary depending on whether we considered the residential or the nonresidential parent: closeness to either parent was associated with lower feelings of being caught. These findings, of course, raise questions about the direction of effect. It very well may be that adolescents who feel caught between their parents are thereby pre-cluded from feeling very close to one or both parents, whereas adoles-cents who do not feel caught between their parents are free to maintain good relationships with both.

Finally, does the presence of a new partner for one or both parents increase the likelihood of loyalty conflicts among adolescents? Lutz (1983) identified divided loyalties as the most stressful issue for adoles-cents in stepfamilies, and other authors have speculated about the impor-tance of divided loyalties among children whose parents remarry. The entrance of new partners may lead to loyalty conflicts because these newcomers potentially represent new and additional parent figures; children may see these new partners as competitors for their affection with the biological parent of the same sex. Our findings suggest, however, that in the usual case a mother's remarriage does not alienate mother-resident children from their fathers (see Chapter 7), nor does it augment adolescents' feelings of being caught between their parents (see Figure 11.4). Rather than feeling more caught between their parents as a result of the presence of two—perhaps competing—father figures, adolescents whose mothers had remarried felt less caught than adolescents whose mothers had not remarried.[3] Among father-resident adolescents, those whose fathers were dating felt less caught between their parents than did those

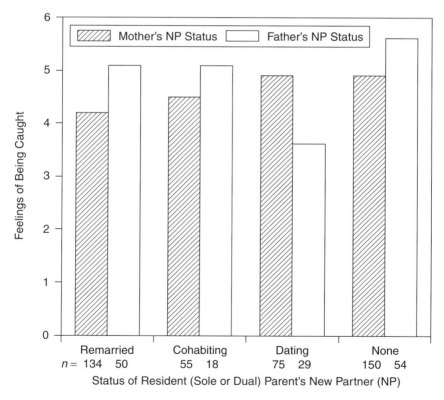

Figure 11.4 Feelings of being caught between one's parents by residential parent's new partner status. Means are adjusted for age and sex of adolescent and residential parent's education.

in the other three groups. Divided loyalties appear to be an issue faced by children of divorce regardless of whether their parents form new relationships; the residential parent's involvement with a new person per se does not appear to intensify those feelings—at least not four and a half years after parental separation.

Did a residential parent's involvement with a new partner lead to loyalty conflicts if the adolescent was especially close to the nonresidential parent? To the extent that we can address this question, the answer is no. In line with the findings just reported, greater closeness to a nonresidential parent was linked to a lower likelihood of feeling caught regardless of whether the residential parent had a new partner.

Feeling Caught between One's Parents and Adolescent Adjustment

In the absence of longitudinal data, we cannot truly talk about consequences of feelings of being caught. Conceptually, however, loyalty conflicts are presumed to lead to negative outcomes, particularly anxiety and emotional stress, for children. We expected, then, that more feelings of being caught between one's parents would be associated with poorer adjustment, especially "internalizing" aspects of adjustment. Indeed, we found this to be the case. Feelings of being caught were clearly related to higher levels of depression/anxiety ($r = .39$,[4] $p \le .0001$). This link was the same for both genders (although somewhat stronger for girls than for boys) and in all residence groups. Feelings of being caught were also related to higher levels of deviant behavior ($r = .19$,[5] $p \le .0001$), although the link between feeling caught and deviance was not as high as that for feeling caught and depression/anxiety. Feelings of being caught were not related to school adjustment as measured by grades or school effort.

Do feelings of being caught between one's parents help to explain why interparental conflict more often than not has negative effects on children's adjustment? In other words, do feelings of being caught "mediate" a relation between the quality of the interparental relationship and adolescent adjustment? We have some evidence that they do. Although the direct relations between measures of the interparental relationship and adolescent adjustment were not very strong in our sample—certainly not as strong as we had expected them to be based on previous work (see Chapter 6 for discussion)—we investigated whether the links that did exist were reduced or eliminated if we introduced feelings of being caught into analyses predicting adjustment with interparental conflict or

Table 11.3 Relations between the interparental relationship and adolescent adjustment, with and without controlling for feelings of being caught between parents[a]

	Relation to depression		Relation to deviance	
	Without "feeling caught"	With "feeling caught"	Without "feeling caught"	With "feeling caught"
Measure of the interparental relationship	β	β	β	β
Discord (T3)	.09+	−.01	.07	.02
Cooperative communication (T3)	−.00	.07	.01	.05
Maximum hostility (T3)	.02	−.04	.08*	.05
Frequency of arguing (T4)	.18****	.06	.19****	.15***
Parental agreement (T4)	−.16****	−.10*	−.10**	−.07+
Cooperation (T4)	−.09+	−.02	−.06	−.03

a. Statistics are from regression equations that control for age and sex of adolescent and residential arrangement.

$+p \leq .10$. $*p \leq .05$. $**p \leq .01$. $***p \leq .001$. $****p \leq .0001$.

cooperation. If introducing feelings of being caught into these analyses decreased the link between the quality of the interparental relationship and adolescent adjustment, we would have evidence that the effects of interparental conflict on children are due, at least in part, to the fact that conflict leads to loyalty conflicts (Baron and Kenny, 1986).

Table 11.3 shows the magnitude of the relations between various measures of the interparental relationship and both depression/anxiety and deviance, with and without the inclusion of feelings of being caught between one's parents in the same analysis.[6] The results suggest that feelings of being caught do partly explain the relation between frequency of parental arguing at T4 and depression, as well as the smaller relations between both discord at T3 and cooperation at T4 and depression. The evidence that feelings of being caught mediate the link between interparental conflict or cooperation and deviance is weaker, although there is a small reduction in the magnitude of the relation between deviance and five of the six measures of interparental functioning (all except cooperative communication at T3) when "feeling caught" is also included in the predictive equation.

Figures 11.5 and 11.6 depict the role of "feeling caught" as a mediator of discord at T3 (Figure 11.5) and frequency of arguing at T4 (Figure 11.6)

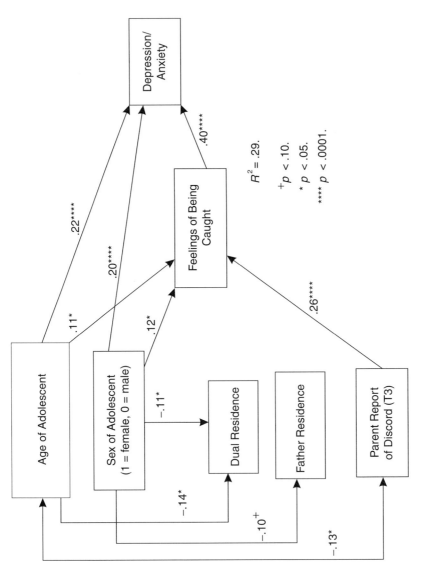

Figure 11.5 Model predicting depression/anxiety with feelings of being caught between one's parents and interparental discord at T3. Adapted with permission from Buchanan, Maccoby, and Dornbusch (1991), © The Society for Research in Child Development, Inc.

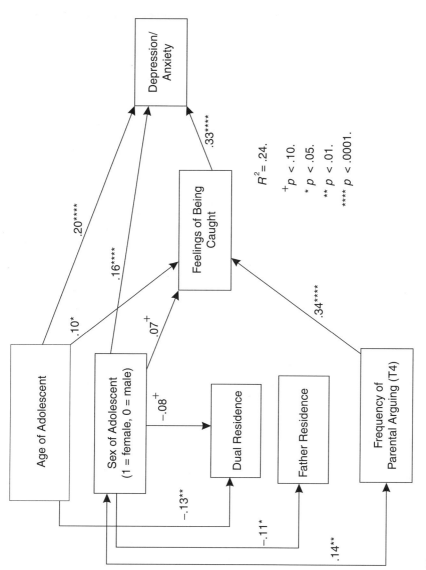

Figure 11.6 Model predicting depression/anxiety with feelings of being caught between one's parents and frequency of parental arguing at T4.

and adolescent depression/anxiety. These figures illustrate two of the instances in which we found no direct relation between the interparental measures and adolescent adjustment once feelings of being caught were accounted for, indicating that when interparental conflict does have an impact on adjustment, it does so by generating feelings in the adolescent of being caught between his or her parents.

Because the magnitude of the association between the interparental relationship and adjustment varied for boys and girls, and for adolescents in the different residential arrangements (see Chapter 6), we also looked at evidence for mediation in each subgroup of adolescents. We found more instances of mediation for girls than for boys, especially for girls in dual or father residence. Thus we did find some evidence that feelings of being caught mediate a relation between interparental conflict and adjustment, although we would expect this evidence to be stronger if we had better distinguished between general parental conflict prior to Time 4 and instances of conflict to which the adolescents were currently being exposed when we interviewed them at T4.

In summary, the fact that children (in this case, adolescent children) are more likely to feel caught between their parents when the adults have a great deal of conflict between them may help to explain why adjustment problems are often found among children in high-conflict situations. As we noted in an earlier report, parental conflict may change interactions among family members in such a way that "either the child is explicitly drawn into the conflict and/or becomes fearful of what effect a positive relationship with one parent will have on the other parent. Stress from the parent-parent relationship is, in this sense, shared with or diverted to the parent-child relationships, and this stress appears to have negative consequences in terms of adjustment" (Buchanan, Maccoby, and Dornbusch, 1991), particularly in regard to internalizing symptoms like depression or anxiety. These results also imply, however, that even if parents are in conflict, if they can avoid actions that lead children to feel caught—for example, avoid using the child as a go-between or an informer, or avoid denigrating the former spouse—the impact of that conflict on the child might be reduced.

Summary

Feeling caught between their parents is an issue many children face when parents divorce. A number of our adolescents told us graphically and in detail how difficult it was to deal with parents competing for their loyalty, using them as intermediaries or openly disparaging each other. The more intense the interparental conflict, the more likely it was that the children would feel caught up in the conflict in some way. And those adolescents who reported being caught between their parents showed more symptoms of maladjustment (depression and deviance).

What, besides interparental conflict, increases or diminishes the likelihood that adolescents will feel caught between their parents? Gender is one factor: girls are more likely to experience this problem. We expected that such feelings might be especially common among those children who had high levels of contact with both parents, either through dual residence or high levels of visitation, but this did not turn out to be the case. Dual residence was associated with higher levels of feeling caught if the parents were in high conflict, but dual-resident adolescents had the lowest "caught" feelings of all residential groups when their parents were cooperative. Spending substantial time with both parents thus does not automatically lead to being caught between them. Considering just the three residential arrangements by themselves, adolescents living with their fathers were the most likely to feel caught between their parents; this may have something to do with the unique circumstances under which father residence often comes about (see Chapter 5 for a more detailed discussion), in particular the higher levels of conflict in the history of these families. We also might have attributed the greater tendency of father-resident adolescents to feel caught between their parents to adolescents' stronger emotional ties to their mothers (see Chapters 5 and 10), except that we found no evidence to support a link between greater closeness to parents and greater feelings of being caught. The closer adolescents were to their parents—residential or nonresidential—the less likely they were to report feeling caught. In fact, adolescents were least likely to feel caught if they were close to both parents.

We conclude that loyalty conflicts, though common, are not by any means a necessary accompaniment of divorce. We have pointed to several individual and family factors that increase the likelihood that children will experience loyalty conflicts, the most important of which is the level of conflict parents maintain with each other during the postdivorce period and how careful they are to insulate the children from whatever conflict does continue to occur. In Chapter 12, we will see that inconsistencies in parental standards across the two households constitute another risk factor.

12

Inconsistency in Parenting

Consistency of parenting—with regard to how rules are created, what the rules are, methods of discipline, and expectations for behavior—is thought to be an important influence on a child's behavioral and emotional development. Consistency can be thought of as a within-parent phenomenon (how consistent is a mother over time, or a father over time?) or a between-parent phenomenon (how similar are a mother and father in their child-rearing behavior?). In keeping with our interest in adolescents' experience in two homes, this chapter is concerned with the latter: consistency between mother and father. Most research on consistency of parenting has been done with nondivorced families (see, for example, Block, Block, and Morrison, 1981; Deal, Halverson, and Wampler, 1989; Gjerde, 1988; Stoneman, Brody, and Burke, 1989; Vaughn, Block, and Block, 1988). Yet after divorce, opportunities and inclinations for parents to communicate about their rules and expectations are greatly reduced, raising the probability of inconsistent parenting. Among parents interviewed in the Stanford Child Custody Study at T3, only about one-third of the parents said that they were attempting to coordinate rules between the two households (Maccoby and Mnookin, 1992). When children interact with parents who live in separate homes, inconsistency between parents regarding rules and expectations for behavior may become a central issue in the child's life.

Consistency across parents might be important with regard to children's adjustment for several reasons. Disagreement between parents in their child-rearing may send confusing messages, so that the child does not know the true standards for appropriate behavior. One early-adolescent girl complained: "I don't like it 'cause all the rules are different," and went on to describe differences in expectations for how she dressed, what she ate, and the chores she had to do. Such confusion may be disconcerting to children who are trying to learn appropriate standards for behavior. In addition, it may be frustrating, even anxiety provoking, to try to remember or predict which behavior is appropriate in which situation as a child moves back and forth between homes.

Different rules on the part of each parent may also interfere with the child's relationship with one or the other parent—say, distancing the child from the parent whose rules or methods of parenting the child likes least, or creating conflict between the child and this parent. For instance, Stoneman and colleagues (1989) found that parental disagreement over discipline among married parents was related to increased conflict between mothers and daughters.

It is also possible that children, especially older children and adolescents, realize that they can manipulate parents who don't agree with each other. By using one parent against the other, children can end up setting their own standards and rules for behavior or at least evading discipline for deviating from parental standards. For example, if a parent establishes rules that the child does not like, children are more likely to be able to manipulate that parent into changing—or not enforcing—those rules if they can say that the other parent would not require the same behavior. Or, in situations of divorce, children may choose to spend more time with a more lenient parent. One late-adolescent male was quite open about how he took advantage of the situation:

> "I like that the supervision isn't so strong. I can get away with much more. I can take advantage of my parents. If one is being bad, I can go live with the other for a few weeks. It seems that parent tries harder to win your respect."

In nondivorced families where parents do not provide clear, consistent limits and expectations—where children are left to define their own limits—children are more likely to show both behavioral and emotional problems (Patterson, 1982). Adolescent children of divorce who are capable of manipulating parents in these ways may be more susceptible to becoming involved in the norm-breaking or risk-taking behavior common among adolescents who are not expected to abide by clear, reasonable expectations. Thus one might find higher levels of both minor and major forms of deviance among adolescent children in such situations, as they either openly or covertly manipulate parents' differences about rules and expectations to take part in those activities and behaviors that appear most appealing.

Finally, disunity between parents may cause a child to experience loyalty conflicts. Many of the elements of feeling caught between parents, described in Chapter 11, may be exacerbated by inconsistent parenting across homes. For instance, children may simply feel torn between the differing expectations of the two parents. Or they may be afraid to talk about one parent in front of the other for fear that disclosure of one parent's behavior or standards (or lack thereof) will anger the other parent. Parents who differ in their rules may also be more likely to use the child to carry messages or to spy on the other household. As seen in Chapter 11, feelings of conflicted loyalties are associated with more problems in adjustment among adolescents, especially higher levels of depression and anxiety.

Although the consistency of parenting across homes in which the child spends time after a divorce has not generally been considered by researchers, it seems that this aspect of a child's postdivorce experience might be a critical factor in understanding how the child adjusts. Consistency across homes in terms of rules and expectations would be expected to facilitate more quick and positive adjustment to the upheaval of divorce; inconsistency should make adjustment more difficult. Furthermore, consistency may be more important for certain children (for example, for boys) or in certain situations (for example, when a child spends a great deal of time in both homes).

In this chapter, we look first at how often consistency in parenting was present four and a half years after divorce. Second, we examine the relation between various demographic and family factors and consistency in parenting, including the age and sex of the adolescent, the level of the parents' education, the residential arrangement, and the quality of the interparental relationship. Third, we looked at whether consistency was related to better emotional and behavioral adjustment, and if so, whether consistency predicted adjustment by promoting better relationships and interactions between parents and adolescents, less manipulation of parents, or a lower likelihood of feeling caught between parents. Figure 12.1 shows our hypothesized model. Although Figure 12.1 does not indicate direct links between background variables (for example, age of adolescent or interparental conflict) and indices of the parent-adolescent relationship or adolescent adjustment, we know that these direct links exist and have discussed many of them in previous chapters. We did not include these in the figure in order to make it easier to focus on the links central to this chapter. Finally, we examined whether any links between inconsistency and either parent-child interaction or adolescent adjustment varied depending on age or sex of the child, parental education,

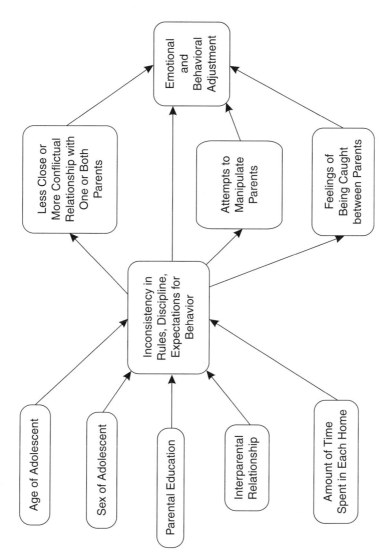

Figure 12.1 Hypothesized associations between inconsistency of parenting across homes, parent-adolescent relationships, and adolescent adjustment.

amount of time spent in each home, or the quality of the interparental relationship.

Defining Inconsistency in Parenting Practices

Inconsistency in parenting was measured from the adolescent's perspective. This represents an important divergence from previous data on the topic, which has measured inconsistency as the difference in parents' reports of their child-rearing practices (see Johnson, Shulman, and Collins, 1991, for an exception). Inconsistency in our study was measured by comparing adolescents' reports of specific parenting practices in the mother's home and the father's home.

The specific aspects of parenting used to examine differences were a subset of those we have referred to as indicators of parental management and control. Specifically, we compared adolescents' reports of mothers' and fathers' monitoring, youth-alone decision making (the practice of letting adolescents make decisions completely on their own, without discussion with parents), organization of the household and household routines, and each parent's use of consistent and fair rules. Scores were created by taking the absolute value of the difference in scores for the mother's and father's home on each of these four parenting variables and averaging these differences;[1] higher scores indicate higher inconsistency, or discrepancies, in parenting. We were only able to assess discrepancies for those adolescents who spent substantial time (at minimum, one month of vacation time) in both homes and who had, therefore, reported on the parenting practices of both homes ($n = 333$). Adolescents who rarely or never saw one parent could not report on specific practices for that parent's home and were excluded from analyses for this chapter.

Level of Inconsistency

To what degree were parents inconsistent in their parenting practices four and a half years after their divorce, from the adolescent's point of view? Reported inconsistency in actual parenting practices was quite low: the average score was only .91, on a scale that ranged from 0 to 5.17. Obviously the large majority of scores were toward the low end of the range. As another confirmation that parents were generally similar to each other in parenting practices, correlations between mothers and fathers on the four specific aspects of parenting that constituted the discrepancy score ranged from .51 to .85.

Correlates of Inconsistencies in Parenting

Demographic Variables

Of the demographic variables we examined, only sex of the adolescent was related to parenting discrepancy. Compared with boys, girls reported higher levels of parenting discrepancy (M_{girls} = 1.01, M_{boys} = .82). Neither age of adolescent nor level of parental education was related to discrepancies in parenting.

Time Spent with Each Parent

Two measures of contact were used to examine whether parenting inconsistency was related to the amount of time adolescents spent in each home. The first was residential arrangement. Using this measure, we found that parenting discrepancies were indeed related to the division of time in each home: parenting discrepancy was markedly lower in dual residence (M = .63) than in either mother (M = .93) or father (M = 1.04) residence. This is consistent with the results reported in Chapter 4, that dual-resident parents were seen as more cooperative at T4 than other parents—they talked with each other more frequently, and they tried to cooperate in making decisions concerning the child, including the rules in each home.[2]

The second measure of contact distinguished among levels of visitation within mother and father residence. Dual-resident adolescents constituted the individuals with the highest score on this measure of contact (a "5"); the remainder of the scale points indicated the amount of time spent with the nonresidential parent for adolescents in either mother or father residence. Specifically, a "2" indicated one month of vacation-time contact with the nonresidential parent but little or no contact throughout the school year; a "3" indicated low contact throughout the school year; and a "4" indicated high contact throughout the school year. (Adolescents with a "1" on this measure were those who had little or no contact with the nonresidential parent and were excluded from these analyses.) As indicated in Figure 12.2, parental inconsistency was generally lower the more time that adolescents spent with a nonresidential parent.[3] The biggest difference, however, was between the lowest-contact categories as a group and the highest-contact categories as a group. Adolescents who had high levels of school-year visitation or who were in dual residence reported more consistency between their parents than did adolescents with lower levels of contact.

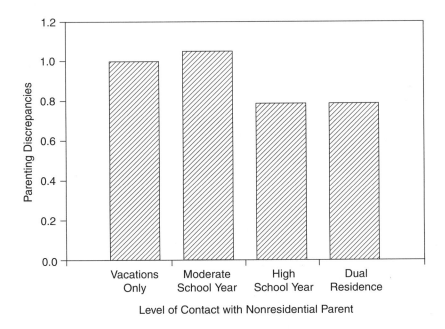

Figure 12.2 Parenting discrepancies by level of contact with the nonresidential parent.

Quality of Interparental Relationship

Parenting discrepancies were not related to any T3 parent-reported measures of conflict or cooperation (see Table 12.1). Adolescent reports of higher parental arguing and lower parental cooperation, however, were significantly correlated with more discrepant parenting. Although it is possible that parenting discrepancy is more highly related to current, rather than past, parental conflict and cooperation, it is also possible that the significant correlations only for T4 measures of the interparental relationship are due to the fact that adolescents reported on both the interparental relationship and parenting practices. In other words, an adolescent's tendency to view their parents as quite similar or quite different could have influenced both measures.

Predicting Parenting Inconsistency with Multiple Factors

Having described the relations between parenting inconsistency and each of the above factors individually, we were interested in (a) which of these

Table 12.1 Zero-order correlations between the interparental relationship
and parenting discrepancies

Measure of interparental relationship	(*n*)	Parenting discrepancies
Discord (T3)	(260)	.02
Cooperative communication (T3)	(259)	−.05
Maximum hostility (T3)	(328)	.03
Frequency of arguing (T4)	(326)	.12*
Cooperation (T4)	(332)	−.24****

p ≤ .05.   ****p* ≤ .0001.

factors were the strongest predictors of parenting inconsistency, and (b) whether the relation between any one factor and discrepancy varied depending on any other factor.[4] Appendix Table B.11 summarizes the results of our analysis using multiple predictors simultaneously. Higher levels of adolescent-reported parental cooperation (T4) and higher levels of contact with the nonresidential parent at T4 continued to be directly related to fewer parenting discrepancies. In addition, parental arguing and parental cooperation were more strongly related to parenting discrepancy among parents with lower levels of education.[5]

Inconsistency in Parenting, Adolescents' Relationships with Parents, and Adolescents' Adjustment

In considering the relation of inconsistency to adjustment, we needed to account for the fact that greater discrepancies were related to a greater likelihood that at least one parent was using poor parenting practices (for example, not monitoring well, allowing the adolescent to make many decisions without parental input or discussion, maintaining a disorganized household). We needed to make sure that poor adjustment or poor parent-child relationships were related to inconsistency, not merely to poor parenting. To achieve this, we controlled for the quality, or level, of parenting in analyses relating discrepancy to aspects of relationships and adjustment.[6] Thus we are able to speak about the effects of parenting inconsistency over and above the quality of parenting being experienced by the adolescent in the two parental households.

High parenting discrepancies were related to more conflict with the residential parent and to a greater likelihood of feeling caught between one's parents (see Table 12.2). Parenting consistency was not related to the likelihood of using one parent against the other, at least as we measured it. This fact, together with the fact that using parents against each other was least likely to remain related to adjustment measures once the other relationship variables (feelings of being caught between one's parents and level of parent-child conflict) were controlled, led us to exclude "using parents against one another" from further analyses.

More discrepancies in parenting were also directly related to higher levels of depression/anxiety (see Table 12.2). Discrepancies were not related to overall deviance, but this was because they were related in different ways to different forms of deviance. The strongest association was between parenting discrepancy and antisocial behavior, with more discrepancies related to more antisocial acts. There were only very weak relations between discrepancies and school deviance or substance use, with more discrepancy marginally associated with higher levels of substance use but lower levels of school deviance. Neither school performance nor school effort were related to parenting differences.

Table 12.2 Associations between parenting discrepancies and various aspects of the parent-adolescent relationship and adolescent adjustment[a]

Measure of relationship or adjustment	β	n
Parent-Adolescent Relationship		
Conflict with residential parent	.16**	325
Using parents against one another	−.03	325
Feelings of being caught	.19**	333
Adjustment		
Depression/anxiety	.16**	333
Overall deviant behavior	.06	333
Substance use	.09+	333
School deviance	−.10+	333
Antisocial behavior	.24****	333
School grades	−.08	333
School effort	.05	316
Worst problem	.11*	333

a. The measures of association are standardized regression coefficients for parental discrepancy regressed on each of the parent-child relationships and adjustment measures individually, controlling for sex of adolescent and for absolute levels of parenting in each home.

$+p \leq .10$. $*p \leq .05$. $**p \leq .01$. $****p \leq .0001$.

A Closer Look at the Link between Parenting Discrepancies and Adjustment

For depression/anxiety and antisocial behavior—the adjustment measures that were most strongly associated with parenting discrepancies—we were interested in whether parenting discrepancy would continue to be associated with adjustment once measures of the parent-child relationship (parent-child conflict, feeling caught) were simultaneously considered or whether the link would decline or disappear, indicating that discrepancies affect adjustment by altering these aspects of the parent-adolescent relationship. In addition, we wanted to know whether the link between discrepancies and adjustment depended on any other factor. For example, was parenting discrepancy more highly linked to depression for adolescent girls, who are more prone to depression to begin with? And although discrepancies did not appear to be related in a direct way to overall deviance, school grades, or school effort, we were still interested in finding out whether discrepancies were linked to these aspects of adjustment for any subgroup of adolescents.[7] The results for the central parts of the models predicting depression/anxiety are presented in Figure 12.3.

Depression/Anxiety

As Figure 12.3 shows, both feelings of being caught between parents (primarily) and parent-child conflict (secondarily) were mediators of the relation between parenting discrepancies and depression/anxiety. In other words, when parents were dissimilar in their parenting, adolescents were more likely to feel caught between parents; in turn, adolescents who felt caught were more likely to report being depressed and anxious. Similarly, the more discrepant the parenting in the two homes, the more conflict there was between the adolescent and the residential parent (especially for older adolescents); this conflict was, in turn, related to higher levels of depression/anxiety.[8] Apart from the fact that discrepancies interfered with the parent-child relationship, discrepancies had no independent link to depression/anxiety, except for certain subgroups of adolescents: girls, younger adolescents, and adolescents whose parents were low in hostility.

Antisocial Behavior

Higher levels of parenting discrepancies were strongly related to higher levels of antisocial behavior in a direct way, even when the indicators of

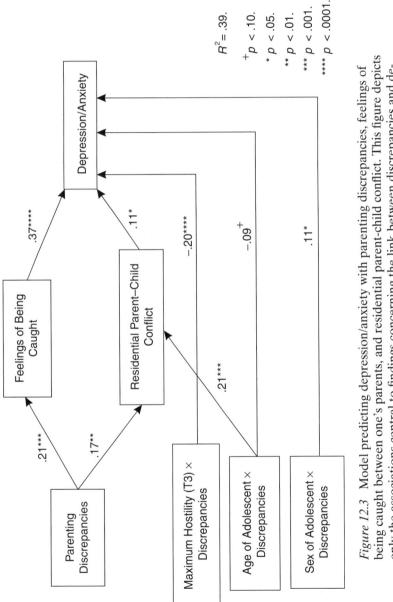

Figure 12.3 Model predicting depression/anxiety with parenting discrepancies, feelings of being caught between one's parents, and residential parent–child conflict. This figure depicts only the associations central to findings concerning the link between discrepancies and depression/anxiety; excluded are main effects of age or sex of adolescent, average parental education, interparental conflict or cooperation, contact with the nonresidential parent, and parenting quality on the main variables of interest.

the parent-adolescent relationship were taken into account. Unlike with depression, we had little evidence that discrepancies led to antisocial behavior by creating conflict between residential parents and their adolescents or by increasing the likelihood that adolescents would feel caught between their parents. Including these "mediators" in the analysis did not alter the strong relation between discrepancies and antisocial behavior (see Baron and Kenny, 1986). Dissimilarity in parenting was especially likely to be related to antisocial behavior for adolescents who had relatively low contact with their nonresidential parent.

Overall Deviance and School Adjustment

Parenting discrepancies were in fact related to higher levels of deviant behavior for adolescents who had low levels of contact with the nonresidential parent, and under conditions of high parental arguing (T4). Similarly, grades and school effort were also lower when parenting was discrepant and there was frequent parental arguing.

The Relative Importance of Discrepancy and Quality of Parenting

Our results thus far suggest that discrepant parenting after divorce has negative implications for certain aspects of adolescent adjustment. A question not directly addressed by our discussion up to this point, however, is whether consistency in parenting is beneficial even when parents are consistently *poor* in their parenting. Is a situation in which only one parent is using positive parenting practices better or worse than a situation in which neither parent does? To more directly address this issue, we classified our families into "high-discrepant" (scoring in the top third on the discrepancy scale) and "low-discrepant" (scoring in the bottom third on the discrepancy scale) families. We further classified these families according to the kind of parenting practiced by mothers and by fathers. If both mother and father had high scores on quality of parenting (in other words, they scored in the top half on the composite measuring levels of monitoring, decision making, household organization, and fairness and consistency of rules), the family was classified as "both parents good." Families in which both mother and father scored in the bottom half of the parenting measure were classified as "both parents poor." If one parent scored in the top half and the other parent scored in the bottom half of the parenting measure, the family was classified as "mixed." Table 12.3 shows the number of families in our sample that fell

Table 12.3 Number of adolescents in each category of parenting discrepancy by parenting quality

Level of parenting discrepancy	Quality of parenting of the two parents		
	Both parents good	Both parents poor	Mixed parenting
High discrepancy	20	46	47
Low discrepancy	72	28	

into each of the five possible categories. Note that it was possible for parents to be fairly discrepant from each other in parenting and yet both fall into the range of good (for example, one parent scores very high and the other scores just above the cut-off for "good parenting"), or both to fall into the range of poor, parenting practices. Of course, the range of discrepancy scores was restricted for the "both good" and "both poor" groups, compared with the range for the "mixed" group. No parents fell into the category of being "mixed" in their quality of parenting and yet low in discrepancy.

Parent-Child Relationship

When parents were both using poor parenting practices, but were also discrepant from each other, we found the highest levels of conflict between adolescents and their residential parents (see Figure 12.4). When at least one parent was using good parenting practices, discrepancies didn't appear to matter much with respect to residential parent-child conflict. Discrepant parenting in general was related to heightened levels of feeling caught between one's parents, particularly in the context of poor parenting by both parents or mixed-quality parenting (see Figure 12.5). There was no benefit from only one parent exercising good parenting in reducing loyalty conflicts. There was some benefit from both parents exercising good parenting—even if the parenting differed somewhat between the parents—but even more benefit from consistent parenting.

Adolescent Adjustment

Depression was lowest among those adolescents who had both highly consistent and good parents (see Figure 12.6). Depression was lower in

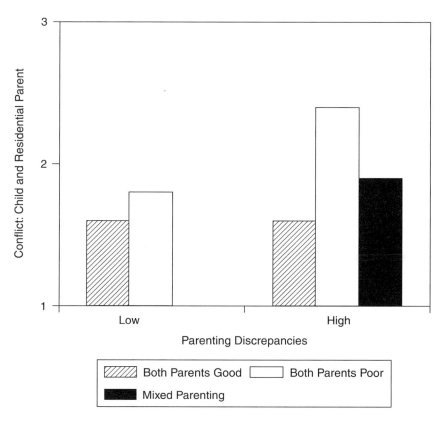

Figure 12.4 Conflict between residential parent and child as a function of parenting discrepancies and parenting quality. Means are adjusted for age and sex of adolescent and the average education of the two parents.

this group than in any other group, indicating that both discrepancies (even when both parents fall within the range of good parenting overall) and poor parenting are associated with increased levels of depression. With regard to deviance, however, good parenting on the part of both parents was the most important factor and discrepancies between parents were less important (see Figure 12.7). For overall deviance, and for school deviance and antisocial behavior, if both parents practiced good parenting—whether parents were similar to each other or not in the degree of good parenting—adolescents were involved in less deviant behavior than when both parents exercised poor parenting. The effects of mixed parenting (one parent good and one parent poor) fell between

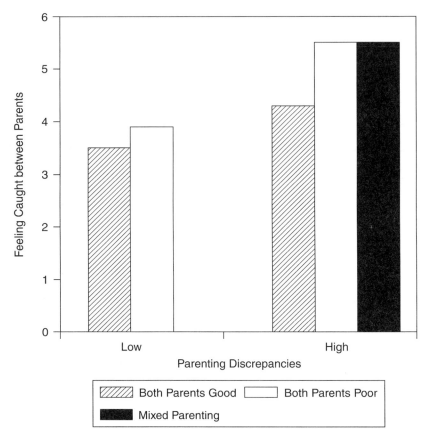

Figure 12.5 Feelings of being caught between one's parents as a function of parenting discrepancies and parenting quality. Means are adjusted for age and sex of adolescent and the average education of the two parents.

these two extremes, and only for antisocial behavior was having mixed-quality parenting significantly worse than having two "good" parents (consistent or not). Parenting, as defined by consistency and quality of parenting, was not related to school grades or school effort.

Summary

One might have expected that discrepancies in parenting would be fairly high among a group of divorced mothers and fathers. Our adolescents, however, did not perceive a high level of discrepancy. Adolescents in our

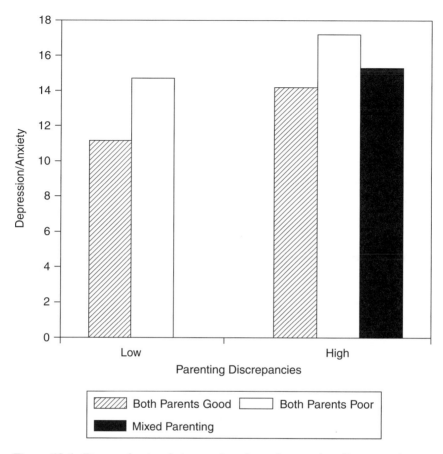

Figure 12.6 Depression/anxiety as a function of parenting discrepancies and parenting quality. Means are adjusted for age and sex of adolescent and the average education of the two parents.

sample reported a surprisingly high degree of similarity in how those parents went about managing their homes. No doubt because reports of both parents were obtained from the adolescents themselves, there is some reporting bias involved, with adolescents tending to see their parents as more similar than they really are. Further evidence of reporting bias comes from only adolescents' reports of interparental conflict (and not parents' own reports) being related to discrepancies in parenting. Even so, the degree of discrepancy between parents was much lower than we would have predicted.

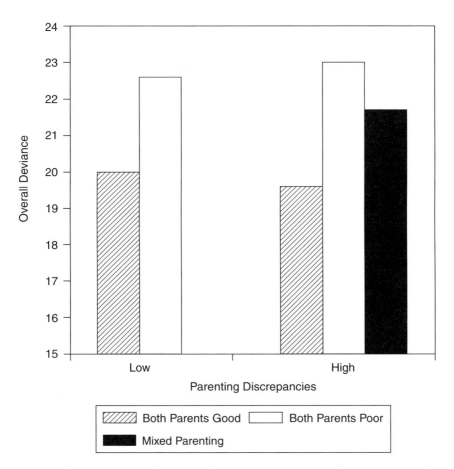

Figure 12.7 Overall deviance as a function of parenting discrepancies and parenting quality. Means are adjusted for age and sex of adolescent and the average education of the two parents.

Discrepancies between parents were lower in families where adolescents had high levels of contact with both parents than they were in families where contact with the nonresidential parent was low. This may indicate a drift toward less visitation in those situations where residential parents are unhappy with the parenting style of the nonresidential parent, or where adolescents find that discrepancies in parenting expectations make spending much time in the nonresidential home uncomfortable.

As we expected, inconsistency in parenting between homes was related to more negative parent-child relationships. In particular, discrepant parenting was related to higher levels of conflict between adolescents and their residential parents if the overall quality of the parenting in both homes was relatively poor. When parents differ in their expectations and rules for adolescents, adolescents are, no doubt, more likely to question or challenge the rules that they like least. In situations of divorce, this may lead to challenges of the residential parent in particular, given that most of the adolescent's time is spent with the residential parent, and residential parents are more likely than nonresidential parents to exercise more control and place more restrictions on the adolescent (see Chapter 10). The fact that this scenario only appeared to hold in situations of relatively poor parenting by both parents, however, indicates that good parenting on the part of one parent may be effective in stifling such challenges.

We also found that inconsistent parenting practices were related to a higher likelihood that children would feel caught between parents. As noted earlier, children may simply feel torn about the differing expectations, feeling that they have to act in different ways to please different parents. When parents differ in their standards, however, they may also engage in other kinds of behavior that leads to loyalty conflicts, for example, asking the child to carry messages to the other parent or interrogating the child about activities with the other parent or the standards maintained in the other household.

Inconsistent parenting was not linked to a greater tendency to use parents against each other, as we had thought it would be. The possible link between parenting differences and adolescent manipulation of one's parents seems so plausible that we are hesitant to discount it based on our results. More likely, our one-item measure ("How often do you use your parents against each other?") was not an adequate indicator of the tendency to manipulate parents.

Parenting discrepancies were, as expected, related to higher levels of adjustment problems—depression/anxiety and antisocial behavior, in particular. The link between discrepancies and depression/anxiety was explained by the fact that both residential parent-child conflict and feelings of being caught were higher when discrepancies were high, and parent-child conflict and feelings of being caught were both linked to depression. That feelings of being caught only mattered in the case of depression is consistent with results reported in Chapter 11 indicating that loyalty conflicts have their greatest impact on internalizing kinds of problems and less impact on externalizing problems.

In addition to evidence for the indirect effects of parenting inconsistency on adolescent adjustment, via parent-child conflict and feelings of being caught between one's parents, direct effects of inconsistency for some measures and some subgroups of adolescents were also found. For instance, inconsistency was a direct and strong predictor of antisocial behavior. Antisocial behavior represents some of the more extreme forms of misbehavior (destroying property, carrying weapons); the link between such forms of behavior and parenting discrepancies indicates either that disagreement between parents provides the inclination and opportunity for such extreme behavior or that, when adolescents participate in such behavior, parents are likely to differ in how they respond to it. In the latter case, we would expect that the differing reactions between parents cause them to become less effective in dealing with the adolescent's deviance.

Inconsistency in parenting also had direct associations with depression for girls and younger adolescents. This may reflect the fact that adolescent girls are more susceptible to depression in response to stress (Buchanan, Maccoby, and Dornbusch, 1992; Compas, 1987; Gore, Aseltine, and Colten, 1993; Petersen, Sarigiani, and Kennedy, 1991). Younger adolescents may have more emotional trouble with discrepant parenting because of their generally greater investment in the family. Older adolescents, however, have more conflict with their residential parent than younger adolescents as a result of discrepancies; thus younger adolescents may be internalizing the stress of parenting discrepancies while older adolescents may react, not by becoming sad or depressed or anxious directly, but by fighting about what they want or trying to use the inconsistencies to their advantage.

Inconsistency was also more strongly related to various forms of deviance (antisocial behavior, overall deviance) if the adolescent had low levels of contact with the nonresidential parent. We might have thought that parenting discrepancies would be more stressful under conditions of high levels of contact with each parent, because in such cases adolescents would be continually exposed to the differences. We are not sure what to make of this set of findings, except to note that both low visitation and discrepancies are negative factors for the adolescent. Although neither in itself was related to deviance as a measure of adjustment (see also Chapter 9), the existence of both may be detrimental for adolescents. Also, it may be that relatively high contact with both parents provides more opportunities for adolescents to learn their parents' different styles and adapt to the differences.

With regard to the interparental relationship and parenting discrepancies, we obtained mixed findings. Inconsistency was linked to more depression when parents were less hostile toward one another at T3. Yet inconsistency was related to more overall deviance and lower school performance if parents argued frequently (according to adolescents at T4). Why this particular pattern of results should appear is not clear.

Was consistency in parenting more important than absolute quality of parenting? No. In general, consistently poor parenting was of no benefit to adolescents. Furthermore, when considering deviance, consistent good parenting was no better for the adolescent than inconsistent good parenting. "Good parenting," as we measured it, means that parents are aware of their adolescents' activities, that parents stay involved in decision making concerning the adolescent while still allowing the adolescent to have quite a bit of input into those decisions, and that they generally have fair and consistent rules and routines in the home. Two parents who generally stay involved with their adolescents in these ways, even when the absolute level at which they do so differs, have adolescents who are unlikely to become involved in deviant activities.

Consistently good parenting did have some benefits over inconsistent parenting, even when both parents were generally good parents, with regard to adolescent depression. In this case, we see the potential benefits of experiencing consistent and good parenting, over and above inconsistent but good parenting. Consistently poor parenting, in line with what was said above, was not of significant benefit in reducing depression. The findings for depression are in line with those of Johnson and colleagues (1991), who found benefits for adolescents in what they called "congruent" authoritative ("good") parenting over both congruent permissive parenting (a less desirable parenting style) and incongruent parenting. When parents both fall into the range of what we would consider "good" parenting, but are still different from one another, this seems to take at least a modest emotional toll on the adolescent, even though it reduces the risk of deviance.

Of course, as we have acknowledged throughout this book, we cannot specify cause and effect with certainty. We have argued that parenting inconsistency can, for many reasons, lead to emotional and behavioral problems among adolescents. It is also possible, however, that more troubled adolescents are more difficult to parent, and therefore the two parents are more likely to come up with different ways of handling such children. Further research should investigate this question, using a longitudinal design to provide more insight into the processes taking place. In general, however, we found support for our hypotheses that inconsistency between households in parenting is associated with negative characteristics in family relationships, as well as with lower levels of adjustment among adolescents.

13

Conclusion

In this chapter we present our interpretation of the most important empirical findings from our study of adolescents four and a half years after their parents' separation. Before delving into the empirical results, however, we begin with an impression. The impression is that most of the adolescents we talked to appeared to be adjusting quite well to their family situation. For the most part, they talked easily and openly with us about their homes, their relationships, and their feelings. And most of the adolescents impressed us with their insight, understanding, and acceptance of the circumstances in their families. This impression should not be viewed as minimizing the pain that these children felt in the years immediately surrounding the estrangement of their parents, nor indeed the pain they sometimes still felt. Most studies have concluded that the first two years after divorce are the most difficult for children, and we intentionally chose to study a period when the children had had time to build a new life and to integrate their relationships with two parents who were no longer together. Thus we most certainly would have heard of more distress had we interviewed the adolescents earlier in the divorce process. And even after four and a half years, some adolescents were unhappy and still struggling with the breakup of their original family. What was remarkable, however, was that even in those instances in which adolescents communicated ongoing hardship or pain, they often did so in a way that indicated a mature understanding of the situation.

Our purpose in conducting this study, however, was not to assess the adjustment of these adolescents taken as a group. Rather, our central interest was to uncover the conditions under which adolescents functioned well or poorly after their parents divorced. It was the variability in adjustment among the adolescents in our sample that was of most interest to us: it provided us with the opportunity to study the circumstances and processes that are associated with more or less successful adjustment after divorce.

Adjustment in the Three Residential Arrangements

A central question for our study was whether the well-being of adolescents depended on where they lived—in other words, whether adolescents appeared to be better off when living with their mothers, with their fathers, or in a shared arrangement in which they spent substantial time in both parental households. Dual residence (also sometimes called joint custody) has been a particularly controversial arrangement. Its advocates have insisted that it offers great benefits to children by shielding them from the loss of either parent and by providing support from both parents. Its opponents have warned about the potential dangers of the instability involved in moving constantly from one home to another, the loyalty conflicts that would surely stem from maintaining close relationships with two mutually hostile parents, and the difficulty for parents in keeping track of youngsters who are away so much of the time. We have found, however, only minor differences among the residential groups, on the average, in adolescent adjustment. What differences there were favored the adolescents in dual residence, and indicated somewhat more adjustment difficulties among father-resident adolescents.

Does the similarity among residential groups mean that it hardly matters where or with whom an adolescent lives after parents divorce? Not at all. Parents came to their initial agreement about physical custody on the basis of their intimate knowledge of themselves and their children, usually attempting to put the children in the household they thought would provide the most supportive environment (Maccoby and Mnookin, 1992). Following these initial arrangements, there was considerable shifting of residence, with nearly a third of the sample moving from one residential arrangement to another during the four-and-a-half postdivorce years prior to our study. This means that families selected and reselected the arrangements they considered most suited to their family circumstances. Their choices appear to have been about equally good—from the standpoint of the well-being of their adolescent children—whether they ended up with mother, father, or dual residence. This does not mean that the residential choices were unimportant. If one arbitrarily assigned children to one of the three arrangements, without the benefit of any effort to match residence to individual family circumstances, there is no reason to believe that the differences in outcomes would still be as small as they have proved to be in our study.

The modest differences that we did find among residential groups are to some extent a reflection of self-selection into these groups. When there had been residential shifts, we asked the adolescents to tell us why the changes had occurred. Moves into mother residence, more often than moves into father or dual residence, occurred when one parent or the other relocated. When adolescents had moved into dual residence, they usually explained the move in terms of their missing one or the other parent, and the implication is that the parents responded to their children's wish to spend time with both parents by making the effort to maintain a dual-resident arrangement. Moves into father residence, by contrast, more often occurred because of family conflicts. Thus we have evidence that moves into mother or dual residence occur for more benign or positive reasons than do moves into father custody.

The implication is that over the course of the postdivorce period, fathers probably were taking into their households somewhat more troubled children—children who had had difficulty adapting to other residential arrangements—compared with families in which children moved into mother or dual residence. This conclusion is supported by the finding that adolescents currently living with their fathers who had shifted residential arrangements one or more times since the parental separation were more likely to have problems in adjustment than other father-resident adolescents. Instability of residence was linked to negative adjustment only for this one group.

We wanted to know whether there were factors, however, over and above self-selection, that might affect adolescent adjustment in each of the three residential groups. We expected that certain family processes would support adolescent adjustment and that others would weaken it. The question then was: were adolescents in the three residential groups being exposed to different living situations—different environmental inputs or different family processes in their primary residential households? And if so, did these differences in process account for any differences in adjustment among the residential groups? After describing some of the ways in which family processes were linked to adolescent adjustment, we will be in a position to see whether the processes linked to good or problematic outcomes were more prevalent in one residential group than another.

Life Situation, Family Processes, and Adolescent Adjustment

Life Stresses

The more life stresses experienced by the adolescents in the previous year, the more adjustment problems they had. The life stresses we assessed ranged from financial hardships, to losing a pet, to having a serious fight with a good friend. In line with other research on stress in general (Rutter, 1979; Simmons et al., 1987) and stress for children of divorce specifically (Amato, 1993), the total number of life stresses was a powerful and pervasive predictor of adjustment for adolescents in all residence arrangements.

Parents' Repartnering

For adolescents in sole-residence arrangements,[1] one of the more consistent predictors of good adjustment was having a remarried residential parent. In contrast, when the residential parent was living with a new partner to whom he or she was not married, adjustment was worse in a number of ways, particularly for boys. These findings are partly at odds with other research on adolescents, which has suggested that adolescents are more poorly adjusted in stepfamilies than they are in divorced families where a remarriage has not occurred (Ferri, 1984; Furstenberg, 1987; Hetherington and Clingempeel, 1992). For mother-resident adolescents, better adjustment in situations of remarriage was partly due to closer relationships between adolescents and remarried mothers. In addition, the better adjustment of mother-resident adolescents—and to some extent father-resident adolescents as well—in situations of remarriage occurred because remarried new partners were accorded more acceptance by the adolescents. Although it was easier for some adolescents to accept parents' new partners than for others, on average, acceptance was greater if the parent and new partner were remarried than if the parent and new partner were cohabiting or only dating on a regular basis. An adolescent's acceptance of a new partner, and of that person as an authority figure in the home, means that there are now two adults available for effective supervision, monitoring, and development of rapport with the adolescent. Other studies have indicated that the presence of two parents means higher levels of parental supervision for adolescents (Dornbusch et al., 1985; Hetherington, 1987), but results conflict concerning whether two parents necessarily provide a greater degree of protection against risky or unhealthy types of behavior than does the presence of only one (Dornbusch et al., 1985; Steinberg, 1987). Our results suggest that the benefits of two parents, and any accompanying increases in supervision, for adolescents' behavior are more likely to emerge when the second adult is accepted by the adolescent. In situations where a new partner is simply cohabiting, the same degree of acceptance and authority is not accorded, and the same benefits in terms of adjustment do not accrue.

Interparental Conflict

Interparental conflict after divorce had much smaller direct relations to adolescent adjustment than we had expected on the basis of previous research (Amato, 1993; Emery, 1982; Johnston and Campbell, 1988). Yet recent reviewers of the research on marital conflict have noted that there is, in fact, variability in the impact of conflict, and that the task of researchers is to identify conditions under which, or individuals for whom, conflict has the most detrimental effects (Cummings and Davies, 1994; Depner, Leino, and Chun, 1992). Our data can begin to address this question.

Interparental conflict as reported by adolescents was more strongly related to adjustment than conflict as reported independently by parents over the first three and a half years since their separation. Of course, to some extent this may reflect a reporting bias on the part of adolescents; those adolescents who are not doing well may have a more negative outlook and report their parents' relationships as more negative than they really are. Instead or in addition, however, adolescents' reports may reflect the conflict to which the adolescent has been exposed (as distinct from the conflict that occurs between parents privately), a factor that others have identified as important in anticipating conflict's impact on the child (Cummings and Davies, 1994; Davies and Cummings, 1994).

Interparental conflict was also more likely to be related to poor adjustment for boys than for girls. Among boys, conflict was related both to higher levels of deviance and to higher levels of depression. Why boys should be more affected by conflict is not clear; our findings add more diversity to an already diverse body of literature on sex differences in response to conflict. Conflict was also more likely to predict negative adjustment for father-resident adolescents than for other adolescents.

Other research has suggested that conflict between parents can be especially detrimental for children who continue to spend time with both parents after divorce. Recommendations for policy have sometimes been made based on this assumption—that children should be encouraged to maintain contact with both parents unless those parents cannot get along. In our study, however, conflict between parents did not appear to affect children more negatively the more time they spent with each parent, with one potentially important exception. Adolescents who lived in dual residence were more strongly affected by interparental conflict in terms of their feelings of being caught between their parents. When parents were in high conflict, dual-resident adolescents were more likely to feel caught up in this conflict than were adolescents living primarily with either their mothers or their fathers. When parents were not in conflict, dual-resident adolescents were the group least likely to feel caught between their parents. Although feelings of being caught between one's parents were related to problems in adjustment (particularly depression), we did not find that dual-resident adolescents were especially prone to adjustment difficulties under situations of high interparental conflict. It seems that other factors intervene in determining the dual-resident adolescent's ultimate adjustment—for example, the benefits of maintaining close relationships with both parents in dual residence may offset the negative effects of conflict and loyalty problems even when parents are in high conflict.

Among sole-resident adolescents, we found no evidence that adolescents who visited the nonresidential parent frequently were more likely to suffer negative consequences of interparental conflict. Our results are different from those of several other studies (see, for example, Amato and Rezac, 1994; Hetherington, Cox, and Cox, 1978, 1982; Johnston and Campbell, 1988), most of which focus on preadolescent children (see Amato and Rezac, 1994, for an exception). On the one hand, adolescents may be better able than younger children to understand that they are not responsible for their parents' conflict (Wallerstein and Kelly, 1980), and thus may be more able to benefit from maintaining a relationship with the nonresidential parent. On the other hand, feelings of being caught between parents increased with age in our sample, which suggests that as children get older it may become more difficult in some respects to avoid becoming involved in interparental conflict. Thus it is unclear whether the age of our sample accounts to any extent for our failure to replicate the earlier findings. There are, in fact, a few studies other than our own that also provide no support for the hypothesis of worsened outcomes in situations of high interparental conflict and high visitation (for example, Crosbie-Burnett, 1991), and yet others suggest that high visitation may buffer the effects of high interparental conflict (Forehand et al., 1991). This mixture of findings in the literature suggests that the impact of visitation in high-conflict situations probably depends on yet other factors (for example, the extent to which parents use the child to carry messages or spy on the other home). Our own findings regarding dual-resident adolescents are evidence that multiple factors (amount of contact with each parent, degree of interparental conflict, and the adolescent's closeness to each parent) are in fact important.

Parent-Child Relationships and Parenting Style in the Residential Home

A great deal of previous research points to the importance for adolescents' adjustment of continued positive relationships with their parents. More specifically, adolescents, like younger children, benefit from warm, affectionate, responsive relationships with their parents. They also adjust better when their parents continue to make maturity demands—when they set clear and reasonable rules, maintaining expectations for good behavior while also allowing for growing input and negotiation on the part of the adolescent (see, for example, Baumrind, 1991a, 1991b; Eccles et al., 1993; Lamborn et al., 1991; Maccoby and Martin, 1983). Thus we expected positive adjustment to be associated both with parent-child closeness and with the extent of parental management and control, that is, with the degree to which parents were involved in setting limits and making decisions, as opposed to adolescents' being completely in control of such things, and the degree to which parents established reasonable and predictable household routines.

In general, our results supported these expectations. Of all of the aspects of the household context and family relationships that we considered, the affective closeness of the relationship between the residential parent and the child and the extent of management and control a parent exercised were the strongest and most consistent predictors of a range of adjustment indices. There were some qualifications, however. First of all, the benefits of close father-child relationships were somewhat weaker in father residence than in the other arrangements, and the benefits of parental management and control for girls were limited to certain aspects of that management (to monitoring, in particular). Why might good parenting on the part of a sole-resident father have less of an impact on the adolescents in his care than good parenting on the part of other residential parents? One reason may concern the nonresidential mother.

As we will discuss later, the adjustment of father-resident adolescents depended to a greater extent—relative to adolescents in other arrangements—on their continuing relationship with their nonresidential parent. Another reason, no doubt, is that father-resident adolescents are more likely to represent more difficult adolescents, from more difficult family circumstances. There may be other reasons as well. In any case, although there were still clear benefits to fathers' exercising warm, responsive, involved, demanding parenting—and sole-resident fathers should be encouraged to engage in this kind of parenting—the benefits appear to be moderated, more so than in other arrangements, by other factors.

A second important qualification is that the closeness of the relationship between the residential parent and the child, and the parent's management and control, were highly related to each other. The closer and more trusting the relationship between parents and adolescents, the more well managed and controlled was the household. In other words, when parents had good relationships with their adolescents, they were better able to stay in touch with the activities and concerns of their adolescents, discuss important matters with them concerning their decision making and behavior, and, no doubt, be accorded more respect and authority regarding rules and decisions. Of these two aspects of parenting, the degree to which a parent managed the household well and stayed involved in rule-setting and decision making was a stronger and more direct predictor of several aspects of adjustment, especially deviant kinds of behavior, than was closeness considered separately. When it comes to reducing the likelihood that adolescents will act out or will be susceptible to peer pressure to participate in such acts as cutting class or taking drugs, a parent's continued knowledge of and involvement in decisions concerning the adolescent's behavior play a highly important role. The closeness of the relationship, in many cases, played only an indirect role, in the sense that it facilitated such knowledge and involvement on the part of the parent.

Was a positive parent-child relationship (feeling close to the residential parent, engaging in activities together, and trusting and identifying with that parent) of primary importance for any aspect of adjustment, over and above the role of management and control? For mother-resident adolescents, closer mother-child relationships were associated with less depression and less school deviance (which reflects rather minor forms of deviance like class-cutting and being tardy). For father-resident adolescents, a closer father-daughter relationship was related to the use of compromise in peer conflicts by those girls and less substance use. There were thus some direct relations between closeness and adjustment, but the number of significant relations was smaller than we would have predicted.

Adolescents who felt disengaged from the residential home (didn't enjoy being there, tried to spend time away from the home or at least away from others in the home) were also more likely to show indications of poor adjustment. In particular, they were more likely to be depressed. It may be that depressed adolescents withdraw from the home, or that not feeling integrated into the home leads to depression. Either way, our data suggest that such signs of withdrawal from the family and home are a warning sign of emotional distress. Disengagement from the home was also linked to higher levels of deviance—especially antisocial behavior—among boys. As we noted earlier, continued parental supervision and monitoring during adolescence is of benefit with regard to "acting out" kinds of behaviors. Boys who withdraw from the home, and therefore do not have that supervision, are at risk for some of the more serious forms of deviant behavior.

In general, our data point to the importance of continued engaged and involved parenting after divorce. Hetherington and her colleagues have documented the "diminished parenting" that often takes place in the first year or two following divorce (Hetherington, Cox, and Cox, 1982). Certainly devoting the time and attention to children—even adolescent children—that they require is a difficult task for a parent who, after divorce, is usually working full time and parenting very much alone. Our data indicate, however, that at four and a half years after divorce, some parents are finding a way to maintain involved and vigilant parenting and some are not. These variations among primary residential parents depend hardly at all on the amount of time adolescents spend in each parent's home. In other words, some parents who have little or no "relief" from parenting by virtue of their adolescents' spending time with the other parent, as well as some parents whose adolescents spend a great deal of time out of their own home, find ways to stay responsive and involved with their adolescents. As difficult as such responsive parenting might be, our data indicate that it is one of the most important facilitators of adolescents' adjustment after divorce; parents' efforts in this area should have high payoffs.

Role Reversal

A concern that has been voiced about children of divorce is that they will be drawn into "playing parent" to their own parents. There is fear that parents, in the absence of a spouse with whom they can share their troubles, concerns, or joys, will turn to children as confidants. There is also concern about the danger that children will feel the need to help, or take care of, a parent who is lonely, discouraged, angry, helpless, frightened, or in any of a number of negative emotional states that can arise as a result of separation and divorce. To investigate this, we looked separately at the extent of parents' confiding in their adolescent children, and the adolescents' feelings of worry or needing to take care of that parent. Our findings did not indicate any negative ramifications of parental confiding. Among sole-resident adolescents, however, feeling worried about the residential parent or feeling that the parent needed to be cared for by the adolescent was related to negative adjustment indices. The critical factor appears to be whether the parent conveys that she or he is weak and vulnerable and needs the adolescent to be strong, to be the caretaker. Seemingly, there are parents who confide in their adolescents without having such an effect: either they confide about more positive things, or in confiding negative information they leave the child feeling that the parent is capable of coping with hardship. But the confiding in and of itself did not appear to be a problem.

The Nonresidential Parent: How Important Is Continuing Contact?

Early in the book we raised the issue of parental loss. It was reassuring for us to find that in our sample, few parents completely dropped out of their adolescents' lives. Most continued to have some kind of contact. Even so, there was a great deal of variability in the extent of that contact over the course of a year, with some nonresidential parents having very little and others having a great deal of contact. Was that variability in contact related to any indices of adolescent functioning? The level of visitation in and of itself turned out not to be important with respect to an adolescent's adjustment. Even adolescents who rarely or never saw their nonresidential parents were, on average, adjusting as well as adolescents who saw their nonresidential parents on a regular basis. Not surprisingly, however, adolescents who visited their nonresidential parents on a regular basis maintained closer relationships with those parents than did adolescents who rarely or never visited. What was more surprising was that the level of visitation required to sustain feelings of closeness was quite low: adolescents who visited their nonresidential parent for as little as two weeks in the summer felt about as close to that parent as did adolescents who visited regularly and frequently throughout the school year. Having at least a few weeks of contact each year, then, appeared to permit, but by no means guarantee, a close relationship with the nonresidential parent. Given the fact that we could document no negative effects of visitation, even in the face of continuing conflict between parents (as we will see below, visitation also did not interfere with the functioning of the residential home), the closeness that nonresidential parents and their children can sustain through visitation may be a goal worth pursuing in and of itself.

Furthermore, closeness with the nonresidential parent appears to have some beneficial effects on the adolescent—at least in the context of a close relationship with the residential parent. In fact, for father-resident adolescents, a good relationship with their mother appeared crucial: without a close relationship with their mother, a close relationship with their father was of little benefit. Even father-resident girls, whose relationships with their nonresidential mothers frequently appeared strained, benefited when the mother-daughter relationship remained close. For mother-resident adolescents, maintaining a close relationship with their father also had modest benefits, but the importance of the mother-child relationship did not depend on that continued closeness.

In neither mother nor father residence, however, did adolescents benefit by being close only to the nonresidential parent. The benefits of a close father-child relationship for mother-resident adolescents were too modest to make up for a loss in closeness to their mother. And the benefits of a close mother-child relationship for father-resident adolescents depended on being close to their father as well. For father-resident adolescents, then, it was especially important to maintain a good relationship with both parents: a poor relationship with either mother or father led to noticeable deficits in adjustment.

Interestingly, the ability and willingness of the nonresidential parent to remember special days (holidays, birthdays) was also linked to several aspects of better adjustment. The benefits of a nonresidential parent's remembering special days rivaled those of having a close relationship and superseded any other aspect of the relationship between the nonresidential parent and child. By remembering special days, the nonresidential parent communicates that the child is still important and not forgotten, regardless of how frequent the contact or how emotionally close the relationship between parent and child. Apparently the symbolic value of a parent's love and commitment has noticeable rewards with regard to adolescents' well-being.

Residence Differences in Life Situations and Family Processes

We now return to the modest differences among the three residential groups in adolescent adjustment, and consider whether there were differences in the life situations, or family or household conditions, experienced by adolescents in these three groups that might help to account for the differences in adjustment. In doing so, we continue to keep in mind that there is not a great deal to be explained: the three groups were quite similar in adjustment. Still, on the average, dual-resident adolescents were doing somewhat better, and father-resident adolescents somewhat worse, and we have attempted to understand why this is so.

Dual-resident adolescents were a relatively advantaged group, in that their parents had more education and higher incomes than parents in the other groups. But their adjustment advantage remained after we controlled for parental socioeconomic status. We expected that dual-resident adolescents might be benefiting from greater cooperation between their parents, but these adolescents reported only slightly higher levels of cooperation, and there had been equivalent amounts of interparental conflict in the three residential groups since the divorce. What about the kind of control and organization that prevailed in the two parental households where dual-resident adolescents spent their time? We had expected that dual-resident adolescents might be worse off in this respect. We thought that life might be relatively unorganized and chaotic in households where children were moving in and out, and that it might be easier for dual-resident children to slip between the cracks of parental supervision. We found, however, that the households of dual-resident parents were as well organized as any others, and it appeared that all family members had adjusted to whatever patterns of alternation had been adopted for the children. As far as monitoring was concerned, dual-resident boys were somewhat less closely monitored than their sole-resident counterparts, but dual-resident girls were more closely monitored, and considering boys and girls together, the dual-resident adolescents did not appear to be advantaged in this respect.

What stands out for dual-resident adolescents is that they were able to maintain closer relationships with both parents than the other groups. Indeed, girls in dual residence felt closer to their fathers than did girls who actually lived with their fathers most of the time. Their closeness to both parents undoubtedly reflects some self-selection into the dual-resident group. That is, parents who maintained dual residence four and a half years after divorce were probably more child-centered and therefore more willing to make the extra effort that this arrangement entails. Parents who earlier tried dual residence but did not maintain it, or parents who never tried it, probably were less willing or able to set aside some of their personal concerns and goals for the sake of enabling their children to maintain a close relationship with the other parent. Furthermore, adolescents who moved into a dual-residence arrangement after initially being in sole custody commonly said they did so because they missed the less-seen parent. Dual residence is thus more likely to be implemented among families where parents and children are initially close; subsequently, the high levels of contact with both parents allow those close relationships to be maintained. Being able to maintain close relationships with two parents after a divorce, in turn, appears to benefit adolescents' well-being.

In general, dual-resident adolescents did not appear to be paying a price in terms of loyalty conflicts for their closeness to both parents. In fact, being close to both parents was, overall, linked with lower levels of loyalty conflicts. And when the parents of dual-resident adolescents were not in active conflict, those adolescents reported feeling caught between their parents less frequently than any other group. When their parents were still hostile and in conflict, these adolescents were more susceptible to feeling caught between their parents than other adolescents, although we did not find that the high levels of loyalty conflicts translated directly into their being the worst-adjusted group. The benefits of maintaining a close relationship with both parents appeared to soften the impact of torn loyalties even among dual-resident adolescents whose parents were highly conflicted. We must emphasize again at this point that our dual-resident families represent a small group of families whose dual-resident arrangements had survived over time or had been adopted voluntarily since the divorce. Our results concerning the well-being of adolescents in even the high-conflict families should not be construed to suggest that adolescents would benefit from court-imposed dual residence for parents who are highly hostile or in which the relationships between children and parents are not likely to be close or positive.

Why did we find somewhat more problems in adjustment among adolescents living with their fathers? For one thing, fathers in this group expressed relatively high levels of hostility toward their former spouses, and this was a source of distress for the adolescents in their care even more so than adolescents in other arrangements. Adolescents in father residence also reported less close relationships with their fathers than did adolescents in the other groups with their residential parents. The lower level of closeness to residential fathers was particularly true for the small group of girls who lived with their fathers. Similarly, as far as monitoring is concerned, it was once again the father-resident girls who were least likely to report that their fathers really knew about their interests, activities, and whereabouts. We return below to the special case of father-resident girls, but note here merely that the greater incidence of adjustment problems among father-resident adolescents can be traced, at least in part, to the higher number of cases in this group in which the adolescent felt emotionally alienated from the custodial parent and in which monitoring was weak.

Same-Sex Parents: Do Children Need Their Same-Sex Parent More?

Other researchers have claimed that it is optimal for children, when their parents divorce, to be in the custody of their same-sex parent, or at least to maintain a close relationship with that parent (Santrock and Warshak, 1979; Santrock, Warshak, and Elliott, 1982; Zaslow, 1989). In our study, we find only weak evidence to support this hypothesis, and it is limited to girls. When adolescents live with their mothers, we do not find that boys benefit more than girls from maintaining contact with a nonresident father—neither sex appeared to benefit significantly from such contact alone. Adolescents did benefit somewhat from a continuing relationships with nonresidential fathers if the relationship was a close, trusting one, but this benefit accrued equally to mother-resident boys and girls. In addition, the boys in our sample were not better adjusted when living with their fathers than when living with their mothers. If anything, the balance tipped slightly toward the advantages of mother residence for boys, although generally speaking, mother-resident and father-resident boys were very similar on our measures of adjustment. It might be thought that boys would have more interests in common with their fathers (for example, in sports) and that this would mean a greater compatibility between fathers and sons; there may be some truth to this, but we were surprised to find that all parents—mothers, fathers, stepmothers, and stepfathers—engaged in higher levels of joint activities with boys than with girls. There was no pattern of more joint activities for same-sex parent-child pairs.

The situation was somewhat different for girls. Out of our sample of 522 adolescents, only 38 were girls living with their fathers. Most of these girls (all but 9) had changed residences at least once since their parents had separated. In some ways, this group of girls represents a unique subgroup among the population of adolescents with divorced parents. They reported more adjustment problems than any other group (see Appendix Table B.6).[2] They felt less emotionally close to their residential parent and received less monitoring and supervision from their residential parent than did other groups. Some of the emotional distance between fathers and their resident daughters reflects processes that occur in families whether or not divorce has occurred. We know that in many families, fathers withdraw to some degree from interaction with adolescent daughters; at least, fathers feel less free to show physical affection toward daughters who are becoming physically mature. Some fathers have told us, too, that there are certain topics or activities that arise in parenting daughters (for example, helping them to braid their hair, discussing their choice of clothes, dealing with the physical changes of puberty) that don't come as naturally to fathers as they would to mothers (Maccoby and Mnookin, 1992). Mothers, by contrast, don't seem to encounter as many uncomfortable issues in raising adolescent boys.

The lower levels of emotional closeness in the father-daughter relationship were linked with lower levels of monitoring, which in turn predicted more problems among father-resident girls. Like all other adolescents, father-resident girls benefit from a parent's awareness of activities and behavior that can come from having a close relationship with that parent. We were surprised to find, however, that other aspects of parental management and control—specifically, curfews and parental involvement in decision making—were not as beneficial for this group of girls (see Chapter 6) as for other adolescents. Although we believe that these girls do benefit from their fathers' involvement and supervision, it would appear that there is something about their background or emotional state that makes certain controls more difficult for residential fathers to maintain and less effective when fathers do impose them.

Father-resident girls stood out, too, with respect to their relationship with their nonresidential mothers. For instance, they had more conflict with their mothers than did father-resident boys or than mother-resident children of either sex had with their nonresidential fathers. And although boys were closer to nonresidential mothers than to nonresidential fathers on several dimensions, this was not true of girls. Girls' relationships with nonresidential mothers were not especially warm, and they were conflictual. In addition, it was only among father-resident girls that closeness to father was unrelated to closeness to mother. For all other groups, a good relationship with one parent was predictive of—and may have facilitated—a good relationship with the other. Furthermore, the relationships between father-resident girls and their nonresident mothers appeared to be especially sensitive to the presence of ongoing interparental conflict. Although both boys and girls in both mother and father residence reported less close relationships with their nonresidential parents in situations of ongoing parental conflict, this was especially true of father-resident girls. These findings may indicate that the father's hostility toward the mother—which was especially high among sole-resident fathers—contributed to the problems between these girls and their mothers. It is still true, however, that when a father-resident girl was able to sustain a close relationship with her mother, this was especially beneficial. For example, a positive relationship with the nonresidential parent was associated with lower levels of deviance for father-resident girls only.

There are strong social norms leading to mother residence for children in divorcing families. It is unusual for children of either sex to live with their fathers, but especially unusual for girls to do so. It is not surprising, then, that father-resident girls should be different in important ways, because in many cases there would necessarily have been a special reason for their residential situation. Although it was not true of all father-resident girls, some had especially troubled relationships with their mothers; others had had trouble with a stepfather and had moved into the father's residence more to escape an unwelcome situation in the mother's household than out of any positive desire to be with their fathers. Boys, more often than girls, when they moved in with their fathers, did so because they wanted to be with them. And boys, by and large, sustained positive relationships with their nonresidential mothers. It would appear that a number of the father-resident girls in our sample were relatively alienated from both parents—more, at least, than the number of adolescents who were so alienated in other arrangements.

These findings have made us acutely aware that girls who live with their fathers after divorce are an important group to understand. They are relatively uncommon, so they are not an easy or representative group to study. However, we need more information about the circumstances under which they come to be in the custody of their fathers, and how the circumstances of living with their fathers and apart from their mothers influence their development.

The Impact of Parents' Repartnering on Home and Relationships

We have already noted that a residential parent's remarriage was associated with positive adjustment, and that cohabiting was associated with negative adjustment. We also looked at how a parent's involvement with a new partner affected relationships within the family as well as the degree of parental control and management. In terms of relationships between the ex-spouses, the earlier study of the parents of these adolescents noted that remarriage typically led either to a more disengaged or a more conflictual co-parenting style (Maccoby and Mnookin, 1992). In our study, the parent's stage of repartnering had little to do with the quality of the relationship between the two parents as the adolescents reported it.

Parent-child relationships did depend, however, on a residential parent's repartnering status, and this effect differed depending on whether it was a mother or a father who was involved with the new partner. Adolescents who lived with their mothers in either mother or dual residence had closer relationships with their mothers if either the mother was not involved in a new relationship at all or the mother was remarried. Previous research has demonstrated that mothers and preadolescent children (daughters in particular) often become very close when the mother is a single parent (Hetherington, 1993). Some of the problems that preadolescent girls have with remarriage have been attributed to interference with this close bond. Our data indicate, however, that the quality of the mother-child relationship with both sons and daughters may suffer most when mothers are in the earliest stages of repartnering: dating or living with a person to whom they are not remarried. It is, perhaps, in these stages of a new relationship that a mother reduces the time spent with her children most significantly, as she develops and establishes the new relationship. The fact that mothers were reported to be lower in management and control of the household during the dating stages of a relationship is further evidence for lowered maternal involvement with their children during this period. By the time they are remarried, mothers appear to be more settled in the new relationship and therefore able to spend more time with their children than they did in the earlier repartnering stages. In addition, by the time a mother remarries, her children may have had more time to accept this new partner and may see him as less threatening to their relationship with their mother.

Mothers' serious involvement with a new partner had another potential benefit. Adolescents were less likely to worry about, or feel the need to take care of, mothers who had a live-in partner (either remarried or not).

For both mothers and fathers, involvement with a new partner reduced the amount of confiding that that parent did with the opposite-sex adolescent. Mothers confided less in sons when they had a live-in new partner (cohabiting or remarried) and fathers confided less in daughters. The new partner, especially when available in the home on a daily basis, appears to take the place of an opposite-sex child as confidant. Of course, because our data were not longitudinal, we cannot rule out the possibility that parents who are less prone to confiding in their opposite-sex children are more likely to seek out or find a new partner. Further research is needed to clarify which of these processes takes place.

We found no evidence that the presence of a new partner interfered with adolescents' relationships with their nonresident biological parents. For adolescents living with their mothers (in sole or dual residence) there were no differences in the quality of the father-adolescent relationship depending on the mother's repartnering status. For adolescents living with their fathers (again, in sole or dual residence) the presence of a new partner was related to a better relationship between adolescents and their mothers. Our data thus provide no reason for nonresidential parents to fear the arrival of a new partner, at least when the new partner has been present for less than four years, as was the case in our study.

Integrating Life in Two Homes

As long as both parents are still alive, many children of divorce face the reality of being a part of two families. When they spend time in both households on a regular basis, they also face the task of actively integrating life in two separate homes. How is it that children integrate—or fail to integrate—life in two homes after divorce?

Our overriding impression was that there was no one way to handle visitation or transitions between homes that was ideal for all adolescents. Adolescents and their families appeared to be adapting equally well to many different forms of family life after divorce, whether with regard to residential arrangement or visitation schedules. For example, the amount of time spent in the nonresidential home had virtually no bearing on the relationships in or functioning of the residential home. We also found that when adolescents spent time with both parents, and especially when those parents were not in conflict, adolescents were able to sustain close relationships with both parents. Love is not a zero-sum game. Emotional ties to one parent do not subvert ties to the other parent.

We did identify two potential difficulties in integrating life in the two homes and two families, however. First, a majority of adolescents said that they at least sometimes experienced the feeling of being caught between their parents, and we found that the more loyalty conflicts the adolescents felt, the more depression they experienced, and the more likely they were to be involved in deviant behavior (although the link with deviance was less strong than the link with depression).

How can parents reduce the chances that adolescents will experience such torn loyalties? Above all, they can try to limit the amount of conflict in their relationship with the ex-spouse, and in the event that such conflict cannot be limited, they can take steps to make sure that their children are not drawn into it. For example, when ex-spouses communicate directly with each other about matters concerning their children or their ongoing parenting relationship, rather than passing messages through the children, this is of benefit to the children. Even when the issues seem harmless, having to carry messages from one parent to the other can be a stressful experience. Parents can also reduce the chances of stimulating loyalty conflicts in their children by refraining from asking questions about the other parent or other home—especially if those questions are motivated by jealousy or criticism of the other parent—and from derogating the other parent in the child's presence. In the end, parents must try to allow the child to develop and maintain a good relationship with the other parent if that is what the child wants, and the problems and hostilities within the marital relationship should be contained there as much as possible. Otherwise, children may react by withdrawing from one or both parents (children who felt most caught said they were not close to either parent; perhaps withdrawal from both relationships represents an attempt to relieve the stress of loyalty conflicts).

Of course, our data on loyalty conflicts are preliminary; our measures were limited, and our cross-sectional data preclude conclusions about cause and effect. Given the association between feelings of being caught and adjustment (especially depression), however, we believe this is an aspect of children's postdivorce experience that merits focused attention.

A second potential difficulty in integrating life in two homes arises when the two parents are inconsistent with respect to management and control. Inconsistent parenting has been identified as a risk factor for negative adjustment among children in nondivorced families (Block, Block, and Morrison, 1981; Stoneman, Brody, and Burke, 1989). Our data suggest that, after divorce, when parents' rules and expectations for the child are inconsistent, this can generate conflict between the residential parent and child as well as loyalty conflicts. Parent-child conflict and loyalty conflicts are particularly likely, in turn, to be associated with depression in the adolescent; in fact, they account for the relation between inconsistency and depression. Furthermore, inconsistent parenting by itself (regardless of any associations with parent-child conflict or loyalty conflicts) is linked to higher levels of antisocial deviant behavior on the part of the adolescent. Again, this finding merits further investigation to identify the extent to which inconsistencies allow antisocial behavior to emerge versus the extent to which inconsistencies emerge as a parental response to antisocial behavior in the child. In any case, it appears that adolescents do have difficulty—particularly emotional difficulty—when parents do not establish consistent routines and styles of control in the two postdivorce homes.

It is not an easy matter for divorced parents to maintain consistency between the two households. With the passage of time, there is a rapid drop-off in the frequency with which the two parents talk to one another about the children (Maccoby and Mnookin, 1992). At Time 1 of the initial study (about six months after parental separation), 68 percent of parents reported that they talked together about the children at least once a week; by Time 3 (three and a half years after separation), this proportion had dropped to 40 percent. Even as early as Time 1, only about half of the parents said that they were attempting to coordinate rules between the two households, and by Time 3, only about a third were doing so. As parents remarry and residential moves take place, it becomes ever more difficult to reach and sustain any explicit agreements about what adolescents' curfews should be, what decisions they can make on their own, where they may go after school or in the evenings, and how much supervision they require. More and more, it is a question of whether the two parents (and their new partners) happen to have the same kinds of values and standards, independent of each other. Yet consistency does benefit the children, and parents should be aware of its influence and attempt not to diverge too greatly from each other's standards if the children are spending time in both households. Among the families in our study, dual-resident parents were generally more successful at maintaining consistency than other parents, perhaps because they communicated with each other more often.

Summary

In general, we are encouraged by the results of our endeavor. Four and a half years after their parents had separated, many adolescents were functioning well and could talk to us frankly and articulately about their experiences as members of divorced families. Furthermore, our findings have allowed us to identify actions that parents can take to enhance their children's adjustment to the divorce. Some of these actions may not be easy. It requires effort and self-discipline not to disparage an ex-spouse; to maintain an involved, affectionate, supervisory parental role; to take steps to prevent children from feeling the need to move into a caretaking role; or to work out consistent rules and standards across homes in which the adolescent spends time. For parents who feel they must divorce, however, but who care deeply about their children's functioning, these achievements are possible.

Resolving Discrepancies in Reports of New Partners

In the course of our study, we encountered discrepancies between siblings, and between adolescents and parents, in reports of the presence of new partners or the duration of new relationships. With regard to the *existence* of new partners, discrepancies between siblings were resolved as follows: (1) if the adolescents lived with different parents, we took the answer of the adolescent living with the parent in question; (2) if one adolescent gave information that clearly conflicted with earlier information given by one or both parents and one did not, we took the nonconflicting answer; and (3) if we could not resolve the discrepancy, we took the affirmative answer (for example, that the parent was remarried, was dating someone, or was living with someone). Although there were some disagreements between children and parents over the *existence* of new partners, we always took the adolescent's answer in such cases because of the possibility of change between the time of the last parent interview and the adolescent interview. Discrepancies about whether a parent was living with a new partner were also resolved in the adolescent's favor for the same reason. When parent and adolescent disagreed over the *remarriage status* of a parent, we coded the parent as remarried (if the adolescent said that the parent was remarried and the parent said that he or she was not remarried, the remarriage could have occurred since the parent interview; if the parent responded positively regarding remarriage but the adolescent answered negatively—yet identified the same new partner—we assumed that the parent knew best).

Disagreements between siblings or between parent and adolescent concerning the length of time the parent had been involved with or remarried to the new partner were resolved as follows:

•If the adolescent said that the new partner had been around for a long time (longer than parent's T3 interview) but the parent indicated no special new partner at T3, we counted this person as a new partner (as explained above), but categorized time of involvement as "1" (less than two years), even if the time given by the adolescent had been two years or longer.

•If the time period for which the adolescent said that the parent and new partner had been dating was longer than the time period since the parent's Time 3 interview but shorter than the time period since the parent's Time 2 interview, and the parent's interviews did not contradict this (in other words, the parent said he or she was not involved at T2 but was involved at T3), we categorized the couple's time of involvement based on the number of months the adolescent said this couple had been dating. If more than one adolescent was interviewed and their answers fell into different categories, we averaged (for two adolescents) or took the majority answer (for more than two adolescents).

•If the parent indicated that he or she was "seriously involved" or "dating one person frequently" at both Times 2 and 3, yet the adolescent gave the time of involvement as less than two years, we took the adolescent's answer since we could not discern from the parent's interview whether the new partners of Time 2 and Time 3 were the same.

•If the adolescent and parent disagreed on the time the couple had lived together (for remarried or cohabiting new partners), and we could tell by the names given that they were talking about the same new partner, we used the date given by the parent (for remarriage or start of time living together) to compute time. If the adolescent and parent were talking about different people, we took the adolescent's answer to reflect the most recent situation. If names weren't available, and the discrepancy in times given by parent and child was large enough to place the answers in different categories (with the adolescent giving a length of time as less than two years, and data from the parent indicating a relationship of two or more years), we took the adolescent's answer on the assumption that things could have changed within the year prior to our talking to the adolescent.

•If the adolescent said he or she did not know the length of a new relationship, we used parent information to compute the length. If there was no parent information, or if parent information was not specific enough, data were left as missing.

•If we had no information at all from parents, we took the adolescent's answer to be correct. Where there was more than one sibling and the answers conflicted, the same procedures for resolution as described above were used (in other words, taking the average or majority answer depending on the number of siblings).

•If we had information only from the ex-spouse of the parent whose new partner was at issue, and that information conflicted with information given by the adolescent, we took the adolescent's answer.

•With the exceptions listed above, disagreements between adolescent and parent at issue were resolved in favor of the parent, even in cases where we had information from the other parent that more closely agreed with the adolescent.

APPENDIX B

Supplementary Tables

Table B.1 Descriptive statistics for measures

Measure	Time measured	n	Mean	S.D.	Min.	Max.	Cronbach's alpha
Demographics							
Age of adolescent	4	522	14.1	2.5	10	18	N/A
Sex of adolescent	1	522	1.49	.50	1	2	N/A
Mother's education	1	519	5.1	1.3	2	8	N/A
Father's education	1	521	5.4	1.6	2	8	N/A
Mother's earnings	Average T1–T3	507	19,214	12,156	0	82,333	N/A
Father's earnings	Average T1–T3	495	43,871	28,296	0	204,976	N/A
Family size	1	522	2.3	.87	1	6	N/A
Mother's working hours	3	431	36.6	16.8	0	84	N/A
Father's working hours	3	377	46.2	12.3	0	85	N/A
Stability of Residential Arrangement	4	522	.68	.47	0	1	N/A
Life Stresses	4	522	4.9	2.6	0	14	N/A
Interparental Relationship							
Discord	2	361	4.6	2.0	1	10	.72
Discord	3	339	4.1	1.5	1.2	8.5	.69
Cooperative communication	2	369	4.6	1.7	1	8	.52
Cooperative communication	3	338	4.5	1.9	2	9.3	.56
Mother's hostility	1	349	5.6	2.1	1	10	N/A
Father's hostility	1	282	5.3	2.1	1	10	N/A
Mother's hostility	2	416	5.3	2.4	1	10	N/A
Father's hostility	2	324	5.1	2.6	1	10	N/A
Mother's hostility	3	447	5.1	2.3	1	10	N/A
Father's hostility	3	378	4.9	2.3	1	10	N/A
Parental arguing	4	514	2.0	.99	1	4	N/A
Parental cooperation	4	334	6.2	2.2	.80	10.49	.57
Parental agreement on child rearing	4	520	15.4	5.0	5	25	.83
Overall parental conflict[a]	T1–T3	381	99.5	11.2	75	131	.81
Parent-Child Relationship							
Closeness to mother	4	521	36.1	7.5	10	45	.89
Closeness to father	4	494	33.0	8.1	9	45	.90
Trust of mother	4	522	9.5	2.5	2	12	.70
Trust of father	4	518	8.6	3.0	2	12	.78
Identification with mother	4	520	7.2	2.3	2	10	.79

Table B.1 (continued)

Measure	Time measured	n	Mean	S.D.	Min.	Max.	Cronbach's alpha
Identification with father	4	520	6.4	2.5	2	10	.82
Joint activities with mother	4	468	4.2	1.9	0	8	N/A
Joint activities with father	4	390	4.2	2.2	0	8	N/A
Mother remembers special days	4	519	2.9	.35	1	3	N/A
Father remembers special days	4	518	2.7	.60	1	3	N/A
Eager to see mother	4	468	3.6	1.1	1	5	N/A
Eager to see father	4	468	3.4	1.2	1	5	N/A
Overall closeness to mother[b]	4	521	102.0	12.0	60	122	.80
Overall closeness to father[b]	4	491	98.2	13.4	61	122	.79
Average conflict with mother	4	444	1.8	.93	1	5	.83
Average conflict with father	4	312	1.7	.91	1	5	.89
Maximum conflict with mother	4	444	2.4	1.4	1	5	N/A
Maximum conflict with father	4	312	2.1	1.3	1	5	N/A
Disengagement from mother's home	4	486	7.1	2.4	3	14	.55
Disengagement from father's home	4	360	6.5	2.4	3	14	.57
Considered moving out	4	494	.38	.49	0	1	N/A
Both places feel like home	4	468	.27	.44	0	1	N/A
Mother confides	4	520	3.7	1.9	0	7	.74
Father confides	4	496	2.2	1.9	0	7	.76
Adolescent nurtures mother	4	522	3.2	1.6	0	6	.63
Adolescent nurtures father	4	522	2.5	1.7	0	6	.66
Feels caught between parents	4	522	4.8	2.9	0	12	.64
Uses parents against each other	4	499	1.5	.71	1	4	N/A

Table B.1   (continued)

Measure	Time measured	n	Mean	S.D.	Min.	Max.	Cronbach's alpha
Parental Control and Management							
Monitoring–mother	4	447	11.8	2.4	5	15	.75
Monitoring–father	4	315	10.8	2.6	5	15	.75
School night curfew–mother	4	423	2.2	2.0	0	6	N/A
School night curfew–father	4	212	1.9	1.9	0	6	N/A
Weekend night curfew–mother	4	459	3.5	2.6	0	8	N/A
Weekend night curfew–father	4	339	3.1	2.6	0	8	N/A
Adult home after school–mother	4	382	.48	.50	0	1	N/A
Adult home after school–father	4	198	.51	.50	0	1	N/A
Youth-alone decisions–mother	4	464	.45	.27	0	1	N/A
Youth-alone decisions–father	4	351	.42	.26	0	1	N/A
Youth decides–mother	4	464	.61	.26	0	1	N/A
Youth decides–father	4	351	.59	.25	0	1	N/A
Joint decisions–mother	4	464	.70	.44	0	1	N/A
Joint decisions–father	4	351	.73	.42	0	1	N/A
Household organization–mother	4	486	38.1	8.9	9	54	.79
Household organization–father	4	360	38.8	8.2	13	54	.74
Acceptance of rules–mother	4	487	19.0	3.8	5	25	.68
Acceptance of rules–father	4	368	18.7	3.8	5	25	.67
Chores–mother	4	486	26.3	5.8	11	43	N/A
Chores–father	4	360	23.3	6.4	11	44	N/A
Household management–mother[c]	4	444	100.1	10.7	68	121	.75
Household management–father[c]	4	301	100.0	10.2	69	121	.71
Adolescents' Satisfaction with Time Spent with Each Parent	4	521	6.9	2.6	1	10	N/A

Table B.1 (continued)

Measure	Time measured	*n*	Mean	S.D.	Min.	Max.	Cronbach's alpha
Adolescent Adjustment							
Depression/anxiety	4	522	15.2	7.0	0	30	.83
Overall deviance	4	522	21.8	5.7	16	46	.83
Substance use	4	522	7.9	3.3	6	24	.83
School deviance	4	521	7.2	2.5	4	16	.70
Antisocial behavior	4	522	5.7	1.2	5	13	.53
School grades	4	522	5.8	1.6	1	8	N/A
School effort	4	477	14.6	3.2	5	24	.55
Worst problem	4	522	111.3	14.9	83.7	168.1	N/A
Attacking conflict resolution style	4	522	1.6	.33	1	2.88	.67
Compromising conflict resolution style	4	522	2.6	.38	1.25	3	.58
Avoiding conflict resolution style	4	522	2.0	.33	1	3	.50
Enjoyment of activities	4	522	5.8	1.7	1	9	N/A
Closeness to same-sex friend	4	519	36.3	5.8	16	45	.79

N/A = Not applicable.

a. A composite combining several of the "interparental relationship" scales (discord at T2 and T3, cooperative communication at T2 and T3, and both mother's and father's hostility at T1 and T3). See Chapter 5 for further explanation.

b. A composite combining several of the "parent-child relationship" scales (closeness, trust, identification, and joint activities). See Chapter 5.

c. A composite combining several of the "parental control and management" scales (monitoring, school night curfew, weekend night curfew, youth-alone decisions, household organization, and acceptance of rules). See Chapter 5.

Table B.2 Age and school grade of the adolescent respondents ($N = 522$)

Age		Grade in school	
10½–11	19.7%	Fifth–sixth	26.5%
12–13	25.6	Seventh–eighth	23.2
14–15	21.5	Ninth–tenth	21.9
16–17	19.2	Eleventh–twelfth	17.9
18	14.0	Dropped out before	
	100.0%	completing high school	1.9
		Completed high school,	
		not now in school	2.3
		Taking college courses	6.3
			100.0%

Table B.3 Characteristics of the adolescents' parents

Characteristic	Mothers	Fathers
Highest Education Attained		
Eighth grade or less	1.0%	1.9%
Less than high school graduate	5.0	6.0
Graduated high school	27.3	22.3
Some college	39.7	28.0
College graduate	13.8	18.1
Some postgraduate education	5.2	5.8
Completed advanced degree	8.0	17.9
	100.0%	100.0%
	n = (363)	(364)
Working Hours at Time 3		
Not employed for pay	17.2%	6.2%
Under 30 hours per week	5.9	1.1
30–39 hours	11.3	2.2
40–44 hours	41.2	35.4
45 hours or more	24.4	55.1
	100.0%	100.0%
	n = (320)	(274)
Yearly Earnings at Time 3		
(for employed parents)		
Less than $10,000	8.8%	00.0%
$10,000–$19,999	41.3	10.6
$20,000–$29,999	30.0	14.2
$30,000–$39,999	12.9	24.8
$40,000–$49,999	4.7	17.9
$50,000 or more	2.3	32.5
	100.0%	100.0%
	n = (317)	(330)

Table B.4 Composition of the parental households[a]

Persons in household	Percentage of households including indicated person	
	Mothers' households	Fathers' households
Stepparent (married to natural parent)	31.6%	36.8%
Parent's new partner (unmarried)	15.4	18.7
Natural sibling	60.4	27.7
Stepsibling[b]	6.6	21.2
Half-sibling	8.5	9.3
Adult relative	6.6	7.7
Unrelated adult female	6.3	3.3
Unrelated adult male	2.7	6.9
Child of adolescent subject	.8	0.0
Child cousin	1.9	1.6
Unrelated child	1.6	1.1
Composition not known	.5	4.4

a. This table excludes cases of adolescents not living with either parent. Columns add to more than 100 percent because some households included persons in more than one category.

b. Children of unmarried but cohabiting new partners are included in the count of stepsiblings.

Table B.5 Adolescents' personal resources by residential arrangement and sex of adolescent[a]

Measure of personal resources	Mother residence M	(n)	Dual residence M	(n)	Father residence M	(n)	F_{sex}	$F_{residence}$	$F_{interaction}$
Conflict resolution styles									
Attacking style (range: 1–3)[b]									
Boys	1.58	(168)	1.59	(32)	1.60	(62)	.16	1.43	.82
Girls	1.54	(197)	1.65	(19)	1.63	(38)			
Compromising style (range: 1–3)									
Boys	2.55	(168)	2.45	(32)	2.49	(62)	7.09**	1.13	.15
Girls	2.64	(197)	2.60	(19)	2.61	(38)			
Avoidant style (range: 1–3)									
Boys	1.94	(168)	1.88	(32)	2.02	(62)	.01	.20	1.93
Girls	1.96	(197)	1.96	(19)	1.90	(38)			
Enjoyment of activities (range: 1–10)									
Boys	5.9	(168)	5.4	(32)	6.2	(62)	.50	.74	1.50
Girls	5.7	(197)	5.7	(19)	5.6	(38)			
Closeness to same-sex friend (range: 9–45)									
Boys	34.7	(167)	35.4	(32)	35.3	(61)	17.68****	.89	.70
Girls	37.8	(197)	39.3	(19)	37.1	(37)			

a. All means are adjusted for age and sex of adolescent and average parental education.
b. The ranges given are possible, not actual, ranges.
**$p \leq .01$.   ****$p \leq .0001$.

Table B.6 Adolescents' internalizing problems, externalizing problems, school adjustment, and "worst problem" by residential arrangement and sex of adolescent[a]

Measure of adjustment	Mother residence		Dual residence		Father residence		F_{sex}	$F_{residence}$	$F_{interaction}$	Significant differences
	M	(n)	M	(n)	M	(n)				
Internalizing Problems										
Depression/anxiety (range: 0–30)[b]										
Boys	14.0	(168)	13.0	(32)	13.3	(62)	12.59***	2.10	2.10	
Girls	16.5	(197)	14.0	(19)	18.5	(38)				
Externalizing Problems										
Substance use (range: 6–24)										
Boys	7.8	(168)	7.8	(32)	8.5	(62)	.64	3.77*,c	.25	F > M, D
Girls	7.6	(197)	7.2	(19)	8.5	(38)				
School deviance (range: 4–16)										
Boys	7.2	(168)	7.5	(32)	7.5	(62)	1.09	1.00	.03	
Girls	6.9	(196)	7.2	(19)	7.3	(38)				
Antisocial behavior (range: 5–20)										
Boys	5.9	(168)	6.2	(32)	6.0	(62)	21.59****	1.50	1.28	
Girls	5.3	(197)	5.2	(19)	5.6	(38)				

							F	F	F	
Overall deviance (range: 15–68)										
Boys	22.0	(168)	22.6	(32)	23.1	(62)	3.85+	3.58*		F > M
Girls	20.9	(197)	20.6	(19)	22.7	(38)			.46	
School Adjustment										
Grades (range: 1–8)										
Boys	5.6	(168)	6.1	(32)	5.4	(62)	2.14	2.87+,d		F < D
Girls	6.0	(197)	6.2	(19)	5.6	(38)			.43	
School effort (range: 2–24)										
Boys	14.2	(153)	14.2	(32)	14.7	(59)	1.07	.58		
Girls	15.1	(176)	15.4	(17)	13.9	(35)			3.01+,e	
"Worst Problem" (standardized)										
Boys	111.4	(168)	109.3	(32)	112.4	(62)	.09	5.39**		F > M, D
Girls	110.2	(197)	104.5	(19)	116.9	(38)			2.32+,e	

a. All means are adjusted for age and sex of adolescent and mid-parent education.
b. The ranges given are possible, not actual, ranges.
c. The effect weakens in random subsamples.
d. The effect gets stronger when residence effects are examined controlling for sex.
e. The effect drops out in three random subsamples.
+$p \leq .10$. *$p \leq .05$. **$p \leq .01$. ***$p \leq .001$. ****$p \leq .0001$.

Table B.7 Selected indices of family context by new-partner status

Demographic factor	No new partner	Dating	Cohabiting	Remarried	p
Residential Mothers[a]					
Mean age of adolescent	14.2	14.5	13.9	13.7	+
Mother's education[b]	5.5	5.2	5.2	5.0	+
Mother's earnings (T1–T3)[b,c]	20.7	22.6	18.7	19.7	n.s.
Mother's working hours (T3)[b]	40.8	40.8	30.4	33.2	***
Residential Fathers[d]					
Mean age of adolescent	13.9	14.7	14.1	13.3	+
Father's education[b]	5.4	5.8	4.7	5.6	n.s.
Father's earnings (T1–T3)[b,c]	44.1	37.1	44.2	57.2	+
Father's working hours (T3)[b]	44.9	39.7	48.6	49.5	*

Column header spanning: New-partner status

a. Included here are cases in which the adolescents lived with their mothers (in sole or dual residence).

b. Numbers are based on a sample of only one adolescent per family selected randomly.

c. In thousands of dollars per year. Based on average over T1, T2, and T3.

d. Included here are cases in which the adolescents lived with their fathers (in sole or dual residence).

$^+p = \leq .10.$ $^*p = \leq .05.$ $^{***}p = \leq .001.$ n.s. = not significant.

Table B.8 Relation of visitation levels to demographic characteristics

	Level of visitation				
Demographic characteristic	Little or none (1)	Vacation only (2)	Moderate (3)	High (4)	$F_{\text{visitation}}$
Mother-Resident Adolescents					
Maximum *n*	(116)	(63)	(75)	(93)	
Mean age of adolescents	14.5	14.0	14.1	13.1	6.50^{***} (4 < 1,2,3)
Percentage male	41.4	39.7	50.7	54.8	1.85
Mother's education[a]	4.9	5.1	5.2	5.3	1.15
Father's education[a]	5.0	5.8	5.3	5.6	2.39^{+} (1 < 2,4)
Mid-parent education[a]	5.0	5.4	5.3	5.5	2.14^{+} (1 < 4)
Percentage with mother remarried[a,b]	33.6	36.3	20.7	38.0	1.42
Percentage with father remarried[a,b]	38.8	49.3	28.8	33.9	1.37
Percentage who have been in same residence since divorce[b]	77.8	71.9	84.3	81.7	1.22
Father-Resident Adolescents					
Maximum *n*	(23)	(28)	(22)	(25)	
Mean age of adolescents	15.4	14.0	14.7	12.9	5.29^{**} (4 < 1,2,3; 2 < 1)
Percentage male	56.5	60.7	59.1	76.0	.80
Mother's education[a]	4.4	5.0	4.4	4.7	1.65
Father's education[a]	4.9	5.9	5.2	4.8	3.10^{*} (2 > 1,4)
Mid-parent education[a]	4.7	5.5	4.8	4.7	3.23^{*} (2 > 1,3,4)
Percentage with mother remarried[a,b]	24.9	48.8	27.4	24.1	1.11
Percentage with father remarried[a,b]	22.5	46.6	34.4	50.6	1.10
Percentage who have been in same residence since divorce[b]	54.8	32.5	21.3	30.4	2.06

a. Values taken from a random sample where only one adolescent per family is represented.
b. Means are controlled for age and sex of adolescent and mid-parent education.
$^{+}p \leq .10.$ $^{*}p \leq .05.$ $^{**}p \leq .01.$ $^{***}p \leq .001.$

Table B.9 Parent-adolescent relationships in three residential arrangements, by sex of adolescent[a]

Measure of parent-adolescent relationship	Mother residence		Dual residence		Father residence	
	M	(n)	M	(n)	M	(n)
Closeness to mother (range: 9–45)[b]						
Boys	37.3	(168)	37.4	(31)	**35.7**	(61)
Girls	35.9	(197)	39.4	(18)	**30.5**	(38)
Closeness to father (range: 9–45)						
Boys	**33.5**	(151)	35.7	(32)	35.6	(62)
Girls	**31.1**	(186)	37.8	(19)	32.6	(38)
Trust of mother (range: 2–12)						
Boys	9.8	(168)	10.0	(31)	**9.6**	(62)
Girls	9.3	(197)	10.1	(18)	**8.0**	(38)
Trust of father (range: 2–12)						
Boys	**8.4**	(168)	9.5	(32)	9.8	(61)
Girls	**8.1**	(194)	9.6	(19)	9.5	(38)
Identification with mother (range: 2–10)						
Boys	7.6	(168)	8.3	(31)	**7.3**	(61)
Girls	7.0	(196)	7.8	(18)	**5.4**	(38)
Identification with father (range: 2–10)						
Boys	**6.5**	(168)	7.7	(32)	7.0	(62)
Girls	**5.8**	(195)	7.5	(19)	6.8	(38)
Joint activities with mother (range: 0–11)						
Boys	4.1	(162)	4.9	(31)	**4.2**	(41)
Girls	4.3	(184)	3.9	(16)	**3.4**	(27)
Joint activities with father (range: 0–11)						
Boys	**4.2**	(113)	5.1	(32)	5.0	(62)
Girls	**3.5**	(126)	4.4	(17)	4.0	(36)
Average conflict with mother (range: 0–5)						
Boys	1.9	(162)	1.6	(31)	**1.5**	(30)
Girls	1.9	(184)	1.8	(16)	**2.2**	(14)

Table B.9 (continued)

Measure of parent-adolescent relationship	Mother residence		Dual residence		Father residence	
	M	(*n*)	*M*	(*n*)	*M*	(*n*)
Average conflict with father (range 0–5)						
Boys	**1.6**	(89)	1.6	(32)	1.9	(62)
Girls	**1.5**	(74)	1.7	(17)	1.8	(36)
Maximum conflict with mother (range: 0–5)						
Boys	2.5	(162)	2.1	(31)	**1.8**	(30)
Girls	2.6	(184)	2.4	(16)	**2.8**	(14)
Maximum conflict with father (range: 0–5)						
Boys	**1.9**	(89)	2.1	(32)	2.4	(62)
Girls	**1.8**	(74)	2.3	(17)	2.5	(36)
Disengagement from mother's household (range: 3–14)						
Boys	7.2	(168)	6.9	(31)	**5.6**	(44)
Girls	7.4	(197)	5.9	(18)	**7.2**	(21)
Disengagement from father's household (range: 3–14)						
Boys	**6.0**	(106)	7.0	(32)	7.2	(62)
Girls	**5.9**	(101)	6.1	(19)	7.8	(38)
Mother confides (standardized; actual range: 0–7)						
Boys	3.7	(168)	4.0	(31)	**3.4**	(61)
Girls	3.8	(197)	3.8	(18)	**3.3**	(37)
Father confides (standardized; actual range: 0–7)						
Boys	**2.1**	(152)	3.2	(32)	3.0	(62)
Girls	**1.7**	(187)	3.2	(19)	2.2	(38)
Adolescent nurtures mother (standardized; actual range: 0–6)						
Boys	3.4	(168)	2.8	(31)	**2.9**	(62)
Girls	3.3	(197)	3.2	(18)	**3.0**	(38)

Table B.9 (continued)

Measure of parent-adolescent relationship	Mother residence		Dual residence		Father residence	
	M	*(n)*	*M*	*(n)*	*M*	*(n)*
Adolescent nurtures father (standardized; actual range: 0–6)						
Boys	**2.4**	(168)	2.3	(32)	2.8	(62)
Girls	**2.5**	(197)	2.9	(19)	2.7	(38)
Mother remembers special days (range: 1–3)						
Boys	2.93	(168)	2.91	(31)	**2.89**	(61)
Girls	2.91	(195)	3.00	(18)	**2.71**	(38)
Father remembers special days (range: 1–3)						
Boys	**2.63**	(167)	2.74	(32)	2.85	(61)
Girls	**2.63**	(195)	3.00	(19)	2.83	(38)
Eagerness to see mother (range: 1–5)						
Boys	3.5	(146)	3.6	(31)	**3.7**	(58)
Girls	3.7	(173)	3.5	(16)	**3.5**	(36)
Eagerness to see father (range: 1–5)						
Boys	**3.4**	(146)	3.3	(32)	3.4	(58)
Girls	**3.3**	(173)	3.2	(17)	3.6	(36)

Note: Means for nonresidential parents are presented in boldface.

a. Means are adjusted for age of adolescent and the appropriate form of parental education (mother's education when comparing relationships with mother, father's education when comparing relationships with father) by entering these variables as covariates in the analysis.

b. Unless otherwise noted, range of scores indicates possible, not actual, range.

Table B.10 Parental management and control in three residential
arrangements, by sex of adolescent[a]

Measure of parental management/control	Mother residence M	Mother residence (n)	Dual residence M	Dual residence (n)	Father residence M	Father residence (n)
Monitoring by mother (range: 5–15)[b]						
Boys	11.7	(162)	11.6	(31)	**10.9**	(32)
Girls	12.1	(184)	12.6	(16)	**9.9**	(15)
Monitoring by father (range: 5–15)						
Boys	**10.3**	(88)	11.4	(32)	11.9	(61)
Girls	**10.1**	(79)	12.2	(17)	10.9	(36)
Youth alone–mother (range: 0–1)						
Boys	.46	(162)	.51	(31)	**.46**	(44)
Girls	.41	(184)	.37	(16)	**.51**	(20)
Youth alone–father (range: 0–1)						
Boys	**.42**	(103)	.50	(32)	.44	(62)
Girls	**.40**	(99)	.38	(17)	.41	(36)
Youth decides–mother (range: 0–1)						
Boys	.62	(162)	.70	(31)	**.64**	(44)
Girls	.58	(184)	.51	(16)	**.67**	(20)
Youth decides–father (range: 0–1)						
Boys	**.60**	(103)	.70	(32)	.61	(62)
Girls	**.55**	(99)	.50	(17)	.57	(36)
Joint decisions–mother (range: 0–1)						
Boys	.68	(162)	.57	(31)	**.68**	(44)
Girls	.76	(184)	.79	(16)	**.63**	(20)
Joint decisions–father (range: 0–1)						
Boys	**.73**	(103)	.60	(32)	.70	(62)
Girls	**.77**	(99)	.82	(17)	.72	(36)
School night curfew–mother (range: 0–6)						
Boys	2.1	(162)	2.4	(30)	**2.1**	(17)
Girls	2.2	(184)	2.2	(16)	**1.9**	(9)

Table B.10 (continued)

Measure of parental management/control	Mother residence		Dual residence		Father residence	
	M	(n)	M	(n)	M	(n)
School night curfew– father (range: 0–6)						
Boys	**2.1**	(37)	2.5	(28)	1.8	(62)
Girls	**1.6**	(38)	1.8	(12)	1.9	(35)
Weekend night curfew– mother (range: 0–8)						
Boys	3.5	(162)	3.9	(28)	**3.3**	(43)
Girls	3.6	(184)	2.8	(15)	**3.5**	(20)
Weekend night curfew– father (range: 0–8)						
Boys	**3.2**	(98)	4.2	(31)	3.2	(62)
Girls	**2.7**	(95)	3.0	(17)	3.3	(35)
Household organization– mother (range: 9–54)						
Boys	38.6	(168)	40.4	(31)	**39.6**	(44)
Girls	36.9	(197)	40.8	(18)	**37.4**	(21)
Household organization– father (range: 9–54)						
Boys	**39.4**	(106)	40.4	(32)	39.3	(62)
Girls	**37.8**	(101)	40.2	(19)	37.4	(38)
Chores–mother (range: 11–48)						
Boys	27.6	(168)	25.6	(31)	**22.1**	(44)
Girls	26.5	(197)	25.8	(18)	**23.9**	(21)
Chores–father (range: 11–48)						
Boys	**21.4**	(152)	24.4	(32)	27.5	(62)
Girls	**21.3**	(187)	23.9	(19)	26.2	(38)
Acceptance of rules– mother (range: 5–25)						
Boys	19.2	(168)	19.1	(31)	**19.4**	(44)
Girls	18.9	(197)	19.6	(18)	**18.2**	(22)
Acceptance of rules– father (range: 5–25)						
Boys	**19.2**	(109)	18.8	(32)	18.8	(62)
Girls	**18.3**	(106)	19.3	(19)	17.8	(38)

Table B.10   (continued)

Measure of parental management/control	Mother residence		Dual residence		Father residence	
	M	(*n*)	*M*	(*n*)	*M*	(*n*)
Adult home after school– mother (range: 0–1)						
Boys	.46	(145)	.41	(30)	**.59**	(14)
Girls	.50	(168)	.45	(14)	**.17**	(7)
Adult home after school– father (range: 0–1)						
Boys	**.62**	(37)	.52	(27)	.44	(57)
Girls	**.66**	(35)	.44	(11)	.36	(31)

Note: Means for nonresidential parents are presented in boldface.

a. Means are adjusted for age of adolescent and the appropriate form of parental education (mother's education when comparing relationships with mother, father's education when comparing relationships with father) by entering these variables as covariates in the analysis.

b. Range of scores indicates possible, not actual, range.

Table B.11   Results of multivariate regression predicting parenting discrepancies

Predictor variables	Parenting discrepancies	
	b	β
Constant	1.16	
Female	.10	.07
Parental education	.04	.07
Frequency of parental arguing (T4)	.06	.08
Parental cooperation (T4)	−.07****	−.23
Contact with nonresidential parent (T4)	−.12**	−.17
Education × arguing (T4)	−.07*	−.11
Education × cooperation (T4)	.03*	.11
Total R^2 = .12, F = 7.08****		

$*p \leq .05.$ $**p \leq .01.$ $****p \leq .0001.$

NOTES

1. Introduction

1. An additional factor that has been emphasized as important in understanding the effects of divorce is economic stress. Even among fairly affluent families, divorce can mean economic stringency. Families currently spend a much higher proportion of their incomes on housing than was the case twenty-five or more years ago. At present, supporting two residences is substantially more costly than supporting one, and the postdivorce standard of living of one or both parents must reflect this fact. For some families, one or both parents simply live less well, and perhaps must work longer hours. For other families, however, one or both households will fall below the poverty line. Most commonly, it is the mother's household—usually including the children—that becomes impoverished. Although economic factors, per se, are not a central focus of this book, we take these and related factors into account as we examine the importance of the other more interpersonal factors.

2. The processes whereby parents negotiate their custodial decisions are described and analyzed in Mnookin et al. (1989) and in Maccoby and Mnookin (1992).

3. In Study 1, "residence" and "residential arrangement" were used to describe a child's physical custody arrangement, which in a number of cases was not the same as the custody arrangement specified in the divorce decree. We continue the practice of using "residence," rather than "custody," when we are referring to the adolescents' physical custody arrangements.

4. See the early work of Wallerstein and Kelly (1980) and Hetherington and colleagues (for example, Hetherington, Cox, and Cox, 1982). More recent evidence and reviews of the growing body of research may be found in Hetherington and Clingempeel (1992) and in Emery (1988).

2. Methods

1. The findings from these parent interviews are reported in Maccoby and Mnookin (1992).
2. Detailed information about how each scale was constructed can be obtained from the first author.

3. The Adolescents

1. Maccoby and Mnookin (1992) report similar findings for the overall sample from which our adolescents were drawn. For example, Study 1 children who were under age six when their parents separated were more likely to lose contact with nonresidential fathers over time than children six years and older. Thus our adolescent sample was drawn from those age groups most likely to maintain or increase contact with nonresidential fathers over time (see Maccoby and Mnookin, 1992, p. 180, Figure 8.6).
2. We did compare the adjustment of our adolescents with adolescents of comparable age from another large study of adolescents in the same geographic area (Dornbusch et al., 1991; Steinberg et al., 1991). The comparison adolescents had answered the same questions concerning depression/anxiety and deviance that our adolescents answered, except that they answered using a written questionnaire. We found that our adolescents were more depressed and anxious than the comparison group from nondivorced families, and similar in depression to a comparison group from divorced families. Adolescents in our study, however, reported lower levels of deviance than either the divorced or nondivorced comparison samples, leading us to believe that the method of data collection influenced reporting of deviance.
3. The means and ranges for each of the scales we discuss in the following section are among those recorded in Appendix Table B.1.
4. Schoenbach and colleagues (1983) asked a junior high school sample (twelve- to fifteen-year-olds) questions similar to ours, but focusing on "the last week" rather than "the past month." They found that between 10 percent and 20 percent of the early adolescent sample experienced a variety of symptoms of depression "a lot of the time" or "most of the time," while over 50 percent experienced them "rarely or none of the time."
5. Two-fifths said that their most heated discussion with their mothers in the last two weeks had been "pretty angry," "very angry," or "extremely angry." Fewer (30 percent) reported conflicts of this intensity with fathers.

4. Adolescent Adjustment

1. The difference in father's earnings between dual residence and father residence did not quite reach statistical significance but, as Table 4.1

shows, was almost as substantial as the difference between dual residence and mother residence.

2. We realized that using the average across the two parents as a control may not have adequately accounted for differences in the residential parent's resources across arrangements. In addition, controlling for education—although more strongly related to residence than income—may not have captured the income differentials completely. Thus, in additional analyses, we compared adjustment scores across residential arrangements, controlling for both income and education of the residential parent, thus statistically equating residential mothers' and residential fathers' socioeconomic status. Because of the difficulty in defining a "residential parent" for adolescents in dual residence, dual-resident adolescents were excluded from some of these analyses; in others, we continued to use average parental education as the measure of education for dual-resident adolescents. In general, controlling for the residential parent's resources made little difference in the results. In the couple of instances where results changed slightly, we note this fact in the appropriate section of the text.

3. Controlling for residential parent's income and education (rather than average parental education) strengthened the residence difference.

4. The standardized score ($M = 100$, $S.D. = 16$) for each of these scales was summed to create the "worst problem" score.

5. The difference between mother- and dual-resident adolescents was significant at $p \leq .10$.

5. Life in the Residential Home

1. For analyses of residence differences concerning factors that were measured at the child or family level (in other words, there was only one measure of the construct for each adolescent respondent; examples are the number of life stresses and the amount of cooperation between parents), we compared all three residential groups in one analysis. However, when we examined residence differences in aspects of context or family functioning that were measured separately for each parent or each parent's household (constructs for which each adolescent could potentially have two scores, one for mother's home and one for father's home; examples include the number of people living in each household, the adolescent's closeness to each parent, and the level of monitoring in each home), we made three sets of comparisons. First, we compared households of mothers for adolescents in mother versus dual residence and households of fathers for adolescents in father versus dual residence. Then we excluded dual-resident households and directly compared homes of the residential parent for adolescents in mother and father residence.

2. Analyses for contextual factors were conducted with and without controlling for the demographic factors identified in Chapter 4 as linked to residence (age and sex of adolescent, education of parent). Adding controls never changed the results substantially. Because we were less interested in reasons for any differences in context than we were in whether such differences in fact existed, we discuss results obtained without controls.

3. The overall equation predicting father's hostility at Time 3 (using sex and age of adolescent and father's education, as well as residence) was not significant. The main effect of residence, however, was significant, and the differences among means for this main effect were consistent with the differences described for hostility measured at the other time points, and with what we would have predicted given the circumstances under which fathers often get custody. Thus we consider the results obtained at Time 3 as significant and meaningful.

4. However, over all ages (not just among the adolescents), according to the parents' own reports of the closeness of their predivorce involvement with the children, fathers who obtained sole physical custody were not more closely involved than other fathers before the parental separation.

5. Although the contrast between dual- and sole-resident fathers was not significant, the magnitude of the difference between means was the same as that for the significant contrast between dual- and sole-resident mothers.

6. Linking Home Life and Adjustment

1. Details about the derivation of these scores can be obtained from the first author.

2. For boys in mother residence, girls in mother residence, and boys in father residence, we used a modified hierarchical regression procedure whereby variables in the "context" set were entered first, followed by variables in the "interparental" relationship set, then variables in the "parent-child relationship" and "parental control and management" sets (see Cohen and Cohen, 1983, for a description of hierarchical regression using sets of variables). Yet even in the larger groups (for example, mother-resident boys) we did not have enough cases to legitimately enter all variables representing all four sets of constructs. We therefore used a "modified" procedure, as follows. Given that there is a strong theoretical basis for expecting that context variables influence process variables, rather than vice versa, we first entered the set of context variables. Any context variables that were not significant in predicting adjustment when just the context set was entered were dropped from subsequent analyses. In other words, our first analysis considered all context variables in

predicting each adjustment variable, but when we moved to include the interparental relationship set, we controlled only for those context variables that had been statistically significant in the first analysis, with the exception that age of adolescent was retained in all analyses. (The initial analysis of context variables was done both including and excluding parental working hours. Because including parental working hours reduced the number of cases available for analysis significantly, we only proceeded on the basis of the analysis including working hours if in fact working hours was a significant predictor of the adjustment measure in question. If working hours was not a significant predictor, we proceeded with further steps based on the analysis excluding working hours.) Entry of "interparental relationship" variables was done in three different ways: entering only the parent-reported variable (T3 maximum hostility or the parental conflict composite), entering just the two adolescent-reported (T4) measures of the relationship as a set, and entering parent-reported and adolescent-reported variables together as a set. If both parent-reported and adolescent-reported measures were significant predictors of a particular adjustment outcome (and the variables as a set added significant variance to the prediction at hand), both were retained for further analysis. If only the parent report or only the adolescent report added significant variance to the prediction of the adjustment measure, just that measure (or set, in the case of the adolescent-reported measures) was retained. In a similar fashion, we then entered the "parent-child relationship" set and the "parental control and management" set, both separately and together, controlling for context variables that had been significant, and any interparental relationship sets that had added significant variance to the context variables. In the description of results, we focus on whichever equation provided the best prediction of the adjustment measure at hand.

Note that this analysis strategy does not test explicitly for interactions of the predictor variables with sex or residence. When it appeared from the by-group analyses that a predictor of adjustment was different for boys and girls, or for mother- and father-resident adolescents, we then tested for interactions by entering multiplicative terms into a regression equation that included all of the main effect predictors that had been significant for each group separately.

3. In Table 6.2, we show the correlations of parent's new partner status with "worst problem" with only the adolescent's age and residential parent's education controlled. The predictive power of the residential parent's new partner status—for both presence of a stepparent and presence of an unmarried new partner—was stronger, however, when the other contextual variables (set 1) were controlled in regression analyses.

4. The presence of a cohabiting new partner was linked to attacking conflict

resolution, substance use, overall deviance, school grades, and "worst problem" for both mother- and father-resident boys; the links to attacking conflict resolution, antisocial behavior, and school effort were strongest for father-resident boys; and the link with school deviance was strongest for mother-resident boys.

5. The association between the presence of a cohabiting new partner and adolescent adjustment is no longer significant, although the residual correlations are in the same direction as before.

6. Table 6.2 shows significant relations between parent-child conflict and "worst problem," but these do not hold up in multivariate analyses when other aspects of the parent-child relationship are also included.

7. The relations were not statistically significant for father-resident girls, but were similar in magnitude to the relations for mother-resident girls.

8. This association was only significant for mother-resident girls, but went in the same direction for mother- and father-resident boys.

9. We examined the correlations separately for younger and older girls because we noted that when we correlated household management with "worst problem" without partialling the adolescent's age, the correlation went in the predicted direction.

10. The correlations between "worst problem" and the different components of household management for the fourteen father-resident girls who were fifteen or older were not significant, and several were close to zero.

11. Given the weakness of most direct associations between parent-child closeness and adolescent adjustment among father-resident adolescents, this interpretation may have less validity for this group. Even among father-resident adolescents, however, father-child closeness was highly related to the father's household management. The father's management, in turn, was clearly related to better adjustment among boys living with their fathers, and most likely related to better adjustment of girls as well (with the caveats already noted in the text).

12. The colinearity between measures for the two parents meant that when they were entered together in a multiple regression, the highest first-order correlation would absorb the variance common to both, and the beta coefficient for the second parent's scores was drastically reduced, or indeed in many instances switched signs, leading to a very misleading picture of the role of the parent with the initially lower correlation.

13. The links between the affective quality of the parent-child relationship and household management for the very small group of dual-resident girls were different in some ways from those in every other group. For example, the correlation between the averaged (across parents) scores for "household management" and "overall closeness" was .05 for these girls, making them the only group in which these two constructs were not

significantly and positively associated. However, the two main components of each of these composites—parent-child emotional closeness and
parental monitoring—were, in fact, positively and significantly correlated ($r = .52$). It turns out that other aspects of "overall closeness" and
"household management" were negatively related for these girls (for
example, more closeness was related to later curfews; more joint activities between parent and child were related to feelings that rules were less
fair and consistent). It appears that among this small group of girls, it is
still the case that close relationships facilitate more effective monitoring,
but that this relation is not apparent when we use the "overall closeness"
and "household management" composites.

7. Adaptation to New Partners

1. This strategy means that we had many fewer new partnerships to study
for fathers (a maximum of 151 cases) than we had for mothers (a maximum of 417). When we subdivided our sample by residence, sex of
adolescent, and our fourfold grouping of new-partner status, cell sizes
became quite small in some instances, especially for the father-resident
group. For example, there were only eighteen adolescents—nine boys
and nine girls—living with their fathers in sole or dual residence whose
fathers had a cohabiting partner. Cell sizes dropped even further when
some of the cases did not provide data on certain questions of interest,
or when we attempted to check our results in random subsamples using
only one sibling per family. We dealt with these issues by first subdividing
our cases by our four categories of new-partner status and sex of adolescent, and noting how or whether these subgroups differed with respect
to family process. We also, however, contrasted the remarried group with
the other three new-partner groups combined, and contrasted the families in which a new partner was living in the home (cohabiting or remarried) with the other two new-partner groups combined.

Throughout this chapter, analyses predicting "child-level" variables (in
other words, variables on which siblings in the same family could differ)
were first conducted using all adolescents, despite the fact that a parent's
new-partner status (the independent variable) was the same for all siblings in a family. Because siblings may differ in their reaction to the same
new-partnering situation, we felt that analyses using the full sample were
appropriate, especially given the low cell sizes that resulted in some of
the analyses using random subsamples. We did, however, follow the
procedure outlined in Chapter 2 for checking results in random subsamples where only one adolescent per family was represented, and thus any
results that did not hold up in subsamples are noted or considered
nonsignificant.

2. Mother's education was used as the control when examining mother's new-partner status, and father's education for father's new-partner status, with a few exceptions. When using measures of one parent's new-partner status to predict the relationship between adolescents and the other biological parent, we used the other parent's education as the control if it was related to the outcome measure of interest. New-partner status was not related to the number of children of the marriage, to the number of moves that adolescents had made from one household to the other, or to the number of life stresses adolescents had encountered. These factors, therefore, did not need to be controlled in the analyses of new-partner status and family processes.

3. In two random subsamples contrasting all four repartnering groups, and in the whole-sample analysis contrasting those who had live-in new partners (both cohabiting and remarried) with those who didn't, there was a significant repartnering status by sex interaction.

4. In a comparison of remarried versus nonremarried mothers, there was a trend-level interaction of mother's remarriage and sex of adolescent, indicating a tendency for girls to feel closer to their fathers if the mother was remarried than if she was not. There was also a trend-level relation between the mother's remarriage and lower levels of disengagement from the father's home for both sexes.

5. The differences for boys in closeness to their fathers were significant only for the original closeness composite, not for "overall closeness," although it is apparent in Figure 7.3 that the stated trend exists for "overall closeness" as well.

6. On several measures of the parent-adolescent relationship, we also found that adolescents, especially girls, experienced better relationships with their fathers when they did not have a new partner living in the home (there was no new partner or only regular dating) than when they did (the father was remarried or cohabiting with the new partner).

7. There was a significant sex by new-partner status interaction when contrasting the group that had live-in new partners (remarried or cohabiting) with the group that did not have such partners.

8. Household management was also high among dating fathers, particularly when we used the full sample of adolescents. But in all subsamples of adolescents where we used only one adolescent per family, selected randomly, the level of management in the "dating only" group was reduced and was not significantly higher than the household management of fathers who had no new partner or a cohabiting new partner. Also, the level of management in the "dating only" group was reduced to the level of the "no new partner" group when we took into account the fewer working hours among fathers in the "dating only" group. Thus the most robust finding was the difference in management between

remarried fathers and fathers with no new partner or a cohabiting new partner.

9. Although when all four groups were contrasted with one another the effect of father's repartnering status on "adult home after school" was not significant, there was a significant difference on this variable between remarried fathers and the other three groups combined.

10. When adolescents are quoted, their ages are identified only as "early adolescent" (ages ten to thirteen), "mid-adolescent" (ages fourteen to sixteen), and "late adolescent" (ages seventeen to eighteen) in order to further conceal their identity. Gender or residence may be omitted for the same reason.

11. The interaction of age and sex of adolescent is not significant, but post-hoc t-tests indicate that there is a sex difference in the acceptance of mother's new partner's authority only for thirteen- and fourteen-year-olds.

12. There was a significant interaction of closeness to the residential parent and sex of the adolescent when predicting acceptance of the new partner's authority in the following instances: predicting acceptance of the new father for mother- and dual-resident adolescents combined, and predicting acceptance of the new mother for father-resident adolescents alone. The sex difference did not apply to dual-resident adolescents' acceptance of a new mother's authority.

13. The three scales with negative correlations are of course not independent of one another, and so must be taken together in indicating a weak negative trend.

14. When we repeated these analyses using the adolescent's closeness to the parent's new partner, rather than acceptance of the new partner's authority, the results were in the same direction, but somewhat weaker.

15. The relation between remarriage and adjustment was somewhat weaker in the analyses presented in Table 7.8 than in the analyses reported in Chapter 6. The change in magnitude of the relations among the father- and dual-resident adolescents is due to the somewhat different subset of adolescents used in Chapter 6 and in the present analyses. If dual-resident adolescents are excluded from the current analyses, the associations between father's remarriage and the adjustment indices are stronger. Among the mother- and dual-resident group, however, the findings indicate that the better adjustment of adolescents with a stepfather is partially a result of the fact that these adolescents have closer relationships with their mothers. As we noted in Chapter 6, the positive effects of parental remarriage are attenuated when the affective quality of the residential parent-child relationship is considered.

16. With regard to compromising conflict resolution, accounting for acceptance of the authority of the new partner reduced the importance of

remarriage itself. In addition, although acceptance of the new partner's authority was not a significant predictor of compromising, the relation between acceptance and compromise was as large for the acceptance of new mothers as it was for the acceptance of new fathers. Thus if there had been larger numbers of adolescents living with their fathers in sole or dual residence, we might have found the relation between acceptance of the new mother's authority and compromising in conflict situations to be significant.

9. Visitation

1. If regression analyses were required, we dummy coded the visitation scale to represent the different categories of interest, unless we had determined that the scale did bear a linear relation to the variable under study.
2. The residence difference was significant using all subjects but was of borderline significance in random samples.
3. These correlations are partialed for sex of adolescent and average parent education.
4. The differences in means for the father-resident adolescents are not significant, but are roughly the same magnitude as the differences for mother-resident adolescents.

10. Life in the Nonresidential Home

1. When using all subjects in our sample, there was a trend-level interaction between residence and sex, indicating that average conflict with mother did not differ by residential arrangement for girls, but that for boys, conflict was highest in mother residence. The interaction was not significant in random subsamples, although the means went in the same direction.
2. Dual-resident adolescents were excluded from analyses comparing only nonresidential parents, because dual-resident adolescents do not have a nonresidential parent.
3. Although the statistical results indicated that adolescents of both sexes reported more trust in nonresidential mothers than nonresidential fathers, the means clearly show that the effect is carried by boys.
4. Statistical tests generally did not reveal that boys and girls differed in the *difference between* relationships with residential fathers and nonresidential mothers; however, the means for some of the measures suggest that girls' relationships with each parent were less similar than those of boys (see the means for trust, conflict, and remembering special days). In each of these cases, the evidence indicates a somewhat troubled relationship

between girls and their nonresidential mothers, at least in comparison to the relationship between boys and nonresidential mothers.

5. When mother- and father-resident adolescents were analyzed separately, the difference between conflict with the residential parent and nonresidential parent was significant for mother-resident adolescents and not significant for father-resident adolescents. However, in analyses incorporating residential arrangement, the interaction between residence and type of parent was not significant.

6. The adjustment indices were regressed on each characteristic of the nonresidential parent–child relationship, controlling for that same characteristic of the adolescent's relationship with the residential parent. Age of adolescent was also accounted for in each analysis. Dual-resident adolescents were excluded from these analyses.

7. We also explicitly tested for interactions between gender of adolescent, residential arrangement, and relationships with the nonresidential parent as this set of factors related to adolescent adjustment. The analyses used were stepwise regressions, in which main effects were entered in the first step, all two-way interactions in a second step, and the three-way interaction in the third step.

8. In only two instances was there an indication of a link, and these emerged only in random subsamples and for specific subgroups of the sample.

9. Statistically, the relation between eagerness to see the nonresidential parent and adolescent deviance was significant for all father-resident adolescents, but an examination of the relations separately for boys and girls makes it clear that the effect is carried by girls.

10. The correlations for father-resident girls are no longer negative if we use only the component of "overall closeness" that we have called "emotional closeness," although they are still close to zero.

11. The analyses used were stepwise regressions, with adjustment measures as the dependent variables, and the following sets of predictor variables: (1) main effects of overall closeness to the residential parent and overall closeness to the nonresidential parent; (2) two-way interactions, including the central one of closeness to residential parent by closeness to nonresidential parent; and (3) the three-way interaction of closeness to residential parent by closeness to nonresidential parent by residential arrangement.

12. Analyses using categorical versions of parent-child "overall closeness" indicated that the adjustment of adolescents who experienced low closeness in their relationships with both father and mother was not different from that of adolescents who experienced low closeness to father but high closeness to mother.

13. Analyses using categorical versions of parent-child "overall closeness" indicated that the difference in adolescent adjustment between experi-

encing a close relationship with both parents and experiencing a close relationship with only the mother was not significant. In addition, these analyses indicated that the adjustment of adolescents who experienced low closeness in their relationships with both their mother and their father was not different from that of adolescents who experienced low closeness with their mother but high closeness with their father.

14. "Worst problem" was predicted with a dummy variable indicating dual (1) versus sole (0) residence, controlling for age and sex of adolescent, average parental education, and the sum of closeness to two parents.

15. These remaining analyses in this chapter use, as the predicted variable, the "emotional closeness" component of the "overall closeness" composite that included emotional closeness, activities, trust, and identification.

16. The significance of the effects of parental conflict (and any interactions of conflict with sex, residence, or sex and residence) on closeness to the residential parent or the nonresidential parent were tested using stepwise multiple regression. The dependent variable in these regressions was either closeness to the nonresidential parent or closeness to the residential parent. The independent variables were age of adolescent, sex of adolescent, residential arrangement (mother versus father), interparental conflict (step one); two-way interactions between sex of adolescent and conflict, residential arrangement and conflict, and sex of adolescent and residential arrangement (step two); and the three-way interaction of sex, residential arrangement, and conflict (step three).

17. The interaction of sex and nonresidential parent's hostility was significant when using all cases but not in random subsamples. The three-way interaction of sex, residence, and nonresidential parent's hostility was significant using all cases and marginally significant in random subsamples, but the correlation between hostility and closeness to the nonresidential mother remained strong for father-resident girls.

18. The effect for girls in father residence was significantly greater than that for any other group of adolescents for hostility of the residential parent and frequency of parental arguing, and nonsignificant but of the same pattern for T3 discord and T3 cooperative communication.

19. Any apparent differences in the magnitude of the relation between the interparental relationship and closeness to the nonresidential parent between boys and girls in mother residence were not statistically significant, with the exception of cooperation at T4.

20. For hostility of residential parent, the interaction with age was significant at $p \leq .05$; for hostility of nonresidential parent, the interaction was significant at $p \leq .10$.

21. We explicitly tested whether the difference in the association between the interparental relationship and closeness to the residential versus nonresidential parent was significant. Overall there was a differential

effect of interparental conflict on closeness to the residential versus the nonresidential parent for residential parent hostility, nonresidential parent hostility, and frequency of parental arguing. The differential negative impact of the nonresidential parent's hostility only emerged when the hostility measure was dichotomized, and is not evident using the correlational analysis depicted in Table 10.2. Among adolescents in father residence, however, T3 cooperation, residential parent hostility, nonresidential parent hostility, and T4 frequency of arguing had their greatest negative impact on closeness to nonresidential mothers for girls: only for girls in father residence was the impact of interparental conflict on closeness to the nonresidential parent consistently greater than it was on closeness to the residential parent.

22. The interactions of closeness to the nonresidential parent, interparental conflict, and residential arrangement were tested using stepwise multiple regression. In the first step, the main effects of age, sex, residential arrangement, closeness to the nonresidential parent, and interparental conflict were entered. In the second step, all two-way interactions were entered, including the interaction of central interest, closeness to the nonresidential parent by interparental conflict. Finally, in the third step, the three-way interaction of closeness by conflict by residential arrangement was entered.

23. See Chapter 6 for a more detailed discussion of the importance of mother-child closeness. It was noted there that some of the effects of closeness on adjustment are indirect, mediated by the mother's monitoring of her adolescent's activities and whereabouts.

11. Feeling Caught between One's Parents

1. Feelings of being caught were predicted, in an analysis of variance, by residence, sex of adolescent, and the interaction of residence and sex, with age of adolescent and parental education as controls. In Buchanan, Maccoby, and Dornbusch (1991), we reported that residence was essentially unrelated to feelings of being caught, because we did not control for parental education in that instance. Although parental education was not significantly related to feelings of being caught ($r = .06$, $p > .10$), it was related to residential arrangement (see Chapter 4); analyses employing parental education as a control were therefore conducted for exploratory purposes. We found, in fact, that this control did increase the magnitude of the differences between residence groups, although the significance of the difference was reduced to trend level ($p \leq .10$) in random samples.

2. Regression analyses were used to address this question. Feelings of being caught were predicted with age of adolescent, sex of adolescent, one of

the co-parenting measures, a dummy variable indicating whether the adolescent was in dual residence or in sole residence (either mother or father), and the interaction of being in dual residence with the co-parenting measure. Only the parent-reported measures of co-parenting were used in these analyses.

3. Although there was not a significant relation of feeling caught to parents' new-partner status when the four separate groups were compared, a two-group comparison of remarried mothers with those not remarried showed significantly higher levels of feeling caught in the nonremarried group. Feelings of being caught were also significantly lower in mother's households that had a new partner in the home (whether remarried or only cohabiting) than in those without a new partner.

4. This correlation is partialed for age of adolescent and sex of adolescent.

5. This correlation is partialed for age of adolescent and sex of adolescent.

6. In all of these analyses, we controlled for age and gender of the adolescent, as well as residential arrangement.

12. Inconsistency in Parenting

1. These four discrepancy scores loaded above .60 on a single factor, in a factor analysis of discrepancies in seven aspects of household management and control (in addition to the four noted, assignment of chores, school-night curfews, and weekend-night curfews were included). These four highly related discrepancy scores were standardized before averaging to create the parental discrepancy composite. A constant was added to bring all scores above zero.

2. See also Chapter 6, where we noted that the high correspondence between adolescents' reports of parent-child relationships and parental control and management in the two homes precluded using indicators of family process in both homes together in analyses predicting adolescent adjustment.

3. A significant linear progression was indicated in regression analyses treating the contact measure as a continuous variable.

4. This involved testing two-way interactions between the various demographic, contact, and interparental relationship variables. Individual interactions that remained significant at $p \leq .10$ in analyses controlling for all significant main effects were entered into a multiple regression analysis predicting parental discrepancy, with all significant main effects and interactions entered simultaneously. Subsequently, the model was re-run eliminating all nonsignificant predictors except sex, which remained as a control in all analyses. Interactions involving contact were tested by treating the contact variables as categorical as well as continuous variables. Because results of the two types of analyses were similar, we report

only the results of analyses in which contact was treated as a continuous variable.

5. When parents had higher levels of education, a higher frequency of arguing was not related to more discrepancies in parenting, and lower levels of cooperation were not as strongly related to more discrepancies in parenting.

6. The control variables were composites of the level of monitoring, youth-alone decision making, household organization, and consistency and fairness of rules in mother's and father's homes.

7. To address these questions, each of the adjustment measures (depression, antisocial behavior, and "worst problem") was predicted, in turn, with a full set of factors, including (a) parent-child relationship factors (feelings of being caught, conflict with the residential parent); (b) parenting discrepancies, and interactions of parenting discrepancies with background variables that were significant predictors of either the adjustment index or relationship factors; and (c) background variables that had been shown earlier to be related to parental discrepancies. Only those interaction terms that remained significant at $p \leq .10$ when controlling for all background factors related to discrepancy were included in the full models predicting adjustment. If an interaction term does not appear in the model, the reader may assume that it was not significant.

8. Evidence that "feeling caught" and "parent-child conflict" mediated the relation between parenting discrepancies and depression/anxiety was provided by examining the link between parenting discrepancies and depression/anxiety with and without the hypothesized mediators in the model. Without "feeling caught" and "parent-child conflict" in the model, discrepancies were significantly related to depression ($\beta = .16$, $p < .01$). With these two variables in the model, the link between discrepancies and depression was no longer significant ($\beta = .07$).

13. Conclusion

1. We could not test this for dual-resident adolescents, given the low numbers of individuals in the remarried and cohabiting groups.

2. As noted in Chapter 4, in statistical terms the residence differences indicating poorer adjustment applied equally to both boys and girls; however, the difference is generally larger for girls, and father-resident girls have the highest mean on the "worst problem" scale.

REFERENCES

Abarbanel, A. 1979. Shared parenting after separation and divorce: A study of joint custody. *American Journal of Orthopsychiatry, 49,* 320–329.

——— 1993. Children's adjustment to divorce: Theories, hypotheses, and empirical support. *Journal of Marriage and the Family, 55,* 23–38.

Amato, P. R., and B. Keith. 1991. Parental divorce and the well-being of children: A meta-analysis. *Psychological Bulletin, 110,* 26–46.

Amato, P. R., and S. J. Rezac. 1994. Contact with nonresident parents, interparental conflict, and children's behavior. *Journal of Family Issues, 15,* 191–207.

Aponte, J. J., and J. M. Van Deusen. 1981. Structural family therapy. In A. S. Gurman and D. P. Kniskern, eds., *Handbook of family therapy,* pp. 310–360. New York: Brunner/Mazel.

Barber, B. L., and J. S. Eccles. 1992. Long-term influence of divorce and single parenting on adolescent family- and work-related values, behaviors, and aspirations. *Psychological Bulletin, 111,* 108–126.

Barber, B. L., and J. M. Lyons. 1994. Family processes and adolescent adjustment in intact and remarried families. *Journal of Youth and Adolescence, 23,* 421–436.

Baron, R. M., and D. A. Kenny. 1986. The moderator-mediator variable distinction in social psychological research: Conceptual, strategic, and statistical considerations. *Journal of Personality and Social Psychology, 51,* 1173–1182.

Baumrind, D. 1991a. Effective parenting during the early adolescent transition. In P. A. Cowan and M. Hetherington, eds., *Family transitions,* pp. 111–163. Hillsdale, N.J.: Lawrence Erlbaum Associates.

——— 1991b. The influence of parenting style on adolescent competence and substance use. *Journal of Early Adolescence, 11,* 56–95.

Block, J. H., J. Block, and P. F. Gjerde. 1986. The personality of children prior to divorce: A prospective study. *Child Development, 57,* 827–840.

Block, J. H., J. Block, and A. Morrison. 1981. Parenting agreement-disagreement on child-rearing orientations and gender-related personality correlates in children. *Child Development, 52,* 965–974.

Bowlby, J. 1973. *Attachment and loss,* vol. 2, *Separation.* New York: Basic Books.

Braver, S. L., S. A. Wolchik, I. N. Sandler, B. S. Fogas, and D. Zvetina. 1991. Frequency of visitation by divorced fathers: Differences in reports by fathers and mothers. *American Journal of Orthopsychiatry, 61,* 448–454.

Bray, J. H. 1991. Psychosocial factors affecting custodial and visitation arrangements. *Behavioral Sciences and the Law, 9,* 419–437.

Bray, J. H., and S. H. Berger. 1990. Noncustodial father and paternal grandparent relationships in step-families. *Family Relations, 39,* 414–419.

——— 1993a. Developmental issues in StepFamilies Research Project: Family relationships and parent-child interactions. *Journal of Family Psychology, 7,* 76–90.

——— 1993b. Nonresidential family-child relationships following divorce and remarriage. In C. E. Depner and J. H. Bray, eds., *Nonresidential parenting: New vistas in family living,* pp. 156–181. Newbury Park, Calif.: Sage.

Buchanan, C. M., J. S. Eccles, and J. B. Becker. 1992. Are adolescents the victims of raging hormones: Evidence for activational effects of hormones on moods and behavior at adolescence. *Psychological Bulletin, 111,* 62–107.

Buchanan, C. M., E. E. Maccoby, and S. M. Dornbusch. 1991. Caught between parents: Adolescents' experience in divorced homes. *Child Development, 62,* 1008–1029.

——— 1992. Adolescents and their families after divorce: Three residential arrangements compared. *Journal of Research on Adolescence, 2,* 261–291.

Camara, K. A., and G. Resnick. 1988. Interparental conflict and cooperation: Factors moderating children's post-divorce adjustment. In E. M. Hetherington and J. D. Arasteh, eds., *Impact of Divorce, Single Parenting, and Stepparenting on Children,* pp. 169–195. Hillsdale, N.J.: Lawrence Erlbaum Associates.

Chase-Lansdale, P. L., A. J. Cherlin, and K. E. Kiernan. 1995. The long-term effects of parental divorce on the mental health of young adults: A developmental perspective. *Child Development, 66,* 1614–1634.

Cherlin, A. J., and F. F. Furstenberg. 1994. Stepfamilies in the United States: A reconsideration. In J. Hagan and K. Cook, eds., *Annual Review of Sociology,* vol. 20, pp. 359–381. Palo Alto, Calif.: Annual Reviews.

Cherlin, A. J., F. F. Furstenberg, P. L. Chase-Lansdale, K. E. Kiernan, P. K. Robins, D. R. Morrison, and J. O. Teitler. 1991. Longitudinal studies of effects of divorce on children in Great Britain and the United States. *Science, 252,* 1386–1389.

Clingempeel, W. G., E. Brand, and R. Ievoli. 1984. Stepparent-stepchild relationships in stepmother and stepfather families: A multimethod study. *Family Relations, 33,* 465–473.

Clingempeel, W. G., and S. Segal. 1986. Stepparent-stepchild relationships and the psychological adjustment of children in stepmother and stepfather families. *Child Development, 57,* 474–484.

Cohen, J., and P. Cohen. 1983. *Applied multiple regression/correlation analysis for the behavioral sciences.* Hillsdale, N.J.: Lawrence Erlbaum Associates.

Collins, W. A., and G. Russell. 1991. Mother-child and father-child relationships in middle childhood and adolescence: A developmental analysis. *Developmental Review, 11,* 99–136.

Compas, B. E. 1987. Stress and life events during childhood and adolescence. *Clinical Psychology Review, 7,* 275–302.

Crosbie-Burnett, M. 1991. Impact of joint versus sole custody and quality of co-parental relationship on adjustment of adolescents in remarried families. *Behavioral Sciences and the Law, 9,* 439–449.

Cummings, E. M., and P. Davies. 1994. *Children and marital conflict: The impact of family dispute and resolution.* New York: Guilford Press.

Davies, P. T., and E. M. Cummings. 1994. Marital conflict and child adjustment: An emotional security hypothesis. *Psychological Bulletin, 116,* 387–411.

Deal, J. E., C. F. Halverson, Jr., and K. S. Wampler. 1989. Parental agreement on child-rearing orientations: Relations to parental, marital, family, and child characteristics. *Child Development, 60,* 1025–1034.

Depner, C. E., E. V. Leino, and A. Chun. 1992. Interparental conflict and child adjustment: A decade review and meta-analysis. *Family and Conciliation Courts Review, 30,* 323–341.

Dornbusch, S. M., J. M. Carlsmith, S. J. Bushwall, P. L. Ritter, H. Leiderman, A. H. Hastorf, and R. T. Gross. 1985. Single parents, extended households, and the control of adolescents. *Child Development, 56,* 326–341.

Dornbusch, S. M., R. Mont-Reynaud, P. L. Ritter, Z. Chen, and L. Steinberg. 1991. Stressful events and their correlates among adolescents of diverse backgrounds. In M. E. Colten and S. Gore, eds., *Adolescent stress: Causes and consequences,* pp. 111–130. Hawthorne, N.Y.: Aldine de Gruyter.

Dornbusch, S. M., P. L. Ritter, P. H. Leiderman, D. F. Roberts, and M. J. Fraleigh. 1987. The relation of parenting style to adolescent school performance. *Child Development, 58,* 1244–1257.

Duncan, G. J., and S. D. Hoffman. 1985. Economic consequences of marital instability. In M. David and T. Smeeding, eds., *Horizontal equity, uncertainty, and well-being,* pp. 427–469. Chicago: University of Chicago Press.

Dunn, J. 1990. *Separate lives: Why siblings are so different.* New York: Basic Books.

Eagly, A. H., and V. J. Steffen. 1986. Gender and aggressive behavior: A meta-analytic review of the social psychological literature. *Psychological Bulletin, 100,* 309–330.

Eccles, J. S., C. Midgley, A. Wigfield, C. M. Buchanan, D. Reuman, C. Flanagan, and D. MacIver. 1993. Development during adolescence: The impact of stage/environment fit on young adolescents' experiences in schools and families. *American Psychologist, 48,* 90–101.

Emery, R. E. 1982. Interparental conflict and the children of discord and divorce. *Psychological Bulletin, 92,* 310–330.

———— 1988. *Marriage, divorce, and children's adjustment.* Newbury Park, Calif.: Sage Publications.

Espenshade, T. J. 1979. The economic consequences of divorce. *Journal of Marriage and the Family, 41,* 615–625.

Fauber, R., R. Forehand, A. M. Thomas, and M. Wierson. 1990. A mediational model of the impact of marital conflict on adolescent adjustment in intact and divorced families: The role of disrupted parenting. *Child Development, 61,* 1112–1123.

Ferri, E. 1984. *Stepchildren: A national study.* Windsor, Berkshire, U.K.: NFER-Nelson Publishing Co.

Flanagan, C., J. Schulenberg, and A. Fuligni. 1993. Residential setting and parent-adolescent relationships during the college years. *Journal of Youth and Adolescence, 22,* 171–189.

Funder, K. 1991. Children's constructions of their post-divorce families: A family sculpture approach. In K. Funder, ed., *Images of Australian families,* pp. 73–87. Melbourne: Longman-Cheshire.

Furman, W., and D. Buhrmester. 1985a. Children's perceptions of the personal relationships in their social networks. *Developmental Psychology, 21,* 1016–1024.

———— 1985b. Children's perceptions of the qualities of sibling relationships. *Child Development, 56,* 448–461.

Furstenberg, F. F. 1987. The new extended family: The experience of parents and children after remarriage. In K. Pasley and M. Ihinger-Tallman, eds., *Remarriage and stepparenting: Current research and theory,* pp. 42–61. New York: Guilford Press.

———— 1990. Coming of age in a changing family system. In S. S. Feldman and G. R. Elliott, eds., *At the threshold: The developing adolescent,* pp. 147–170. Cambridge, Mass.: Harvard University Press.

Furstenberg, F. F., Jr., S. P. Morgan, and P. D. Allison. 1987. Paternal participation and children's well-being after marital dissolution. *American Sociological Review, 52,* 695–701.

Furstenberg, F. F., Jr., C. W. Nord, J. L. Peterson, and N. Zill. 1983. The life course of children of divorce. *American Sociological Review, 48,* 656–668.

Furstenberg, F. F., Jr., and G. Spanier. 1984. *Recycling the family: Remarriage after divorce.* Beverly Hills, Calif.: Sage.

Galambos, N. L., H. A. Sears, D. M. Almeida, and N. L. Kolaric. 1995. Parents' work overload and problem behavior in young adolescents. *Journal of Research on Adolescence, 5,* 201–224.

Ganong, L. H., and M. Coleman. 1984. The effects of remarriage on children: A review of the empirical literature. *Family Relations, 33,* 389–406.

Garmezy, N., A. S. Masten, and A. Tellegen. 1984. The study of stress and competence in children: A building block for developmental psychopathology. *Child Development, 55,* 97–111.

Gilligan, C. 1982. *In a different voice: Psychological theory and women's development.* Cambridge, Mass.: Harvard University Press.

Gjerde, P. F. 1986. The interpersonal structure of family interaction settings: Parent-adolescent relations in dyads and triads. *Developmental Psychology, 22,* 297–304.

———— 1988. Parental concordance on child-rearing and the interactive emphases of parents: Sex-differentiated relationships during the preschool years. *Developmental Psychology, 24,* 700–706.

Glover, R. J., and C. Steele. 1989. Comparing the effects on the child of post-divorce parenting arrangements. *Journal of Divorce, 12,* 185–201.

Goldstein, J., A. Freud, and A. J. Solnit. 1979. *Beyond the best interests of the child.* New York: Free Press.

Gore, S., Aseltine, R. H., Jr., and Colten, M. E. 1993. Gender, social-relational involvement, and depression. *Journal of Research on Adolescence, 3,* 101–125.

Grief, J. B. 1979. Fathers, children, and joint custody. *American Journal of Orthopsychiatry, 49,* 311–319.

Groves, R. M., and R. L. Kahn. 1979. *Surveys by telephone: A natural comparison with personal interviews.* New York: Academic Press.

Gunnoe, M. L. 1994. Noncustodial mothers' and fathers' contributions to the adjustment of adolescents in stabilized stepfamilies. Paper presented in J. Bray, chair, Family transitions and adolescent adjustment: Impact of divorce, remarriage, and repartnering. Symposium conducted at the biennial meetings of the Society for Research in Adolescence, San Diego. February.

Hartup, W. W., D. C. French, B. Laursen, M. K. Johnston, and J. R. Ogawa. 1993. Conflict and friendship relations in middle childhood: Behavior in a closed-field situation. *Child Development, 64,* 445–454.

Heider, F. 1958. *The psychology of interpersonal relations.* New York: John Wiley.

Hess, R. D., and K. A. Camara. 1979. Post-divorce family relationships as mediating factors in the consequences of divorce for children. *Journal of Social Issues, 35,* 79–96.

Hetherington, E. M. 1987. Family relations six years after divorce. In K. Pasley and M. Ihinger-Tallman, eds., *Remarriage and stepparenting today: Research and theory,* pp. 185–205. New York: Guilford.

———— 1993. An overview of the Virginia Longitudinal Study of Divorce and Remarriage with a focus on early adolescence. *Journal of Family Psychology, 7,* 39–56.

Hetherington, E. M., and W. G. Clingempeel. 1992. Coping with marital transitions: A family systems perspective. *Monographs of the Society for Research in Child Development, 57.*

Hetherington, E. M., M. Cox, and R. Cox. 1978. The aftermath of divorce. In J. H. Stevens, Jr., and M. Matthews, eds., *Mother-child, father-child relations,* pp. 149–176. Washington, D.C.: NAEYC.

——— 1982. Effects of divorce on parents and children. In M. E. Lamb, ed., *Nontraditional families,* pp. 233–288. Hillsdale, N.J.: Erlbaum.

Hill, J. P., and G. N. Holmbeck. 1986. Attachment and autonomy during adolescence. *Annals of Child Development, 3,* 145–189.

Hyde, J. S. 1984. How large are gender differences in aggression? A developmental meta-analysis. *Developmental Psychology, 20,* 722–736.

Ihinger-Tallman, M. 1988. Research on stepfamilies. In W. R. Scott and J. Blake, eds., *Annual Review of Sociology,* vol. 14, pp. 25–48. Palo Alto, Calif.: Annual Reviews.

Irving, H. H., M. Benjamin, and N. Trocme. 1984. Shared parenting: An empirical analysis utilizing a large data base. *Family Process, 23,* 561–569.

Johnson, B. M., S. Shulman, and W. A. Collins. 1991. Systemic patterns of parenting as reported by adolescents: Developmental differences and implications for psychosocial outcomes. *Journal of Adolescent Research, 6,* 235–252.

Johnston, J. R., and L. E. G. Campbell. 1987. Instability in family networks of divorced and disputing parents. In E. J. Lawler, ed., *Advances in group processes,* vol. 4, pp. 243–269, Greenwich, Conn.: JAI Press.

——— 1988. *Impasses of divorce: The dynamics and resolution of family conflict.* New York: Free Press.

Johnston, J. R., M. Kline, and J. M. Tschann. 1989. Ongoing post-divorce conflict in families contesting custody: Effects on children of joint custody and frequent access. *American Journal of Orthopsychiatry, 59,* 576–592.

Kalter, N., and J. Rembar. 1981. The significance of a child's age at the time of parental divorce. *American Journal of Orthopsychiatry, 51,* 85–100.

Kelly, J. B. 1993. Current research on children's postdivorce adjustment: No simple answers. *Family and Conciliation Courts Reviews, 31,* 29–49.

King, V. 1994. Nonresident father involvement and child well-being. *Journal of Family Issues, 15,* 78–96.

Kline, M., J. M. Tschann, J. R. Johnston, and J. Wallerstein. 1989. Children's adjustment in joint and sole physical custody families. *Developmental Psychology, 25,* 430–438.

Kurdek, L. A. 1987. Children's adjustment to parental divorce: An ecological perspective. In J. P. Vincent, ed., *Advances in family intervention, assessment, and theory,* vol. 4, pp. 1–31. Greenwich, Conn.: JAI Press.

Kurdek, L. A., D. Blisk, and A. Siesky, Jr. 1981. Correlates of children's long-term adjustment to their parents' divorce. *Developmental Psychology, 17,* 565–579.

Lamb, M. E., J. H. Pleck, E. L. Charnov, and J. A. Levine. 1987. A biosocial perspective on paternal behavior and involvement. In J. B. Lancaster, J. Altman, A. S. Rossi, and L. R. Sherrod, eds., *Parenting across the lifespan: Biosocial dimensions.* New York: Aldine de Gruyter.

Lamborn, S. D., N. S. Mounts, L. Steinberg, and S. M. Dornbusch. 1991. Patterns of competence and adjustment among adolescents from authoritative, authoritarian, indulgent, and neglectful families. *Child Development, 62,* 1049–1065.

Levy, B., and C. Chambers. 1981. The folly of joint custody. *Family Advocate, 3,* 6–10.

Luepnitz, D. A. 1982. *Child custody: A study of families after divorce.* Lexington, Mass.: Lexington Books/D. C. Heath and Company.

——— 1986. A comparison of maternal, paternal, and joint custody: Understanding the varieties of post-divorce family life. *Journal of Divorce, 9,* 1–12.

Lutz, P. 1983. The stepfamily: An adolescent perspective. *Family Relations, 32,* 367–375.

Maccoby, E. E. 1990. Gender and relationships. *American Psychologist, 45,* 513–520.

——— 1995. Divorce and custody: The rights, needs, and obligations of mothers, fathers, and children. In G. Melton, ed., *The individual, the family, and social good: Personal fulfillment in times of change,* Nebraska Symposium on Motivation, vol. 42, pp. 135–172. Lincoln: University of Nebraska Press.

Maccoby, E. E., C. E. Depner, and R. H. Mnookin. 1990. Coparenting in the second year after divorce. *Journal of Marriage and the Family, 52,* 141–155.

Maccoby, E. E., and C. N. Jacklin. 1974. *The psychology of sex differences.* Stanford, Calif.: Stanford University Press.

Maccoby, E. E., and J. Martin. 1983. Socialization in the context of the family: Parent-child interaction. In P. H. Mussen, ed., *Handbook of child psychology,* vol. 4, *Socialization, personality, and social development,* pp. 1–102. New York: John Wiley and Sons.

Maccoby, E. E., and R. H. Mnookin. 1992. *Dividing the child: Social and legal dilemmas of custody.* Cambridge, Mass.: Harvard University Press.

McCormick, M. C., K. Workman-Daniels, J. Brooks-Gunn, and G. J. Peckham. 1993. When you're only a phone call away: A comparison of the information in telephone and face-to-face interviews. *Developmental and Behavioral Pediatrics, 14,* 250–257.

Miller, P. M., D. L. Danaher, and D. Forbes. 1986. Sex-related strategies for coping with interpersonal conflict in children aged five and seven. *Developmental Psychology, 22,* 543–548.

Minuchin, S. 1974. *Families and family therapy.* Cambridge, Mass.: Harvard University Press.

Mnookin, R. H., E. E. Maccoby, C. R. Albiston, and C. E. Depner. 1989. Private ordering revisited: What custodial arrangements are parents negotiating? In S. D. Sugarman and H. H. Kay, eds., *Divorce reform at the crossroads,* pp. 37–74. New Haven, Conn.: Yale University Press.

Montemayor, R. 1983. Parents and adolescents in conflict: All families some of the time and some families most of the time. *Journal of Early Adolescence, 3,* 83–103.

Montemayor, R., and J. R. Brownlee. 1987. Fathers, mothers, and adolescents: Gender-based differences in parental roles during adolescence. *Journal of Youth and Adolescence, 16,* 281–291.

Mussen, P., and N. Eisenberg-Berg. 1977. *Roots of caring, sharing, and helping.* San Francisco: W. H. Freeman.

Natriello, G., and S. M. Dornbusch. 1984. *Teacher evaluative standards and student effort.* New York: Longman.

Nelson, R. 1989. Parental hostility, conflict, and communication in joint and sole custody families. *Journal of Divorce, 13,* 145–157.

Neugebauer, R. 1989. Divorce, custody, and visitation: The child's point of view. *Journal of Divorce, 12,* 153–168.

Nolen-Hoeksema, S., and J. S. Girgus. 1994. The emergence of gender differences in depression during adolescence. *Psychological Bulletin, 115,* 424–443.

Noller, P. 1994. Relationships with parents in adolescence: Process and outcome. In R. Montemayor, G. R. Adams, and T. P. Gullotta, eds., *Personal relationships during adolescence,* pp. 37–77. Thousand Oaks, Calif.: Sage Publications.

Oppawsky, J. 1989. Family dysfunctional patterns during divorce—from the view of the children. In C. A. Everett, ed., *Children of divorce: Developmental and clinical issues,* pp. 139–152. Binghamton, N.Y.: Haworth Press.

Parke, R. D., and B. R. Tinsley. 1981. The father's role in infancy: Determinants of involvement in caregiving and play. In M. E. Lamb, ed., *The role of the father in child development,* pp. 429–457. New York: John Wiley and Sons.

Pasley, K., and M. Ihinger-Tallman, eds. 1987. *Remarriage and stepparenting: Current research and theory.* New York: Guilford Press.

Patterson, G. R. 1982. *Coercive family process.* Eugene, Ore.: Castalia.

Pearson, J., and N. Thoennes. 1990. Custody after divorce: Demographic and attitudinal patterns. *American Journal of Orthopsychiatry, 60,* 233–249.

Petersen, A. C., P. A. Sarigiani, and R. E. Kennedy. 1991. Adolescent depression: Why more girls? *Journal of Youth and Adolescence, 20,* 247–271.

Peterson, J. L., and N. Zill. 1986. Marital disruption, parent-child relationships, and behavior problems in children. *Journal of Marriage and the Family, 48,* 295–307.

Rosemond, J. K. 1994. Helping children with the before and after of divorce. *Hemispheres,* May: 99–103.

Russell, G., and A. Russell. 1987. Mother-child and father-child relationships in middle childhood. *Child Development, 58,* 1573–1585.

Rutter, M. 1979. Protective factors in children's responses to stress and disadvantage. In M. W. Kent and J. E. Rolf, eds., *Primary prevention of pathology: Social competence in children.* Hanover, N.H.: University Press of New England.

Rutter, M., P. Graham, O. F. D. Chadwick, and W. Yule. 1976. Adolescent turmoil: Fact or fiction? *Journal of Child Psychology and Psychiatry, 17,* 35–56.

Santrock, J. W. 1970. Paternal absence, sex typing, and identification. *Developmental Psychology, 2,* 262–274.

Santrock, J. W., and R. A. Warshak. 1979. Father custody and social development in boys and girls. *Journal of Social Issues, 35,* 112–125.

Santrock, J. W., R. A. Warshak, and G. L. Elliott. 1982. Social development and parent-child interaction in father custody and step-mother families. In M. E. Lamb, ed., *Nontraditional families.* Hillsdale, N.J.: Lawrence Erlbaum Associates.

Santrock, J. W., R. A. Warshak, C. Lindberg, and L. Meadows. 1982. Children's and parent's observed social behavior in stepfather families. *Child Development, 53,* 472–480.

Schoenbach, V. J., B. H. Kaplan, E. H. Wagner, R. C. Grimson, and F. T. Miller. 1983. Prevalence of self-reported depressive symptoms in young adolescents. *American Journal of Public Health, 73,* 1281–1287.

Seltzer, J. A. 1991. Relationships between fathers and children who live apart: The father's role after separation. *Journal of Marriage and Family, 53,* 79–101.

Sessa, F. M., and L. Steinberg. 1991. Family structure and the development of autonomy during adolescence. *Journal of Early Adolescence, 11,* 38–55.

Shiller, V. M. 1986a. Joint vs. maternal physical custody for families with latency age boys: Parent characteristics and child adjustment. *American Journal of Orthopsychiatry, 56,* 486–489.

——— 1986b. Loyalty conflicts and family relationships in latency age boys: A comparison of joint and maternal custody. *Journal of Divorce, 9,* 17–38.

Simmons, R. G., R. Burgeson, S. Carlton-Ford, and D. A. Blyth. 1987. The impact of cumulative change in early adolescence. *Child Development, 58,* 1220–1234.

Simring, S. 1984. Joint custody best alternative when ex-spouses are hostile:

New research. *Marriage and divorce today: The professional newsletter for family therapy practitioners, 9,* 1.

Smollar, J., and J. Youniss. 1985. Parent-adolescent relations in adolescents whose parents are divorced. *Journal of Early Adolescence, 5,* 129–144.

Steinberg, L. 1987. Single parents, stepparents, and the susceptibility of adolescents to antisocial peer pressure. *Child Development, 58,* 269–275.

Steinberg, L., N. S. Mounts, S. D. Lamborn, and S. M. Dornbusch. 1991. Authoritative parenting and adolescent adjustment across varied ecological niches. *Journal of Research on Adolescence, 1,* 19–36.

Steinman, S. B. 1981. The experience of children in a joint-custody arrangement: A report of a study. *American Journal of Orthopsychiatry, 51,* 403–414.

Stolberg, A. L., and P. M. Cullen. 1983. Preventive interventions for families of divorce: The divorce adjustment project. In L. A. Kurdek, ed., *New Directions for Child Development,* no. 19, *Children and Divorce,* pp. 71–82. San Francisco: Jossey-Bass.

Stoneman, Z., G. H. Brody, and M. Burke. 1989. Marital quality, depression, and inconsistent parenting: Relationships with observed mother-child conflict. *American Journal of Orthopsychiatry, 59,* 105–117.

Sweet, J. A., and L. L. Bumpass. 1987. *American families and households.* New York: Russell Sage Foundation.

Vaughn, B. E., J. H. Block, and J. Block. 1988. Parental agreement on child-rearing during early childhood and the psychological characteristics of adolescents. *Child Development, 59,* 1020–1033.

Wallerstein, J. S., and S. Blakeslee. 1989. *Second chances: Men, women, and children a decade after divorce.* New York: Ticknor and Fields.

Wallerstein, J. S., and J. B. Kelly. 1980. *Surviving the breakup: How children and parents cope with divorce.* New York: Basic Books.

Warshak, R. A., and J. W. Santrock. 1983. The impact of divorce in father-custody and mother-custody homes: The child's perspective. In L. A. Kurdek, ed., *New Directions for Child Development,* no. 19, *Children and Divorce,* pp. 29–46. San Francisco: Jossey-Bass.

Werner, E. E., and R. S. Smith. 1982. *Vulnerable but invincible: A study of resilient children.* New York: McGraw-Hill.

Whitehead, B. D. 1993. Dan Quayle was right. *Atlantic Monthly, 271,* 47–84.

Whiting, B. B., and J. W. M. Whiting. 1975. *Children of six cultures: A psychocultural analysis.* Cambridge, Mass.: Harvard University Press.

Youniss, J., and J. Smollar. 1983. *Adolescent relations with mothers, fathers, and friends.* Chicago: University of Chicago Press.

Zaslow, M. J. 1988. Sex differences in children's response to parental divorce: 1. Research methodology and post-divorce family forms. *American Journal of Orthopsychiatry, 58,* 355–378.

――― 1989. Sex differences in children's response to parental divorce: 2.

Samples, variables, ages, and sources. *American Journal of Orthopsychiatry, 59,* 118–141.

Zill, N. 1988. Behavior, achievement, and health problems among children in stepfamilies: Findings from a national survey of child health. In E. M. Hetherington and J. Arasteh, eds., *The impact of divorce, single parenting, and stepparenting on children.* Hillsdale, N.J.: Erlbaum.

INDEX

Adjustment, adolescents in our sample: 37–42, 253–254; as related to acceptance of new partner, 135–138, 140, 256–257; as related to visitation with nonresidential parent, 181–184; as related to loyalty conflicts, 226–230; as related to inconsistency in parenting, 240, 241–243, 244–246, 249. *See also specific indices of family relationships and family functioning, including* Residential arrangement

Adjustment, children of divorce: 4–7

Age of adolescents: in sample, 9, 16, 26–27; as factors in residence and visitation, 46, 166; as factor in acceptance of new partners, 126–127, 140; and feelings about visitation, 168, 174; and impact of visitation, 179, 181; and impact of interparental conflict, 208, 258; and loyalty conflicts, 219, 221, 258; and impact of inconsistency in parenting, 241, 250

Analysis strategies, 19–20, 25, 46, 48–49, 81–84, 98, 110–111, 136, 161–162, 193, 206, 239

Authoritarian parenting, 94–95. *See also specific indices of parenting, including* Closeness, child and residential parent, *and* Household management

Authoritative parenting, 94–95. *See also specific indices of parenting, including* Closeness, child and residential parent, *and* Household management

Birth order, of adolescents in sample, 27

Chores, 97–98, 192

Closeness, child and nonresidential parent: and residential parent's repartnering status, 114–116, 118–119, 132–134, 139–140, 270; and adolescent adjustment, 146–147, 193, 198, 199–200, 201–205, 210–212, 213, 263; and level of visitation, 176–179, 185–186, 208, 262–263; and sex of nonresidential parent, 188–189, 212; and impact of residential parent's repartnering on loyalty conflicts, 226. *See also* Closeness, parent-child

Closeness, child and residential parent: and residential arrangement, 70, 71–72, 264, 265–266; and adolescent adjustment, 90–91, 93–96, 101–102, 103, 105–106, 146, 201–205, 259–261, 263; and parent's repartnering status, 113–114, 116–117, 139, 269; and acceptance of parent's new partner, 131–132, 140; and closeness to nonresidential parent, 146, 200–201; and visitation with nonresidential parent, 180. *See also* Closeness, parent-child

Closeness, parent-child: measure, 24; in sample, 41, 67–70; as related to parent's residential status, 187–188, 212; and loyalty conflicts, 223–224, 231. *See also* Closeness, child and nonresidential parent; Closeness, child and residential parent

Cohabitation. *See* Remarriage and repartnering

Conflict and cooperation, interparental: and adolescent adjustment, 5, 89–90,